Review for the third edition

"This book is a reference for those interested in innovation management and entrepreneurship. Standing on the shoulders of the second edition, Bessant and Tidd have incorporated current debates such as sustainability-led innovation, entrepreneurial creativity and the growing importance of ICTs in shaping the innovation model, e.g. crowd sourcing, crowd funding and innovation communities. What makes this edition even more outstanding is the way theories are combined with case studies, media links and other online learning and revision material."

Dolores Añon Higon, Associate Professor, Faculty of Economics,
Universitat de València, Spain

Reviews for the second edition

"Bessant and Tidd's *Innovation and Entrepreneurship* 2nd Edition is an ideal undergraduate textbook. It successfully synthesises relevant frameworks from previously segmented fields of inquiry and presents them within a practical and logical process model which is packed with illustrative material and useful aids to learning."

John Storey, Professor of Management,
The Open University Business School

"This is a comprehensive and authoritative text prepared by an authoritative team – professors John Bessant and Joe Tidd. They both have an excellent grounding and credible presence in innovation studies and have been at the forefront of research in the field for many years.

The text is an extremely timely melding of insights about innovation and about entrepreneurship. Around the world today it is being increasingly recognised that innovation – the commercial exploitation of new ideas – is a crucial driver for improving economic and social wellbeing across both public and private sectors. At the same time, recognition is also growing that effective and successful innovation requires the ingenious involvement of individuals with the energy and commitment to build appropriate organisational arrangements to deliver the potential of innovation. This text explains and illustrates in a very accessible manner just how this can be done. It will prove to be an extremely effective anchor text for any undergraduate courses in the area, and indeed is worthwhile reading for researchers and practitioners who would like authoritative confirmation that what they are doing makes sense."

Professor James Fleck, Dean of the Open University Business
School and Professor of Innovation Dynamics

Innovation and Entrepreneurship

Innovation and Entrepreneurship

Third Edition

John Bessant and Joe Tidd

WILEY

Library of Congress Cataloging-in-Publication Data

Bessant, J. R.
  Innovation and entrepreneurship / John Bessant and Joe Tidd. — Third Edition.
      pages cm
   Includes index.
  ISBN 978-1-118-99309-5 (pbk.)
  1. Creative ability in business. 2. Entrepreneurship. I. Tidd, Joseph, 1960- II. Title.
  HD53.B476 2015
  658.4'21—dc23

                                                             2014048328

ISBN: 9781118993095 (pbk)
ISBN: 9781119126522 (ebk)
ISBN: 9781119088752 (ebk)

A catalogue record for this book is available from the British Library

Set in 10/12 Sabon LT Std Roman by Thomson Digital, India
Printed in Italy by Printer Trento Srl.

Contents

Preface to third edition

Organizations which innovate are much more likely to create value, both private and social.[1] However, few new ventures are successful, and very few manage to grow and prosper.[2]

This book has been developed specifically for students of Business and Management Studies, and for Science and Engineering students studying courses on innovation and/or entrepreneurship. It is designed to complement our best-selling text *Managing Innovation: Integrating Technological, Market and Organizational Change* (5th edn, John Wiley & Sons Ltd, 2013), which is focused more on the needs of specialist postgraduate and post-experience audiences.

In this third edition, we were inspired by the pioneering scholars of entrepreneurship and innovation, such as Joseph Schumpeter and Peter Drucker, to attempt to re-integrate these two fields. For too long the two subjects have diverged into narrow disciplines, each suffering as a result: entrepreneurship has become preoccupied with small business creation and innovation dominated by new product development.[3] In this text, we aim to reunite the study and practice of entrepreneurship and innovation.

We believe that this text is unique in two significant respects. First, how it treats and applies the key theories and research on innovation and entrepreneurship. Second, the pedagogy and approach to learning. In this text we review and synthesize the theory and research, where relevant, but put far greater emphasis on the practice of innovation and entrepreneurship applied in a much broader context, including the corporate and public services, emerging technologies and economies, and for sustainability and development. Research has shifted from a narrow focus on individuals and inventions to a broader process perspective.[4] Therefore, in this third edition, we continue to adopt an explicit process model to help organize the material:

- Entrepreneurial Goals and Context
- Recognizing the Opportunity
- Finding the Resources
- Developing the Venture
- Creating Value.

In the first section, Entrepreneurial Goals and Context, we review the key theories and recent research relevant to understanding the dynamics and practice of innovation and entrepreneurship. In the first chapter, we begin with mapping out different definitions and types of innovation, and identify the relationships between innovation, entrepreneurship and the performance of organizations in the private and public sectors. We develop a process for innovation and entrepreneurship that consists of four phases: Recognizing the Opportunity; Finding the Resources; Developing the Venture and Creating Value. In Chapter 2 we explore the context and goals of social entrepreneurship and innovation, including public organizations and other third-sector bodies such as non-governmental organizations (NGOs), which includes charities and the voluntary sectors. In many advanced economies the service sector, broadly defined, accounts for 60–75% of employment, and more than half of this is in public- and third-sector services. Chapter 3 examines the contributions of innovation and entrepreneurship in emerging and developing economies, and for sustainability in the more advanced nations.

The rest of the text is organized by the process model. Part II, Recognizing the Opportunity, includes chapters on the sources of and searching for opportunities, with a focus on the respective roles of individuals, groups and organizations in innovation and entrepreneurship, and identifies the key characteristics of creative people, and the factors which contribute to an innovative organization, including trust, challenge, support, conflict and debate, risk-taking and freedom. In Part III, Finding the Resources, we discuss how to develop a business plan and how to use this to identify and manage uncertainty, and the critical contributions of personal and organizational networks. Part IV, Developing the Venture, focuses on how to develop new, innovative products, services and businesses, including corporate entrepreneurship and ventures. Finally, in Part V, Creating Value, we identify paths to create and capture value, in the broadest sense. This includes creating and sharing knowledge and intellectual property, novel business models and factors which influence the success and growth of new ventures. The final chapter reviews the steps and resources necessary to make innovation and entrepreneurship happen, and provides an action plan for translating ideas into practice.

The text is also fully integrated with our interactive Web resources, available at www.innovation-portal.info, which features:

- additional, full-length case studies
- tools to support innovation and entrepreneurship
- video and audio media
- flash interactive exercises
- self-test bank of questions and answers.

We welcome your feedback and invite you to share your experiences.

John Bessant and Joe Tidd

References

1. Tidd, J. and J. Bessant (2014) *Strategic Innovation Management*, Chichester: John Wiley & Sons Ltd.

2. Coad, A., S.-O. Daunfeldt, W. Hölzl *et al.* (2014) High-growth firms: Introduction to the special section, *Industrial and Corporate Change*, **23**(1): 91–112.

3. Tidd, J. (2014) Conjoint innovation: Building a bridge between innovation and entrepreneurship, *International Journal of Innovation Management*, **18**(1): 1–20.

4. Landström, H., G. Harirchi and F. Åström, F. (2012) Entrepreneurship: Exploring the knowledge base, *Research Policy*, **41**(7): 1154–81.

Acknowledgements

We would like to thank all those colleagues and students at SPRU, Exeter, CENTRIM, Imperial College and elsewhere who have provided feedback on our work. We are also grateful for the more formal reviews by various anonymous reviewers whose comments and suggestions helped develop this new edition.

Thanks are also due to Dave Francis, Howard Rush, Stefan Kohn, Girish Prabhu, Richard Philpott, David Simoes-Brown, Alastair Ross, Suzana Moreira, Michael Bartl, Roy Sandbach, Lynne Maher, Philip Cullimore, Helle-Vibeke Carstensen, Helen King, Patrick McLaughlin, Melissa Clark-Reynolds, Boyi Li, Simon Tucker, Ana Sena, Victor Cui, Emma Taylor, Armin Rau, Francisco Pinheiro, David Overton, Michelle Lowe, Gerard Harkin, Dorothea Seebode, Fabian Schlage, Catherina van Delden, John Thesmer, Tim Craft, Bettina von Stamm, Mike Pitts and Kathrin Moeslein for their help in creating case studies and podcast/video material for the text and website. Particular thanks are due to Anna Trifilova for her help in background research and assembling many of the Web-based cases.

As always we're really grateful for the help and support of the extended team at Wiley, who have practised what we preach with their seamless cross-functional working, especially Steve Hardman, Georgia King, Deb Egleton, Juliet Booker, Tim Bettsworth, Sarah Booth and Gladys Famoriyo.

How to Use This Book

Features in the Book

INNOVATION IN ACTION 5.2

Sticky Success

It was during a flight in 1967 that Wolfgang Dierichs, a scientist working for the German company Henkel, had a flash of creative insight. The company made a wide range of stationery products and one area in which he worked was in adhesives. As he sat waiting for the plane to take off he noticed the woman next to him applying lipstick. His insight was to see the potential of the lipstick tube as a new way to deliver glue. Put some solid glue in a tube, twist the cap and apply it to any surface.

The company launched the 'Pritt Stick' in 1969, and within two years it was available in 38 countries around the world. Today, around 130 million Pritt Sticks are sold each year in 120 countries and the product has sold over 2.5 billion units since its invention.

Innovation In Action:
Real-life case studies contextualize the topics covered

ENTREPRENEURSHIP IN ACTION 5.2

Snakes on a Bus

The 19th-century chemist Friedrich August Kekulé is credited with having unravelled one of the keys to the development of organic chemistry, the structure of the benzene ring. This arrangement of atoms is central to understanding how to make a range of chemicals, from fertilizers and medicines to explosives, and enabled the rapid acceleration of growth in the field. Having wrestled for a long period with the problem, he eventually had a flash of inspiration on waking from a dream in which he had seen the atoms dance and then, like a snake, begin eating its own tail. This weird dream picture nudged him towards the key insight that the atoms in benzene were arranged in a ring.

He later reported on another dream which he had had while dozing on a London bus in which atoms were dancing in different formations, which gave him further insight into the key components of chemical structure.

Entrepreneurship In Action:
Practical implications and advice through evidence-based examples

 Deeper Dive explanations of innovation concepts and ideas are available on the Innovation Portal at **www.innovation-portal.info**

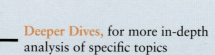

Deeper Dives, for more in-depth analysis of specific topics

Web Resources

Innovation Portal

The **Innovation Portal** at www.innovation-portal.info houses all the online resources for the book. This fully searchable resource contains a wealth of material including a complete compendium of **videos, audio clips, cases, activities** and a fully searchable **innovation toolkit**, and is an essential resource for anyone wishing to deepen their understanding of innovation concepts. Signposts to this material can be found in the relevant book chapters wherever you see the icon boxes as shown below:

 Tools to help you explore prototyping are available on the Innovation Portal at **www.innovation-portal.info**

 **Audio Clips** of a talk by Wikipedia founder Jimmy Wales and of Charles Leadbeater talking about the power of the crowd in innovation are available on the Innovation Portal at **www.innovation-portal.info**

 Activities to help you try some of these prototyping tools are available on the Innovation Portal at **www.innovation-portal.info**

 Video Clips using the Honey Bee network in India and Blackstone Entrepreneur Networks as examples of these issues are available on the Innovation Portal at **www.innovation-portal.info**

 Case Studies of the NHS RED and Open Door projects, which made use of prototyping, are available on the Innovation Portal at **www.innovation-portal.info**

Additional Resources for Instructors

The authors have compiled an extensive range of resources to help lecturers teach their innovation and entrepreneurship courses including a teaching guide and course outline that provides a template for courses, seminars and assessments built around specific themes, together with linked media such as lecture slides, seminar exercises, cases, tools and assessments. There is also a comprehensive test bank and shorter quizzes to help test student understanding. All this material can also be accessed via the Innovation Portal at www.innovation-portal.info.

PART I

ENTREPRENEURIAL GOALS AND CONTEXT

The national, regional and sectoral contexts can have a significant influence on the rate and direction of innovation and entrepreneurship through the availability or scarcity of resources, talent, opportunities, infrastructure and support. However, while context influences the rate and direction, it does not determine outcomes. The education, training, experience and aptitude of individuals also have a profound effect on the goals and outcomes of innovation and entrepreneurship.

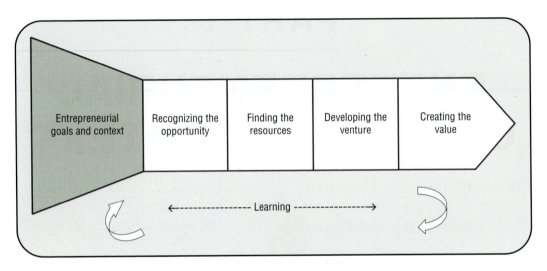

Chapter 1

The Innovation Imperative

LEARNING OBJECTIVES

By the end of this chapter you will develop an understanding of:

- what 'innovation' and 'entrepreneurship' mean – and how they are essential for survival and growth
- innovation as a process rather than a single flash of inspiration
- the difficulties in managing what is an uncertain and risky process
- the key themes in thinking about how to manage this process effectively.

Innovation Matters

You don't have to look far before you bump into the innovation imperative. It leaps out at you from a thousand mission statements and strategy documents, each stressing how important **innovation** is to 'our customers/our shareholders/our business/our future' and, most often, 'our survival and growth'. Innovation shouts at you from advertisements for products ranging from hairspray to hospital care. It nestles deep in the heart of our history books, pointing out how far and for how long it has shaped our lives. And it is on the lips of every politician, recognizing that our lifestyles are constantly shaped and reshaped by the process of innovation.

INNOVATION IN ACTION 1.1

Everybody's Talking about It

- 'We have the strongest innovation programme that I can remember in my 30-year career at P&G, and we are investing behind it to drive growth across our business' – Bob McDonald, Chairman, President and CEO, Procter & Gamble
- 'We believe in making a difference. Virgin stands for value for money, quality, innovation, fun and a sense of competitive challenge. We deliver a quality service by empowering our employees and we facilitate and monitor customer feedback to continually improve the customer's experience through innovation' – Virgin Life Care (http://www.virginlifecare.co.za/aboutus/aboutVirgin.aspx)
- 'Adi Dassler had a clear, simple, and unwavering passion for sport. Which is why with the benefit of 50 years of relentless innovation created in his spirit, we continue to stay at the forefront of technology' – Adidas (www.adidas.com)
- 'Innovation is our lifeblood' – Siemens (www.siemens.com)
- 'We're measuring GE's top leaders on how imaginative they are. Imaginative leaders are the ones who have the courage to fund new ideas, lead teams to discover better ideas, and lead people to take more educated risks' – J. Immelt, chairman and CEO, General Electric
- 'We are always saying to ourselves. We have to innovate. We've got to come up with that breakthrough' – Bill Gates, former chairman and CEO, Microsoft
- 'Innovation distinguishes between a leader and a follower' – Steve Jobs, co-founder and former chairman and CEO, Apple
- 'John Deere's ability to keep inventing new products that are useful to customers is still the key to the company's growth' – Robert Lane, CEO, John Deere

This isn't just hype or advertising babble. Innovation does make a huge difference to organizations of all shapes and sizes. The logic is simple: if we don't change what we offer the world (products and services) and how we create and deliver them, we risk being overtaken by others who do. At the limit it's about survival, and history is very clear on this point: survival is not compulsory! Those enterprises which survive do so because they are capable of regular and focused change. (It's worth noting that Bill Gates used to say of Microsoft that it was always only two years away from extinction. Or, as Andy Grove, one of the founders of Intel, pointed out, 'Only the paranoid survive!')

INNOVATION IN ACTION 1.2

...and It's a Big Issue

- OECD countries spend $1500 billion/yr on R&D.
- More than 16 000 firms in the USA currently operate their own industrial research labs, and there are at least 20 firms that have annual R&D budgets in excess of $1 billion.
- In 2008, 16.8% of all firms' turnover in Germany was earned with newly introduced products; in the research-intensive sector this figure was 38%. During the same year, the German economy was able to save costs of 3.9% per piece by means of process innovations.
- 'Companies that do not invest in innovation put their future at risk. Their business is unlikely to prosper, and they are unlikely to be able to compete if they do not seek innovative solutions to emerging problems' – Australian government website, 2006.
- 'Innovation is the motor of the modern economy, turning ideas and knowledge into products and services' – UK Office of Science and Technology, 2000.
- According to Statistics Canada, the following factors characterize successful small and medium-sized enterprises SMEs:
  - Innovation is consistently found to be the most important characteristic associated with success.
  - Innovative enterprises typically achieve stronger growth or are more successful than those that do not innovate.
  - Enterprises that gain market share and increasing profitability are those that are innovative.

On the plus side innovation is also strongly associated with growth. New business is created by new ideas, by the process of creating competitive advantage in what a firm can offer. Economists have argued for decades over the exact nature of the relationship but they are generally agreed that innovation accounts for a sizeable proportion of economic growth. William Baumol points out that 'virtually all of the economic growth that has occurred since the eighteenth century is ultimately attributable to innovation.'[1]

INNOVATION IN ACTION 1.3

Growth Champions and the Return from Innovation

Tim Jones has been studying successful innovating organizations for some time (see http://growthchampions.org/about-us/). His most recent work has built on this, looking to try to establish a link between those organizations which invest consistently in innovation and their

(continued)

Audio Clip of an interview with Tim Jones discussing the link between innovation and growth is available on the Innovation Portal at **www.innovation-portal.info**

subsequent performance.[2] His findings show that over a sustained period of time there is a strongly positive link between the two; innovative organizations are more profitable and more successful.

Survival and growth poses a problem for established players but a huge opportunity for newcomers to rewrite the rules of the game. One person's problem is another's opportunity and the nature of innovation is that it is fundamentally about **entrepreneurship**. The skill to spot opportunities and create new ways to exploit them is at the heart of the innovation process. Entrepreneurs are risk-takers, but they calculate the costs of taking a bright idea forward against the potential gains if they succeed in doing something different – especially if that involves upstaging the players already in the game.

INNOVATION IN ACTION 1.4

Global Innovation Performance

The consultancy Arthur D. Little conducts a regular survey of senior executives around the world exploring innovation.[3] In its 2012 survey of 650 organizations, the following emerged:

- Top quartile innovation performers obtain on average 13% more profit from new products and services than average performers do, and 30% shorter time-to-break-even, although the gap is narrowing.
- There is a clear correlation between capability in innovation measurement and innovation success.
- A number of key innovation management practices have a particularly strong impact on innovation performance across industries.

Of course, not all games are about win/lose outcomes. Public services like healthcare, education and social security may not generate profits but they do affect the quality of life for millions of people. Bright ideas when implemented well can lead to valued new services and the efficient delivery of existing ones at a time when pressure on national purse strings is becoming ever tighter. New ideas – whether wind-up radios in Tanzania or micro-credit financing schemes in Bangladesh – have the potential to change the quality of life and the availability of opportunity for people in some of the poorest regions of the world. There's plenty of scope for innovation and entrepreneurship and sometimes this really is about life and death. Table 1.1 gives some examples.

TABLE 1.1 Where innovation makes a difference

Innovation is about ….	Examples
Identifying or creating opportunities	Innovation is driven by the ability to see connections, to spot opportunities and to take advantage of them. Sometimes this is about completely new possibilities, for example by exploiting radical breakthroughs in technology. New drugs based on genetic manipulation have opened a major new front in the war against disease. Mobile phones, tablets and other devices have revolutionized where and when we communicate. Even the humble window pane is the result of radical technological innovation – almost all the window glass in the world is made these days by the Pilkington float glass process which moved the industry away from the time-consuming process of grinding and polishing to get a flat surface

Case Study of James Dyson and his innovation-led business is available on the Innovation Portal at **www.innovation-portal.info**

New ways of serving existing markets	Innovation isn't just about opening up new markets; it can also offer new ways of serving established and mature ones. Low-cost airlines are still about transportation, but the innovations firms like Southwest Airlines, easyJet and Ryanair have introduced have revolutionized air travel and grown the market in the process. Despite a global shift in textile and clothing manufacture towards developing countries, the Spanish company Inditex (through its retail outlets under various names, including Zara) has pioneered a highly flexible, fast turnaround clothing operation with over 2000 outlets in 52 countries. It was founded by Amancio Ortega Gaona, who set up a small operation in the west of Spain in La Coruña – a region not previously noted for textile production – and the first store opened there in 1975. The company now has over 5000 stores worldwide and is the world's biggest clothing retailer; significantly, it is also the only manufacturer to offer specific collections for northern and southern hemisphere markets. Central to the Inditex philosophy is close linkage between design, manufacture and retailing and its network of stores constantly feeds back information about trends, which are used to generate new designs. It also experiments with new ideas directly on the public, trying samples of cloth or design and quickly getting back indications of what is going to catch on. Despite its global orientation, most manufacturing is still done in Spain, and it has managed to reduce the turnaround time between a trigger signal for an innovation and responding to it to around 15 days

(continued)

TABLE 1.1   *(Continued)*

Innovation is about ….	Examples

Case Study of Zara and how it has used innovation around design and 'fast fashion' to create new opportunities in a crowded and mature marketplace is available on the Innovation Portal at **www.innovation-portal.info**

Growing new markets

Equally important is the ability to spot where and how new markets can be created and grown. Alexander Bell's invention of the telephone didn't lead to an overnight revolution in communications – that depended on developing the market for person-to-person communications. Henry Ford may not have invented the motor car but in making the Model T – 'a car for Everyman' at a price most people could afford – he grew the mass market for personal transportation. And eBay justifies its multi-billion-dollar price tag not because of the technology behind its online auction idea but because it created and grew the market

Case Study of the Model T Ford is available on the Innovation Portal at **www.innovation-portal.info**

Rethinking services

In most economies the service sector accounts for the vast majority of activity, so there is likely to be plenty of scope. And the lower capital costs often mean that the opportunities for new entrants and radical change are greatest in the service sector. Online banking and insurance have become commonplace but they have radically transformed the efficiencies with which those sectors work and the range of services they can provide. New entrants riding the Internet wave have rewritten the rule book for a wide range of industrial games, for example Amazon in retailing, eBay in market trading and auctions, Google in advertising and Skype in telephony

Case Study of Alibaba and the Taobao online shopping mall, one of the world's top ten most visited websites, is available on the Innovation Portal at **www.innovation-portal.info**

TABLE 1.1 *(Continued)*

Innovation is about ….	Examples
Meeting social needs	Innovation offers huge challenges – and opportunities – for the public sector. Pressure to deliver more and better services without increasing the tax burden is a puzzle likely to keep many civil servants awake at night. But it's not an impossible dream: right across the spectrum there are examples of innovation changing the way the sector works. For example, in healthcare there have been major improvements in efficiencies around key targets such as waiting times. Hospitals like the Leicester Royal Infirmary in the UK or the Karolinska Hospital in Stockholm, Sweden have managed to make radical improvements in the speed, quality and effectiveness of their care services, such as cutting waiting lists for elective surgery by 75% and cancellations by 80%, through innovation

Case Studies of innovation in public services, Karolinska Hospital, Aravind Eye Clinics and Narayana Hrudayalaya Hospitals (NHL), are available on the Innovation Portal at **www.innovation-portal.info**

Improving operations – doing what we do but better	At the other end of the scale Kumba Resources is a large South African mining company which makes another dramatic claim: 'We move mountains.' In Kumba's case, the mountains contain iron ore and the company's huge operations require large-scale excavation – and restitution of the landscape afterwards. Much of its business involves complex large-scale machinery – and its ability to keep it running and productive depends on a workforce able to contribute innovative ideas on a continuing basis

Case Study of Kumba's innovation activities is available on the Innovation Portal at **www.innovation-portal.info**

INNOVATION IN ACTION 1.5

Finding Opportunities

- When the Tasman Bridge collapsed in Hobart, Tasmania in 1975, Robert Clifford was running a small ferry company and saw an opportunity to capitalize on the increased demand

(continued)

for ferries – and to differentiate his by selling drinks to thirsty cross-city commuters. The same entrepreneurial flair later helped him build a company – Incat – that pioneered the wave-piercing design which helped the company capture over half the world market for fast catamaran ferries. Continuing investment in innovation has helped this company from a relatively isolated island build a key niche in highly competitive international military and civilian markets.

- 'We always eat elephants' is a surprising claim made by Carlos Broens, founder and head of a successful tool-making and precision engineering firm in Australia with an enviable growth record. Broens Industries is a small/medium-sized company of 130 employees which survives in a highly competitive world by exporting over 70% of its products and services to technologically demanding firms in aerospace, medical and other advanced markets. The quote doesn't refer to strange dietary habits but to the company's confidence in 'taking on the challenges normally seen as impossible for firms of our size' – a capability which is grounded in a culture of innovation in products and the processes that go to produce them.

- There has always been a need for artificial limbs and the demand has, sadly, significantly increased as a result of high-technology weaponry such as mines. The problem is compounded by the fact that many of those requiring new limbs are also in the poorest regions of the world and unable to afford expensive prosthetics. The chance meeting of a young surgeon, Dr Pramod Karan Sethi, and a sculptor, Ram Chandra, in a hospital in Jaipur, India has led to the development of a solution to this problem: the Jaipur Foot. This artificial limb was developed using Chandra's skill as a sculptor and Sethi's expertise and is so effective that those who wear it can run, climb trees and pedal bicycles. It was designed to make use of low-tech materials and be simple to assemble, for example in Afghanistan craftsmen hammer the foot together out of spent artillery shells, while in Cambodia part of the foot's rubber components are scavenged from truck tyres. Perhaps the greatest achievement has been to do all of this for a low cost: the Jaipur Foot costs only $28 in India. Since 1975, nearly one million people worldwide have been fitted for the Jaipur limb and the design is being developed and refined, for example using advanced new materials.

- Not all innovation is necessarily good for everyone. One of the most vibrant entrepreneurial communities is in the criminal world where there is a constant search for new ways of committing crime without being caught. The race between the forces of crime and law and order is a powerful innovation arena – as work by Howard Rush and colleagues have shown in their studies of cybercrime.

 Case Study detailing a report on cybercrime is available on the Innovation Portal at **www.innovation-portal.info**

Innovation and Entrepreneurship

Innovation matters – but it doesn't happen automatically. It is driven by entrepreneurship – a potent mixture of vision, passion, energy, enthusiasm, insight, judgement and plain hard work which enables good ideas to become reality. The power behind changing products, processes and services comes from individuals – whether acting alone or embedded within organizations – who make innovation happen. As the famous management writer Peter Drucker put it:[4]

> Innovation is the specific tool of entrepreneurs, the means by which they exploit change as an opportunity for a different business or service. It is capable of being presented as a discipline, capable of being learned, capable of being practised.

INNOVATION IN ACTION 1.6

Joseph Schumpeter

One of the most significant figures in this area of economic theory was Joseph Schumpeter, who wrote extensively on the subject. He had a distinguished career as an economist and served as Minister for Finance in the Austrian government. His argument was simple: entrepreneurs will seek to use technological innovation – a new product/service or a new process for making it – to get strategic advantage. For a while, this may be the only example of the innovation so the entrepreneur can expect to make a lot of money – what Schumpeter calls 'monopoly profits'. But of course, other entrepreneurs will see what he has done and try to imitate it – with the result that other innovations emerge, and the resulting 'swarm' of new ideas chips away at the monopoly profits until an equilibrium is reached. At this point the cycle repeats itself: our original entrepreneur or someone else looks for the next innovation that will rewrite the rules of the game, and off we go again. Schumpeter talks of a process of 'creative destruction', where there is a constant search to create something new which simultaneously destroys the old rules and establishes new ones – all driven by the search for new sources of profits.

In his view '[what counts is] competition from the new commodity, the new technology, the new source of supply, the new type of organization … competition which … strikes not at the margins of the profits and the outputs of the existing firms but at their foundations and their very lives.'[5]

Entrepreneurship plays out on different stages in practice. One obvious example is the start-up venture in which the lone entrepreneur takes a calculated risk to bring something new into the world. But entrepreneurship matters just as much to the established organization which needs to renew itself in what it offers and how it creates and delivers that offering. Internal entrepreneurs – often labelled as 'intrapreneurs' or working in 'corporate entrepreneurship' or 'corporate venture' departments – provide the drive, energy and vision to take risky new ideas forward within that context.[6] And of course, the passion to change things may not be focused on creating commercial value but rather on improving conditions or enabling change in the wider social sphere or in the direction of environmental sustainability – a field which has become known as 'social entrepreneurship' (see Chapter 2).

This idea of entrepreneurship driving innovation to create value – social and commercial – across the lifecycle of organizations is central to this book. Table 1.2 gives some examples.

In the rest of the book, we use this lens to look at managing innovation and entrepreneurship. We'll use three core concepts:

- **innovation.** As a process which can be organized and managed, whether in a start-up venture or in renewing a 100-year-old business
- **entrepreneurship.** As the motive power to drive this process through the efforts of passionate individuals, engaged teams and focused networks
- **creating value.** As the purpose for innovation, whether expressed in financial terms, employment or growth, sustainability or improvement of social welfare.

TABLE 1.2   Entrepreneurship and innovation

Stage in lifecycle of an organization	Start-up	Growth	Sustain/scale	Renew
Creating commercial value	Individual entrepreneur exploiting new technology or market opportunity	Growing the business through adding new products/services or moving into new markets	Building a portfolio of incremental and radical innovation to sustain the business and/or spread its influence into new markets	Returning to the radical frame-breaking kind of innovation which began the business and enables it to move forward as something very different
Creating social value	Social entrepreneur, passionately concerned to improve or change something in their immediate environment	Developing the ideas and engaging others in a network for change – perhaps in a region or around a key issue	Spreading the idea widely, diffusing it to other communities of social entrepreneurs, engaging links with main-stream players like public sector agencies	Changing the system – and then acting as agent for the next wave of change

Innovation Isn't Easy!

Coming up with good ideas is what human beings are good at – we have this facility already fitted as standard equipment in our brains! But taking those ideas forward is not quite so simple, and most new ideas fail. It takes a particular mix of energy, insight, belief and determination to push against these odds; it also requires judgement to know when to stop banging against the brick wall and move on to something else.

It's important here to remember a key point: new ventures often fail, but it is the ventures which are failures rather than the people who launched them. Successful entrepreneurs recognize that failure is an intrinsic part of the process. They learn from their mistakes, understanding where and when timing, market conditions, technological uncertainties, etc. mean that even a great idea isn't going to work. But they also recognize that the idea may have had its weaknesses but that they have not failed themselves but rather learnt some useful insights to carry over to their next venture.

INNOVATION IN ACTION 1.7

Failure Breeds Success

Thomas Edison was a pretty successful entrepreneur with over 1000 patents to his name and the reputation for bringing many key technologies into widespread use, including the phonograph, the electric telegraph and the light bulb; he also founded the General Electric Company, which is still a major player today. He is famous for his attitude towards failure, typified by the search for the right material to make the filament for his incandescent light bulb, where he explored over 1000 different options. He is reported as having said that the process did not involve failure so much as 'the elimination of a design that didn't work, so we must be getting close'.

While the road for an individual entrepreneur may be very rocky with a high risk of hitting potholes, running into roadblocks or careering off the edge, it doesn't get any easier if you are a large established company. It's a disturbing thought but the majority of companies have a lifespan significantly less than that of a human being. Even the largest firms can show worrying signs of vulnerability, and for the smaller firm the mortality statistics are bleak.

Many SMEs fail because they don't see or recognize the need for change. They are inward looking, too busy fighting fires and dealing with today's crises to worry about storm clouds on the horizon. Even if they do talk to others about the wider issues, it is very often to people in the same network and with the same perspectives, for example the people who supply them with goods and services or their immediate customers. The trouble is that by the time they realize there is a need to change it may be too late.

But it isn't just a small firm problem. There is no guaranteed security in size or in previous technological success. Take the case of IBM – a giant firm which can justly claim to have laid the foundations of the IT industry and came to dominate the architecture of hardware and software and the ways in which computers were marketed. But such core strength can sometimes become an obstacle to seeing the need for change – as proved to be the case when, in the early 1990s, the company moved too slowly to counter the threat of networking technologies – and nearly lost the business in the process. Thousands of jobs and billions of dollars were lost and it took years of hard work to bring the share price back to the high levels which investors had come to expect.

One problem for successful companies occurs when the very things which helped them achieve success – their 'core competencies' – become the things which make it hard to see or accept the need for change. Sometimes the response is 'not invented here': the new idea is recognized as good but in some way not suited to the business.

INNOVATION IN ACTION 1.8

The 'Not Invented Here' Problem

A famous example of 'not invented here' was the case of Western Union, which, in the 19th century, was probably the biggest communications company in the world. It was approached by one Alexander Graham Bell, who wanted the company to consider helping him commercialize his new invention. After mounting a demonstration to senior executives, he received a written reply which said, 'after careful consideration of your invention, which is a very interesting novelty, we have come to the conclusion that it has no commercial possibilities … We see no future for an electrical toy.' Within four years of the invention, there were 50 000 telephones in the USA and within 20 years five million. Over the next 20 years, the company which Bell formed grew to become the largest corporation in the USA.

Sometimes the pace of change appears slow and the old responses seem to work well. It appears, to those within the industry that they understand the rules of the game and have a good grasp of the relevant technological developments likely to change things. But what can sometimes happen here is that change comes along from *outside* the industry – and by the time the main players inside have reacted it is often too late.

INNOVATION IN ACTION 1.9

The Melting of the Ice Industry

In the late 19th century, there was a thriving industry in New England based upon the harvesting and distribution of ice. In its heyday, it was possible for ice harvesters to ship hundreds of tons of ice around the world on voyages that lasted as long as six months – and still have over half the cargo available for sale. By the late 1870s, the 14 major firms in the Boston area of the USA were cutting around 700 000 tons per year and employing several thousand people. But the industry was completely overthrown by the new developments which followed from the invention of refrigeration and the growth of the modern cold storage industry.

Case Study of the ice industry is available on the Innovation Portal at **www.innovation-portal.info**

Of course, for others these conditions provide an opportunity for moving ahead of the game and writing a new set of rules. Think about what has happened in online banking, call-centre-linked insurance or low-cost airlines. In each case, the existing stable pattern has been overthrown, disrupted by new entrants coming in with new and challenging business models. For many managers business model innovation is seen as the biggest threat to their competitive position, precisely because they need to learn to let go of their old models as well as learn new ones. We also need to see that while for established organizations these crises are a problem, they represent a rich source of opportunity for entrepreneurs looking to disrupt an established order and create value in new ways.

In many cases the individual enterprise can renew itself, adapting to its environment and moving into new things. Consider the example of the Stora company in Sweden: founded in the 13th century as a timber cutting and processing operation it still thrives today – albeit in the very different areas of food processing and electronics.

Case Study of how innovation has helped a 100-year-old company, Marshalls, develop and grow is available on the Innovation Portal at **www.innovation-portal.info**

All of these examples point to the same conclusion. Organizations need entrepreneurship at all stages in their lifecycle, from start-up to long-lived survival. The ability to recognize opportunities, pull resources together in creative ways, implement good ideas and capture the value from them are core skills.

Managing Innovation and Entrepreneurship

The dictionary defines 'innovation' as 'change'; it comes from Latin *in* and *novare*, meaning 'to make something new'. That's a bit vague if we're trying to manage it; perhaps a more useful definition would be 'the successful exploitation of new ideas'. Those ideas don't necessarily have to be completely new to the world, or particularly radical; as one definition has it: 'innovation does not necessarily imply the commercialization of only a major advance in the technological state of the art (a **radical innovation**) but it includes also the utilization of even small-scale changes in technological know-how (an improvement or **incremental innovation**).'[7] Whatever the nature of the change the key issue is how to bring it about, in other words how to *manage* innovation.

Can we do it? One answer comes from the experiences of organizations that have survived for an extended period of time. While most organizations have comparatively modest lifespans, some have survived at least one and sometimes multiple centuries. Looking at the experience of these '100 club' members – firms like 3M, Corning, Procter and Gamble, Reuters,

Siemens, Philips and Rolls-Royce – we can see that much of their longevity is down to having developed a capacity to innovate on a continuing basis. They have learnt, often the hard way, how to manage the process and, importantly, how to repeat the trick. Any organization can get lucky once but sustaining it for a century or more suggests there's a bit more to it than that.

Case Studies about long-term innovation success in businesses, 3M, Corning and Philips Lighting, are available on the Innovation Portal at **www.innovation-portal.info**

It's the same with individuals: 'serial entrepreneurs' may start many different businesses and what they bring to the party is an accumulated understanding of how to do it better. They have learnt and built long-term capability into a robust set of skills.

Over the past hundred years, there have been many attempts to answer the question of whether we can manage innovation. Researchers have looked at case examples, at sectors, at entrepreneurs, at big firms and small firms, at success and failure. Practising entrepreneurs and innovation managers in large businesses have tried to reflect on the 'how' of what they do. The key messages come from the world of experience. What we've learnt comes from the laboratory of practice rather than some deeply rooted theory.

The key messages from this knowledge base are that successful innovators:

- explore and understand different dimensions of innovation (ways in which we can change things)
- manage innovation as a process
- create conditions to enable them to repeat the innovation trick (building capability)
- focus this capability to move their organizations forward (innovation strategy)
- build dynamic capability (the ability to rest and adapt their approaches in the face of a changing environment).

In the following sections we'll explore each of these themes in a little more detail.

Dimensions of Innovation: What Can We Change?

One approach to finding an answer to the question of where we could innovate is to use a kind of 'innovation compass' exploring different possible directions.

Innovation can take many forms but we can map the options along four dimensions, as shown in Table 1.3.

TABLE 1.3 Dimensions for innovation[8]

Dimension	Type of change
Product	Changes in the things (products/services) an organization offers
Process	Changes in the ways these offerings are created and delivered
Position	Changes in the context into which the products/services are introduced
Paradigm	Changes in the underlying mental models which frame what the organization does

For example, a new design of car, a new insurance package for accident-prone babies and a new home-entertainment system would all be examples of product innovation. And change in the manufacturing methods and equipment used to produce the car or the home-entertainment system, or in the office procedures and sequencing in the insurance case, would be examples of process innovation.

Sometimes the dividing line is somewhat blurred. For example, a new jet-powered sea ferry is both a product and a process innovation. Services represent a particular case of this where the product and process aspects often merge. For example, is a new holiday package a product or process change?

Innovation can also take place by repositioning the perception of an established product or process in a particular user context. For example, an old-established product in the UK is Lucozade, originally developed as a glucose-based drink to help children and invalids in convalescence. These associations with sickness were abandoned by the brand owner, Beechams (part of GlaxoSmithKline), when it relaunched the product as a health drink aimed at the growing fitness market, where it is now presented as a performance-enhancing aid to healthy exercise. In 2014, the brand was sold to Suntory for around $1.35bn. This shift is a good example of 'position' innovation. In similar fashion Häagen Dazs created a new market for ice cream, essentially targeted at adults, through position innovation rather than changing the product or core manufacturing process.

Sometimes opportunities for innovation emerge when we reframe the way we look at something. Henry Ford fundamentally changed the face of transportation not because he invented the motor car (he was a comparative latecomer to the new industry) or because he developed the manufacturing process to put one together (as a craft-based specialist industry car-making had been established for around 20 years). His contribution was to change the underlying model from one which offered a hand-made specialist product to a few wealthy customers to one which offered a car for Everyman at a price he could afford. The ensuing shift from craft to mass production was nothing short of a revolution in the way cars (and later countless other products and services) were created and delivered. Of course, making the new approach work in practice also required

Video Clip about the Model T Ford is available on the Innovation Portal at **www.innovation-portal.info**

extensive product and process innovation, for example in component design, in machinery building, in factory layout and particularly in the social system around which work was organized.

Examples of 'paradigm' innovation – changes in mental models – include the shift to low-cost airlines, the provision of online insurance and other financial services and the repositioning of drinks like coffee and fruit juice as premium 'designer' products. They involve a shift in the underlying vision about how innovation can create social or commercial value. The term 'business model' is increasingly used and this is another way of thinking about 'paradigm innovation'. We explore this theme in detail in Chapter 16.

Table 1.4 gives some examples of paradigm innovation.

TABLE 1.4   Examples of paradigm innovation

Business model innovation	How it changes the rules of the game
'Servitization'	Traditionally, manufacturing was about producing and then selling a product. But, increasingly, manufacturers are bundling various support services around their products, particularly for major capital goods. Rolls-Royce, the aircraft engine maker, still produces high-quality engines but it has an increasingly large business around services to ensure those engines keep delivering power over the 30-plus-year life of many aircraft. Caterpillar, the specialist machinery company, now earns as much from service contracts, which help keep its machines running productively, as it does from the original sale
Ownership to rental	Spotify is one of the most successful music-streaming companies with around eight million subscribers. It shifted the model from people's desire to own the music they listened to towards one in which they rented access to a huge library of music. In similar fashion, Zipcar and other car rental businesses have transformed the need for car ownership in many large cities
Offline to online	Many businesses have grown up around the Internet and enabled substitution of physical encounters, for example in retailing, with virtual ones
Mass customization and co-creation	New technologies and a growing desire for customization have enabled the emergence not only of personalized products but platforms on which users can engage and co-create everything from toys (e.g. Lego), clothing (e.g. Adidas) to complex equipment like cars (Local Motors).

TABLE 1.4 *(Continued)*

Business model innovation	How it changes the rules of the game
	Case Studies of these companies are available on the Innovation Portal at **www.innovation-portal.info**
Experience innovation	Moving from commodity through offering a service towards creating an experience around a core product, for example Starbucks making a coffee shop into a place where people can meet and chat, use Wi-Fi, read books and do a host of activities as well as buy and drink coffee.

Paradigm innovation can be triggered by many different things: new technologies, the emergence of new markets with different value expectations, new legal rules of the game, new environmental conditions (climate change, energy crises), etc. For example, the emergence of Internet technologies made possible a complete reframing of how we carry out many businesses. In the past, similar revolutions in thinking were triggered by technologies like steam power, electricity, mass transportation (via railways and, with motor cars, roads) and microelectronics. And it seems very likely that similar reframing will happen as we get to grips with new technologies like nanotechnology or genetic engineering.

Video Clip of Finnegan's Fish Bar showing the ideas around 4Ps model applied to a simple food business is available on the Innovation Portal at **www.innovation-portal.info**

Tool to help you explore the 4Ps approach is available on the Innovation Portal at **www.innovation-portal.info**

From Incremental to Radical Innovation...

Another thing to think about is the degree of novelty involved. Clearly, updating the styling on our car is not the same as coming up with a completely new concept car which has an electric engine and is made of new composite materials as opposed to steel and glass. Similarly, increasing the speed and accuracy of a lathe is not the same thing

Activities to explore incremental and radical innovation are available on the Innovation Portal at **www.innovation-portal.info**

as replacing it with a computer-controlled laser forming process. There are degrees of novelty in these, running from minor, incremental improvements right through to radical changes, which transform the way we think about and use them. Sometimes these changes are common to a particular sector or activity, but sometimes they are so radical and far-reaching that they change the basis of society, for example the role played by steam power in the Industrial Revolution or the ubiquitous changes resulting from today's communications and computing technologies.

...to Components and Systems

Innovation is often like a set of Russian dolls: we can change things at the level of components or we can change a whole system. For example, we can put a faster transistor on a microchip on a circuit board for the graphics display in a computer. Or we can change the way several boards are put together into the computer to give it particular capabilities – a games box, an e-book, a media PC. Or we can link the computers into a network to drive a small business or office. Or we can link the networks to others into the Internet. There's scope for innovation at each level – but changes in the higher-level systems often have implications for lower down. For example, if cars, as a complex assembly, were suddenly designed to be made out of plastic instead of metal, it would still leave scope for car assemblers but would pose some sleepless nights for producers of metal components!

Figure 1.1 illustrates the range of choices, highlighting the point that such change can happen at the component or sub-system level or across the whole system.

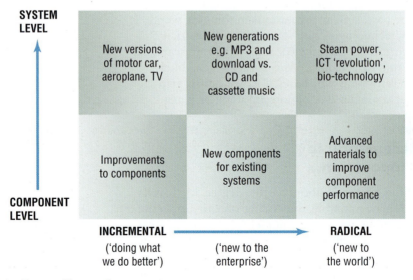

FIGURE 1.1 Types of innovation

A Process Model for Innovation and Entrepreneurship

Rather than the cartoon image of a light bulb flashing on above someone's head, we need to think about innovation as an extended sequence of activities – as a process. Whether we are looking at an individual entrepreneur bringing their idea into action or a multi-million-dollar corporation launching the latest in a stream of new products, the same basic framework applies.

We can break it down to the four key steps we mentioned earlier:

- recognizing the opportunity
- finding the resources
- developing the idea
- capturing value.

Figure 1.2 illustrates this model.

Recognizing the Opportunity

Innovation triggers come in all shapes and sizes and from all sorts of directions. They could take the form of new technological opportunities or changing requirements on the part of markets. They could be the result of legislative pressure or competitor action. They could be a bright idea occurring to someone as they sit, Archimedes-like, in their bathtub. They could come as a result of buying in a good idea from someone outside the organization. Or they could arise from dissatisfaction with social conditions or a desire to make the world a better place in some way.

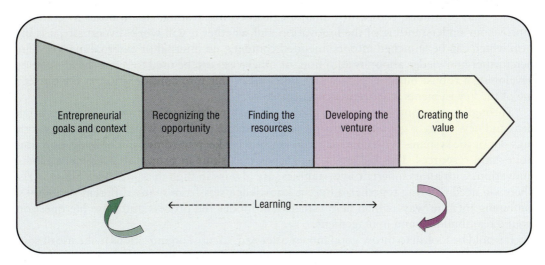

FIGURE 1.2   A model of the entrepreneurial process

The message here is clear: if we are going to pick up these trigger signals then we need to develop some pretty extensive antennae for searching and scanning around us – and that includes some capability for looking into the future.

Finding the Resources

The trouble with innovation is that it is by its nature a risky business. You don't know at the outset whether what you decide to do is going to work out or even that it will run at all. Yet you have to commit some resources to begin the process. So how do you build a portfolio of projects which balance the risks and the potential rewards? (Of course, this decision is even tougher for the first-time entrepreneur trying to launch a business based on his or her great new idea – the choice there is whether to go forward and commit what may be a huge investment of personal time, the mortgage, family life, etc. Even if they succeed, there is then the problem of trying to grow the business and needing to develop more good ideas to follow the first.)

So this stage is very much about *strategic* choices. Does the idea fit a business strategy, does it build on something we know about (or where we can get access to that knowledge easily) and do we have the skills and resources to take it forward? And if we don't have those resources, which is often the case with the lone entrepreneur at start-up, how will we find and mobilize them?

Developing the Idea

Having picked up relevant trigger signals, made a strategic decision to pursue some of them and found and mobilized the resources we need, the next key phase is actually turning those potential ideas into some kind of reality. In some ways this implementation phase is a bit like making a kind of 'knowledge tapestry', by gradually weaving the different threads of knowledge (about technologies, markets, competitor behaviour, etc.) into a successful innovation.

Early on it is full of uncertainty but gradually the picture becomes clearer – but at a cost. We have to invest time and money and find people to research and develop ideas and conduct market studies, competitor analysis, prototyping, testing, etc. in order to gradually improve our understanding of the innovation and whether it will work. Eventually, it is in a form which can be launched into its intended context – an internal or external market – and then further knowledge about its adoption (or otherwise) can be used to refine the innovation. Developing a robust business plan which takes all of this into consideration at the outset is one of the key elements in entrepreneurial success.

Throughout this implementation phase, we have to balance creativity – finding bright ideas and new ways to get around the thousand and one problems which emerge and get the bugs out of the system – with control – making sure we keep to some kind of budget on time, money and resources. This balancing act means that skills in project management around innovation, with all its inherent uncertainties, are always in high demand! This phase is also where we need to bring together different knowledge sets from many different people – so combining them in ways which help rather than hinder the process and raise big questions around teambuilding and management.

It would be foolish to throw good money after bad, so most organizations make use of some kind of risk management as they implement innovation projects. By installing a series of 'gates' as the project moves from a gleam in the eye to an expensive commitment of time and money, it becomes possible to review and if necessary redirect or even stop something which is going off the rails. For the solo entrepreneur it is in this stage that judgement is needed – and sometimes the courage to know when to stop and move on, to let go and start again on something else.

Eventually, the project is launched into some kind of marketplace: externally, people who might use the product or service or, internally, people who make the choice about whether to buy into the new process being presented to them. Either way, we don't have a guarantee that just because the innovation works and we think it the best thing since sliced bread they will feel the same way. Innovations diffuse across user populations over time. Usually, the process follows some kind of S-curve shape. A few brave souls take on the new idea and then gradually, assuming it works for them, others get on the bandwagon until finally there are just a few diehards (laggards) who resist the temptation to change. Managing this stage well means we need to think ahead about how people are likely to react and build these insights into our project before we reach the launch stage – or else work hard at persuading them after we have launched it!

Capture Value

Despite all our efforts in recognizing opportunities, finding resources and developing the venture, there is no guarantee we will be able to capture the value from all our hard work. We also need to think about, and manage, the process to maximize our chances – through protecting our intellectual property and the financial returns if we are engaged in commercial innovation or in scaling and spreading our ideas for social change so that they are sustainable and really do make a difference. We also have an opportunity at the end of an innovation project to look back and reflect on what we have learnt and how that knowledge could help us do things better next time. In other words, we could capture valuable learning about how to build our innovation capability.

The Context of Success

It's all very well putting a basic process for turning ideas into reality in place. But it doesn't take place in a vacuum. It is subject to a range of internal and external influences that shape what is possible and what actually emerges. This process doesn't take place in a vacuum; it is shaped and influenced by a variety of factors. In particular, innovation needs:

- *Clear strategic leadership and direction*, plus the commitment of resources to make this happen. Innovation is about taking risks, about going into new and sometimes completely unexplored spaces. We don't want to gamble, simply changing things for their own sake or because the fancy takes us. No organization has resources to waste in that scattergun fashion: innovation needs a strategy. But, equally, we need to have a degree of courage and leadership, steering the organization away from what everyone else is doing or what we've always done and towards new spaces.

   In the case of the individual entrepreneur this challenge translates to one in which a clear personal vision can be shared in ways which engage and motivate others to buy into it and to contribute their time, energy, money, etc. to help make it happen. Without a compelling vision, it is unlikely the venture will get off the ground.

- *An innovative organization* in which the structure and climate enables people to deploy their creativity and share their knowledge to bring about change. It's easy to find prescriptions for innovative organizations which highlight the need to eliminate stifling bureaucracy, unhelpful structures, brick walls blocking communication and other factors stopping good ideas getting through. But we must be careful not to fall into the chaos trap. Not all innovation works in organic, loose, informal environments or 'skunk works'; indeed, these types of organization can sometimes act against the interests of successful innovation. We need to determine appropriate organization, that is the most suitable organization given the operating contingencies. Too little order and structure may be as bad as too much.

This is one area where start-ups often have a major advantage – by definition they are small organizations (often one-person ventures) with a high degree of communication and cohesion. They are bound together by a shared vision and they have high levels of cooperation and trust, giving them enormous flexibility. But the downside of being small is a lack of resources, and so successful start-ups are very often those which can build a network around them through which they can tap into the key resources they need. Building and managing such networks is a key factor in creating an extended form of organization.

- *Proactive links* across boundaries inside the organization and to the many external agencies who can play a part in the innovation process: suppliers, customers, sources of finance, skilled resources and of knowledge, etc. Twenty-first-century innovation is most certainly not a solo act but a multiplayer game across boundaries inside the organization and to the many external agencies who can play a part in the innovation process. These days it's about a global game and one where connections and the ability to find, form and deploy creative relationships is of the essence. Once again, this idea of successful lone entrepreneurs and small-scale start-ups as network builders is critical. It's not necessary to know or have everything to hand but to know where and how to get it.

Figure 1.3 shows the resulting model: what we need to pay attention to if we are going to manage innovation well.

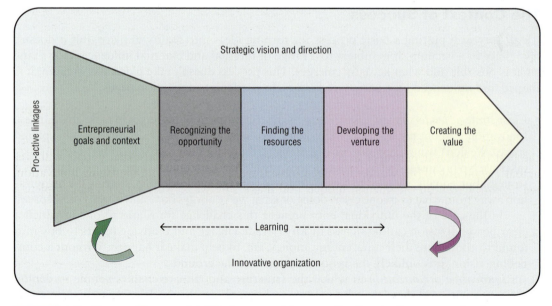

FIGURE 1.3   The resulting model: What we need to pay attention to if we are going to manage innovation well

How Can We Make Change Happen?

What are the actions involved in innovation and how can we use this understanding to help us manage the process better? What comes into our minds when we think of innovation taking place?

INNOVATION IN ACTION 1.10

Making Ideas Happen

If someone asked you, 'When did you last use your Spengler?' they might well be greeted by a quizzical look. But if they asked you when you last used your 'Hoover', the answer would be fairly easy. Yet it was not Mr Hoover who invented the vacuum cleaner in the late 19th century but one J. Murray Spengler. Hoover's genius lay in taking that idea and making it a commercial reality. In similar vein, the father of the modern sewing machine was not Mr Singer, whose name jumps to mind and is emblazoned on millions of machines all round the world. It was Elias Howe, who invented the machine in 1846 and Singer who brought it to technical and commercial fruition. Perhaps the godfather of them all in terms of turning ideas into reality was Thomas Edison, who during his life registered over 1000 patents. Products for which his organization was responsible include the light bulb, 35mm cinema film and even the electric chair. Many of the inventions for which he is famous weren't in fact invented by him – the electric light bulb, for example – but were developed and polished technically and their markets opened up by Edison and his team. More than anyone else Edison understood that invention is not enough – simply having a good idea is not going to lead to its widespread adoption and use.

One of the problems we have in managing anything is that how we think about it shapes what we do about it. So if we have a simplistic model of how innovation works, for example that it's just about **invention**, that's what we will organize and manage. We may end up with the best invention department in the world, but there is no guarantee that people will ever actually want any of our wonderful inventions! If we are serious about managing innovation, we need to check on our mental models and make sure we're working with as complete a picture as possible. Otherwise, we run risks like those in Table 1.5.

Configuring the Innovation Process: Building Capability

Whatever their size or sector, all organizations are trying to find ways of managing this process of growth and renewal. There is no right answer: every organization needs to aim for the most appropriate solution for its particular circumstances. They develop their own particular ways of doing things and some work better than others. Any organization can get lucky once but the real skill in innovation management is being able to repeat the trick. And while there

TABLE 1.5   The problem with partial models

If innovation is only seen as...	...the result can be
Strong R&D capability	Technology which fails to meet user needs and may not be accepted: 'the better mousetrap nobody wants'
The province of specialists in white coats in the R&D laboratory	Lack of involvement of others, and a lack of key knowledge and experience input from other perspectives
Meeting customer needs	Lack of technical progression, leading to inability to gain competitive edge
Technological advances	Producing products the market does not want or designing processes which do not meet the needs of the user and are opposed
The province of large firms	Weak small firms with too high a dependence on large customers
Breakthrough changes	Neglect of the potential of incremental innovation. Also an inability to secure and reinforce the gains from radical change because the incremental performance ratchet is not working well
Associated with key individuals	Failure to utilize the creativity of the remainder of employees, and to secure their inputs and perspectives to improve innovation
Internally generated	The 'not invented here' effect, where good ideas from outside are resisted or rejected
Externally generated	Innovation becomes simply a matter of filling a shopping list of needs from outside and there is little internal learning or development of technological competence

are no guarantees, there is plenty of evidence to suggest that firms can and do learn to manage the process for success, by consciously building and developing their innovation capability.

These issues apply across the board, though solutions to them may take us in different directions depending on where we start from. A start-up business may not need much in the way of a formal and structured process for organizing and managing innovation. But a firm the size of Nokia will need to pay careful attention to structures and procedures for building a strategic portfolio of projects to explore and for managing the risks as the project moves from ideas into technical and commercial reality. Equally, a large firm may have extensive resources to build a global set of networks to support its activities, whereas a start-up may be vulnerable to threats from elements in its environment it simply didn't know about, never mind being connected to.

This core process runs through any successful innovation, from a lone entrepreneur right up to IBM or GlaxoSmithKline. Of course, making the model work in practice requires configuring it for different situations, for example in a large company 'recognizing the opportunity' may involve a large R&D department, a market research team, a design studio, etc., whereas all of this could go on in a lone entrepreneur's head. Finding the resources may involve bringing different departments together in a large organization, but a lone innovator will have to create networks. Attracting support may involve a lone entrepreneur making a pitch to venture capitalists, whereas in a large organization the business case may be put to a monthly project portfolio meeting.

Allowing for the fact that we will organize and manage in different ways depending on different kinds of organizations, it is still possible to identify some generic recipes or conditions that help the innovation process to happen effectively. As we mentioned earlier, there has been plenty of research around this question and the Further Reading and Resources section at the end of the chapter lists some good examples of these studies. But one of the most important points to make at the outset is that organizations and individuals aren't born with the capability to organize and manage this process: they learn and develop it over time, and mainly through a process of trial and error. They hang on to what works and develop their capabilities in that – and they try to drop those things which don't work.

For example, successful innovation correlates strongly with how a firm selects and manages projects, how it coordinates the inputs of different functions, how it links up with its customers, etc. Successful innovators acquire and accumulate technical resources and managerial capabilities over time; there are plenty of opportunities for learning – through doing, using, working with other firms, asking the customers, etc. – but they all depend upon the readiness of the organization to see innovation less as a lottery than as a process which can be continuously improved.

Another critical point to emerge from research is that innovation needs managing in an *integrated* way; it is not enough just to be good at one thing. It's less like running a 100-metre sprint than developing the range of skills to compete effectively in a range of events in the pentathlon.

Tool to help you assess areas where an organization may need to improve its innovation management capability, the Innovation Fitness Test, is available on the Innovation Portal at **www.innovation-portal.info**

What, Why and When: The Challenge of Innovation Strategy

Building a capability to organize and manage innovation is a great achievement, but unless that capability is pointed in a suitable direction the organization risks being all dressed up with nowhere to go! And for entrepreneurs starting a new venture the challenge is even greater: without a clear sense of direction, a vision you can share with others to excite and focus them, the whole thing may never take off.

So the last theme we need to consider is where and how innovation can be used to strategic advantage. Table 1.6 gives some examples of the different ways in which this can be achieved, and you may like to add your own ideas to the list.

Activity to explore this theme, strategic advantage through innovation, is available on the Innovation Portal at **www.innovation-portal.info**

TABLE 1.6   Strategic advantages through innovation

Mechanism	Strategic advantage	Examples
Novelty in product or service offering	Offering something no one else can	Introducing the first (Walkman, fountain pen, camera, dishwasher, telephone bank, online retailer, etc.) to the world
Novelty in process	Offering it in ways others cannot match – faster, cheaper, more customized, etc.	Pilkington's float glass process, Bessemer's steel process, Internet banking, online bookselling, etc.
Complexity	Offering something others find difficult to master	Rolls-Royce and aircraft engines (only a handful of competitors can master the complex machining and metallurgy involved)
Legal protection of intellectual property	Offering something others cannot do unless they pay a licence or other fee	Blockbuster drugs like Zantac, Prozac, Viagra, etc.
Add/extend range of competitive factors	Move basis of competition (e.g. from price of product to price and quality, or price, quality, choice)	Japanese car manufacturing, which systematically moved the competitive agenda from price to quality, to flexibility and choice, to shorter times between launch of new models, and so on – each time not trading these off against each other but offering them all
Timing	First-mover advantage (being first can be worth significant market share in new product fields)	Amazon.com, Yahoo – others can follow, but the advantage sticks to the early movers
	Fast-follower advantage (sometimes being first means you encounter many unexpected teething problems, and it makes better sense to watch someone else make the early mistakes and move fast into a follow-up product)	Personal digital assistants (iPads) and smartphones have captured a huge and growing share of the market. In fact, the concept and design were articulated in Apple's ill-fated Newton product some five years before Palm launched its successful Pilot range – but problems with software and especially handwriting recognition meant it flopped. By contrast, Apple's success with iPod as an MP3 player came because it was quite late into the market and could learn and include key features into its dominant design

TABLE 1.6 (*Continued*)

Mechanism	Strategic advantage	Examples
Robust/platform design	Offering something which provides the platform on which other variations and generations can be built	Sony's original Walkman architecture which has spawned several generations of personal audio equipment (minidisk, CD, DVD, MP3, iPod)
		Boeing 737 (over 30 years old, the design is still being adapted and configured to suit different users) remains one of the most successful aircraft in the world in terms of sales
		Intel and AMD with different variants of their microprocessor families
Rewriting the rules	Offering something which represents a completely new product or process concept – a different way of doing things – and makes the old ones redundant	Typewriters vs. computer word processing, ice vs. refrigerators, electric vs. gas or oil lamps
Reconfiguring the parts of the process	Rethinking the way in which bits of the system work together (e.g. building more effective networks, outsourcing and coordination of a virtual company)	Zara and Benetton in clothing, Dell in computers, Toyota in its supply chain management
Transferring across different application contexts	Recombining established elements for different markets	Polycarbonate wheels transferred from application market like rolling luggage into children's toys – lightweight micro-scooters
Others	Innovation is all about finding new ways to do things and to obtain strategic advantage – so there will be room for new ways of gaining and retaining advantage	Napster began by writing software which would enable music fans to swap their favourite pieces via the Internet – the Napster program essentially connected person-to-person by providing a fast link. Its potential to change the architecture and mode of operation of the Internet was much greater, and although Napster suffered from legal issues followers developed a huge industry based on downloading and file sharing

The problem isn't the shortage of ways of gaining competitive advantage through innovation but rather which ones to choose and why. It's a decision all organizations have to take, be it a start-up deciding the (relatively) simple question of go/no go in terms of trying to enter a hostile marketplace with its new idea or a giant firm trying to open up new market space through innovation. And it's not just about commercial competition. The same idea of strategic advantage plays out in public services and social innovation. For example, police forces need to think strategically about how to deploy scarce resources to contain crime and maintain law and order, while hospital managements are concerned to balance limited resources against the increasing demands of healthcare expectations.

Creating an Innovation Strategy

Putting an innovation strategy together involves three key steps, pulling together ideas around core themes and inviting discussion and argument to sharpen and shape them. These are:

- Strategic analysis: what could we do?
- Strategic selection: what are we going to do, and why?
- Strategic implementation: how are we going to make it happen?

Let's look at each of these in more detail.

Strategic Analysis

Strategic analysis begins with exploration of innovation space: where could we innovate and why would it be worth doing so? A useful place to start is to build some sense of the overall environment, to explore the current threats and opportunities and the likely changes to these in the future. Typically, questions here relate to technologies, to markets, to underlying political trends, to emerging customer needs, to competitors and to social and economic forces. It's also useful to add to this map some sense of who the players are in the environment: the particular customers and markets, the key suppliers and the number and type of competitors.

Within this framework it's also important to reflect on what resources the organization can bring to bear. What are its relative strengths and weaknesses and how may it build and sustain a competitive advantage?

Tools to help with this mapping exercise, such as PEST analysis, Rich pictures, SWOT and Five forces strategic analysis, are available on the Innovation Portal at **www.innovation-portal.info**

Activity to map the innovation environment using these tools is available on the Innovation Portal at **www.innovation-portal.info**

(It's important to remember that these are tools to help start a discussion – not accurate measuring devices. There are real limitations to how much we can know about an environment which is complex, interactive and constantly changing, and there are often wide differences about where the strengths and weaknesses actually lie.)

Having explored this environment, we need to understand the range of possibilities. Where can we innovate to advantage? What kinds of opportunities exist for use to create something different and capture value from bringing those ideas into the world?

We can think about strategy as a process of exploring the space defined by our four innovation types – the

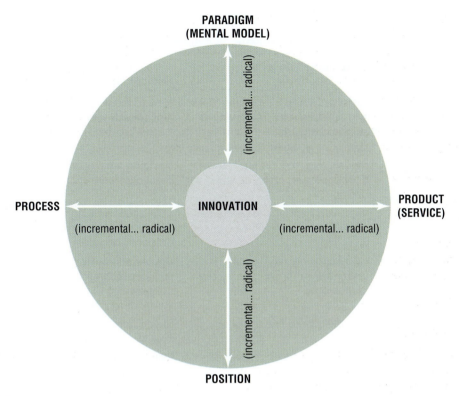

FIGURE 1.4   Exploring innovation space

4Ps mentioned earlier. Each of our 4Ps of innovation can take place along an axis running from incremental through to radical change; the area indicated by the circle in Figure 1.4 is the potential innovation space within which an organization can operate.

Where it actually explores and why – and which areas it leaves alone – are all questions for innovation strategy. And for new-entrant entrepreneurs this can provide a map of explored and unexplored territory, showing where there is open opportunity, where and how to tackle existing players, etc. It also provides a useful map for social innovation: where could we create new social value, where is there unexplored territory, where and how could we do things differently?

Table 1.7 gives some examples of innovations mapped onto this 4Ps model.

Strategic Selection

The issue here is choosing out of all the things we could do which ones we will do – and why? We have scarce resources so we need to place our bets carefully, balancing the risks and rewards across a portfolio of projects. There are plenty of tools to help us do this, from simple financial measures like payback time or return on investment through to complex frameworks which compare projects across many dimensions. We look more closely at this toolkit and the different ways we can make decisions under uncertainty in Chapter 8.

TABLE 1.7   Some examples of innovations mapped onto the 4Ps model

Innovation type	Incremental: do what we do but better	Radical: do something different
'Product': what we offer the world	Windows 7 and 8 replacing Vista and XP, essentially improving existing software	New to the world software (e.g. the first speech-recognition program)
	New versions of established car models (e.g. the VW Golf essentially improving on established car design)	Toyota Prius's hybrid engines (bringing a new concept) and the Tesla high-performance electric car
	Improved performance incandescent light bulbs	LED-based lighting (using completely different and more energy efficient principles)
	CDs replacing vinyl records (essentially improving on storage technology)	Spotify and other music-streaming services (changing the pattern from owning to renting a vast library of music)
Process: how we create and deliver that offering	Improved fixed-line telephone services	Skype and other VOIP systems
	Extended range of stock-brokering services	Online share trading
	Improved auction house operations	eBay
	Improved factory operations efficiency through upgraded equipment	Toyota Production System and other 'lean' approaches
	Improved range of banking services delivered at branch banks	Online banking and now mobile banking in Kenya and the Philippines (using phones as an alternative to banking systems)
	Improved retailing logistics	Online shopping
Position: where we target that offering and the story we tell about it	Häagen Dazs changing the target market for ice cream from children to consenting adults	Addressing underserved markets – for example the Tata Nano aimed at emerging but relatively poor Indian market with car priced around $2000
	Airlines segmenting service offering for different passenger groups – Virgin Upper Class, BA Premium Economy, etc.	Low-cost airlines opening up air travel to those previously unable to afford it (create new market and disrupt existing one)

TABLE 1.7 *(Continued)*

Innovation type	Incremental: do what we do but better	Radical: do something different
	Dell and others segmenting and customizing computer configuration for individual users	Variations on the 'One laptop per child' project (e.g. Indian government $20 computer for schools)
	Online support for traditional higher education courses	University of Phoenix and others building large education businesses via online approaches to reach different markets
	Banking services targeted at key segments (e.g. students, retired people)	'Bottom of the pyramid' approaches using a similar principle but tapping into huge and very different high-volume/low-margin markets (e.g. Aravind Eye Clinics, Cemex construction products)
Paradigm: how we frame what we do	Bausch & Lomb moved from 'eye wear' to 'eye care' as its business model, effectively letting go of the old business of spectacles, sunglasses (Raybans) and contact lenses, all of which were becoming commodity businesses and moved into newer high-tech fields like laser surgery equipment, specialist optical devices and research in artificial eyesight	Grameen Bank and other microfinance models (rethinking the assumptions about credit and the poor)
	Dyson redefining the home appliance market in terms of high-performance engineered products	iTunes platform (a complete system of personalized entertainment)
	Rolls-Royce (from high-quality aero engines to becoming a service company offering 'power by the hour')	Amazon, Google, Skype (redefining industries like retailing, advertising and telecoms through online models)
	IBM (from being a machine maker to a service and solution company, selling off its computer making and building up its consultancy and service side)	Linux, Mozilla, Apache (moving from passive users to active communities of users co-creating new products and services)

Tool to help you with strategic selection, competency mapping, is available on the Innovation Portal at **www.innovation-portal.info**

Activity designed to help you explore this tool, harvesting knowledge crops, is available on the Innovation Portal at **www.innovation-portal.info**

Case Studies of Kodak and Fujifilm, (who faced significant challenges when redeploying core technological knowledge into new markets) and are available on the Innovation Portal at **www.innovation-portal.info**

Case Study Philips Lighting, which used novel lighting technologies to enhance its position in the global lighting market, is available on the Innovation Portal at **www.innovation-portal.info**

Case Study describing Tesco's approach to building a deep understanding of its customers' changing needs is available on the Innovation Portal at **www.innovation-portal.info**

The challenge is for individuals and organizations to be aware of the extensive space within which innovation possibilities exist and to try to develop a strategic portfolio which covers this territory effectively, balancing risks and resources. So how can we choose which options will make sense for us? It's helpful to consider two complementary themes in answering this question:

- What is our overall business strategy (where we are trying to go as an organization) and how will innovation help us get there?
- Do we *know* anything about the direction we want to go in – does it build on something we have some competence in (or have access to)?

Of course, competencies may become superseded by shifts in the technological area. Sometimes they can destroy the basis of competitiveness (competence-destroying), but they can also be reconfigured to enhance a competitive position (competence enhancing). A famous study by Tushman and Anderson gives a wide range of examples of these types of change.[9]

But it isn't just technical knowledge. Google's expertise is based not only on a powerful search engine but also on using the data that helps it build to offer services in advertising. Major retailers like Tesco and Wal-Mart have rich and detailed understanding of customers and their shopping preferences and behaviour.

Strengths can also come from specific capabilities, things which an organization has learnt to do to help it stay agile and able to move into new fields. Virgin as a group of companies is represented across many different sectors but the underlying approach is essentially the original entrepreneurial one which Richard Branson used when setting up his music business.

INNOVATION IN ACTION 1.11

Assessing Competencies and Assets

Richard Hall is an experienced coach and researcher on innovation and entrepreneurship. He distinguishes between intangible assets and intangible competencies. Assets include intellectual property rights and reputation. Competencies include the skills and know-how of employees, suppliers and distributors, and the collective attributes which constitute organizational culture. His empirical work, based on a survey and case studies, indicates that managers believe the most significant of these intangible resources to be company reputation and employee know-how, both of which may be a function of organizational culture. Thus, organizational culture, defined as the shared values and beliefs of members of an organizational unit, and the associated artefacts become central to organizational learning. This framework provides a useful way to assess the competencies of an organization, and to identify how these contribute to performance.

Strategic Implementation

Having explored what we could do and decided what we are going to do, the third stage in innovation strategy development is to plan for implementation. Thinking through what we are going to need and how we will get these resources, who we may need to partner with, what likely roadblocks may we find on the way – all of these questions feed into this step.

Of course, it isn't a simple linear process. In practice, there will be plenty of discussion of these issues as we explore options and argue for particular choices, But that's the essence of strategy: a conversation and a rehearsal, imagining and thinking forward about uncertain activities into the future.

Tools to help with strategic planning, such as FMEA, potential problem analysis and project management, are available on the Innovation Portal at **www.innovation-portal.info**

To help do this we have a number of tools, again ranging from the simple to the complex. We could, for example, make a simple project plan which sets out the sequence of activities we need to carry out to make our innovation come alive. That would help us identify which resources we need and when and could also highlight some of the potential trouble spots so we could think through how we would deal with them. Many tools add a dimension of 'What if?' planning to such project models – trying to anticipate key difficulties and take a worst-case view so suitable contingency plans can be made.

Activity to help you explore strategic planning for implementation is available on the Innovation Portal at **www.innovation-portal.info**

Activity to help you explore some of the challenges in preparing and presenting a business case, Dragons' Den, is available on the Innovation Portal at **www.innovation-portal.info**

It's also worth thinking through and challenging the underlying strategic concept – the business case for doing whatever it is we have in mind. Once again, building a business case or thinking through the underlying business model provides a powerful way of making our assumptions explicit and opening them up for discussion and challenge. (We look in detail at the role of business models as a way of capturing value in Chapter 16, but the tools for working with these ideas are very helpful at this early strategic planning stage.)

Tools to help you with this activity, such as the business model canvas, are available on the Innovation Portal at **www.innovation-portal.info**

Beyond the Steady State: The Challenge of Discontinuous Change and the Need for Dynamic Capability

Most of the time innovation takes place within a set of rules of the game which are clearly understood, and involves players trying to innovate by doing what they do (product, process, position, etc.) but better. Some manage this more effectively than others do, but the rules of the game are accepted and do not change.

But occasionally something happens which dislocates this framework and changes the rules of the game. By definition, these are not everyday events but have the capacity to redefine the space and the boundary conditions. They open up new opportunities but also challenge existing players to reframe what they are doing in the light of new conditions. Taking advantage of the opportunities – or seeing the threats early enough and doing something different to help deal with them – requires an entrepreneurial approach which new entrants have but which may be difficult to revive in an established organization. So under these conditions we often see disruption of the old market and technological order and new rules of the game.

The important message is that under such conditions (which don't emerge every day) we need different approaches to organizing and managing innovation. If they try to use established models which work under steady-state conditions, organizations are likely to find themselves increasingly out of their depth and risk being upstaged by new and more agile players. The risk is clear if organizations fail to keep pace: there are plenty of examples of major corporations which began with an innovative flourish but ended up beaten by their failure to innovate fast enough or in the right directions. The examples of great photographic pioneers Kodak and Polaroid are graphic reminders that competitive advantage doesn't always last even if you are a major spender on R&D and have powerful marketing skills.

That raises a general point. We have spent a long time in this chapter talking about building innovation management capability. But in a changing world we also need to be able to step back and review our position, looking at our capability and fine-tuning it. There are some behaviours which we should keep on with, maybe increasing our commitment to them. And there may be others which worked in the past but are no longer so relevant. Importantly, there will always be new tricks to learn, new skills to acquire. (Think about the ways in which the Internet has changed the innovation game, opening up many more players, allowing rich links and connections, enabling knowledge flows. That simply wasn't the case thirty years ago and an organization trying to manage innovation today using its recipe book from back then would be in deep trouble!)

This idea of reviewing and resetting our innovation management approaches is termed **dynamic capability** and building it is a core theme which will run through the book.

Finally, it's worth remembering some useful advice from an old but wise source. In his famous book *The Prince* Niccolò Machiavelli gave a warning to would-be innovators.

> It must be remembered that there is nothing more difficult to plan, more doubtful of success, nor more dangerous to management than the creation of a new system. For the initiator has the enmity of all who would profit by the preservation of the old institution and merely luke-warm defenders in those who gain by the new ones.

Chapter Summary

- Innovation is about growth, about recognizing opportunities for doing something new and implementing those ideas to create some kind of value. It could be business growth; it could be social change. But at its heart is the creative human spirit, the urge to make change in our environment.

- Innovation is also a survival imperative. If an organization doesn't change what it offers the world and the ways in which it creates and delivers its offerings, it may well be in trouble. And innovation contributes to competitive success in many different ways: it's a *strategic* resource to getting the organization where it is trying to go, be it delivering shareholder value for private sector firms, providing better public services or enabling the start-up and growth of new enterprises.

- Innovation doesn't just happen. It is driven by *entrepreneurship*. This powerful mixture of energy, vision, passion, commitment, judgement and risk taking provides the motive power behind the innovation process. It's the same whether we are talking about a solo start-up venture or a key group within an established organization trying to renew its products or services.

- Innovation doesn't happen simply because we hope it will. It's a complex process which carries risks and needs careful and systematic *management*. Innovation isn't a single event, like the light bulb going off above a cartoon character's head. It's an extended process of picking up on ideas for change and turning them through into effective reality. The core process involves four steps:
  - recognizing opportunities
  - finding resources
  - developing the venture
  - capturing value.

  The challenge comes in doing this in an organized fashion and in being able to repeat the trick.

- This core process doesn't take place in a vacuum. We also know that it is strongly influenced by many factors. In particular, innovation needs:
  - clear strategic leadership and direction, plus the commitment of resources to make this happen
  - an innovative organization in which the structure and climate enables people to deploy their creativity and share their knowledge to bring about change
  - proactive links across boundaries inside the organization and to the many external agencies who can play a part in the innovation process (suppliers, customers, sources of finance, skilled resources and of knowledge, etc.).

- Research repeatedly suggests that if we want to succeed in managing innovation we need to:
  - explore and understand different dimensions of innovation (ways in which we can change things)

- manage innovation as a *process*
- create enabling conditions to enable them to repeat the innovation trick (building capability)
- focus this capability to move their organizations forward (innovation strategy)
- build *dynamic capability* (the ability to rest and adapt their approaches in the face of a changing environment).

- Innovation can take many forms but they can be reduced to four directions of change:
  - **product innovation:** changes in the things (products/services) an organization offers
  - **process innovation:** changes in the ways in which they are created and delivered
  - **position innovation:** changes in the context in which the products/services are introduced
  - **paradigm innovation:** changes in the underlying mental models which frame what the organization does.

- Within any of these dimensions innovations can be positioned on a spectrum from 'incremental' (doing what we do but better) through to 'radical' (doing something completely different). And they can be stand-alone (**component innovations**) or form part of a linked 'architecture' or system which brings many different components together in a particular way.

- Building a capability to organize and manage innovation is a great achievement, but we also need to consider where and how innovation can be used to strategic advantage. Putting an innovation strategy together involves three key steps, pulling together ideas around core themes and inviting discussion and argument to sharpen and shape them. These are:
  - Strategic analysis: what could we do?
  - Strategic selection: what are we going to do, and why?
  - Strategic implementation: how are we going to make it happen?

- Any organization can get lucky once but the real skill in innovation management is being able to repeat the trick. So if we want to manage innovation we ought to ask ourselves the following check questions:
  - Do we have effective enabling mechanisms for the core process?
  - Do we have strategic direction and commitment for innovation?
  - Do we have an innovative organization?
  - Do we build rich, proactive links?
  - Do we learn and develop our innovation capability?

- Most of the time innovation takes place within a set of rules of the game which are clearly understood, and involves players trying to innovate by doing what they do (product, process, position, etc.) but better. But occasionally something happens which changes the rules of the game (e.g. when radical change takes place along the technological frontier or when completely new markets emerge). When this happens, we need different approaches to organizing and managing innovation. If we try to use established models which work under steady-state conditions we find ourselves increasingly out of our depth and risk being upstaged by new and more agile players.

- For this reason, a key skill lies in building 'dynamic capability' (the ability to review and reset the approach which the organization takes to managing innovation in the face of a constantly shifting environment).

Key Terms Defined

Component innovation   changes at the level of components in a bigger system, for example a faster transistor in a microchip in a computer.

Creating value   implementing an idea which makes an economic or social difference.

Discontinuous innovation   radical innovations which change the rules of the game and open up a new game in which new players are often at an advantage.

Dynamic capability   the ability to review and reset the approach which the organization takes to managing innovation in the face of a changing environment.

Entrepreneurship   the powerful mixture of energy, vision, passion, commitment, judgement and risk taking which provides the motive power behind the innovation process.

Incremental innovation   small improvements to existing products, services or processes – 'doing what we do but better'.

Innovation   the process of translating ideas into useful new products, processes or services.

Invention   coming up with a new idea.

Paradigm innovation   changes in the underlying mental models which frame what the organization does.

Position innovation   changes in the context in which the products/services are introduced.

Process innovation   changes in the ways in which products/services are created and delivered.

Product innovation   changes in products/services an organization offers.

Radical innovation   significantly different changes to products, services or processes – 'doing something completely different'.

Discussion Questions

1. Is innovation manageable or just a random gambling activity where you sometimes get lucky? If it is manageable, how can firms organize and manage it – what general principles could they use?

2. 'Build a better mousetrap and the world will beat a path to your door!' Will it? What are the limitations of seeing innovation simply as coming up with bright ideas? Illustrate your answer with examples drawn from manufacturing and services.

3. What are the key stages involved in an innovation process? And what are the characteristic sets of activities which take place at each stage? How could such an innovation process look for:
    a. a fast food restaurant chain?
    b. an electronic test equipment maker?
    c. a hospital?
    d. an insurance company?
    e. a new entrant biotechnology firm?

4. Fred Bloggs was a bright young PhD scientist with a patent on a new algorithm for monitoring brainwave activity and predicting the early onset of a stroke. He was convinced of the value of his idea and took it to market having sold his car, borrowed money from family and friends and taken out a large loan. He went bankrupt despite having a demonstration version which doctors he showed it to were impressed by. Why might his failure be linked to having a partial model of how innovation works – and how could he avoid making the same mistake in the future?

5. How does innovation contribute to competitive advantage? Support your answer with illustrations from both manufacturing and services.

6. Does innovation matter for public services? Using examples, indicate how and where it can be an important strategic issue.

7. You are a newly appointed director for a small charity which supports homeless people. How could innovation improve the ways in which your charity operates?

8. Innovation can take many forms. Give examples of product/service, process, position and paradigm (mental model) innovations.

9. The low-cost airline approach has massively changed the way people choose and use air travel – and has been both a source of growth for new players and a life-threatening challenge for some existing players. What types of innovation have been involved in this?

10. You have been called in as a consultant to a medium-sized toy manufacturer whose range of construction toys (building bricks, etc.) has been losing market share to other types of toys. What innovation directions would you recommend to this company to restore its competitive position? (Use the 4Ps framework to think about possibilities.)

11. Innovation is about big leaps forward, eureka moments and radical breakthroughs – or is it? Using examples from manufacturing and services, make a case for the importance of incremental innovation.

12. Describe, with examples, the concept of platforms in product and process innovation and suggest how such an approach could help spread the high costs of innovation over a longer period.

13. What are the challenges managers could face in trying to organize a long-term steady stream of incremental innovation?

Further Reading and Resources

Peter Drucker's famous *Innovation and Entrepreneurship* (1985) provides an accessible introduction to the subject, but perhaps relies more on intuition and experience than on empirical research. A number of writers have looked at innovation from a process perspective; good examples include Keith Goffin and Rick Mitchell's *Innovation Management* (Pearson, 2010), Paul Trott's *Innovation and New Product Development* (Pearson, 2011) and Andrew Van de Ven's *Innovation Journey* (Oxford University Press, 1999). Case studies provide a good lens through which this process can be seen and there are several useful collections including Bettina von Stamm's *Innovation, Design and Creativity* (2nd edn, John Wiley & Sons Ltd, 2008), Roland Kaye and David Hawkridge's *Case Studies of Innovation* (Kogan Page, 2003) and Roger Miller and Marcel Côté's *Innovation Reinvented: Six Games that Drive Growth* (University of Toronto Press, 2012).

Some books cover company histories in detail and give an insight into the particular ways in which firms develop their own bundles of routines, for example David Vise's *The Google Story* (Pan, 2008), Graham and Shuldiner's *Corning and the Craft of Innovation* (Oxford University Press, 2001) and Gundling's *The 3M Way to Innovation: Balancing People and Profit* (Kodansha International, 2000).

Autobiographies and biographies of key innovation leaders provide a similar, if sometimes personally biased, insight into this, for example Richard Brandt's *One Click: Jeff Bezos and the Rise of Amazon.com* (Viking, 2011), Walter Issacson's *Steve Jobs: The Authorized Biography* (Little Brown, 2011) and James Dyson's *Against the Odds* (Texere, 2003). In addition, several websites – such as the Product Development Management Association (www.pdma.org) and www.innovationmanagement.se – carry case studies on a regular basis.

Many books and articles focus on particular aspects of the process, for example on technology strategy, Burgelman *et al.*'s *Strategic Management of Technology* (McGraw-Hill Irwin, 2004). On product or service development, Robert Cooper's *Winning at New Products* (Kogan Page, 2001), Rosenau *et al.*'s *The PDMA Handbook of New Product Development*' (John Wiley & Sons Ltd, 1996) and Tidd and Hull's *Service Innovation: Organizational Responses to Technological Opportunities and Market Imperatives* (Imperial College Press, 2003). On process innovation, Lager's *Managing Process Innovation* (Imperial College Press, 2011), Zairi and Duggan's *Best Practice Process Innovation Management*

(Butterworth-Heinemann, 2012) and Gary Pisano's *The Development Factory: Unlocking the Potential of Process Innovation* (Harvard Business School Press, 1996). On technology transfer, Mohammed Saad's *Development through Technology Transfer* (Intellect, 2000). On implementation, Alan Afuah's *Innovation Management: Strategies, Implementation and Profits* (Oxford University Press, 2003), Osborne and Brown's *Managing Change and Innovation in Public Service Organizations* (Psychology Press, 2010) and Bason's *Managing Public Sector Innovation* (Policy Press, 2011). On learning, Kim and Nelson's *Technology, Learning, and Innovation: Experiences of Newly Industrializing Countries* (Cambridge University Press, 2003), Nooteboom's *Learning and Innovation in Organizations and Economies* (Oxford University Press, 2000), Leonard's *Wellsprings of Knowledge* (Harvard Business School Press, 1995) and Nonaka's *The Knowledge Creating Company* (Harvard Business School Press, 1991).

For recent reviews of the core competence and dynamic capability perspectives, see David Teece's *Dynamic Capabilities and Strategic Management: Organizing for Innovation and Growth* (Oxford University Press, 2011), Joe Tidd's (editor) *From Knowledge Management to Strategic Competence* (3rd edn, Imperial College Press, 2012) and Connie Helfat's *Dynamic Capabilities: Understanding Strategic Change in Organizations* (Blackwell, 2006). Lockett, Thompson and Morgenstern (2009) provide a useful review in 'The development of the resource-based view of the firm: A critical appraisal' (*International Journal of Management Reviews*, 11(1)), as do Wang and Ahmed (2007) in 'Dynamic capabilities: A review and research agenda' (*International Journal of Management Reviews*, 9(1)). Davenport, Leibold and Voelpel provide an edited compilation of leading strategy writers in *Strategic Management in the Innovation Economy* (2nd edn, John Wiley & Sons Ltd, 2006), and the review edited by Galavan, Murray and Markides, *Strategy, Innovation and Change* (Oxford University Press, 2008) is excellent. On the more specific issue of technology strategy Chiesa's *R&D Strategy and Organization* (Imperial College Press, 2001) is a good place to start.

Websites such as AIM (www.aimresearch.org), NESTA (www.nesta.org) and ISPIM (http://ispim.org/) regularly report academic research around innovation. Others explore the challenges posed to future entrepreneurs. The site www.thefutureofinnovation.org offers the views of nearly 400 researchers in the area of future challenges, while www.innovation-futures.org presents a number of different scenarios for the future, each with significant innovation and entrepreneurship challenges.

References

1. Baumol, W. (2002) *The Free-Market Innovation Machine: Analyzing the Growth Miracle of Capitalism*, Princeton: Princeton University Press.
2. Jones, T., D. McCormick and C. Dewing (2012) *Growth Champions: The Battle for Sustained Innovation Leadership*, Chichester: John Wiley & Sons Ltd.

3. Little, A.D. (2012) *Global Innovation Excellence Survey*, Frankfurt: ADL Consultants.

4. Drucker, P. (1985) *Innovation and Entrepreneurship*, New York: Harper & Row.

5. Schumpeter, J. (1943) *Capitalism, Socialism and Democracy*, New York: Harper.

6. Pinchot, G. (1999) *Intrapreneuring in Action: Why You Don't Have to Leave a Corporation to Become an Entrepreneur*, New York: Berrett-Koehler Publishers.

7. Rothwell, R. and P. Gardiner (1984) Design and competition in engineering. *Long Range Planning*, **17**(3): 30–91.

8. Francis, D. and J. Bessant (2006) Targetting innovation and implications for capability development, *Technovation*, **25**: 171–83.

9. Tushman, M. and P. Anderson (1987) Technological discontinuities and organizational environments, *Administrative Science Quarterly*, **31**(3): 439–65.

Deeper Dive explanations of innovation concepts and ideas are available on the Innovation Portal at **www.innovation-portal.info**

Quizzes to test yourself further are available online via the Innovation Portal at **www.innovation-portal.info**

Summary of online resources for Chapter 1 –
all material is available via the Innovation Portal at
www.innovation-portal.info

Cases	**Media**	**Tools**	**Activities**	**Deeper Dives**

Cases
- James Dyson
- Zara
- Model T Ford
- Alibaba
- Taobao
- Karolinska Hospital
- Aravind Eye Clinics
- Narayana Hrudayalaya Hospitals (NHL)
- Kumba Resources
- Cybercrime
- Ice industry
- Marshalls
- 3M
- Corning
- Philips Lighting
- Lego
- Adidas
- Local Motors
- Kodak
- Fujifilm
- Tesco

Media
- Model T Ford
- Finnegan's Fish Bar
- Tim Jones

Tools
- 4Ps for innovation strategy
- Innovation Fitness Test
- PEST analysis
- Rich pictures
- SWOT
- Five forces strategic analysis
- Competency mapping
- FMEA
- Potential problem analysis
- Project management
- Business model canvas

Activities
- Incremental and radical innovation
- Strategic advantage through innovation
- Mapping the strategic environment
- Harvesting knowledge crops
- Strategic planning for implementation
- Dragons' Den

Deeper Dives
- Servitization

Chapter 2

Social Innovation

LEARNING OBJECTIVES

By the end of this chapter you will develop an understanding of:

- social entrepreneurship and social innovation
- social entrepreneurship as an organized and disciplined process rather than a well-meaning but unfocused intervention
- the difficulties in managing what is just as much an uncertain and risky process as 'conventional' economically motivated innovation
- the key themes needed to manage this process effectively.

INNOVATION IN ACTION 2.1

Grameen Bank and the Development of Microfinance

One of the biggest problems facing people living below the poverty line is the difficulty of getting access to banking and financial services. As a result they are often dependent on moneylenders and other unofficial sources – and are often charged at exorbitant rates if they do borrow. This makes it hard to save and invest, and puts a major barrier in the way of breaking out of this spiral through starting new entrepreneurial ventures. Awareness of this problem led Muhammad Yunus, Head of the Rural Economics Programme at the University of Chittagong, to launch a project to examine the possibility of designing a credit delivery system to provide banking

(continued)

services targeted at the rural poor. In 1976, the Grameen Bank Project (*grameen* means 'rural' or 'village' in Bengali) was established, aiming to:

- extend banking facilities to the poor
- eliminate the exploitation of the poor by moneylenders
- create opportunities for self-employment for unemployed people in rural Bangladesh
- offer the disadvantaged an organizational format which they can understand and manage by themselves
- reverse the age-old vicious circle of 'low income, low saving and low investment' into a virtuous circle of 'low income, injection of credit, investment, more income, more savings, more investment, more income'.

The original project was set up in Jobra (a village adjacent to Chittagong University) and some neighbouring villages and ran during 1976–1979. The core concept was of 'microfinance' – enabling people (and a major success was with women) to take tiny loans to start and grow tiny businesses. With the sponsorship of the central bank of the country and support of the nationalized commercial banks, the project was extended to Tangail district (a district north of Dhaka, the capital city of Bangladesh) in 1979. Its further success there led to the model being extended to several other districts in the country, and in 1983 it became an independent bank as a result of government legislation. Today, Grameen Bank is owned by the rural poor, whom it serves. Borrowers of the bank own 90% of its shares, while the remaining 10% is owned by the government. It now serves over five million clients and every month enables 10 000 new families to escape the poverty trap.

Grameen Bank has moved into other areas where the same model applies, for example Grameen Phone is one of the largest mobile telephone operators in Asia but bases its model on providing communication access to the poorest members of society through innovative pricing models.

What Is 'Social Innovation'?

In this book, we're looking at the challenge of *change* – and how individuals and groups of entrepreneurs, working alone or inside organizations, try to bring this about. We've seen that innovation is not a simple flash of inspiration but an extended and organized process of turning bright ideas into successful realities, changing the offering (product/service), the ways in which it is created and delivered (process innovation), the context and the ways in which it is introduced to that context (position innovation) and the overall mental models for thinking about what we are doing (business model or 'paradigm' innovation).

Above all, we've seen that getting innovation to happen depends on a focused and determined drive – a passion to change things, which we call 'entrepreneurship'. Essentially, this is about being prepared to challenge and change, to take (calculated) risks and put energy and enthusiasm into the venture, picking up and enthusing other supporters along the way. If we think about successful entrepreneurs they are typically ambitious, mission-driven, passionate, strategic (not just impulsive), resourceful and results-oriented. And we can think of plenty of names to fit this frame: Bill Gates (Microsoft), Richard Branson (Virgin), James Dyson (Dyson), Larry Page and Sergey Brin (Google) and Jeff Bezos (Amazon).

But we could also apply these terms to describe people like Florence Nightingale, Elizabeth Fry or Albert Schweitzer. And while less famous than Gates or Bezos, there are some impressive individuals around today who have made a significant mark on the world through getting their ideas into action. As the Ashoka Foundation comments, 'Unlike traditional business entrepreneurs, social entrepreneurs primarily seek to generate "social value" rather than profits. And unlike the majority of non-profit organizations, their work is targeted not only towards immediate, small-scale effects, but sweeping, long-term change.'

For example, as well as Muhammad Yunus, the founder of Grameen Bank (that has now been replicated in 58 countries around the world), Dr Venkataswamy founded the Aravind Eye Clinics. His passion for finding ways of giving eyesight back to people with cataracts in his home state of Tamil Nadu eventually led to the development of an eye care system which has helped thousands of people around the country.

Case Study of Aravind Eye Clinics is available on the Innovation Portal at **www.innovation-portal.info**

A social entrepreneur uses the same process of entrepreneurship that we saw in Chapter 1 but does so to meet social needs and create value for society. These are people who undoubtedly fit our entrepreneur mould but target their efforts in a different, socially valuable direction. Key characteristics of this group include:

Video Clip of Aravind Eye Clinics is available on the Innovation Portal at **www.innovation-portal.info**

- *Ambitious*. Social entrepreneurs tackle major social issues – poverty, healthcare, equal opportunities, etc. – with the underlying desire, passion even, to make a change. They may work alone or from within a wide range of existing organizations, including those which mix elements of non-profit and for-profit activity.
- *Mission driven*. their primary concern is generating social value rather than wealth; wealth creation may be part of the process but it is not an end in itself. Just like business entrepreneurs, social entrepreneurs are intensely focused and driven, even relentless, in their pursuit of a social vision.
- *Strategic*. Like business entrepreneurs, social entrepreneurs see and act upon what others miss: opportunities to improve systems, create solutions and invent new approaches that create social value.
- *Resourceful*. Social entrepreneurs are often in situations where they have limited access to capital and traditional market support systems. As a result, they must be exceptionally skilled at mustering and mobilizing human, financial and political resources.
- *Results-oriented*. Again, like business entrepreneurs, social entrepreneurs are motivated by a desire to see things change and to produce measurable returns. The results they seek are essentially linked to 'making the world a better place', for example through improving quality of life, access to basic resources or supporting disadvantaged groups.

Social innovation has a long tradition, with examples dating back to some of the great social reformers. For example, in the 19th century in the UK the strong Quaker values held by key entrepreneurial figures like George Cadbury led to innovations in social housing, community development and education as well as in the factories which they organized and managed. As Geoff Mulgan and colleagues point out: 'The great wave of industrialization and urbanization in the nineteenth century was accompanied by an extraordinary upsurge of **social enterprise** and innovation: mutual self-help, microcredit, building societies, cooperatives, trade unions.'[1]

ENTREPRENEURSHIP IN ACTION 2.1

Tateni Home Care

Veronica Khosa was frustrated with the system of healthcare in South Africa. A nurse by trade, she saw sick people getting sicker, elderly people unable to get to a doctor and hospitals with empty beds that would not admit patients with HIV. So Veronica started Tateni Home Care Nursing Services and instituted the concept of 'home care' in her country. Beginning with practically nothing, her team took to the streets providing care to people in a way they had never received it: in the comfort and security of their own homes. Just years later, the government had adopted her plan and through the recognition of leading health organizations the idea is spreading beyond South Africa.

Source: Ashoka Foundation website, https://www.ashoka.org/fellow/veronica-khosa, accessed 20th December 2014.

Major social innovations include the kindergarten, the cooperative movement, first aid and the Fair Trade movement, all of which began with social entrepreneurs and spread internationally.

Video Clips of Grameen Bank and Anil Gupta's Honey Bee network are available on the Innovation Portal at **www.innovation-portal.info**

Case Study of the rare diseases project is available on the Innovation Portal at **www.innovation-portal.info**

The growth in social innovation has also been accelerated through enabling technologies around information and communication. These days, it becomes easier to reach many different players and to combine their innovative efforts into rich and new types of solution, for example mobilizing patients and carers in an online community concerned with rare diseases or using mobile communications to help deal with the aftermath of humanitarian crises – reuniting families, establishing communications, providing financial aid quickly via mobile money transfers, etc.

ENTREPRENEURSHIP IN ACTION 2.2

Samasource

An innovative application of mobile communications has been to create employment opportunities for disadvantaged groups using 'microwork' principles. 'Impact sourcing' is the term increasingly used to describe the use of advanced communication technologies to permit participation in global labour markets by disadvantaged groups. Increasingly, many tasks – such as translation, proofreading, optical character recognition (OCR) clean-up or data entry– can be carried out using crowd-sourcing approaches. Amazon's Mechanical Turk is extensively used in this fashion. Social entrepreneurs like Leila Janah saw the potential for applying this approach, and her Samasource organization now provides employment for around 2000 people on very low incomes in rural areas.[2] The increasing availability of mobile communications allows for mobilizing and empowering this group and an increasing number of US high-tech companies are sourcing work through her organization.

The model is not simply low-cost outsourcing; through a network of local agencies Samasource provides not only direct employment opportunities but also training and development such that workers become better able to participate in the growing network of online knowledge work. Organizations like Samasource recognize the risk that the model could simply be used to exploit very low wage rate workers. Its business model requires partners to employ people earning less than $3/day and reinvest 40% of revenues in training, salaries and community programmes.

There are similarities to microfinance: the underlying business model is essentially extending a well-known principle (business process outsourcing) to a new context (educated but marginalized people on low incomes who could play a role as knowledge workers). Samasource mobilizes people in a variety of countries and contexts, including rural villages, urban slums and even refugee camps. The model is diffusing widely; other organizations such as DigitalDivideData[3] (originally established in S.E. Asia in 2001 and now employing nearly 1000 people in Cambodia, Laos and Kenya) and Crowdflower[4] perform similar integrating roles, bringing disadvantaged groups into the online workforce.

Video Clips of an interview with Leila and another from a user's perspective on Samasource are available on the Innovation Portal at **www.innovation-portal.info**

Different Players

Social innovation involves the same core entrepreneurial process of finding opportunities, choosing amongst them, implementing and capturing value, but it plays out in a number of different ways, which we explore briefly.

Individual Start-ups…

In many cases, social innovation is an individual-driven thing, where a passion for change leads to remarkable and sustainable results. They include people like:

- Amitabha Sadangi of International Development Enterprises (India), who develops low-cost irrigation technologies to help subsistence farmers survive dry seasons
- Anshu Gupta, who has formed a channel for recycling clothes and fabric to meet the needs of rural poor in India. He initiated Goonj in 1998 with just 67 items of clothing; today, his organization sends out over 40 000 kg of material every month, in 21 states.
- Mitch Besser, founder and medical director of the Cape Town-based programme, mothers2mothers (m2m), which aims to reduce mother-to-child transmission of HIV and provide care to women living with HIV. He founded mothers2mothers with one site in South Africa in 2001. It has grown to more than 645 sites in South Africa, Kenya, Lesotho, Malawi, Rwanda, Swaziland and Zambia.
- Tri Mumpuni, executive director of Indonesian NGO IBEKA (People Centred Economic and Business Institute), strives to bring light and energy into the lives of rural populations through the introduction of micro-hydropower plants to more than 50 villages.

 Video Clips of interviews with Melissa Clark-Reynolds and Suzana Moreira, both of whom set up social innovation projects, are available on the Innovation Portal at **www.innovation-portal.info**

(These and other examples can be found on the Ashoka website, www.ashoka.org, website which links a global community of social entrepreneurs.)

Not Just Passionate Individuals

But **social entrepreneurship** of this kind is also an increasingly important component of 'big business', as large organizations realize that they only secure a licence to operate if they can demonstrate some concern for the wider communities in which they are located. 'Corporate social responsibility' (CSR) is becoming a major function in many businesses and many make use of formal measures – such as the **triple bottom line** – to monitor and communicate their focus on more than simple profit-making.

INNOVATION IN ACTION 2.2

Innovation and Assisted Living

BT, the UK telecommunications firm, has – under strong pressure from the regulator – a responsibility to provide services for all elements of society but it has used the connections in this 'stakeholder network' to move early into understanding and creating services for what will be a major expansion in the future with an ageing population. By 2026, 30% of the UK population will be more than 60 years old. The pilot innovation is based on placing sensors in the home to monitor movement and the use of power and water: if something goes wrong, it triggers an alarm. It has already begun to generate significant revenues for BT but has also opened up the possibility of relieving pressure on the NHS for beds and services. Estimates suggest savings of around £700 million of this kind if fully deployed. Most significantly, the initial project can be seen as a stepping stone, a transitional object to help BT learn about what will be a huge and very different market in the future.

By engaging stakeholders directly, companies are also better able to avoid conflicts, or to resolve them when they arise. In some cases, this involves directly engaging with activists who are leading campaigns or protests against a company.

INNOVATION IN ACTION 2.3

Opening up Markets through Social Innovation

The UK 'do-it-yourself' home and garden retailer B&Q has been honoured for its work on disability where it has used CSR to drive improvements in customer services. What in retrospect looks like a successful business strategy has in fact evolved through real-time learning from partnerships between individual stores and local disability organizations. Following on from its pioneering experiments in having stores entirely staffed by older people, B&Q wanted to ensure that disabled people were able to shop in confidence and that they would be able to access goods and services easily. In the UK alone, there are eight million disabled people. It is estimated that the 'disabled pound' is worth £30 billion and is growing. However, B&Q also saw this initiative as a way to improve wider customer care competencies: 'If we can get it right for disabled people we can get it right for most people.' To begin the process of understanding what it was like to shop and work in B&Q as a disabled person, the company started by talking to disabled people in a single store. It now has established 300 partnerships between store 'disability champions' and local disability groups to understand local needs and develop training on disability awareness and service provision. B&Q sees these partnerships as a way for it to access 'the incredible amount of knowledge, commitment and enthusiasm which exists in this wide variety of organizations'. As a result all B&Q staff now take part in disability awareness training, they are improving store design and provide printed material in Braille, audio type, large print and CD-ROM. They are also developing their 'Daily Living Made Easier' range of products from grab rails and bath chairs through to visual smoke alarms and lightweight garden tools.

Sometimes there is scope for social entrepreneurship to spin out of mainstream innovative activity. Procter and Gamble's PUR water purification system offers radical improvements to point-of-use drinking water delivery. Estimates are that it has reduced intestinal infections by 30–50%. The product grew out of research in the mainstream detergents business but the initial conclusion was that the market potential of the product was not high enough to justify investment; by reframing it as a development aid, the company has improved its image and opened up a radical new area for working.

In some cases, the process begins with an individual but gradually a trend is established which other players see as relevant to follow, in the process bringing their resources and experience to the game. An example here is the Fair Trade range of products, which were originally a minority idea but have now become a mainstream item in many supermarkets.

Public Sector Innovation

Providing basic services like education, healthcare and a safe society are all hallmarks of a 'civilized society'. But they are produced by an army of people working in what is loosely called 'the public sector' – and as we saw at the start of this book, there is huge scope for innovation in this space. In many ways this sector represents a major application field for social innovation: while there may be concerns about costs and using resources wisely, the fundamental driver is around social change.[5]

 Video Clips of interviews with Helle-Vibeke Carstensen, describing efforts to improve the Danish Ministry of Taxation, and Lynne Maher, discussing involving patients as 'user innovators', are available on the Innovation Portal at **www.innovation-portal.info**

 Case Studies giving examples in the healthcare setting, such as NHS RED and Open Door, are available on the Innovation Portal at **www.innovation-portal.info**

Occasionally there is a radical innovation, for example in the UK the setting up of a National Health Service to provide healthcare for all, free at the point of delivery or the establishment of the Open University, which brought higher education within reach of everyone. But most of the time social innovation in the public sector consists of thousands of small incremental improvements to core services.

Innovation in the 'Third Sector'

There is also a long tradition of innovation in the so-called third sector: the voluntary and charitable organizations which operate to provide various forms of social welfare and service. Some of these – for example Cancer Research UK and Macmillan Cancer Relief – have created innovation management groups which work to use the kind of approaches we have been exploring in the book to help improve their operations.

 Case Studies of crisis-driven innovation describing activities in the humanitarian sector are available on the Innovation Portal at **www.innovation-portal.info**

Supporting and Enabling Social Innovation

Social innovation is seen as having a major role in improving living standards, and so it has attracted growing attention from a variety of agencies aiming to support and stimulate it. For example, there are investment vehicles, like the Big Society Capital fund in the UK and specialist venture funds like Acumen in the USA, which provide an alternative source of capital.

And there are coordinating agencies – like the Young Foundation in the UK, which provide further support for the mobilization and institutionalization of social innovation.

Another increasingly significant development is the setting-up by established organizations and successful business entrepreneurs of charitable foundations whose aim is explicitly to enable social entrepreneurship and the scaling of ideas with potential benefits. Examples include the Nike Foundation, the Schwab Foundation, the Skoll Foundation (established by Jeffrey Skoll, founder of eBay) and the Gates Foundation (established by Microsoft founder Bill Gates and which increasingly receives support from financier Warren Buffett).

Video Clip of an interview with Simon Tucker of the Young Foundation describing its social innovation approaches is available on the Innovation Portal at **www.innovation-portal.info**

Motivation: Why Do It?

It's worth pausing for a moment to reflect on the underlying motivation for social innovation, whether we are talking about passionate individuals, enlightened corporations, public sector institutions or 'third sector' organizations.

Just as mountaineers climb peaks simply 'because they are there', sometimes the motivation for innovating comes because of a desire to make a difference. Psychological studies of entrepreneurs (see Chapter 9) suggest they often have a high need for achievement (n-Ach), which is a measure of how far they want to make their mark on the world. High n-Ach requires some evidence that a mark has been made – but this doesn't have to be in terms of profit or loss on a balance sheet. As we saw earlier, many people find entrepreneurial satisfaction through social value creation, and even those with a long track record of building successful businesses may find themselves drawn into this territory. For example, Bill Gates' withdrawal from running Microsoft to concentrate on the Gates Foundation and other activities is the latest in a long line. Back in the early 17th century, James Coram, a successful businessman who had made his fortune in transatlantic trade, was so concerned with infant mortality in London that he set up the Foundling Hospital, pestering his friends and colleagues to raise the funding to support the project.

Video Clip of a talk by Jeff Church, founder of NEKA, a social enterprise supporting clean water projects in impoverished countries, is available on the Innovation Portal at **www.innovation-portal.info**

INNOVATION IN ACTION 2.4

Different Types of Entrepreneurs

In an award-winning paper, Emmanuelle Fauchart and Marc Gruber studied the motivations and underlying psychological drivers amongst entrepreneurial founders of businesses in

(continued)

the sports equipment sector. Their study used social identity theory to explore the underlying self-perceptions and aspirations and found three distinct types of role identity amongst their sample. 'Darwinians' were primarily concerned with competing and creating business success, 'Communitarians' were much more concerned with social identities which related to participating in and contributing to a community and 'Missionaries' had a strong inner vision, a desire to change the world, and their entrepreneurial activity was an expression of this.

Case Study of Eastville Community Shop highlighting different but complementary motivations of social entrepreneurs is available on the Innovation Portal at **www.innovation-portal.info**

Source: Derived from Fauchart, E. and M. Gruber (2011) Darwinians, Communitarians, and Missionaries: The role of founder identity in entrepreneurship, *Academy of Management Journal*, 54(5): 935–57.

Another important area where individuals have been a powerful source of social innovation comes from the world of 'user-innovators'. As we argue in Chapter 6, this class of innovator is increasingly important and has often been at the heart of major social change. Experiencing problems first-hand can often provide the trigger for change, for example in the area of healthcare.

INNOVATION IN ACTION 2.5

User-led Social Innovation

One day, Louis Plante, a sufferer from cystic fibrosis, had to leave a concert because of excessive coughing while sitting in proximity to a large speaker. Using his skills as an electronics technician, Louis developed a device that could generate the low frequency vibrations. His primary goal was to develop a treatment he would benefit from but he realized that his efforts could be valuable for others and so he created a firm (Dymedso) to commercialize his solution.

Another CF affected person, Hanna Boguslawska, developed chest percussion with electrical percussion and founded a firm named eper ltd to commercialize it: 'My daughter, 26 with CF, depended for most of her life on us, her parents to do her chest physiotherapy. So her independence was constantly compromised and she hated it. On the other hand, we not always delivered the best physiotherapy; simply because we were tired, or didn't have all this time required, or were sick. Sure, you know all of this … Many times

Video Clip of and links to a major patient innovation project are available on the Innovation Portal at **www.innovation-portal.info**

I was thinking about a simple solution, which would deliver a good physiotherapy and wouldn't require a caregiver. And I am very happy I could do it. My daughter uses my eper 100 (stands for electrical percussor, and 100 symbolizes all my percussion ideas which were never realized) all the time. According to her it is much better than the human hand and she can do it alone.'

Video Clip of a talk by Tad Golesworthy, who was diagnosed with a terminal heart condition that spurred him to design a new heart valve, saving his and many other lives, is available on the Innovation Portal at **www.innovation-portal.info**

Source: Habicht, H., P. Oliveira and V. Scherbatuik (2012) User innovators: When patients set out to help themselves and end up helping many, *Die Unternehmung – Swiss Journal of Management Research*, **66**(3): 277–94.

Why Organizations Do It

As we've seen, it isn't just individuals who undertake social innovation: it is increasingly part of the offering by all kinds of business organization. There are several reasons for this, and we focus on three:

- social innovation as securing a 'licence to operate'
- social innovation as aligning values
- social innovation as a learning laboratory.

Licence to Operate

There is growing pressure on established businesses to work to a more socially responsible agenda, with many operating a key function around CSR. The concept is simple: firms need to secure a 'licence to operate' from the stakeholders in the various constituencies in which they work. Unless they take notice of the concerns and values of those communities, they risk passive, and increasingly active, resistance and their operations can be severely affected. CSR goes beyond public relations in many cases with genuine efforts to ensure social value is created alongside economic value, and that stakeholders benefit as widely as possible and not simply as consumers. CSR thinking has led to the development of formal measures and frameworks like the 'triple bottom line', which many firms use as a way of expanding the traditional company reporting framework to take into account not just financial outcomes but also environmental and social performance.

It is easy to become cynical about CSR activity, seeing it as a cosmetic overlay on what are basically the same old business practices. But there is a growing recognition that pursuing social entrepreneurship-linked goals may not be incompatible with developing a viable and commercially successful business.

This value is in both intangible domains like brand and reputation and increasingly in bottom line benefits like market share and product/service innovation. And the downside of a failure in CSR is that public perception of the organization can shift with a negative impact on brands, reputation and ultimately performance. Concern in the UK over the tax arrangements of Amazon, Starbucks and Google forced changes in their operating agenda, while the backlash against fast-food meant that players like McDonald's and KFC had to rethink their approach.

Aligning Values

A second reason for engaging in social innovation on the part of organizations is the motivational effects they get from aligning their values with those of their staff. Most people want to work for organizations in which there is a positive benefit to society. Many see this as a way of fulfilling themselves. Think of the motives for working in healthcare or education and the sense is often one of vocation (a calling) rather than because of the more formal rewards.

Video Clips of interviews with staff at a UK hospital working on various innovation projects to improve patient care are available on the Innovation Portal at **www.innovation-portal.info**

Organizations which align with the values of their staff tend to have better retention and the chance to build on the ideas and suggestions of their staff – high involvement innovation. This is also critical in those organizations which operate with a small core staff and a large number of volunteers, for example in the charity sector or in the case of social care.

Learning Laboratory

One other area where participating in social innovation may be valuable is in using it as an extension of innovation search possibilities. Social innovations often arise out of a combination of widespread and often urgent need *and* severe resource limitations. Existing solutions may not be viable in such situations and instead new solutions emerge which are better suited to the extreme conditions.

As we have seen, meeting the needs of a different group with very different characteristics to those of the mainstream population can provide a laboratory for the emergence of innovations which may well diffuse later to the wider population. There is clearly enormous demand for such innovation to meet widespread demand for healthcare, education, sanitation, energy and food across populations which do not have the disposable income to purchase these goods and services via conventional routes.[6]

Humanitarian emergencies – such as earthquakes, tsunami, flood and drought or man-made crises such as war and the consequent refugee problems – provide another example of urgent and widespread need which cannot be met through conventional routes. Instead, agencies working in this space are characterized by high rates of innovation, often improvising solutions which can then be shared across other agencies and provide radically different routes to innovation in logistics, communication and healthcare.

Case Studies of innovations triggered by social needs that have application in other areas, such as Aravind Eye Clinics, Narayana Hrudayalaya Hospitals (NHL) and Lifespring Hospitals, are available on the Innovation Portal at **www.innovation-portal.info**

Learning from such experiments can lead to the wider application of the underlying concepts, for example GE's best-selling portable ultrasound scanner emerged from a small project to meet the needs of midwives working in rural villages in India. Other examples include changing business models in banking (based on the Grameen experience) and resilient logistics using lessons originally learned in humanitarian crises.[7]

INNOVATION IN ACTION 2.6

Mobilizing Stakeholder Innovation

The Danish pharmaceutical firm Novo Nordisk is deploying stakeholder innovation through expansion and reframing of the role of its CSR activities. It has been consistently highly rated on this, not least because it is a board-level strategic responsibility (specified in the company's articles of association) with significant resources committed to projects to sustain and enhance good practice. It was one of the first companies to introduce the concept of the triple bottom line performance measurement, recognizing the need to take into account wider social and societal concerns and to be clear about its values.

But there is now growing recognition that this investment is also a powerful innovation resource which offers a way of complementing its 'mainstream' R&D. For example, its DAWN (Diabetes Attitudes, Wishes and Needs) programme, initiated in 2001, tried to explore attitudes, wishes and needs of both diabetes sufferers and healthcare professionals to identify critical gaps in the overall care offering. Its findings showed in quantitative fashion how people with diabetes suffered from different types of emotional distress and poor psychological well-being, and that such factors were a major contributing factor to impaired health outcomes. Insights from the programme opened up new areas for innovation across the system. For example, a key focus was on the ways in which healthcare professionals presented therapeutic options involving a combination of insulin treatment and lifestyle elements – and on developing new approaches to this.

Søren Skovlund, senior adviser at Corporate Health Partnerships, sees the key element as 'the use of the DAWN study as a vehicle to get all the different people round the same table … to bring patients, health professionals, politicians, payers, the media together to find new ways to work more effectively together on the same task … You can't avoid getting some innovation because you're bringing together different baskets of knowledge in the room!'

DAWN provides an input to another set of activities operated by Novo Nordisk under the banner of National Diabetes Programmes (NDPs). This initiative began in 2001 when the company set about building a network of relationships in key geographical areas helping devise and configure relevant holistic care programmes. Rather than a product focus, NDPs offer a range of inputs, for example supporting the education of healthcare professionals or establishing clinics for care of diabetic ulcers. Its CEO, Lars Rebien Sørensen, argues that 'only by offering and advocating the right solutions for diabetes care will we be seen as a responsible company. If we just say "drugs, drugs, drugs", they will say "give us a break!"' This is clearly good CSR practice – but the potential learning about new approaches to care, especially under resource-constrained conditions, also represents an important 'hidden R&D' investment.

(*continued*)

For example, Tanzania was an early pilot. It was initially difficult to convince authorities to take chronic diseases like diabetes into account since they had no budget for them and were already fighting hard with infectious diseases. With little likelihood of new investment, Novo Nordisk began working with local diabetes associations to establish demonstration projects. It set up clinics in hospitals and villages, trained staff and provided relevant equipment and materials. This gave visibility to the possibilities in a chronic disease management approach, for example before the programme someone with diabetes might have had to travel 200 km to the major hospital in Dar es Salaam, whereas now they could be dealt with locally. The value to the national healthcare system is significant in terms of savings on the costs of treating complications such as blindness and amputations, which are tragic and expensive results of poor and delayed treatment. As a result, the Ministry of Health is able to deal with diabetes management without the need for new investment in hospital capacity or recruitment of new doctors and nurses.

NDPs represent an experience-sharing network across over 40 countries. Much of the learning is about the context of different national healthcare systems and how to work within them to bring about significant change – essentially positioning the company for the co-evolution of novel models.

Enabling Social Innovation

We'll see throughout the book how innovation doesn't simply happen: it is a process which can be organized and managed. Figure 2.1 reminds us of the model we introduced in Chapter 1:

The process begins with seeking out opportunities, often new or different combinations which no one else has seen, and working them up into viable concepts which can be taken

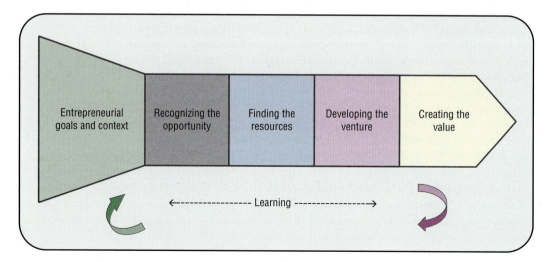

FIGURE 2.1   Process model of innovation and entrepreneurship

forward. It's then a matter of persuading various people – venture capitalists, senior management, etc. – to choose to put resources behind the idea rather than backing off or backing something else. If we get past this hurdle, the next step is beginning to transform the idea into reality, weaving together a variety of different knowledge and resource streams before finally launching the new thing – product, process or service – into a market. Whether they choose to adopt and use it, and spread the word to others so the innovation diffuses, depends a lot on how we manage using other knowledge and resource streams to understand, shape and develop the market. We also know that the whole process is influenced and shaped by having clear strategic direction and support, an underlying innovative and enthusiastic organization willing to commit its creativity and energy, and extensive and rich links to other players who can help with the knowledge and resource flows we need. Fuelling the whole is the underlying creativity, drive, foresight and intuition to make it happen – entrepreneurship – to undertake and take the risks.

So how does this play out in the case of social entrepreneurship? Table 2.1 gives some examples of the challenges

TABLE 2.1   Challenges in social entrepreneurship

What has to be managed…	Challenges in social entrepreneurship
Recognizing opportunities	Many potential social entrepreneurs (SEs) have the passion to change something in the world – and there are plenty of targets to choose from, like poverty, access to education and healthcare. But passion isn't enough. They also need the classic entrepreneur's skill of spotting an opportunity, a connection, a possibility which could develop. It's about searching for new ideas that could bring a different solution to an existing problem, for example the microfinance alternative to conventional banking or street-level moneylending
	As we've seen elsewhere in the book the skill is often not so much discovery (finding something completely new) as connection (making links between disparate things). In the SE field, the gaps may be very wide, for example connecting rural farmers to high-tech international stock markets requires considerably more vision to bridge the gap than spotting the need for a new variant of futures trading software. So SEs need both passion and vision, plus considerable broking and connecting skills
Finding resources	Spotting an opportunity is one thing, but getting others to believe in it and, more importantly, back it is something else. Whether it's an inventor approaching a venture capitalist or an internal team pitching a new product idea to the strategic management in a large organization the story of successful entrepreneurship is about convincing other people

(continued)

TABLE 2.1 (Continued)	
What has to be managed…	**Challenges in social entrepreneurship**
	In the case of SE the problem is compounded by the fact that the targets for such a pitch may not be immediately apparent. Even if you can make a strong business case and have thought through the likely concerns and questions, who do you approach to try to get backing? There are some foundations and non-profit organizations but in many cases one of the important skill sets of an SE is networking, the ability to chase down potential funders and backers and engage them in the project
	Even within an established organization, the presence of a structure may not be sufficient. For many SE projects the challenge is that they take the firm in very different directions, some of which fundamentally challenge its core business. For example, a proposal to make drugs cheaply available in the developing world may sound a wonderful idea from an SE perspective but it poses huge challenges to the structure and operations of a large pharmaceutical firm with complex economics around R&D funding, distribution and so on
	It's also important to build coalitions of support. Securing support for social innovation is often a distributed process, but power and resources are often not concentrated in the hands of a single decision-maker. There may also not be a board or venture capitalist to pitch the ideas to. Instead, it is a case of building momentum and groundswell
	And there is a need to provide practical demonstrations of what otherwise may be seen as idealistic pipedreams. The role of pilots which then get taken up and gather support is well-proven, for example the Fair Trade model or microfinance
Developing the venture	Social innovation requires extensive creativity in getting hold of the diverse resources to make things happen, especially since the funding base may be limited. Networking skills become critical here, engaging different players and aligning them with the core vision
	One of the most important elements in much social innovation is scaling up, taking what may be a good idea implemented by one person or in a local community and amplifying it so that it has widespread social impact. For example, Anshu Gupta's original idea was to recycle old clothes found on rubbish dumps or cast away to help poor people in his local community. Beginning with 67 items of clothing, the idea has now been scaled up so that his organization collects and recycles 40 000 kg of cloth every month across 23 states in India. The principle has been applied to other materials, for example recycling old cassettes to make mats and soft furnishings (see www.goonj.org/)

TABLE 2.1 *(Continued)*	
What has to be managed...	**Challenges in social entrepreneurship**
Innovation strategy	Here the overall vision is critical: the passionate commitment to a clear vision can engage others, but social entrepreneurs can also be accused of idealism and 'having their head in the clouds'. Consequently, there is a need for a clear plan to translate the vision step-by-step into reality
Innovative organization/ rich networking	Social innovation depends on loose and organic structures where the main linkages are through a sense of shared purpose. At the same time there is a need to ensure some degree of structure to allow for effective implementation. The history of many successful social innovations is essentially one of networking, mobilizing support and accessing diverse resources through rich networks. This places a premium on networking and broking skills

Audio Clip of a talk about using business skills in a social context given by Carmel McConnel is available on the Innovation Portal at **www.innovation-portal.info**

The Challenges of Social Entrepreneurship

While changing the world with social innovation is possible, it isn't easy! Just because there is no direct profit motive doesn't take the commercial challenges out of the equation. If any-thing, it becomes harder to be an entrepreneur when the challenge is not only to convince people that it can be done (and use all the tricks of the entrepreneur's trade to do so) but also to do so in a form that makes it commercially sustainable. Bringing a radio within reach of rural poor across Africa is a great idea – but someone still has to pay for raw materials, build and run a factory, arrange for distribution and collect the small money from the sales. None of this comes cheap, and setting up such a venture faces economic, political and business obstacles every bit as hard as a bright start-up company in medical devices or computer software working in a developed country environment.

Case Study of Lifeline Energy, a social innovation, describing the difficulties in moving from a 'good idea' to building a sustainable, scalable venture is available on the Innovation Portal at **www.innovation-portal.info**

Video Clip of Red Button highlighting some of the challenges facing social entrepreneurship is available on the Innovation Portal at **www.innovation-portal.info**

Case Study of Red Button is available on the Innovation Portal at **www.innovation-portal.info**

The problem isn't just the difficulty of finding resources. Table 2.2 lists some other examples of the difficulties social entrepreneurs face when trying to innovate for the greater good.

TABLE 2.2 Challenges in social innovation

Problem area	Challenges
Resources	Not easily available and may need to cast the net widely to secure funding and other support
Conflicts	While the overall goal may be to meet a social need, there may be conflicts in how this can be balanced against the need to generate revenue. For example, Lifeline Energy wanted to provide simple communication devices for the developing world and provide employment to disabled people. The costs of the latter made the former difficult to achieve competitively and set up a major conflict for the management of the enterprise
Voluntary nature	Many people involved in social innovation are there because of core values and beliefs and contribute their time and energy in a voluntary way. This means that 'traditional' forms of organization and motivation may not be available, posing a significant human resource management challenge
'Lumpy' funding	Unlike commercial businesses where a stream of revenue can be sued to fund innovation in a consistent fashion, many social enterprises rely on grants, donations and other sources which are intermittent and unpredictable
Scale of the challenge	The sheer size of many of the issues being addressed – how to provide clean drinking water, how to deliver reliable low-cost healthcare, how to combat illiteracy – means that having a clear focus is essential. Without a targeted innovation strategy, social enterprises risk dissipating their efforts

Video Clips of talks given by social entrepreneurs in India, Jane Chen and Arunachalam Muruganantham, describing their challenges and ultimate success are available on the Innovation Portal at **www.innovation-portal.info**

Chapter Summary

- Innovation is about creating value and one important dimension of this is making change happen in a socially valuable direction.

- 'Social entrepreneurs' – individuals and organizations – recognize a social problem and organize an innovation process to enable social change.

- Just because there is no direct profit motive doesn't take the commercial challenges out of the equation. If anything, it becomes harder to be an entrepreneur when the challenge is to convince people not only that it can be done (and use all the tricks of the entrepreneur's trade to do so) but also that it can be done in a form which makes it commercially sustainable.

- Social entrepreneurship of this kind is also an increasingly important component of 'big business', as large organizations realize they only secure a licence to operate if they can demonstrate some concern for the wider communities in which they are located.

- There are also benefits which emerge through aligning corporate values with those of employees within organizations.

- And there are significant learning opportunities through experiments in social innovation which may have impacts on mainstream innovation.

- Making social entrepreneurship happen will require learning and absorbing a new set of skills to sit alongside our current ways of thinking about and managing innovation. How do we find opportunities which deliver social as well as economic benefits? How do we identify and engage a wide range of stakeholders – and understand and meet their very diverse expectations? How do we mobilize resources across networks? How do we build coalitions of support for socially valuable ideas?

Key Terms Defined

Social enterprise   an organization that tries to pursue a double bottom line or a triple bottom line.

Social entrepreneurship   applying entrepreneurship to achieve social goals rather than (but not excluding) financial reward.

Triple bottom line   simultaneous assessment of a company's performance against its financial and shareholder performance, its internal and external stakeholder expectations and responsibilities, and its environmental responsibilities.

Discussion Questions

1. Give a man a fish and you feed him for a day. Teach a man to fish and he can feed himself for life. How could you put this principle into practice through a social entrepreneurship venture – and what would stop you making a success of this?

2. 'Some problems have no solution' – a somewhat pessimistic Japanese saying. How could a social entrepreneur challenge this?

3. Jasmine Chang has approached you – as an innovation adviser – with a novel treatment for childhood diarrhoea. How would you advise her to take this idea forward to make a difference?

4. In many ways, taking a socially valuable concept to market has much in common with 'conventional' new product development. Where do you see the similarities and differences?

Further Reading and Resources

There is a wealth of information about social entrepreneurship, including useful websites for the Ashoka Foundation (www.ashoka.org), the Skoll Foundation (www.skollfoundation.com) and the Institute for Social Entrepreneurs (www.socialent.org). Chapter 12 has a case example of the UK organization UnLtd and web links to its site. Stanford University's Entrepreneurs website has a number of resources, including videos of social entrepreneurs explaining their projects (http://edcorner.stanford.edu).

A number of books describing approaches and tools include David Bornstein's *How to Change the World: Social Entrepreneurs and the Power of New Ideas* (Oxford, 2004), Peter Brinckerhoff's *Social Entrepreneurship: The Art of Mission-Based Venture Development* (John Wiley & Sons Ltd, 2000), Gregory Dees *et al.*'s *Enterprising Nonprofits: A Tool-kit for Social Entrepreneurs* (John Wiley & Sons Ltd, 2001) and Robin Murray *et al.*'s *The Open Book of Social Innovation* (The Young Foundation, 2010).

Case studies of projects like Grameen bank (www.grameen-info.org) and the wind-up radio (www.freeplayenergy.com) also give insights into the process and the difficulties confronting social entrepreneurs. A useful website here is www.howtochangetheworld.org/, as is that of the Ashoka Foundation, www.ashoka.org. Prahalad's book *The Fortune at the Bottom of the Pyramid* is a useful collection of cases in this direction.

References

1. Mulgan, G. (2007) *Ready or Not? Taking Innovation in the Public Sector Seriously*, London: NESTA.

2. http://samasource.org/, accessed 20th December 2014.

3. www.digitaldividedata.org/, accessed 20th December 2014.

4. http://crowdflower.com/, accessed 20th December 2014.

5. Ramalingam, B., K. Scriven and C. Foley (2010) *Innovations in International Humanitarian Action*, London: ALNAP.

6. Prahalad, C.K. (2006) *The Fortune at the Bottom of the Pyramid*, Upper Saddle River, NJ: Wharton School Publishing.

7. Bessant, J., H. Rush and A. Trifilova (2012) Jumping the tracks: Crisis-driven social innovation and the development of novel trajectories. *Die Unternehmung – Swiss Journal of Business Research and Practice*, **66**(3): 221–42.

Deeper Dive explanations of innovation concepts and ideas are available on the Innovation Portal at **www.innovation-portal.info**

Quizzes to test yourself further are available online via the Innovation Portal at **www.innovation-portal.info**

Summary of online resources for Chapter 2 –
all material is available via the Innovation Portal at
www.innovation-portal.info

Cases	**Media**	**Tools**	**Activities**	**Deeper Dives**
• Aravind Eye Clinics • Rare diseases project • NHS RED • Open Door • Crisis-driven innovation • Eastville Community Shop • Narayana Hrudayalaya Hospitals (NHL) • Lifespring Hospitals • Lifeline Energy • Red Button	• Aravind Eye Clinics • Grameen Bank • Honey Bee • Leila Janah • User's perspective of Samasource • Melissa Clark-Reynolds • Suzana Moreira • Helle-Vibeke Carstensen • Lynne Maher • Simon Tucker • Jeff Church • Patient innovation project • Tad Golesworthy • Patient care • Carmel McConnel • Red Button • Jane Chen • Arunachalam Muruganantham	—	—	• Responsible innovation framework

Chapter 3

Innovation, Globalization and Development

LEARNING OBJECTIVES

By the end of this chapter you will develop an understanding of:

* the reasons for, and implications of, the uneven global distribution of innovation
* the main components of a national system of innovation, and how these interact to influence the degree and direction of innovation in a country
* the challenges faced and the opportunities offered by emerging markets, in particular meeting needs at 'the bottom of the pyramid'.

Globalization of Innovation

Innovation and enterprise are central to the development and growth of emerging economies, and yet their contribution is usually considered in terms of the most appropriate national policy and institutions, or the regulation of international trade. Macroeconomic issues are important and national systems of innovation, including formal policy, institutions and governance, can have a profound influence on the degree and direction of innovation and enterprise in a country or region. Four factors have a major influence on the ability of a firm to develop and create value through innovation:

- The *national system of innovation* in which the firm is embedded, and which in part defines its range of choices in dealing with opportunities and threats.
- Its power and *market position* within the international value chain, which in part defines the innovation-based opportunities and threats that it faces.
- The *capability and processes* of the firm, including research, design, development, production, marketing and distribution.
- The ability to identify and exploit *external sources of innovation*, especially international networks.

However, it is equally critical to consider a more micro perspective, in particular innovation by firms and the entrepreneurship of individuals. Therefore in this chapter we examine the respective roles of national systems and policy, the capabilities of firms, the initiative of individual entrepreneurs and the interactions between these three perspectives.

In his best-selling book, *The World is Flat: The Globalized World in the 21st Century* (Penguin, 2007), Thomas Friedman argues that developments in technology and trade, in particular information and communications technologies (ICTs), are spreading the benefits of globalization to the emerging economies, promoting their development and growth. This optimistic thesis is appealing, but the evidence suggests the reality is rather more complex.

First, technology and innovation are not evenly distributed globally, and are not easily packaged and transferred across regions or firms. For example, only about a quarter of the innovative activities of the world's largest 500 technologically active firms are located outside their home countries.[1] Second, different national contexts influence significantly the ability of firms to absorb and exploit such technology and innovation. For example, state ownership and the availability of venture capital both influence entrepreneurship.[2] Third, the position of firms in international value chains can constrain profoundly their ability to capture the benefits of their innovation and entrepreneurship. Many firms in emerging economies have become trapped in dependent relationships as low-cost providers of low-technology, low-value manufactured goods or services, and have failed to develop their own design or new products.[3]

Since the 1980s, some analysts and practitioners have argued that, following the 'globalization' of product markets, financial transactions and direct investment, innovation activities should also become globalized. However, although striking examples of the internationalization of R&D can be found (e.g. the large Dutch firms, particularly Philips, and some more progressive German firms, such as Siemens), more comprehensive evidence casts doubt on the strength of such a trend. The evidence from patent files and R&D data suggests that innovation remains unevenly distributed across the world:

- The world's largest firms perform about only 25% of their innovative activities outside their home country. Overall, the proportion of R&D expenditure made outside the home nation is growing, albeit slowly, from less than 15% in 1995.

- Since the late 1990s, European firms – and especially those from France, Germany and Switzerland – have been performing an increasing share of their innovative activities in the USA, in large part in order to tap into local skills and knowledge in such fields as biotechnology and IT.
- The most important factor explaining each firm's share of foreign innovative activities is its share of foreign production. Firms from smaller countries in general have higher shares of foreign innovative activities. On average, foreign production is less innovation-intensive than home production.

Controversy remains both in the interpretation of this general picture and in the identification of implications for the future. Our own views are as follows:[4]

- There are major efficiency advantages in the geographic concentration in one place of strategic R&D for launching major new products and processes (first model and production line). These include dealing with unforeseen problems, since proximity allows quick, adaptive decisions; and integrating R&D, production and marketing, since proximity allows integration of tacit knowledge through close personal contacts.
- The nature and degree of the international dispersion of R&D will also depend on the company's major technological trajectory, and the strategically important points for integration and learning that relate to it. Thus, whereas automobile firms find it difficult to separate their R&D geographically from production when launching a major new product, drug firms can do so and instead locate their R&D close to strategically important basic research and testing procedures.
- In deciding about the internationalization of their R&D, managers must distinguish between becoming part of global knowledge networks, in other words being aware of, and able to absorb, the results of R&D being carried out globally. Practising scientists and engineers have always done this, and it is now easier with modern IT. However, business firms are finding it increasingly useful to establish relatively small laboratories in foreign countries in order to become strong members of local research networks and thereby benefit from the person-embodied knowledge behind the published papers; and the launching of major innovations, which remains complex, costly and depends crucially on the integration of tacit knowledge. This remains difficult to achieve across national boundaries. Firms therefore still tend to concentrate major product or process developments in one country.
- Matching global knowledge networks with the localized launching of major innovations will require increasing international mobility amongst technical personnel, and the increasing use of multinational teams in launching innovations.
- Advances in IT have enabled spectacular increases in the international flow of codified knowledge in the form of operating instructions, manuals and software. They may also have some positive impact on international exchanges of tacit knowledge through teleconferencing, but not anywhere near to the same extent. Product development and the first stage of the product cycle will still require frequent and intense personal exchanges, and be facilitated by physical proximity.

- The main factors influencing the decision of where to locate R&D globally are, in order of importance:
  1. the availability of critical competencies for the project
  2. the international credibility (within the organization) of the R&D manager responsible for the project
  3. the importance of external sources of technical and market knowledge (e.g. sources of technology, suppliers and customers)
  4. the importance and costs of internal transactions (e.g. between engineering and production)
  5. cost and disruption of relocating key personnel to the chosen site.

INNOVATION IN ACTION 3.1

Frugal Innovation from Emerging Economies

An *Economist* Special Report argues that emerging economies are fast becoming sources of innovation, rather than simply relying on low-cost labour, and appears to support the popular belief that innovation is increasingly a global phenomenon.

Woolridge estimates that there are more than 20 000 multinational companies (MNCs) originating from the emerging economies, and that the firms in the *Financial Times* 500 list from the BRIC economies – Brazil, Russia, India and China – more than quadrupled in 2006–2008, from 15 to 62. The focus of innovation is not confined to technological breakthroughs, but typically incremental process and product innovations, aimed at the middle or the bottom of the income pyramid, such as the $3,000 car, $300 computer and $30 mobile phone, so-called frugal innovation.

For example, in India Tata Consultancy Services (TCS) has developed a water filter which uses rice husks. It is simple, portable and relatively cheap, giving a large family an abundant supply of bacteria-free water for an initial investment of about $24 and around $4 every few months for a new filter. Similarly, General Electric's Bangalore R&D facility has developed a hand-held electrocardiogram (ECG) called the Mac 400. Through simplification, the Mac 400 can run on batteries and fit in a rucksack, and sells for $800, instead of $2,000 for a conventional ECG, which reduces the cost of an ECG test to just $1 per patient. These innovations target two of India's most common health problems: contaminated water and heart disease, which cause millions of deaths each year.

 Video Clip of C.K. Prahalad's discussion of the potential for innovation at the 'bottom of the pyramid' of market demand is available on the Innovation Portal at **www.innovation-portal.info**

Source: Derived from Wooldridge, A. (2010) 'The world turned upside down', *The Economist*, 15th April, Special Report.

Learning from Foreign Systems of Innovation

While information on competitors' innovations is relatively cheap and easy to obtain, corporate experience shows that knowledge of how to replicate competitors' product and process innovations is much more costly and time-consuming to acquire. Useful and usable knowledge does not come cheap. Such imitation typically costs between 60 and 70% of the original, and typically takes three years to achieve. These conclusions are illustrated by the examples of Japanese, Korean and Taiwanese firms, where very effective imitation has been sustained by heavy and firm-specific investments in education, training and R&D.

Firms can benefit more specifically from the technology generated in foreign systems of innovation. A high proportion of large European firms attach great importance to foreign sources of technical knowledge, whether obtained through affiliated firms (i.e. direct foreign investment) and joint ventures, links with suppliers and customers or reverse engineering. In general, they find it is more difficult to learn from Japan than from North America and elsewhere in Europe, probably because of greater distances – physical, linguistic and cultural. Perhaps more surprising, European firms find it most difficult to learn from foreign publicly funded research. This is because effective learning involves more subtle linkages than straightforward market transactions, for example the membership of informal professional networks. This public knowledge is often seen as a source of potential world innovative advantage and, as we discussed earlier, firms are increasingly active in trying to access foreign sources. In contrast, knowledge obtained through market transactions and reverse engineering enables firms to catch up, and keep up, with competitors. East Asian firms have been very effective over the past 25 years in making these channels an essential feature of their rapid technological learning.

INNOVATION IN ACTION 3.2

Technology Strategies of Latecomer Firms in East Asia

The spectacular modernization in the past 25 years of the East Asian 'dragon' countries – Hong Kong, South Korea, Singapore and Taiwan – has led to lively debate about its causes. Michael Hobday has provided important new insights into how business firms in these countries succeeded in rapid learning and technological catch-up, in spite of underdeveloped domestic systems of science and technology, and of lack of technologically sophisticated domestic customers.

Government policies provided the favourable general economic climate: export orientation; basic and vocational education, with strong emphasis on industrial needs; and a stable economy, with low inflation and high savings. However, of major importance were the strategies and policies of specific business firms for the effective assimilation of foreign technology.

The main mechanism for catching up was the same in electronics, footwear, bicycles, sewing machines and automobiles, namely the OEM (original equipment manufacture) system. OEM is a specific form of subcontracting, where firms in catching-up countries produce goods to the

(continued)

exact specification of a foreign transnational company (TNC) normally based in a richer and technologically more advanced country. For the TNC, the purpose is to cut costs, and to this end it offers assistance to the latecomer firms in quality control, choice of equipment, and engineering and management training. OEM began in the 1960s, and became more sophisticated in the 1970s. The next stage in the mid-1980s was ODM (own design and manufacture), where the latecomer firms learnt to design products for the buyer. The last stage is OBM (own brand manufacture), where latecomer firms market their own products under their own brand name (e.g. Samsung, Acer) and compete head-on with the leaders.

For each stage of catching up, the company's technology position must be matched with a corresponding market position, as is shown in the table.

Stage	Technology position	Market position
1.	Assembly skills	Passive importer pull
	Basic production	Cheap labour
	Mature products	Distribution by buyers
2.	Incremental process change	Active sales to foreign buyer
	Reverse engineering	Quality and cost-based
3.	Full production skills	Advanced production sales
	Process innovation	International marketing department
	Product design	Markets own design
4.	R&D	Product marketing push
	Product innovation	Own brand product range and sales
5.	Frontier R&D	Own brand push
	R&D linked to market needs	In-house market research
	Advanced innovation	Independent distribution

Source: Hobday, M. (1995) *Innovation in East Asia: The challenge to Japan*, Guilford: Edward Elgar.

The slow but significant internationalization of R&D is also a means of firms learning from foreign systems of innovation. There are many reasons why MNCs choose to locate R&D outside their home country, including regulatory regime and incentives, lower cost or more specialized human resources, proximity to lead suppliers or customers, but in many cases a significant motive is to gain access to national or regional innovation networks. However, some countries are more advanced in internationalizing their R&D than others. In this respect, (some) European firms are the most internationalized, and the Japanese the least.

Managers report that the most important methods of learning about competitors' innovations are independent R&D, reverse engineering and licensing, all of which are expensive compared to reading publications and the patent literature. More formal approaches to technology intelligence gathering are less widespread, and the use of different approaches varies by company and sector (Figure 3.1). For example, in the pharmaceutical sector, where much of the knowledge is highly codified in publications and patents, these sources of information are scanned routinely, and the proximity to the science base is reflected in the widespread use of expert panels. In electronics, product technology roadmaps are commonly used, along with the lead users. Surprisingly, long-established and proven methods such as Delphi-studies, S-curve analysis and patent citations are not in widespread use.

Tools to help you explore forecasting techniques, such as the Delphi method and Scenarios, are available on the Innovation Portal at **www.innovation-portal.info**

National Systems of Innovation

In this section we examine how the national and market environment of a firm shapes its innovation strategy. We first show that the 'home country' positions of even global firms have a strong influence on their innovation strategies. The national influences can be grouped into three categories: 'competencies' (workforce education, research), 'economic inducement mechanisms' (local demand and input prices, competitive rivalry) and 'institutions' (methods of funding, controlling and managing business firms). For example, the largest numbers of European firms amongst the technical leaders were to be found in the technological fields of industrial and fine chemicals, and defence-related technologies (i.e. aerospace), which are fields of national technological strength, while the reverse is the case in electronics, capital equipment and consumer goods. Japanese firms predominate in consumer electronics and motor vehicle technologies, and US firms in fine chemicals and in raw-materials-based (i.e. oil, gas and food) and defence-related technologies, again reflecting the technological strengths of their home countries.

The strategic importance to corporations of home countries' technological competencies would matter little if they were all more or less the same, but they are not. Patterns of sectoral specialization differ greatly, for example the Japanese pattern of strengths and weaknesses is almost the opposite of that in the USA. In addition, countries differ in both the level and the rate of increase in the resources devoted by business firms to innovative activities. Compare Finland and Canada, both of whose economies rely heavily on natural resources; Finland's R&D expenditures have increased even more rapidly than Japan's as a share of GDP, while Canada's increased only slightly.

A study of the innovation capabilities of European countries based on two Community Innovation Surveys (which are conducted every four years by all nation-states within the EU) and other data estimated the effects of different macro and micro factors on innovation. Table 3.1 provides a summary of the results. Using patents as an indicator of innovation, innovation at the national level is positively influenced by the size of the economy, foreign competition in the domestic market, public expenditure on R&D and the availability of venture capital. It is negatively influenced by the presence of a relatively large number of small

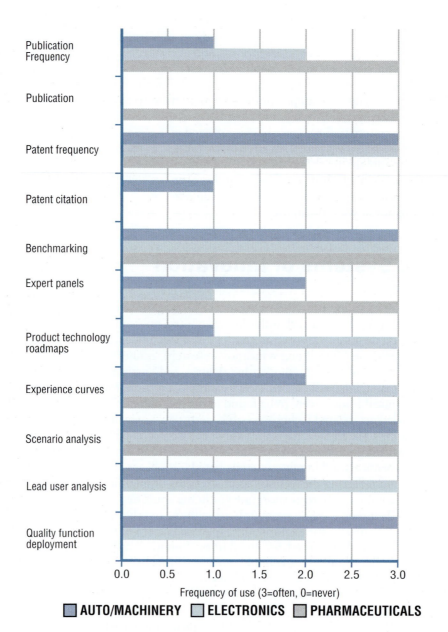

FIGURE 3.1   Use of methods of technology intelligence by sector

Source: Derived from Lichtenthaler, E. (2004) Technology intelligence processes in leading European and North American multinationals, *R&D Management*, **34**(2), 121–34.

TABLE 3.1 European national systems of innovation and innovation capability

NIS variable	Regression coefficient on	
	Patents granted	**Sales of new products**
Public R&D expenditure	+0.839	—
Firm expenditure on R&D	—	+0.421
Gross domestic product (GDP)	+0.691	+0.310
Openness of national economy	+0.319	−0.454
Availability of venture capital	+0.200	—
Presence of SMEs	−0.146	+0.621
External sources of innovation	—	+0.688
Presence of innovative firms	—	+0.591

Source: Derived from Faber, J. and A.B. Hesen (2004) Innovation capabilities of European nations: Cross sectional analyses of patents and sales of product innovations, *Research Policy*, **33**, 193–207.

and medium-sized firms, high company tax and a high level of economic prosperity. Using relative sales of innovative products as an indicator of innovation, firm-level effects become more evident: national innovation is positively influenced by the size of the economy, R&D expenditure of firms, use of external sources of innovation and the presence of small and medium-sized firms, but negatively influenced by economic prosperity and foreign competition in the home market. Put another way, macroeconomic conditions in a country and the structure of the national economy have significant effects on innovation, measured by patenting and sales of innovative products. At the national level, the innovative activities of firms appear to have a stronger influence on sales of innovative products than patenting does.

In conclusion, the national system of innovation in which a firm is embedded matters greatly, since it strongly influences both the direction and the vigour of its own innovative activities. However, managements still have ample influence over their firms' innovation strategies, and firms can benefit from foreign systems of innovation through a variety of mechanisms. Next, we identify and discuss the main national factors that influence the rate and direction of technological innovation in a country: more specifically, the national market 'incentives and pressures' to which firms have to respond, and the 'institutions of corporate governance'.

Incentives and Pressures: National Demand and Competitive Rivalry

Patterns of National Demands

Those concerned to explain international patterns of innovative activities have long recognized the important influence of local demand and price conditions on patterns of innovation in local firms. Strong local 'demand pull' for certain types of products generates innovation opportunities for local firms, especially when the demand depends on face-to-face interactions with customers. In Table 3.2 we identify the main factors that influence local demands for innovation, and give some examples. In addition to the obvious examples of local buyers' tastes, we identify:

- Local (private and public) investment activities, which create innovative opportunities for local suppliers of machinery and production inputs, where competence is accumulated mainly through experience in designing, building and operating machinery.
- Local production input prices, where international differences can help generate very different pressures for innovation (e.g. the effects of different petrol prices on the design and related competencies in automobiles in the USA and Europe). High prices can also generate pressure for substitute products, like synthetic fertilizers in Germany at the beginning of the 20th century.
- Local natural resources, which create opportunities for innovation in both upstream extraction and downstream processing.

A more subtle, but increasingly significant influence is the role of social concerns and pressure about the environment, safety and governance. For example, nuclear power as a technological innovation has evolved in very different ways in countries like the USA, the UK, France and Japan. Similarly, innovation in genetically modified crops and foods has taken radically different paths in the USA and Europe, mainly because of public concerns and political pressure.

TABLE 3.2   Local factors that influence the rate and direction of innovation

Factors in	Examples
Local buyers' tastes	Quality food and clothing in France and Italy
	Reliable machinery in Germany
Private investment activities	Automobile and other downstream investments stimulating innovation in computer-aided design and robots in Japan, Italy, Sweden and Germany
Public investment activities	Railways in France
	Medical instruments in Sweden
	Coal-mining machinery in the UK (<1979)
Input prices	Labour-saving innovations in the USA
	Europe–USA differences in automobile technology
	Environmental technology in Scandinavia
	Synthetic fertilizers in Germany
Local natural resources	Innovations in oil and gas, mineral ores, and food and agriculture in North America, Scandinavia and Australia

Competitive Rivalry

Innovation is always difficult and often upsetting to established interests and habits, and so local demands by themselves do not create the necessary conditions for innovation. Both case studies and statistical analysis show that competitive rivalry stimulates firms to invest in innovation and change, since their very existence will be threatened if they do not. For example, comparison of public policies towards the pharmaceutical industries in Britain and France show that the former was more successful in creating a demanding local competitive environment conducive to the emergence of British firms amongst global leaders. German strength in chemicals is based on three large and technologically dynamic firms – BASF, Bayer and Hoechst – rather than on one super-large national champion. Similarly, the Japanese strengths in consumer electronics and automobiles is based on numerous technologically active firms rather than a few giants (despite the early efforts of the Ministry of International Trade and Industry, MITI, to promote national champions and mergers; however, neither Sony nor Honda was a member of the Japanese industrial groups, or *zaibatsu*). A relatively smaller size also reduces the severity of the task of management to maintain corporate entrepreneurship. This is because managers can spend more time familiarizing themselves with the innovative potentialities of the various businesses, and can thereby avoid the dangers of managing divisions purely through financial indicators.

Thus although corporate policy-makers in large firms may often be tempted in the short term to avoid strong competition – and to reap extra monopoly profits – by merging with their competitors, the long-term costs could be considerable. Public policy-makers should be persuaded by the evidence that creating gigantic national champions does not increase innovation, quite the contrary, and therefore take countervailing measures. Lack of competitive rivalry makes firms less fit to compete on global markets through innovation.

In many countries, national advantages in natural resources and traditional industries have been fused with related competencies in broad technological fields that then become the basis for technological advantage in new product fields (Figure 3.2). For example, in Denmark, Sweden and Switzerland linkages with established fields of strength were the basis of local technological accumulation: metallurgy and materials in Sweden, machinery in Switzerland and Sweden, and chemistry and (more recently) biology in Switzerland and Denmark. Another example is the development of chemical engineering in the USA in response to the challenges and opportunities of refining petrol.

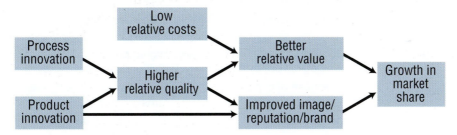

FIGURE 3.2   Evolution from natural endowment to national specialization of innovation

Source: Clayton, T. and G. Turner (2012) Brands, innovation and growth. In Tidd, J. (ed.) *From Knowledge Management to Strategic competence: Measuring Technological, Market and Organizational Innovation.* Imperial College Press, London. Copyright Imperial College Press/World Scientific Publishing Co.

Similarly, firms in the UK and the USA are particularly strong in software and pharmaceuticals, both of which require strong basic research and graduate skills, but few production skills; they are therefore particularly well matched to local skill structures. Japanese strength in consumer electronics and automobiles is particularly well matched to its local strength in production skills, as is the German strength in mechanical engineering.

Institutions: Finance, Management and Corporate Governance

Firms' innovative behaviours are strongly influenced by the competencies of their managers and the ways in which their performance is judged and rewarded (and punished). Methods of judgement and reward vary considerably amongst countries, according to their national systems of **corporate governance,** in other words the systems for exercising and changing corporate ownership and control. In broad terms, we can distinguish two systems: one practised in the USA and the UK and the other in Japan, Germany and its neighbours, such as Sweden and Switzerland. In his book *Capitalism against Capitalism,* Michel Albert calls the first the 'Anglo-Saxon' and the second the 'Nippon–Rhineland' variety. A lively debate continues about the essential characteristics and performance of the two systems, in terms of innovation and other performance variables. Table 3.3 is based on a variety of sources, and tries to identify the main differences that affect innovative performance.

In the UK and the USA, corporate ownership (shareholders) is separated from corporate control (managers), and the two are mediated through an active stock market. Investors can

TABLE 3.3   National governance structures and innovation

Characteristics	Anglo-Saxon	Nippon–Rhineland
Ownership	Individuals, pension funds, insurers	Companies, individuals, banks
Control	Dispersed, arm's length	Concentrated, close and direct
Management	Business schools (USA), accountants (UK)	Engineers with business training
Evaluation of R&D investments	Published information	Insider knowledge
Strengths	Responsive to radically new technological opportunities	Higher priority to R&D than to dividends for shareholders
	Efficient use of capital	Remedial investment in failing firms
Weaknesses	Short-termism	Slow to deal with poor investment choices
	Inability to evaluate firm-specific intangible assets	Slow to exploit radically new technologies

be persuaded to hold shares only if there is an expectation of increasing profits and share values. They can shift their investments relatively easily. On the other hand, in countries with governance structures like those of Germany or Japan, banks, suppliers and customers are more heavily locked into the firms in which they invest. Until the 1990s, countries strongly influenced by German and Japanese traditions persisted in investing heavily in R&D in established firms and technologies, while the US system has since been more effective in generating resources to exploit radically new opportunities in IT and biotechnology.

During the 1980s, the Nippon–Rhineland model seemed to be performing better. R&D expenditures were on a healthy upward trend, and so were indicators of aggregate economic performance. Since then, there have been growing doubts. The technological and economic indicators have been performing less well. Japanese firms have proved unable to repeat in telecommunications, software, microprocessors and computing their technological and competitive successes in consumer electronics. German firms have been slow to exploit radically new possibilities in IT and biotechnology, and there has been criticism of expensive and unrewarding choices in corporate strategy, like the entry of Daimler-Benz into aerospace. At the same time, US firms appear to have learnt important lessons, especially from the Japanese in manufacturing technology, and to have reasserted their eminence in IT and biotechnology. The 1990s also saw sustained increases in productivity in US industry.

However, some observers have concluded that the strong US performance in innovation cannot be satisfactorily explained simply by the combination of entrepreneurial management, a flexible labour force and a well-developed stock market. They argue that the groundwork for US corporate success in exploiting IT and biotechnology was laid initially by the US Federal Government, with the large-scale investments by the Defense Department in California in electronics, and by the National Institutes of Health in the scientific fields underlying biotechnology.[5] The influences institutions, incentives and competition have on innovation and entrepreneurship are complex, as illustrated by the case of Russia.

INNOVATION IN ACTION 3.3

Building BRICs – Capabilities in Russia

Industry in Russia is still dominated by heavy industry, including oil, gas, defence and aerospace. Consumer and service sectors are relatively poorly developed, reflecting national endowments and the legacy of the communist, centrally planned era. For example, in 2001 oil and energy accounted for about 70% of all industrial output, and 40% of total GDP. Similarly, hydrocarbons account for more than half of exports, followed by metals, which make up about a quarter of overseas sales. Some higher-technology sectors have emerged from the earlier specialization of the Soviet economy, such as space-launches, aviation and lasers, but these remain relatively small niches. This absence of significant innovations is an interesting paradox, given the strong national emphasis given to investment and training in science and technology.

(continued)

In the year 2000, Russia had more than 4000 formal organizations dedicated to science and technology, including 2600 public R&D centres employing almost a million qualified scientists and engineers. However, historically, the focus of these numerous organizations has been on basic scientific research rather than on technological or commercial innovation. The focus has been on 'big science' and the science-push model of innovation and growth, rather than a market or demand coupled model. On the supply side, the prestigious Russian Academy of Sciences dominates this system, and emphasizes disciplines traditionally seen as Soviet strengths in the theoretical and physical, such as mathematics, chemistry and physics. The Academy has never had the responsibility or role to commercialize scientific research or to support the development of new processes or products. While overall investment in science and technology has declined in Russia, the investment in basic sciences has proportionally declined far less than investment in the applied sciences and technologies. On the demand side, the traditional centrally planned, target-based structure did not provide incentives or resources for firms to develop or seek such innovations. Given this industrial structure and political legacy, the industrial research and design centres have failed to flourish: in 2000, there were fewer than 300 industrial R&D enterprises and around 400 design organizations.

Russia also has an unusual industrial structure by the size of enterprise. Compared to other industrial economies, very large firms and very small enterprises are relatively underrepresented, and instead in Russia medium-sized firms are the most common and economically significant. In most advanced economies the very large firms are the main investors in formal R&D and development of commercially significant innovations, whereas the microbusinesses provide a continuous outlet for more entrepreneurial behaviour. Typically, medium-sized enterprises are less important as they lack sufficient resources, but suffer from most of the disadvantages of size. They are also less likely to participate in international joint ventures and alliances, or to receive foreign direct investment (FDI).

Unlike the case of many other emerging economies, FDI and international joint ventures have played only a minor part in the development of the Russian economy. It accounts for only around 5% of total investment in Russia, compared to more than 20% in other former Soviet economies such as Hungary, Poland and Romania. The main foreign investments and associated transfers of technological and managerial know-how have been in the oil industry, because of its significance to the Russian economy, and the food industry, which historically has been a low national priority and has performed poorly. However, in most manufacturing and service sectors there has been little foreign investment or influence, and little improvement or innovation. There are many reasons for this relative isolation from international investment and innovation, including problems of governance, including legal restrictions on ownership and the dominance of dynastic insiders in the main industries. Therefore the institutional structure of Russia continues to constrain domestic and international innovation and entrepreneurship.

There are many cases of transfer of hard technologies in the oil and aerospace industries, both into and out of Russia, but these are usually rather conventional licensing agreements, with very little transfer or upgrading of critical managerial or commercial know-how. However, there are examples of successful innovation, often as a result of individual technical entrepreneurs or spin-offs from public research organizations working with firms overseas. For example, the Moscow Centre for SPARC Technology, founded by Boris Babayan, is funded by Sun Microsystems and is active in the workstation market, but is based on supercomputer technology used in the Soviet space and nuclear industries. Similarly, ParaGraph, a Russian software company, is based on technology used by the military for pattern recognition, but works with Apple to commercialize the technology.

Sources: Derived from D.A. Dyker (2006) *Closing the EU East–West Productivity Gap*, Imperial College Press, London; and D.A. Dyker (2004) *Catching Up and Falling Behind: Post-Communist Transformation in Historical Perspective*, Imperial College Press, London.

ENTREPRENEURSHIP IN ACTION 3.1

Russian Spirit

Spirit DSP is a world-leading provider of embedded voice and communication software products. More than 200 million embedded voice channels in over 80 countries are based on Spirit's technology (www.spiritdsp.com). Spirit's award-winning multi-point full-duplex voice conferencing engine is now inside collaboration solutions lately rolled out by Oracle and Macromedia. During the past 10 years Spirit served over 200 global telecom OEMs and software vendors, including Agere, Atmel, Ericsson, Furuno, HTC, Hyundai, Iwatsu, JRC, Kyocera, LG, Macromedia, Marconi, Namco, NEC, Nortel Networks, Oracle, Panasonic, Philips, Samsung, Siemens, Tadiran, Texas Instruments and Toshiba. Global top seven semiconductor vendors have installed Spirit voice and

communication software right on their processors. This example may certainly be an exception for emerging R&D sources but the fact is that the R&D centre is located in Moscow and the founder and chairman of Spirit is Andrew Sviridenko.

Case Study of Spirit is available on the Innovation Portal at **www.innovation-portal.info**

ENTREPRENEURSHIP IN ACTION 3.2

Russia's Internet Ventures

Russia's large domestic market, high barriers to entry and strong technical education have provided a unique opportunity for domestic Internet businesses.

Ozon is Russia's equivalent of Amazon, established during the first Internet bubble in 1999. It began selling books online within Russia, and has since expanded into broader e-commerce

(continued)

and has entered into Kazakhstan and Latvia. In 2013, it had 2100 employees and had sales of $492 million.

Yandex is a Russian search engine business, similar to Google. The company was launched in 1997, only eight days after Google. It expanded into Ukraine, Kazakhstan, Belarus and most recently Turkey. In 2013, it had a domestic market share of 62%, reached 90 million users monthly and employed 4300 across seven countries.

AlterGeo is a location-based social networking business. It's most recent service is a restaurant mobile app, similar to the USA Foursquare service. However, Altergeo launched a year before Foursquare. It won the best Russian start-up in 2013.

Source: J. Nickerson (2013) Russia's next tech titans, *Financial Times*, 19th September, 10–11.

Positions in International Value Chains

Development of firms from emerging economies is much more than simply catching up with those in the more advanced economies, and is not (only) the challenge of moving from 'followers' to 'leaders'. Global standards and position in international **value chains** can constrain the ability of firms based in emerging economies to upgrade their capabilities and appropriate greater value, but they also present ways in which these firms can innovate to overcome these hurdles, for example by using international standards as a catalyst for change, or by repositioning themselves in local clusters or global networks. By **position**, we refer to the current endowment of technology and intellectual property of a firm, as well as its relations with customers and suppliers.

INNOVATION IN ACTION 3.4

Globetronics – Evolution of Global Supply Chains

Globetronics Bhd. was formed in 1990 by two Malaysians formerly employed by Intel. The Malaysian Technology Development Corporation (MTDC) provided 30% of the venture capital, and the company was subsequently floated in 1997 to raise additional capital for growth. The company's primary activities are similar to the majority of transnational semiconductor firms based in Malaysia, and involve post-fabrication manufacture of semiconductors, including assembly and packaging. Indeed, the company's main customers are American and Japanese transnationals. The significant difference is that domestic ownership and management have allowed Globetronics to more easily capture value-added activities such as development and marketing.

The company now has seven business divisions and a new plant in the Philippines. Two of the businesses are joint ventures with the Japanese firm Sumitomo. The relationship with

Sumitomo began as a simple subcontracting agreement, but over the years a high level of trust has been achieved and two joint ventures have been established. The first, SGT, was created in 1994, and is 49% owned by Globetronics. It is the largest manufacturer in the world and the only company outside of Japan to produce ceramic substrate semiconductor packages. The second joint venture, SGTI, was created in 1996, and is 30% owned by Globetronics. In both cases the Japanese partner has maintained majority ownership, but it is clear that the Malaysian partner has made some progress in assimilating the technological and design capabilities. This provides a promising model for companies in developing countries, to escape dependent subcontracting relationships by using joint ventures to upgrade their technological and market competencies.

Source: Tidd, J. and M. Brocklehurst (1999) Routes to technological learning and development: An assessment of Malaysia's innovation policy and performance, *Technological Forecasting and Social Change*, **63**(2), 239–57.

Case Study of Aravind Eye Clinics as an example of the importance of accumulated tacit knowledge and learning is available on the Innovation Portal at **www.innovation-portal.info**

INNOVATION IN ACTION 3.5

Chip Design in Asia

In the case of complex innovations, physical proximity is normally an advantage in the organization and location of design and development. However, a study of 60 electronics firms and 15 research organizations found that in the design and development of electronic chips there has been a growing geographic dispersion of organization and location. Over a decade, Asia's share of world chip design grew from almost nothing to around a third. It was forecast to reach a 50% world share by 2008, led by Japan, South Korea, Taiwan and Singapore, with Malaysia, India and China following fast.

The study concludes that two of the drivers of this trend are specific to the technology: changes in design methodology, which allow the de-coupling of design stages and the design of related components and sub-systems, and greater outsourcing and vertical specialization within global innovation systems. Therefore, any generalizations regarding the globalization of innovation are unwise.

Source: Derived from Ernst, D. (2005) Complexity and Internationalisation of Innovation: Why is Chip Design Moving to Asia? *International Journal of Innovation Management*, **9**(1), 47–74.

Building Capabilities and Creating Value

In this section, we discuss the importance of developing firm-level capabilities. Firms in emerging economies may pursue different routes to upgrading through innovation:[6]

- Process upgrading: incremental process improvements to adapt to local inputs, reduce costs or to improve quality.
- Product upgrading: through adaptation, differentiation, design and product development.
- Capability upgrading: improving the range of functions undertaken, or changing the mix of functions (e.g. production versus development or marketing).
- Inter-sectoral upgrading: moving to different sectors (e.g. to those with higher value-added).

To some extent firms in emerging economies face a reverse product–process innovation lifecycle. We saw earlier that the most common pattern of evolution of technological innovation in the industrialized world has been from product to process innovation on the one hand and from radical to incremental innovation on the other. Initially, a series of different radical product innovations emerge and compete in the market, but as the innovations and markets evolve together a 'dominant design' begins to emerge, and the locus of innovation shifts from product to process, and from radical to more incremental improvements in cost and quality.

In contrast, in emerging economies the path of evolution is often reversed, and begins with incremental process innovations, to produce an existing product at a lower cost or at a lower quality for different market needs. As firms improve their capabilities they may then begin to make product adaptations and changes in design, and eventually move towards more radical product innovation. This has important implications for the type of capabilities firms need to develop. For example, at first, the emphasis should be on incremental process improvement and development, which suggests innovation in production and organization, rather than technological development or formal R&D. This suggests a hierarchy of capabilities or learning, each adding greater value.

Therefore, upgrading consists of improvements and changes in the operation of complex technical and organizational systems. This involves trial, error and learning. Learning tends to be incremental, since major step changes in too many parameters both increase uncertainty and reduce the capacity to learn. As a consequence, firms' learning processes are path-dependent, with the directions of search strongly conditioned by the competencies accumulated for the development and exploitation of their existing product base. Moving from one path of learning to another can be costly, even impossible, given cognitive limits – think of the problems of learning a foreign language from scratch.

However, dynamic capabilities typically involve long-term commitments to specialized resources, and consist of patterned activity to relatively specific objectives. Therefore, dynamic capabilities involve both the exploitation of existing competencies and the development of new ones. For example, leveraging existing competencies through new product development can consist of de-linking existing technological or commercial competencies from one set of current products and linking them in a different way to create new products. However, new product development can also help to develop new competencies. For example, an existing technological competence may demand new commercial competencies to reach a new market, or conversely a new technological competence may be necessary to service an existing customer.

The trick is to get the right balance between exploitation of existing competencies and the exploitation and development of new competencies. Research suggests that over time some firms are more successful at this than others, and that a significant reason for this variation in performance is due to difference in the ability of managers to build, integrate and reconfigure organizational competencies and resources. These 'dynamic' managerial capabilities are influenced by managerial cognition, human capital and social capital. 'Cognition' refers to the beliefs and mental models which influence decision-making. These affect the knowledge and assumptions about future events, available alternatives and association between cause and effect. This will restrict a manager's field of vision, and influence perceptions and interpretations. 'Human capital' refers to the learnt skills that require some investment in education, training experience and socialization, and these can be generic, industry- or firm-specific. It is the firm-specific factors that appear to be the most significant in dynamic managerial capability, which can lead to different decisions when faced with the same environment. 'Social capital' refers to the internal and external relationships which affect a manager's access to information, their influence, control and power.

Tool to help organizations identify and develop capabilities to create value, Identifying innovative capabilities, is available on the Innovation Portal at **www.innovation-portal.info**

Building BRICs: The Rise of New Players on the Innovation Stage

The current wave of innovation expansion has seen a focus on key countries known as the BRICs – Brazil, Russia, India and China – but there are many other smaller economies surging into the same space, for example Kazakhstan or South Africa. They share a mixture of rich resource endowments, relatively young populations, large potential domestic markets, reasonably developed infrastructure and a technological base which provides them with a platform for growing and building innovation capability to play on the wider global stage.

Video Clips of talks by Nirmalya Kumar about India's hidden innovation contribution and Nandan Nilekani about the rise of software services are available on the Innovation Portal at **www.innovation-portal.info**

INNOVATION IN ACTION 3.6

Building BRICs – Capabilities in India

India has a population of around 1.1 billion, a large proportion of which is English-speaking, a relatively stable political and legal regime, and a good national system of education, especially in science and engineering. It has some 250 universities and listed 1500 R&D centres (although care needs to be taken in the definitions used in both cases), and this has translated into international strengths in the fields of biotechnology, pharmaceuticals and software. As a result Indian firms have benefited greatly from the increasing international division of labour in some services and the support and development of software and services. India is now a global centre for outsourcing and offshoring. Until the mid-1980s, the software industry was dominated by government and public research organizations, but the introduction of export processing zones provided tax breaks and allowed the import of foreign computer technology for the first time. The market liberalization of 1991 accelerated development and inward investment, and in 2005 India attracted inward investment of $6 billion (significant, but still only around a tenth of that attracted by China). Since then the software and services industry in India grew by around 50% each year to reach $8.3 billion by 2000, and employed 400 000, second only to the USA. In 2014, the IT services sector generated revenues of US$ 108 billion. Unusually for India, which has historically pursued a policy of national self-reliance, the industry is very export-oriented, with around 70% of output being traded internationally.

There are three broad types of software firms in India. First, those that specialize in a specific sector or domain, for example accounting, gaming or film production, and these develop capabilities and relationships specific to those users. Second, those that develop methods and tools to provide low-cost and timely software support and solutions. The majority of the industry is in this lower-value-added part of the supply chain, and is involved in low-level coding, maintenance and design, and relies on a large pool of English-speaking talent which costs around 10% of that in the USA or the EU. However, a third segment of firms is emerging that is more involved with new product and service development.

India's version of Silicon Valley is around the southern city of Bangalore. This is home to a large number of firms from the USA, as well as indigenous Indian firms. Large employers include Infosys, and call and service centres here employ 250 000 operatives, including support services for firms such as Cisco, Microsoft and Dell. IBM, Intel, Motorola, Oracle, Sun Microsystems, Texas Instruments and GE all now have technology centres there. Texas Instruments was one of the few major foreign firms to start up a development unit, in 1985, prior to the opening up of the India economy in 1991. GE Medical Systems followed in the late 1980s and established a development centre in Bangalore in 1990, which later resulted in a joint venture with the India firm Wipro Technologies. GE now employs 20 000 people in India, who generate sales of $500 million. IBM was one of the first investors in India, but later withdrew because of the onerous government policy and restrictions in the 1980s. It returned after the government liberalized the economy, and its Indian operations contributed $510 million in sales in 2005, employing 43 000 in India following the acquisition of the Indian outsourcing company Daksh in 2004. In 2014, IBM announced plans to invest over $1.2 billion in India to expand its global cloud computing services.

One of the challenges of the software and services industry in India is to increase value-added through product and service development. To date the impressive growth has been based on winning more outsourcing business from overseas and employing more staff, rather than on increasing the value-added by new services and products. For example, the Indian software and service firm Tata plans to increase the proportion of its revenue from new products from around 5% to 40%, to make it less reliant on low-cost human capital, which is likely to become more expensive, and more mobile. Ramco Systems developed an ERP system in the 1990s, which cost a billion rupees to develop and involved 400 developers. By 2000, the company was profitable, with 150 customers, half overseas. It has established sales and support offices in the USA, Europe and Singapore. In 2006, the Indian outsourcing company Genpact (40% owned by GE of the USA) launched a joint venture with New Delhi Television (NDTV) to offer digital video editing, post-production and archiving services to media firms. The industry is worth $1 trillion, and 70% of all media work is now digital.

Based on patent citations, Indian firms rely much more on linkages with the science base and technology from the developed countries, whereas China has a broader reliance, which includes its Asian neighbours in other emerging economies, and specializes on more applied fields of technology. Indian firms rely on technologies from USA firms most – about 60% of all patent citations, followed by (in order of importance), Japan, Germany, France and the UK. In many cases, these linkages have been reinforced by inward investment by MNCs, but in other cases they are the result of Indians trained or employed overseas who have returned to India to create new ventures.

Infosys was one of the first and now one of the largest software and IT services firms in India. It was created by entrepreneur N. R. Narayana Murthy with six colleagues in 1981 with only $250, but revenues in 2014 were more than $8 billion in 2014. Murthy believes that 'entrepreneurship is the only instrument for countries like India to solve the problem of its poverty … it is our responsibility to ensure that those who have not made that kind of money have an opportunity to do so.'

Sources: Woo, J. (2012) *Technological Upgrading in China and India: What Do We Know?* OECD Development Centre Working Paper no. 308; N. Forbes and D. Wield (2002) *From Followers to Leaders: Managing Technology and Innovation*, Routledge, London; IEEE (2006) International Conference on Management of Innovation and Technology, Singapore; T.L. Friedman (2007) *The World is Flat: The Globalized World in the Twenty-First Century*, Penguin, London; India Brand Equity Foundation (2014), www.ibef.org.

INNOVATION IN ACTION 3.7

Building BRICs: Capabilities in Brazil

In his research, Fernando Perini examined the structure and dynamics of the knowledge networks in the IT and telecommunications sectors in Brazil. The Brazilian government promoted the development of the industry between 1997 and 2003 by the 'ICT Law' which provided tax incentives for

(continued)

collaborative R&D, following the liberalization of the economy in the early 1990s and the unsuccessful period of import substitution. This policy promoted an overall private investment of more than $2 billion in innovation, supporting partnerships in innovation projects inside a network of 216 companies and 235 universities and research institutes, but the lasting effects on firm and national capabilities are more mixed. While the policy of tax incentives promoted a higher level of investments in innovation, it did not determine the direction or organization of innovation in the sector.

The study concludes that the effect of the tax incentives depends on the nature of the technology and industry structure. They were important in helping to create knowledge networks in system and software technologies where MNCs were key players, but much less successful in equipment, semiconductors, production process and hardware, where MNCs relied most on internal R&D and their own international networks. However, the MNCs did develop new partnerships in product development in IT systems and software, mainly with new private research institutes, rather than with established universities and research centres. Many of these private research institutes have become network integrators in the Brazilian ICT sector, and act as technological partners in activities such as training, technological services and research.

However, a small number of MNCs still dominate the Brazilian market. More than 70% of the total investments under the ICT Law were conducted by the top 15 MNC subsidiaries.

For example, Lucent entered Brazil through the acquisition of two main national telecom companies, Zetax and Batik. In 2011 Alcatel-Lucent opened a new 15 400 square feet technology centre in São Paulo, to support the expansion of broadband and 4G mobile in Brazil, and in 2014 announced the start of construction of the Seabras-1 submarine fibre optic cable system between the US and Brazil. The lab has competencies in both hardware and software, but there has been a shift towards software because it is less influenced by the regulation of international trade. The lab includes a new group of 50 engineers created in 2004 to develop competencies in optical access, specifically an optical concentrator for public commutation networks. The interaction with the global R&D community is very strong, in particular through the exchange of personnel. For example, the new optical unit involved the exchange of 35 people for two months. In addition, Lucent has developed local supply and research networks, and approximately 85% of its external activities are outsourced to FITec. FITec has facilities throughout Brazil, including Campinas, Belo Horizonte and Recife.

Siemens Mercosur has the longest and largest MNC presence in Brazil. The subsidiary has developed technological capabilities mainly in telecommunications and since the ICT law expired continues to invest more than twice that required by legislation. R&D at the subsidiary is divided into six groups; the largest in Manaus, has 300 technical staff and specializes in Mobile Handsets that supply global markets. In addition, the Networks development group in Curitiba has around 120 engineers and the Enterprise group 100 engineers. In relation to local technological partners, Siemens has focused on the upgrading of partnerships in the south, including two local universities (UTF-PR and PUC-PR) and one private institute (CITS), but the removal of public incentives and shifts in the technology have increased

Case Study of Instituto Nokia de Tecnologia (INdT), a joint venture with the Brazilian government to work on solutions for local and global ICT needs, is available on the Innovation Portal at **www.innovation-portal.info**

the importance of the partnership with CITS. However, the subsidiary has also invested in enabling institutes and post-graduate courses, for example it helped to create a new postgraduate degree in computer science in Manaus. Another initiative is the creation of an Innovation Portal to register and process innovative ideas from Brazilian companies and researchers.

Source: Perini, F. (2010) *The Structure and Dynamics of the Knowledge Networks: Incentives to Innovation and R&D Spillovers in the Brazilian ICT Sector*, DPhil dissertation, SPRU, University of Sussex, UK.

Video Clip of Ana Sena describing the work of INdT in its Living Lab aiming to meet the needs of the largely rural population of Amazonas is available on the Innovation Portal at **www.innovation-portal.info**

Case Study of Natura, a cosmetics company using a similar model to the Body Shop's, aiming to bring natural cosmetic products to a rapidly growing international market is available on the Innovation Portal at **www.innovation-portal.info**

INNOVATION IN ACTION 3.8

Building BRICs — Innovation Capabilities in China

Since economic reform began in 1978, the Chinese economy has grown by about 9–10% each year, compared to 2–3% for the industrialized countries. As a result, its GDP overtook Italy in 2004, France and the UK in 2005 and in 2014 was second only to the USA.

After two decades of providing the world economy with inexpensive labour, China is becoming a platform for innovation, research and development. The formal R&D expenditure reached about 1.8% of GDP in 2014 (compared to an average of 2.4% of GDP in the advanced economies of the OECD, although Japan exceeds 3%), and the Chinese government aims to increase R&D expenditure to 2.5% of GDP by 2020, and to make China a scientific power by 2050.

China's policy has followed the East Asian model in which success has depended on technological and commercial investment by and collaboration with foreign firms. Typically, companies in the East Asian tiger economies such as South Korea and Taiwan developed technological capabilities on a foundation of manufacturing competence based on low-tech production, and developed higher levels of capability such as design and new product development, for example, through OEM (own equipment manufacture) production for international firms. However, the flow of technology and development of capabilities are not automatic. Economists refer to **spillovers** of know-how from foreign investment and collaboration, but this demands a significant effort by domestic firms.

Most significantly, China has encouraged foreign MNCs to invest in China, and these are now also beginning to conduct some R&D in China. Motorola opened the first foreign R&D

(continued)

lab in 1992, and estimates indicate there were more than 1000 R&D centres in China by 2014, although care needs to be taken in the definitions used. In 2014, the Chinese PC manufacturer Lenovo acquired Motorola from Google. The transfer of technology to China, especially in the manufacturing sector, is considered a major contributor to its recent economic growth. Around 80% of China's inward FDI is 'technology' (hardware and software), and FDI inflows have continued to grow. However, we must distinguish between technology transferred by foreign companies into their wholly or majority-owned subsidiaries in China versus the technology acquired by indigenous enterprises. It is only through the successful acquisition of technological capability by indigenous enterprises, many of which still remain state-owned, that China can become a really innovative and competitive economic power.

The import of foreign technology can have a positive impact on innovation, and for large enterprises the more foreign technology is imported, the more conducive to its own patenting. However, for the small and medium-sized enterprises this is not the case. This probably implies that larger enterprises possess certain absorptive capacity to take advantage of foreign technology, which in turn leads to an enhancement of innovation capacity, whereas small and medium-sized enterprises are more likely to rely on foreign technology owing to the lack of appropriate absorptive capacity and the possibly huge gap between imported and its own technology. Buying bundles of technology has been encouraged. These included 'embodied' and 'codified' technology: hardware and licences. If innovation expenditure is broken down by class of innovative activity, the costs of acquisition for embodied technology, such as machines and production equipment, account for about 58% of the total innovation expenditures, compared with 17% internal R&D, 5% external R&D, 3% marketing of new product, 2% training cost and 15% engineering and manufacturing start-up.

It is clear that the large foreign MNCs are the most active in patenting in China. Foreign patenting began in around 1995, and since 2000 patent applications have increased annually by around 50%. MNCs' patenting activities are highly correlated with total revenue, or the overall Chinese market size. This strongly supports the standpoint that foreign patents in China are largely driven by demand factors. China's specialization in patenting does not correspond to its export specialization. Automobiles, household durables, software, communication equipment, computer peripherals, semiconductors and telecommunication services are the primary areas. The semiconductor industry in 2005, for example, was granted as many as fourfold inventions of the previous year. Patents by foreign MNCs account for almost 90% of all patents in China, the most active being firms from Japan, the USA and South Korea. Thirty MNCs have been granted more than 1000 patents, and eight of these each have more than 5000: Samsung, Matsushita, Sony, LG, Mitsubishi, Hitachi, Toshiba and Siemens. Almost half of these patents are for the application of an existing technology, a fifth for inventions and the rest for industrial designs. Among the 18 000 patents for inventions with no prior overseas rights, only 924 originate from Chinese subsidiaries of these MNCs, accounting for only 0.75% of the total. The average lag between patenting in the home country and in China is more than three years, which is an indicator of the technology lag between China and MNCs.

Examples of companies which have gone through significant changes in governance or financial structure include Tianjin FAW Xiali, which was transformed into a joint venture with Toyota, TPCO, where debt funding was changed into equity and shareholding, which allowed higher investment in production capacity and technology development, and Tianjin Metal Forming, restructured to remove debt and in a stronger position to invest and be a more attractive candidate for a foreign investment. Private firms like Lenovo, TCL, (Ningbo) Bird and Huawei have since prospered and with belated government help are successful overseas. As a result of its success in telecommunications networks and mobile, Huawei achieved global sales of US $40 billion in 2014.

However, there are significant differences of innovation and entrepreneurial activity in different areas of China. The eastern coastal region is higher than the other regions, especially in Shanghai, Beijing, Tianjin, whose entrepreneurial activity level is higher and continues to grow. Beijing and the Tianjin Region, Yangtze River Delta Region (Shanghai, Jiangsu, Zhejiang) and Zhu Jiang Delta Region (Guangdong) are the most active regions. Shanghai ranks first in most surveys, followed by Beijing, but the disparity of the two areas has been expanding. The western and north-western region is the lowest and least-improving area for entrepreneurial activity level, and shows little change. Econometric models indicate that the main determinants for entrepreneurial activity are explained by regional market demand, industrial structure, availability of financing, entrepreneurial culture and human capital. Technology innovation and rate of consumption growth have no significant effects on the entrepreneurship in China.

Studies comparing successful and unsuccessful new ventures in China confirm the significance of entrepreneurial quality in explaining the success of new ventures, especially business and management skills, industrial experience and strength of social networks, the ubiquitous *guanxi*. However, there remain significant regulatory and institutional challenges with complex ownership structures, poor corporate governance and ambiguous intellectual property rights issues, especially with public research, former state enterprises and university spin-offs and academic-run enterprises.

Sources: Woo, J. (2012) *Technological Upgrading in China and India: What Do We Know?* OECD Development Centre Working Paper no. 308; Wang, Q., S. Collinson and X. Wu (eds) (2010) Special Issue on Innovation in China, *International Journal of Innovation Management* **14**(1); *East meets West: 15th International Conference on Management of Technology*, Beijing, May 2006.

Innovation for Development

A characteristic of BRICS and other emerging economies is that they can be simultaneously very advanced in terms of industrial and market development in some areas but also still at a relatively early stage of development in others. India, for example, has satellite technology, a global pharmaceuticals industry and some market-leading corporations but it also has huge problems of healthcare, illiteracy and basic infrastructure. And other countries – notably in Africa and much of Latin America – are still at a relatively early stage in their development of innovation capability.

But these conditions do not mean there is no scope for innovation. Indeed, there has been something of a revolution in thinking as we have come to realize that learning to meet the particular needs for goods and services in these spaces may actually offer radical new alternative pathways for innovation in more industrialized settings.

In his influential 2006 book *The Fortune at the Bottom of the Pyramid*, C.K. Prahalad points out that most of the world's population – around four billion people – live close to or below the poverty line, with an average income of less than \$2/day.[7] In 2013, nearly half of the world's population, more than three billion people, still lived on less than \$2.50 a day. It is easy to make assumptions about this group along the lines of 'they can't afford it so why innovate?' In fact, the challenge of meeting their basic needs for food, water, shelter and healthcare requires high levels of creativity – but beyond this social agenda lies a considerable innovation opportunity. However, it requires a reframing of the 'normal' rules of the market game and a challenging of core assumptions. Table 3.4 provides some examples.

Solutions to meeting these needs will have to be highly innovative but the prize is equally high: access to a high-volume, low-margin marketplace. For example, Unilever realized the potential of selling its shampoos and other cosmetic products not in 250 ml bottles (which were beyond the price range of most 'bottom of the pyramid' (BoP) customers but in single sachets. The resulting market growth has been phenomenal – and examples like this are fuelling major activity amongst large corporations looking to adapt their products and services to serve the BoP market.

TABLE 3.4   Challenging assumptions about the bottom of the pyramid

Assumption	Reality – and opportunity
The poor have no purchasing power and do not represent a viable market	Although low income the sheer scale of this market makes it interesting. And the poor often pay a premium for access to many goods and services (e.g. borrowing money, clean water, telecommunications and basic medicines) because they cannot address mainstream channels like shops and banks. The innovation challenge is to offer low-cost, low-margin but high-quality goods and services across a potential market of four billion people
The poor are not brand-conscious	Evidence suggests a high degree of brand and value consciousness, so if an entrepreneur can come up with a high-quality, low-cost solution it will be subject to hard testing in this market. Learning to deal with this can help migrate to other markets, essentially the classic pattern of 'disruptive innovation'
The poor are hard to reach	By 2015, there are likely to be nearly 400 cities in the developing world with populations of over one million and 23 with over 10 million. Around 35% of these will be poor, so the potential market access is considerable. Innovative thinking around distribution via new networks or agents (such as the women village entrepreneurs used by Hindustan Lever in India or the 'Avon ladies' in rural Brazil) can open up untapped markets
The poor are unable to use and not interested in advanced technology	Experience with PC kiosks, low-cost mobile phone sharing and access to the Internet suggests that take-up rates are extremely fast amongst this group. In India the e-Choupal (e-meeting place) set up by the tobacco company ITC enabled farmers to check prices for their products at the local markets and auction houses. Very shortly after that the same farmers were using the Web to access prices of their soybeans at the Chicago Board of Trade and strengthen their negotiating hand!

For example, in the Philippines there is little in the way of a formal banking system for the majority of people – and this has led to users creating very different applications for their mobile phones where pay-as-you-go credits become a unit of currency to be transferred between people and used as currency for various goods and services. In Kenya, the M-PESA system is used to increase security: if a traveller wishes to move between cities he or she will not take money but instead forward it via mobile phone in the form of credits which can then be collected from the person at the other end. Apple Pay began to be introduced into the USA and Europe in 2014, but Africa leads the world in mobile payment use, with nine African countries having more mobile cash accounts like M-PESA, than conventional bank accounts.[8]

The potential exists to use this kind of extreme environment as a laboratory to test and develop concepts for wider application, for example Citicorp has been experimenting with a design of ATM-based on biometrics for use with the illiterate population in rural India. The pilot involves some 50 000 people but as a spokesman for the company explained, 'We see this as having the potential for global application.'

ENTREPRENEURSHIP IN ACTION 3.3

Entrepreneurship for Sustainable Development

The annual FT/IFC Transformational Business Awards attracted 237 entries in 2014, from 214 companies representing 61 countries. The Awards focus on businesses which provide fundamental development needs, such as healthcare, food, water, housing, energy and infrastructure. The focus has broadened from a firm's social and environmental footprint, to its external impact in such areas.

For example, Engro Foods is a Pakistan-based business which provides real-time data collection and processing for 1800 smallholder farmers in order to reduce waste and promote faster payments. Jain Irrigation Systems (Jains), a family-run Indian business, is another case. It pioneered micro-irrigation systems such as drip systems, sprinklers, valves and water filters to pre-serve water use and improve crop yields.

Video Clip of an interview with Suzana Moreira giving an example of BoP social innovation using mobile phones is available on the Innovation Portal at **www.innovation-portal.info**

Source: Murray, S. (2014) Development groups can drive commercial innovation, *Financial Times*, 13th June, 1–3.

Significantly, the needs of this BoP market cover the entire range of human wants and needs, from cosmetics and consumer goods through to basic healthcare and education. Prahalad's original book contains a wide range of case examples where this is beginning to happen and which indicate the huge potential of this group – but also the radical nature of the innovation challenge. Subsequently, there has been significant expansion of innovative activity in these emerging market areas – driven in part by a realization that the major growth in global markets will come from regions with a high BoP profile.

Importantly, many companies are actively using BoP markets as places to search for weak signals of potentially interesting new developments. For example, Nokia sent scouts to study how people in rural Africa and India are using mobile phones and the potential for new services which this could offer, while the pharmaceutical firm Novo-Nordisk has been learning about the low-cost provision of diabetes care in Tanzania as an input to a better understanding of how such models could be developed for different regions.

Meeting the needs of people at the bottom of the pyramid is not about charity but rather about a fundamental rethink of the business model – 'paradigm innovation' in the 4Ps model we looked at in Chapter 2 – to create sustainable alternative systems.

INNOVATION IN ACTION 3.9

Changing the Game at the Bottom of the Pyramid

Pretty high on anyone's list of wants is a quality home, but financing more than basic shelter is often beyond the means of most of the world's population. But CEMEX, the Mexican cement and building materials producer, has pioneered an innovative approach to changing this. Triggered by a domestic financial crisis in the mid-1990s, CEMEX saw a big drop in sales in Mexico. But closer inspection revealed that the market segment of do-it-yourself, especially amongst the less wealthy, had sustained demand levels. In fact, the market was worth a great deal – nearly a billion dollars per year – but it was made up of many small purchases rather than large construction projects. Since over 60% of the Mexican population earn less than $5/day, the challenge was to find ways to work with this market in the future.

The response was a novel financing approach, built on the fact that many communities operate a 'savings club' type of scheme to help finance major purchases: the tanda network. CEMEX set up Patrimonio Hoy – a version of the tanda system which allowed poor people to save and access credit for building projects. It relies on social networks, replacing traditional distributors with 'promoters' who work on a commission but also help set up and run the tandas; significantly 98% of these promoters are women. The scheme allows access not just to materials but also to architects and other support services. It has effectively changed the way a large segment of society can manage its own construction projects. Success with the home improvements area has led to its extension to village infrastructure projects linked to drainage, lighting and other community facilities.

Case Studies of innovative solutions to the challenges posed by healthcare provision in India, such as Lifespring Hospitals, Narayana Hrudayalaya Hospitals (NHL) and Aravind Eye Clinics, are available on the Innovation Portal at **www.innovation-portal.info**

Audio Clip of an interview with Girish Prabhu, director of Srishti Labs in Bangalore, which specializes in developing BoP solutions is available on the Innovation Portal at **www.innovation-portal.info**

Chapter Summary

- In formulating and executing their development and innovation strategies, business firms cannot ignore the national systems of innovation and international value chains in which they are embedded.

- Through their strong influences on demand and competitive conditions, the provision of human resources, and forms of corporate governance, national systems of innovation both open opportunities and impose constraints on what firms can do.

- However, although firms' strategies are *influenced* by their own national systems of innovation, and their position in international value chains, they are not *determined* by them.

- Learning (i.e. assimilating knowledge) from competitors and external sources of innovation is essential for developing capabilities, but does require costly investments in R&D, training and skills development to develop the necessary absorptive capacity.

- This depends in part on what management itself does, by way of investing in complementary assets in production, marketing, service and support, and its position in local and international systems of innovation. It also depends on a variety of factors that make it more or less difficult to appropriate the benefits from innovation, such as intellectual property and international trading regimes, and over which management can sometimes have very little influence.

Key Terms Defined

Corporate governance   the systems for exercising and changing corporate ownership and control.

Position   the current endowment of technology and intellectual property of a firm, as well as its relations with customers and suppliers.

Spillovers   a term used by economists to describe the flow of know-how and other benefits from firm-specific investments, for example by MNCs, to the broader economy or between firms or sectors. This is often presented as being automatic, but demands a significant effort by domestic firms.

Value chain (or value network)   the system of relationships to create and capture value, for example between suppliers and customers. These can constrain profoundly their ability to capture the benefits of their innovation and entrepreneurship.

Discussion Questions

1. What factors influence the location of innovation, and how could these constrain the globalization of innovation?

2. What are the main components of a national innovation system, and how do these interact?

3. How can firms learn from overseas sources of innovation?

4. How can firms limit the scope for competitors imitating their innovations, and therefore better appropriate the benefits of their innovations?

5. Beyond formal R&D investment, what types of capabilities and competencies do firms need in order to innovate?

6. Compare the development of capabilities in China and India. What are the key lessons for developing economies?

Further Reading and Resources

There are a number of texts which describe and compare different systems of national innovation policy. In the edited text *National Systems of Innovation: Toward a Theory of Innovation and Interactive Learning*, Bengt-Åke Lundvall provides an excellent up-to-date overview of the key theories and research (Anthem Press, 2010), and for a more specific focus see *Small Country Innovation Systems: Globalization, Change and Policy in Asia and Europe*, edited by Charles Edquist and Leif Hommen (Edward Elgar, 2008). A more classic contribution is *National Innovation Systems* (Oxford University Press, 1993), edited by Richard Nelson, but all these have an emphasis on public policy rather than corporate strategy. For more polemic perspectives, try David Landes' *Wealth and Poverty of Nations* (Little Brown, 1998) and Marianna Mazzucato's *The Entrepreneurial State: Debunking Public vs. Private Sector Myths* (Anthem Press, 2013).

   More relevant to firms from emerging economies, and our favourite text on the subject, is Naushad Forbes and David Wield's *From Followers to Leaders: Managing Technology and Innovation* (Routledge, 2002), which includes numerous case examples; and *Innovative Firms in Emerging Market Countries*, edited by Edmund Amann and John Cantwell (Oxford University Press, 2014), provides firm-level evidence from emerging economies in Asia and Latin America. Mammo Muchie and Angathevar Baskaran edit a useful collection, *Creating Systems of Innovation in Africa: Country Case Studies* (Africa Institute of South Africa, 2013).

References

1. Ujjual, V. and P. Patel (2011) *Performance Characteristics of Large Firms at the Forefront of Globalization of Technology*, SPRU Electronic Working Paper Series, SWEPS No. 191, Brighton: University of Sussex; Cantwell, J. and J. Molero (2003) *Multinational Enterprises, Innovative Systems and Systems of Innovation*, Cheltenham: Edward Elgar; Granstrand, O., L. Hêakanson and S. Sjèolander (1992) *Technology Management and International Business: Internationalization of R&D and Technology*, Chichester: John Wiley & Sons Ltd.

2. Mytelka, L.K. (2007) *Innovation and Economic Development*, Cheltenham: Edward Elgar; Kim, L. and R.R. Nelson (2000) *Technology, Learning and Innovation: Experiences of Newly Industrializing Economies*, Cambridge: Cambridge University Press; Viotti, E.B. (2002) National learning systems: A new approach on technological change in late industrializing economies and evidence from the cases of Brazil and South Korea, *Technological Forecasting and Social Change*, **69**: 653–80; Bell, M. and K. Pavitt (1993) Technological accumulation and industrial growth: Contrasts between developed and developing countries, *Industrial and Corporate Change*, **2**(2): 157–210.

3. Kaplinsky, R. (2005) *Globalisation, Poverty and Inequality*, London: Polity Press; Schimtz, H. (2004) *Local Enterprises in the Global Economy*, Cheltenham: Edward Elgar; Sahay, A. and D. Riley (2003) The role of resource access, market conditions, and the nature of innovation in the pursuit of standards in the new product development process, *Journal of Product Innovation Management*, **20**: 338–55.

4. Tidd, J. and J. Bessant (2014) *Strategic Innovation Management*, Chichester: John Wiley & Sons Ltd; Tidd, J. and J. Bessant (2013) *Managing Innovation: Integrating Technological, Market and Organizational Change*, 5th edn, Chichester: John Wiley & Sons Ltd; Herstad, S.J., H.W. Aslesen and B. Ebersberger (2014) On industrial knowledge bases, commercial opportunities and global innovation network linkages, *Research Policy*, **43**(3): 495–504.

5. Mazzucato, M. (2013) *The Entrepreneurial State: Debunking Public vs. Private Sector Myths*, London: Anthem Press; Edquist, C. and M. McKelvey (2000) *Systems of Innovation: Growth, Competitiveness and Employment*, Cheltenham: Edward Elgar; Nelson, R. (1993) *National Innovation Systems*, Oxford: Oxford University Press; Lundvall, B.A. (1992) *National Systems of Innovation*, London: Pinter.

6. Woo, J. (2012) *Technological Upgrading in China and India: What Do We Know?* OECD Development Centre, Working Paper no. 308; Forbes, N. and D. Wield (2002) *From Followers to Leaders: Managing Technology and Innovation*, London: Routledge.

7. Prahalad, C.K. (2006) *The Fortune at the Bottom of the Pyramid*, Upper Saddle River, NJ: Wharton School Publishing.

8. Bhan, N. (2014) Mobile money is driving Africa's cashless future, *Harvard Business Review*, 19th September.

 Deeper Dive explanations of innovation concepts and ideas are available on the Innovation Portal at **www.innovation-portal.info**

 Quizzes to test yourself further are available online via the Innovation Portal at **www.innovation-portal.info**

Summary of online resources for Chapter 3 –
all material is available via the Innovation Portal at
www.innovation-portal.info

Cases	 Media	Tools	Activities	Deeper Dives
• Spirit • Aravind Eye Clinics • Instituto Nokia de Tecnologia (INdT) • Natura • Lifespring Hospitals • Narayana Hrudayalaya Hospitals (NHL)	• C.K. Prahalad • Nirmalya Kumar • Nandan Nilekani • Ana Sena • Suzana Moreira • Girish Prabhu	• Delphi method • Scenarios • Identifying innovative capabilities	—	• Building BRICS – Innovation capabilities in China

Chapter 4

Sustainability-led Innovation

LEARNING OBJECTIVES

By the end of this chapter you will develop an understanding of:

- the challenges which sustainability raises for innovation
- the different types of innovation which can contribute to improved sustainability
- a model framework for positioning sustainability-led innovation with three levels:
  - doing what we do better
  - opening up new opportunity at enterprise level
  - system-level change
- the key issues in the process of moving towards sustainability-led innovation
- some tools to help with the journey.

The Challenge of Sustainability-led Innovation

The Threat...

Sustainability is becoming a major driver of innovation. In an influential report the WWF points out that lifestyles in the developed world at present require the resources of around two planets and if emerging economies follow the same trajectory this will rise to 2.5 by 2050.[1] Many key energy and raw material resources are close to passing their peak of availability and will become increasingly scarce.[2] At the same time the dangers of global warming have moved to centre stage and climate change (and how to deal with it) is an urgent political as well as economic issue. This translates to increasingly strong legislation forcing organizations to change their products and processes to reduce carbon footprint, greenhouse gas emission and energy consumption. Behind this is the growing challenge of environmental pollution and the concern not only to stop the increasing damage being done to the natural environment but also to reverse the impacts of earlier practices.[3]

...and the Opportunity

It's not necessarily all doom and gloom. Considerable opportunities are also opening up, both for process innovations that increase operating efficiencies and reduce costs and for product innovations that exploit the huge potential market space represented by the 'green economy'. For example, the global market for 'green products and services' was recently estimated as a $3.2 trillion business opportunity, while UK consumer spending on 'sustainable' products and services was last reported at more than £36 billion – bigger even than alcohol and tobacco sales combined.

The provision of alternative goods and services, more efficient approaches to resource and energy management and new partnerships and ways of working could help unleash a new era of economic development. A recent PricewaterhouseCoopers report suggests significant market potential in the provision of green goods and services; its estimate was as high as 3% of global GDP.[4] A United Nations (2011) report illustrates how 'greening the economy' is already becoming a powerful new engine of growth in the 21st century.[5] The World Business Council for Sustainable Development's (WBCSD) Vision 2050 sets out new opportunities for businesses in responding to sustainability challenges, promoting whole system perspectives.[6]

As management guru C. K. Prahalad and colleagues put it, 'sustainability is a mother lode of organizational and technological innovations that yield both bottom-line and top-line returns. Becoming environment-friendly lowers costs because companies end up reducing the inputs they use. In addition, the process generates additional revenues from better products or enables companies to create new businesses. In fact, because [growing the top and bottom lines] are the goals of corporate innovation, we find that smart companies now treat sustainability as innovation's new frontier.'[7]

INNOVATION IN ACTION 4.1

Sustainability-led Innovation at Interface

One of the success stories in sustainability-led innovation (SLI) has been the growth of floorings business Interface, which has made radical changes to its business and operating model

 Video Clip of Ray Anderson talking about the potential of sustainability-led innovation is available on the Innovation Portal at **www.innovation-portal.info**

and secured significant business growth. Interface has cut greenhouse gas emissions by 82%, fossil fuel consumption by 60%, waste by 66%, water use by 75% and increased sales by 66%, doubled earnings and raised profit margins. To quote Ray

Anderson, founder and chairman: 'As we climb Mount Sustainability with the four sustainability principles on top, we are doing better than ever on bottom-line business. This is not at the cost of social or ecological systems, but at the cost of our competitors who still haven't got it.'

Activity to help you explore this topic further, Innovation challenges in sustainability, is available on the Innovation Portal at **www.innovation-portal.info**

We've Seen This Before

Preoccupation with sustainability and the need for innovation to deal with it is, of course, not new. Back in the 1970s an influential report called *The Limits to Growth* triggered a long-running and high-profile debate around these issues and this led to a continuing stream of research and advocacy around the need for change and the best ways to drive the innovation agenda.[8] Organizations such as the WWF and Greenpeace emerged out of this and continue to play a key role in raising awareness, exploring issues and challenging policymakers and organizations to improve sustainability.

Whatever the perspective adopted it is clear that change – innovation – will be needed. Growing concern of the kind described above is driving a combination of increasingly strong legislation, international environmental management standards, new sustainability metrics and reporting standards that will force business to adopt greener approaches if they are to retain a licence to operate. At the same time the opportunities opened up for 'doing what we do better' (through 'lean, green' investments in improving efficiencies around resources, energy, logistics, etc.) and 'doing different' – radical new moves towards systems change – make it an increasingly significant item in strategic planning amongst progressive organizations of all sizes.

Sustainability-led Innovation

So what are organizations doing about this? Early activity centred on cosmetic activity with which organizations sought to improve their image or strengthen their corporate social responsibility image through high-profile activities designed to show their green credentials. But now it has moved to a second phase in which increasingly strong legislation provides a degree of forced **compliance**. The frontier is now one along which leading organizations are seeking to exploit opportunities, as they recognize the need for innovation to deal with resource instability and scarcity, energy security and systemic efficiencies across their supply chains.

INNOVATION IN ACTION 4.2

Managing Innovation for Sustainability

In their review of the field, Frans Berkhout and Ken Green argue that 'technological and organizational innovation stands at the heart of the most popular and policy discourses about sustainability.

Innovation is regarded as both a cause and solution … yet, very little attempt has been made in the business and environment, environmental management and environmental policy literatures to systematically draw on the concepts, theories and empirical evidence developed over the past three decades of innovation studies.' They identify a number of limitations in the innovation literature, and suggest potential ways to link innovation and sustainability research, policy and management:

1. A focus on managers, the firm or the supply chain is too narrow. Innovation is a distributed process across many actors, firms and other organizations, and is influenced by regulation, policy and social pressure.
2. A focus on a specific technology or product is inappropriate. Instead, the unit of analysis must be on technological systems or regimes, and their evolution rather than management.
3. The assumption that innovation is the consequence of coupling technological opportunity and market demand is too limited. It needs to include the less obvious social concerns, expectations and pressures. These may appear to contradict stronger but misleading market signals.

They present empirical studies of industrial production, air transportation and energy to illustrate their arguments, and conclude that 'greater awareness and interaction between research and management of innovation, environmental management, corporate social responsibility and innovation and the environment will prove fruitful'.

Source: Berkhout, F. and K. Green (eds) (2002) Special issue on managing innovation for sustainability, *International Journal of Innovation Management*, **6**(3).

A number of frameworks have been proposed to take account of this – for example, Prahalad and Nidumolo suggest five steps moving from 'viewing compliance as an opportunity', through 'making value chains sustainable' and 'designing sustainable products and services' to 'designing new business models'. Their fifth stage focuses on 'creating next practice platforms' – implying a system-level change.[9] For entrepreneurs these opportunities offer significant options for new ventures in the sustainability space around resources, energy and environmental management.

We can use the 4Ps framework from Chapter 1 to classify the kinds of activity going on around SLI. Table 4.1 gives some examples.

TABLE 4.1 Examples of sustainability-led innovation

Innovation target	Examples
Product/service offering	Green products, design for greener manufacture and recycling, service models replacing consumption/ownership models
Process innovation	Improved and novel manufacturing processes, lean systems inside the organization and across supply chain, green logistics
Position innovation	Rebranding the organization as green, meeting needs of underserved communities (e.g. bottom of pyramid)
Paradigm innovation – changing business models	System-level change, multi-organization innovation, servitization (moving from manufacturing to service emphasis)

A Framework Model for Sustainability-led Innovation

We can see the journey towards full sustainability as involving three dimensions which under-pin a change in the overall approach from treating the symptoms of a problem to eventually working with the system in which the problem origi-nates (Figure 4.1).

In particular, we can think of three stages in the evolu-tion of SLI, from simple compliance and 'doing what we do better' innovation through to more radical exploration of new business opportunities. The third stage is all about system change, where significant effects can be achieved but which rely on cooperation and co-evolution of innova-tive solutions across a group of stakeholders.

Case Study of a research project carried out with the Network for Business Sustainability, which works with companies like RIM, Suncor and Unilever and academic institutions like the Richard Ivey School of Business is available on the Innovation Portal at **www.innovation-portal.info**

FIGURE 4.1 The journey towards sustainability-led innovation

Step 1 is **Operational optimization,** essentially doing what we do but better. Table 4.2 gives some examples.

Approach	**1.** **OPERATIONAL OPTIMIZATION** 'Eco-Efficiency'	
Innovation Objective	Compliance, efficiency • 'Doing the same things better'	
Innovation Outcome	Reduces harm	
Innovation's Relationship to the Firm	Incremental improvements to business as usual	

TABLE 4.2 Examples of paradigm innovation

Definition	Characteristics	Examples
Compliance with regulations or optimized performance through increased efficiency	In the stage of operational optimization, the organization actively reduces its current environmental and social impacts without fundamentally changing its business model. In other words, an optimizer innovates in order to 'do less harm'. Innovations are typically incremental, addressing a single issue at a time. And they tend to favour the 'technofix' – focusing on new technologies as ways to reduce impacts while maintaining business as usual. Innovation tends to be inward-focused in both development and outcome; at this stage, companies typically	Pollution controls Flexible work hours/ telecommuting Waste diversion Shutting or consolidating facilities Energy-efficient lighting Use of renewable energy Reduced paper consumption Reduced packaging Decreased use of raw materials Reduced use/elimination of hazardous materials

TABLE 4.2 *(Continued)*

Definition	Characteristics	Examples
	rely on internal resources to innovate, and the resulting innovations are company-centric: their intent is primarily to reduce costs or maximize profits.	Optimization of product size/weight for shipping Hybrid electric fleet vehicles Delivery boxes redesigned from single to multi-use

> **Case Studies** of companies like TetraPak, Volvo, Lafarge, Nokia Solutions and Networks (NSN) and Fairmount Hotels working in China to reduce greenhouse gas emissions are available on the Innovation Portal at **www.innovation-portal.info**

> **Video Clip** of Fabian Schlage (NSN) illustrating some of these themes is available on the Innovation Portal at **www.innovation-portal.info**

Step 2 is **Organizational transformation,** essentially doing things differently different at the level of the organization. Table 4.3 gives more detail.

2.

ORGANIZATIONAL TRANSFORMATION
'New Market Opportunities'

Novel products, services or business models
• 'Doing good by doing new things'

Creates shared value

Fundamental shift in firm purpose

TABLE 4.3 Organizational transformation

Definition	Characteristics	Examples
The creation of often disruptive new products and services by viewing sustainability as a market opportunity	Rather than focusing on 'doing less harm', organizational transformers believe their organization can benefit financially from 'doing good'. They see opportunities to serve new markets with novel, sustainable products, or they are new entrants with business models predicated on creating value by lifting people out of poverty or producing renewable energy. Organizational transformers may focus less on creating products and more on delivering services, which often have a lower environmental impact. They often produce innovations that are both technological and sociotechnical – designed to improve quality of life for people inside or outside the firm. Transformers are still primarily internally focused in that they see their organization as an independent figure in the economy. However, they do work up and down the value chain and collaborate closely with external stakeholders. The move from operational optimization to organizational transformation requires a radical shift in mindset from doing things better to doing new things	Disruptive new products that change consumption habits (e.g. a camp stove that turns any biomass into a hyper-efficient) heat source whose sales subsidize cheaper models distributed in developing countries

Disruptive new products that benefit people (e.g. CT scanners that are portable, durable and have minimum functionality – making them affordable and useful for health care providers in developing countries)

Replacing products with services (e.g. leasing and maintaining carpets over a prescribed lifetime rather than selling them)

Introducing car- and bike-sharing services in urban centres to reduce pollution caused by individual car ownership while increasing overall mobility

Replacing physical services with electronic services (e.g. reducing paper consumption by delivering bills electronically rather than by mail)

Services with social benefits (e.g. a smartphone app that rewards people with coupons for local merchants when they make charitable donations) |

INNOVATION IN ACTION 4.3

Sustainability-led Innovation within Philips

Philips is a Dutch multinational company, founded in 1891 and now operating in over 100 countries and employing 118 000 people. It has a long-standing commitment to sustainability principles, for example in the early 20th century Philips' employees benefited from schools, housing and pension schemes. It has also been a key actor in several international sustainability initiatives; back in the early 1970s, Philips participated in the Club of Rome's 'The Limits to Growth' dialogue and in 1974 the first corporate environmental function was established. In 1992, it was one of 29 multinational companies participating in the World Council for Sustainable Business Development which developed 'Vision 2050' – a roadmap for future development towards a more sustainable position.

Its own 'EcoVision' programmes were first launched in 1998, setting corporate sustainability-related targets and the first green innovation targets were introduced in 2007, in EcoVision4. In parallel, in 2003, the Philips Environmental Report (first published in 1999) was extended into a Sustainability Report and in 2009 this was integrated into the Philips Annual Report, signalling the full embedding of sustainability in Philips' business practices.

Philips EcoVision5 programme for 2010–2015 establishes concrete targets for sustainable innovation:

- To bring care to 500 million people.
- To improve the energy efficiency of our overall portfolio by 50%.
- To double the amount of recycled materials in our products as well as to double the collection and recycling of Philips products.

Like many other long-lived companies, Philips has adjusted its innovation approach several times, anticipating major changes in society. In recent decades, this has resulted in the opening of an Experience Lab in Eindhoven and the extension of the traditional technology-driven product-creation process towards end-user driven innovation. 'Open innovation' has also changed its way of working: in the late 1990s, the former Research Laboratories were transformed into a vibrant High Tech Campus, now hosting over 80 non-Philips business entities. During the last decade, its focus was 'inside-out' based on teaming up, incubation and spin-outs and the emphasis is now on co-creating sustainable systems solutions.

With the launch of EcoVision4 Philips introduced a target on green innovation, spending a total of €1 billion on developing green products and processes. These are defined as offering significant environmental improvements in one or more 'Green Key Focal Areas': energy efficiency, packaging, hazardous substances, packaging, weight, recycling and disposal and lifetime reliability. In 2010, green products accounted for 37.5% of the Philips sales. The target for 2015 is 50%.

For example, the Consumer Lifestyle division recently launched the first **cradle-to-cradle** inspired products, such as the Performer EnergyCare vacuum cleaner, 50% made from post-industrial plastics and 25% from bio-based plastics. It is extremely energy-efficient, but it earns its designations as a green product primarily because it scores so highly in the focal area of recycling.

Another example is the award-winning Canova LED TV. This high-performance LED TV consumes 60% less power than its predecessor. Even the remote control is efficient: it's powered by solar energy. In addition, the TV is completely free of PVC and brominated flame retardants, and 60% of the aluminium used in the set is recycled.

(continued)

More information to be found at: http://www.philips.com/about/sustainability/index.page

Case Study of Natura, a Brazilian cosmetics company, which takes sustainability as a core foundation for its products, services and processes, is available on the Innovation Portal at **www.innovation-portal.info**

Step 3 is **systems building,** essentially changing the system, coevolving solutions with different stakeholders to create new and sustainable alternatives. Table 4.4 explores this in more detail.

3.

SYSTEMS BUILDING
'Societal Change'

Novel products, services or business models that are impossible to achieve alone
• 'Doing good by doing new things with others'

Creates net positive impact

Extends beyond the firm to drive institutional change

TABLE 4.4   Systems building

Definition	Characteristics	Examples
The interdependent collaborations between many disparate organizations that create positive impacts on people and the planet	Systems builders perceive their economic activity as being part of society, not distinct from it. Individually, almost every organization is unsustainable. But taken as a collective, systems can sustain each other. Systems	Industrial symbiosis: Disparate organizations cooperate to create a 'circular economy' in which one firm's waste is another's resources (e.g. a construction company uses other companies' glass waste: the synergies lead

TABLE 4.4 *(Continued)*

Definition	Characteristics	Examples
	builders extend their thinking beyond the boundaries of the organization to include partners in previously unrelated areas or industries. Because the concept of systems building reflects an unconventional economic paradigm, very few organizations or industries occupy this realm The move from organizational transformation to systems building requires another radical shift in mindset – this time from doing new things and serving new markets to thinking beyond the firm	to environmental and economic benefits for all) B Corporations: conceived in the United States but now existing in dozens of countries worldwide, B Corporations are organizations legally obliged to deliver societal benefits. Well-known examples include ice-cream producer Ben & Jerry's, e-commerce platform Etsy and cleaning product manufacturers Method and Seventh Generation

Case Studies of Green supply chains, Desso and other organizations which are attempting to innovate across their supply networks and move towards a systems level approach are available on the Innovation Portal at **www.innovation-portal.info**

Case Study outlining a total design approach to construction, Green Buildings, is available on the Innovation Portal at **www.innovation-portal.info**

INNOVATION IN ACTION 4.4

An Environmental Innovation Network for IKEA

The catalogue of IKEA has one of the world's highest circulations, with a print run of more than 100 million per year, needing 50 000 tonnes of high-quality paper each year. However, in the 1990s there were growing environmental concerns about the discharge of chlorinated compounds from the processes used to create the relatively high-quality paper used in such

(continued)

promotional materials, as well as the more general issue of paper recycling. In response to these concerns, in 1992 IKEA introduced two new goals for the production of its catalogue: to be printed on paper that was totally chlorine-free (TCF) and to include a high proportion of recycled paper.

However, these goals demanded significant innovation. No such paper product existed at the time, and the dominant industry suppliers believed that it would be impossible to combine chlorine-free materials with high levels of recycled pulp. To achieve the necessary paper brightness for catalogue printing, a minimum of 50% chlorine-dioxide-bleached pulp had been used. Chlorine had been used for 50 years as the bleaching agent for high-quality paper. Moreover, the high-quality paper used for such catalogues consisted of a very thin paper base, which is coated with clay, which makes the insertion of recycled fibre very difficult. The manager of R&D at Svenska Cellulosa Aktiebolaget (SCA), one of Europe's largest producers of high-quality paper, argued that 'the high-quality demands and the large volume of filling substances is the main reason that it is neither realistic nor necessary to use recycled fibre'. SCA reinforced this view with the decision to build a new SKr2.4 billion (£200 million) plant to produce conventional high-quality coated paper. At that time SCA was not a supplier to IKEA.

In Sweden, the paper manufacturer Aspa worked with the chemical firm Eka Nobel to develop an environmentally acceptable bleaching process with less damaging discharges, but this was still based on chlorine dioxide and failed to achieve the necessary brightness for use in high-quality paper, and was marketed as 'semi-bleached'. Following customer demand for a true TCF product, including a request from Greenpeace for TCF paper for production of its newsletter, Aspa was forced to develop a stable product with secure supplies. At this stage the pulp and fibre company Södra Cell became involved, and identified the need to reach full brightness to create a broader market for TCF paper. Södra worked with the German company Kværner to develop an alternative but equally effective bleaching process, and Kværner established a research project on ozone bleaching with Lenzing and Stora Billerud. The ozone bleaching process was adapted from an established process for water purification with the help of AGA Gas. However, the use of ozone in place of chlorine for bleaching required the quality of the pulpwood to be improved, so the harvesting system had to be changed to ensure that wood was better sorted and available within weeks of harvesting. To improve the brightness and strength of the paper, the impurities in the pulp from de-inked recycled paper had to be reduced, which required a new washing process. The changes in the chemistry of the pulp subsequently reduced the strength of the paper, which required changes in the paper production process. The printing processes had to be adapted to the characteristics of the new paper. Initially, Södra Cell supplied the new product to SCA through its relationship with Aspa, but also to the Italian paper producer Burgo, which provided the paper for the IKEA catalogue.

Video Clip of an interview with Michael Pitts of the UK's Technology Strategy Board on the challenges of sustainability-led innovation is available on the Innovation Portal at **www.innovation-portal.info**

Thus, the organization evolved beyond a simple industrial supply relationship to an innovation network including customers, printers, paper manufacturers, pulp and fibre producers, forestry companies, research institutes and environmental lobby groups across many different countries. At the same time, the intended innovation shifted from a high-quality TCF clay-coated paper to a TCF uncoated fresh pulp and 10% de-inked recycled pulp product.

Source: Derived from Hakansson, H. and A. Waluszewski (2003) *Managing Technological Development: IKEA, the Environment and Technology*, London: Routledge.

The whole model looks like this:

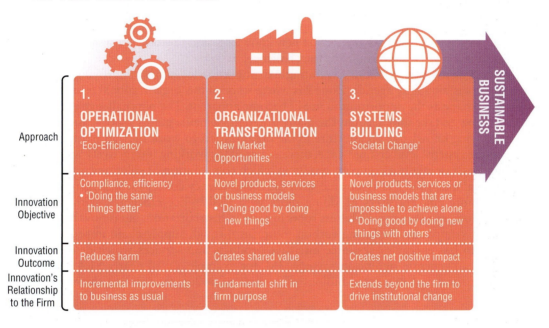

Managing the Innovation Process for Sustainability

While there is plenty of discussion about the need for innovation in the direction of sustainability, it is less clear *how* this process can be managed. What do these changes mean for the innovation process and how does consideration of sustainability change the routines we put in place for innovation management? Are our current models for handling the process are sufficient – or will the nature and pace of change be so disruptive that it requires radically new approaches? What kinds of innovation ecosystem may emerge and how will current players position themselves within it? What opportunities exist for entrepreneurs and how can they best frame their activities to ride the waves of radical change? What new skills will we need within – and between – our organizations? What tools, techniques and approaches will help equip established players and aspiring new entrants to manage effectively? In the face of radical change, what do we need to do more of, less of and differently in the ways we manage innovation?

Case Study of how Philips Lighting reconfigured its innovation process to support its sustainability ambitions is available on the Innovation Portal at **www.innovation-portal.info**

We suggest that SLI highlights once again the challenge of 'dynamic capability' in that it forces firms to learn new approaches and let go of old ones around the core search, select and implement questions. By its nature, SLI involves working with different knowledge components – new technologies, new markets, new environmental or regulatory conditions, etc. – and firms need to develop enhanced 'absorptive capacity' for handling this. In particular, they need capability (and enabling tools and methods) to acquire, assimilate and exploit new knowledge and to work at a systems level.

Figure 4.2 gives a simple map of the challenge.

Zone 1 is essentially about exploiting existing knowledge and improving efficiencies around the sustainability agenda. Zone 2 is where some of the 'organizational transformation' ideas take shape as the opportunities in SLI become apparent. The big challenge in SLI comes in 'reframing' to take into account the many different elements in this space – and to rethink the underlying knowledge architecture in the organization to work in it. In particular, as we move to the systems-level change stage, there is a need for working interactively with multiple stakeholders, essentially a complex system in which co-evolution of solutions is the model.

For example, zone 3 is associated with the **eco-efficiency** concept which involves finding new and more efficient ways of 'doing more with less'.[10] Eco-efficiency, with its famous '3 Rs' – reduce, re-use, recycle – has its roots in early industrialization, but is now being widely adopted by companies. Reducing carbon footprint through supply chain improvements or switching to less energy or resource-intensive products and services which deliver equivalent value can generate significant savings. 3M, for example, saved nearly $1.4 billion over a 34-year period and prevented billions of pounds of pollutants entering the environment

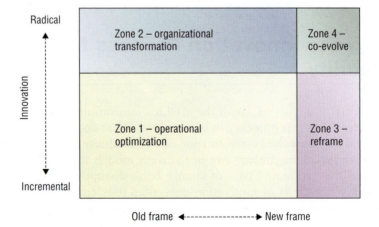

FIGURE 4.2 Sustainability-led innovation challenges

through its Pollution-Prevention-Pays (3P) programmes. GE Industrial saved $12.8 million per year by using high-efficiency lights in its plants. One of Alcoa's facilities in France achieved an 85% reduction in water consumption leading to a $40 000-a-year reduction in operating costs.[11]

Zone 4 involves significant 'systems level thinking' around emergent and radically different solutions. Such system-level innovation has the capacity to generate positive social and environmental impacts rather than simply minimizing negative ones, representing a shift from eco-efficiency to 'eco-effectiveness'. One aspect of this is the involvement of multiple players, which have traditionally not worked together, in co-creating system-level change. For instance, Grameen Shakti, a rural renewable energy initiative in Bangladesh, fosters collaboration between the microfinance sector, suppliers of solar-energy equipment and consumers, enabling millions of poor households to leapfrog to new energy systems. It is generating new employment opportunities, increasing rural incomes, empowering women and reducing the use of environmentally polluting kerosene. Grameen Shakti is the world's largest and fastest-growing rural renewable energy company in the world.[12]

INNOVATION IN ACTION 4.5

Sustainability-led innovation in Novo Nordisk

Novo Nordisk, a major Danish pharmaceuticals business, makes use of a company-wide scenario-based programme to explore radical futures around its core business. Its 'Diabetes 2020' process involved exploring radical alternative scenarios for chronic disease treatment and the roles which a player like Novo Nordisk could play. As part of the follow-up from this initiative, in 2003 the company helped set up the Oxford Health Alliance, a non-profit collaborative entity which brought together key stakeholders – medical scientists, doctors, patients and government officials – with views and perspectives which were sometimes quite widely separated. To make it happen, Novo Nordisk made clear that its goal was nothing less than the prevention or cure of diabetes – a goal which if it were achieved would potentially kill off the company's main line of business. As Lars Rebien Sørensen, the CEO of Novo Nordisk, explains:

> In moving from intervention to prevention – that's challenging the business model where the pharmaceuticals industry is deriving its revenues! … We believe that we can focus on some major global health issue – mainly diabetes – and at the same time create business opportunities for our company.

Unilever's Sustainable Living Plan, which builds partnerships with multiple stakeholders – including suppliers, NGOs and consumers – aims to create a better future in which billions of people can increase their quality of life without increasing their environmental footprint. The new plan is fuelling innovation, generating markets and saving money.

Innovations can arise from developing unusual partnerships across sectors. For example, the GreenZone, in Umea, Sweden, designed by architect Anders Nyquist, is an early example of holistic planning. It involves a block of interconnected businesses, including a car dealership, a petrol station and carwash and a fast-food restaurant. The buildings are connected, allowing a recycling and sharing of heat.

Table 4.5 highlights some of the emerging challenges to innovation management routines as organizations move into the sustainability space.

TABLE 4.5 Key innovation management challenges associated with sustainability-led innovation

Innovation activity	Challenges in zone 3 and 4
Search	Peripheral vision – searching in unfamiliar fields (sectors, technologies, markets, etc.) Reframing Finding, forming, performing new networks
Selection	Resource allocation under high uncertainty Cognitive dissonance Not invented here
Implementation	Internal mobilization – new skills, structures, etc. Crossing the chasm and the diffusion problem New appropriate language
Innovation strategy	Need for a clear framework within which to locate search, select, implement – a 'roadmap for the future' New corporate paradigm – criteria based on sustainability (people, profit, planet, etc.)

Tools to help organizations work with sustainability-led innovation are available on the Innovation Portal at **www.innovation-portal.info**

Video Clip of Deborah Meaden (a successful entrepreneur) and David Nussbaum (chief executive of WWF) discussing the challenges for businesses embracing sustainability-led innovation is available on the Innovation Portal at **www.innovation-portal.info**

Responsible Innovation

One message from this theme of SLI is that we will need to look at some of the questions we ask during our innovation process. In particular, at the 'select' stage what criteria will we use to ensure the project is worth pursuing? We need to consider carefully whether to take possible innovation ideas forward but current frameworks for innovation project selection mainly deal with risks and rewards. In the public sector there is additional concern around the 'reliability' theme: will the changes we introduce have an impact on our ability to deliver the public services people depend on like healthcare and education? But in this chapter we have seen that there are now urgent additional questions which we should bring into our decision process around the question of sustainability and wider impact.

Interestingly, much of the academic and policy-oriented innovation research tradition evolved around such concerns, riding on the back of the 'science and society' movement of the 1970s. This led to key institutes (like the Science Policy Research unit at Sussex University) being established. Their concern – and the many tools which they developed – remained one of challenging the innovation process and particularly questioning the targets towards which it worked.

For example, although the global pharmaceutical industry has done much to improve healthcare through a highly efficient innovation process there are questions which can be raised around it. Evidence suggests that 90% of its innovation efforts are devoted to the concerns of the richest 10% of the world's population. In similar fashion questions can be asked about innovation systems, which can produce impressive consumer electronics yet leave many people in the world short of clean water or without access to basic medical care.

The argument is that despite the good intentions of individual researchers and corporations, innovation can sometimes be irresponsible. Products like the insecticide DDT (developed as a powerful aid to controlling pests) or Thalidomide (a useful anti-nausea drug) turned out to have unforeseen and seriously negative consequences. In other cases (like BSE) pursuit of innovation without adequate safeguards or questions being raised led to major crises. One of the major causes of the global financial crisis – with all the misery it has brought – lay in irresponsible and sometimes reckless financial innovation around tools and techniques. And the current debates around genetically modified (GM) foods and reinvestment in nuclear power to cope with energy shortages remind us of the need to ask questions around innovation.

For these reasons there is growing interest in developing frameworks which can bring a series of 'responsibility' questions into the innovation process and ensure that careful consideration takes place around major change programmes.[13]

Chapter Summary

- Sustainability is becoming a key factor in innovation, representing both a significant threat and a source of opportunity.

- Sustainability-led innovation (SLI) involves changes across the 'innovation space' – in products/services, in processes, in positions and in paradigms.

- SLI can involve incremental improvements – 'do better' – and more radical changes. We have explored a three-level model which maps the nature of SLI into three areas:
  - Operational optimization
  - Organizational transformation
  - Systems building.

- SLI poses challenges across the innovation process model – how we search, select and implement. In particular, working at the higher levels of the model, towards organizational transformation and systems building, will require developing new routines.

- Part of the dynamic capability challenge in dealing with SLI is to introduce some elements of a **responsible innovation** framework to our decision making around innovation selection and implementation.

Key Terms Defined

Compliance   the requirement for organizations to comply with an increasingly wide range of regulations covering emissions, carbon footprint, material recycling, etc.

Cradle-to-cradle   an approach to sustainable products which looks to re-use component materials, recycling as much as possible.

Eco-efficiency   improvements to products/services or processes which improve one or more dimensions of their ecological impact.

Operational optimization   compliance with regulations or optimized performance through increased efficiency.

Organizational transformation   the creation of often-disruptive new products and services by viewing sustainability as a market opportunity.

Responsible innovation   an approach which looks at the wider consequences of innovation decisions and tries to anticipate negative impacts.

Systems building   the interdependent collaborations between many disparate organizations that create positive impacts on people and the planet.

Discussion Questions

1. You have been asked to develop a sustainability-led innovation strategy for your business which makes children's toys. Using the framework model in the chapter, outline how you would carry this out.

2. Using examples of innovations which may have had unexpected negative consequences, outline what factors you would build into a framework for ensuring 'responsible innovation'.

3. Where could the sustainability space open up new opportunities for an entrepreneur? And where would the challenges lie in exploiting those opportunities?

4. How would an organization obtain competitive advantage through following a strategy of sustainability-led innovation? Give examples to support your case.

Further Reading and Resources

For a general introduction to the key issues in sustainable development, our favourite text is *The Principles of Sustainability* by Simon Dresner (Earthscan, 2002). Unlike most of the literature on the subject, this treatment is well balanced and even includes some humour. Jennifer Elliott's *An Introduction to Sustainable Development* (Routledge, 2nd edn, 2005) is a more conventional academic approach, and focuses on the implications for developing nations. However, neither text is strong on the links between sustainability and innovation. The Special Issue of the *International Journal of Innovation Management* (2002) **6**(3) on 'Innovation for Sustainability' is a useful place to begin, and is edited by two leading scholars in the field, Frans Berkhout and Ken Green. Richard Adams and colleagues conducted an extensive literature review for the NBS report which contains a wealth of useful resources.[14]

The Natural Advantage of Nations: Business Opportunities, Innovations and Governance in the 21st Century by Amory B. Lovins (Earthscan Publications, 2005) is a collection of papers by leading authors, including Michael Porter, and makes the business case for sustainable development, including technological, structural and social change. The book has a useful companion website. *Sustainable Business Development: Inventing the Future Through Strategy, Innovation, and Leadership* by David L. Rainey (Cambridge University Press, 2006) provides a practical analysis of what sustainable business development (SBD) is and how companies do it, and includes many case studies from the USA, Europe, Pacific Rim and South America. *Sustainable Innovation: The Organisational, Human and Knowledge Dimension* by Rene J. Jorna (Greenleaf Publishing, 2006) is a more theoretical and philosophical book.

Responsible innovation is a theme of increasing interest and the edited book of the same name by Richard Owen and colleagues is a good place to start exploring this theme (John Wiley & Sons Ltd, 2013).

References

1. WWF (2010) *Living Planet Report 2010: Biodiversity, Biocapacity and Development*, Gland, Switzerland: WWF International.

2. Brown, L. (2011) *World on the Edge: How to Prevent Environmental and Economic Collapse*, New York: Norton.

3. Heinberg, R. (2007) *Peak Everything: Waking up to the Century of Decline in Earth's Resources*, London: Clairview.

4. PricewaterhouseCoopers (2010) *Green Products: Using Sustainable Attributes to Drive Growth and Value*, http://www.pwc.com/us/en/corporate-sustainability-climate-change/assets/green-products-paper.pdf, accessed 20th December 2014.

5. UNEP (2011) *Towards a Green Economy: Pathways to Sustainable Development and Poverty Eradication*, 2011, United Nations Environment Programme: Online version http://hqweb.unep.org/greeneconomy/Portals/88/documents/ger/GER_synthesis_en.pdf, accessed 20th November 2014.

6. WBCSD (2010) *Vison 2050*, Geneva: World Business Council for Sustainable Development.

7. Nidumolo, R., C. Prahalad and M. Rangaswami (2009) Why sustainability is now the key driver of innovation, *Harvard Business Review*, **September**: 57–61.

8. Meadows, D. and J. Forrester (1972) *The Limits to Growth*, New York: Universe Books.

9. Adams, R., S. Jeanrenaud, J. Bessant *et al.* (2012) *Innovating for sustainability: A guide for executives*, London, Ontario, Canada: Network for Business Sustainability.

10. WBCSD (2000) *Eco-efficiency: Doing More with Less*, Geneva: World Business Council for Sustainable Development.

11. Senge, P., B. Smith, N. Kruschwitz, *et al.* (2008) *The Necessary Revolution: How Individuals and Organizations Are Working Together to Create a Sustainable World*, New York: Doubleday.

12. Shakti, G. (2011) *Grameen Shakti*, www.gshakti.org, accessed 20th December 2014.

13. Owen, R., J. Bessant and M. Heintz (eds) (2013) *Responsible Innovation*, Chichester: John Wiley & Sons Ltd.

14. Adams, R., S. Jeanrenaud *et al.* (2013) *Sustainability-oriented Innovation: A Systematic Review of the Literature*, Ottawa, Canada: Network for Business Sustainability.

Deeper Dive explanations of innovation concepts and ideas are available on the Innovation Portal at **www.innovation-portal.info**

Quizzes to test yourself further are available online via the Innovation Portal at **www.innovation-portal.info**

Summary of online resources for Chapter 4 –
all material is available via the Innovation Portal at
www.innovation-portal.info

Cases	**Media**	**Tools**	**Activities**	**Deeper Dives**
• Network for Business Sustainability • TetraPak • Volvo • Lafarge • NSN • Fairmount Hotels • Natura • Green supply chains • Desso • Green buildings • Philips Lighting	• Ray Anderson • Fabian Schlage • Michael Pitts • Deborah Meaden and David Nussbaum	• SLI tools	• Innovation challenges in sustainability	• Responsible innovation framework

PART II

RECOGNIZING THE OPPORTUNITY

Innovative ideas can come from a wide range of sources and situations: from inspiration, transfer from another context, from listening to customer needs, from frontier research or by combining existing ideas into something new. And they could come through building alternative models of the future and exploring options opened up within these alternative worlds. But, if we are to succeed, we need to build rich and varied ways of picking up on all of the potential trigger signals that offer us interesting variation opportunities. What marks out successful individual entrepreneurs is often this ability to spot the key opportunity from a forest of possibilities.

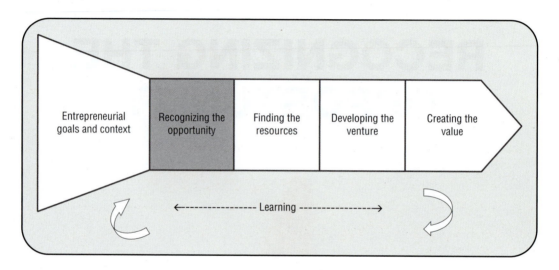

Chapter 5

Entrepreneurial Creativity

ods. This chapter looks at the nature of creativity and explores ways in which a better understanding of the creative process to enhance

What is Creativity?

Introduction

Close your eyes and imagine someone being creative. What do you see? The chances are you have begun to picture an artist, maybe a composer, perhaps a sculptor or a poet wrestling with his or her imagination? Maybe you have a mad scientist in mind, a crazy white-haired professor who has questionable dress sense but a brilliant mind and is working out solutions to the problems of the universe?

These are common pictures which remind us that we tend to think of creativity as something rather special, very important in the worlds of art and science but somehow the province of exceptional and rare individuals working on their own. The reality is a bit different: what we know about creativity is that everyone is capable of it and it can be developed and parts of brain function relate to these different areas. Work originally carried out by Nobel Prize winner Roger Sperry and colleagues back in the 1960s (and confirmed by more recent neuroimaging techniques) shows that the left hemisphere is particularly associated with activities like language and calculation. While our 'left brain' seems linked to what we might call 'logical' processing, the role of the 'right brain' was, for a long time, much less well understood. Gradually it became clear that it is involved in associations, patterns and emotional links; people with damage to the right hemisphere are often incapable of understanding humour or of feeling moved by painting or music. Our ability to think in metaphors and to visualize and imagine in novel ways is strongly linked to activity on this side of the brain.

It's not a case of 'creativity = right brain thinking' but rather that we need to recognize that both hemispheres are involved and they play different roles. This has important implications for developing the skills of creative thinking, as we'll see later, because we need to find ways to enable this interconnection between the two.

Pattern Recognition

Creativity is particularly about patterns and our ability to see these. In its simplest form if we see a pattern, which we recognize, we have access to solutions which worked in the past and which we can apply again. But sometimes it is a case of recognizing a similarity between a new problem and something like it which we have seen before. For example, Johannes Gutenberg saw the connection between the way winepresses worked and his idea for the printing press. Alastair Pilkington saw a link between the way fat floated on the surface of water and the way his company could make glass, eventually leading to the revolutionary 'float glass' process with which most of the world's windows are now made. And James Dyson applied ideas about the large-scale industrial cyclones used to capture factory emissions to the world of domestic vacuum cleaners.

INNOVATION IN ACTION 5.2

Sticky Success

It was during a flight in 1967 that Wolfgang Dierichs, a scientist working for the German company Henkel, had a flash of creative insight. The company made a wide range of stationery products and one area in which he worked was in adhesives. As he sat waiting for the plane to take off he noticed the woman next to him applying lipstick. His insight was to see the potential of the lipstick tube as a new way to deliver glue. Put some solid glue in a tube, twist the cap and apply it to any surface.

The company launched the 'Pritt Stick' in 1969, and within two years it was available in 38 countries around the world. Today, around 130 million Pritt Sticks are sold each year in 120 countries and the product has sold over 2.5 billion units since its invention.

Sometimes it is about finding a new pattern which makes sense. One of the challenges in creativity is that it sometimes involves breaking rules, changing perspectives, seeing things differently. And this can set up tensions between the person coming up with this new way of seeing and the rest of the world, who still have the old view.

That's not always a comfortable position since it can involve going head to head with an established view of the world. Those who hold it are likely to defend their view strongly. Being creative is often linked to breaking the rules and challenging the conventional view – and it isn't always popular. When Galileo, the astronomer, proposed a different view for the way the sun and planets operated, he was imprisoned and threatened with death by the Inquisition. And in a version of this which was not quite so life threatening, when Bob Dylan performed his new electric music at the Newport festival he was booed off the stage. Not for nothing did successful entrepreneur James Dyson title his autobiography *Against the Odds*![2]
As the 16th-century writer Machiavelli put it:

> It must be remembered that there is nothing more difficult to plan, more doubtful of success, nor more dangerous to management than the creation of a new system. For the initiator has the enmity of all who would profit by the preservation of the old institution and merely lukewarm defenders in those who gain by the new ones.

Case Study of Dyson is available on the Innovation Portal at **www.innovation-portal.info**

If we are to manage creativity effectively, we need to think about how to bridge these two worlds.

Individual and Group Creativity

So far we have been talking about individual creativity but it is also important to recognize the power of interaction with others. We are all different in personality, experience and approach, and these differences mean we see problems and solutions from different perspectives. Combining our approaches, sparking ideas off each other and building on shared insights are all-powerful ways of amplifying creativity. The old proverb that 'two heads are better than one' is often true; think of the many successful creative partnerships in the world of music or theatre, for example.

Activities around shared problem-solving are available on the Innovation Portal at **www.innovation-portal.info**

ENTREPRENEURSHIP IN ACTION 5.1

The Power of Groups

Take any group of people and ask them to think of different uses for an everyday item – a cup, a brick, a ball, etc. Working alone, they will usually develop an extensive list – but then ask them to

(continued)

share the ideas they have generated. The resulting list will not only be much longer but will also contain much greater diversity of possible classes of solution to the problem. For example, uses for a cup could include using it as a container (vase, pencil holder, drinking vessel, etc.), a mould (for sandcastles, cakes, etc.), a musical instrument, a measure, a template around which one could draw, a device for eavesdropping (when pressed against a wall) and even, when thrown, a weapon!

The psychologist J.P. Guilford classed these two traits as **fluency** – the ability to produce ideas – and **flexibility** – the ability to come up with different types of idea.[3] The above experiment will quickly show that, when working as a group, people are usually much more fluent and flexible than any single individual. When working together, people spark each other off, jump on and develop each other's ideas, encourage and support each other through positive emotional mechanisms like laughter and agreement – and in a variety of ways stimulate a high level of shared creativity.

 Tools to help you explore brainstorming and creativity enhancement techniques are available on the Innovation Portal at **www.innovation-portal.info**

Creativity in Practice

One way of exploring the nature of creativity is to ask people about it, and Table 5.1 gives some examples. It is based on asking new product development engineers how they come up with creative insights and shows the importance of several behaviours rather than a single magic ingredient. It also underlines a key point; creativity is about behavioural skills which we can learn and develop.

TABLE 5.1   Creative behaviours in NPD engineers

Behavioural skills	Examples
Coming up with ideas	'Having many and different ideas'
Thinking differently	'Using a different way of seeing things'
Integrating differences	'Transferring a principle from another field'
Analysing problems	'Getting a deep understanding of the functionality of the machine'
	'Redefining the question or the problem'
Collaboration with other people	'Discussing the problem with my colleagues'
Having expertise/know-how	'Having a lot of experience in the field'

Source: Based on private communication with Ian Goller.

Creativity as a Process

It's easy to see creativity as being that wonderful moment where we have a flash of inspiration. The light bulb goes on and suddenly everything becomes clear. But research has shown it is not as simple as this; there is an underlying *process* which starts a long way before that light bulb moment.[4]

Activity to help you explore this, recollecting creativity, is available on the Innovation Portal at **www.innovation-portal.info**

It begins with our recognizing we have a puzzle or a problem to solve. If it is something we have seen before, we can often switch straight to applying a solution. But if it is something trickier, we need to explore it further. This can be frustrating; we may wrestle with it for some time without coming up with any insight about possible solutions. Or we may try out various ideas and realize they don't or won't work. Importantly, what's going on here is a process of recognizing and preparing the problem.

We could give up on the struggle and switch off our attention – but the reality is that we don't let the problem go. Our brain continues to process and explore, trying out different connections, playing with different options. When we walk away from the problem, or decide to sleep on it, we are not leaving it behind but rather passing the work of trying to solve it over to our unconscious minds. This 'incubation stage' is important; as the name suggests, we are allowing something to develop and grow.

At some stage, there is a moment when the insight is born. It may be that we wake up with a fresh idea in our head, or we suddenly get that flash of inspiration. The 'aha!' moment is often accompanied by feelings of certainty; even if we can't explain why, we just *know* this is the right solution. There's a flow of energy and a sense of direction to our thinking. The idea may still need a lot of work to elaborate on and develop it but the underlying breakthrough has been made.

Figure 5.1 shows a model of this process.

This pattern can be seen in many accounts of creativity where people talk about how they came up with apparently radical new solutions. And it's a key resource for us in thinking

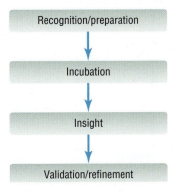

FIGURE 5.1 A model of the creative process

about how we can build creativity. If it's a process then we can map the stages, understand what's going on and provide some resources to help.

ENTREPRENEURSHIP IN ACTION 5.2

Snakes on a Bus

The 19th-century chemist Friedrich August Kekulé is credited with having unravelled one of the keys to the development of organic chemistry, the structure of the benzene ring. This arrangement of atoms is central to understanding how to make a range of chemicals, from fertilizers and medicines to explosives, and enabled the rapid acceleration of growth in the field. Having wrestled for a long period with the problem, he eventually had a flash of inspiration on waking from a dream in which he had seen the atoms dance and then, like a snake, begin eating its own tail. This weird dream picture nudged him towards the key insight that the atoms in benzene were arranged in a ring.

He later reported on another dream which he had had while dozing on a London bus in which atoms were dancing in different formations, which gave him further insight into the key components of chemical structure.

Sometimes this process takes place almost instantaneously; we recognize the problem and can retrieve a solution almost simultaneously. But sometimes we need to work through the process in a more systematic fashion, allowing time for each stage. We mentioned divergent and convergent thinking a little earlier and one way of seeing the creativity process is as a mixture of divergent and convergent cycles. Figure 5.2 gives an illustration.

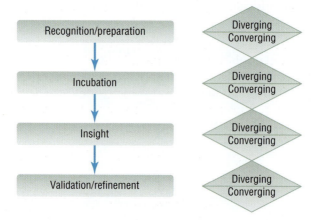

FIGURE 5.2 Cycles of divergence and convergence in creativity

We can link this to our earlier point about the two hemispheres of the brain. 'Left brain' thinking involves assembling facts and processing them in a logical fashion, whereas the right hemisphere is about seeing patterns and making new associations. Both are involved in these different stages of the creative process – the left side early on in preparing and recognizing and the right in the incubating and insight stages.

In practice, this means we need to find ways to engage both hemispheres and to practise skills and use tools to help us open up and close down ideas around the core problem.

Video Clip of IDEO describing and enacting this process in its design methodology is available on the Innovation Portal at **www.innovation-portal.info**

(Why, When and Where) Does Creativity Matter?

Of course creativity matters. Evolutionary psychologists point out the stage at which human beings began to accelerate in their development and link it to the evolution of the brain, especially the frontal cortex and the underlying 'theory of mind' which accompanied it.[5] Being able to imagine, to simulate and to play with ideas and possibilities gave us a huge advantage when dealing with a complex and dangerous environment.

Today's environment may be physically less threatening but it's still filled with uncertainty and complex problems with which we have to wrestle on a daily basis. We need as much creativity as we can get, whether in starting up a new venture or in steering an established organization through an increasingly turbulent sea.

Activity to help you explore where and why creativity matters is available on the Innovation Portal at **www.innovation-portal.info**

And we need different types of creativity, ranging from the occasional breakthrough to the systematic deployment of new solutions in incremental fashion. For example, in healthcare we have seen breakthroughs, like the flashes of inspiration behind the discovery of antibiotics or the structure of DNA. But these have been followed by decades of systematic, incremental creativity, opening up the field, refining and configuring solutions based on these breakthrough ideas.

That's important because it highlights the need to think about managing creativity right across the novelty spectrum and to find ways in which people can deploy their natural skills in support of the process. Companies like Toyota wrestle with the continuing challenge of remaining productive in the face of rising costs, complex and uncertain markets, challenging new technologies and a host of other threats. It has achieved its position as the most productive carmaker in the world and sustained it for over thirty years not by relying on occasional breakthrough ideas (although it has had its fair share of them) but because it has learnt to mobilize and deploy incremental creativity across its workforce.

Case Studies of high involvement innovation at Veeder-Root, Denso Systems, Innocent Fruit Juices, Redgate Software, Devon and Cornwall Police and the UK Meteorological Office are available on the Innovation Portal at **www.innovation-portal.info**

TABLE 5.2　Where and when we may need creativity in different contexts

Stage in development	Start-up	Growth	Maturity	Crisis
Need for creativity	How to develop a creative vision followed by incremental improvement and refinement around the core idea – 'pivoting' and learning via experiment	How to solve the problems of keeping the entrepreneurial advantages of speed and flexibility while growing in size, in opening new markets, in increasing control over processes	How to improve across the broad frontier, mobilizing everyone to help with continuous development	How to 'get out of the box'

Every day, thousands of employees engage their brains in systematic incremental creativity problem-solving in a process called 'kaizen'. (We will discuss this later in the chapter.)

It's exactly the same pattern for the individual entrepreneur. The initial flash of insight, the wonderful new idea for a business or social venture is followed by a long journey of problem-solving, applying creative thinking to get the bugs out of the core idea, pivoting and changing as the venture develops. The process involves recruiting all sorts of people into a network, which adds its own creative energy and insight to the underlying development process.

The point is there is a huge demand for creativity… we can never have enough new thinking. And the good news is we have plenty of evidence that it can be harnessed and focused in both radical and incremental ways. As we'll see, there are many different ways in which the process can be helped along, from simple tools to enhance incremental problem-solving to some power tools for the 'heavy lifting' work of generating radical new concepts. Table 5.2 gives some examples.

Who Is Creative?

The exercise we did earlier, imagining people being creative, usually leads to pictures of exceptional individuals, gifted (and often troubled) geniuses who possess the magic ingredient of 'creativity'. In reality, every human being has the capacity for creativity – watch any group of children in a playground to be reminded of this wonderful facility fitted as standard equipment! The question is not whether people are creative but how to unlock what is already there and then hone and develop the skill.

It's also important to recognize that, while we are all capable of creativity, we differ in how comfortable we feel about playing with new ideas or loosening up our minds to allow new thought patterns. We have a mental 'comfort zone' within which we can be creative and we can occasionally push the boundaries and explore something significantly novel. But few of us would want to spend all of our time wrestling with the pain of trying to create something radically new. (One of the characteristics associated with stereotypes of 'creative' people is that they are often troubled and unhappy, struggling with the pain of constantly trying to break through to something new. Think of van Gogh or Tchaikovsky as examples.)

ENTREPRENEURSHIP IN ACTION 5.3

The Kirton Adaptor/Innovator Scale

Everyone is creative but we all have different preferred styles of behaviour – how we like to express it and what we feel comfortable with. The UK psychologist Michael Kirton carried out extensive work and developed an instrument to measure these differences.[6] He defined two points on a scale running from 'innovators', who were open to considerable flexibility in their creative thinking, to 'adaptors', who were more comfortable with incremental creativity.

We discuss the Kirton model in more detail in Chapter 9.

Another personal dimension of creativity is linked to experience and expertise. Creative people are often highly experienced in a field and thus able to see patterns and identify variations on a core theme which others won't see. Dorothy Leonard calls these 'deep smarts' and many studies in psychology have shown the importance of such deep knowledge as a part of creativity.[7] But this raises the idea of 'domain specificity': people who may be highly creative in one field may not be so in another.

As we saw earlier, a lot of creativity research has been around convergent and divergent thinking. Studies suggest that people differ in their approaches; some are more comfortable in divergent thinking than others. Attempts have been made to map these to personality types and characteristics like introversion and extraversion. But the emerging conclusion is that people need both sets of skills for effective creativity, and these can be trained and developed.

What all of this means for our challenge of mobilizing creativity is that we need to find multiple ways of doing so. It's not simply a matter of finding an 'on/off' switch but rather one of building the context in which people can deliver their particular skills. Much of what we have learnt about managing creativity is about configuring tools and resources to enable different people to feel comfortable and supported in the process. For some this may be a very loose unstructured environment where crazy ideas fly around the room and bounce off each other in wild flights of fancy. For others it may be more structured and systematic, supporting people in a guided process in which they can find and solve problems in an incremental fashion.

Activity to find out about your creativity, How creative are you?, based on a self-assessment questionnaire is available on the Innovation Portal at **www.innovation-portal.info**

How to Enable Creativity

So how do we make it happen? As we've seen, everyone is already capable of creativity – it's not a case of injecting them with some magic new ingredient. Instead, we need to look for ways in which this natural capability can be drawn out, developed and extended. It's useful to start by thinking about what blocks this natural ability?

Activity to build your own map of the ways in which we stifle creativity, Blocks to creativity, is available on the Innovation Portal at **www.innovation-portal.info**

Video Clip of Ken Robinson talking about creativity and how we block it is available on the Innovation Portal at **www.innovation-portal.info**

It doesn't take long to see that there are all sorts of pressures, inside and outside our minds, which can act to block creativity. Figure 5.3 summarizes some of these.

If we are going to enable creativity, we need to provide ways of tackling these different areas and developing skills and resources to deal with them. We could use the metaphor of a 'mental gym' in which there are various pieces of equipment to help us develop the muscles and techniques for creativity. There's no single solution but our overall aim is improving fitness across the board.

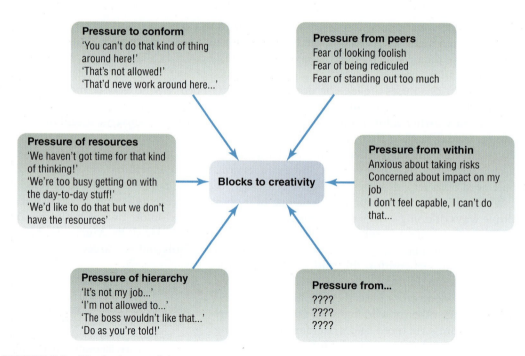

FIGURE 5.3 Blocks to creativity

In the following section, we look at four areas in which we could do this:

- developing thinking skills
- developing personal skills
- developing group-level creativity
- developing the environment.

Developing Thinking Skills

Research into creativity has moved us a long way from the notion that there is some magic spark in a few gifted individuals. We understand a lot more about the neuropsychological processes which underpin the creative process, and this gives us some useful clues about how we could develop skills to enhance our ability to think creatively.

It's worth going back to our simple model of the creative process (Figure 5.1) and looking at ways in which we could help support the thinking processes at each of these. Table 5.3 gives some examples of tools to help develop skills.

It's important to remember that our creative process is a series of cycles of divergence and convergence gradually closing in on a useful solution which we can apply. Let's look at some of the tools for each stage in a little more detail.

TABLE 5.3   Examples of tools to help develop creative thinking skills

Stage in creative process	Useful thinking skills to support this	Stage in creative process
Recognition/ preparation	Redefining and exploring the problem	Five whys
		Fishbone chart
		Levels of abstraction
		'How to' statements
		Reframing tools
Incubation	Supporting development of new insights	Attribute listing
		Metaphor and analogy
		Mind-mapping
		Brainstorming
		Lateral thinking
Insight	Making insights available to others	Visualization tools
Validation/ refinement	Testing and adapting, modifying the core insight	Continuous improvement tools
		Prototyping

Tools to help you explore creativity are available in the creativity toolkit on the Innovation Portal at **www.innovation-portal.info**

 Activities linked to using these tools are available on the Innovation Portal at **www.innovation-portal.info**

Preparation

Imagine we have a problem with a banging door. We can't sleep at night because the door keeps banging and rattling in the frame. We decide we need to fix the door, maybe even replace it, and so we get the carpenter in to look at it. He spends the day, shaves and planes the wood, adjusts the hinges, tinkers with the latch. That night the problem comes again, waking us up just as annoyingly. Eventually, we realize that the problem is not with the door at all but with the wind blowing through a hole in the roof, swirling around the house. The answer lies in fixing the roof not in mending the door.

That's a trivial example of problem recognition. Creativity starts with recognizing we have a problem or puzzle to solve and then exploring its dimensions. Working out the real problem, the underlying issue, is an important skill in arriving at a solution which works. Redefining and reframing are key skills here, being able to see the wood for the trees, the underlying pattern of the core problem.

There are several simple ways to develop skills around problem definition.

INNOVATION IN ACTION 5.3

Five Whys and a How

This simple but powerful tool can help strip away the apparent problem to get through to the root problem which is the one we need to solve. For example, a big problem in UK hospitals at the moment is in waiting times and delays, putting pressure on already scarce resources. Here's how the tool could be applied to help.

Apparent problem was that a patient arrived late in the operating theatre, causing a delay.

- *Why?* – Because they had to wait for a trolley to take them from the ward to the theatre.
- *Why?* – Because they had to find a replacement trolley.
- *Why?* – Because the original trolley had a defect – the safety rail had broken.
- *Why?* – Because it had not been regularly checked for wear and tear.
- *Why?* – Because there was no organized system of checking and maintenance.

Arriving at this root cause – the real problem is in the lack of systematic maintenance – gives plenty of clues about the 'how', the potential solutions to the problem. Setting up a simple maintenance schedule could ensure that all trolleys were regularly checked and available for use. This would mean future delays would be avoided, flow would improve and overall system efficiency would be better. Importantly, if we had just focused on the apparent problem – a single broken trolley – we would have solved that by repairing the trolley, but the underlying problem would mean it would happen again.

Activity to help you explore ways of improving a service process is available on the Innovation Portal at **www.innovation-portal.info**

There are plenty of tools to help develop this skill in exploring problems and focusing in on the core issue to be solved. The five whys discussed in Innovation in Action 5.3, cause and effect diagrams (fishbone chart), levels of abstraction, etc. offer ways of looking more closely at the challenge and framing the problem clearly so we can get to grips with solving it.

Tools such as the fishbone chart, Levels of abstraction and other reframing tools are available on the Innovation Portal at **www.innovation-portal.info**

Models of problem-solving suggest we are good at **pattern recognition** and when confronted with a new problem the first thing we do is to look for a pattern we have seen before. If we can find that then we have the basis for a solution, even if we have to adapt it. (This is what experienced people with 'deep smarts' often do: they bring their deep knowledge and intuition and 'see' a solution based on their intuitive pattern recognition.)

Activities to help you practise using these tools are available on the Innovation Portal at **www.innovation-portal.info**

So another set of useful thinking tools to help creativity is all about the patterns – the 'morphology' – of the problem and how to find similarities. For example, where will we have seen a similar-shaped problem in a different context? Can we find similar attributes, ways in which the two problems are like each other? These points of similarity can then give us clues about ways in which we could explore solutions: what works in the one context could be usefully applied in the other.

Case Study about DOME, which used different levels of abstraction to transfer innovations between sectors, is available on the Innovation Portal at **www.innovation-portal.info**

Tools to help you with pattern recognition (Levels of abstraction) and for playing with patterns (SCAMPER and Attribute listing) are available on the Innovation Portal at **www.innovation-portal.info**

Activities to help you try these pattern-recognition tools are available on the Innovation Portal at **www.innovation-portal.info**

ENTREPRENEURSHIP IN ACTION 5.4

TRIZ (Theory of Inventive Problem-Solving)

TRIZ was developed by the Russian Genrich S. Altshuller who worked on reviewing patents to derive his principles around which a wide range of apparently different problems could be solved. His approach classified solutions into five groups:

- *Level one.* Routine design problems solved by methods well known within the specialty. No invention needed. About 32% of the solutions fell into this level.
- *Level two.* Minor improvements to an existing system, by methods known within the industry. Usually with some compromise. About 45% of the solutions fell into this level.
- *Level three.* Fundamental improvement to an existing system, by methods known outside the industry. Contradictions resolved. About 18% of the solutions fell into this category.
- *Level four.* A new generation that uses a new principle to perform the primary functions of the system. Solution found more in science than in technology. About 4% of the solutions fell into this category.
- *Level five.* A rare scientific discovery or pioneering invention of essentially a new system. About 1% of the solutions fell into this category.

From this analysis he suggested that over 90% of the problems engineers faced had been solved somewhere before. If engineers could follow a path to an ideal solution, starting with the lowest level, their personal knowledge and experience and working their way to higher levels, most of the solutions could be derived from knowledge already present in the company, industry or in another industry.

Tool giving you a full description of TRIZ is available on the Innovation Portal at **www.innovation-portal.info**

The risk in pattern recognition is that we are sometimes too quick to categorize a problem – 'we've seen it before; it's one of those…'. For much of the time this is helpful but occasionally we may miss something, some way in which the pattern is not the same, and we need to search for a different solution. Sometimes we need jolting out of pattern recognition because we are framing the problem in ways we want to see it. This challenge of 'mindset' is important and there are tools to help reframe, to look at the problem through new eyes.

Activities highlighting the problems of mindset are available on the Innovation Portal at **www.innovation-portal.info**

Once again, we have some tools and techniques available to help deal with the challenge of reframing. Essentially, they are based on the idea of looking at the problem with fresh eyes, for example asking what

Tools to help you explore reframing, from simple 'New eyes' lenses to more structured techniques like soft systems analysis, are available on the Innovation Portal at **www.innovation-portal.info**

would this look like if you were from another planet? What if you were a three-year-old child? How would someone famous (an artist, a musician, a successful general) look at it?

For entrepreneurs this is a key set of skills. They face the challenge of finding opportunities – and sometimes this will involve creating completely new ones, while in other cases it will be a case of recognizing something which is already there but which no one may have seen before. As we saw earlier, research suggests these 'discovery' skills are of key importance and so it makes sense to try to apply tools to help develop these skills. For example, the start-up team behind Spotify reframed the music question as one in which people were asked if they really needed to own all the songs they enjoyed listening to. Airbnb reframed the idea of a spare room to being a business opportunity for many homeowners. And Google spent a large amount buying home automation company NEST. The challenge here for the entrepreneurs involved (and so for Google) is how to grow a business around an idea which is not particularly exciting. NEST's core product was a thermostat, a heating controller which sits on the wall. How could the company reframe this to make it interesting and exciting, to help people see it not as a passive device but as the heart of a futuristic automated home, one that would give them control and save them money?

Incubation

Sometimes redefining and exploring the problem is enough to lead to a solution – but very often we are left with a problem and no obvious answer. Wrestling with it, pulling it into different shapes and trying to force fit it to something we've seen before simply doesn't work. This is where we need to let go with our conscious minds and allow the brain some time to play around, to incubate. It needs to allow new connections to be made, and typical ways of helping this include relaxing, doing something different, going for a walk, sleeping on the problem, etc. What's going on underneath is a fascinating process of association and connecting in ways which may appear to be illogical. Think about your dreams and the amazing and unlikely events which take place in them; connections are established between random elements which simply wouldn't normally be linked. This is an important part of the unconscious creative process and one of the powerful ways of supporting this stage is to give the brain some help in making new connections.

Tools to help you explore lateral thinking methods are available on the Innovation Portal at **www.innovation-portal.info**

Activities involving lateral thinking puzzles are available on the Innovation Portal at **www.innovation-portal.info**

This also links with our earlier discussion of divergent and convergent thinking; divergence is very much about finding new links and connections. To help with this we need to find ways to enable the right hemisphere of the brain to play a more active role, to shut down temporarily the left brain with its logic and systematic approach and allow for new patterns and associations to emerge.

One approach, associated with the work of Edward de Bono, is called **lateral thinking**. He coined the term back in 1967 to explain a style of thinking aimed at moving away from linear step-by-step thinking and taking a step sideways to re-examine a problem from a different viewpoint.[8] Rather than digging a deeper hole in one place, we need to move sideways and start excavating somewhere new; in the process we may enable a new insight, a new perspective on the original problem.

Lateral thinking tools are systematic aids to moving sideways in our approach to problems. One example is the **intermediate impossible**, where we come up with an idea which is itself impossible but may provide the stepping stone to a practical and novel answer. Just like a stepping stone, the idea itself may be wobbly and poorly shaped but it helps us get to our goal.

For example, in trying to improve the food and service in a company canteen someone could suggest providing fresh foods where possible. One intermediate impossible suggestion would then be to bring cows into the workplace – not in itself very practical! But it provides the stepping stone to ideas about how to get fresh milk as opposed to using long-life packages, for example by making arrangements with a local dairy for daily deliveries.

Many techniques to assist incubation make use of the right brain hemisphere and its ability to make patterns and connections. One rich area lies around the use of 'metaphor'. Metaphor is a figure of speech in which we make connections between things, for example we can talk about someone being 'the light of my life'. We don't mean that they are literally a light bulb but rather that they brighten everything around them in a way a light bulb does. Other examples may be 'drowning in a sea of troubles', 'swimming in dangerous waters' or 'trying to boil the ocean'. In none of these are we meant to take the comparison literally but rather to see a connection where the image of one thing becomes superimposed on the other. Poetry and drama are full of powerful metaphors and that's one reason why they work so well; metaphor creates a rich picture gallery in our minds and engages our imagination far more than direct description could.

Metaphors work well in creativity because they map the properties of one thing onto another, building the kind of associations which we know are important. Famous examples of metaphors include Charles Darwin using the idea of a branching tree to help him get to the theory of evolution and Albert Einstein imagining himself riding on a beam of light holding a mirror in front of him.

We discussed the idea of pattern recognition and finding examples of things which were similar to our problem earlier. Analogies and similes offer another helpful route to pattern recognition by highlighting ways in which something is like something else. They can stimulate our thinking towards new insights; for example, if we say 'this organization is like a cheetah', we begin to think about how that animal is fast and agile, how it has the ability to accelerate and turn quickly, how it can focus on the challenge of bringing down its prey and concentrate its energies on this. From this set of mental pictures we can draw some inspiration for new ways of looking at our organization and how we could improve it.

Or if we want to explore how to make our organization more resilient we could look at the analogy of a rubber ball and explore its characteristics: it bounces back, it is elastic, it can hold and release compressed energy, etc.

Thinking about the way in which other organizations could approach our business is also a useful technique, for example asking questions like:

- How would Google manage our data?
- How would Disney engage with our consumers?
- How could Southwest Airlines cut our costs?
- How would Zara redesign our supply chain?
- How would Apple design and launch our product/service offering?

Activity that allows you to try this, metaphorical thinking, is available on the Innovation Portal at **www.innovation-portal.info**

Tool to help you try these techniques, using metaphor, is available on the Innovation Portal at **www.innovation-portal.info**

Another approach is to use the fact that we store memories as patterns, whole systems of connected elements. When we hear a piece of music we can often reconstruct what was going on in our lives when we heard it in rich detail. Famously, when the French writer Marcel Proust took a bite of a madeleine cake one afternoon the taste took him back to childhood and the sensation was so rich in detail that he used it to write a seven-volume book based on his memories!

Once again, we can make use of this patterning to evoke systems of thought and explore opportunities in there. If we imagine an organization to be like an orchestra then we may enrich this picture by trying to remember when we had been moved by that kind of experience. What elements made that special and powerful for us, and can we transpose some of them to our problem of designing a new organization?

ENTREPRENEURSHIP IN ACTION 5.5

Synectics

Characteristic of these approaches is a style of thinking which aims to 'make the familiar strange and the strange familiar'. In the 1970s, two researchers within the Arthur D. Little consultancy, George Prince and William Gordon, used this phrase to underpin their methodology of 'synectics'. This approach derives from the Greek word meaning 'the joining together of different and apparently irrelevant elements'. Synectics involves various techniques – metaphor, analogy and simulation – which are designed to help people explore and develop insights from new associations.[9]

Tool to help you explore this, analogies, is available on the Innovation Portal at **www.innovation-portal.info**

As we mentioned earlier, one place where creativity often happens is in our dreams; we get flashes of inspiration from the rich and odd associations which can happen when we are sleeping or in a trance. And it's significant that in our dreams the 'normal' rules don't apply; anything can become connected with anything else, often in bizarre and strange ways. Such apparently strange connections often form the basis of a powerful new insight; it's what the writer Arthur Koestler called 'bisociation' and it is essentially about surprise connections. (This is the basis of a great deal of humour. A good joke often depends on a punch line which makes a surprising connection.)

We can use this idea of bisociation to force new connections between elements and in the process get our minds thinking along new pathways. One powerful tool for this is 'random juxtaposition' which involves taking two random elements and forcing a relationship between them. For example, we may be trying to find a solution to a problem of traffic management in a busy city. To help generate ideas we may take a random element – say a seagull – and try to find a relationship between our problem and that element. There is no obvious link but our brains often generate interesting new lines of thinking by trying to force the connection.

ENTREPRENEURSHIP IN ACTION 5.6

Unloved Fruit

Creativity tools in this area require a high level of playfulness, of suspending disbelief and allowing things to happen and emerge. A food company made, amongst other items in its range, fruit pies and was concerned about the high level of wastage by not being able to use fruit which was fresh but damaged. During a creativity workshop, participants were asked to imagine what it felt like to be a piece of damaged fruit – a cherry with its skin ripped off, a strawberry torn in half by a clumsy picker. Playing the role of such fruit, a number of insights emerged: 'I feel lonely, unconnected to the rest', 'I feel incomplete and the others won't let me join their game', 'If only I could wear an artificial skin, then I'd be able to play with them'.

Such images drew on a strong emotional line linked to joining in and playing with other children. Viewed from outside, it would seem very strange to watch a group of adults bemoaning this forced isolation while playing at being pieces of fruit! But it generated an insight around finding something – artificial skin – which could render the damaged fruit whole again. Carrageenan, a substance found naturally in seaweed, has this kind of property, forming a layer around the damaged fruit and effectively giving it an artificial but edible skin. The result was a significant increase in the proportion of fruit the company was able to use in the millions of pies it manufactured every year.

Another way in which we can explore different associations is by creating a space in which anything can happen. Thinking about the future allows this and developing scenarios – rich stories about future worlds – allows us to explore and play with new ideas. Since the future hasn't happened yet, anything could happen – and such simulations can provide powerful ways of releasing constraints on our thinking. Science fiction stories can provide a powerful breeding ground for this kind of creative thinking, for example Arthur C. Clarke wrote wonderful pieces about the future including the short story on which the classic film *2001: A Space Odyssey* was based. One of his ideas, published in a scientific paper back in the 1960s, foresaw communication via satellites allowing us to talk to anyone anywhere on the planet. This futuristic daydreaming has become a reality sixty years later with global satellite-based communications an everyday reality.

Tools to help you think about the future are available in the futures toolkit on the Innovation Portal at **www.innovation-portal.info**

Activities to help you try some of these tools, such as scenario generation, are available on the Innovation Portal at **www.innovation-portal.info**

Insight

The most common picture of creativity is the light bulb moment – and it's an apt description for what it often feels like to come up with a new insight. It's not just the awareness of a solution; there is often a strong emotional charge, a deeps sense of *the* answer, a certainty. According to the story, Archimedes was so excited about the flash of insight he had while sitting in his bath tub trying to understand hydrodynamics that he jumped out and ran naked through the streets crying out 'Eureka!', which, roughly translated, means 'I have it!'

Interestingly, people describing such moments are often not entirely clear about the full extent of their solution, they just 'know' it is right and they then spend time (validation) tidying up the idea and building on their initial insight.

Sometimes their idea is half formed. It's alive but hasn't got a full shape yet. And so making it visible and available to others is an important part of this stage and offers us another area where skills and tools may help. Even if the idea is only a few scrambled words scribbled down on waking from a dream, or an outline sketch, or a key phrase, it may be enough to catch the core idea and allow for its development.

Tools for supporting this kind of thinking are available in the design methods toolkit on the Innovation Portal at **www.innovation-portal.info**

Techniques like **brainstorming** make much of the act of writing down ideas, and variations on the theme use pictures and sketches to capture the insights. Making 'sculptures' out of everyday items to represent elements in a different way and make this available to

Activities to help you try some of these tools, such as visualizing the invisible, are available on the Innovation Portal at **www.innovation-portal.info**

others is another route. Within the field of design methods, many powerful tools and techniques are based on the idea of helping people articulate what they can't fully express – allowing for 'visualizing the invisible'.

Validation

Striking a Light

Although creativity is often pictured as a flash of inspiration, the reality is that it is a lot of hard work, building on that insight and improving and debating with yourself about the idea to make it work. For example, Thomas Edison, when working to develop the light bulb, spent weeks in the laboratory trying to find the right material for the filament for his incandescent bulb, experimenting and learning about the core idea. His painstaking work (some reports suggest he tried over 10 000 different materials) led to the famous phrase attributed to him that 'genius is one per cent inspiration, ninety-nine per cent perspiration!'

Tools to help you explore prototyping are available on the Innovation Portal at **www.innovation-portal.info**

Activities to help you try some of these prototyping tools are available on the Innovation Portal at **www.innovation-portal.info**

Case Studies of the NHS RED and Open Door projects, which made use of prototyping, are available on the Innovation Portal at **www.innovation-portal.info**

This is the stage at which the idea, the core insight, becomes refined and developed. It involves trying the idea out – prototyping – and using feedback from that to adapt and develop it. For example, the 'lean start-up' methodology for new venture entrepreneurs places strong emphasis on the idea of designing experiments around a 'minimum viable product' (MVP). The idea is to use the MVP as a probe, a prototype around which we can gather information to help refine and focus the initial insight. Central to the approach is the idea of the 'pivot' – not changing direction completely but rotating around the core idea to find the most suitable configuration which works.

Prototyping can be done in various ways and forms the core of design methods aimed at bringing new ideas into widespread use. A key point here is that this represents the end of one cycle and the beginning of the next. As we saw earlier, creativity is a process of alternately opening up and closing in on the core solution. By sharing the original idea we can explore its different dimensions from many perspectives and open up the idea for further development.

Developing Personal Skills

So far, we've been looking at thinking skills and some tools to help develop these. But creativity is also about motivation and communication. We need to feel comfortable about taking the risk of trying out something new or trusting our intuition. For a few people, creativity is their way of life. They are constantly challenging and questioning, but for most people there is an element of self-imposed limitation to it. Am I allowed to think this way? What if my idea is wrong? Will I look/sound foolish for suggesting this? Can I trust my instincts which are leading me to think in this way?

Building confidence in our own ideas and then developing skills in communicating them and handling the feedback we get on them is another area where we can develop our creative capabilities. Successful entrepreneurs are not just able to come up with creative insights; they are also resilient in the face of feedback, using this to help shape and adapt their ideas. They have a strong sense of vision and can communicate and engage others in sharing that insight. And they are skilled at 'pitching': communicating the core idea to others in ways which get past their critical comments and engage their interest (and hopefully their resource support).

One key point is to understand the nature of the creative process as we have described it and to recognize that it isn't entirely rational, that emotions, intuitions and odd insights are a valuable part of it, and that ideas which emerge can be useful stepping stones or valuable in their own right. 'If it's worth thinking, it's worth saying' is a useful motto. But understanding the process also reminds us of different kinds of thinking associated with different stages – from divergent activities opening our minds to new connections through to convergent thinking helping us focus in and whittle many wild ideas down to the ones with real potential value. We need to develop the flexibility in our thinking – and as we'll see in the following section in the thinking we do with other people – to deal with these different stages in creativity.

Edward de Bono offers a very practical approach to help with this. His 'Six thinking hats' model uses the metaphor of wearing different hats when we undertake different kinds of thinking.[10] For example, a green hat is all about a freewheeling, 'anything goes' kind of thinking which is essentially opening up and allowing ideas to emerge. By contrast, a black hat is about judgement, evaluating and criticizing ideas to winnow out the less valuable ones and focus on the core. He suggests we need six different modes of thinking and offers helpful tools to develop the ability to recognize when they are needed and the flexibility to move between them.

Tool to help you explore the six thinking hats tool is available on the Innovation Portal at **www.innovation-portal.info**

Activity to help you try this approach is available on the Innovation Portal at **www.innovation-portal.info**

As we'll see in the following sections, there are useful structures and tools to help build on this positive approach to coming up with new ideas and to strengthen self-belief in our ability to play a part in the process.

Developing Group-Level Creativity

Creativity is something we are all capable of; we can all come up with novel and useful ideas on our own. But working together with others can amplify that process, leading to more ideas and more different insights, which can lead to novel solutions. People differ in their experience, their personality and their perspectives on the world, and this diversity is a rich resource for helping creativity to happen. Think about creative partnerships in the musical world like Lennon and McCartney, Rogers and Hammerstein, Rice and Lloyd Webber, the Gershwin brothers. Look at the world of theatre and film and see how much success is the product not of a lone genius but of a team of co-creators front and back stage who help make it happen. Look at business ventures and very often you'll find a team – Eric Schmidt and Sergei Brin (Google), Bill Gates and Paul Allen (Microsoft), Andy Grove and Gordon Moore (Intel).

Activity to help you explore aspects of group creativity, the egg game, is available on the Innovation Portal at **www.innovation-portal.info**

(In Chapter 9, we explore the idea of 'conjoint innovation', where the secret behind many successful innovating organizations lies in a complementary partnership.)

So there's a lot to be said for working with others and there's plenty of research to support the potential of doing so. But it's not as easy as it looks. There are many downsides to working in a group, as Table 5.4 shows. Social pressures can act as a damper on individual sparks of ideas. Diversity can lead to conflict about the 'right' solutions. Groups can quickly become political. As we demonstrate in Chapter 9, simply throwing people together does not make them a team and the wrong mix can easily lead to the whole performing much less well than the sum of the parts.

This suggests that we need to look for ways we can amplify the positive aspects and minimize the negative, and there are various tools which can help in this process.

TABLE 5.4   Advantages and disadvantages of group-level creativity

Advantages	Disadvantages
Diversity – more different ideas	'Groupthink' – social pressures to conform
Volume of ideas – 'many hands make light work'	Lack of focus – 'too many cooks spoil the broth'
Elaboration – multiple resources to explore around the problem	Group dynamics and hierarchy
Rich variety of prior experience	Political behaviour, people following different agendas

Activities around teambuilding are available on the Innovation Portal at **www.innovation-portal.info**

Tool to help you explore teambuilding is available on the Innovation Portal at **www.innovation-portal.info**

Brainstorming is one of the most widely used approaches and has its origins in this space. Originally developed in the 1950s by an advertising executive, Alex Osborn, brainstorming is basically an approach to group idea generation.[11] It recognizes that we have a tendency to judge ideas quickly and that in a group setting this can be negative; without meaning to, we can quickly pour cold water on the sparks. This may come from a simple reaction to the idea itself: 'That's stupid', 'That won't work', etc. Or it can come from hierarchy effects: 'Junior employees should be seen and not heard', 'The best ideas come from the senior people', 'Listen to the experts; they have the experience to solve this', etc. Or it can come from politics and interpersonal rivalries. For whatever reason, the judgement of ideas when they surface can quickly kill them off.

Given what we know about the creative process, sometimes those ideas can be half-formed, we don't quite know what we're suggesting, we haven't through it through, they are new-born insights. So they are at high risk from being surfaced in this group context. Brainstorming provides a simple set of rules to protect them mainly based on postponing judgement. Instead of reacting to ideas, people are encouraged to share them and build on them, exploring and adding to them. Only later does the group move into a judgement phase, winnowing out the novel and useful ideas from the many others which have been suggested.

Tool to help you explore brainstorming is available on the Innovation Portal at **www.innovation-portal.info**

Activities to help you with brainstorming are available on the Innovation Portal at **www.innovation-portal.info**

The power of brainstorming (which is available in many different forms) is that it counters some of the negative effects of working in a group and builds on the positives like diversity. It enables practices like improvisation around a theme, acceptance and building on whatever comes up; a core principle is that 'quantity breeds quality', so generating many possible ideas statistically allows for the emergence of more good ones.

ENTREPRENEURSHIP IN ACTION 5.8

Improving the Climate for Creativity

The consultancy ?Whatif! specializes in creative problem-solving for and with clients. It makes use of many techniques linked to brainstorming and has a simple framework using the analogy of nurturing the fragile early shoots of ideas.[12]

They need plenty of SUN:

S = support, encourage
U = understand, listen to the ideas
N = nurture, help them grow

(continued)

and avoid too much RAIN:

R = react, respond directly and judge the ideas rather than listen to them
A = assume, bringing your preconceptions and your interpretation too quickly
I = insist on your viewpoint, be closed in your mind to other ways of seeing the problem
N = negative, closing down and shutting out possible new directions, saying 'no' to the idea in
     its early undeveloped form.

Beyond brainstorming, many of the tools which we explored in the section on developing thinking skills above can be deployed in a group setting and the diversity can amplify the effect. Within a session the process leader may well throw in such techniques as a way of 'stirring the pot' to try to trigger new direction for thinking or move the group into new search space.

It's important not to see the group as the solution to everything. While there are positive effects arising from interaction with others, there is also value in individual creativity. Many creativity workshops make use of both options, for example encouraging people to work individually on a problem and write down their ideas before sharing those with a group and allowing for creative exploration of them. 'Nominal group' approaches try to build in the complementary advantages of individual and group creativity. Approaches like these help balance out the tendency within groups for some people to dominate while others remain in the background.

One powerful new resource is the online forums and communities which allow many people to come together as a virtual group or community. This can capture some of the positive effects like diversity without some of the negative social effects in a face-to-face context. The downside is that such groups don't get the non-verbal or emotional charge, so it's a case of a complementary approach rather than a replacement.

Brainstorming has its limits. It's not always effective and sometimes the benefits in a group wear out over time. Think again of the examples of creative partnerships we explored earlier. Many of these have a short creative phase but then fall apart, with the members often acknowledging that they need to move on and find new combinations. Even in a simple brainstorming session, there is a phase where ideas come thick and fast, but this gradually dries up as the effects of group stimulation and interaction tail off. Under these conditions, it's often valuable for the session process leader to inject some new stimuli, perhaps bringing in some of the lateral thinking or metaphor techniques described earlier.

Another important feature is the approach to conflict. The 'rules' of brainstorming say that ideas shouldn't be attacked or criticized and that judgement should be suspended. But in many creative situations arguments and debate are a powerful feature for moving things forward – think of a theatre or a music group, for example. It's the differences and debate which help create the edge and provide the spark which makes the difference. Research suggests that a degree of creative conflict is valuable; the secret is not to attack the person but to challenge the idea and this often depends on having someone to moderate and guide the debate.

Studies of creativity in groups suggest there is an inverted U-shape to their effectiveness. Too little time together and they don't deliver much because they are lacking in trust and experience of each other; too long together and a degree of groupthink sets in and the ideas become stale. Similarly, too little conflict and everyone agrees and the frontiers of thinking do not get pushed; too much conflict and ideas get killed off too readily.[13]

All of this suggests we need a contingency approach to managing groups to ensure we get the best out of their shared creativity. Balancing the positives in Table 5.4 with the negatives requires a degree of process leadership and moderation.

Developing the Environment

Creativity doesn't happen in a vacuum. Being able to come up with different new ideas is a process which is influenced by a whole series of external pressures which can act as a barrier, pushing our creative ideas back into the bottle.

ENTREPRENEURSHIP IN ACTION 5.9

Killer Phrases

One of the problems in creativity is that people react quickly to new things with reasons for why they won't work. Such 'killer phrases' are part of the aural landscape; we hear them wherever we go in organizations. They have the same basic structure: 'That's a great idea, but...' Here are some typical examples and you can almost certainly add your own to the list:

- We've never tried that before...
- We've always done it this way...
- The boss won't like it...
- We don't have the time for that...
- It's too expensive...
- You can't do that here...
- We're not that kind of organization...
- That's a brave suggestion...
- Etc., etc.

If we want to enable creativity, we can do a lot by working with these levers to create a physical and mental environment which is supportive. Table 5.5 summarizes some of the key approaches and we'll discuss a few in the following section.

TABLE 5.5   Building a creative environment

Environmental barrier	Ways of dealing with this
Physical environment	Make the workplace stimulating
	Allow for interaction and bumping into new ideas
	Make ideas visible
	Get outside the work environment and experience the problem from a different perspective
	Build a virtual environment (an ICT platform)
Time and permission to play	Allow and even require that employees take time to explore and be curious, to enable incubation
Climate	Create the supporting 'rules of the game'
	SUN/RAIN
	LIFE (little improvements from everyone)
	'No blame' culture – encourage experiment
	Mistakes = opportunities
	Chance favours the prepared mind
Reward and recognition	Reinforce the behaviour
Establish a process	Make creative problem-solving explicit
Training and skills development	Train in creativity tools and techniques
Leadership	Coaching and supporting the process, moderating and facilitating at different stages, providing an overall direction and focus

Physical Environment

The city of Munich in Germany is home to a complex glass and steel structure which houses the BMW research centre where the designs for cars and motorbikes which populate the highways of the world are first created. It was one of the reasons that *Business Week* magazine named BMW one of the world's most innovative companies in 2006.

   The R&D centre is not like a conventional office building but more closely resembles a giant glass cloverleaf with a huge central atrium around which glass-walled offices are spread, each of which looks into the centre and where everyone can see new designs and prototypes whatever they are doing. Walking past them to visit the canteen or use the bathroom, it is impossible not to notice the prototypes and the walls are full of sketch boards and spaces for commenting and suggesting ideas. The whole environment seems constructed to bring many people in contact with emerging new ideas and to encourage their contribution.

Which is exactly what was in the mind of the architect, Gunter Henn. He was strongly influenced by the work of Thomas Allen in the 1970s (see Innovation in Action 5.4) and believed that people interacting was at the heart of creativity and that architecture could force these collisions.[14]

INNOVATION IN ACTION 5.4

Managing the Flow of Ideas

During the 1970s, Tom Allen, a professor at MIT, was interested in how ideas emerged during large complex technical projects. He began studying organizations working for the innovation challenge around the US space programme – finding ways to deliver on Kennedy's original target of putting a man on the moon and bringing him home again safely.

He studied how people shared ideas and how they moved around and across organizations and laid the foundations for what we now call 'social network analysis' as a way of mapping these interactions. He found, for example, the importance of key individuals ('technological gatekeepers') through whom ideas travelled and were disseminated to relevant people. His book contains a wealth of insights which are of continuing importance in designing today's network-based innovation processes.[15]

One project he undertook explored how the distance between engineers' offices coincided with the level of regular technical communication between them. The results of that research, now known as the Allen Curve, revealed a distinct correlation between distance and frequency of communication (i.e. the more distance there is between people – 50 metres or more to be exact – the less they will communicate). This principle has been incorporated into forward-thinking commercial design ever since, in, for example, the Decker Engineering Building in New York, the Steelcase Corporate Development Centre in Michigan and BMW's Research Centre in Germany.

It's a long way (10 000 km) from Munich to the west coast of the USA but in Emeryville, California you'd find a similar model of architecture supporting creativity. Pixar Studios is one of the most consistently successful companies in the film business, producing award-winning animated films like *Toy Story*, *Finding Nemo* and *The Incredibles*. Its ability to repeat its success stands in contrast to most studios; its fourteen films have all been both commercial and critical successes and, as of December 2013, have earned over $8 billion. This is not a matter of luck; at work is a well-understood and managed creative process which keeps the ideas flowing and the output fresh and exciting. One key principle, originating with Steve Jobs (who was a key figure in the early days of Pixar before returning to Apple), was to make the physical geography of the place work to enable the same kind of creative collisions which Gunter Henn uses.

Case Study detailing Pixar's creative process is available on the Innovation Portal at **www.innovation-portal.info**

These days, organizations are increasingly recognizing that physical environments which provide space for interaction and offer stimulation and different perspectives to their employees can act as a powerful catalyst for creativity. The Googleplex is not simply a designer's whim or an attempt to improve employee morale; it is aimed at encouraging creative insights as a part of daily activity.

It's not simply about high-tech California companies; the UK's Meteorological (Met) Office is one of the world's leading scientific institutes and is housed in an open glass-framed building with dedicated spaces to encourage creative interchange. The Danish public sector has an innovation support agency 'owned' by the Ministries of Taxation, Economics and Employee Affairs. 'Mindlab' is located in a traditional government building, but inside it resembles the same kind of open playful space which Gunter Henn and Steve Jobs were aiming for in their designs.

Case Study on the Met Office is available on the Innovation Portal at www.innovation-portal.info

Video Clip of Natalie Wilkie and Gary Holpin explaining some of the philosophy behind their 'Think Up!' approach to stimulating creativity is available on the Innovation Portal at www.innovation-portal.info

One important development in this is the use of virtual space to bring people together and allow for creative interchange. Innovation platforms are now common to many organizations and provide ways in which thousands of employees can engage with each other, and suggest, comment and focus on their innovation efforts. While many of these operate within companies, there is also a growing trend towards bringing in outsiders to the process – 'crowd-sourcing' creative ideas. (We discuss this in more detail in Chapter 6.)

Time, Space and Permission to Play

We've seen throughout this chapter that creativity is about long periods of incubation and exploration punctuated by flashes of insight. That's not a process that lends itself to being switched on and off to order, and organizations are increasingly realizing that if they want creativity to happen they must make space for it. 3M is a business with a long tradition of breakthrough innovation – think about Post-it notes, Scotch tape, industrial masking tape and a host of other products we now take for granted. They came out of an organization which has recognized that it needs its employees to be curious, to play and explore, to make odd connections. And in order to do so they need a sense of time being allowed for this and permission to play within that time. 3M operates what it calls the '15% policy': employees can use up to 15% of their time on personal projects which don't have to be linked to specific company outputs or productivity targets. This time is not accounted for on timesheets, it's more a signal to employees that creativity is important and that the company trusts them to use the time well.

Much attention has been paid in recent years to Google and its 'innovation machine'. While the business began with a powerful search engine, the company has diversified into many new areas: advertising, Web analytics, driverless cars, home automation and retailing. Underpinning Google's approach is the same recognition that people need time and space to explore, and so the company requires its engineers to spend at least 20% of their time working on non-core projects. Major successes like Gmail came out of this process of 'permitted play'.

Not all organizations can afford the luxury of giving employees the freedom to take their own time; Toyota, for example, is driven by the huge commitment of keeping its production lines running as interrupting them is costly and disruptive. But it too has its version of allowing time and space for creativity. Every team spends fifteen minutes each day before and after its shift in group problem-solving, identifying issues to be worked on and coming up with new ideas to try out during the day. This constant high-frequency, short burst approach to creativity is called 'kaizen' and is central to the company's success as the world's most productive car maker. Process innovation keeps happening, driven by the creativity of thousands of employees; it's estimated that the company receives on average one useful idea per worker per week and has done so since the 1960s, when it began this approach to continuous improvement.

Video Clips of Veeder-Root, Redgate Software and Innocent Fruit Juices highlighting various aspects of high involvement innovation systems are available on the Innovation Portal at **www.innovation-portal.info**

Case Studies of Kumba Resources, Redgate Software and Innocent Fruit Juices exploring high involvement innovation systems are available on the Innovation Portal at **www.innovation-portal.info**

Creative Climate

Organizations, as we show in Chapter 9, are much more than a collection of people working together. They have shared beliefs and values and an underlying agreement about 'the way we do things around here'. Whether we are talking about a small start-up or a large corporation, the underlying culture is important since it shapes how people will behave. We can use the metaphor of organizational climate to describe the kind of 'weather system' which provides the context in which they work.

For example, a core belief underpinning the Toyota model mentioned above is 'Little ideas matter'. This sends out a clear message that every employee can make a contribution and, indeed, is expected to share his or her creativity. Another example could be an organization which sends out a clear message that mistakes are OK since they provide learning opportunities. We know creativity is about trying things out and experiments often fail; their value lies in helping us move closer towards a useful solution. So building a climate in which people believe they won't be punished for making mistakes (as long as they don't repeat them!) is an important building block supporting their creativity.

The difficulty with creating this kind of environment is that organizations need to be consistent. Saying, 'We're a blame-free organization' and then punishing people who do try things out and make mistakes is not a consistent message and people quickly see through it.

Successful organizations which have a clear culture for creativity are well aware of the behaviours they want people to practise and the underlying beliefs they want to foster. They make these explicit and they

Case Studies exploring how organizations like Hosiden and NPI try to build a creative environment are available on the Innovation Portal at **www.innovation-portal.info**

Tool to help you explore the climate for supporting creativity, the high involvement innovation audit, is available on the Innovation Portal at **www.innovation-portal.info**

communicate and reinforce them so that they become 'the way we do things around here'. 3M's 15% policy, Pixar's approach to creative debate, Toyota's kaizen philosophy and Google's 'perpetual beta' approach are all company-specific examples of building a creative climate.

Reward and Recognition

One important aspect of a climate which supports creativity is the use of reward and recognition. While everyone is potentially creative, they may not choose to deploy their skills in the context of the organization unless they feel it is worthwhile doing so. Motivation at this level is not so much about paying for ideas as in giving people a sense of being recognized and valued for providing them. (Indeed, one problem with many suggestion schemes is that they can sometimes be divisive; by focusing on the size of the reward people often hoard ideas rather than share them.) Recognition is often a powerful motivator and many organizations like 3M make a feature out of celebrating their creative individuals and the maverick behaviour which they often exhibit.

At its most basic the ability to implement an idea is a key factor in building a climate for creativity. If people feel they have autonomy, they can choose what they do – they feel in control. Whereas in organizations which limit the exercise of individual thinking the overall effect can be to switch off people's creativity and turn them into robots. In a small start-up or in a creative context like an R&D laboratory or an advertising agency this isn't a problem; the need for a steady flow of interesting new ideas means that people are encouraged to contribute.

But it is a challenge for many organizations which rely on procedures and rules for coordinating work – production lines, call centres and retail order-processing, for example. Giving people the opportunity to make suggestions and implement improvements risks compromising the systems which ensure productivity and quality. Yet without those suggestions there is little opportunity to make the system better and the resulting impact on morale and motivation is likely to make things worse.

Tool to help you explore this, policy deployment, is available on the Innovation Portal at **www.innovation-portal.info**

Case Studies exploring this, policy deployment cases, are available on the Innovation Portal at **www.innovation-portal.info**

As we've seen, organizations like Toyota or France Telecom (whose 'idClic' online suggestion scheme has around 30 000 participants every day, building on new ideas) have managed to resolve this paradox by simultaneously putting in place frameworks for creative idea input and specifying where those should be directed. This idea – of **policy deployment** – means there is an understanding of where improvements are needed and rewards and recognizes creativity in these areas. (For example, it would not be a good idea for a worker in a pharmaceutical factory to experiment with the formulation of the drug he or she is making (!), but the same person could have and implement some great ideas around improving workflow or quality.)

Establish a Process

We've seen that creativity involves a process. One useful way of supporting it is to make the process explicit. Organizations like IDEO make use of a formal and disciplined approach to solving problems which their clients bring, building on their own versions of techniques for redefining and preparing problems, exploring and incubating and finally closing in and refining solutions.

Tools to help you explore this, such as Deming Wheel and Six Sigma, are available on the Innovation Portal at **www.innovation-portal.info**

Having an explicit process is particularly important where people may not have much experience of a structured approach to problem finding and solving. Many high-involvement innovation systems, such as the Toyota model, make use of simple frameworks which everyone is trained to use. The 'quality' revolution which

Case Studies of these tools in action, like Torbay Hospital, Gordon Murray Design and Forte's Bakery, are available on the Innovation Portal at **www.innovation-portal.info**

did so much to strengthen the competiveness of Japanese industry in the 1970s emerged from systematic application of models like the Deming Wheel, and more recent impact has come in manufacturing and service organizations through the use of Six Sigma as a formal process.

Training and Skills Development

We've seen that creativity is a natural capability but also that it can be unlocked and developed through the use of tools and techniques. So it makes sense within organizations not only to provide structures and frameworks which support people being creative but also to invest in extending and developing those skills. Creativity training is a large field and ranges from simple inputs designed to give people a sense of the core process and experience when applying it (Six Sigma, Deming Wheel, for example) through to more elaborate inputs designed to stretch thinking skills (lateral thinking, TRIZ, synectics, for example).

Leadership

It is easy to see creativity as a democratic open process in which everyone's ideas are exchanged and built upon. The reality is that without a degree of focus such sessions can quickly degenerate into chaos. There is a need for leadership – not in the sense of strong authoritative direction but in the sense of guiding and shaping the process towards a goal and doing so while balancing resource demands like time and money. We explore the theme of leadership in more detail in Chapter 9, but for now it is worth noting the need for leaders as coaches, facilitators and enablers of the creative process.

Video Clip of interview with Emma Taylor and a transcript of an interview with Hugh Chapman talking about their approach to guiding and supporting creativity are available on the Innovation Portal at **www.innovation-portal.info**

Putting It All Together: Developing Entrepreneurial Creativity

Creativity matters, whether we are starting a new entrepreneurial venture, trying to improve performance of an established organization or help a mature one find new directions and 'get out of the box'. In this chapter we've looked at some of the factors which affect our ability to draw out that creativity. People already have the capacity but there is good evidence that this natural capability can be enhanced and developed through inputs targeted at individual, group and environment. There is no single injection of magic which will make people more creative but rather the need for an integrated approach, creating the conditions and providing the framework within which they can sharpen and develop their skills.

INNOVATION IN ACTION 5.5

Employee-led Innovation

In a study of a wide range of UK organizations in which employees at all levels were regularly contributing creative ideas, Julian Birkinshaw and Lisa Duke identified four key sets of enabling factors:

Time out: to give employees the space in their working day for creative thought.
Expansive roles: to help employees move beyond the confines of their assigned job.
Competitions: to stimulate action and to get the creative juices flowing.
Open forums: to give employees a sense of direction and to foster collaboration.

Source: See www.engageforsuccess and http://uk.ukwon.eu/euwin-knowledge-bank-menu-new for examples of the kind of organizations putting these ideas into practice.

Chapter Summary

- The dictionary defines creativity as 'the use of imagination or original ideas to create something'; in practice, we can see it as the ability to produce work that is both novel and *useful*.

- It is a combination of thinking skills including associating, pattern recognition and divergent and convergent thinking. Its application can range from incremental to radical, from simple problem-solving to breakthrough insights.

- An important area for developing creativity is in high-involvement systems designed to engage 'ordinary' employees in the process of contributing ideas.

- Although often portrayed as a flash of inspiration, creativity actually follows a process of recognition/preparation, incubation, insight and validation/refinement.

- Everyone is naturally capable of creative thinking but there are differences in the ways people prefer to express their creativity (creative style) and differences associated with personality and prior experience.

- Developing creativity is less about injecting something new than in creating enabling conditions to support a natural process. At the individual level, thinking skills can be enhanced through the use of techniques aimed at developing new ways of dealing with the core process.

- Group-level creativity recognizes the potential of diversity and interaction and tools to support this include those which enable 'creative collisions'. Brainstorming is the best known but there are many others; developments in information technology provide new ways of bringing groups together.

- Building an environment to support creativity includes paying attention to factors like physical space, time and 'permission', reward and recognition, establishing a process and training and skills development.

Key Terms Defined

Brainstorming   approach to idea generation, developed by Alex Osborn, in which judgement of new ideas is suspended. Can be used individually or in groups.

Convergent thinking   a style of thinking which emphasizes focus, homing in on a single 'best' answer.

Creativity   the use of imagination or original ideas to create something which is novel and useful.

Divergent thinking   a style of thinking which is about making associations, often exploring round the edges of a problem.

Flexibility   a measure of creativity, the number of different classes of idea produced in a given time.

Fluency   a measure of creativity, the number of new ideas produced in a given time.

Intermediate impossible   concept associated with lateral thinking where we come up with an idea which is itself impossible but may provide the stepping stone to a practical and novel answer.

Lateral thinking   a style of thinking originally developed by Edward de Bono aimed at moving away from linear step-by-step thinking and taking a step sideways to re-examine a problem from a different viewpoint.

Pattern recognition   in its simplest form if we see a pattern that we recognize we have access to solutions which worked in the past and we can apply again. But sometimes it is a case of recognizing a similarity between a new problem and something like it which we have seen before.

Policy deployment   breaking down high-level strategic goals into small elements on which employees can work with their own innovative ideas.

TRIZ   Theory of Inventive Problem Solving – a technique developed by the Russian Genrich S. Altshuller, who worked on reviewing patents to derive principles around which a wide range of apparently different problems could be solved.

Discussion Questions

1. 'You have to be a genius like Einstein or Leonardo da Vinci to be creative'. Is this true?

2. You've been appointed to help an organization develop its creative capability amongst the workforce. How would you go about doing this?

3. Creativity is more than just a light bulb flash of inspiration. How could you use a process view of creativity to support and enhance this capability in an organization?

4. An entrepreneur friend has complained to you about being stuck for new ideas to help grow her business. How could you use ideas about enhancing and developing creativity to offer some advice?

Further Reading and Resources

There are many books on creativity and how to develop it – see, for example, Tudor Rickards, *Creativity and Problem Solving at Work* (Gower, 1997) or P. Cook, *Best Practice Creativity* (Gower, 1999). On the academic side, Teresa Amabile has worked extensively in the area ('How to Kill Creativity', *Harvard Business Review*, **76**(5): 76) and Dorothy Leonard offers some helpful case-based insights *When Sparks Fly: Igniting Creativity in Groups* (Harvard Business School Press, 1999). The main theoretical insights from psychology are available in Sternberg's *Handbook of Creativity* (Cambridge University Press, 1999). Jonah Lehrer offers a very readable review of current thinking in the field in *Imagine: How Creativity Works* (Canongate, 2012) and Tom Kelley reflects on how IDEO makes extensive use of creative thinking approaches in *The Art of Innovation: Lessons in Creativity from IDEO: America's Leading Design Firm* (Currency, 2001).

Employee involvement is covered in John Bessant's *High Involvement Innovation* (John Wiley & Sons Ltd, 2003), Dean Schroeder and Alan Robinson, *Ideas Are Free: How the Idea Revolution Is Liberating People and Transforming Organizations* (Berrett Koehler, 2003) and Boer *et al.*'s *CI Changes: From Suggestion Box to the Learning Organisation* (Ashgate, 1999).

Specific techniques are described in several books such as de Bono's *Serious Creativity* (Harper Collins, 1999), Tony Buzan's *Use Your Head* (BBC Active, 2006) and Roger Von Oech's *A Whack on the Side of the Head: How You Can Be More Creative* (Business Plus, 2008).

References

1. Christensen, C., J. Dyer and H. Gregerson (2011) *The Innovator's DNA*, Boston: Harvard Business School Press.

2. Dyson, J. (1997) *Against the Odds*, London: Orion.

3. Guilford, J. (1967) *The Nature of Human Intelligence*, New York: McGraw-Hill.

4. Sternberg, R. (1999) *Handbook of Creativity*, Cambridge: Cambridge University Press.

5. Baron-Cohen, S. (1999) *The Evolution of a Theory of Mind*, Oxford: Oxford University Press.

6. Kirton, M. (1980) Adaptors and innovators, *Human Relations*, 3: 213–24.

7. Leonard, D. and W. Swap (2005) *Deep Smarts: How to Cultivate and Transfer Enduring Business Wisdom*, Boston: Harvard Business school Press.

8. de Bono, E. (1971) *The Use of Lateral Thinking*, Harmondsworth: Penguin.

9. Prince, G. (1970) *The Practice of Creativity*, New York: Collier.

10. de Bono, E. (1985) *Six Thinking Hats*, Harmondsworth: Penguin.

11. Osborn, A. (1953) *Applied Imagination: Principles and Procedures of Creative Problem Solving*, New York: Charles Scribner and Sons.

12. Kingdon, M.E. (2002) *Sticky Wisdom: How to Start a Creative Revolution at Work*, London: Capstone.

13. Lehrer, J. (2012) *Imagine: How Creativity Works*, Edinburgh: Canongate.

14. Allen, T. and G. Henn (2007) *The Organization and Architecture of Innovation*, Oxford: Elsevier.

15. Allen, T. (1977) *Managing the Flow of Technology*, Cambridge, MA: MIT Press.

Deeper Dive explanations of innovation concepts and ideas are available on the Innovation Portal at **www.innovation-portal.info**

Quizzes to test yourself further are available online via the Innovation Portal at **www.innovation-portal.info**

Summary of online resources for Chapter 5 –
all material is available via the Innovation Portal at
www.innovation-portal.info

Cases	**Media**	**Tools**	**Activities**	**Deeper Dives**

Cases

- Dyson
- Veeder-Root
- Denso Systems
- Innocent Fruit Juices
- Redgate Software
- Devon and Cornwall Police
- UK Meteorological Office
- DOME
- NHS RED
- Open Door
- Pixar
- Kumba Resources
- Hosiden
- NPI
- Policy deployment cases
- Torbay Hospital
- Gordon Murray Design
- Forte's Bakery

Media

- IDEO
- Ken Robinson
- Natalie Wilkie and Gary Holpin
- Veeder-Root
- Redgate Software
- Innocent Fruit Juices
- Hugh Chapman
- Emma Taylor

Tools

- Brainstorming
- Creativity enhancement
- Creativity toolkit
- Fishbone chart
- Levels of abstraction
- SCAMPER
- Attribute listing
- TRIZ
- 'New eyes' lenses
- Soft systems analysis
- Lateral thinking
- Using metaphor
- Analogies
- Futures toolkit
- Design methods
- Prototyping
- Six thinking hats
- Teambuilding
- High involvement innovation audit
- Policy deployment
- Deming Wheel
- Six Sigma

Activities

- Creativity puzzles
- Problem-solving
- Recollecting creativity
- Creativity matters
- How creative are you?
- Blocks to creativity
- Using the Creativity toolkit
- Improving service processes
- Pattern recognition
- Mindset
- Lateral thinking puzzles
- Metaphorical thinking
- Scenario generation
- Visualizing the invisible
- Prototyping
- Six thinking hats
- Egg game
- Teambuilding
- Brainstorming

Deeper Dives

- Theories of creativity
- High involvement innovation
- Personality theories of creativity
- Lean start-up

Chapter 6

Sources of Innovation

LEARNING OBJECTIVES

By the end of this chapter you will develop an understanding of:

- where innovations come from – the wide range of different sources which offer opportunities to entrepreneurs
- the idea of 'push' and 'pull' forces and their interaction
- innovation as a pattern of occasional breakthrough and long periods of incremental improvement
- the importance of different sources over time
- where and when you could search for opportunities to innovate.

Introduction

One definition of an entrepreneur is someone who sees an opportunity – and does something about it. Whether it's an individual looking to find a new product or service to make his or her fortune, a social entrepreneur trying to change the world or a large established organization looking for new market space, the challenge is one of finding opportunities for innovation.

So where do innovations come from? Do they just flash into life like the light bulb popping up above a cartoon character's head? Or strike with sudden inspiration, like Archimedes jumping up from his bath and running down the street, so enthused by his new idea that he forgot to get dressed? Such 'Eureka!' moments are certainly a part of innovation folklore – and from time to time they do lead somewhere. For example, Percy Shaw's observation of the reflection in a cat's eye at night led to the development of one of the most widely used road

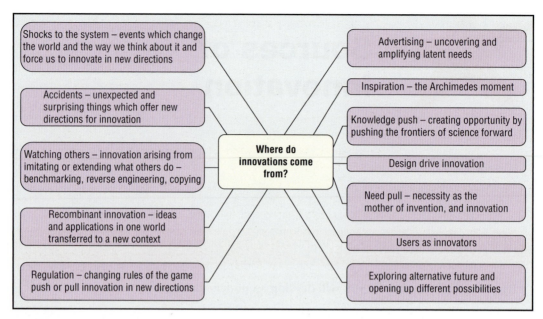

FIGURE 6.1   Where do innovations come from?

safety innovations in the world. Or George de Mestral, on a walk in the Swiss Alps, noticing the way plant burrs became attached to his dog's fur and developing from that inspiration the highly successful Velcro fastener.

Activity to explore sources of innovation, the Innovation family tree, is available on the Innovation Portal at **www.innovation-portal.info**

Audio Clip of Stephen Johnson talking about where innovations come from is available on the Innovation Portal at **www.innovation-portal.info**

But in reality there's much more to innovation than simple inspiration or flashes of bright ideas, although these can be useful starting points. Most of the time it involves a process of taking ideas forward, revising and refining them, weaving the different strands of 'knowledge spaghetti' together towards a useful product, process or service. Triggering that process happens in many different ways; and if we are to manage it effectively, we need to recognize this diversity and target our search for opportunities as widely as possible. Figure 6.1 indicates the wide range of stimuli which can begin the innovation journey.

Let's look at some of these in more detail.

Knowledge Push

Around the world, we spend something like $1500 billion every year on research and development (R&D). All this activity in laboratories and science facilities in the public and private sector isn't for the sheer fun of discovery. It's driven by a clear understanding of the importance of R&D

as a source of innovation. Although there have always been solo researchers, from a very early stage the process of exploring and codifying at the frontiers of knowledge has been a systematic activity involving a wide network of people sharing their ideas. In the 20th century the rise of the large corporate research laboratory was a key instrument of progress: Bell Labs, ICI, Bayer, BASF, Philips, Ford, Western Electric, DuPont (all founded in the early 1900s) are good examples of such 'idea powerhouses'. Their output wasn't simply around product innovation: many of the key technologies underpinning *process* innovations, especially around the growing field of automation and information/communications technology, also came from such organized R&D effort.

Now we are in a new era in which R&D is becoming more open and distributed and the large central laboratory is giving way to networks of collaborating groups inside and between firms. This involves some big changes, for example the giant Philips research complex at Eindhoven in the Netherlands, established a hundred years ago, has moved away from white-coated armies of company researchers in a corporate laboratory to operating as a science campus on the site involving many different research groups. Some work directly for Philips, others are independent small firms and yet others are joint ventures. But the underlying idea is still the same: generate ideas and they will provide the basis for a steady stream of innovations.

Activity to explore knowledge push innovation further, the harvesting knowledge crops, is available on the Innovation Portal at **www.innovation-portal.info**

This model of 'knowledge push' has a strong track record. For example, the rise of the global pharmaceutical industry was essentially about big R&D expenditure, (often running at 15–20% of turnover) in search of new blockbuster drugs.* While there are spectacular success

Case Studies of companies (like 3M and Corning) founded over a hundred years ago who built their strength on extensive R&D investments are available on the Innovation Portal at **www.innovation-portal.info**

stories (the top twenty drugs in the USA in 2011 had earned nearly $320 billion), the real value from such R&D investment comes in the systematic improvement across a broad frontier of products and the processes which created them. We can see the same pattern in many industries (for example semiconductors) in which there is a long-term trajectory of continuous improvement interspersed with occasional breakthroughs. It's a story of occasional breakthrough punctuated by long periods of incremental innovation, consolidating around that idea.

A good illustration would be the camera. Originally invented in the late 19th century, the dominant design gradually emerged with an architecture which we would recognize (shutter and lens arrangement, focusing principles, back plate for film or plates, etc.). But this design was then modified, for example with different lenses, motorized drives, flash technology – and, in the case of George Eastman's work, to creating a simple and relatively idiot-proof model camera (the Box Brownie) which opened up photography to a mass market. This pattern stabilized for an extended period in the 20th century, but by the 1980s there was another surge in research around new imaging technologies and the product changed dramatically with the growth of digital cameras and then a host of other imaging devices like mobile phones and tablets. Although the core players in the industry have shifted positions,

---

* A blockbuster drug is usually defined as one which earns in excess of $1 billion for its manufacturers over its lifetime.

Case Study of the imaging industry is available on the Innovation Portal at **www.innovation-portal.info**

Case Studies of entrepreneur-driven successes, like Spirit and Dyson, are available on the Innovation Portal at **www.innovation-portal.info**

the underlying process of innovation driven by scientific research remains the same, and there are still plenty of patents being registered around this. (The legal battles between Apple and Samsung, for example, are one illustration of the strategic importance of such knowledge in playing out the innovation game.)

Knowledge push has long been a source of innovative start-ups where entrepreneurs have used ideas based on their own research (or that of others) to create new ventures. This model underpins the success of many high-tech regions – for example Silicon Valley and Route 128 in the USA, 'medical valley' around the city of Nuremburg in Germany or the Cambridge area in the UK where giant technology businesses like ARM (whose chips are at the heart of most mobile phones) were founded as spin-outs from the university. (We discuss the creation of new ventures in more detail in Chapter 12.)

Need Pull...

Knowledge push creates a field of possibilities – but not every idea finds successful application. The American writer Ralph Waldo Emerson is supposed to have said 'build a better mousetrap and the world will beat a path to your door'; unfortunately, the reality is that there are plenty of bankrupt mousetrap salesmen around! Bright ideas are not, in themselves, enough: they may not meet a real or perceived need and people may not feel motivated to change. Innovation requires some form of demand if it is to take root.

In its simplest form this idea of 'need pull' innovation is captured in the saying 'Necessity is the Mother of invention'. For example, Henry Ford was able to turn the luxury plaything that was the early automobile into something which became 'a car for Everyman', while Procter and Gamble began a business meeting needs for domestic lighting (via candles) and moved across into an ever-widening range of household needs from soap to nappies to cleaners, toothpaste and beyond. Low-cost airlines have found innovative solutions to the problem of making flying available to a much wider market, while microfinance institutions have developed radical new approaches to help bring banking and credit within the reach of the poor.

INNOVATION IN ACTION 6.1

Maintaining a Stream of Ideas

Two hundred years ago, Churchill Potteries began life in the UK making a range of crockery and tableware. That it is still able to do so today, despite a turbulent and highly competitive global market, says much for the approach which it has taken to ensure a steady stream of innovation. Its chief executive, Andrew Roper, highlights the way in which listening to users and understanding their needs has changed the business. 'We have taken on a lot of service disciplines, so you could think of us as less of a pure manufacturer and more as a service company with a manufacturing arm.' Staff spend a significant proportion of their time talking to chefs, hoteliers and others: 'sales, marketing and technical people spend far more of their time than I could ever have imagined checking out what happens to the product in use and asking the customer, professional or otherwise, what they really want next.'

Source: 'Ingredients for success on a plate', Peter Marsh, *Financial Times*, 26th March 2008: 16.

Just as the knowledge push model involves a mixture of occasional breakthrough followed by extensive elaboration, so the same is true of need pull. Occasionally, it involves a 'new to the world' idea but mostly it is extensions, variations and adaptations around those core ideas. Figure 6.2 indicates a typical breakdown of product innovation along these lines and we could construct a similar picture for process innovations.

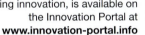

Activity to explore this idea, classifying innovation, is available on the Innovation Portal at **www.innovation-portal.info**

Need pull innovation is particularly important at mature stages in industry or product lifecycles when there is more than one offering to choose from – competing depends on differentiating on the basis of needs and attributes, and/or segmenting the offering to suit different adopter types. But it's also a key source of opportunity for entrepreneurial start-ups. Identifying a need which no one has worked on before or finding novel ways to meet an existing need lies behind many new business ideas. For example, Jeff Bezos picked up on the needs (and frustrations) around conventional retail and has built the Amazon empire on the back of using new technologies to meet these in a different way. Airbnb ('I need

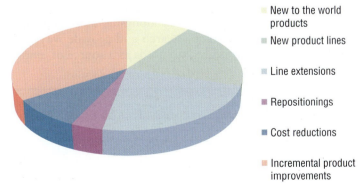

- New to the world products
- New product lines
- Line extensions
- Repositionings
- Cost reductions
- Incremental product improvements

FIGURE 6.2   Types of new product

Source: Based on Griffin, A. (1997) PDMA research on new product development practices. *Journal of Product Innovation Management,* 14: 429. Reproduced by permission of John Wiley & Sons Ltd.

to find somewhere to stay'), nextbike, Zipcar ('I need easy short-term access to transport') and WhatsApp ('I need to communicate with my friends') are other well-known examples.

A good source of opportunity for entrepreneurs is to look at the underlying need which people have for goods and services – and then to ask if there are different ways of expressing or meeting this need. For example, the huge industry around selling drills and screws and other devices to the domestic market is not about a desire for owning power tools but reflects a more basic need – how can I put a picture or photograph on the wall? Maybe there are other ways of meeting this need and new business opportunities behind that?

Activity to explore this approach to finding innovation opportunities using the outcome-oriented innovation tool is available on the Innovation Portal at **www.innovation-portal.info**

It's also important to recognize that innovation is not always about commercial markets or consumer needs; social innovation is also important. Whether it's providing healthcare or clean water in developing countries or more effective education or social services in established industrial economies, the need for change is clear and provides an engine for increasing innovation. Some examples of major social innovations which grew out of meeting needs are the kindergarten (providing childcare when both parents are working), the National Childbirth Trust (providing education and information to new parents about all aspects of childbirth), the Open University (providing access to higher education to students once excluded by the barriers of wealth and work) and the Big Issue (providing employment and identity to homeless people).

Video Clip of an interview with Michael Bartl of Hyve illustrating these approaches to uncovering 'hidden needs' is available on the Innovation Portal at **www.innovation-portal.info**

As we'll see in the next chapter, understanding user needs requires getting as close as we can to those users. Recent years have seen a growth in using tools drawn originally from anthropology to watch and understand how people actually behave rather than simply asking them. Tools like 'empathic design' and 'ethnography' now sit alongside more conventional methods of market research and provide ways of getting a clearer insight into needs as a source of innovation ideas.

Case Studies illustrating this approach (RED, Tesco and Open Door) are available on the Innovation Portal at **www.innovation-portal.info**

Tools to help you with this (Kano method and other design methods) are available on the Innovation Portal at **www.innovation-portal.info**

INNOVATION IN ACTION 6.2

Understanding User Needs in Hyundai Motor

One of the problems facing global manufacturers is how to tailor their products to suit the needs of local markets. For Hyundai, this has meant paying considerable attention to getting deep insights into customer needs and aspirations – an approach which it used to good effect in developing the Santa Fe, reintroduced to the US market in 2007. The headline for its development programme was 'touch the market' and it deployed a number of tools and techniques to enable it. For example, it visited an ice rink and watched an Olympic medallist skate around to help it gain an insight into the ideas of grace and speed which it wanted to embed in its car. This provided a metaphor – 'assertive grace' – which the development teams in Korea and the US were able to use.

Analysis of existing vehicles suggested some aspects of design were not being covered, for example many sport/utility vehicles (SUVs) were rather 'boxy' so there was scope to enhance the image of the car. Market research suggested a target segment of 'glamour mums' who would find this attractive and the teams then began an intensive study of how this group lived their lives. Ethnographic methods looked at their homes, their activities and their lifestyles, for example team members spent a day shopping with some target women to gain an understanding of their purchases and what motivated them. The list of key motivators which emerged from this shopping study included durability, versatility, uniqueness, child-friendliness and good customer service from knowledgeable staff. Another approach was to make all members of the team experience driving routes around southern California, making journeys similar to those popular with the target segment and in the process getting first-hand experience of comfort, features and fixtures inside the car, etc.[1]

Making Processes Better

Of course, needs aren't just about products and services – they also apply as drivers for *process* innovation. 'Squeaking wheels' and other sources of frustration with the way current processes operate can provide rich signals for change, both in terms of incremental improvement and in finding radically new ways of working. For example, this approach provided the basic philosophy behind the 'total quality management' movement in the 1980s, the 'business process re-engineering' ideas of the 1990s and the current widespread application of concepts based on the idea of 'lean thinking'. All of these are essentially about taking the waste out of existing processes.

Video Clip of an interview with Emma Taylor of Denso Corporation talking about establishing this kind of approach is available on the Innovation Portal at **www.innovation-portal.info**

Case Studies of continuous improvement are available on the Innovation Portal at **www.innovation-portal.info**

Tools like process mapping highlighting opportunities for process innovation (search for 'continuous improvement toolkit' to find others) are available on the Innovation Portal at **www.innovation-portal.info**

Video Clips showing how employee engagement in innovation can make a difference in organizations like Innocent Fruit Juices, Redgate Software, the UK Meteorological Office and the Devon and Cornwall Police are available on the Innovation Portal at **www.innovation-portal.info**

INNOVATION IN ACTION 6.3

'Pretty in Pink'

Walking through the plant belonging to Ace Trucks (a major producer of forklift trucks) in Japan, the first thing which strikes you is the colour scheme. In fact, you would need to be blind not to notice it – amongst the usual rather dull greys and greens of machine tools and other equipment there are flashes of pink. Not just a quiet pastel tone but a full-blooded, shocking pink which would do credit to even the most image-conscious flamingo. Closer inspection shows these flashes and splashes of pink are not random but associated with particular sections and parts of machines – and the eye-catching effect comes in part from the sheer number of pink-painted bits, distributed right across the factory floor and all over the different machines.

What is going on here is not a bizarre attempt to redecorate the factory or a failed piece of interior design. The effect of catching the eye is quite deliberate: the colour is there to draw attention to the machines and other equipment which have been modified. Every pink splash is the result of a kaizen project to improve some aspect of the equipment, much of it in support of the drive towards 'total productive maintenance', (TPM) in which every item of plant is available and ready for use 100% of the time. This is a goal like 'zero defects' in total quality – certainly ambitious, possibly an impossibility in the statistical sense, but one which focuses the minds of everyone involved and leads to extensive and impressive problem-finding and problem-solving. TPM programmes have accounted for year-on-year cost savings of 10–15% in many Japanese firms and these savings are being ground out of a system which is already renowned for its lean characteristics.

Painting the improvements pink plays an important role in drawing attention to the underlying activity in this factory, in which systematic problem-finding and problem-solving is part of 'the way we do things around here'. The visual cues remind everyone of the continuing search for new ideas and improvements, and often provide stimulus for other ideas or for places where the displayed pink idea can be transferred to. Closer inspection around the plant shows other forms of display – less visually striking but powerful nonetheless – charts and graphs of all shapes and sizes which focus attention on trends and problems as well as celebrating successful improvements, photographs and graphics which pose problems or offer suggested improvements in methods or working practices and flipcharts and whiteboards covered with symbols and shapes of fish bones and other tools being used to drive the improvement process forward.

This kind of process improvement is of particular relevance in the public sector where the issue is not about creating wealth but rather providing value for money in service delivery. Many applications of 'lean' and similar concepts can be found which apply this principle, for example in reducing waiting times or improving patient safety in hospitals, in speeding up delivery of services like car taxation and passport issuing and even in improving the collection of taxes!

INNOVATION IN ACTION 6.4

MindLab

MindLab is a Danish organization set up to promote and enable public sector innovation in Denmark. 'Owned' by the Ministries of Taxation, Employment and Economic Affairs, it has pioneered a series of initiatives engaging civil servants and members of the public in a wide range of social innovation which have raised productivity, improved service quality and cut costs across the public sector. Case studies of its activities can be found on its website (www.mind-lab.dk/en).

Video Clip of an interview with Helle-Vibeke Carstensen discussing applying this approach in the Danish public sector is available on the Innovation Portal at **www.innovation-portal.info**

Case Studies of various process innovations in healthcare are available on the Innovation Portal at **www.innovation-portal.info**

One important aspect of process innovation is that it relates to how organizations create and deliver whatever they offer. Improving and sometimes radically changing these processes is something with which all employees can potentially engage since they are all users and operators of these processes. Such high involvement innovation lies behind the success of companies like Toyota in terms of their long-term productivity improvement; it is largely based on the idea of regular improvement ideas – kaizen – collected from the majority of the workforce.

Whose Needs? Working at the Edge

And sometimes what has relevance for the fringe begins to be of interest to the mainstream. US professor Clayton Christensen shows this has been the pattern across industries as diverse as computer disk drives, earth-moving equipment, steel making and low-cost air travel.[2]

It poses a problem for existing players because the needs of such fringe groups are not seen as relevant to their mainstream activities – and so they tend to ignore or dismiss them as not being important. As we've seen, for much of the time there is stability around markets where innovation of the 'do better' variety takes place and is well managed. Close relationships with existing customers are fostered and the system is configured to deliver a steady stream of what the market wants – and often a great deal more! (What Christensen calls 'technology overshoot' is often a characteristic of this, where markets are offered more and more features which they may not ever use or place much value on but which come as part of the package.)

But somewhere else there is another group of potential users who have very different needs – usually for something much simpler and cheaper – which will help them get something done. Meeting these needs not only creates a new market but also destabilizes the existing one as customers there realize their needs can be met with a different approach. This phenomenon is known as **disruptive innovation** and focuses our attention on the need to look for needs which are not being met, or poorly met, or sometimes where there is an overshoot. Each of these can provide a trigger for innovation – and often involves disruption because existing players don't see the different patterns of needs.

Video Clip in which Clayton Christensen explains his theory of disruptive innovation is available on the Innovation Portal at **www.innovation-portal.info**

INNOVATION IN ACTION 6.5

Gaining Competitive Edge through Meeting Unserved Needs

The Nintendo Wii opened up radically new competitive space in the computer games industry and for a while gave it market leadership. The Wii console is not a particularly sophisticated piece of technology – compared to the rivals Sony PS3 or the Microsoft Xbox it has less computing power, storage or other features and the games' graphics are much lower resolution than major sellers like *Call of Duty*. But the key to the phenomenal success of the Wii has been its appeal to an underserved market. Where computer games were traditionally targeted at boys the Wii extends – by means of a simple interface wand – their interest to all members of the family. Add-ons to the platform like the Wii board for keep-fit and other applications and the market reach extends, for example, to include the elderly or patients suffering the after effects of stroke.

The success of the Wii led others to introduce technologies supporting interaction, and Microsoft's Kinect has opened up a huge range of new applications both within and beyond the games sector.

Nintendo performed a similar act of opening up the marketplace with its DS handheld device – again by targeting unmet needs across a different segment of the population. Many DS users are middle-aged or retired and the best-selling games are for brain training and puzzles.

Emerging New Markets at 'the Base of the Pyramid'

One powerful source of ideas at the edge comes from what are often termed 'emerging markets' – countries like India, China and those in the Latin American and African regions. As we saw in Chapter 3, these are huge markets in terms of population and often very young in age profile, and while there may be limited disposable income they represent significant opportunities. The writer C. K. Prahalad first drew attention to this idea in his book *The Fortune at the Bottom of the Pyramid*, in which he argues that nearly 80% of the world's population lived on less than $2/day but could represent a huge market of unserved needs for goods and services. Since its publication in 2005, there has been an explosion of interest in exploring the innovation opportunities in meeting the needs of this significant population involving billions of people.

Audio Clip of an interview with Girish Prabhu of Sristi Labs, an organization specializing in this kind of innovation, is available on the Innovation Portal at **www.innovation-portal.info**

This is not simply a matter of opening up new markets; finding different solutions to the needs of those markets may have big implications for mainstream markets. For example, think what a producer in China could do to an industry like pump manufacturing if it began to offer a simple, low-cost 'good enough' household pump for $10 instead of the high-tech, high-performance variants available from today's industry at prices ten to fifty times higher.

INNOVATION IN ACTION 6.6

Jugaad Innovation

In their book *Jugaad Innovation* Navi Radjou, Jaideep Prabhu and Simone Ahuja explore an approach to innovation which is rooted in emerging economies like India, China and Latin America – but which draws on some long-established principles. Through a variety of case studies they suggest that crisis conditions often trigger new approaches to innovation, and that the pressure to be frugal and flexible often leads to novel and sometimes breakthrough solutions. The phrase 'scarcity is the mother of invention' could be applied to examples such as the low-technology design for a fridge which keeps food and liquid cool yet is based on a simple ceramic pot – the 'mitticool'. While this may seem a low-tech solution, the problem in India is that around 500 million people have to live with an unreliable electricity supply which means that conventional refrigerators are unusable. The simple device has been so successful it is now mass produced and sold worldwide providing employment for the village in which the idea originated.

Jugaad is a Hindi word which roughly translates as 'an innovative fix, an improvised solution born from ingenuity and cleverness'. Such an approach characterizes entrepreneurship – and examples of such innovation can be found throughout history. But the authors argue that

(continued)

the very different conditions across much of the emerging world are creating opportunities for *jugaad* innovators finding solutions to meet the needs of a large population for an increasingly wide range of good and services. In the process they are marrying very different needs with an increasingly wide range of networked technological options, for example evolving new forms of banking based on mobile phones or deploying telemedicine to help deal with the problems of distance and skills shortage in healthcare.

Of particular significance is the potential for such solutions to then find their way back to the industrialized world as simpler, ingenious solutions which challenge existing high-technology approaches. The potential for such reverse innovation to act as a disruptive force is significant.

Source: Radjou, N., J. Prabhu and S. Ahuja (2012) *Jugaad Innovation: Think Frugal, Be Flexible, Generate Breakthrough Innovation*, San Francisco: Jossey-Bass.

The idea of 'reverse innovation' where innovations migrate back from these emerging markets is of growing interest, for example General Electric developed a simple low-cost version of its ultrasound scanner for use in the emerging market context of rural India. Designed to be easy to use and rugged enough for travelling midwives to carry round on their bicycles from village to village, the unit was not only very successful in those markets but also attracted considerable attention elsewhere in the world. While maternity care in major economies is currently delivered in highly specialized hospitals and clinics using sophisticated machinery, there is a clear demand for something simpler and GE has found this to be a surprising growth market. In 2009, it announced its intention to spend at least $3 billion to develop 100 low-cost healthcare innovations, targeted at emerging economies but with potential for such reverse innovation.

Audio Clip of a talk by Jane Chen about developing a low-cost baby incubator is available on the Innovation Portal at **www.innovation-portal.info**

Case Study of the GE simple scanner is available on the Innovation Portal at **www.innovation-portal.info**

INNOVATION IN ACTION 6.7

Low-cost Innovation: The Akash Computer

India represents an interesting laboratory for the development of radically different products and services configured for a large but not particularly wealthy population. Examples include the Tata Nano car, developed and now on sale for around $3000, and a mobile phone which retails at $20. In 2010, the country's Human Resources Development minister unveiled a $35 computer, targeted first at the school market (which is huge, around 110 million children in the first instance) and to be followed by higher education students. The minister commented: 'The solutions for tomorrow will emerge from India. We have reached a stage that today, the motherboard, its chip, the processing, connectivity, all of them cumulatively cost around $35 [£23], including memory, display, everything.'

The Akash 1 was launched in 2011 and an updated version, the Akash 2, in 2012. A tablet-style device, it competes with Apple's iPad currently retailing in the USA for $450. It runs on an open source Linux operating system, using Open Office software and can be powered by solar panel or batteries as well as mains electricity. It has no hard drive but additional functionality can be provided via a USB port.

Innovation in these emerging market conditions is not confined to product ideas; there is also considerable scope for finding alternative solutions to process innovation problems in delivering key services like healthcare and education.

Importantly, it isn't just the case that fringe markets trigger simpler and cheaper innovations. Sometimes the novel conditions spawn completely new trajectories. For example, the emergence of 'mobile money' in Africa came about because of the security risks of carrying cash, which meant that people began to use the mobile phone system to provide an alternative way of moving money around. Systems like M-PESA have now grown in sophistication and enjoy widespread application in emerging markets like Africa and Latin America – but they also offer a template for existing markets back in the industrialized world.

Case Studies illustrating the potential of new approaches to process innovation in public services (Aravind Eye Clinics, NHL, Lifespring Hospitals) are available on the Innovation Portal at **www.innovation-portal.info**

Video Clip of an interview with Dr Venkataswamy, founder of the Aravind Eye Clinics, is available on the Innovation Portal at **www.innovation-portal.info**

Audio Clip of an interview with Suzana Moreira, whose company, Mowoza, uses a version of this mobile money platform, is available on the Innovation Portal at **www.innovation-portal.info**

Case Study of M-PESA, the mobile money platform, is available on the Innovation Portal at **www.innovation-portal.info**

INNOVATION IN ACTION 6.8

Living Labs

One approach being used by an increasing number of companies involves setting up 'Living Labs' which allow experimentation with and learning from users to generate ideas and perspectives on innovation. These could be amongst particular groups, for example in Denmark a network of such laboratories (http://www.openlivinglabs.eu/ourlabs/Denmark) is particularly concerned with the experience of ageing and the likely products and services which an increasingly elderly population will need. A description of the Lab and its operation can be found at http://www.edengene.co.uk/article/living-labs/.

 Case Study of Living Labs is available on the Innovation Portal at **www.innovation-portal.info**

 Video Clip of an interview with Ana Sena, Innovation Manager at INdT, is available on the Innovation Portal at **www.innovation-portal.info**

In Brazil the Nokia Institute of Technology (INdT) develops user-driven innovation platforms to support mobile products and services and as part of that process aims to enable large-scale involvement of motivated communities (www.indt.org/). Its Mobile Work Spaces Living Lab is working in several technological fields and with communities across rural and urban environments.

Crisis-driven Innovation

Sometimes the urgency of a need can have a forcing effect on innovation – the example of wartime and other crises supports this view. For example, the demand for iron and iron products increased hugely in the Industrial Revolution and exposed the limitations of the old methods of smelting with charcoal – it created the pull which led to developments like the Bessemer converter. In similar fashion the energy crisis has created a significant pull for innovation around alternative energy sources – and an investment boom for such work.

 **Case Studies** of crisis-driven innovations are available on the Innovation Portal at **www.innovation-portal.info**

A powerful example of the impact crisis can have on driving innovation can be seen in the context of major humanitarian crises, for example after devastating earthquakes or hurricanes. The need to improvise solutions around logistics, shelter, healthcare, water and sanitation and energy forces a rapid pace of innovation.

Towards Mass Customization

Another important source of innovation results from our desire for 'customization'. Markets are not made up of people wanting the same thing – we all want variety and some degree of personalization. And as we move from conditions where products are in short supply to one of mass production so the demand for differentiation increases. We can see this in the case of the motor car as one simple example. Arguably, Henry Ford's plant, based on principles of mass production, represented the most efficient response to the market environment of its time. But that environment changed rapidly during the 1920s, so that what had begun as a winning formula for manufacturing began gradually to represent a major obstacle to change. Production of the Model T began in 1909 and for

fifteen years or so it was the market leader. Despite falling margins, the company managed to exploit its blueprint for factory technology and organization to ensure continuing profits. But growing competition (particularly from General Motors with its strategy of product differentiation) was shifting away from trying to offer the customer low-cost personal transportation and towards other design features – such as the closed body – and Ford was increasingly forced to add features to the Model T. Eventually, it was clear that a new model was needed and production of the Model T stopped in 1927.

Case Study of the Model T Ford is available on the Innovation Portal at **www.innovation-portal.info**

Video Clip about the Model T Ford is available on the Innovation Portal at **www.innovation-portal.info**

There has always been a market for personalized custom-made goods (like tailored clothes) and services (for example personal shoppers, personal travel agents, personal physicians). But until recently there was an acceptance that this customization carried a high price tag and that mass markets could only be served with relatively standard product and service offerings.

However, a combination of enabling technologies and rising expectations has begun to shift this balance and resolve the trade-off between price and customization. **Mass customization** (MC) is a widely used term which captures some elements of this. MC is the ability to offer highly configured bundles of non-price factors to suit different market segments (with the ideal target of total customization – i.e. a market size of 1) – but to do this without incurring cost penalties and the setting-up of a trade-off of agility vs. prices.

Of course, there are different levels of customizing – from simply putting a label 'specially made for . . . (insert your name here)' on a standard product right through to sitting down with a designer and co-creating something truly unique. Table 6.1 gives some examples of this range of options.

TABLE 6.1   Options in customization

Type of customization	Characteristics	Examples
Distribution customization	Customers may customize product/service packaging, delivery schedule and delivery location but the actual product/service is standardized	Sending a book to a friend from Amazon. com. They will receive an individually wrapped gift with a personalized message from you – but it's actually all been done online and in distribution warehouses. iTunes appears to offer personalization of a music experience but in fact it does so right at the end of the production and distribution chain
Assembly customization	Customers are offered a number of pre-defined options. Products/services are made to order using standardized components	Buying a computer from Dell or another online retailer. Customers choose and configure to suit their exact requirements from a rich menu of options – but Dell only starts to assemble this (from standard modules and components) when the order is finalized. Banks offering tailor-made insurance and financial products are actually configuring these from a relatively standard set of options
Fabrication customization	Customers are offered a number of pre-defined designs. Products/services are manufactured to order	Buying a luxury car like a BMW, where the customer is involved in choosing ('designing') the configuration which best meets their needs and wishes (for engine size, trim levels, colour, fixtures and extras, etc.

TABLE 6.1   *(Continued)*

Type of customization	Characteristics	Examples
		Only when they are satisfied with the virtual model they have chosen does the manufacturing process begin – and they can even visit the factory to watch their car being built. Services allow a much higher level of such customization since there is less of an asset base needed to set up for 'manufacturing' the service – examples here would include made to measure tailoring, personal planning for holidays, pensions, etc.
Design customization	Customer input stretches to the start of the production process. Products do not exist until initiated by a customer order	Co-creation, where end users may not even be sure what it is they want but where, sitting down with a designer, they co-create the concept and elaborate it. It's a little like having some clothes made but rather than choosing from a pattern book they actually have a designer with them and create the concept together. Only when it exists as a firm design idea is it then made. Co-creation of services can be found in fields like entertainment (where user-led models like YouTube are posing significant challenges to mainstream providers) and in healthcare (where experiments towards radical alternatives for healthcare delivery are being explored)

Source: Derived from Lampel, J. and H. Mintzberg (1996) Customizing, customization, *Sloan Management Review*, **38**(1): 21–30.

Video Clip of an interview with Frank Piller, who runs a fascinating blog around mass customization, is available on the Innovation Portal at **www.innovation-portal.info**

Case Studies of companies using this approach (Adidas, Lego, Threadless.com) are available on the Innovation Portal at **www.innovation-portal.info**

Video Clip of Chris Anderson of *Wired* magazine discussing the new industrial revolution around the possibilities offered by technologies like 3D printing is available on the Innovation Portal at **www.innovation-portal.info**

Mass customization has taken on particular relevance as the enabling technologies of design and manufacture have matured. With technologies like 3D printing becoming widely available, it becomes possible to customize and configure pretty much anything – from personalizing your choice of cola from a vending machine through to creating spare parts for village pumps in rural Africa and even printing a gun using designs from the Internet!

Understanding what it is that customers value and need is critical in pursuing a customization strategy, and it leads, inevitably, to the next source of innovation in which the users themselves become the source of ideas.

Users as Innovators

It is easy to fall into the trap of thinking about need pull innovation as involving a process in which user needs are identified and then something is created to meet those needs. This assumes that users are passive recipients, but this is often not the case. In many cases users are ahead of the game. Their ideas plus their frustrations with existing solutions lead them to experiment and create something new. And sometimes these prototypes eventually become mainstream innovations.

Eric von Hippel of Massachusetts Institute of Technology has made a lifelong study of this phenomenon and gives the example of the pickup truck – a long-time staple of the world automobile industry.[3] This major category did not begin life on the drawing boards of Detroit but rather on the farms and homesteads of a wide range of users who wanted more than a family saloon. They adapted their cars by removing seats, welding new pieces on and cutting off the roof – in the process prototyping and developing the early model of the pickup. Only later did Detroit pick up on the idea and then begin the incremental innovation process to refine and mass produce the vehicle. A host of other examples support the view that user-led innovation matters, for example petroleum refining, medical devices, semiconductor equipment, scientific instruments and a wide range of sports goods and the Polaroid camera. Importantly, active and interested users (**lead users**) are often well ahead of the market in terms of innovation needs.

Central to their role in the innovation process is that they are very early on the adoption curve for new ideas. They are concerned with getting solutions to particular needs and prepared to experiment and tolerate failure in their search for a better solution. One strategy (which we explore in more detail in the next chapter) is thus to identify and engage with such lead users to co-create innovative solutions.

ENTREPRENEURSHIP IN ACTION 6.1

User-led Innovation

Although we have known about user innovation for a long time, it has recently become a powerful source of innovation in both social and commercial contexts. Below are links to some examples on the Portal (www.innovation-portal.info) of entrepreneurs who have begun to exploit this approach:

- Eric von Hippel describes lead user methods and their application in the 3M company.
- Tim Craft describes how he developed a range of connectors and other equipment following concerns about safety in operating theatres.
- Yellowberry is a case example of an underwear company founded to cater for the 'tween' market.
- Tad Golesworthy was diagnosed with a terminal heart condition and that spurred him to design a new heart valve, saving his and many other lives.
- Opening up healthcare innovation describes the role played by patients and carers in generating ideas for innovation.
- Charles Leadbeater talks about the opening up of innovation opportunities through engaging with users.

'User-led innovation' is becoming increasingly significant, for example the Linux software which lies at the heart of mobile phones did not originate with a traditional Linux Corporation. Instead it is the product of a community of frustrated users who began to share (and continue to do so) their expertise and ideas to co-create solutions which major companies like IBM then take forward. Studies of 'hidden innovation' suggest that a significant and growing number of people are involved in such innovation and it accounts for a surprising number of new ideas. And the idea doesn't stop with products. It is very relevant to services and the public sector. For example, the Danish government has had considerable success with engaging users in innovations around the tax system!

INNOVATION IN ACTION 6.10

User Involvement in Innovation

One of the key lessons about successful innovation is the need to get close to the customer. At the limit the user can become a key part of the innovation process, feeding in ideas and improvements to help define and shape the innovation. The Danish medical devices company

(continued)

Coloplast was founded in 1954 on these principles when nurse Elise Sorensen developed the first self-adhering ostomy bag as a way of helping her sister, a stomach cancer patient. She took her idea to various plastics manufacturers, but none showed interest at first. Eventually one, Aage Louis-Hansen, discussed the concept with his wife, also a nurse, who saw the potential of such a device and persuaded her husband to give the product a chance. Hansen's company, Dansk Plastic Emballage, produced the world's first disposable ostomy bag in 1955. Sales exceeded expectations and in 1957, after having taken out a patent for the bag in several countries, the Coloplast company was established. Today the company has subsidiaries in 20 factories in five countries around the world, with specialist divisions dealing with incontinence care, wound care, skin care, mastectomy care, consumer products (specialist clothing etc.) as well as the original ostomy care division.

Keeping close to users in a field like this is crucial, and Coloplast has developed novel ways of building in such insights by making use of panels of users, specialist nurses and other health-care professionals located in different countries. This has the advantage of getting an informed perspective from those involved in post-operative care and treatment who can articulate needs which may for the individual patient be difficult or embarrassing to express. By setting up panels in different countries, the varying cultural attitudes and concerns could also be built into product design and development.

An example is the Coloplast Ostomy Forum (COF) board approach. The core objective within COF boards is to try to create a sense of partnership with key players, either as key customers or key influencers. Selection is based on an assessment of their technical experience and competence but also on the degree to which they will act as opinion leaders and gatekeepers, for example by influencing colleagues, authorities, hospitals and patients. They are also a key link in the clinical trials process. Over the years, Coloplast has become quite skilled in identifying relevant people who would be good COF board members, for example by tracking people who author clinical articles or who have a wide range of experience across different operation types. Their specific role is particularly to help with two elements in innovation:

- identify, discuss and prioritize user needs
- evaluate product development projects from idea generation right through to international marketing.

Importantly, COF boards are seen as integrated with the company's product development system and they provide valuable market and technical information into the decision process. This input is mainly associated with early stages around concept formulation (where the input is helpful in testing and refining perceptions about real user needs and fit with new concepts). There is also significant involvement around project development, where involvement is concerned with evaluating and responding to prototypes, suggesting detailed design improvements, design for usability, etc.

Sometimes, user-led innovation involves a community which creates and uses innovative solutions on a continuing basis. Good examples of this include the Apache server community around Web server development applications, Mozilla (browser software), Propellerhead and other music software communities and the emergent group around Apple's i-platform devices like the iPhone.

Within some communities, users will freely share innovations with peers, termed **free revealing**. For example, online communities for open source software, music hobbyists, sports equipment and professional networks. Participation is driven mostly by intrinsic motivations, such as the pleasure of being able to help others or to improve or develop better products, but also by peer-recognition and community-status. The elements valued are social ties and opportunities to learn new things rather than concrete awards or esteem. Such knowledge-sharing and innovation tends to be more collective and collaborative than idea-competitions.

Public sector applications of this idea are growing as citizens act as user innovators for the services which they consume. **Citizen sourcing** is increasingly being used; an example is the UK website fixmystreet.com in which citizens are able to report problems and suggest solutions linked to the road network. The approach also opens up significant options in the area of social innovation, for example, the crisis response tool 'Ushahidi' emerged out of the Kenyan post-election unrest and involves using crowdsourcing to create and update rich maps which can help direct resources and avoid problem areas. It has subsequently been used in the Brisbane floods of 2011, several snow emergencies in Washington and the aftermath of the 2011 tsunami in Japan.

Case Study of Coloplast is available on the Innovation Portal at **www.innovation-portal.info**

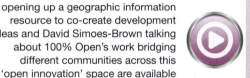

Video Clips of interviews with Michael Bartl discussing crowdsourcing and innovation contests and Catherina van Delden of Innosabi, which mobilizes communities of innovators across a Facebook platform to co-create a range of products, are available on the Innovation Portal at **www.innovation-portal.info**

Audio Clips of David Overton (Ordnance Survey) talking about opening up a geographic information resource to co-create development ideas and David Simoes-Brown talking about 100% Open's work bridging different communities across this 'open innovation' space are available on the Innovation Portal at **www.innovation-portal.info**

INNOVATION IN ACTION 6.11

Collective User Innovation

An increasingly important element in the innovation equation is co-creation – using the ideas, experience and insights of many people across a community to generate innovation. For example, *Encyclopaedia Britannica* was founded in 1768 and currently has around 65 000 articles. Until 1999, it was available only in print version but, in response to a growing number of CD and online-

(continued)

based competitors (such as Microsoft's Encarta), it now has an online version. Encarta was launched in 1993 and offered many new additions to the Britannica model, through multimedia illustrations carried on a CD/DVD; like Britannica it was available in a limited number of different languages.

By contrast, Wikipedia is a relative newcomer, launched in 2004 and available free on the Internet. It has become the dominant player in terms of online searches for information and is currently the sixth-most-visited site in the world. Its business model is fundamentally different – it is available free and is constructed through the shared contributions and updates offered by members of the public.

A criticism of Wikipedia is that this model means that inaccuracies are likely to appear but although the risk remains there are self-correcting systems in play, which mean that if it is wrong it will be updated and corrected quickly. A study by the journal *Nature* in 2005 (15th December) found it to be as accurate as *Encyclopaedia Britannica*, yet the latter employs around 4000 expert reviewers and a rewrite (including corrections) takes around five years to complete.

Encarta closed at the end of 2009 but *Encyclopaedia Britannica* continues to compete in this knowledge market. After three hundred years of an expert-driven model it moved, in January 2009, to extend its model and invite users to edit content using a variant on the Wikipedia approach.

 **Case Study** of open collective innovation is available on the Innovation Portal at **www.innovation-portal.info**

Shortly after that (February 2010), it discovered an error in its coverage of a key event in Irish history which had gone uncorrected in all its previous editions and only emerged when users pointed it out!

Extreme Users

An important variant which picks up on both the lead user and the fringe needs concepts lies in the idea of extreme environments as a source of innovation. The argument here is that the users in the toughest environments may have needs which by definition are at the edge – so any innovative solution which meets those needs has possible applications back into the mainstream. An example would be antilock braking systems (ABS) which are now a commonplace feature of cars but began life as a special add-on for premium high-performance cars. The origins of this innovation came from a more extreme case, though: the need to stop aircraft safely under difficult conditions where traditional braking could lead to skidding or other loss of control. ABS was developed for this extreme environment and then migrated across to the (comparatively) easier world of automobiles.

Looking for extreme environments or users can be a powerful source of stretch in terms of innovation, meeting challenges which can then provide new opportunity space. As Roy Rothwell puts it in the title of a famous paper, 'tough customers mean good designs'. For example, stealth technology arose out of a very specific and extreme need for creating an invisible aeroplane, essentially something which did not have a radar signature. It provided a powerful pull for some radical innovation which challenged fundamental assumptions about aircraft design, materials, power sources etc. and opened up a wide frontier for changes in aerospace and related fields. The 'bottom of the pyramid' concept mentioned earlier also offers some powerful extreme environments in which very different patterns of innovation are emerging. And the crisis innovations emerging from sites of disasters via humanitarian agencies offer another powerful set of examples.

Using the Crowd

Not everyone is an active user but the idea of the crowd as a source of different perspectives is an important one. Sometimes people with very different ideas, perspectives or expertise can contribute new directions to our sources of ideas, essentially amplifying. Using the wider population has always been an idea but until recently it was difficult to organize their contribution simply because of the logistics of information processing and communication. By using the Internet, new horizons open up to extend the reach of involvement as well as the richness of the contribution people can make.

In 2006, journalist Jeff Howe coined the term **crowdsourcing** in his book *Crowdsourcing: How the Power of the Crowd is Driving the Future of Business*. Crowdsourcing is where an organization makes an open call to a large network to provide some voluntary input or perform some function. The core requirements are that the call is open, and that the network is sufficiently large, the 'crowd'. Crowdsourcing of this kind can be enabled via a number of routes – for example innovation contests, innovation markets, innovation communities – which we discuss in detail in Chapter 10. But it is worth commenting here that opening up to the crowd can amplify not only the volume of ideas but also their diversity, and evidence is emerging that it is particularly this feature which makes the crowd a useful additional source of innovation.

INNOVATION IN ACTION 6.12

Online Innovation Markets

Karim Lakhani (of the Harvard Business School) and Lars Bo Jepessen (of the Copenhagen Business School) studied the ways in which businesses are making use of the innovation market platform Innocentive.com. The core model at Innocentive is to host 'challenges' put up by 'seekers' for ideas which 'solvers' offer. They examined 166 challenges and carried out a Web-based survey of solvers and found that the model offered around a 30% solution rate – of particular value to seekers looking to diversify the perspectives and approaches to solving their problems. The approach was particularly relevant for problems that large and well-known R&D-intensive firms had been unsuccessful in solving internally. Innocentive currently has around 200 000 solvers and as a result considerable diversity; its study suggested that as the number of unique scientific interests in the overall submitter population increased the higher the probability that a challenge was successfully solved. In other words, diversity of potential scientific approaches to a problem was a significant predictor of problem-solving success. Interestingly, the survey also found that solvers were often bridging knowledge fields – taking solutions and approaches from one area (their own specialty) and applying them to other different areas. This study offers systematic evidence for the premise that innovation occurs at the boundary of disciplines.

Prototyping

We've emphasized the importance of understanding user needs as a key source of innovation. But one challenge is that the new idea – whether knowledge push or need pull – may not be perfectly formed. Innovations are made rather than born, and this means we need to think about modifying, adapting and configuring the original idea. Feedback and learning early on can help shape it to make sure it meets the needs of the widest group and has features which people understand and value. For this reason, a core principle in sourcing innovation is to work with potential users as early as possible. One way of doing this is to create a simple prototype. It serves as a 'boundary object', something everyone can get around and give their ideas, and in the process innovation becomes a shared project.

INNOVATION IN ACTION 6.13

Learning from Users at IDEO

IDEO is one of the most successful design consultancies in the world, based in Palo Alto, California and London, UK, it helps large consumer and industrial companies worldwide design and develop innovative new products and services. Behind its rather typical Californian wacki-ness lies a tried-and-tested process for successful design and development:

1. Understand the market, client and technology.
2. Observe users and potential users in real-life situations.
3. Visualize new concepts and the customers who could use them, using prototyping, models and simulations.
4. Evaluate and refine the prototypes in a series of quick iterations.
5. Implement the new concept for commercialization.

The first critical step is achieved through close observation of potential users in context. As Tom Kelly of IDEO argues, 'We're not big fans of focus groups. We don't much care for traditional market research either. We go to the source. Not the "experts" inside a (client) company, but the actual people who use the product or something similar to what we're hoping to create . . . we believe you have to go beyond putting yourself in your customers' shoes. Indeed, we believe it's not even enough to ask people what they think about a product or idea . . . customers may lack the vocabulary or the palate to explain what's wrong, and especially what's missing.'

The next step is to develop prototypes to help evaluate and refine the ideas captured from users. 'An iterative approach to problems is one of the foundations of our culture of prototyping . . . you can prototype just about anything – a new product or service, or a special promotion. What counts is moving the ball forward, achieving some part of your goal.'

Source: Kelly, T. (2002) *The Art of Innovation: Lessons in Creativity from IDEO*, New York: HarperCollinsBusiness.

This approach is widely used by entrepreneurs trying to start new ventures. The 'lean start-up' method, for example, argues that the process needs to be one of fast learning and modifying of the original idea. By putting a 'minimum viable product' out into the market-place it becomes possible to test and adapt the idea, and it may well be that there is a need to 'pivot' around that idea to a new way of delivering it. This prototype doesn't have to be perfect but it provides a live experiment to help learn about what things in the new venture need to change.

Tools to help you explore prototyping innovation are available on the Innovation Portal at **www.innovation-portal.info**

Prototyping is widely used, for example beta testing of software or pilot projects which are deliberately set up to explore and learn rather than provide the finished product or service.

Watching Others – and Learning from Them

Another important source of innovation comes from watching others: imitation is not only the sincerest form of flattery but also a viable and successful strategy for sourcing innova-tion. For example, reverse engineering of products and processes and development of imitations – even around impregnable patents – is a well-known route to find ideas. Much of the rapid progress of Asian economies in the post-war years was based on a strategy of 'copy and develop', taking Western ideas and improving on them.

Tools which provide structured ways for learning of this kind, such as competitiveness profiling and benchmarking, are available on the Innovation Portal at **www.innovation-portal.info**

A powerful variation on this theme is the concept of **benchmarking**. In this process enterprises make structured comparisons with others to try to identify new ways of carrying out particular processes or to explore new product or service concepts. The learning trig-gered by benchmarking may arise from comparing between similar organizations (same firm, same sector, etc.), or it may come from looking outside the sector but at similar products or processes.

For example, Southwest Airlines became the most successful carrier in the USA by dra-matically reducing the turnaround times at airports – an innovation which it learnt from studying pit-stop techniques at Formula 1 Grand Prix events. Similarly, Karolinska Hospital in Stockholm made significant improvements to its cost and time performance through study-ing inventory management techniques in advanced fac-tories.

Case Studies of organizations (like Karolinska Hospital) and sectors (like the global automotive industry) which have made use of benchmarking are available on the Innovation Portal at **www.innovation-portal.info**

Benchmarking of this kind is increasingly being used to drive change across the public sector, both via league tables linked to performance metrics, which aim to encourage the fast transfer of good practice between schools or hospitals, and also via secondment, visits and other mechanisms designed to facilitate learning from other sectors managing similar process issues such as logistics and distribution. One of the most successful applications of benchmarking has been in the development of the concept of 'lean thinking', now widely applied to many public- and private-sector organizations. The origins were in a detailed benchmarking study of car manufacturing plants during the 1980s which identified significant performance differences and triggered a search for the underlying process innovations driving the differences.

Recombinant Innovation

An assumption which we often make about innovation is that it always has to involve something new to the world. The reality is that there is plenty of scope for crossover; ideas and applications which are commonplace in one world may be perceived as new and exciting in another. This is an important principle in sourcing innovation where transferring or combining old ideas in new contexts – a process called 'recombinant innovation' by US researcher Andrew Hargadon – can be a powerful resource.[4] The Reebok pump running shoe, for example, was a significant product innovation in the highly competitive world of sports equipment – yet although this represented a breakthrough in that field it drew on core ideas which were widely used in a different world. Design Works, the agency which came up with the design, brought together a team which included people with prior experience in fields like paramedic equipment (from which it took the idea of an inflatable splint providing support and minimizing shock to bones) and operating theatre equipment (from which it took the micro-bladder valve at the heart of the pump mechanisms.

Many businesses – as Hargadon points out – are able to offer rich innovation possibilities primarily because they have deliberately recruited teams with diverse industrial and professional backgrounds and thus bring very different perspectives to the problem in hand. His studies of the design company IDEO show the potential for such recombinant innovation work.

Nor is this a new idea. Thomas Edison's famous 'Invention Factory' in New Jersey was founded in 1876 with the grand promise of 'a minor invention every ten days and a big thing every six months or so'. It was able to deliver on that promise not because of the lone genius of Edison but rather from taking on board the recombinant lesson: Edison hired scientists and engineers from all the emerging new industries of early-20th-century America. In doing so, he brought experience in technologies and applications like mass production and precision machining (gun industry), telegraphy and telecommunications, food processing and canning, automobile manufacture, etc. Some of the early innovations which built the reputation of the business, for example the teleprinter for the New York Stock Exchange, were really simple crossover applications of well-known innovations in other sectors.

Case Study of recombinant innovation in the area of patient safety, DOME, is available on the Innovation Portal at **www.innovation-portal.info**

Regulation

Photographs of many industrial towns of the UK taken in the early part of the 20th century would not be much use in tracing landmarks or spotting key geographical features. The images would reveal very little at all – not because the technology was limited but simply because the subject was rendered largely invisible by the thick smog which regularly enveloped the area. Yet sixty years later the same images would show up crystal clear because of the continuing effects of the Clean Air Act and other legislation. They provide a reminder of another important source of innovation: the stimulus given by changes in the rules and regulations which define the various 'games' for business and society. The Clean Air Act didn't specify how but only what had to change. Achieving the reduction in pollutants emitted to the atmosphere involved extensive innovation in materials, processes and even in product design made by the factories.

Regulation in this way provides a double-edged sword. It closes off avenues along which innovation had been taking place but also opens up new ones along which change needs to happen. One of the powerful drivers for moving into environmentally sustainable 'clean' technologies is the increasingly tough legislation in areas like carbon emissions and pollution.

And it works the other way – deregulation, the slackening-off of controls – may open up new innovation space. The liberalization and then privatization of telecommunications in many countries led to the rapid growth in competition and high rates of innovation, for example.

Given the pervasiveness of legal frameworks in our lives we shouldn't be surprised to see this source of innovation. From the moment we get up and turn the radio on (regulation of broadcasting shaping the range and availability of the programmes we listen to) to eating our breakfast (food and drink is highly regulated in terms of what can and can't be included in ingredients, how foods are tested before being allowed for sale, etc.) to climbing into our cars and buckling on our safety belt while switching on our hands-free phones (both the result of safety legislation), the role of regulation in shaping innovation can be seen. Chapter 4 showed how powerful a force regulation has become in driving innovation around the sustainability agenda.

Case Studies highlighting the role played by regulation in shaping the innovation agenda of companies like Volvo, Nokia Solutions and Networks (NSN) and Lafarge are available on the Innovation Portal at **www.innovation-portal.info**

Video Clip of Fabian Schlage (NSN) illustrating some of these themes is available on the Innovation Portal at **www.innovation-portal.info**

Regulation can also trigger counter innovation – solutions designed to get round existing rules or at least bend them to advantage. The rapid growth in speed cameras as a means of enforcing safety legislation on roads throughout Europe has led to the healthy growth of an industry providing products or services for detecting and avoiding cameras. And at the limit, changes in the regulatory environment can create radical new space and opportunity. Although Enron ended its days as a corporation in disgrace owing to financial impropriety, it is worth asking how a small gas pipeline services company rose to become such a powerful beast in the first place. The answer was its rapid and entrepreneurial take-up of the opportunities opened up by deregulation of markets for utilities like gas and electricity.

Futures and Forecasting

Audio Clip of an interview with Helen King, describing how the Irish Food Board uses futures to alert the industry to new challenges is available on the Innovation Portal at **www.innovation-portal.info**

Video Clip of of Shell's GameChanger programme is available on the Innovation Portal at **www.innovation-portal.info**

Another way we can identify innovation possibilities is to imagine and explore into the future. What might be the key trends, where might the threats and opportunities lie? For example, Shell has a long history of exploring future options and driving innovations, most recently through its 'GameChanger' programme. Various tools and techniques for forecasting and imagining alternative futures have been developed to help work with these rich sources of innovation and we look at them in detail in Chapter 7.

Case Study of Philips Lighting showing how a large company makes use of futures is available on the Innovation Portal at **www.innovation-portal.info**

Tools relating to these issues can be found in the toolkit on the Innovation Portal at **www.innovation-portal.**

Design-driven Innovation

One increasingly significant source of innovation is what researcher Roberto Verganti calls 'design driven innovation'.[5] Examples include many of the successful Apple products where the user experience is one of surprise and pleasure at the look and feel, the intuitive beauty, of the product. This emerges not as a result of analysis of user needs but rather through a design process which seeks to give meaning to the shape and form of products – features and characteristics which they didn't know they wanted. But it is also not another version of knowledge or technology push in which powerful new functions are installed – in many ways design-led products are deceptively simple in their usability. Apple's iPod was a comparative latecomer to the mp3 player market yet it created the standard for the others to follow because of the uniqueness of the look and feel – the design attributes. Its subsequent success with its iPad and iPhone devices owes a great deal to the design ideas of Jonathan Ive, which brought a philosophy to the whole product range and provided one of the key competitiveness factors for the company.

As Verganti points out, people do not buy things only to meet their needs: there are important psychological and cultural factors at work as well. In essence, we need to ask about the meaning of products in people's lives – and then develop ways of bringing this into the innovation process. This is the role of design – to use tools and skills to articulate and create meaning in products – and it has increasing implications in the world of services as well. He suggests a map in which both knowledge/ technology push and market pull can be positioned and where design-driven innovation represents a third space around creating radical new concepts which have meaning in people's lives (Figure 6.3).

Audio Clip of Lynne Maher discussing patient-centred healthcare is available on the Innovation Portal at **www.innovation-portal.info**

Case Studies cardiac care (NHS RED) and hospital design (Open Door) are available on the Innovation Portal at **www.innovation-portal.info**

Design features increasingly in the area of services and design methods and tools are being used to identify and work with user needs in a variety of contexts. One example is in the field of healthcare where inputs from patients and carers are beginning to be seen as valuable sources of innovation.

Related to the design idea is that of **experience innovation**, a concept first explored by Joseph Pine.[6] In an increasingly competitive world differentiation comes increasingly from creating experience innovation, especially in services where fulfilling needs takes second place to the meaning and psychological importance of the experience. For example, the restaurant business moves from emphasis on food as an essential human need towards increasingly

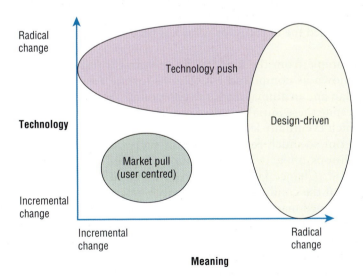

FIGURE 6.3   The role of design-driven innovation

Source: Verganti, R. (2009) *Design-driven Innovation*, Boston: Harvard Business School Press.

Case Study of a report on intelligent design describing how design and innovation are linked is available on the Innovation Portal at **www.innovation-portal.info**

significant experience innovation around restaurants as systems of consumption involving the product, its delivery, the physical and cultural context, etc. Increasingly, service providers such as airlines, hotels or entertainment businesses are differentiating themselves along such experience innovation lines.

Video Clips of several examples of intelligent design are available on the Innovation Portal at **www.innovation-portal.info**

Accidents

Accidents and unexpected events happen – and in the course of a carefully planned R&D project they could be seen as annoying disruptions. But on occasions accidents can also trigger innovation, opening up surprisingly new lines of attack. The famous example of Fleming's discovery of penicillin is but one of many stories in which mistakes and accidents turned out to trigger important innovation directions. 3M's Post-it notes began when a polymer chemist mixed an experimental batch of what should have been a good adhesive but which turned out to have rather weak properties – sticky but not very sticky. This failure in terms of the original project provided the impetus for what has become a billion-dollar product platform for the company.

In another example from the late 1980s, scientists working for Pfizer began testing what was then known as compound UK-92,480 for the treatment of angina. Although promising in the lab and in animal tests, the compound showed little benefit in clinical trials in humans. Despite these initial negative results, the team pursued what was an interesting side effect which eventually led to UK-92,480 becoming the blockbuster drug Viagra.

The secret is not so much recognizing that such stimuli are available but rather in creating the conditions under which they can be noticed and acted upon. As Pasteur is reputed to have said, 'Chance favours the prepared mind!' Using mistakes as a source of ideas only happens if the conditions exist to help it emerge. A study of Xerox highlighted the fact that it developed many technologies in its laboratories in Palo Alto which did not easily fit its image of itself as 'the document company'. These included Ethernet (later successfully commercialized by 3Com and others) and PostScript language (taken forward by Adobe Systems). In fact, eleven of 35 rejected projects from Xerox's labs were later commercialized with the resulting businesses having a market capitalization of twice that of Xerox itself.

INNOVATION IN ACTION 6.14

Cleaning up by Accident

Audley Williamson is not a household name of the Thomas Edison variety but he was a successful innovator whose UK business sold for £135 million in 2004. The core product which he invented was called Swarfega and offered a widely used and dermatologically safe cleaner for skin. It is a greenish gel which has achieved widespread use in households as a simple and robust aid with the advertising slogan 'Clean hands in a flash!' But the original product was not designed for this market at all – it was developed in 1941 as a mild detergent to wash silk stockings. Unfortunately, the invention of Nylon and its rapid application in stockings meant that the market quickly disappeared and he was forced to find an alternative. Watching workers in a factory trying to clean their hands with an abrasive mixture of petrol, paraffin and sand which left their hands cracked and sore led him to rethink the use of his gel as a safer alternative.

Source: The Independent, 28th February 2006, 7.

Chapter Summary

- Innovations don't just appear perfectly formed – and the process is not simply a spark of imagination giving rise to changing the world. Instead, innovations come from a number of sources and these interact over time.

- Sources of innovation can be resolved into two broad classes – knowledge push and need pull – although they almost always act in tandem. Innovation arises from their interplay.

- There are many variations on this theme, for example 'need pull' can include social needs, market needs, latent needs, 'squeaking wheels', crisis needs, etc.

- While the basic forces pushing and pulling have been a feature of the innovation landscape for a long time, it involves a moving frontier in which new sources of push and pull come into play. Examples include the emerging demand pull from the 'bottom of the pyramid' and the opportunities opened up by an acceleration in knowledge production in R&D systems around the world.

- User-led innovation has always been important but developments in communications technology have enabled much higher levels of engagement – via crowdsourcing, user communities, co-creation platforms, etc.

- Regulation is also an important element in shaping and directing innovative activity. By restricting what can and can't be done for legal reasons, new trajectories for change are established which entrepreneurs can take advantage of.

- Design-driven approaches and the related toolkit around prototyping are of growing importance.

- Accidents have always been a potential source of innovation – but converting them to opportunities requires an open mind. As Pasteur is reputed to have said, 'Chance favours the prepared mind!'

Key Terms Defined

Benchmarking   systematic comparison of products, processes or services to identify areas for innovation.

Citizen sourcing   as crowdsourcing but particularly related to acquiring ideas for improving public services.

Crowdsourcing   acquiring ideas from a wide range of people as inputs to the innovation process, usually across an internet-based platform.

Disruptive innovation   innovation which occurs at the periphery of a mainstream market and which has the potential to change the 'rules of the game' in terms of price, performance and other characteristics.

Experience innovation innovation based on engaging customers through creating experiences (rather than just products or services) which they value.

Free revealing in open innovation communities the practice of sharing ideas with others without trying to protect intellectual property rights.

Lead users group of very early adopters of new ideas who are enthusiastic for changes and who can be used as a test-bed for prototypes and early-stage concept development.

Mass customization providing a high degree of personalization to products or services without incurring the traditional costs of tailoring to specific needs.

Discussion Questions

1. Where do innovations come from? Generate a list of as many categories of trigger as you can think of, with examples for each one.

2. Push and pull – which is more important? This question has worried managers and policy-makers for decades, and having an idea of the answer would help focus support for the innovation process more effectively. Using examples try to show how each is important under certain conditions but that it is their interplay which really shapes innovation.

3. Taking each of the '4Ps' of innovation which we introduced in Chapter 1, try to identify examples of 'product', 'process', 'position' and 'paradigm' innovation – and in each case list the sources which gave rise to those innovations.

4. Julia Wilson is keen to use her skills in creating social enterprises. Where could she look for sources of inspiration on which to focus her entrepreneurial enthusiasm?

Further Reading and Resources

The long-running debate about which source – demand pull or knowledge push – is more important is well covered in Freeman and Soete's book *The Economics of Industrial Innovation* (3rd edn, MIT Press, 1997). Particular discussion of fringe markets and unmet or poorly met needs as a source of innovation is covered by Christensen *et al.* (Christensen, C., S. Anthony and E. Roth, *Seeing What's Next*, Harvard Business School Press, 2007), Utterback (Utterback, J., High End Disruption, *International Journal of Innovation Management*, 2007) and Ulnwick (Ulnwick, A., *What Customers Want: Using Outcome-driven Innovation to Create Breakthrough Products and Services*, McGraw-Hill, 2005), while the 'bottom of the pyramid' and extreme user potential is explored in C.K. Prahalad's *The Fortune at the Bottom of the Pyramid* (Wharton School Publishing, 2006) and in Navi Radjou, Jaideep Prabhu and Simone Ahuja's *Jugaad Innovation: Think Frugal, Be Flexible, Generate Breathrough Innovation* (Jossey-Bass, 2012). Keith Goffin, Fred Lemke and Ursula Koeners cover the challenge of identifying hidden needs (*Identifying Hidden Needs Creating Breakthrough Products* (Palgrave Macmillan, 2010), while Kelley offers a description of how this approach is used in IDEO (*The Art of Innovation: Lessons in Creativity from Ideo: America's Leading Design Firm,* Currency, 2001).

User-led innovation has been researched extensively by Eric von Hippel (http://web.mit.edu/evhippel/www/). Frank Piller, Professor at Aachen University in Germany, has a rich website around the theme of mass customization with extensive case examples and other resources (www.mass-customization.de/); the original work on the topic is covered in Joseph Pine's book (*Mass Customisation: The New Frontier in Business Competition*, Harvard University Press, 1993). High involvement innovation is covered in John Bessant's *High Involvement Innovation* (John Wiley & Sons Ltd, 2003) and lean thinking ideas and tools in Dan Jones and Jim Womack's *Lean Solutions* (Free Press, 2005). Andrew Hargadon has done extensive work on 'recombinant innovation' (*How Breakthroughs Happen*, Harvard Business School Press, 2003) and Mohammed Zairi provides a good overview of benchmarking (*Effective Benchmarking: Learning from the Best* (Chapman & Hall, 1996). And open innovation is extensively explored, for example by Henry Chesbrough, Wim Vanhaverbeke and Joel West (eds) in *Open Innovation: Researching a New Paradigm* (Oxford University Press, 2008) and Kathrin Möslein, Ralf Reichwald and Anne Sigismund Huff's *Leading Open Innovation* (MIT Press, 2013).

References

1. Kluter, H. and D. Mottram (2007) Hyundai uses 'Touch the market' to create clarity in product concepts, in *PDMA Visions*, Mount Laurel, NJ: Product Development Management Association, 16–19.

2. Christensen, C. (1997) *The Innovator's Dilemma*, Cambridge, MA: Harvard Business School Press.

3. Von Hippel, E. (2005) *The Democratization of Innovation*, Cambridge, MA: MIT Press.

4. Hargadon, A. (2003) *How Breakthroughs Happen*, Boston: Harvard Business School Press.

5. Verganti, R. (2009) *Design-driven Innovation*, Boston: Harvard Business School Press.

6. Pine, J. and J. Gilmore (1999) *The Experience Economy*, Boston: Harvard Business School Press.

Deeper Dive explanations of innovation concepts and ideas are available on the Innovation Portal at **www.innovation-portal.info**

Quizzes to test yourself further are available online via the Innovation Portal at **www.innovation-portal.info**

Summary of online resources for Chapter 6 –
all material is available via the Innovation Portal at
www.innovation-portal.info

Cases	**Media**	**Tools**	**Activities**	**Deeper Dives**
• 3M • Corning • Imaging industry • Spirit • Dyson • Philips Lighting • NHS RED • Tesco • Open Door • Continuous improvement • Process innovations in healthcare • GE simple scanner • Aravind Eye Clinics • NHL • Lifespring Hospitals	• Stephen Johnson • Michael Bartl • Emma Taylor • Innocent Fruit Juices • Redgate Software • UK Meteorological Office • Devon and Cornwall Police • Helle-Vibeke Carstensen • Clayton Christensen • Girish Prabhu • Jane Chen • Dr Venkataswamy	• Kano method • Design methods • Process mapping • Prototyping innovation • Competitiveness profiling • Benchmarking • Futures	• Innovation family tree • Harvesting knowledge crops • Classifying innovation • Outcome-oriented innovation tool	• Discontinuous innovation • Disruptive innovation • Frugal innovation • Mass customization • Open user innovation • Search strategies for peripheral vision

(continued)

Summary of online resources for Chapter 6 –
all material is available via the Innovation Portal at
www.innovation-portal.info

 Cases

 Media

 Tools

 Activities

 Deeper Dives

Cases	Media
• M-PESA	• Suzana Moreira
• Living Labs	• Ana Sena
• Crisis-driven innovation	• Model T Ford
• Model T Ford	• Frank Piller
• Adidas	• Chris Anderson
• Lego	• Eric von Hippel
• Threadless.com	• Tim Craft
• Yellowberry	• Tad Golesworthy
• Opening up healthcare innovation	• Charles Leadbeater
• Coloplast	• Michael Bartl
• Open Collective Innovation	• Catherina van Delden
• Karolinska Hospital	• David Overton
• DOME	• David Simoes-Brown
• Volvo	• Fabian Schlage
• NSN	• Helen King
• Lafarge	• Shell's GameChanger programme
• Intelligent design	• Lynne Maher
	• Intelligent design

Chapter 7

Search Strategies for Innovation

LEARNING OBJECTIVES

By the end of this chapter you will develop an understanding of:

- the need for a strategy to guide search for opportunities
- dimensions of search space – incremental/radical and old/new frame
- strategies for covering the space – exploit and explore
- tools and structures to support these strategies
- opening up and amplifying search capabilities through networks
- the role of entrepreneurship as a mindset underpinning search, whether in start-ups or established organizations
- the concept of absorptive capacity and building search capability.

Making Sense of the Sources

It's clear from the last chapter that opportunities for innovation are not in short supply. The key challenge for innovation management is how to spot the potential in a sea of possibilities. It's a difficult choice because it involves limited resources. No organization can hope to cover all the bases, so there needs to be some underlying strategy to how the search process is undertaken. And for a solo start-up entrepreneur there simply isn't the 'bandwidth' to explore in so many directions at the same time. So how can we make sense of all the sources out there?

TABLE 7.1 (*Continued*)

Innovation type	Incremental (do what we do but better)	Radical (do something different)
Position – where we target that offering and the story we tell about it	Häagen Dazs changing the target market for ice cream from children to consenting adults Low-cost airlines University of Phoenix and others, building large education businesses via online approaches to reach different markets Dell and others segmenting and customizing computer configuration for individual users Banking services targeted at key segments (e.g. students, retired people)	Addressing underserved markets (e.g. Tata Nano targets huge but relatively poor Indian market using the low-cost airline model) 'Bottom of the pyramid' approaches using a similar principle (e.g. Aravind Eye Clinics, Cemex construction products) One laptop per child project – the $100 universal computer Microfinance (Grameen Bank opening up credit for the very poor)
Paradigm – how we frame what we do	Bausch & Lomb moving from 'eye wear' to 'eye care' as its business model, effectively letting go of the old business of spectacles, sunglasses and contact lenses and moving to newer high-tech fields like laser surgery, specialist optical devices and research into artificial eyesight IBM moving from being a machine maker to a service and solution company, selling off its computer making and building up its consultancy and service side VT moving from being a shipbuilder with roots in Victorian England to a service and facilities management business	iTunes platform – a complete system of personalized entertainment Rolls-Royce – from high-quality aero engines to becoming a service company offering 'power by the hour' Cirque du Soleil – redefining the circus experience

For all but the smallest start-up, we will be looking to balance a portfolio of ideas – most of them 'do better' incremental improvements on what has gone before but with a few which are more radical and may even be 'new to the world'. The big advantage of innovation of this kind is that there is a degree of familiarity, that is the risk is lower because we are moving along a well-trodden path. The benefits from doing so may be small in themselves but their effect is cumulative. And the ways in which we can search for such opportunities – tools and directions – are essentially well established and systematic.

By contrast, taking a leap forward could bring big gains – but also carries higher risk. Since we are moving into unknown territory there will be a need to experiment – and a good chance that much of that experimentation will fail. We won't be clear about the directions in which we want to go and so there is a real risk of going up blind alleys or being trapped in one-way systems. Essentially, the kind of searching we do, and the tools we use, will be different.

Activity to help you use the 4Ps approach to explore opportunities in incremental and radical innovation is available on the Innovation Portal at **www.innovation-portal.info**

Exploit or Explore?

One way we can innovate is by moving forward from what we already know. Individuals and organizations can deploy knowledge resources and other assets to secure returns, and a 'safe' way of doing so is to harvest a steady flow of benefits derived from 'doing what we do better'. This has been termed 'exploitation' by innovation researchers, and it essentially involves using what we already know as the foundation for further incremental innovation. It builds strongly on what is already well established, but in the process leads to a high degree of what is called 'path dependency'. Essentially, what we did in the past will play a strong role in shaping what we do next.

The trouble is that in an uncertain environment the potential to secure and defend a competitive position depends on 'doing something different', i.e. radical product or process innovation rather than imitations and variants of what others are also offering. This kind of search had been termed 'exploration' and is the kind which involves big leaps into new knowledge territory – risky but they enable the organization to do new and very different things. Figure 7.2 illustrates this

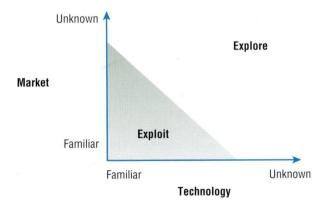

FIGURE 7.2   Exploit and explore options in search

When?

A key issue is around timing. At different stages in the product or industry lifecycle the emphasis may be more or less on push or pull. For example, mature industries will tend to focus on pull, responding to different market needs and differentiating by incremental innovation in key directions of user need. By contrast a new industry, for example the emergent industries based on genetics or nano materials technology, is often about solutions looking for a problem. So we would expect a different balance of resources committed to push or pull within these different stages.

This kind of thinking is reflected in models of the 'innovation lifecycle' which see innovation as moving through different stages. Back in the 1970s two US researchers (William Abernathy and James Utterback) developed a model which has three different phases with important lessons for how we think about managing innovation.[2] In the early stage – the 'fluid' phase – there is a lot of uncertainty, and emphasis is placed on product innovation. Typically, entrepreneurs have lots of ideas (most of which fail) about the ways to use new market and technological opportunities. (Think about the rise of the Internet and the continuing proliferation of entrepreneurial ideas as an example of a fluid phase.)

But after a while there is a stabilization around a particular configuration – the 'dominant design' (which may not always be the best in technical terms but is the one that matches the market's needs and aspirations) – and then emphasis shifts away from more product variety to process innovation. How can we make this in volume, to a low price, consistent quality, etc.? (Think of Henry Ford; he was a latecomer to the business of car design but his Model T became the dominant design and succeeded principally because of the extensive process innovations around mass production.)

Finally, there is a third, 'mature' phase in which innovation is incremental in both product and process, there is extensive competition and the scene is set for another breakthrough and return to the fluid stage. What this model means is that we could particularly look for radical product innovation ideas in the fluid phase but in the mature stage we would be better placed concentrating on incremental improvement innovations.

Case Study of these patterns of innovation associated with the evolution of the bicycle is available on the Innovation Portal at **www.innovation-portal.info**

Figure 7.3 illustrates the basic model.

Adoption and Diffusion

A related issue is around diffusion: the adoption and elaboration of innovation over time. Innovation adoption takes place gradually over time, following some version of an S-curve. In the early stages innovative users with high tolerance for failure will explore to be followed by early adopters. This gives way to the majority following their lead until finally the remnant of a potential adopting population – the laggards – adopt or remain stubbornly resistant. Understanding diffusion processes and the influential factors is important because it helps us understand where and when different kinds of triggers are picked up.

Activity to help you explore sources of innovation and the role of these models of adoption and diffusion is available on the Innovation Portal at **www.innovation-portal.info**

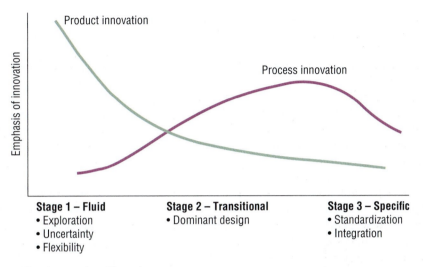

FIGURE 7.3   The innovation lifecycle

Source: Abernathy, W. and J. Utterback (1975) A dynamic model of product and process innovation, *Omega*, **3**(6): 639–56.

Lead users and early adopters are likely to be important sources of ideas and variations which can help shape an innovation in its early life, whereas the early and late majority will be more a source of incremental improvement ideas.[3] (We explore this in detail in Chapter 11.)

Where? The Innovation Treasure Hunt

As we saw in Chapter 1, innovation can take a variety of forms – 'product', 'process', 'position' and 'paradigm'– and comes in incremental or radical flavours. So it would help to have a map of the innovation search space before we start out on our journey. We'll build it with two axes:

- incremental/radical innovation
- existing frame/new frame

and then look at how we can prepare to explore this space effectively. We discussed incremental/radical innovation earlier; the other axis is linked to how we frame the space in which we look.

Established Frame/New Frame

Just as human beings need to develop mental models to simplify the confusion which the rich stimuli in their environment offer them, so individual entrepreneurs and established organizations make use of simplifying frames. They 'look' at the environment and take note of elements which they consider relevant – threats to watch out for, opportunities to take advantage of, competitors and collaborators, etc. Constructing such frames helps give the organization some stability but it also defines the space within which it will search for innovation possibility.

In practice, these models often converge around a core theme, and although organizations may differ, they often share common models about how their world behaves. So most firms in a particular sector will adopt similar ways of **framing**: assuming certain 'rules of the game', following certain trajectories in common. And this shapes where and how they tend to search for opportunities. It emerges over time but once established becomes the 'box' within which further innovation takes place.

It's difficult to think and work outside this box because it is reinforced by the structures, processes and tools which the organization uses in its day-to-day work. The problem is also that such ways of working are linked to a complex web of other players in the organization's 'value network' – its key competitors, customers and suppliers – who reinforce the dominant way of seeing the world.

INNOVATION IN ACTION 7.1

Technological Excellence May Not Be Enough…

In the 1970s, Xerox was the dominant player in photocopiers, having built the industry from its early days when it was founded on the radical technology pioneered by Chester Carlsen and the Battelle Institute. But despite its prowess in the core technologies and continuing investment in maintaining an edge, it found itself seriously threatened by a new generation of small copiers developed by new-entrant Japanese players. Despite the fact that Xerox had enormous experience in the industry and a deep understanding of the core technology, it took the company almost eight years of mishaps and false starts to introduce a competitive product. In that time Xerox lost around half its market share and suffered severe financial problems.

In similar fashion in the 1950s the electronics giant RCA developed a prototype portable transistor-based radio using technologies which it had come to understand well. However, it saw little reason to promote such an apparently inferior technology and continued to develop and build its high range devices. By contrast, Sony used it to gain access to the consumer market and to build a generation of portable consumer devices – and in the process acquired considerable technological experience, which enabled the company to enter and compete successfully in higher-value and more complex markets.

Powerful though they are, such frames are only models of how individuals and organizations think the world works. It is possible to see things differently, take into account new elements, pay attention to different things and come up with alternative solutions. This is, of course, exactly what entrepreneurs do when they try to find opportunities: they look at the world differently and see opportunity in a different way of framing things. And sometimes their new way of looking at things becomes a widely accepted one – and their innovation changes the game.

Rather like the drunk who has lost his keys on the way home and is desperately searching for them under the nearest lamp post 'because there is more light there', firms have a natural tendency to search in spaces which they already know and understand. But we know that the weak early-warning signals of the emergence of totally new possibilities – radically different technologies, new markets with radically different needs, changing public opinion or political context – won't happen under our particular lamp post. Instead, they are out there in the darkness, and so we have to find new ways of searching in space we aren't familiar with.

How can this be done? By luck, sometimes – except that simply being in the right place at the right time doesn't always help. History suggests that even when the new possibility is presented to the firm on a plate its internal capacity to see and act on the possibilities is often lacking. For example, the famous 'not invented here' effect has been observed on many occasions where an otherwise well-established and successful innovative firm rejects a new opportunity which turns out to be of major significance.

A Map of Innovation Search Space

Putting these together gives us the map in Figure 7.4.

Zone 1 corresponds to the exploit area we looked at earlier where we are working in familiar territory and looking to exploit the knowledge base which we already have. Zone 2 is about exploring but within the context of our existing frame, pushing the frontiers but in directions we are familiar with. Zone 3 brings in new elements and combinations and requires a different and more open approach to search. And zone 4 is where the different elements interact with each other to make a complex system which is extremely difficult to explore in systematic fashion. We look at the particular challenges of searching these zones in the next section.

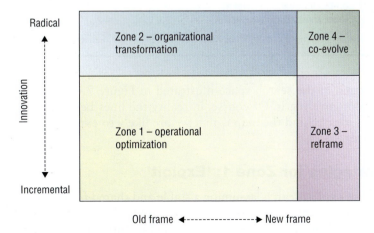

FIGURE 7.4 A map of innovation search space

How?

Case Studies of Tesco and Cerulean giving us clues about the actual approaches organizations take, and the combinations of tools they employ, are available on the Innovation Portal at **www.innovation-portal.info**

So how do we start covering this enormous space looking for innovation opportunities? More importantly, what patterns of behaviour – routines – work to help us do it and repeat the trick? We may get lucky once but being able to find a steady stream of opportunities is the name of the game.

INNOVATION IN ACTION 7.2

How We Search for Innovation

We look in the usual places for our industry. We look at our customers. We look at our suppliers. We go to trade bodies. We go to trade fairs. We present technical papers. We have an input coming from our customers. What we also try to do is develop inputs from other areas. We've done that in a number of ways. Where we're recruiting, we try to bring in people who can bring a different perspective. We don't necessarily want people who've worked in the type of instruments we have in the same industry … certainly in the past we've brought in people who bring a completely different perspective, almost like introducing greensand into the oyster. We deliberately look outside. We will look in other areas. We will look in areas that are perhaps

Video Clip of an interview with Patrick McLaughlin is available on the Innovation Portal at **www.innovation-portal.info**

different technology. We will look in areas that are adjacent to what we do, where we haven't normally looked. And we also do encourage the employees themselves to come forward with ideas.

Source: Patrick McLaughlin, Managing Director, Cerulean.

Let's look again at the search space illustrated in Figure 7.4 and think about how we could we go about covering it. Of course, in reality the lines between these 'zones' are not clear-cut, but the idea behind the map is that we are likely to experience very different challenges in each area.

Search Strategies for Zone 1: 'Exploit'

Zone 1 is all about **exploit** search, assuming a stable and shared frame within which adaptive and incremental development takes place. Search 'routines' here are associated with *refining* tools and methods for technological and market research, deepening relationships with established key players. Examples would be working with key suppliers, getting closer to customers and building key strategic alliances to help deliver established innovations more efficiently. Process innovation is enabled by inviting suggestions for incremental improvement across the organization, a high-involvement kaizen model.

Understanding buyer/adopter behaviour has become a key theme in marketing studies, since it provides us with frameworks and tools for identifying and understanding user needs. Advertising and branding play a key role in this process – essentially using psychology to tune into, or even stimulate and create, basic human needs. Another strand has focused on detailed studies of what people actually do and how they actually use products and services, using the same approaches which anthropologists use to study strange new tribes to uncover hidden and latent needs.

Video Clip looking at how Veeder-Root approaches the challenge of continuous process innovation is available on the Innovation Portal at www.innovation-portal.info

Case Studies illustrating how different organizations (Kumba Resources, NPI and Tesco) manage this 'exploit' search task are available on the Innovation Portal at www.innovation-portal.info

Tools in the market research toolkit and continuous improvement toolkit highlighting ways of carrying out this kind of search are available on the Innovation Portal at www.innovation-portal.info

Search Strategies for Zone 2: 'Explore'

Zone 2 involves search into new territory, pushing the frontiers of what is known and deploying different search techniques for doing so, but still doing so within an established framework. R&D search investments here tend to include big projects with high strategic potential, patenting and intellectual property (IP) strategies aimed at marking out and defending territory, and riding key technological trajectories (such as Moore's Law in semiconductors). Market research similarly aims to get close to customers but to push the frontiers via empathic design, latent needs analysis, etc. Although the activity is risky and exploratory, it is still governed strongly by the frame for the sector.

Explore search strategies are much more about specialist groups and networks inside and outside the organization, for example with university, public and commercial laboratories and other firms. The highly specialized nature of the work makes it difficult for others in the organization to participate – and indeed this gap between worlds can often lead to tensions between the 'operating' and the 'exploring' units, and the boardroom battles between these two camps for resources are often tense. In similar fashion, market research is highly specialized and may include external professional agencies in its network with the task of providing sophisticated business intelligence around a focused frontier.

Case Studies of describing formal R&D and major market research approaches, Philips Lighting and Tesco, are available on the Innovation Portal at www.innovation-portal.info

From the standpoint of the entrepreneur, this zone is interesting since there may be significant opportunities. Individuals and start-up businesses with highly specialized knowledge assets, for example hi-tech spin-outs from universities, may feature strongly on the radar

Tool to help you explore this area, the ADL matrix, is available on the Innovation Portal at www.innovation-portal.info

screens of large established organizations looking to explore. This pattern of 'symbiosis' – mutual dependency and advantage for new and established players – is a common one in fields like pharmaceuticals, electronics, software and biotechnology. (The case study of Chiroscience which we explore in Chapter 12 is a good example of this.)

Search Strategies for Zone 3: 'Reframing'

Zone 3 is essentially associated with **reframing**. It involves searching a space where alternative architectures are generated, exploring different permutations and combinations of elements in the environment. Importantly this often happens by working with elements in the environment not embraced by established business models, for example working with fringe markets, looking at the 'bottom of the pyramid' or collaborating with 'extreme users'.

INNOVATION IN ACTION 7.3

Changing Directions

Sometimes an organization needs to change its perspective in radical fashion – to reframe what it does in order to survive and compete under very different conditions. (This corresponds to radical 'paradigm' innovation of the kind which we saw in Chapter 1.) Fujifilm is a Japanese company which has been a key player in the world of photography and imaging (printers, scanners, cameras, etc.). But in recent years it has been extending its sphere of activity through some radical reframing – using the fact that it has a deep knowledge base underpinning its established business based on particles coated on surfaces. As Stefan Kohn explains in the case on the Innovation Portal, they have begun to play a major role in the world of skin care and in the process of reframing have opened up considerable new innovation space.

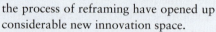

Case Studies of Fujifilm and Kodak are available on the Innovation Portal at **www.innovation-portal.info**

In similar fashion Kodak is now trying to resurrect a business through deploying its knowledge base around coating surfaces to enter the printing industry with radically new technologies.

This zone often favours entrepreneurs on the outside of established organizations because they can see ways of putting the pieces together differently. Importantly, this may not involve pushing the technological frontiers with radical innovation in the core offering or process – it is often about change in the ways the architecture works.

Table 7.2 describes some of the additional approaches which organizations use to try to extend their peripheral vision and find new innovation opportunities.

TABLE 7.2 Developing new ways of searching

Search strategy	Mode of operation
Sending out scouts	Dispatch idea hunters to track down new innovation triggers
Exploring multiple futures	Use futures techniques to explore alternative possible futures, and develop innovation options from that
Using the Web	Through online communities, and virtual worlds, for example to detect new trends
Working with active users	Team up with product and service users to see the ways in which they change and develop existing offerings
Deep diving	Study what people actually do, rather than what they say they do. 'Ethnographic' tools are a key resource in the designer's toolbox to uncover hidden needs
Probe and learn	Use prototyping as a mechanism to explore emergent phenomena and act as boundary object to bring key stakeholders into the innovation process
Mobilize the mainstream	Bring mainstream actors into the product and service development process
Corporate venturing	Create and deploy venture units
Corporate entrepreneurship and intrapreneuring	Stimulate and nurture the entrepreneurial talent inside the organization
Use brokers and bridges	Cast the ideas net far and wide and connect with other industries
Deliberate diversity	Create diverse teams and a diverse workforce
Idea generators	Use creativity tools

Case Study of the full report, Twelve search strategies that may help to save your organisation, is available on the Innovation Portal at **www.innovation-portal.info**

Tool to uncover hidden user needs, the Kano method, is available on the Innovation Portal at **www.innovation-portal.info**

INNOVATION IN ACTION 7.4

Scouting for Ideas

The mobile phone company O2 has a trend-scouting group of about 10 **scouts** who interpret externally identified trends into their specific business context, while BT has a scouting unit in Silicon Valley which assesses some 3000 technology opportunities a year in California. The four-man operation was established in 1999 to make venture investments in promising telecom start-ups, but after the dotcom bubble burst it shifted its mission towards identifying partners and technologies that BT was interested in. The small team looks at more than 1000 companies per year and then, based on their deep knowledge of the issues facing the R&D operations back in England, team members target the small number of cases where there is a direct match between BT's needs and the Silicon Valley company's technology. While the number of successful partnerships that result from this activity is small – typically four or five per year – the unit serves an invaluable role in keeping BT abreast of the latest developments in its technology domain.

 Tool to help you find opportunities for breakthrough innovation, lead user methods, is available on the Innovation Portal at **www.innovation-portal.info**

 Video Clips of Eric von Hippel (of 3M)'s experience with these tools are available on the Innovation Portal at **www.innovation-portal.info**

INNOVATION IN ACTION 7.5

Using Innovation Markets

Karim Lakhani (Harvard Business School) and Lars Bo Jepessen (Copenhagen Business School) studied the ways in which businesses are making use of the innovation market platform Innocentive.com. The core model at Innocentive is to host 'challenges' put up by 'seekers' for ideas which 'solvers' offer. They examined 166 challenges and carried out a Web-based survey of solvers and found that the model offered around a 30% solution rate – of particular value to seekers looking to diversify the perspectives and approaches to solving their problems. The approach was particularly relevant for problems that large and well-known R&D-intensive firms had been unsuccessful in solving internally. Innocentive currently has around 200 000 solvers and as a result considerable diversity. Lakhani and Jepessen's study suggested that as the number of unique scientific interests in the overall submitter population increased so too would the probability that a challenge was successfully solved. In other words, diversity of potential scientific approaches to a problem was a significant predictor of problem-solving success. Interestingly, the survey also found that solvers were often bridging knowledge fields – taking solutions and approaches from one area (their own specialty) and applying them to other different areas. This study offers systematic evidence for the premise that innovation occurs at the boundary of disciplines.

Search Strategies for Zone 4: 'Co-evolution'

Zone 4 represents the kind of complex environment where innovation emerges as a product of a process of **co-evolution**. In this space many different elements are involved and each affects the other so that it becomes impossible to predict the outcome. Think about the emerging future for healthcare. It's unlikely that the current models (whether publicly or privately funded) will survive long into the future because of the pressures of greater demand, ageing population, spending cuts etc. But any new model is going to be hard to predict because so many factors are involved: technology, markets, global distribution, public/private sector split, increasing lobbying by different interest groups, etc. Instead, we should see it as a complex system in which there is extensive interaction and where what happens in one part of the system will affect the others.

Under conditions like these it would be easy to assume there was nothing we could do and, more importantly for our entrepreneurs, nowhere they could find opportunities except by accident or by waiting until the new game had fully emerged. But we do know something about these situations: there is a body of knowledge around 'complexity theory' which specializes in them. And there are some simple principles which can help us work in innovation space of this kind. In particular, there is a pattern of what is called co-evolution in which different interacting elements begin to converge on a particular solution. (An example in nature is the way ice crystals can form into the particular and organized pattern of a snowflake.)

As this pattern begins to emerge, it can be amplified through feedback, making the signal about the pattern clearer than all the other competing background signals. And gradually the system acquires momentum to move in a particular direction – and a dominant pattern emerges. We see this a lot in what is sometimes called the 'fluid phase' in the innovation lifecycle, when new combinations of technologies and markets swirl around and entrepreneurs try out many different ideas. Eventually, out of the turbulent and unpredictable set of possibilities, a dominant design emerges which sets the pattern for future innovation – think about the motor car or the bicycle as simple examples.

So for entrepreneurs to work in this complex space there are some simple rules:

- Be in the game early: the signals about the emergence of the dominant design will be weak at first and hard to spot from the outside.
- Be in there actively and prepared to experiment: there is no right answer but a lot of playing with possibilities.
- Be prepared for failure: essentially working in zone 4 is about probing and learning, mostly about what won't work.
- Be aware of others in the system, picking up weak signals and amplifying what seems to work.

An Overview of Search Strategies

To summarize, Table 7.3 shows the different approaches – search strategies – which can be used to explore innovation space.

TABLE 7.3   Challenges in navigating innovation search space

Zone	Search challenges
1. 'Business as usual': innovation but under 'steady state' conditions, little disturbance around core business model	Exploit: extend in incremental fashion boundaries of technology and market. Refine and improve. Build close links/strong ties with key players. Favours established organizations with resources: start-up entrepreneurs are looking to spot niches within the mainstream
2. 'Business model as usual': bounded exploration within this frame	Exploration: pushing frontiers of technology and market via advanced techniques. Build close links with key strategic knowledge sources, inside and especially outside the organization. Entrepreneurs with key knowledge assets (e.g. spin-off ventures from a university research lab) can benefit from this search process and link their ideas with the resources which a major organization can bring
3. Alternative frame: taking in new/different elements in environment Variety matching, alternative architectures	Reframing: explore alternative options, introduce new elements. Experimentation and open-ended search Breadth and periphery important. Entrepreneurs have a significant advantage here since they can bring fresh thinking and perspectives to an established game. Mainstream organizations often seek to explore here through setting up internal entrepreneurial groups (e.g. corporate venturing, 'intrapreneurs')
4. Radical 'new to the world' possibilities New architecture around as yet unknown and established elements	Emergence: need to co-evolve with stakeholders • Be in there. • Be in there early. • Be in there actively. Entrepreneurs have advantages here since this resembles the 'fluid' state in the innovation lifecycle and requires flexibility in thinking, tolerance for failure, willingness to take risks, etc. Big problem is the high rate of failure here which established organizations have some capacity to absorb but which is an issue for start-up entrepreneurs

Who?

A key question still to answer is who will do all of this search activity. And it's not simply a matter of sending out people to scout for new possibilities: we also have to think about bringing those ideas back into the organization and doing something with them. In this section, we look briefly at the key people involved and some of the ways in which they can be organized to support effective search.

In particular, it makes sense to understand how new knowledge is found or created and moved around our organization and in its wider environment. This idea of 'knowledge management' has been studied for many years and there are some useful pointers emerging around helpful strategies. (We look in more detail at this question in Chapter 15.)

Table 7.4 gives some examples of knowledge management.

TABLE 7.4 Examples of knowledge management

Who and how	Examples
Use specialists in R&D, market research, futures, etc.	A number of organizations have specialists working in the area of futures and forecasting. On the Portal Helen King describes how the Irish Food Board uses futures to alert the industry to new challenges, and there is also a video of Shell's GameChanger programme
Use scouts and venturers	See Innovation in Action 7.4's discussion of scouts
Mobilize the mainstream	Mobilizing employee ideas and knowledge around incremental product and especially process innovation. This has always been a powerful source of innovation but has been given additional impetus through communication and networking technologies which allow for innovation contests, 'innovation jams' and other approaches bringing more people into the game[4]

Video Clips of interviews with organizations which have been working to mobilize **workplace innovation** are available on the Innovation Portal at **www.innovation-portal.info**

Case Studies of organizations (Kumba Resources, Veeder-Root, NPI, Forte's Bakery, Hosiden) which mobilize workplace innovation are available on the Innovation Portal at **www.innovation-portal.info**

(continued)

TABLE 7.4 *(Continued)*

Who and how	Examples
Voice of the customer	Bringing the 'voice of the customer' into all areas of the organization and using that to focus and draw out relevant ideas and knowledge. Amongst recipes for achieving this are to rotate staff so they spend some time out working with and listening to customers, and the introduction of the concept that 'everybody is someone's customer'

 Tool for enabling this approach, quality function deployment (QFD), is available on the Innovation Portal at **www.innovation-portal.info**

 Activity to help you explore QFD at Lexus is available on the Innovation Portal at **www.innovation-portal.info**

| Social networking | Using our understanding of social networks and how ideas flow within and across organizations. Of particular significance in this context is the role played by various forms of **gatekeeper** in the organization. This concept, which goes back to the pioneering work of Thomas Allen in his studies within the aerospace industry of the 1970s, relates to a model of communication in which ideas flow via key individuals to those who can make use of them in developing innovation[5] |

 Case Study of Pixar, which uses some of these approaches, is available on the Innovation Portal at **www.innovation-portal.info**

| Communities of practice | Using **communities of practice** e.g. Procter and Gamble's successes with 'connect and develop' owe much to their mobilizing rich linkages between people who know things *within* their giant global operations and increasingly outside it. They use 'communities of practice' where people with different knowledge sets can converge around core themes. Intranet technology links around 10 000 people in an internal 'ideas market' – and some of their significant successes have come from making better internal connections. 3M put much of its success down to making and managing connections, and Larry Wendling, Vice President for Corporate Research, called the rich formal and informal |

TABLE 7.4   *(Continued)*

Who and how	Examples
	networking which links the thousands of R&D and market-facing people across the organization the company's 'secret weapon'!

Case Studies of 3M and Procter and Gamble, who use these ideas, are available on the Innovation Portal at **www.innovation-portal.info**

Who and how	Examples
Intrapreneurship	**Intrapreneurship**: mobilizing internal entrepreneurship. A rich source lies in the entrepreneurial ideas of employees: projects which are not formally sanctioned by the business but which build on the energy, enthusiasm and inspiration of people passionate enough to want to try out new ideas. Encouraging this kind of activity is increasingly popular and organizations like 3M and Google make attempts to manage it in a semi-formal fashion, allocating a certain amount of time/space to employees to explore their own ideas. Managing this is a delicate balancing act: on the one hand there is a need to give both permission and resources to enable employee-led ideas to flourish, but on the other there is the risk of these resources being dissipated with nothing to show for them. In many cases there is an attempt to create a culture of what can be termed **bootlegging** in which there is tacit support for projects which go against the grain[6]

Case Study of how 3M uses intrapreneurship to help identify breakthrough innovations is available on the Innovation Portal at **www.innovation-portal.info**

Open Innovation

Building rich and extensive linkages with potential sources of innovation has always been important, for example studies in the UK in the 1950s identified one key differentiator between successful and less-successful innovating firms as the degree to which they were 'cosmopolitan' as opposed to 'parochial' in their approach towards sources of innovation. Entrepreneurs starting up new ventures know the importance of building networks; the essence of what they do in spotting opportunities is to make connections which others may have missed.

This is especially true when we move into our 'explore' spaces on the map. We are going to need different knowledge sets and perspectives – and this requires learning new search strategies. Innovation has always been a multiplayer game, one which involves weaving together many different strands of what could be termed 'knowledge spaghetti' to create something new. What's different about today's context is the sheer volume and distribution of that knowledge; for example it's estimated that nearly $1500 billion of new knowledge is being created every year in public- and private-sector R&D around the world. Keeping track of growth on this scale, especially when this R&D is increasingly globalized and coming from an ever-wider range of players, becomes a major headache even for major technology-based firms.

US professor Henry Chesbrough coined the term **open innovation** to describe the challenge facing even large organizations in keeping track of and accessing external knowledge rather than relying on internally generated ideas. Put simply, open innovation involves the recognition that 'not all the smart guys work for us'.

Of course, it is not simply new R&D knowledge about science and technology which is exploding; there are similar seismic shifts on the market demand side, and on the interests of users in greater customization and even participation in the innovation game. Table 7.5 indicates some of the big shifts in the context for innovation.

TABLE 7.5   Changing context for innovation

Context change	Indicative examples
Acceleration of knowledge production	OECD estimates that close to $1500 bn is spent each year (public and private sector) in creating new knowledge, and hence extending the frontier along which 'breakthrough' technological developments can happen
Global distribution of knowledge production	Knowledge production is increasingly involving new players, especially in emerging market fields like the BRIC (Brazil, Russia, India, China) nations, so the need to search for innovation opportunities across a much wider space arises. One consequence of this is that 'knowledge workers' are now much more widely distributed and concentrated in new locations (e.g. Microsoft's third-largest R&D centre employing thousands of scientists and engineers is now in Shanghai)
Market fragmentation	Globalization has massively increased the range of markets and segments so that these are now widely dispersed and locally varied, putting pressure on innovation search activity to cover much more territory, often far from 'traditional' experiences, such as the 'bottom of the pyramid' conditions in many emerging markets

TABLE 7.5 *(Continued)*

Context change	Indicative examples
Market virtualization	Increasing use of the Internet as a marketing channel means different approaches need to be developed. At the same time emergence of large-scale social networks in cyberspace pose challenges in market research approaches (e.g. Facebook currently has over one billion subscribers). Further challenges arise in the emergence of parallel world communities as a research opportunity (e.g. Second Life now has over six million 'residents')
Rise of active users	Although users have long been recognized as a source of innovation there has been an acceleration in the ways in which this is now taking place (e.g. the growth of Linux has been a user-led open community development). In sectors like media the line between consumers and creators is increasingly blurred (e.g. YouTube has around six billion videos viewed each month but also has over 200 000 new videos uploaded every day from its user base)
Development of technological and social infrastructure	Increasing linkages enabled by information and communications technologies around the Internet and broadband have enabled and reinforced alternative social networking possibilities. At the same time the increasing availability of simulation and prototyping tools has reduced separation between users and producers

Source: Bessant, J. and T. Venables (2008) *Creating Wealth from Knowledge: Meeting the Innovation Challenge*, Cheltenham: Edward Elgar.

What we've been seeing in the first part of the 21st century is a big shift towards what can be termed 'open, collective innovation' (OCI).[7] This involves spreading the search net much more widely and engaging a variety of different external players in the innovation process.

The 'open innovation' model essentially involves opening up the enterprise to flows of knowledge into and out from the organization, as indicated in Figure 7.5.

It offers significant opportunities for entrepreneurs since it implies new ways of connecting – small enterprises with key knowledge assets may become attractive to large players who need that knowledge, while small

Audio Clip of an interview with Richard Philpott discussing open innovation is available on the Innovation Portal at **www.innovation-portal.info**

Video Clip of an interview with David Simoes-Brown discussing open innovation is available on the Innovation Portal at **www.innovation-portal.info**

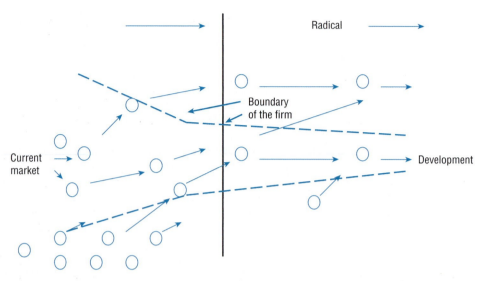

FIGURE 7.5   The open innovation model

Source: Based on Chesbrough, H. (2003) *Open Innovation: The New Imperative for Creating and Profiting from Technology*, Boston: Harvard Business School Press.

enterprises can now access a wide range of knowledge resources providing they are well networked. Inevitably, this raises big questions, though, around how those connections can be made, who and what broker mechanisms come into play – and how intellectual property rights can be managed in such a knowledge-trading world.

Moving to this new model is not without its difficulties. On the one hand, it makes sense to recognize that in a knowledge-rich world 'not all the smart guys work for us'. Even large R&D spenders like Procter and Gamble (annual R&D budget around $3 billion and about 7000 scientists and engineers working globally in R&D) are fundamentally rethinking their models – in their case switching from 'Research and Develop' to 'Connect and Develop' as the dominant slogan, with the strategic aim of moving from closed innovation to sourcing 50% of their innovations from outside the business.

But, on the other, we should recognize the tensions that poses around intellectual property (how do we protect and hold onto knowledge when it is now much more mobile – and how do we access other people's knowledge?), around appropriability (how do we ensure a return on our investment in creating knowledge?) and around the mechanisms to make sure we can find and use relevant knowledge (are we now effectively sourcing it from across the globe and exploring all sorts of unlikely locations?). In this context innovation management emphasis shifts from knowledge creation to knowledge trading and managing knowledge flows.

We return to this theme in more detail in Chapter 10, where we look at the key role being played by networks as a source of ideas and resources.

INNOVATION IN ACTION 7.6

Connect and Develop at P&G

Creating and combining different knowledge sets has always been the name of the game both inside and outside the firm. But there has been a dramatic acceleration in recent years led by major firms like Procter and Gamble, GSK, 3M, Siemens and GE exploring ways of making open innovation happen. For example, P&G in the late 1990s was concerned that its traditional inward-focused model for R&D was declining in effectiveness while representing a major cost. As CEO Alan Lafley explained: 'Our R&D productivity had levelled off, and our innovation success rate—the percentage of new products that met financial objectives—had stagnated at about 35 percent. Squeezed by nimble competitors, flattening sales, lacklustre new launches, and a quarterly earnings miss, we lost more than half our market cap when our stock slid from $118 to $52 a share. Talk about a wake-up call' (*Harvard Business Review*, March 2006).

The company recognized that much important innovation was being carried out in small entrepreneurial firms, or by individuals or in university labs and that other major players like IBM, Cisco, Eli Lilly and Microsoft were beginning to open up their innovation systems.

As a result P&G moved to what it calls 'Connect And Develop' – its version of an innovation process based on the principles of 'open innovation'.

Audio Clip of Roy Sandbach, of P&G, discussing how networking in a large corporation enables innovation is available on the Innovation Portal at **www.innovation-portal.info**

Enabling Open Innovation

The idea behind open innovation is deceptively simple: recognize that not all the smart guys work for you and find ways to connect with others. But making it happen requires a strategic approach, and organizations have spent the past ten years since the publication of Chesbrough's book working out their own particular ways of using the rich opportunities offered by open innovation.[8]

Having a totally open strategy for innovation is rarely the best option, rather different degrees and ways of openness can be pursued successfully, including adopting a totally closed approach.[9] For example, some firms will passively respond to external opportunities when these occur, whereas others will proactively seek out such opportunities, a so-called prospector strategy.[10]

Some have made use of external scouts, sending out ambassadors to look across sectors to find suitable opportunities. Others have made use of third-party organizations offering various kinds of **brokering** and **bridging** activity. Examples include mainstream design

Video Clip of an interview with Michael Bartl of Hyve discussing working in this space is available on the Innovation Portal at **www.innovation-portal.info**

houses like IDEO and ?Whatif! which help to link clients with new ideas and connections on the technology and market side, technology brokers aiming at match-making between different needs and means (both Web-enabled and on a face-to-face basis) and intellectual property transfer agents like the Innovation Exchange which seek to identify, value and exploit internal IP which may be underutilized.

Case Study of Joseph's, a shop in Germany that enables people to contribute ideas for new products and services, is available on the Innovation Portal at **www.innovation-portal.info**

Others have gone further down the road towards creating open-source communities in which co-creation amongst different stakeholders takes place. Google's support for the Android platform is a good example: the expectation is that the collective innovation across such a space allows for rapid acceleration and diffusion of innovation.

INNOVATION IN ACTION 7.7

Models for Open Innovation

A number of models are emerging around enabling open innovation – for example, Nambisan and Sawhney identify four.[11] The 'orchestra' model is typified by a firm like Boeing, which has created an active global network around the 787 Dreamliner with suppliers as both partners and investors and moving from 'build to print' to 'design and build to performance'. In this mode they retain considerable autonomy around their specialist tasks, while Boeing retains the final integrating and decision making, analogous to professional musicians in an orchestra working under a conductor.

By contrast, the 'creative bazaar' model involves more of a 'crowdsourcing' approach in which a major firm goes shopping for innovation inputs – and then integrates and develops them further. Examples here would include aspects of the Innocentive.com approach being used by P&G, Eli Lilly and others, or the Dial Corporation in the US which launched a 'Partners in innovation' website where inventors could submit ideas. BMW's Virtual Innovation Agency operates a similar model.

A third model is what it terms 'Jam central' which involves creating a central vision and then mobilizing a wide variety of players to contribute towards reaching it. It is the kind of approach found in many pre-competitive alliances and consortia where difficult technological or market challenges are used – such as the 5th Generation Computer project in Japan – to focus efforts of many different organizations. Once the challenges are met, the process shifts to an exploitation mode, for example in the 5th Generation programme the pre-competitive efforts by researchers from all the major electronics and IT firms led to generation of over 1000 patents which were then shared out amongst the players and exploited in 'traditional' competitive fashion. Philips deploys a similar model via its InnoHub, which selects a team from internal and external businesses and staff and covering technology, marketing and other elements. It deliberately encourages fusion of people with varied expertise in the hope that this will enhance the chances of 'breakthrough' thinking.

Its fourth model is called 'Mod Station', drawing on a term from the personal computer industry which allows users to make modifications to games and other soft and hardware. This is typified by many open-source projects – such as Sun Microsystems's OpenSPARC, Google's Android developer platform and before that Nokia's release of the Symbian operating system – which open up to the developer community in an attempt to establish an open platform for creating mobile applications. It reflects models used by the BBC, by Lego and many other organizations trying to mobilize external communities and amplify their own research efforts while retaining an ability to exploit the new and growing space.

Other models which could be added include NASA's 'infusion' approach in which a major public agency uses its Innovative Partnerships Programme (IPP) to co-develop key technologies such as robotics. The model is essentially one of drawing in partners who work alongside NASA scientists, a process of 'infusion' in which ideas developed by NASA or by one or more of the partners are worked on. There is particular emphasis on spreading the net widely and seeking partnerships with 'unusual suspects': companies, university departments and others that may not immediately recognize that they have something of value to offer.[12]

Learning to Search

As we saw in Chapter 1, managing innovation is something which individuals and organizations learn to do through a mixture of trial and error, imitation and borrowing of good practices, improvisation, etc. Over time, they accumulate experience about what works best for them, and this becomes a highly specific approach, almost like a personality. The idea of 'routines' – repeated, learnt and embedded patterns of behaviour – very much applies here in the area of search tools. Individuals and organizations develop and refine the tools they use to trawl the innovation space, building on tried-and-tested techniques but also experimenting and adding new ones to deal with new challenges in their search space.

For example, much experience has been gained in how R&D units can be structured to enable a balance between applied research (supporting the 'exploit' type of search) and more wide-ranging, 'blue sky' activities (which facilitate the 'explore' side of the equation). These approaches have been refined further along 'open innovation' lines where the R&D work of others is brought into play, and by ways of dealing with the increasingly global production of knowledge, for example the pharmaceutical giant GSK deliberately pursues a policy of R&D competition across several major facilities distributed around the world.

In similar fashion market research has evolved to produce a rich portfolio of tools for building a deep understanding of user needs – and continues to develop new and further refined techniques, for example empathic design, lead user methods and increasing use of **ethnography**.

The choice of techniques and structures depends on a variety of strategic factors like those explored above, balancing their costs and risks against the quality and quantity of knowledge they bring in. Throughout the book, we stress the idea that managing innovation is a *dynamic* capability, something which needs to be updated and extended on a continuing basis to deal with the 'moving frontier' problem. As markets, technologies, competitors, regulations and all sorts of other elements in a complex environment shift so we need to learn new tricks and sometimes let go of older ones which are no longer appropriate.

The label **absorptive capacity** has been widely used to describe this learning capability and it can be expressed as 'the ability of a firm to recognize the value of new, external information, assimilate it, and apply it'.[13] It's an important concept because it is easy to make the assumption that because there is a rich environment full of potential sources of innovation every organization will find and make use of these. The reality is, of course, that they differ widely in their ability to make use of such trigger signals; for various reasons organizations may find difficulties in growing through acquiring and using new knowledge.

Some may simply be unaware of the need to change, never mind having the capability to manage such change. Such firms – a classic problem of small business growth, for example – differ from those which recognize in some strategic way the need to change, to acquire and use new knowledge but lack the capability to target their search or to assimilate and make effective use of new knowledge once identified. Others may be clear about what they need but lack the capability to find and acquire it. And others may have well-developed routines for dealing with all of these issues and represent resources on which less-experienced firms may draw – as is the case with some major supply chains focused around a core central player.

The key message from research on absorptive capacity is that acquiring and using new knowledge involves multiple and different activities around search, acquisition, assimilation and implementation.[14] It's essentially about learning to learn, building capabilities which allow organizations to repeat the innovation trick. Developing absorptive capacity involves two complementary kinds of learning. Type 1 – adaptive learning – is about reinforcing and establishing relevant routines for dealing with a particular level of environmental complexity and type 2 – generative learning – for taking on new levels of complexity.[15]

 Tool to help an organization reflect on and develop this, absorptive capacity audit, is available on the Innovation Portal at **www.innovation-portal.info**

Chapter Summary

- Faced with a rich environment full of potential sources of innovation, individuals and organizations need a strategic approach to searching for opportunities.

- We can imagine a search space for innovation within which we look for opportunities. There are two dimensions: 'incremental/do better vs. radical/do different innovation' and 'existing frame/new frame'.

- Looking for opportunities can take us into the realms of 'exploit' – innovations built on moving forward form what we already know in a mainly incremental fashion. Or it can involve 'explore' innovation, making risky but sometimes valuable leaps into new fields and opening up innovation space.

- Exploit innovation favours established organizations, and start-up entrepreneurs mostly find opportunities within niches in an established framework.

- Bounded exploration involves radical search but within an established frame. This requires extensive resources, for example in R&D, but although this again favours established organizations there is also scope for knowledge-rich entrepreneurs, for example in high-tech start-up businesses.

- Reframing innovation requires a different mindset, a new way of seeing opportunities – and often favours start-up entrepreneurs. Established organizations find this area difficult to search in because it requires them to let go of the ways they have traditionally worked. In response, many set up internal entrepreneurial groups to bring the fresh thinking they need.

- Exploring at the edge of chaos requires skills in trying to 'manage' processes of co-evolution. Again, this favours start-up entrepreneurs with the flexibility, risk taking and tolerance for failure to create new combinations and the agility to pick up on emerging new trends and ride them.

- Search strategies require a combination of exploit and explore approaches, but these often need different organizational arrangements.

- There are many tools and techniques available to support search in exploit and explore directions; increasingly, the game is being opened up and networks (and networking approaches and technologies) are becoming increasingly important.

- Absorptive capacity – the ability to absorb new knowledge – is a key factor in the development of innovation management capability. It is essentially about learning to learn.

Key Terms Defined

Absorptive capacity   the ability of an organization to take on and use new knowledge from outside.

Bootlegging   innovation projects which take place without the formal backing of the host organization.

Bridging   refers to mechanisms for connecting players in an increasingly open innovation landscape, for example by using innovation markets or contests running across an internet platform.

Brokering   ways of connecting different players in a network, for example linking start-up entrepreneurs with sources of resources.

Co-evolution   situation where multiple elements interact with each other making it impossible to predict their future development. Instead, it emerges as a result of interaction: co-evolution.

Communities of practice   groups of individuals with common interest who cooperate to share knowledge within and across organizations.

Corporate entrepreneurship   attempt on the part of established organizations to recreate entrepreneurial. characteristics like agility, new perspectives and risk taking by licensing a specific group to operate in a different fashion.

Deep diving   deep immersion in the context within which innovations could be used.

Ethnography   approaches to understanding user needs through observation, using approaches similar to those employed by anthropologists.

Exploit   innovation based on doing what we do but better, moving forward along established trajectories.

Explore   innovation involving jumps and leaps into new fields and opening up new space for innovation.

Framing/reframing   the ways in which organizations and individuals make sense of a complex environment by simplifying it, using mental lenses to decide on what they pay attention to and what solutions they look at.

Gatekeeper   person within an organization or network who helps facilitate connections to others.

Intrapreneurship   internal entrepreneurship, as corporate entrepreneurship.

Lead users   early and active users within a population who can contribute ideas which shape the final version of an innovation.

Open innovation   model of innovation which allows for much more emphasis on knowledge flows rather than on knowledge production.

Scouts   individuals or groups who search out new technologies and/or markets.

Workplace innovation   innovation which involves a high proportion of the workforce or other population in contributing their ideas for change.

Discussion Questions

1. Where and how would you organize search for innovation opportunities for the following businesses:
   a. A fast food restaurant chain?
   b. An electronic test equipment maker?
   c. A hospital?
   d. An insurance company?
   e. A new-entrant biotechnology firm?

2. Using the list of innovation sources in Chapter 6, how would you organize search to pick up trigger signals from these?

3. If innovation is increasingly a matter of knowledge management, what sorts of challenges does this approach pose for managing the process?

4. How would you search for innovation opportunities in the public sector? Using examples, indicate how and where it can be an important strategic issue.

5. You are a newly appointed director for a small charity which supports homeless people. How could innovation improve the ways in which your charity operates in terms of finding new opportunities for raising support?

6. What are the challenges which managers face in trying to organize to find a long-term steady stream of incremental innovation ideas?

Further Reading and Resources

The concept of 'exploit' vs. 'explore' was first discussed by James March and has formed the basis for many studies since then; see March, J., 'Exploration and exploitation in organizational learning' (*Organization Science*, 1991, **2**(1), 71–87) and Benner, M.J. and M.L. Tushman, 'Exploitation, exploration, and process management: The productivity dilemma revisited' (*The Academy of Management Review*, 2003, **28**(2), 238).

Tushman and Anderson explore the challenges for organizations in the midst of major technological upheavals (Tushman, M. and P. Anderson, 'Technological discontinuities and organizational environments', *Administrative Science Quarterly*, 1987, **31**(3), 439–65).

The difficulties of reframing are well explored by Day and Shoemaker, who argue the need for 'peripheral vision' amongst entrepreneurs (Day, G. and P. Schoemaker, *Peripheral Vision: Detecting the Weak Signals that Will Make or Break Your Company*, Boston: Harvard Business School Press, 2006). This theme is also picked up in Foster, R. and S. Kaplan, *Creative Destruction* (Harvard University Press, 2002) and Christensen, C., S. Anthony and E. Roth, *Seeing What's Next* (Harvard Business School Press, 2007).

Searching at the frontier is one of the questions addressed by the Discontinuous Innovation Laboratory, a network of around 30 academic institutions and 150 companies, see Augsdorfer *et al.*'s *Discontinuous Innovation* (Imperial College Press, 2014).

Looking at the edge of familiar markets to find unexploited space is discussed in Ulnwick, A., *What Customers Want: Using Outcome-Driven Innovation to Create Breakthrough Products and Services* (McGraw-Hill, 2005) and Kim, W. and R. Mauborgne, *Blue Ocean Strategy: How to Create Uncontested Market Space and Make the Competition Irrelevant* (Harvard Business School Press, 2005).

Open innovation was originated by Henry Chesbrough but has been elaborated in a number of other studies – see, for example, Reichwald, R., A. Huff and K. Moeslein, *Leading Open Innovation* (MIT Press, 2013). Case examples include the Procter and Gamble story, and Alan Lafley's book provides a readable account from the perspective of the CEO (Lafley, A. and R. Charan, *The Game Changer*, Profile, 2008).

The concept of absorptive capacity was originated by Cohen and Levinthal and developed by Zahra and George (Zahra, S.A. and G. George, 'Absorptive capacity: A review, reconceptualization and extension', *Academy of Management Review*, 2002, **27**, 185–94).

References

1. Freeman, C. and L. Soete (1997) *The Economics of Industrial Innovation*, 3rd edn, Cambridge, MA: MIT Press.

2. Abernathy, W. and J. Utterback (1975) A dynamic model of product and process innovation, *Omega*, 3(6): 639–56.

3. Rogers, E. (2003) *Diffusion of Innovations*, 5th edn, New York: Free Press.

4. Bessant, J. (2003) *High Involvement Innovation*, Chichester: John Wiley & Sons Ltd.

5. Allen, T. and G. Henn (2007) *The Organization and Architecture of Innovation*, Oxford: Elsevier.

6. Augsdorfer, P. (1996) *Forbidden Fruit*, Aldershot: Avebury.

7. Bessant, J. and K. Moeslein (2011) *Open Collective Innovation*, London: Advanced Institute of Management Research.

8. Chesbrough, H. (2003) *Open Innovation: The New Imperative for Creating and Profiting from Technology*, Boston: Harvard Business School Press.

9. Enkel, E. and K. Bader (2014) How to balance open and closed innovation: Strategy and culture as influencing factors, in: J. Tidd (ed.), *Open Innovation Research, Management and Practice*, London: Imperial College Press.

10. Nambisan, S. and M. Sawhney (2007) *The Global Brain: Your Roadmap for Innovating Smarter and Faster in a Networked World*, Philadelphia: Wharton School Publishing.

11. Nambisan, S. and M. Sawhney (2007) *The Global Brain: Your Roadmap for Innovating Smarter and Faster in a Networked World*, Philadelphia: Wharton School Publishing.

12. Cheeks, N. (2007) H*ow NASA Uses 'Infusion Partnerships'*, Mount Laurel, NJ: Product Development Management Association, 9–12.

13. Cohen, W. and D. Levinthal (1990) Absorptive capacity: A new perspective on learning and innovation, *Administrative Science Quarterly*, 35(1): 128–52.

14. Zahra, S.A. and G. George (2002) Absorptive capacity: A review, reconceptualization and extension, *Academy of Management Review*, 27: 185–94.

15. Senge, P. (1990) *The Fifth Discipline*, New York: Doubleday.

Deeper Dive explanations of innovation concepts and ideas are available on the Innovation Portal at **www.innovation-portal.info**

Quizzes to test yourself further are available online via the Innovation Portal at **www.innovation-portal.info**

Summary of online resources for Chapter 7 –
all material is available via the Innovation Portal at
www.innovation-portal.info

Cases	**Media**	**Tools**	**Activities**	**Deeper Dives**

Cases	Media	Tools	Activities	Deeper Dives
• Evolution of the bicycle • Tesco • Cerulean • Kumba Resources • NPI • Philips Lighting • Fujifilm • Kodak • Twelve search strategies • Kumba Resources • Veeder-Root • Forte's Bakery • Hosiden • Pixar • 3M • Procter and Gamble • Joseph's	• Patrick McLaughlin • Veeder-Root • Mobilizing workplace innovation • Eric von Hippel • Helen King • Shell's GameChanger programme • Richard Philpott • David Simoes-Brown • Roy Sandbach • Michael Bartl	• Market research toolkit • Continuous improvement toolkit • ADL matrix • Kano method • Lead user methods • Quality function deployment • Absorptive capacity audit	• 4Ps • Adoption and diffusion • Quality function deployment	• Searching for innovation • Open collective innovation • Absorptive capacity

PART III

FINDING THE RESOURCES

more than 20 pages. Begin with an executive summary and include sections on the product, markets, technology, development, production, marketing, human resources, financial estimates with contingency plans and timetable and funding requirements. A typical formal business plan will include:[3]

- details of the product or service
- assessment of the market opportunity
- identification of target customers
- barriers to entry and competitor analysis
- experience, expertise and commitment of the management team
- strategy for pricing, distribution and sales
- identification and planning for key risks
- cash-flow calculation, including break-even points and sensitivity
- financial and other resource requirements of the business.

Most business plans submitted to venture capitalists are strong on the technical considerations, often placing too much emphasis on the technology relative to other issues. As Roberts notes, 'entrepreneurs propose that they can do it better than anyone else, but may forget to demonstrate that anyone wants it'.[4] He identifies a number of common problems with business plans submitted to venture capitalists: marketing plan, management team, technology plan and financial plan. The management team will be assessed against their commitment, experience and expertise, normally in that order. Unfortunately, many potential entrepreneurs place too much emphasis on their expertise, but have insufficient experience in the team, and fail to demonstrate the passion and commitment to the venture (Table 8.1).

There are common serious inadequacies in all four of these areas, but the worst are in marketing and finance. Less than half of the plans examined provide a detailed marketing strategy, and just half include any sales plan. Three-quarters of the plans fail to identify or analyse any potential competitors. As a result most business plans contain only basic financial forecasts, and just 10% conduct any sensitivity analysis on the forecasts. The lack of attention to marketing and competitor analysis is particularly problematic as research indicates that both factors are associated with subsequent success.

 Case Study illustrating the difficulties in developing a business plan, even in mature markets and technologies, Clearvue, is available on the Innovation Portal at **www.innovation-portal.info**

For example, in the early stages many new ventures rely too much on a few major customers for sales, and are therefore very vulnerable commercially. As an extreme example, around half of technology ventures rely on a single customer for more than half of their first-year sales. An overdependence on a small number of customers has three major drawbacks:

- Vulnerability to changes in the strategy and health of the dominant customer.
- A loss of negotiating power, which may reduce profit margins.

TABLE 8.1   Criteria used by venture capitalists to assess proposals

Criteria	European (n = 195)	American (n = 100)	Asian (n = 53)
Entrepreneur able to evaluate and react to risk	3.6	3.3	3.5
Entrepreneur capable of sustained effort	3.6	3.6	3.7
Entrepreneur familiar with the market	3.5	3.6	3.6
Entrepreneur demonstrated leadership ability*	3.2	3.4	3.0
Entrepreneur has relevant track record*	3.0	3.2	2.9
Product prototype exists and functions*	3.0	2.4	2.9
Product demonstrated market acceptance*	2.9	2.5	2.8
Product proprietary or can be protected*	2.7	3.1	2.6
Product is 'high technology'*	1.5	2.3	1.4
Target market has high growth rate*	3.0	3.3	3.2
Venture will stimulate an existing market	2.4	2.4	2.5
Little threat of competition within three years	2.2	2.4	2.4
Venture will create a new market*	1.8	1.8	2.2
Financial return > 10 times within 10 years*	2.9	3.4	2.9
Investment is easily made liquid* (e.g. made public or acquired)	2.7	3.2	2.7
Financial return > 10 times within 5 years*	2.1	2.3	2.1

1 = irrelevant, 2 = desirable, 3 = important, 4 = essential. * Denotes significant at the 0.05 level.

Source: Adapted from Knight, R. (1992) Criteria used by venture capitalists, in: T. Khalil and B. Bayraktar (eds), *Management of Technology III: The Key to Global Competitiveness*, Norcross, GA: Industrial Engineering & Management Press, 574–83.

- Little incentive to develop marketing and sales functions, which may limit future growth.

Therefore, it is essential to develop a better understanding of the market and technological inputs to a business plan. The financial estimates flow from these critical inputs relatively easily, although risk and uncertainty still need to be assessed. This chapter focuses only on the most important, but often poorly executed, aspects of business planning for innovations. We first discuss approaches to forecasting markets and technologies, and then identify how a better understanding of the adoption and diffusion of innovations can help us to develop more successful business plans. Finally, we look at how to assess the risks and resources required to finalize a plan.

ENTREPRENEURSHIP IN ACTION 8.1

What Is the 'Fuzzy Front End', Why Is It Important and How Can It Be Managed?

Technically, new product development (NPD) projects often fail at the end of a development process. The foundations for failure, however, often seem to be established at the very beginning of the NPD process, often referred to as the **fuzzy front end**. Broadly speaking, the fuzzy front end is defined as the period between when an opportunity for a new product is first considered and when the product idea is judged ready to enter formal development. Hence, the fuzzy front end starts with a firm having an idea for a new product and ends with the firm deciding to launch a formal development project or, alternatively, deciding not to launch such a project.

In comparison with the subsequent development phase, knowledge on the fuzzy front end is severely limited. Hence, relatively little is known about the key activities that constitute the fuzzy front end, how these activities can be managed, which actors participate as well as the time needed to complete this phase. Many firms also seem to have great difficulties managing the fuzzy front end in practice. In a sense this is not surprising: the fuzzy front end is a crossroads of complex information processing, tacit knowledge, conflicting organizational pressures and considerable uncertainty and equivocality. In addition, this phase is also often ill defined and characterized by ad hoc decision making in many firms. It is therefore important to identify success factors which allow firms to increase their proficiency in managing the fuzzy front end. This is the purpose of this research note.

In order to increase knowledge on how the fuzzy front end can be better managed, we conducted a large-scale survey of the empirical literature on the fuzzy front end. In total, 39 research articles constitute the base of our review. Analysis of these articles identified 17 success factors for managing the fuzzy front end. The factors are not presented in order of importance, as the present state of knowledge makes such an ordering judgemental at best.

- *The presence of idea visionaries or product champions.* Such persons can overcome stability and inertia and thus secure the progress of an emerging product concept.
- *An adequate degree of formalization.* Formalization promotes stability and reduces uncertainty. The fuzzy front end process should be explicit, widely known among members of the organization, characterized by clear decision-making responsibilities and contain specific performance measures.
- *Idea refinement and adequate screening of ideas.* Firms need mechanisms to separate good ideas from the less good ones, but also to screen ideas by means of both business and feasibility analysis.
- *Early customer involvement.* Customers can help to construct clear project objectives, reduce uncertainty and equivocality, and facilitate the evaluation of a product concept.
- *Internal cooperation among functions and departments.* A new product concept must be able to survive criticism from different functional perspectives, but cooperation among functions

and departments also creates legitimacy for a new concept and facilitates the subsequent development phase.

- *Information processing other than cross-functional integration and early customer involvement.* Firms need to pay attention to product ideas of competitors, as well as legally mandated issues in their emerging product concepts.
- *Senior management involvement.* A pre-development team needs support from senior management to succeed, but senior management can also align individual activities which cut across functional boundaries.
- *Preliminary technology assessment.* Technology assessment means asking early whether the product can be developed, what technical solutions will be required and at what cost. Firms need also to judge whether the product concept, once turned into a product, can be manufactured.
- *Alignment between NPD and strategy.* New concepts must capitalize on the core competence of their firms, and synergy among projects is important.
- *An early and well-defined product definition.* Product concepts are representations of the goals for the development process. A product definition includes a product concept, but in addition provides information about target markets, customer needs, competitors, technology, resources, etc. A well-defined product definition facilitates the subsequent development phase.
- *Beneficial external cooperation with stakeholders other than customers.* Many firms benefit from a 'value-chain perspective' during the fuzzy front end, e.g. through collaboration with suppliers. This factor is in line with the emerging literature on 'open innovation'.
- *Learning from experience capabilities of the pre-project team.* Pre-project team members need to identify critical areas and forecast their influence on project performance, i.e. through learning from experience.
- *Project priorities.* The pre-project team needs to be able to make trade-offs among the competing virtues of scope (product functionality), scheduling (timing) and resources (cost). In addition, the team also needs to use a priority criteria list, i.e. a rank ordering of key product features, should it be forced to disregard certain attributes owing to, say, cost concerns.
- *Project management and the presence of a project manager.* A project manager can lobby for support and resources and coordinate technical as well as design issues.
- *A creative organizational culture.* Such a culture allows a firm to utilize the creativity and talents of employees, as well as maintaining a steady stream of ideas feeding into the fuzzy front end.
- *A cross-functional executive review committee.* A cross-functional team for development is not enough; cross-functional competence is also needed when evaluating product definitions.
- *Product portfolio planning.* The firm needs to assure sufficient resources to develop the planned projects, as well as balancing its portfolio of new product ideas.

Although successful management of the fuzzy front end requires firms to excel in individual factors and activities, this is a necessary rather than sufficient condition. Firms must also be able to integrate or align different activities and factors, as reciprocal interdependencies exist among

(continued)

different success factors. This is often referred to as 'a holistic perspective', 'interdependencies among factors' or simply as 'fit'. To date, however, nobody seems to know exactly which factors should be integrated, and how this should be achieved. In addition, specific guidelines on how to measure performance in the fuzzy front end are also lacking. Hence, only fragments of a 'theory' for managing the fuzzy front end can be said to be in place.

To make things even more complicated, the fuzzy front end process seems to vary not only among firms but also among projects within the same firm where activities, their sequencing, degree of overlap and relative time duration differ from project to project. Therefore, capabilities for managing the fuzzy front end are both highly valuable yet difficult to obtain. Developing firms therefore need first to obtain proficiency in individual success factors. Second, they need to integrate and arrange these factors into a coherent whole aligned to the circumstances of the firm. And finally, they need to master several trade-off situations which we refer to as 'balancing acts'.

As a first balancing act, firms need to ask if the screening of ideas should be made gentle or harsh. On the one hand, firms need to get rid of bad ideas quickly, to save the costs associated with their further development. On the other hand, harsh screening may also kill good ideas too early. Ideas for new products often refine and gain momentum through informal discussion, a fact which forces firms to balance too gentle and too harsh screening. Another balancing act concerns formalization. The basic proposition is that formalization is good because it facilitates transparency, order and predictability. However, in striving to enforce effectiveness, formalization also risks inhibiting innovation and flexibility. Even if evidence is still scarce, the relationship between formality and performance seems to obey an inverted U-shaped curve, where both too little and too much formality has a negative effect on performance. From this it follows that firms need to carefully consider the level of formalization they impose on the fuzzy front end.

A third balancing act concerns the trade-off between uncertainty and equivocality reduction. Market and technological uncertainty can often be reduced through environmental scanning and increased information processing in the development team, but more information often increases the level of equivocality. An equivocal situation is one where multiple meanings exist, and such a situation implies that a firm needs to construct, cohere or enact a reasonable interpretation to be able to move on, rather than to engage in information seeking and analysis. Therefore, firms need to balance their need to reduce uncertainty with the need to reduce equivocality, as trying to reduce one often implies increasing the other. Furthermore, firms need to balance the need for allowing for flexibility in the product definition with the need to push it to closure. A key objective in the fuzzy front end is a clear, robust and unambiguous product definition as such a definition facilitates the subsequent development phase. However, product features often need to be changed during development as market needs change or problems with underlying technologies are experienced. Finally, a final balancing act concerns the trade-off between the competing virtues of innovation and resource efficiency. In essence, this concerns balancing competing value orientations, where innovation and creativity in the front end are enabled by organizational slack and an emphasis on people management, while resource efficiency is enabled by discipline and an emphasis on process management.

In addition, the fuzzy front end process needs to be adapted to the type of product under development. For physical products, different logics apply to assembled and non-assembled products. Emerging research shows that a third logic applies to the development of new service concepts. To conclude, managing the fuzzy front end is indeed no easy task, but can have an enormous positive impact on performance for those firms that succeed.

Case Study illustrating the uncertainties in translating product concept into a business, Gordon Murray Design, is available on the Innovation Portal at **www.innovation-portal.info**

Source: Florén, H. and J. Frishammar (2012) From preliminary ideas to corroborated product definition: Managing the front-end of new product development, *California Management Review*, 54(4), 20–43.

Forecasting Innovation

Forecasting the future has a pretty bad track record, but nevertheless has a central role in business planning for innovation. In most cases the outputs, that is the predictions made, are less valuable than the process of forecasting itself. If conducted in the right spirit, forecasting should provide a framework for gathering and sharing data, debating interpretations and making assumptions, challenges and risks more explicit.

Forecasting the future has a central role in business planning for innovation. In most cases the outputs, that is the predictions made, are less valuable than the process of forecasting itself. If conducted in the right spirit, forecasting should provide a framework for gathering and sharing data, debating interpretations and making assumptions, challenges and risks more explicit.

There are many different methods to support forecasting, each with different benefits and limitations (Table 8.2).

There is no single best method. In practice, there will be a trade-off between the cost, time and robustness of a forecast. The most appropriate choice of forecasting method will depend on:

- what we are trying to forecast
- rate of technological and market change
- availability and accuracy of information
- the company's planning horizon
- the resources available for forecasting.

In practice, there will be a trade-off between the cost and robustness of a forecast. The more common methods of forecasting, such as trend extrapolation and time series, are of limited use for new products, because of the lack of past data. However, regression analysis can be used to identify the main factors driving demand for a given product, and therefore provide some estimate of future demand, given data on the underlying drivers.

TABLE 8.2 Types, uses and limitations of different methods of forecasting

Method	Uses	Limitations
Trend extrapolation	Short-term, stable environment	Relies on past data and assumes past patterns
Product and technology road mapping	Medium-term, stable platform and clear trajectory	Incremental, fails to identify future uncertainties
Regression, econometric models and simulation	Medium-term, where relationship between independent and dependent variables understood	Identification and behaviour of independent variables limited
Customer and marketing methods	Medium-term, product attributes and market segments understood	Sophistication of users, limitation of tools to distinguish noise and information
Benchmarking	Medium-term, product and process improvement	Identifying relevant benchmarking candidates
Delphi and experts	Long-term, consensus-building	Expensive, experts disagree or consensus wrong
Scenarios	Long-term, high uncertainty	Time-consuming, unpalatable outcomes

For example, a regression could express the likely demand for the next generation of digital mobile phones in terms of rate of economic growth, price relative to competing systems, rate of new business formation, and so on. Data are collected for each of the chosen variables and coefficients for each derived from the curve that best describes the past data. Thus, the reliability of the forecast depends a great deal on selecting the right variables in the first place. The advantage of regression is that, unlike simple extrapolation or time-series analysis, the forecast is based on cause and effect relations. Econometric models are simply bundles of regression equations, including their interrelationship. However, regression analysis is of little use where future values of an explanatory value are unknown or where the relationship between the explanatory and forecast variables may change.

Leading indicators and analogues can improve the reliability of forecasts, and are useful guideposts to future trends in some sectors. In both cases there is a historical relationship between two trends. For example, new business start-ups may be a leading indicator of the demand for fax machines in six months' time. Similarly, business users of mobile telephones may be an analogue for subsequent patterns of domestic use.

Such normative techniques are useful for estimating the future demand for existing products, or perhaps

Tools including forecasting techniques, such as scenario planning and the Delphi method, are available on the Innovation Portal at **www.innovation-portal.info**

alternative technologies or novel niches, but are of limited utility in the case of more radical systems innovation. Exploratory forecasting, in contrast, attempts to explore the range of future possibilities. The most common methods are:

Audio Clip of Helen King of the Irish Food Board talking about forecasting to help shape innovation priorities within the sector is available on the Innovation Portal at **www.innovation-portal.info**

- customer or market surveys
- internal analysis, e.g. brainstorming
- Delphi or expert opinion
- scenario development.

ENTREPRENEURSHIP IN ACTION 8.2

Limits of Forecasting

A number of predictions of future innovations were made by government agencies and consultants in the 1960s. Several predictions did become technological realities, such as electric cars, fuel cells and using grains for fuel, but even these took much longer to become commercial products than predicted, more than fifty years rather than the forecast of less than a decade. Moreover, most of the predictions have never materialized, including:

- Turbine cars
- Jet-powered ships
- Family helicopters
- Home dry cleaner
- Tooth decay vaccine
- End of cinema
- Plastic housing
- Passenger rockets (yet!)

Customer or Market Surveys

Most companies conduct customer surveys of some sort. In consumer markets this can be problematic simply because customers are unable to articulate their future needs. For example, Apple's iPod was not the result of extensive market research or customer demand, but largely because of the vision and commitment of Steve Jobs. In industrial markets, customers tend to be better equipped to communicate their future requirements, and consequently business-to-business innovations often originate from customers. Companies can also consult their direct sales force, but these may not always be the best guide to future customer requirements. Information is often filtered in terms of existing products and services, and biased in terms of current sales performance rather than long-term development potential.

There is no 'one best way' to identify novel niches, but rather a range of alternatives. For example, where new products or services are very novel or complex, potential users may not be aware of, or able to articulate, their needs. In such cases, traditional methods of market research are of little use, and there will be a greater burden on developers of radical new products and services to 'educate' potential users.

Our own research confirms that different managerial processes, structures and tools are appropriate for routine and novel development projects. We discuss this in detail in Chapter 9, when we examine new product and service development. For example, in terms of frequency of use, the most common methods used for high novelty projects are segmentation, prototyping, market experimentation and industry experts, whereas for the less novel projects the most common methods are partnering customers, trend extrapolation and segmentation. The use of market experimentation and industry experts may be expected where market requirements or technologies are uncertain, but the common use of segmentation for such projects is harder to justify. However, in terms of usefulness, there are statistically significant differences in the ratings for segmentation, prototyping, industry experts, market surveys and latent needs analysis. Segmentation is more effective for routine development projects, and prototyping, industry experts, focus groups and latent needs analysis are all more effective for novel development projects.[5]

Internal Analysis (e.g. Brainstorming)

Structured idea generation, or brainstorming, aims to solve specific problems or to identify new products or services. Typically, a small group of experts are gathered together and allowed to interact. A chairman records all suggestions without comment or criticism. The aim is to identify, but not evaluate, as many opportunities or solutions as possible. Finally, members of the group vote on the various suggestions. The best results are obtained when representatives from different functions are present, but this can be difficult to manage. Brainstorming does not produce a forecast as such, but can provide useful input to other types of forecasting.

We discussed a range of approaches to creative problem-solving and idea generation in Chapter 5. Most of these are relevant here, and include ways of:[6]

- *Understanding the problem.* The active construction by the individual or group through analysing the task at hand (including outcomes, people, context and methodological options) to determine whether and when deliberate problem-structuring efforts are needed. This stage includes constructing opportunities, exploring data and framing problems.
- *Generating ideas.* To create options in answer to an open-ended problem. This includes generating and focusing phases. During the generating phase of this stage, the person or group produces many options (fluent thinking), a variety of possible options (flexible thinking), novel or unusual options (original thinking) or a number of detailed or refined options (elaborative thinking). The focusing phase provides an opportunity for examining, reviewing, clustering and selecting promising options.

- *Planning for action.* This is appropriate when a person or group recognizes a number of interesting or promising options that may not necessarily be useful, valuable or valid. The aim is to make or develop effective choices, and to prepare for successful implementation and social acceptance.

External Assessment, e.g. Delphi

The opinion of outside experts, or **Delphi method,** is useful where there is a great deal of uncertainty or for long time horizons.[7] Delphi is used where a consensus of expert opinion is required on the timing, probability and identification of future technological goals or consumer needs and the factors likely to affect their achievement. It is best used in making long-term forecasts and revealing how new technologies and other factors could trigger discontinuities in technological trajectories. The choice of experts and the identification of their level and area of expertise are important; the structuring of the questions is even more so. The relevant experts may include suppliers, dealers, customers, consultants and academics. Experts in non-technological fields can be included to ensure that trends in economic, social and environmental fields are not overlooked.

The Delphi method begins with a postal survey of expert opinion on what the future key issues will be, and the likelihood of the developments. The response is then analysed, and the same sample of experts resurveyed with a new, more focused questionnaire. This procedure is repeated until some convergence of opinion is observed, or conversely if no consensus is reached. The exercise usually consists of an iterative process of questionnaire and feedback among the respondents; this process finally yields a Delphi forecast of the range of experts' opinions on the probabilities of certain events occurring by a quoted time. The method seeks to nullify the disadvantage of face-to-face meetings at which there could be deference to authority or reputation, a reluctance to admit error, a desire to conform or differences in persuasive ability. All of these could lead to an inaccurate consensus of opinion. The quality of the forecast is highly dependent on the expertise and calibre of the experts; how the experts are selected and how many should be consulted are important questions to be answered. If international experts are used, the exercise can take a considerable length of time or the number of iterations may have to be curtailed. Although seeking a consensus may be important, adequate attention should be paid to views that differ radically 'from the norm' as there may be important underlying reasons to justify such maverick views. With sufficient design, understanding and resources, most of the shortcomings of the Delphi method can be overcome and it is a popular technique, particularly for national foresight programmes.

In Europe, governments and transnational agencies use Delphi studies to help formulate policy, usually under the guise of 'Foresight' exercises. In Japan, large companies and the government routinely survey expert opinion in order to reach some consensus in those areas with the greatest potential for long-term development. Used in this way, the Delphi method can to a large extent become a self-fulfilling prophecy.

Scenario Development

Scenarios are internally consistent descriptions of alternative possible futures, based upon different assumptions and interpretations of the driving forces of change.[8] Inputs include quantitative data and analysis, and qualitative assumptions and assessments, such as societal, technological, economic, environmental and political drivers. Scenario development is not, strictly speaking, prediction, as it assumes that the future is uncertain and that the path of current developments can range from the conventional to the revolutionary. It is particularly good at incorporating potential critical events which may result in divergent paths or branches being pursued.

Scenario development can be normative or explorative. The normative perspective defines a preferred vision of the future and outlines different pathways from the goal to the present. For example, this is commonly used in energy futures and sustainable futures scenarios. The explorative approach defines the drivers of change, and creates scenarios from these without explicit goals or agendas.

For scenarios to be effective they need to be inclusive, plausible and compelling (as opposed to being exclusive, implausible or obvious), as well as being challenging to the assumptions of the stakeholders. They should make the assumptions and inputs used explicit, and form the basis of a process of discussion, debate, policy, strategy and ultimately action. The output is typically two or three contrasting scenarios, but the process of development and discussion of scenarios is much more valuable.

A strong scenario will be:

- *Consistent.* Each scenario must be internally logical and consistent to be credible.
- *Plausible.* To be persuasive and support action the scenarios and underlying assumptions must be realistic.
- *Transparent.* The assumptions, sources and goals should be made explicit. Without such transparency, emotive or doomsday-style scenarios with catchy titles can be convincing but highly misleading.
- *Differentiated.* Scenarios should be structurally or qualitatively different, in terms of assumptions and outcomes, not simply degree or magnitude. Probability assessment of scenarios should be avoided, such as 'most or least probable'. Different subjective assessments of probability will be made by different stakeholders, so probability assessment can close rather than open debate on the range of possible futures.
- *Communicable.* Typically develop between three and five scenarios, each with vivid titles to promote memory and dissemination.
- *Practical, to support action.* Scenarios should be an input to strategic or policy decision making and so should have clear implications and recommendations for action.

INNOVATION IN ACTION 8.1

Internet Scenarios at Cisco

Cisco develops much of the infrastructure for the Internet and so has a strategic need to explore potential future scenarios. However, almost all organizations rely on the Internet, so these scenarios are relevant to most, including those who provide technology, connectivity, devices, software, content or services.

They began with three focal questions:

1. What will the Internet be like in 2025?
2. How much bigger will the Internet have grown from today's two billion users and $3 trillion market?
3. Will the Internet have achieved its full potential to connect the world's entire population in ways that advance global prosperity, business productivity, education and social interaction?

Next, they then identified three critical drivers:

1. Size and scope of broadband network build out.
2. Incremental or breakthrough technological progress.
3. Unbridled or constrained demand from Internet users.

This analysis resulted in four contrasting scenarios:

- *Fluid Frontiers.* The Internet becomes pervasive, connectivity and devices are ever-more available and affordable while global entrepreneurship and competition create a wide range of diverse businesses and services.
- *Insecure Growth.* Internet demand stalls because users fear security breaches and cyber-attacks result in increasing regulation.
- *Short of the Promise.* Prolonged economic stagnation in many countries reduces the diffusion of the Internet, with no compensating technological breakthroughs.
- *Bursting at the Seams.* Demand for IP-based services is boundless, but capacity constraints and occasional bottlenecks create a gap between the expectations and reality of Internet use.

If you're interested in the implications and potential strategies which flow from these four scenarios, see the full report on the Cisco website.

Source: Olsen, E. (2011) *Strategic Planning Kit for Dummies*, Chichester: John Wiley & Sons Ltd, http://www.dummies.com/how-to/content/strategic-planning-case-study-ciscos-internet-scen.html, accessed 20th December 2014.

Organizations using scenario techniques confirm that these are useful to explore future risks in the business environment, to identify trends, understand interdependent forces and to evaluate the implications of different strategic decisions. Building scenarios with broad organizational inputs helps to stretch people's thinking collectively and individually.[9]

The concept of an entrepreneurial 'pivot' has become popular in research and practice. The term is adapted from financial investment analysis, but essentially describes how young (and sometimes not

Case Study of VeryPC, which is a good example of the need to learn from (initial) failure, is available on the Innovation Portal at **www.innovation-portal.info**

Audio Clip of Minimonos founder Melissa Clark-Reynolds discussing the novel business model she developed for her new venture is available on the Innovation Portal at **www.innovation-portal.info**

so young) organizations often have to challenge their assumptions, revise their initial plans and change direction and business model.[10] We discuss business model innovation in Chapter 16, but the idea of a pivot is relevant here because any business plan is simply work in progress, and has to be revised in response to feedback from the environment, such as customer responses, competitor behaviour and regulatory challenges and new opportunities. So the key to a successful pivot is to test the model continually, adapting and adjusting as necessary.[11]

Assessing Risk and Recognizing Uncertainty

Dealing with **risk** and **uncertainty** is central to the assessment of most innovative projects. It is usually considered possible to estimate risk, either qualitatively – high, medium, low – or ideally by probability estimates. Uncertainty is by definition unknowable, but nonetheless the fields and degree of uncertainty should be identified to help to select the most appropriate methods of assessment and plan for contingencies. Traditional approaches to assessing risk focus on the probability of foreseeable risks, rather than true uncertainty, or complete ignorance – what Donald Rumsfeld memorably called the 'unknown unknowns' (12th February 2002, US Department of Defense news briefing).

Research on new product development and R&D project management has identified a broad range of strategies for dealing with risk. Both individual characteristics and organizational climate influence perceptions of risk and propensities to avoid, accept or seek risks. Formal techniques such as failure mode and effects analysis (FMEA), potential problem analysis (PPA) and fault tree analysis (FTA) have a role, but the broader signals and support from the organizational climate are more important than the specific tools or methods used.

Tools for assessing risk, both at the project and portfolio levels, are available on the Innovation Portal at **www.innovation-portal.info**

For example, too many organizations emphasize project management in order to contain internal risks in the organization, but as a result fail to identify or exploit opportunities to take acceptable risks and to innovate.

There are many approaches to risk assessment, but the most common issues to be managed include:

- probabilistic estimates of technical and commercial success
- psychological (cognitive) and sociological perceptions of risk.

A number of approaches exist to help entrepreneurs assess risk in a balanced way.

Risk as Probability

Research indicates that 30–45% of all projects fail to be completed, and over half of projects overrun their budgets or schedules by up to 200%. Figure 8.1 presents the results of a survey

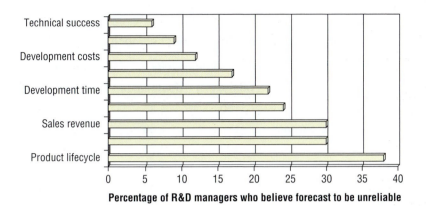

FIGURE 8.1   Managers' perceptions of sources of uncertainty

Source: Based on data from Freeman, C. and L. Soete (1997) *The Economics of Innovation*, Cambridge, MA: MIT Press.

of R&D managers. While most appear to be relatively confident when predicting technical issues such as development time and costs, a much smaller proportion are confident when forecasting the commercial aspects of the projects.

We examined how commonly different approaches to project assessment were used in practice. We surveyed 50 projects in 25 companies, and assessed how often different criteria were used and how useful they were thought to be. Table 8.3 summarizes some of the results. Clearly, probabilistic estimates of technical and commercial success are near universal, and considered to be of critical importance in all types of project assessment. These are usually combined with some form of financial assessment, and fit with the company strategy and capabilities.

Given the complexities involved, the outcomes of investments in innovation are uncertain, so that the forecasts (of costs, prices, sales volume, etc.) that underlie project and programme evaluations can be unreliable. According to Joseph Bower, management finds it easier, when appraising investment proposals, to make more accurate forecasts of reductions in production cost than of expansion in sales, while their ability to forecast the financial consequences of new product introductions is very limited indeed.[12] This last conclusion is confirmed by the study by Edwin Mansfield and his colleagues of project selection in large US firms.[13] By comparing project forecasts with outcomes, Mansfield showed that managers find it difficult to pick technological and commercial winners:

- Probability of *technical* success of projects $(P_t) = 0.80$
- Subsequent probability of *commercial* success $(P_c) = 0.20$
- Combined probability for all stages: $0.8 \times 0.2 = 0.16$.

He also found that managers and technical managers cannot predict accurately the development costs, time periods, markets and profits of R&D projects. On average, costs were

TABLE 8.3 Use and usefulness of criteria project screening and selection

	High novelty		Low novelty	
	Usage (%)	Usefulness	Usage (%)	Usefulness
Probability of technical success	100	4.37	100	4.32
Probability of commercial success	100	4.68	95	4.50
Market share*	100	3.63	84	4.00
Core competencies*	95	3.61	79	3.00
Degree of internal commitment	89	3.82	79	3.67
Market size	89	3.76	84	3.94
Competition	89	3.76	84	3.81
NPV/IRR	79	3.47	68	3.92
Payback period/break-even*	79	3.20	58	4.27

Usefulness score: 5 = critical; 0 = irrelevant.

* Denotes difference in usefulness rating is statistically significant at 5% level.

Source: Adapted from Tidd, J. and K. Bodley (2002) Effect of novelty on new product development processes and tools, *R&D Management*, **32**(2), 127–38.

greatly *underestimated*, and time periods *overestimated* by 140–280% in incremental product improvements, and by 350–600% in major new products. Other studies have found that:

- About half of business R&D expenditure is on *failed* R&D projects. The higher rate of success in *expenditures* than in *projects* reflects the weeding-out of unsuccessful projects at their early stages and before large-scale commercial commitments are made to them.
- R&D scientists and engineers are often deliberately overoptimistic in their estimates, in order to give the illusion of a high rate of return to accountants and managers.

Trying to get involved in the right projects is worth an effort, both to avoid wasting time and resources in meaningless activities, and to improve the chances of success. Project appraisal and evaluation aims to:

1. Profile and gain an overall understanding of potential projects.
2. Prioritize a given set of projects, and where necessary reject projects.
3. Monitor projects, e.g. by following up the criteria chosen when the project was selected.
4. Where necessary, terminate a project.
5. Evaluate the results of completed projects.
6. Review successful and unsuccessful projects to gain insights and improve future project management, i.e. learning.

Project evaluation usually assumes there is a choice of projects to pursue, but where there is no choice project evaluation is still important to help to assess the opportunity costs and what could be expected from pursuing a project. Different situations and contexts demand different approaches to project evaluation. We argued earlier that complexity and uncertainty are two of the most important dimensions for assessing projects. Different types of project will demand specific techniques, or at least different criteria for assessment. A large number of techniques have been developed over the years, and are still being developed and used today. Most of these can be described by means of some common elements which form the core of any project evaluation technique:

- *Inputs* into the assessment include likely costs and benefits in financial terms, probability of technical and market success, market attractiveness and the strategic importance to the organization.
- *Weighting*: as certain data may be given more relevance than others (e.g. of market inputs compared with technical factors), in order to reflect the company's strategy or the company's particular views. The data are then processed to arrive at the outcomes.
- *Balancing* a range of projects, as the relative value of a project with respect to other projects, is an important factor in situations of competition for limited resources. Portfolio management techniques are specifically devoted to deal with this factor.

Economic and **cost–benefit approaches** are usually based on a combination of expected utility or **Bayesian analysis** assumptions. Expected utility theory can take into account probabilistic estimates and subjective preferences, and therefore deals well with risk aversion, but in practice utility curves are almost impossible to construct and individual preferences are different and highly subjective. Bayesian probability is excellent at incorporating the effects of new information, as we discussed earlier under the diffusion of innovations, but is very sensitive to the choice of relevant inputs and the weights attached to these.

As a result no technique should be allowed to determine outcomes, as these decisions are a management responsibility. Many techniques used today are totally or partially software based, which has some additional benefits in automating the process. In any case, the most important issue, for any method, is the manager's interpretation.

There is no single best technique. The extent to which different techniques for project evaluation can be used will depend upon the nature of the project, the information availability, the company's culture and several other factors. This is clear from the variety of techniques that are theoretically available and the extent to which they have been used in practice. In any case, no matter which technique is selected by a company, it should be implemented, and probably adapted, according to the particular needs of that organization. Most of the techniques in practical use incorporate a mixture of financial assessment and human judgement.

Perceptions of Risk

Probability estimates are only the starting point of risk assessment. Such relatively objective criteria are usually significantly moderated by psychological (cognitive) perceptions and bias, or overwhelmed altogether by sociological factors, such as peer pressure and cultural context.

Studies suggest that different people (and animals) have different perceptions and tolerances for risk taking. For example, a study comparing the behaviours of chimpanzees and bonobo apes found that the chimps were more prepared to gamble and take risks.[14] At first sight this appears to support the personality explanation for risk taking, but actually the two types of ape share more than 99% of their DNA. A more likely explanation is the very different environments in which they have evolved: in the chimp environment, food is scarce and uncertain, but in the bonobo habitats, food is plentiful. We are not suggesting that entrepreneurs are chimp-like or accountants ape-like but rather that experience and context have a profound influence on the assessment of, and appetite for, risk.

At the individual, cognitive level, risk assessment is characterized by overconfidence, loss aversion and bias. Overconfidence in our ability to make accurate assessments is a common failing, and results in unrealistic assumptions and uncritical assessment. Loss aversion is well documented in psychology, and essentially means that we tend to prefer to avoid loss rather than to risk gain. Finally, cognitive bias is widespread and has profound implications for the identification and assessment of risk. Cognitive bias results in our seeking and overemphasizing evidence which supports our beliefs and reinforces our bias, but at the same time leads us to avoid and undervalue any information which contradicts our view. Therefore, we need to be aware of and challenge our own biases, and encourage others to debate and critique our data, methods and decisions.

Studies of research and development confirm that measures of cognitive ability are associated with project performance. In particular, differences in reflection, reasoning, interpretation and sense making influence the quality of problem formulation, evaluation and solution, and therefore ultimately the performance of research and development. A common weakness is the oversimplification of problems characterized by complexity or uncertainty, and the simplification of problem-framing and evaluation of alternatives. This includes adopting a single prior hypothesis, selective use of information that supports this, and devaluing alternatives, and illusion of control and predictability. Similarly, marketing managers are likely to share similar cognitive maps, and make the same assumptions concerning the relative importance of different factors contributing to new product success, such as the degree of customer orientation versus competitor orientation, and the implications of relationship between these factors, such as the degree of interfunctional coordination. So the evidence indicates the importance of cognitive processes at the senior management, functional, group and individual levels of an organization. More generally, problems of limited cognition include:[15]

- *Reasoning by analogy*, which oversimplifies complex problems.
- *Adopting a single, prior hypothesis bias*, even where information and trails suggest this is wrong.
- *Limited problem set*, the repeated use of a narrow problem-solving strategy.
- *Single outcome calculation*, which focuses on a simple single goal and a course of action to achieve it, while denying value trade-offs.
- *Illusion of control and predictability*, based on an overconfidence in the chosen strategy, a partial understanding of the problem and limited appreciation of the uncertainty of the environment.
- *Devaluation of alternatives*, emphasizing the negative aspects of alternatives.

At the group or social level, other factors also influence our perception and response to risk. How managers assess and manage risk is also a social and political process. It is influenced by prior experience of risk, perceptions of capability, status and authority, and the confidence and ability to communicate with relevant people at the appropriate times. In the context of managing innovation, risk is less about personal propensity for risk taking or rational assessments of probability and more about the interaction of experience, authority and context. In practice, managers deal with risk in different ways in different situations. General strategies include delaying or delegating decisions, or sharing risk and responsibilities. Generally, when managers are performing well, and achieving their targets, they have less incentive to take risks. Conversely, when under pressure to perform, managers will often accept higher risks, unless these threaten their survival in the firm.

The inherent uncertainty in some projects limits the ability of managers to predict the outcomes and benefits of projects. In such cases changes to project plans and goals are commonplace, being driven by external factors, such as technological breakthroughs or changes in markets, as well as internal factors, such as changes in organizational goals. Together the impact of changes to project plans and goals can overwhelm the benefits of formal project planning and management.

Anticipating the Resources

Given their mathematical skills, one might have expected R&D managers to be enthusiastic users of quantitative methods for allocating resources to innovative activities. The evidence suggests otherwise: practising R&D managers have been sceptical for a long time. An exhaustive report by practising European managers on R&D project evaluation classifies and assesses more than 100 methods of evaluation and presents 21 case studies on their use.[16] However, it concludes that no method can guarantee success, that no single approach to preevaluation meets all circumstances and that, whichever method is used, the most important outcome of a properly structured evaluation is improved communication. These conclusions reflect three of the characteristics of investments in innovative activities:

- *They are uncertain*, so that success cannot be assured.
- *They involve different stages* that have different outputs that require different methods of evaluation.
- *Many of the variables in an evaluation cannot be reduced to a reliable set of figures* to be plugged into a formula, but depend on expert judgements, hence the importance of communication, especially between the corporate functions concerned with R&D and related innovative activities on the one hand and with the allocation of financial resources on the other.

Financial Assessment of Projects

As we showed earlier, financial methods are still the most commonly used method of assessing innovative projects, but usually in combination with other, often more qualitative, approaches.

The financial methods range from simple calculation of payback period or return on investment to more complex assessments of net present value (NPV) through discounted cash flow (DCF).

Project appraisal by means of DCF is based on the concept that money today is worth more than money in the future. This is not because of the effect of inflation but reflects the difference in potential investment earnings, that is the opportunity cost of the capital invested.

The NPV of a project is calculated using:

$$NPV = \sum_{0}^{T} P_t/(1 + i)^t - C$$

where:

P_t = Forecast cash flow in time period t
T = Project life
i = Expected rate of return on securities equivalent in risk to project being evaluated
C = Cost of project at time $t = 0$

In practice, rather than use this formula, it is easy to create standard NPV templates in a spreadsheet package such as Excel.

A simple checklist could be one made up of a range of factors which have been formed to affect the success of a project and need to be considered at the outset. In the evaluation procedure a project is evaluated against each of these factors using a linear scale, usually 1 to 5 or 1 to 10. The factors can be weighted to indicate their relative importance to the organization.

The value in this technique lies in its simplicity, but by the appropriate choice of factors it is possible to ensure that the questions address, and are answered by, all functional areas. When used effectively, this guarantees a useful discussion, an identification and clarification of areas of disagreement and a stronger commitment, by all involved, to the ultimate outcome. Table 8.4 shows an example of a checklist, developed by the Industrial Research Institute, which can be adapted to almost any type of project.

TABLE 8.4 List of potential factors for project evaluation

	Score (1–5)	Weight (%)	S × W
Corporate objectives			
Fits into overall objectives and strategy			
Corporate image			
Marketing and distribution			
Size of potential market			
Capability to market product			
Market trend and growth			
Customer acceptance			
Relationship with existing markets			

TABLE 8.4 *(Continued)*

	Score (1–5)	Weight (%)	S × W
Market share			
Market risk during development period			
Pricing trend, proprietary problem, etc.			
Complete product line			
Quality improvement			
Timing of introduction of new product			
Expected product sales life			
Production			
Cost savings			
Capability of manufacturing product			
Facility and equipment requirements			
Availability of raw material			
Manufacturing safety			
Research and development			
Likelihood of technical success			
Cost			
Development time			
Capability of available skills			
Availability of R&D resources			
Availability of R&D facilities			
Patent status			
Compatibility with other projects			
Regulatory and legal factors			
Potential product liability			
Regulatory clearance			
Financial			
Profitability			
Capital investment required			
Annual (or unit) cost			
Rate of return on investment			
Unit price			
Payout period			
Utilization of assets, cost reduction and cash-flow			

As with all techniques, there is a danger that project appraisal becomes a routine that a project has to suffer rather than an aid to designing and selecting appropriate projects. If this happens, people may fail to apply the techniques with the rigour and honesty required, and can waste time and energy trying to 'cheat' the system. Care needs to be taken to communicate the reasons behind the methods and criteria used, and where necessary these should be adapted to different types of project and to changes in the environment (Table 8.5).[17]

INNOVATION IN ACTION 8.2

Limitations of Conventional Project and Product Assessment

Clayton Christensen and colleagues argue that three commonly used means of assessment discourage expenditure on innovation. First, conventional means of assessing projects, such as discounted cash flow (DCF) and the treatment of fixed costs, favour the incremental exploitation of existing assets rather than the more risky development of new capabilities. Second, methods such as the stage-gate process demand data on estimated markets, revenues and costs, which are much more difficult to generate for more radical innovations. Finally, senior managers and publically quoted firms are typically assessed by improvements in the earning per share (EPS), which encourages short-term investments and returns – most institutional investors hold shares for only 10 months in the USA, and the tenure of CEOs is shrinking.

While they appreciate the benefits of such financial methods of assessment, they argue that such techniques should be adjusted to redress the balance for risk taking and expenditure on innovation. For example, when using DCF, comparative assessments should be made with the option of doing nothing, or not investing in an innovative project, rather than assuming a decision not to invest will result in no loss of competitiveness. Similarly, for the stage-gate process, they propose focusing less on the (unreliable) quantitative forecasts and much more on challenging and testing the assumptions made in business planning. Finally, they believe that the use of short-term measurers such as EPS is no longer appropriate because it provides perverse incentives. The original rationale for this type of approach was the principal–agent problem: to try to align the interests of the principals (owners/shareholders) and their agents (managers). However, the growth of the collective institutional ownership of most public firms has created an agent–agent problem, and the interests of the agents need to be more aligned to promote innovation.

 Audio Clip exploring how Web-based businesses can reduce risk by expanding using a scalable business model, Glasses Direct, is available on the Innovation Portal at **www.innovation-portal.info**

Source: Christensen, C.M., S.P. Kaufmann and W.C. Shih (2008) Innovation killers: How financial tools destroy your capacity to do new things, *Harvard Business Review*, **January**, 98–105.

TABLE 8.5   Approaches to project selection

Selection approach	Advantages	Disadvantages
Intuition	Fast	Lacks evidence and analysis. May be wrong
Simple qualitative techniques, e.g. checklists and decision matrix	Fast and easy to share. Provides a useful focus for initial discussions	Lacks factual information and little or no quantitative dimension
Financial measures, e.g. return on investment or payback time	Fast and uses some simple measurement	Doesn't take account of other benefits which may come from the innovation, e.g. learning about new technologies, markets
Complex financial measures, e.g. 'real options' approach	Takes account of learning dimension, e.g. the benefits from projects may lie in improved knowledge which we can use elsewhere as well as in direct profits	More complex and time-consuming. Difficult to predict the benefits which might arise from taking options on the future
Multidimensional measures, e.g. decision matrix	Compares on several dimensions to build an overall score for attractiveness	Allows consideration of different kinds of benefits but level of analysis may be limited
Portfolio methods and business cases	Compares between projects on several dimensions and provides detailed evidence around core themes	Takes a long time to prepare and present

Tools to help with strategic selection, including options, decision matrix, portfolio methods and bubble charts, are available on the Innovation Portal at **www.innovation-portal.info**

Chapter Summary

- The process of innovation is much more complex than technology responding to market signals. Effective business planning under conditions of uncertainty demands a thorough understanding and management of the dynamics of innovation, including conception, development, adoption and diffusion.

- The adoption and diffusion of an innovation depend on the characteristics of the innovation, the nature of potential adopters and the process of communication. The relative advantage, compatibility, complexity, trial-ability and observability of an innovation all affect the rate of diffusion.

- Forecasting the development and adoption of innovations is difficult, but participative methods such as Delphi and scenario planning are highly relevant to innovation and sustainability. In such cases the process of forecasting, including consultation and debate, is probably more important than the precise outcomes of the exercise.

Key Terms Defined

Bayesian analysis   expresses uncertainty about unknown parameters probabilistically, and updates these likelihoods as new knowledge becomes available.

Cost–benefit (or benefit–cost) approach   is simply a systematic comparison of costs and benefits which requires all activities to be captured and given a value. This should include the cost of failure, the cost of not pursuing the project and the opportunity costs, that is preventing an alternative plan.

Delphi method   is a forecasting method which surveys expert opinion on the timing, probability and identification of future technological goals or consumer needs and the factors likely to affect their achievement.

Fuzzy front end   in new product and service development is the very early phase in which an idea is developed into a concept, and is usually poorly managed.

Risk   is usually considered to be possible to estimate, either qualitatively – high, medium, low – or ideally by probability estimates. However, in practice different stakeholders' perceptions of risk and hazard influence decisions more than simple probabilistic assessments.

Scenarios   are internally consistent descriptions of alternative possible futures, based upon different assumptions and interpretations of the driving forces of change. Scenario development can be normative or explorative.

Uncertainty   is by definition unknowable, but nonetheless the sources, fields and degree of uncertainty can be identified to help to select the most appropriate methods of assessment and plan for contingencies.

Discussion Questions

1. Which components of a business plan are most important to attract resources?

2. How can forecasting be used to identify and reduce risk and uncertainty?

3. What is meant by the 'fuzzy front end' and how can it be better managed?

4. What is the difference between risk and uncertainty?

5. What are the relative advantages and disadvantages of using quantitative and qualitative methods for assessing projects?

Further Reading and Resources

There are numerous books and papers on forecasting, but only a finite number of methods to master, so be selective. The article by Paul Saffo ('Six rules for effective forecasting', *Harvard Business Review*, **Jan/Feb**, 2007, 122–31) is a good place to start. For a strong overview of different methods, try Paul Schoemaker's *Profiting from Uncertainty* (Free Press, 2002) or Joseph Martino's *Technological Forecasting for Decision Making* (McGraw-Hill, 1992).

A special issue of the journal *Long Range Planning* (37(2), 2004) is devoted to forecasting and provides a good overview of current thinking. There was a special issue of the journal *Technological Forecasting and Social Change* (**79**(1), January 2012), entitled 'Scenario method: Current developments in theory and practice', and another special issue of the same journal entitled 'Delphi technique: Past, present, and future prospects' (78(9), November 2011). For a comprehensive overview of international research and practice, refer to *The Handbook of Technology Foresight*, edited by Luke Georghiou (Edward Elgar, 2008).

For a practical and applied approach to development, see Mats Lindgren and Hans Bandhold's *Scenario Planning: The Link between Future and Strategy* (2nd edn, Palgrave Macmillan, 2009) or Gill Ringland's *Scenario Planning: Managing for the Future* (John Wiley & Sons Ltd, 1997). Shell also provide a free practical guide to developing scenarios, including detail of its own scenarios for the energy sector: http://s03.static-shell.com/content/dam/shell/static/future-energy/downloads/shell-scenarios/shell-scenarios-explorersguide.pdf.

References

1. Delmar, F. and S. Shane (2003) Does business planning facilitate the development of new ventures? *Strategic Management Journal*, **24**(12): 1165–85.

2. Kirsch, D.B., B. Goldfarb and A. Gera (2009) Form or substance? The role of business plans in venture capital decision making, *Strategic Management Journal*, **30**(5): 487–515.

3. Kaplan, J.M. and A.C. Warren (2013) *Patterns of Entrepreneurship*, New York: John Wiley & Sons, Inc.

4. Roberts, E.B. (1991) *Entrepreneurs in High Technology: Lessons from MIT and Beyond*, Oxford: Oxford University Press.

5. Tidd, J. and K. Bodley (2002) Effect of novelty on new product development processes and tools, *R&D Management*, **32**(2): 127–38.

6. Isaksen, S. and J. Tidd (2006) *Meeting the Innovation Challenge: Leadership for Transformation and Growth*, Chichester: John Wiley & Sons Ltd.

7. Landeta, J. (2006) Current validity of the Delphi method in social sciences, *Technological Forecasting and Social Change*, **73**(5): 467–82; Fuller, T. and L. Warren (2006) Entrepreneurship as foresight: A complex social network perspective on organizational foresight, *Futures*, **38**(8): 956–71; Gupta, U.G. and R.E. Clarke (1996) Theory and applications of the Delphi technique: A bibliography (1975–1994), *Technological Forecasting and Social Change*, **53**(2): 185–212.

8. Chermack, T.J. (2011) *Scenario Planning in Organizations: How to Create, Use, and Assess Scenarios*, San Francisco: Berrett-Koehler Publishers; Lindgren, M. and H. Bandhold (2009) *Scenario Planning: The Link between Future and Strategy*, 2nd edn, Basingstoke: Palgrave Macmillan.

9. Visser, M.P. and T.J. Chermack (2009) Perceptions of the relationship between scenario planning and firm performance: A qualitative study, *Futures*, **41**(9): 581–92; Godet, M. and F. Roubelat (1996) Creating the future: The use and misuse of scenarios, *Long Range Planning*, **29**(2): 164–71.

10. Arteaga, R. and J. Hyland (2013) *Pivot: How Top Entrepreneurs Adapt and Change Course to Find Ultimate Success*, Chichester: John Wiley & Sons Ltd.

11. Ries, E. (2011) *The Lean Startup: How Constant Innovation Creates Radically Successful Businesses*, Harmondsworth: Penguin.

12. Bower, J. (1986) *Managing the Resource Allocation Process*, Boston: Harvard Business School.

13. Mansfield, E., J. Raporport, J. Schnee *et al.* (1972) *Research and Innovation in the Modern Corporation*, London: Macmillan.

14. Heilbronner, S.R. (2008) A fruit in the hand or two in the bush? Divergent risk preferences in chimpanzees and bonobos, *Biology Letters*, **4**(3): 246–49.

15. Walsh, J.P. (1995) Managerial and organizational cognition: Notes from a field trip, *Organization Science*, **6**(1): 1–41; Genus, A. and A.M. Coles (2006) Firm strategies for risk management in innovation, *International Journal of Innovation Management*, **10**(2): 113–26; Berglund, H. (2007) Risk conception and risk management in corporate innovation, *International Journal of Innovation Management*, **11**(4): 497–514.

16. EIRMA (1995) *Evaluation of R&D Projects*, Paris: European Industrial Research Management Association.

17. Laslo, Z. and A.I. Goldberg (2008) Resource allocation under uncertainty in a multi-project matrix environment: Is organizational conflict inevitable? *International Journal of Project Management*, **26**(8): 773–88.

Deeper Dive explanations of innovation concepts and ideas are available on the Innovation Portal at **www.innovation-portal.info**

Quizzes to test yourself further are available online via the Innovation Portal at **www.innovation-portal.info**

Summary of online resources for Chapter 8 –
all material is available via the Innovation Portal at
www.innovation-portal.info

Cases	**Media**	**Tools**	**Activities**	**Deeper Dives**
• Clearvue • Gordon Murray Design • VeryPC	• Helen King • Melissa Clark-Reynolds • Glasses Direct	• Scenario planning • Delphi method • Risk assessment matrix • Options • Decision matrix • Bubble charts • Portfolio analysis	–	• Business Model Canvas

Chapter 9

Leadership and Teams

LEARNING OBJECTIVES

By the end of this chapter you will develop an understanding of:

- how the leadership and organization of innovation is much more than a set of processes, tools and techniques and that the successful practice of innovation and entrepreneurship demands the interaction and integration of three different levels of management: individual, collective and climate

- at the personal or individual level, how different leadership and entrepreneurial styles influence the ability to identify, assess and develop new ideas and concepts

- at the collective or social level, how teams, groups and processes each contribute to successful innovation behaviours and outcomes

- at the context or climate level, how different factors can support or hinder innovation and entrepreneurship.

There is no single universal ideal type of person or organization which promotes innovation and entrepreneurship. However, by studying case studies of entrepreneurs and innovative organizations and comparing these systematically with less successful ventures, we can begin to identify consistent patterns of good leadership and organization. Larger-scale academic research confirms these factors tend to contribute to superior performance (Table 9.1).

In this chapter we focus on the contribution and interaction of three of these critical components: individual characteristics, composition of entrepreneurial teams and influence of the creative context and climate.

TABLE 9.1   Components of the innovative organization

Component	Key features
Shared vision, leadership and the will to innovate	Clearly articulated and shared sense of purpose
	Stretching strategic intent
	Top management commitment
Appropriate structure	Organization design which enables creativity, learning and interaction
	Not always a loose 'skunk works' model
	Key issue is finding appropriate balance between organic and mechanistic options for particular contingencies
Key individuals	Promoters, champions, gatekeepers and other roles which energize or facilitate innovation
Effective team working	Appropriate use of teams (at local, cross-functional and inter-organizational level) to solve problems
	Requires investment in team selection and building
High-involvement innovation	Participation in organization-wide continuous improvement activity
Creative climate	Positive approach to creative ideas, supported by relevant motivation systems
External focus	Internal and external customer orientation

Individual Characteristics

Studies of innovation and entrepreneurship tend to focus on the role of key individuals, in particular the inherent or given traits of inventors or entrepreneurs. Archetypical inventors include Thomas Edison and Alexander Graham Bell, or more recently James Dyson and Steve Jobs. Each of these inventors was also an innovator, translating the original technical inventions into new products, but each was also an entrepreneur, in the sense that they created and developed successful businesses based on the inventions and innovations.

Typical characteristics of an entrepreneur include:[1]

- Passionately seek to identify new opportunities and ways to profit from change and disruption.
- Pursue opportunities with discipline and focus on a limited number of projects, rather than opportunistically chasing every option.
- Focus on action and execution, rather than endless analysis.
- Involve and energize networks of relationships, exploiting the expertise and resources of others, while helping others to achieve their own goals.

These characteristics are consistent with what research tells us about the cognitive abilities necessary for creativity and innovation:

- *Information acquisition and dissemination.* including the capture of information from a wide range of sources, requiring attention and perception.
- *Intelligence.* The ability and capability to interpret, process and manipulate information.
- *Sense making.* Giving meaning to information.
- *Unlearning.* the process of reducing or eliminating existing routines or behaviours, including discarding information.
- *Implementation and improvisation.* Autonomous behaviour, experimentation, reflection and action. Using information to solve problems, for example during new product development or process improvement.

Personal orientation includes what is traditionally thought of as characteristics of creative people as well as the creative abilities associated with creativity. These include personality traits traditionally associated with creativity such as openness to experience, tolerance of ambiguity, resistance to premature closure, curiosity and risk taking, among others. They also include such creative-thinking abilities as fluency, flexibility, originality and elaboration. Expertise, competence and knowledge base also contribute to creative efforts. Traditionally, people have been assessed and selected for different tasks on the basis of such characteristics, for example using psychometric questionnaires or tests. For example, the **Kirton Adaption-Innovation (KAI) scale** assesses different dimensions of creativity, including originality, attention to detail and reliance on rules.

The KAI scale is a psychometric approach for assessing the creativity of individuals. By a series of questions it seeks to identify an individual's attitudes towards originality, attention to detail and following rules. It seeks to differentiate 'adaptive' from 'innovative' styles:

- Adaptors characteristically produce a sufficiency of ideas based closely on existing agreed definitions of a problem and its likely solutions, but stretching the solutions. These ideas help to improve and 'do better'.
- Innovators are more likely to reconstruct the problem, challenge the assumptions and to emerge with a much less expected solution which very probably is also at first less acceptable. Innovators are less concerned with doing things better than with doing things differently.

It is important to recognize that creativity is an attribute that we all possess, but the preferred style of expressing it varies widely. Recognizing the need for different kinds of individual creative styles is an important aspect of developing successful innovations and new ventures. It is clear from a wealth of psychological research that every human being comes with the capability to find and solve complex problems, and where such creative behaviour can be harnessed amongst a group of people with differing skills and perspectives extraordinary things can be achieved. Some people are comfortable with ideas which challenge the whole way in which the universe works, while others prefer smaller increments of change – ideas about how to improve the jobs they do or their working environment. We discuss the role of creativity in more detail in Chapter 5.

ENTREPRENEURSHIP IN ACTION 9.1

Personal Creativity and Entrepreneurship

A study of 800 senior managers revealed that there were significant differences between those in the top quartile (25%) and the rest of the sample. The more successful managers had achieved their goals within eight years, and most were in senior management positions by their early 30s. The key differences associated with the more successful managers were personality and cognitive, in particular the breadth and creativity of their thinking, and their social skills. However, the study does not conclude that creative thinking and social skills are inherent personality traits but rather dispositions, which can be developed and improved significantly.

Such abilities are critical in many contexts, including large organizations and small start-up companies. For example, E.ON, one of the world's largest energy services companies, has created a graduate training programme to help assess and develop new recruits. Following psychometric assessment, graduate recruits follow specific programmes aimed to improve their personal and social skills, including placements in different parts of the business. Alex Oakley, head of human resources at E.ON, believes 'in this way we get a balance between skills and personal attributes that helps people do the job. We don't just concentrate on skills.' Similarly, Jamie Malcolm, an entrepreneur who co-founded the garden centre Shoots in Sussex, argues that 'anything new and innovative, like a start-up business, needs to take risks – you just can't succeed without it. I'll always be prepared to take risk in order to innovate. The innovation required to grow the business is what drives me. Risk can be dangerous if you're taking it because of your personal desire to do so. You don't have to lower your appetite for risk as the business grows – you just have to analyse it more as there's more at stake.'

Activity to assess your creativity is available on the Innovation Portal at **www.innovation-portal.info**

Source: Kaisen Consultants, 2006, www.kaisen.co.uk.

Entrepreneurial Disposition

Research on successful entrepreneurs has identified some of the factors that affect the likelihood of establishing a venture, and these include a combination of those which are largely inherent or given and those which can be more easily learnt or influenced:

* family and ethnic background
* psychological profile
* formal education and early work experience.

Background

A number of other studies confirm that both family background and religion affect an individual's propensity to establish a new venture. A significant majority of technical entrepreneurs have a self-employed or professional parent. Studies indicate that between 50 and 80% have at least one self-employed parent. For example, one seminal study found that four times as many technical entrepreneurs have a parent who is a professional, compared with other groups of scientists and engineers.[2] The most common explanation for this observed bias is that the parent acts as a role model and may provide support for self-employment.

The effect of religious and ethnic background is more controversial, but it is clear that certain groups are over-represented in the population of entrepreneurs. For example, in the USA and Europe, Jews are more likely to establish new ventures, and the Chinese are more likely to in Asia. Whether this observed bias is the result of specific cultural or religious norms or the result of minority status is the subject of much controversy but little research. Research suggests that dominant cultural values are more important than minority status, but even this work indicates the effect of family background is more significant than religion. In any case, and perhaps more importantly, there appears to be no significant relationship between family and religious background and the subsequent probability of success of a new venture.

Psychological Profile

Much of the research on the psychology of entrepreneurs is based on the experience of small firms in the USA, so the generalizability of the findings must be questioned. However, in the specific case of technical entrepreneurs there appears to be some consensus regarding the necessary personal characteristics. The two critical requirements appear to be an internal locus of control and a high need for achievement. The former characteristic is common in scientists and engineers, but the need for high levels of achievement is less common. Entrepreneurs are typically motivated by a high need for achievement (so-called 'n-Ach'), rather than a general desire to succeed. This behaviour is associated with moderate risk taking, but not gambling or irrational risk taking. A person with a high n-Ach:

- likes situations where it is possible to take personal responsibility for finding solutions to problems
- has a tendency to set challenging but realistic personal goals and to take calculated risks
- needs concrete feedback on personal performance.

However, a US study of almost 130 technical entrepreneurs and almost 300 scientists and engineers found that not all entrepreneurs have high n-Ach; only some do.[3] Technical entrepreneurs had only moderate n-Ach, but low need for affiliation (n-Aff). This suggests that the need for independence, rather than success, is the most significant motivator for technical entrepreneurs. Technical entrepreneurs also tend to have an internal locus of control. In other words, technical entrepreneurs believe that they have personal control over outcomes, whereas someone with an external locus of control believes that outcomes are the result of chance, powerful institutions or others. More sophisticated psychometric techniques, such as the Myers–Briggs type indicators (MBTI), confirm the differences between technical entrepreneurs and other scientists and engineers. Attempts to measure more general entrepreneurial traits have been less successful. For example, the General Enterprise Tendency test assesses five types of trait: need for achievement, drive and ambition, risk taking, autonomy, and creativity and potential for innovation. This instrument has proven effective at identifying potential owner-managers but fails to distinguish these from successful entrepreneurs.

Studies of the traits of successful entrepreneurs identify very similar profiles in a wide range of contexts, which typically feature innovativeness, risk taking and an ambition to achieve, compete and grow.[4] However, these are not the same characteristics as those who simply seek self-employment or manage small businesses, where the primary needs appear to be autonomy and independence.[5] These differences are critical, because too often entrepreneurs, the self-employed and SMEs are grouped together, whereas research confirms that these have very different characteristics, motives and outcomes. For example, the Global Entrepreneurship Monitor (GEM) tracks entrepreneurship at the national level, and in addition to cultural, demographic and educational factors includes indicators of infrastructure and national context. However, the focus of the GEM is on start-up activity, rather than subsequent success or growth, so it also fails to differentiate small businesses from successful entrepreneurial activity. For example, despite their evident structural economic problems, the GEM ranked Greece and Ireland top of the EU for 'total entrepreneurial activity'.

Education and Experience

In general, the self-employed and managers of SMEs tend to be under-educated compared to the relevant population. One explanation for this is that either through choice or because of a lack of ability or opportunity, those who do not pursue higher levels of education have fewer career options than those who do. This is often referred to as 'necessity-drive entrepreneurship', in contrast to 'opportunity-driven entrepreneurship'. Opportunity-driven entrepreneurs, in contrast to the self-employed and managers of SMEs, tend to be more educated than the relevant population, and technical entrepreneurs even more so: in general, those with a higher, college or university-level education are twice as likely to be successful entrepreneurs, and 85% of technical entrepreneurs have a degree.[6]

The levels of education of technical entrepreneurs do not differentiate them from other scientists and engineers, but education and training are major factors that distinguish the founders of technical ventures from other types of entrepreneur. The median level of education of technical entrepreneurs is a master's degree, and, with the important exception of biotechnology-based new ventures, a doctorate is superfluous. Significantly, potential technical entrepreneurs tend to have higher levels of productivity than their technical work colleagues, measured in terms of papers published or patents granted. This suggests that potential entrepreneurs may be more driven than their corporate counterparts.

In addition to a master's-level education, on average, a technical entrepreneur will have around 13 years of work experience before establishing a new venture. In the case of Route

128, the entrepreneur's work experience is typically with a single incubator organization, whereas technical entrepreneurs in Silicon Valley tend to have gained their experience from a larger number of firms before establishing their own venture. This suggests that there is no ideal pattern of previous work experience. However, experience of development work appears to be more important than work in basic research. As a result of the formal education and experience required, a typical technical entrepreneur will be aged between 30 and 40 when establishing his or her first venture. This is relatively late in life compared to other types of venture, and is due to a combination of ability and opportunity. On the one hand, it typically takes between 10 and 15 years for a potential entrepreneur to attain the necessary technical and business experience. On the other hand, many people begin to have greater financial and family responsibilities at this time, which reduces the appetite for risk. Thus, there appears to be a window of opportunity to start a new venture some time in the mid-thirties. Moreover, different fields of technology have different entry and growth potential. Therefore, the choice of a potential entrepreneur will be constrained by the dynamics of the technology and markets. The capital requirements, product lead times and potential for growth are likely to vary significantly between sectors.

Numerous surveys indicate that around three-quarters of technical entrepreneurs claim to have been frustrated in their previous job. This frustration appears to result from the interaction of the psychological predisposition of the potential entrepreneur and poor selection, training and development by the parent organization. Specific events may also trigger the desire or need to establish a new venture, such as a major reorganization or downsizing of the parent organization (Figure 9.1).

Innovation Leadership

The contribution that individuals make to the performance of their organizations can be significant. **Upper echelons theory** argues that decisions and choices by top management have an influence on the performance of an organization (positive or negative!), through their assessment of the environment, strategic decision making and support for innovation. The results of different studies vary, but the reviews of research on leadership and performance suggest leadership directly influences around 15% of the differences found in performance of businesses, and contributes around an additional 35% through the choice of business strategy.[7] So directly and indirectly leadership can account for half of the variance in performance observed across organizations. At higher levels of management the problems to be solved are more likely to be ill defined, demanding that leaders conceptualize more.

Researchers have identified a long list of characteristics that may have something to do with being effective in certain situations, which typically include generic traits such as seeking responsibility, social competence and good communication. Although these lists may describe some characteristics of some leaders in certain situations, measures of these traits yield highly inconsistent relationships with being a good leader.[8] In short, there is no brief and universal list of enduring traits all good leaders must possess under all conditions.

Studies in different contexts identify not only the technical expertise of leadership influencing group performance but also broader cognitive ability, such as creative problem-solving

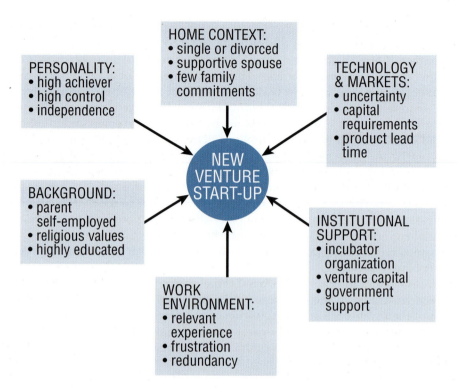

FIGURE 9.1   Factors influencing the creation of a new venture

Source: From Tidd, J. and J. Bessant (2013) *Managing Innovation: Integrating Technological, Market and Organizational Change*, Chichester: John Wiley & Sons Ltd.

and information-processing skills. For example, studies of groups facing novel, ill-defined problems confirm that both expertise and cognitive-processing skills are key components of creative leadership and are associated with effective performance of creative groups.[9] Moreover, this combination of expertise and cognitive capacity is critical for the evaluation of others' ideas. A study of scientists found that they most valued their leader's inputs at the early stages of a new project, when they were formulating their ideas, and defining the problems, and later at the stage where they needed feedback and insights to the implications of their work. Therefore, a key role of creative leadership in such environments is to provide feedback and evaluation, rather than to simply generate ideas.[10] This evaluative role is critical, but is typically seen as not being conducive to creativity and innovation, where the conventional advice is to suspend judgement to foster idea generation. Also, it suggests that the conventional linear view – that evaluation follows idea generation – may be wrong. Evaluation by creative leadership may precede idea generation and conceptual combination.

The quality and nature of the leader–member exchange (LMX) has also been found to influence the creativity of subordinates.[11] A study of 238 knowledge workers from 26 project teams in high-technology firms identified a number of positive aspects of LMX, including monitoring, clarifying and consulting, but also found that the frequency of negative LMX was as high as the positive, around a third of respondents reporting these.[12] Therefore, LMX can either enhance or undermine subordinates' sense of competence and self-determination. However, analysis of exchanges perceived to be negative and positive revealed that it was typically how something was done rather than what was done, which suggests that task and relationship behaviours in leadership support and LMX are intimately intertwined, and that negative behaviours can have a disproportionate negative influence.

Intellectual stimulation by leaders has a stronger effect on organizational performance under conditions of perceived uncertainty. Intellectual stimulation includes behaviours that increase others' awareness of and interest in problems, and develops their propensity and ability to tackle problems in new ways. It is also associated with commitment to an organization.[13] Stratified system theory (SST) focuses on the cognitive aspects of leadership, and argues that conceptual capacity is associated with superior performance in strategic decision making where there is a need to integrate complex information and think abstractly in order to assess the environment. It also is likely to demand a combination of these problem-solving capabilities and social skills, as leaders will depend upon others to identify and implement solutions.[14] This suggests that under conditions of environmental uncertainty the contribution of leadership is not simply, or even primarily, to inspire or build confidence but rather to solve problems and make appropriate strategic decisions.

Rafferty and Griffin propose other sub-dimensions to the concept of transformational leadership that may have a greater influence on creativity and innovation, including articulating a vision and inspirational communication.[15] They define a vision as 'the expression of an idealized picture of the future based around organizational values', and inspirational communication as 'the expression of positive and encouraging messages about the organization, and statements that build motivation and confidence'. They found that the expression of a vision has a negative effect on followers' confidence, unless accompanied with inspirational communication. Mission awareness increases the probability of success of R&D projects, but the effects are stronger at the earlier stages: in the planning and conceptual stage mission awareness explained two-thirds of the subsequent project success.[16] Leadership clarity is associated with clear team objectives, high levels of participation, commitment to excellence and support for innovation.[17]

The creative leader needs to do much more to encourage creative followers than simply provide passive support. Perceptual measures of leaders' performance suggest that in a research environment the perception of a leader's technical skill is the single best predictor of research group performance, explaining around half of innovation performance.[18] Keller found that the type of project moderates the relationships between leadership style and project success, and found that transformational leadership was a stronger predictor in research projects than in development projects.[19] This strongly suggests that certain qualities of transformational leadership may be most appropriate under conditions of high complexity, uncertainty or novelty, whereas a transactional style has a positive effect in an administrative context, but a negative effect in a research context.[20]

A review of 27 empirical studies of the relationship between leadership and innovation investigated when and how leadership influences innovation and identified six factors leaders should focus on:[21]

Case Study of Nokia Solutions and Networks (NSN) illustrating some of these themes is available on the Innovation Portal at **www.innovation-portal.info**

Video Clip of Fabian Schlage (NSN) illustrating some of these themes is available on the Innovation Portal at **www.innovation-portal.info**

- Upper management should establish an innovation policy that is promoted throughout the organization. It is necessary that the organization through its leaders communicates to employees that innovative behaviour will be rewarded.
- When forming teams, some heterogeneity is necessary to promote innovation. However, if the team is too heterogeneous, tensions may arise when heterogeneity is too low, more directive leadership is required to promote team reflection, e.g. by encouraging discussion and disagreement.
- Leaders should promote a team climate of emotional safety, respect and joy through emotional support and shared decision making.
- Individuals and teams have autonomy and space for idea generation and creative problem solving.
- Time limits for idea creation and problem solutions should be set, particularly in the implementation phases.
- Finally, team leaders who have the expertise should engage closely in the evaluation of innovative activities.

Traditionally, people have been assessed and selected for different tasks on the basis of such characteristics, for example using psychometric questionnaires or tests. As we saw earlier, the KAI scale assesses different dimensions of creativity, including originality, attention to detail and reliance on rules. By a series of questions it seeks to identify an individual's attitudes towards originality, attention to detail and following rules. It seeks to differentiate 'adaptive' from 'innovative' styles.

Audio Clip of David Hall discussing the characteristics of entrepreners is available on the Innovation Portal at **www.innovation-portal.info**

It is important to recognize that creativity is an attribute that we all possess, but the preferred style of expressing it varies widely. Recognizing the need for different kinds of individual creative styles is an important aspect of developing successful innovations and new ventures. Expertise, competence and knowledge base also contribute to creative efforts.

ENTREPRENEURSHIP IN ACTION 9.2

Opportunity and Planning at Innocent

Innocent develops and sells fruit smoothies, healthy, premium pulped-fruit drinks, with no additives. The company was created in 1999 by three university friends: Adam Balon, Richard Reed and Jon Wright. The company was founded with the help of £200 000 of venture capital, but Balon, Reed and Wright still own 70% of the company. In 2006, Innocent had sales of around £70 million, representing a market share of 60%, and the company was valued at £175 million. It then recruited more experienced managers from larger firms, employing 100 staff in West London. It also has bases in France and Denmark, and opened offices in Germany and Austria in 2007. All production and packaging is outsourced, and the company focuses on development and marketing.

The company has cultivated a funky liberal image, in contrast to the large multinational firms that dominate the drinks market. It gives 10% of company profits to charities, such as the Rainforest Alliance, and has developed a healthy dialogue with its customers through a weekly email newsletter. In 2005, Reed won the title 'Most Admired Businessman' from the UK National Union of Students (NUS). However, beneath the hippy image there is a well-educated and experienced management team. After university, Reed gained experience in the advertising industry and Balon and Wright both worked for large management consultants, respectively McKinsey and Bain. The likely exit or harvest for the business will be a trade sale, similar to other so-called ethical brands such as Ben & Jerry's, which was bought by Unilever, and Green & Black's, which was acquired by Cadbury. In preparation, in April 2009 the owners sold 18% of the company to Coca-Cola for £30 million.

Entrepreneurial Teams

It takes five years to develop a new car in this country. Heck, we won World War 2 in four years…

Ross Perot's comment on the state of the US car industry in the late 1980s captured some of the frustration with existing ways of designing and building cars. In the years that followed, significant strides were made in reducing the development cycle, with Ford and Chrysler succeeding in dramatically reducing time and improving quality. Much of the advantage was gained through extensive team working; as Lew Varaldi, project manager of Ford's Team Taurus project, put it: '[I]t's amazing the dedication and commitment you get from people … we will never go back to the old ways because we know so much about what they can bring to the party.'[22]

Experiments indicate that teams have more to offer than individuals in terms of both fluency of idea generation and flexibility of solutions developed. Focusing this potential on innovation tasks is the prime driver for the trend towards high levels of team working – in project teams, in cross-functional and inter-organizational problem-solving groups and in cells and work groups where the focus is on incremental, adaptive innovation.

Many use the terms **group** and **team** interchangeably. In general, the word 'group' refers to an assemblage of people who may just be near to each other. Groups can be a number of people who are regarded as some sort of unity or are classed together on account of any sort of similarity. For us, 'team' means a combination of individuals who come together or who have been brought together for a common purpose or goal in their organization. A team is a group that must collaborate in their professional work in some enterprise or on some assignment and share accountability or responsibility for obtaining results. There are a variety of ways to differentiate working groups from teams. One senior executive with whom we have worked described groups as individuals with nothing in common except a zip/postal code. Teams, however, were characterized by a common vision.

Considerable work has been done on the characteristics of high-performance project teams for innovative tasks, and the main findings are that such teams rarely happen by accident.[23] They result from a combination of selection and investment in team building, allied to clear guidance on their roles and tasks, and a concentration on managing group process as well as task aspects.[24] For example, research within the Ashridge Management College developed a model for 'superteams' which included components of building and managing the internal team and its interfaces with the rest of the organization.[25]

Holti, Neumann and Standing provide a useful summary of the key factors involved in developing team working.[26] Although there is considerable current emphasis on team working, we should remember that teams are not always the answer. In particular, there are dangers in putting nominal teams together where unresolved conflicts, personality clashes, lack of effective group processes and other factors can diminish their effectiveness. Tranfield *et al.* look at the issue of team working in a number of different contexts and highlight the importance of selecting and building the appropriate team for the task and the context.[27]

Teams are increasingly being seen as a mechanism for bridging boundaries within the organization – and, indeed, in dealing with inter-organizational issues. Cross-functional teams can bring together the different knowledge sets needed for tasks like product development or process improvement, but they also represent a forum in which often deep-rooted differences in perspectives can be resolved.[28] Successful organizations were those which invested in multiple methods for integrating across groups – and the cross-functional team was one of the most valuable resources.

Self-managed teams working within a defined area of autonomy can be very effective, for example Honeywell's defence avionics factory reports a dramatic improvement in on-time delivery – from below 40% in the 1980s to 99% in 1996 – to the implementation of self-managing teams.[29] In the Netherlands, one of the most successful bus companies is Vancom Zuid-Limburg. It has used self-managing teams to both reduce costs and improve customer satisfaction ratings, and one manager now supervises over 40 drivers, compared to the industry average ratio of 1:8. Drivers are also encouraged to participate in problem finding and solving in areas like maintenance, customer service and planning.[30]

Key elements in effective high-performance team working include:

- clearly defined tasks and objectives
- effective team leadership
- a good balance of team roles matched to individual behavioural style
- effective conflict resolution mechanisms within the group
- continuing liaison with the external organization.

Tool to help you explore teambuilding is available on the Innovation Portal at **www.innovation-portal.info**

Teams typically go through four stages of development, popularly known as 'forming, storming, norming and performing'.[31] That is, they are put together and then go through a phase of resolving internal differences and conflicts around leadership, objectives, etc. Emerging from this process is a commitment to shared values and norms governing the way the team will work, and it is only after this stage that teams can move on to the effective performance of their task. Common approaches to team building can support innovation, but are not sufficient.

Central to team performance is the make-up of the team itself, with good matching between the role requirements of the group and the behavioural preferences of the individuals involved. Belbin's work has been influential here in providing an approach to team role matching. He classifies people into a number of preferred role types, for example 'the plant' (someone who is a source of new ideas), 'the resource investigator', 'the shaper' and the 'completer/finisher'. Research has shown that the most effective teams are those with diversity in background, ability and behavioural style. In one noted experiment highly talented but similar people in 'Apollo' teams consistently performed less well than mixed, average groups.[32]

With increased emphasis on cross-boundary and dispersed team activity, a series of new challenges are emerging. In the extreme case a product development team might begin work in London, pass on to their US counterparts later in the day, who in turn pass on to their Far Eastern colleagues – effectively allowing a 24-hour non-stop development activity. This makes for higher productivity potential, but only if the issues around managing dispersed and virtual teams can be resolved. Similarly, the concept of sharing knowledge across boundaries depends on enabling structures and mechanisms.[33]

Many people who have attempted to use groups for problem solving find out that it is not always easy, pleasurable or effective. Table 9.2 summarizes some of the positive and negative aspects of using groups for innovation.

TABLE 9.2   Potential assets and liabilities of using a group

Potential assets of using a group	Potential liabilities of using a group
1. Greater availability of knowledge and information	1. Social pressure towards uniform thought limits contributions and increases conformity
2. More opportunities for cross-fertilization, increasing the likelihood of building and improving upon ideas of others	2. Groupthink: groups converge on options that have greatest agreement regardless of quality
3. Wider range of experiences and perspectives upon which to draw	3. Dominant individuals influence and exhibit an unequal amount of impact upon outcomes
4. Participation and involvement in problem solving increases understanding, acceptance, commitment and ownership of outcomes	4. Individuals are less accountable in groups, allowing groups to make riskier decisions
5. More opportunities for group development, increasing cohesion, communication and companionship	5. Conflicting individual biases may cause unproductive levels of competition, leading to 'winners' and 'losers'

Source: Isaksen S. and J. Tidd (2006) *Meeting the Innovation Challenge*, Chichester: John Wiley & Sons Ltd.

Case Study exploring some of these issues, Cerulean, is available on the Innovation Portal at **www.innovation-portal.info**

Video Clip of Patrick McLaughlin, Cerulean's MD, exploring some of these issues is available on the Innovation Portal at **www.innovation-portal.info**

A survey of 1207 firms aimed to identify how different organizational practices contributed to innovation performance.[34] It examined the influences of twelve common practices – including cross-functional teams, team incentives, quality circles and ISO 9000 quality standards – on successful new product development. The study found significant differences in the effects of different practices, depending upon the novelty of the development project. For instance, both quality circles and ISO 9000 were associated with the successful development of incremental new products, but both practices had a significant negative influence on the success of radical new products. However, the use of teams and team incentives were found to have a positive effect on both incremental and radical new product development. This suggests that great care needs to be taken when applying so-called universal best practices, as their effects often depend on the nature of the project.

Our own work on high-performance teams, consistent with previous research, suggests a number of characteristics that promote effective teamwork:[35]

- *A clear, common and elevating goal.* Having a clear and elevating goal means having understanding, mutual agreement and identification with respect to the primary task a group faces. Active teamwork towards common goals happens when members of a group share a common vision of the desired future state. Creative teams have clear and common goals. The goals were clear and compelling, but also open and challenging. Less creative teams have conflicting agendas, different missions and no agreement on the result. The tasks for the least creative teams were tightly constrained and considered routine and overly structured.
- *Results-driven structure.* Individuals within high-performing teams feel productive when their efforts take place with a minimum of grief. Open communication, clear coordination of tasks, clear roles and accountabilities, monitoring performance, providing feedback, fact-based judgement, efficiency and strong impartial management combine to create a results-driven structure.
- *Competent team members.* Competent teams are composed of capable and conscientious members. Members must possess essential skills and abilities, a strong desire to contribute, be capable of collaborating effectively and have a sense of responsible idealism. They must have knowledge in the domain surrounding the task (or some other domain which may be relevant) as well as with the process of working together. Creative teams recognize the diverse strengths and talents and use them accordingly.
- *Unified commitment.* Having a shared commitment relates to the way the individual members of the group respond. Effective teams have an organizational unity: members display mutual support, dedication and faithfulness to the shared purpose and vision, and

a productive degree of self-sacrifice to reach organizational goals. Team members enjoy contributing and celebrating their accomplishments.

- *Collaborative climate*. Productive teamwork does not just happen. It requires a climate that supports cooperation and collaboration. This kind of situation is characterized by mutual trust, in which everyone feels comfortable discussing ideas, offering suggestions and being willing to consider multiple approaches.

- *Standards of excellence*. Effective teams establish clear standards of excellence. They embrace individual commitment, motivation, self-esteem, individual performance and constant improvement. Members of teams develop a clear and explicit understanding of the norms upon which they will rely.

- *External support and recognition*. Team members need resources, rewards, recognition, popularity and social success. Being liked and admired as individuals and respected for belonging and contributing to a team is often helpful in maintaining the high level of personal energy required for sustained performance. With the increasing use of cross-functional and inter-departmental teams within larger complex organizations, teams must be able to obtain approval and encouragement.

- *Principled leadership*. Leadership is important for teamwork. Whether it is a formally appointed leader or leadership of the emergent kind, the people who exert influence and encourage the accomplishment of important things usually follow some basic principles. Leaders provide clear guidance, support and encouragement, and keep everyone working together and moving forward. Leaders also work to obtain support and resources from within and outside the group.

- *Appropriate use of the team*. Teamwork is encouraged when the tasks and situations really call for that kind of activity. Sometimes the team itself must set clear boundaries on when and why it should be deployed. One of the easiest ways to destroy a productive team is to overuse it or use it when it is not appropriate to do so.

- *Participation in decision making*. One of the best ways to encourage teamwork is to engage the members of the team in the process of identifying the challenges and opportunities for improvement, generating ideas and transforming ideas into action. Participation in the process of problem solving and decision making actually builds teamwork and improves the likelihood of acceptance and implementation.

- *Team spirit*. Effective teams know how to have a good time, release tension and relax their need for control. The focus at times is on developing friendship, engaging in tasks for mutual pleasure and recreation. This internal team climate extends beyond the need for a collaborative climate. Creative teams have the ability to work together without major conflicts in personalities. There is a high degree of respect for the contributions of others. Less creative teams are characterized by animosity, jealousy and political posturing.

- *Embracing appropriate change*. Teams often face the challenges of organizing and defining tasks. In order for teams to remain productive, they must learn how to make necessary changes to procedures. When there is a fundamental change in how the team must operate, different values and preferences may need to be accommodated.

ENTREPRENEURSHIP IN ACTION 9.3

Entrepreneur Interaction for Innovative New Ventures

Innovation management focuses too much on processes and tools, whereas entrepreneurship is preoccupied with individual personal traits. However, many of the most successful innovations and new ventures were co-created, by multiple entrepreneurs, and it is this interaction of talent that is at the core of radical innovation, what we call **conjoint innovation**. We examined fifteen cases, historical and contemporary, to identify what conjoint innovation is and how it works. We found that a significant number of the most successful were co-created, by multiple entrepreneurs, and it is this interaction of talent that is at the core of conjoint innovation.

Examples of conjoint innovation include:

• Apple*	Steve Jobs and Steve Wozniak
• Google*	Larry Page and Sergey Brin
• Facebook*	Mark Zuckerberg and Eduardo Saverin
• Microsoft*	Bill Gates and Paul Allen
• Netflix*	Marc Randolph and Reed Hastings
• Intel*	Robert Noyce and Gordon Moore
• Marks & Spencer*	Michael Marks and Thomas Spencer
• ARM Holdings	Mike Muller and Tudor Brown
• Skype	Niklas Zennström and Janus Friis
• Sony	Masaru Ibuka and Akio Morita
• Rolls-Royce	Henry Royce and Charles Rolls
• DNA	James Watson and Francis Crick
• Electrification	George Westinghouse and Nikola Tesla
• Steel process	Henry Bessemer and Robert Mushet
• Steam power	James Watt and Matthew Boulton

*Ranked 'world's most innovative' firms, http://www.fastcompany.com/most-innovative-companies/2011/

These examples demonstrate that many radical new ventures are not simply the result of a technical genius or heroic entrepreneur. Instead, all these cases feature a combination of talents and capabilities which interacted to create a radical new venture. Thus it is necessary, but not sufficient, for conjoint innovation that a venture is created by two or more entrepreneurs. We can identify three mechanisms which commonly contribute to the interaction between entrepreneurs and creation of radical new ventures:

- complementary capabilities
- creative conflict
- adjacent networks.

Sources: Tidd, J. (2014) Conjoint innovation: Building a bridge between innovation and entrepreneurship, *International Journal of Innovation Management*, **18**(1), 1–20; Tidd, J. (2012) It takes two to tango: How multiple entrepreneurs interact to innovate, *European Business Review*, **24**(4), 58–61.

There are also many challenges to the effective management of teams. We have all seen teams that have 'gone wrong'. As a team develops, there are certain aspects or guidelines that may be helpful to keep them on track. Hackman identifies a number of themes relevant to those who design, lead and facilitate teams.[36] In examining a variety of organizational work groups, he found some seemingly small factors that if overlooked in the management of teams will have large implications that tend to destroy the capability of a team to function. These small and often hidden 'tripwires' to major problems include:

- *Group versus team.* One of the mistakes often made when managing teams is to call the group a team and to treat it as nothing more than a loose collection of individuals. This is similar to making it a team 'because I said so'. It is important to be very clear about the underlying goal and reward structure. People are often asked to perform tasks as a team, but then have all evaluation of performance based on an individual level. This situation sends conflicting messages, and may negatively affect team performance.

- *Ends versus means.* Managing the source of authority for groups is a delicate balance. Just how much authority can you assign to the team to work out its own issues and challenges? Those who convene teams often 'over manage' them by specifying the results as well as how the team should obtain them. The end, direction or outer limit constraints ought to be specified, but the means to get there ought to be within the authority and responsibility of the group.

- *Structured freedom.* It is a major mistake to assemble a group of people and merely tell them in general and unclear terms what needs to be accomplished and then let them work out their own details. At times, the belief is that if teams are to be creative, they ought not be given any structure. It turns out that most groups would find a little structure quite enabling, if it were the right kind. Teams generally need a well-defined task. They need to be composed of an appropriately small number to be manageable but large enough to be diverse. They need clear limits as to the team's authority and responsibility, and they need sufficient freedom to take initiative and make good use of their diversity. It's about striking the right kind of balance between structure, authority and boundaries – and freedom, autonomy and initiative.

- *Support structures and systems.* Often, challenging team objectives are set but the organization fails to provide adequate support in order to make the objectives a reality. In general, high-performing teams need a reward system that recognizes and reinforces excellent team performance. They also need access to good quality and adequate information, as well as training in team-relevant tools and skills. Good team performance is also dependent on having an adequate level of material and financial resources to get the job done. Calling a group a team does not mean they will automatically obtain all the support needed to accomplish the task.

- *Assumed competence.* Technical skills and domain-relevant expertise, experience and abilities often explain why someone has been included within a group, but these are rarely the only competencies individuals need for effective team performance. Members will undoubtedly require explicit coaching on skills needed to work well in a team.

INNOVATION IN ACTION 9.1

Organizational Climate for Innovation at Google

Google appears to have learnt a few lessons from other innovative organizations, such as 3M. Technical employees are expected to spend 20% of their time on projects other than their core job, and similarly managers are required to spend 20% of their time on projects outside the core business, and 10% to completely new products and businesses. This effort devoted to new, non-core business is not evenly allocated weekly or monthly, but when possible or necessary. These are contractual obligations, reinforced by performance reviews and peer pressure, and integral to the 25 different measures of and targets for employees. Ideas progress through a formal qualification process, which includes prototyping, pilots and tests with actual users. The assessment of new ideas and projects is highly data-driven and aggressively empirical, reflecting the IT basis of the firm, and is based on rigorous experimentation within 300 employee user panels, segments of Google's 132 million users and trusted third parties. The approach is essentially evolutionary in the sense that many ideas are encouraged, most fail but some are successful, depending on the market response. The generation and market testing of many alternatives, and tolerance of (rapid) failure, are central to the process. In this way the company claims to generate around 100 new products each year, including hits such as Gmail, AdSense and Google News.

However, we need to be careful to untangle cause and effect, and determine how much of this is transferable to other companies and contexts. Google's success to date is predicated on dominating the global demand for search engine services through an unprecedented investment in technology infrastructure – estimated at over a million computers. Its business model is based upon 'ubiquity first, revenues later', and is still reliant on search-based advertising. The revenues generated in this way have allowed it to hire the best, and to provide the space and motivation to innovate. Despite this, it is estimated to have only 120 or so product offerings, and the most recent blockbusters have all been acquisitions: YouTube for video content, DoubleClick for Web advertising and Keyhole for mapping (now Google Earth). In this respect, it looks more like Microsoft than 3M.

Source: Iyer B. and T.H. Davenport (2008) Reverse engineering Google's innovation machine, *Harvard Business Review*, **April**, 58–68.

Context and Climate

Climate is defined as the recurring patterns of behaviour, attitudes and feelings that characterize life in the organization. These are the objectively shared perceptions that characterize life within a defined work unit or in the larger organization. Climate is distinct from culture in that it is more observable at a surface level within the organization and more amenable

TABLE 9.3   Climate factors influencing innovation

Climate factor	Most Innovative (score)	Least Innovative (score)	Difference
Trust and openness	253	88	165
Challenge and involvement	260	100	160
Support and space for innovation	218	70	148
Conflict and debate	231	83	148
Risk taking	210	65	145
Freedom	202	110	92

Source: Derived for Isaksen S. and J. Tidd (2006) *Meeting the Innovation Challenge*, Chichester: John Wiley & Sons Ltd.

to change and improvement efforts. **Culture** refers to the deeper and more enduring values, norms and beliefs within the organization. Climate and culture are different: traditionally, studies of organizational culture are more qualitative, whereas research on organizational climate is more quantitative, but a multidimensional approach helps to integrate the benefits of each perspective. What is needed is a common-sense set of levers for change that leaders can exert direct and deliberate influence over.

Table 9.3 summarizes some research of how climate influences innovation. Many dimensions of climate have been shown to influence innovation and entrepreneurship, but here we discuss six of the most critical factors.

Trust and Openness

The trust and openness dimension refers to the emotional safety in relationships. These relationships are considered safe when people are seen as both competent and sharing a common set of values. When there is a strong level of trust, everyone in the organization dares to put forward ideas and opinions. Initiatives can be taken without fear of reprisals and ridicule in case of failure. The communication is open and straightforward. Where trust is missing, count on high expenses for mistakes that may result. People also are afraid of being exploited and robbed of their good ideas.

When trust and openness are too low, you may see people hoarding resources (information, software, materials, etc.). However, trust can bind and blind. If trust and openness are too high, relationships may be so strong that time and resources at work are often spent on personal issues. It may also lead to a lack of questioning each other that, in turn, may lead to mistakes or less productive outcomes. Cliques may form where there are isolated pockets of high trust. In this case it may help to develop forums for interdepartmental and intergroup exchange of information and ideas.

Challenge and Involvement

Challenge and involvement is the degree to which people are involved in daily operations, long-term goals and visions. High levels of challenge and involvement mean that people are intrinsically motivated and committed to making contributions to the success of the organization. The climate has a dynamic, electric and inspiring quality. However, if the challenge and involvement are too high you may observe that people are showing signs of burn out, they are unable to meet project goals and objectives or they spend too many long hours at work. If challenge and involvement are too low, you may see that people are apathetic about their work, are not generally interested in professional development or are frustrated about the future of the organization. One of the ways to improve the situation may be to get people involved in interpreting the vision, mission, purpose and goals of the organization for themselves and their work teams.

Video Clip of interview with Emma Taylor of Denso Systems highlighting some of these issues is available on the Innovation Portal at **www.innovation-portal.info**

Support and Space for Innovation

Idea time is the amount of time people can (and do) use for exploring innovation. In the high idea–time situation, possibilities exist to discuss and test impulses and fresh suggestions that are not planned or included in the task assignment and people tend to use these possibilities. When idea time is low, every minute is booked and specified. If there is insufficient time and space for generating new ideas, you may observe that people are only concerned with their current projects and tasks. Conversely, if there is too much time and space for new ideas you may observe people showing signs of boredom and decisions being made through a slow, bureaucratic process.

Case Studies of Kumba Resources and Hosiden illustrating the building and sustaining of a climate to support high involvement innovation are available on the Innovation Portal at **www.innovation-portal.info**

Video Clip of Veeder-Root illustrating some of these themes is available on the Innovation Portal at **www.innovation-portal.info**

Conflict and Debate

Conflict in an organization refers to the presence of personal, interpersonal or emotional tensions. Although conflict is a negative dimension, all organizations have some level of personal tension. Conflicts can occur over tasks, processes or relationships. Task conflicts focus on disagreements about the goals and content of work, the 'What?' needs to be done and 'Why?' Process conflicts are around 'How?' to achieve a task, means and methods.

Tool to help you explore and reflect on this issue, high involvement innovation audit, is available on the Innovation Portal at **www.innovation-portal.info**

Relationship or affective conflicts are more emotional, and are characterized by hostility and anger. In general, some task and process conflict is constructive, helping to avoid groupthink, and to consider more diverse opinions and alternative strategies. However, task and process conflict only have a positive effect on performance in a climate of openness and collaborative communication; otherwise, it can degenerate into relationship conflict or avoidance.

Relationship conflict generally saps energy and is destructive, as emotional disagreements create anxiety and hostility. If the level of conflict is too high, groups and individuals dislike or hate each other and the climate can be characterized as warfare. Plots and traps are common in the life of the organization. There is gossip and backbiting going on. You may observe gossiping at water coolers (including character assassination), information hoarding, open aggression or people lying or exaggerating about their real needs. In these cases, you may need to take initiative to engender cooperation among key individuals or departments.

So the goal is not necessarily to minimize conflict and maximize consensus but to maintain a level of constructive debate consistent with the need for diversity and a range of different preferences and styles of creative problem solving. Group members with similar creative preferences and problem-solving styles are likely to be more harmonious but much less effective than those with mixed preferences and styles. So if the level of conflict is constructive, people behave in a more mature manner. They have psychological insight and exercise more control over their impulses and emotions.

INNOVATION IN ACTION 9.2

Increasing Challenge and Involvement in an Electrical Engineering Division

The organization was a division of a large, global electrical power and product supply company headquartered in France. The division was located in the south-east of the USA and had 92 employees. Its focus was to help clients automate their processes particularly within the automotive, pharmaceutical, microelectronics, and food and beverage industries. For example, this division would make the robots that put cars together in the automotive industry or provide public filtration systems.

When this division was merged with the parent company, it was losing about $8 million a year. A new general manager was brought in to turn the division around and make it profitable quickly.

An assessment of the organization's climate identified that it was strongest on the debate dimension but was very close to the stagnated norms when it came to challenge and involvement, playfulness and humour, and conflict. The quantitative and qualitative assessment results were consistent with management's own impressions that the division could be characterized as conflict driven and uncommitted to producing results, and that people were generally despondent. The leadership decided, after some debate, that they should target challenge and involvement, which was consistent with their strategic emphasis on a global initiative on employee commitment. It was clear to them that they also needed to soften the climate and drive a warmer, more embracing, communicative and exuberant climate.

The management team re-established training and development and encouraged employees to engage in both personal and business-related skills development. They also provided

(continued)

mandatory safety training for all employees. They committed to increase communication by holding monthly all-employee meetings, sharing quarterly reviews on performance and using cross-functional strategy review sessions. They implemented mandatory 'skip level' meetings to allow more direct interaction between senior managers and all levels of employees. The general manager held 15-minute meetings with all employees at least once a year. Employee suggestions and recommendations were encouraged and managers were told to give feedback on these quickly. A new monthly recognition and rewards programme was launched across the division for both managers and employees that was based on peer nomination. The management team formed employee review teams to challenge and craft the statements in the hopes of encouraging more ownership and involvement in the overall strategic direction of the business.

In 18 months, the division showed a $7 million turnaround, and in 2003 won a worldwide innovation award. The general manager was promoted to a national position.

Source: Isaksen, S. and J. Tidd (2006) *Meeting the Innovation Challenge*, Chichester: John Wiley & Sons Ltd.

Risk Taking

Tolerance of uncertainty and ambiguity constitutes risk taking. In a high-risk-taking climate, bold new initiatives can be taken even when the outcomes are unknown. People feel that they can take a gamble on some of their ideas. People will often go out on a limb and be first to put an idea forward. In a risk-avoiding climate, there is a cautious, hesitant mentality. People try to be on the safe side. They set up committees and cover themselves in many ways before making a decision. If risk taking is too low, employees offer few new ideas or few ideas that are well outside of what is considered safe or ordinary. In risk-avoiding organizations people complain about boring, low-energy jobs and are frustrated by a long, tedious process used to get ideas to action.

Freedom

Freedom is described as the independence in behaviour exerted by the people in the organization. In a climate with much freedom, people are given autonomy to define much of their own work. They are able to exercise discretion in their day-to-day activities. They take the initiative to acquire and share information and make plans and decisions about their work. If there is not enough freedom, people demonstrate very little initiative for suggesting new and better ways of doing things. They may spend a great deal of time and energy obtaining permission and gaining support or perform all their work by the book. If there is too much freedom, people may pursue their own independent directions and have an unbalanced concern weighted towards them rather than the work group or organization.

Case Study of innovation within Philips Lighting highlighting some of these issues is available on the Innovation Portal at **www.innovation-portal.info**

Chapter Summary

- Leadership and organization of innovation are much more than a set of processes, tools and techniques, and the successful practice of innovation demands the interaction and integration of three different levels of management: individual, collective and climate.

- At the personal or individual level, the key is to match the leadership styles with the task requirement and type of teams. General leadership requirements for innovative projects include expertise and experience relevant to the project, articulating a vision and inspirational communication, intellectual stimulation and quality of leader–member exchange (LMX).

- At the collective or social level, there is no universal best practice, but successful teams require clear, common and elevating goals, unified commitment, cross-functional expertise, collaborative climate, external support and recognition, and participation in decision making.

- At the context or climate level, there is no 'best innovation culture', but innovation is promoted or hindered by a number of factors, including trust and openness, challenge and involvement, support and space for ideas, conflict and debate, risk taking and freedom.

Key Terms Defined

Climate   recurring patterns of behaviour, attitudes and feelings that characterize life in the organization. These are the objectively shared perceptions that characterize life within a defined work unit or in the larger organization. Climate is distinct from culture in that it is more observable at a surface level within the organization and more amenable to change and improvement efforts.

Conjoint innovation   is the combination and interaction of two or more entrepreneurs with different capabilities to create a novel technology, product, service or venture.

Culture   the deeper and more enduring values, norms and beliefs within the organization.

Group   simply refers to an assemblage of people who are close to each other.

Kirton Adaption-Innovation (KAI) scale   a psychometric approach for assessing the creativity of individuals. By a series of questions it seeks to identify an individual's attitudes towards originality, attention to detail and following rules. It seeks to differentiate 'adaptive' from 'innovative' styles.

Team   implies a combination of individuals who work together for a common purpose.

Upper echelons theory   asserts that a leader's education, experiences, personality and values influence their framing and interpretation of the challenges they face and, in turn, their decisions.

Discussion Questions

1. What are the key similarities, differences and relationships between entrepreneurship and innovation?

2. Why is the creative style of an individual more important than any assessment of absolute creativity?

3. What are the relevant influences of an individual's characteristics and their environment on entrepreneurship?

4. What is the difference between culture and climate, and why is this distinction critical for innovation and entrepreneurship?

5. What factors contribute to the development of a creative climate – and what factors could block it?

Further Reading and Resources

The relationships between leadership, innovation and organizational renewal are addressed more fully in *Meeting the Innovation Challenge: Leadership for Transformation and Growth*, by Scott Isaksen and Joe Tidd (John Wiley & Sons Ltd, 2006).

Many books and articles look at specific aspects of organizational innovation, for example: the development of creative climates, Lynda Gratton, *Hot Spots: Why Some Companies Buzz with Energy and Innovation, and Others Don't* (Prentice Hall, 2007); team working by T. DeMarco and T. Lister, *Peopleware: Productive Projects and Teams* (Dorset House, 1999); or R. Katz, *The Human Side of Managing Technological Innovation* (Oxford University Press, 2003) is an excellent collection of readings, and Andrew Van de Ven, Douglas Polley and Raghu Garud's *The Innovation Journey* (Oxford University Press, 2008) provides a comprehensive review of a seminal study in the field, and includes a discussion of individual, group and organizational issues. John Bessant's *High Involvement Innovation* (John Wiley & Sons Ltd, 2003) looks in detail at employee involvement and how to enable participation in innovation.

Case studies of innovative organizations focus on many of the issues highlighted in this chapter, and good examples include Ernest Gundling's *The 3M Way to Innovation: Balancing People and Profit* (Kodansha International, 2000) and *Corning and the Craft of Innovation* by Margaret Graham and Alec Shuldiner (Oxford University Press, 2001).

References

1. Kaplan, J.M. and A.C. Warren (2013) *Patterns of Entrepreneurship*, 4th edn, Hoboken, NJ: John Wiley & Sons, Inc.

2. Roberts, E.B. (1991) *Entrepreneurs in High Technology: Lessons from MIT and Beyond*, Oxford: Oxford University Press.

3. Roberts, E.B. (1991) *Entrepreneurs in High Technology: Lessons from MIT and Beyond*, Oxford: Oxford University Press.

4. Mueller, S.L. and A.S. Thomas (2001) Culture and entrepreneurial potential: A nine country study of locus of control and innovativeness, *Journal of Business Venturing*, **16**(1): 51–75; Robichaud, Y., E. McGraw and A. Roger (2001) Towards development of a measuring instrument for entrepreneurial motivation, *Journal of Developmental Entrepreneurship*, **5**(2): 189–202; Shane, S. and S. Venkataraman (2000) The promise of entrepreneurship as a field of research, *Academy of Management Review*, **25**: 217–26; Georgelli, Y.P., B. Joyce and A. Woods (2000) Entrepreneurial action, innovation and business performance, *Journal of Small Business and Enterprise Development*, **7**(1): 7–17; Gartner, W.B. (1988) Who is an entrepreneur is the wrong question, *Entrepreneurship Theory and Practice*, **13**(1): 47–64.

5. Sarason, Y., T. Dean and F. Dillard (2006) Entrepreneurship as the nexus of individual and opportunity, *Journal of Business Venturing*, **21**: 286–305; Feldman, D.C. and M.C. Bolino (2000) Career patterns of the self-employed, *Journal of Small Business Management*, **38**(3): 53–68.

6. Harding, R. (2007) *GEM: Global Entrepreneurship Monitor*, London: London Business School; Storey, D. and B. Tether (1998) New technology-based firms in the European Union, *Research Policy*, **26**: 933–46.

7. Bowman, E.H. and C.E. Helfat (2001) Does corporate strategy matter? *Strategic Management Journal*, **22**: 1–23.

8. Mann, R.D. (1959) A review of the relationships between personality and performance in small groups, *Psychological Bulletin*, **56**: 241–70.

9. Connelly, M.S., J.A. Gilbert, S.J. Zaccaro *et al.* (2000) Exploring the relationship of leader skills and knowledge to leader performance, *The Leadership Quarterly*, **11**: 65–86; Zaccaro, S.J., J.A. Gilbert, K.K. Thor and M.D. Mumford (2000) Assessment of leadership problem-solving capabilities, *The Leadership Quarterly*, **11**: 37–64.

10. Farris, G.F. (1972) The effect of individual role on performance in creative groups, *R&D Management*, **3**: 23–8; Ehrhart, M.G. and K.J. Klein (2001) Predicting

followers' preferences for charismatic leadership: The influence of follower values and personality, *Leadership Quarterly*, **12**: 153–80.

11. Scott, S.G. and R.A. Bruce (1994) Determinants of innovative behavior: A path model of individual innovation in the workplace, *Academy of Management Journal*, **37**(3): 580–607.

12. Amabile, T.M., E.A. Schatzel, G.B. Moneta and S.J. Kramer (2004) Leader behaviors and the work environment for creativity: Perceived leader support, *Leadership Quarterly*, **15**(1): 5–32.

13. Rafferty, A.E. and M.A. Griffin (2004) Dimensions of transformational leadership: Conceptual and empirical extensions, *Leadership Quarterly*, **15**(3): 329–54.

14. Mumford, M.D., S.J. Zaccaro, F.D. Harding *et al.* (2000) Leadership skills for a changing world: Solving complex social problems, *Leadership Quarterly*, **11**: 11–35.

15. Rafferty, A.E. and M.A. Griffin (2004) Dimensions of transformational leadership: Conceptual and empirical extensions, *Leadership Quarterly*, **15**(3): 329–54.

16. Pinto, J. and D. Slevin (1989) Critical success factors in R&D projects. *Research-Technology Management*, **32**: 12–18; Podsakoff, P.M., S.B. Mackenzie, J.B. Paine and D.G. Bachrach (2000) Organizational citizenship behaviors: A critical review of the theoretical and empirical literature and suggestions for future research, *Journal of Management*, **26**(3): 513–63.

17. West, M.A., C.S. Borrill, J.F. Dawson *et al.* (2003) Leadership clarity and team innovation in health care, *Leadership Quarterly*, **14**(4–5): 393–410.

18. Andrews, F.M. and G.F. Farris (1967) Supervisory practices and innovation in scientific teams, *Personnel Psychology*, **20**: 497–515; Barnowe, J.T. (1975) Leadership performance outcomes in research organizations, *Organizational Behavior and Human Performance*, **14**: 264–80; Elkins, T. and R.T. Keller (2003) Leadership in research and development organizations: A literature review and conceptual framework, *Leadership Quarterly*, **14**: 587–606.

19. Keller, R.T. (1992) Transformational leadership and performance of research and development project groups, *Journal of Management*, **18**: 489–501.

20. Berson, Y. and J.D. Linton (2005) An examination of the relationships between leadership style, quality, and employee satisfaction in R&D versus administrative environments, *R&D Management*, **35**(1): 51–60.

21. Denti, L. and S. Hemlin (2012) Leadership and innovation in organizations: A systematic review of factors that mediate or moderate the relationship, *International Journal of Innovation Management*, **16**(3): 1–20.

22. Peters, T. (1988) *Thriving on Chaos*, Free Press, New York.

23. Forrester, R. and A. Drexler (1999) A model for team-based organization performance, *Academy of Management Executive*, **13**(3): 36–49; Conway, S. and R. Forrester (1999) *Innovation and Teamworking: Combining Perspectives through a Focus on Team Boundaries*, Birmingham: University of Aston Business School.

24. Thamhain, H. and D. Wilemon (1987) Building high performing engineering project teams, *Transactions on Engineering Management*, **34**(3): 130–37.

25. Bixby, K. (1987) *Superteams*, London: Fontana.

26. Holti, R., J. Neumann and H. Standing (1995) *Change Everything at Once: The Tavistock Institute's Guide to Developing Teamwork in Manufacturing*, London: Management Books 2000.

27. Tranfield, D., I. Parry, S. Wilson *et al.* (1998) Teamworked organizational engineering: Getting the most out of teamworking, *Management Decision*, **36**(6): 378–84.

28. Jassawalla, A. and H. Sashittal (1999) Building collaborative cross-functional new product teams, *Academy of Management Executive*, **13**(3): 50–3.

29. DTI (1996) *UK Software Purchasing Survey*, London: Department of Trade and Industry.

30. Van Beusekom, M. (1996) *Participation Pays! Cases of Successful Companies with Employee Participation*, The Hague: Netherlands Participation Institute.

31. Tuckman, B. and N. Jensen (1977) Stages of small group development revisited, *Group and Organizational Studies*, **2**: 419–27.

32. Belbin, M. (2004) *Management Teams: Why They Succeed or Fail*, London: Butterworth-Heinemann.

33. Smith, P. and E. Blanck (2002) From experience: Leading dispersed teams, *Journal of Product Innovation Management*, **19**: 294–304.

34. Prester, J. and M.G. Bozac (2012) Are innovative organizational concepts enough for fostering innovation? *International Journal of Innovation Management*, **16**(1): 1–23.

35. Isaksen, S. and J. Tidd (2006) *Meeting the Innovation Challenge: Leadership for Transformation and Growth*, Chichester: John Wiley & Sons Ltd.

36. Hackman J.R. (ed.) (1990) *Groups that Work (And Those that Don't): Creating Conditions for Effective Teamwork*, San Francisco: Jossey-Bass.

Deeper Dive explanations of innovation concepts and ideas are available on the Innovation Portal at **www.innovation-portal.info**

 Quizzes to test yourself further are available online via the Innovation Portal at **www.innovation-portal.info**

Summary of online resources for Chapter 9 –
all material is available via the Innovation Portal at
www.innovation-portal.info

Cases	**Media**	**Tools**	**Activities**	**Deeper Dives**
• NSN • Cerulean • Kumba Resources • Hosiden • Philips Lighting	• Fabian Schlage • David Hall • Patrick McLaughlin • Emma Taylor • Veeder-Root	• Teambuilding • High involvement innovation audit	• Creativity questionnaire	• Creating innovation energy • Team roles • Team diversity

Chapter 10

Exploiting Networks

LEARNING OBJECTIVES

By the end of this chapter you will develop an understanding of:

- how networking helps the process of innovation through improving the range and scale of knowledge interaction
- how different types of network can contribute to the process
- how effective networks can be designed and operated
- how drivers such as globalization and the emergence of Internet infrastructures are shaping an increasingly networked model of innovation.

No Man Is an Island...

Eating out in the days of living in caves was not quite the simple matter it has become today. For a start there was the minor difficulty of finding and gathering the roots and berries – or, being more adventurous, hunting and (hopefully) catching your mammoth for the stew pot. And cold meat isn't necessarily an appetizing or digestible dish so cooking it helps; but for that you need fire and for that you need wood, not to mention cooking pots and utensils. If any single individual tried to accomplish all of these tasks alone they would quickly die of exhaustion, never mind starvation! We could elaborate but the point is clear: like almost all human activity, it is dependent on others. But it's not simply about spreading the workload. For most of our contemporary activities the key is shared creativity: solving problems together and exploiting the fact that different people have different skills and experiences which they can bring to the party.

It's easy to think of innovation as a solo act… the lone genius, slaving away in his or her garret or lying, Archimedes-like, in the bath before that moment of inspiration when they run through the streets proclaiming their 'Eureka!' moment. But although that's a common image, it lies a long way from the reality. In reality, taking any good idea forward relies on all sorts of inputs from different people and perspectives.

For example, the technological breakthrough which makes a better mousetrap is only going to mean something if people can be made aware of it and persuaded that this is something they cannot live without – and this requires all kinds of inputs from the marketing skill set. Making it happen is going to need skills in manufacturing, in procurement of the bits and pieces to make it, in controlling the quality of the final product. None of this will happen without some funding so other skills in getting access to finance – and the understanding of how to spend the money wisely – become important. And coordinating the diverse inputs needed to turn the mousetrap into a successful reality rather than a gleam in the eye will require project management skills, balancing resources against the clock and facilitating a team of people to find and solve the thousand and one little problems which crop up as you make the journey.

Innovation is not a solo act but a multiplayer game. Whether it is the entrepreneur who spots an opportunity or an established organization trying to renew its offerings or sharpen up its processes, making innovation happen depends on working with many different players. This raises questions about team working, bringing the different people together in productive and creative ways inside an organization – a theme we discussed in Chapter 9. But increasingly it's also about links *between* organizations, developing and making use of increasingly wide **networks**. Smart firms and solo entrepreneurs have always recognized the importance of linkages and connections – getting close to customers to understand their needs, working with suppliers to deliver innovative solutions, linking up with collaborators, research centres, even competitors to build and operate innovation systems. But in an era of global operations and high-speed technological infrastructures populated by people with highly mobile skills, building and managing networks and connections becomes *the* key requirement for innovation. It's not about knowledge creation so much as knowledge *flows*. Even major research and development players like Siemens or GlaxoSmithKline are realizing that they can't cover all the knowledge bases they need and instead are looking to build extensive links and relationships with players around the globe.

Networking is important right across the innovation process – from finding opportunities, through pulling together the resources to develop the venture, to making it happen and diffusing the idea – and capturing value at the end of the process. The idea of a solo entrepreneur able to carry all of this out on his/her own is a myth; putting new ventures together depends on securing all kinds of input from many different people and managing this team as a network.

This chapter explores some of the emerging themes around the question of innovation as a network-based multiplayer game. And of course, in the 21st century this game is being played out on a vast global stage but with an underlying networking technology – the Internet – which collapses distances, places geographically far-flung locations right alongside each other in time and enables increasingly exciting collaboration possibilities. However, just because we have the technology to make and live in a global village doesn't necessarily mean we'll be able to do so: much of the challenge, as we'll see, lies in organizing and managing networks so that they perform. Rather than simply being the coming together of different people and organizations, successful networks have what are called **emergent properties** – the whole is greater than the sum of the parts.

The Spaghetti Model of Innovation

As we showed in Chapter 1, innovation is a core process with a defined structure and a number of influences. That's helpful in terms of simplifying the picture into some clear stages and recognizing the key levers we may have to work with if we are going to manage the process successfully. But like any simplification, the model isn't quite as complex as the reality. Figure 10.1 provides an illustration of this complexity.

While our model works as an aerial view of what goes on and has to be managed, the close-up picture can look a lot more like the picture on the right. The ways knowledge actually flows around an innovation project are complex and interactive, woven together in a kind of social spaghetti where different people talk to each other in different ways, more or less frequently, and about different things.

This complex interaction is all about *knowledge* and the ways it flows and is combined and deployed to make innovation happen. Whether it's our entrepreneur building a network to help him get his mousetrap to market or a company like Apple bringing out the latest generation iPhone, the process will involve building and running knowledge networks. And as the innovation becomes more complex so the networks have to involve more and different players, many of whom may lie outside the firm. By the time we get to big complex projects – like building a new aeroplane or hospital facility – the number of players and the management challenges the networks pose get pretty large. There is also the complication that increasingly the networks we have to learn to deal with are becoming more virtual, a rich and global set of human resources distributed and connected by the enabling technologies of the Internet, broadband and mobile communications and shared computer networks.

Innovation and entrepreneurship are evolving – from a world of centuries ago which saw the sole inventor/entrepreneur as the key player through one in the last century in which

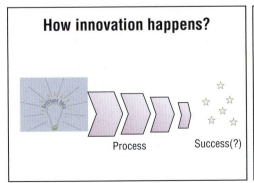
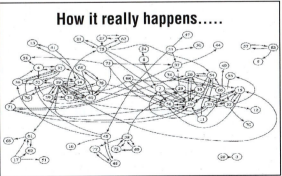

FIGURE 10.1 Spaghetti model of innovation

TABLE 10.1   Rothwell's five generations of innovation models

Generation	Key features
First/second	Simple linear models (need pull, technology push)
Third	Coupling model, recognizing interaction between different elements and feedback loops between them
Fourth	Parallel model, integration within the company, upstream with key suppliers and downstream with demanding and active customers, emphasis on linkages and alliances
Fifth	Systems integration and extensive networking, flexible and customized response, continuous innovation

Video Clip of an interview with Victor Cui founder of OneFC, a global sports entertainment business, exploring how he uses networks is available on the Innovation Portal at **www.innovation-portal.info**

major corporations came to dominate the landscape to today's picture, which is becoming massively networked, globally distributed and connected via communication and information-processing technologies which enable a very different approach.

Networking of this kind is something which Roy Rothwell, for many years a key researcher at Sussex University's Science Policy Research Unit, foresaw in his pioneering work on models of innovation which predicted a gradual move away from thinking about (and organizing) a linear science/technology push or demand pull process to one which saw increasing interactivity.[1] At first, this exists across the company with cross-functional teams and other boundary-spanning activities. Increasingly, it then moves outside it with links to external actors. Rothwell's vision of the 'fifth generation' innovation is essentially the one in which we now need to operate, with rich and diverse network linkages accelerated and enabled by an intensive set of information and communication technologies (Table 10.1).

Types of Innovation Networks

If networking is becoming the dominant mode for innovation and entrepreneurship then it will be useful to begin with a clear understanding of our terms. A network can be defined as

a complex, interconnected group or system

and networking involves using that arrangement to accomplish particular tasks. As we've suggested, innovation has always been a multiplayer game and we can see a growing number of ways in which such networking takes place. At its simplest networking happens in an informal way when people get together and share ideas as a by-product of their social and work interactions. But we'll concentrate our attention on more formal networks which are deliberately set up to help make innovation happen, whether it is creating a new product or service or learning to apply some new process thinking more effectively within organizations.

Innovation networks are more than just ways of assembling and deploying knowledge in a complex world. They can also have emergent properties. Being in an effective innovation network can deliver a wide range of benefits beyond the collective knowledge efficiency mentioned above. These include getting access to different and complementary knowledge sets, reducing risks by sharing them, accessing new markets and technologies and otherwise pooling complementary skills and assets. Without such networks, it would be nearly impossible for the lone inventor to bring his or her idea successfully to market. And it's one of the main reasons why established businesses are increasingly turning to cooperation and alliances: to extend their access to these key innovation resources.

Table 10.2 gives some examples of different types of network in innovation.

We explore these in a little more detail in the following section.

Entrepreneurs' Networks

The idea of the lone inventor pioneering his or her way through to market success is something of a myth, not least because of the huge efforts and different resources needed to make innovation happen. While individual ideas, energy and passion are key requirements, most successful entrepreneurs recognize the need to network extensively and to collect the resources they need via complex webs of relationships. They are essentially highly skilled at networking, both in building and in maintaining those networks to help create a sustainable business model.

If we look at some cases of entrepreneur-driven start-ups, it quickly becomes possible to see their evolution as one of growing networks. Take the wind-up radio story (Lifeline Energy) featured on the Portal – a great idea and an interesting invention required an extensive network of finance, logistics, distribution, marketing and manufacturing to enable it to come to scale and sustainability. Or Mike Lynch's Autonomy – another brilliant technological idea, which provided the basis for what is now a key global player in the information management world, but it began with a process of network building, linking up with key players able to provide the complementary skills and resources to get the innovation established. (This case is discussed in detail in Chapter 12.)

These days one of the most powerful companies in the electronics world is ARM, whose chips are in almost all mobile phones and a host of other devices. Now a global player, ARM began as a spin-off from Cambridge University in the 1980s. But its evolution was not a one-man show but the building and development of a complex network with links across countries, sectors and technologies.

Networking is not just a way of providing leverage for entrepreneurs seeking to access resources. It

Video Clips using the Honey Bee network in India and Blackstone Entrepreneur Networks as examples of these issues are available on the Innovation Portal at **www.innovation-portal.info**

TABLE 10.2   Types of innovation networks

Network type	Characteristics
Entrepreneur-based	Bringing different complementary resources together to help take an opportunity forward. Often a combination of formal and informal, depends a lot on the entrepreneur's energy and enthusiasm in getting people interested to join – and stay in – the network. Networks of this kind provide leverage for obtaining key resources but they can also provide support and mentoring, for example in entrepreneur clubs.
Internal project teams	Formal – and informal – networks of knowledge and key skills within organizations which can be brought together to help enable some opportunity to be taken forward. Essentially like entrepreneur networks but on the inside of established organizations. May run into difficulties because of having to cross internal organizational boundaries.
Internal entrepreneur networks	Aimed at tapping into employee ideas this model has accelerated with the use of online technologies to enable innovation contests and communities. Typically mobilizes on a temporary basis employees into internal ventures – building networks. Not a new idea, comes out of two traditions – employee involvement and 'intrapreneurship' – but social and communications technology has amplified the richness/reach.
Communities of practice	These are networks which can involve players inside and across different organizations – what binds them together is a shared concern with a particular aspect or area of knowledge. They have always been important but with the rise of the Internet there has been an explosion of online communities sharing ideas and accelerating innovation (e.g. Linux, Mozilla and Apache). 'Offline' communities are also important (e.g. the emergence of 'fab-labs' and 'tech-shops' as places where networking around the new ideas of 3D printing and the 'maker movement' is beginning to happen).
Spatial clusters	Networks which form because of the players being close to each other (e.g. in the same geographical region). Silicon Valley is a good example of a cluster which thrives on proximity – knowledge flows amongst and across the members of the network but is hugely helped by the geographical closeness and the ability of key players to meet and talk.
Sectoral networks	Networks which bring different players together because they share a common sector – and often have the purpose of shared innovation to preserve competitiveness. Often organized by sector or business associations on behalf of their members where there is shared concern to adopt and develop innovative good practice across a sector or product market grouping.
New product or process development consortium	Sharing knowledge and perspectives to create and market a new product or process concept (e.g. the Symbian consortium (Sony, Nokia, Ericsson, Motorola and others) worked towards developing a new operating system for mobile phones and PDAs).

TABLE 10.2 *(Continued)*

Network type	Characteristics
New technology development consortium	Sharing and learning around newly emerging technologies (e.g. the pioneering semiconductor research programmes in the US and Japan, or the BLADE server consortium organized by IBM but involving major players in devising new server architectures)
Emerging standards	Exploring and establishing standards around innovative technologies (e.g. the Motion Picture Experts Group (MPEG) working on audio and video compression standards)
Supply chain learning	Developing and sharing innovative good practice and possibly shared product development across a value chain (e.g. the SCRIA initiative in UK aerospace)
Learning networks	Groups of individuals and organizations who converge to learn about new approaches and leverage their shared learning experiences
Recombinant innovation networks	Cross-sectoral groupings which allow for networking across boundaries and the transfer of ideas
Managed open innovation networks	Building on the core idea that 'not all the smart people work for us', organizations are increasingly looking to build external networks in a planned and systematic fashion. Underlying purpose is to amplify their access to ideas and resources. It may involve joining established networks or it may require constructing new ones. In this space there is a growing role for 'brokerage' mechanisms (individuals, software, etc.) which can help make the connections and support the network building process
User networks	Extending the above idea these networks aim to connect to users as a source of innovation input rather than simply as passive markets. Often mobilizes a broadcast approach, opening up to large open networks via crowdsourcing. Problem is converting front-end interest into meaningful long-term co-creation activity
Innovation markets	An extreme version of the open and user networks approach is to broadcast the innovation needs and connect to potential solutions in a marketplace. The Internet has enabled the emergence of such eBay-type models for ideas, allowing connections across a wide area in response to broadcast challenges. This model can often be the precursor to establishing a more formal managed network between key players found on the open market
Crowdfunding and new resource approaches	Another extension of the above ideas is to mobilize the crowd not as sources of ideas but of resources and judgement (e.g. websites like Kickstarter allow comment and discussion around new ideas as well as proving a platform for assembling the resources, and often mobilizing the early market, around innovation)

Video Clip of a talk by Chris Anderson about the 'maker revolution' where increasingly entrepreneurial networks are forming around 'tech shops' and 'fab labs' is available on the Innovation Portal at **www.innovation-portal.info**

also provides valuable support in other ways, from acting as a sounding board through to providing valuable guidance and mentoring. An increasing number of networking clubs, often linked to entrepreneur incubators, are emerging to tap into this need for support networks.

Internal Cross-boundary and Communities of Practice

'If only x knew what x knows…' You can fill the x in with the name of almost any large contemporary organization (Siemens, Philips, GSK, Citibank). They all wrestle with the paradox that they have hundreds or thousands of people spread across their organizations with all sorts of knowledge. The trouble is that, apart from some formal project activities which bring them together, many of these knowledge elements remain unconnected, like a giant jigsaw puzzle in which only a small number of the pieces have so far been fitted together.

This kind of thinking was behind the fashion for 'knowledge management' in the late 1990s and one response, popular then, was to make extensive use of information technology to try to improve the connectivity. Trouble is that, while the computers and database systems were excellent at storage and transmission, they didn't necessarily help make the connections that turned data and information into useful – and used – knowledge. Increasingly, firms are recognizing that, while advanced information and communications technology can support and enhance, the real need is for improved knowledge networks inside the organization. The concept of **communities of practice** is becoming a powerful focal point in designing effective knowledge-sharing systems.[2]

Case Studies of 3M, P&G and Nokia Solutions and Networks (NSN) exploring some of these issues are available on the Innovation Portal at **www.innovation-portal.info**

It's back to the spaghetti model of innovation: how to ensure that people get to talk to others and share and build on each other's ideas. This may not be too hard in a three- or four-person business, but it gets much harder across a typical sprawling multinational company. Although this is a long-standing problem, there has been quite a lot of movement in recent years towards understanding how to build more effective innovation networks within such businesses.

Video Clips of Roy Sandbach (P&G) and Fabian Schlage (NSN) illustrating some of these themes are available on the Innovation Portal at **www.innovation-portal.info**

INNOVATION IN ACTION 10.1

Communities of Practice at Work

For example, Procter and Gamble's successes with 'connect and develop' (which we looked at briefly in Chapter 7) owe much to its mobilizing rich linkages between people who know things within their giant global operations and increasingly outside it. P&G uses communities of practice –

Internet-enabled 'clubs' where people with different knowledge sets can converge around core themes – and deploys a small army of innovation 'scouts' who are licensed to act as prospectors, brokers and gatekeepers for knowledge to flow across the organization's boundaries. Intranet technology links around 10 000 people in an internal 'ideas market', while sites like InnoCentive. com extend the principle outside the firm and enable a world of new collaborative possibilities.

3M – another firm with a strong innovation pedigree dating back over a century – similarly put much of its success down to making and managing connections. Larry Wendling, Vice President for Corporate Research, talks of 3M's 'secret weapon': the rich formal and informal networking which links the thousands of R&D and market-facing people across the organization. Its long history of breakthrough innovations – from masking tape, through Scotchgard, Scotch tape, magnetic recording tape to Post-its and their myriad derivatives – arises primarily out of people making connections.

Clusters and 'Collective Efficiency' in Innovation

Innovation is about taking risks and deploying what are often scarce resources on projects which may not succeed. So, another way in which networking can help is by helping to spread the risk and, in the process, extending the range of things which may be tried. This is particularly useful in the context of smaller businesses where resources are scarce and it is one of the key features behind the success of many industrial **clusters**.[3]

INNOVATION IN ACTION 10.2

Small Can Be Beautiful

'The trouble with small firms isn't that they're small, it's that they're isolated!' A powerful point: we know that small firms have lots of advantages in terms of focus, energy and fast decision making. But they often lack resources to achieve their full potential. This is where a concept the economists call **collective efficiency** comes in – the idea that you don't have to have all the resources under your own roof, only to know where and how to get hold of them. Working with others can get you a lot further. For example, the Italian furniture industry shows how a network of small companies can compete in the high end of the market not through individual excellence but through sharing design expertise and facilities, and with collective materials purchasing and marketing. The same is true around the world. For example, 12% of the world's surgical instruments are made in one town in Pakistan. This isn't a case of low-cost manufacturing; it is a high-precision, design-intensive business and the small firms involved prosper by working together in a cooperative cluster. And the Chinese motorcycle industry is becoming a world leader; most of its manufacturing takes place in the city of Chongqing. Once again, the dominant model is one of networking amongst a wide range of small specialized producers, each taking responsibility for a particular system or component.[4]

Long-lasting innovation networks can create the capability to ride out major waves of change in the technological and economic environment. We think of places like Silicon Valley, Cambridge in the UK or the island of Singapore as powerhouses of innovation but they are just the latest in a long-running list of geographical regions which have grown and sustained themselves through a continuous stream of innovation.

INNOVATION IN ACTION 10.3

Networking for Collective Efficiency

Michael Best's fascinating account of the ways in which the Massachusetts economy managed to reinvent itself several times is one which places innovation networking at its heart.[5] In the 1950s the state suffered heavily from the loss of its traditional industries of textiles and shoes but by the early 1980s the 'Massachusetts miracle' led to the establishment of a new high-tech industrial district. It was a resurgence enabled in no small measure by an underpinning network of specialist skills, high-tech research and training centres (the Boston area has the highest concentration of colleges, universities, research labs and hospitals in the world) and by the rapid establishment of entrepreneurial firms keen to exploit the emerging 'knowledge economy'. But in turn this miracle turned to dust in the years between 1986 and 1992 when around one-third of the manufacturing jobs in the region disappeared as the minicomputer and defence-related industries collapsed. Despite gloomy predictions about its future, the region built again on its rich network of skills, technology sources and a diverse local supply base which allowed rapid new product development to emerge again as a powerhouse in high technology such as special-purpose machinery, optoelectronics, medical laser technology, digital printing equipment and biotech.

Supply Chain and Improvement Networks

Supply chain learning involves building a knowledge-sharing network; good examples can be found in the automotive, aerospace and food industries, and often involve formal arrangements like supplier associations.[6] For example, Toyota has worked over many years to build and manage a learning system based on transferring and improving its core Toyota Production System across local and international suppliers.[7] The model (which has been replicated in Toyota supplier networks outside Japan) is based on:

- a set of institutionalized routines for exchange of tacit and explicit knowledge
- clear rules around intellectual property, e.g. new production process knowledge is the property of the network, though it is derived from the expertise of individual firms
- mechanisms for protecting core proprietary knowledge on product designs and technologies, and to protect the interests of the few suppliers which are direct competitors
- a strong sense of network identity which is actively promoted by Toyota, and evidence of clear benefits accruing to membership which ensures commitment
- effective coordination and facilitation of the network by Toyota.

Similarly, Volvo's and IKEA's experiences in China show how the firms can share their knowledge with their principal suppliers, who then disseminate it further. Key suppliers (in both first and second tiers) learnt parts of Volvo's management systems, especially quality management and supply chain management, and this led to dissemination and positive influence on the next tier of Chinese suppliers.

Case Study of Volvo's approach in China is available on the Innovation Portal at **www.innovation-portal.info**

Another example is the Boeing 787 aircraft. It is manufactured in Japan, Australia, Sweden, India, Italy and France and finally assembled in the USA. In spite of the cultural differences, suppliers must be able to

Case Study exploring supply chain learning is available on the Innovation Portal at **www.innovation-portal.info**

communicate using the same technical language (i.e. common engineering design software, common order/entry systems, etc.). For this reason, it makes sense to try to build an active cooperating network amongst these widely distributed players.

Breakthrough Technology Collaborations

One area where it makes sense to collaborate is in exploring the frontiers of new technology. The advantages of doing this in network fashion include reduced risk and increased resource focused on a learning and experimental process. This is often found in pre-competitive R&D consortia which are convened for a temporary period during which there is considerable experimentation and sharing of both tacit and explicit knowledge. Examples range from the Japanese 5th Generation computer project and the ESPRIT collaborations in the 1980s, through to programmes like the blade server community (www.blade.org) in which networked learning amongst key players led to rapid development and diffusion of key ideas.[8]

Such networks are often organized and supported by government, for example the Magnet programme in Israel encouraged the development of the long-term competitive technological advantage of the industry, by creating clusters in key technological areas as nanotechnology, military systems and software. The DNATF programme in Denmark supports advanced technological research and innovation projects in a variety of sectors like construction, energy and environment, the food chain, biomedical and IT.

Learning Networks

Another way in which networking can help innovation is in providing support for shared learning: **learning networks**. A lot of process innovation is about configuring and adapting what has been developed elsewhere and applying it to your processes, for example in the many efforts which organizations have been making to adopt world-class manufacturing (and increasingly service) practice. While it is possible to go it alone in this process, an increasing number of companies are seeing the value in using networks to give them some extra traction on the learning process.[9]

We saw in Chapter 7 that a problem in innovation arises because, although individuals and organizations operate in a world full of external knowledge which they could access, they are, in practice, limited by their 'absorptive capacity': their ability to make sense of it, acquire it and put it to effective use. They need to learn to learn, building a capability for innovating to take advantage of the open innovation environment. Once again, networking can help enable even very small organizations and individuals to obtain traction on this problem.

Experience and research suggest that shared learning can help deal with some of the barriers to learning which individual firms may face. For example:

- in shared learning there is the potential for challenge and structured critical reflection from different perspectives
- different perspectives can bring in new concepts (or old concepts which are new to the learner)
- shared experimentation can reduce perceived and actual costs or risks in trying new things
- shared experiences can provide support and open new lines of inquiry or exploration
- shared learning helps explicate the systems principles, seeing the patterns (separating the wood from the trees)
- shared learning provides an environment for surfacing assumptions and exploring mental models outside of the normal experience of individual organizations (helps prevent 'not invented here' and other effects)
- shared learning can reduce costs (e.g. in drawing on consultancy services and learning about external markets) which can be particularly useful for small/medium-sized enterprises (SMEs) and for developing country firms.

Recombinant Innovation Networks

Participating in innovation networks can help companies bump into new ideas and creative combinations – even for mature businesses. As we saw in Chapter 5, the process of creativity involves making associations; sometimes, the unexpected conjunction of different perspectives can lead to surprising results. The same is true at the organizational level. Studies of networks indicate that getting together in such a fashion can help open up new and productive territory. Chapter 6 gave some examples of such 'recombinant innovation'; the question it raises is: 'How can we enable connections across sectoral boundaries?'

An increasing number of organizations are offering brokerage services to make these links and to facilitate the building of networks across which organizations can safely exchange ideas and experiences.

INNOVATION IN ACTION 10.4

Many Minds Make Light Work...

Say the name Thomas Edison and people instinctively imagine a great inventor, the lone genius who gave us so many 20th-century products and services – the gramophone, the light bulb, electric power, etc. But he was actually a very smart networker. His 'invention factory' in Menlo Park,

New Jersey employed a team of engineers in a single room filled with workbenches, shelves of chemicals, books and other resources. The key to their undoubted success was to bring together a group of young, entrepreneurial, enthusiastic men from very diverse backgrounds and allow the emerging community to tackle a wide range of problems. Ideas flowed across the group and were combined and recombined into an astonishing array of inventions.

Managed Open Innovation Networks

The logic of **open innovation** (which we discussed in Chapter 7) is that organizations need to open up their innovation processes, searching widely outside their boundaries and working towards managing a rich set of network connections and relationships right across the board. Their challenge becomes one of improving the knowledge *flows* in and out of the organization, trading in knowledge as much as goods and services. Great in theory – but what it implies is that firms need to raise their game around finding and forming relevant connections and networks, and in building high-performance relationships with which to enable innovation.

Similarly this open environment offers rich opportunities for start-up entrepreneurs. They no longer need to have all the knowledge resources in one place; rather, the challenge is knowing where they are and how to get at them. But once again this means learning a whole new set of skills around making and managing connections.

Traditional boundaries are becoming blurred, for example between established organizations and start-ups or between the public and private sectors. Instead, it is a pattern of new relationships across which knowledge spaghetti is combined in new ways. But underlying this is the need to learn new ways of working – or rather new ways of networking.

Case Study of Alibaba and the role its online shopping mall, Taobao, has played in giving entrepreneurs access to markets to grow their businesses is available on the Innovation Portal at **www.innovation-portal.info**

The process of opening up the game is not without its problems – first of all in finding new ways to enable connections. There has been a huge rise in the role played by social and technological networking as mechanisms which enable closer linkages, and with it have sprung up new roles and groupings within organizations (gatekeepers, information managers, knowledge hubs, etc.) and new service businesses on the outside specializing in brokering and connecting. But improving knowledge flows also opens a can of worms as far as managing intellectual property is concerned. In a world of open source, who owns what and how should you protect your hard-won knowledge assets?

For the lone entrepreneur this raises a tantalizing mixture of threat and opportunity. On the one hand, he or she can make effective connections to resources and mobilize them and act on a global basis. We've seen examples of this in the field of Internet businesses which operate often with very small groups of people and amplify their efforts and presence through networking to a global community sometimes running into billions of people. Developments around networking mean that the old problem for small businesses – their isolation – is removed. But on the other hand the sheer scale and number of potential connections requires learning new skills in finding, forming and getting networks to perform.

Choosing the most appropriate form of open innovation network is very much dependent on where an organization sits in terms of its size, sector and stage in its lifecycle. For example, inputs from customers are central when market dynamics are high, suppliers are important in technologically challenging environments, and the inclusion from companies of other industries is effective irrespective of the setting.

Strategy is not limited to the decision whether to open up a project to a wide range of different types of external partners (the breadth dimension), but it is equally important to consider the depth of the relations with different types of external partners (the depth dimension) and the balance between the development of new and long-standing relations with these external partners (the ambidexterity dimension).

For example, higher levels of project novelty are associated with a higher intensity of interaction between actors and the use of more rich mechanisms for knowledge sharing. This suggests that open innovation is not a universal prescription, but may be more relevant to more novel or complex development projects under conditions of uncertainty.

Table 10.3 summarizes some of the key contingency factors in shaping open innovation strategy, based on considerations of:

- conditions and context, e.g. environmental uncertainty and project complexity
- control and ownership of resources
- coordination of knowledge flows
- creation and capture of value.

TABLE 10.3 Potential benefits and challenges of applying open innovation

Six principles of open innovation	Potential benefits	Challenges to apply
Tap into external knowledge	Increase the pool of knowledge	How to search for and identify relevant knowledge sources
	Reduce reliance on limited internal knowledge	How to share or transfer such knowledge, especially tacit and systemic
External R&D has significant value	Can reduce the cost and uncertainty associated with internal R&D, and increase depth and breadth of R&D	Less likely to lead to distinctive capabilities and more difficult to differentiate
		External R&D also available to competitors
Do not have to originate research in order to profit from it	Reduce costs of internal R&D, more resources on external search strategies and relationships	Need sufficient R&D capability in order to identify, evaluate and adapt external R&D

TABLE 10.3 *(Continued)*

Six principles of open innovation	Potential benefits	Challenges to apply
Building a better business model is superior to being first to market	Greater emphasis on capturing rather than creating value	First-mover advantages depend on technology and market context Developing a business model demands time-consuming negotiation with other actors
Best *use* of internal and external ideas, not *generation* of ideas	Better balance of resources to search and identify ideas, rather than generate	Generating ideas is only a small part of the innovation process Most ideas unproven or no value, so cost of evaluation and development high
Profit from others intellectual property (inbound OI) and others' use of our intellectual property (outbound IP)	Value of IP very sensitive to complementary capabilities such as brand, sales network, production, logistics, and complementary products and services	Conflicts of commercial interest or strategic direction Negotiation of acceptable forms and terms of IP licences

OI: open innovation; IP: intellectual property.

Video Clip of David Simoes-Brown of 100% Open exploring innovation management and the challenges and opportunities offered in working in the 'open innovation' space is available on the Innovation Portal at **www.innovation-portal.info**

Mobilizing User Networks

Innovation is not simply about technological knowledge; the other piece of the puzzle is knowledge of user needs. We saw in the previous chapter how users have always been an important source of innovation and this role has accelerated in recent years as the technology and social networks allow for more participating in what is effectively a process of co-creation. However, although the potential of involving users is huge, the experience has often been that actively engaging with and working with communities beyond a front-end process of crowdsourcing ideas requires careful management.

Once again, there are many different ways in which organizations are seeking to build more open networks with users; Figure 10.2 gives an overview of key strategies.

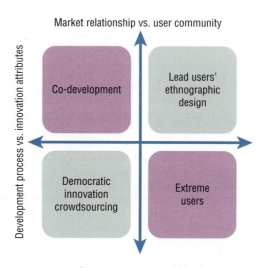

FIGURE 10.2   Strategic options in engaging users in innovation

Lead Users

As their name suggests, lead users demand new requirements ahead of the general market of other users, but are also positioned in the market to significantly benefit from the meeting of those requirements.[10] Where potential users have high levels of sophistication, for example in business-to-business markets such as scientific instruments, capital equipment and IT systems, lead users can help to co-develop innovations, and are therefore often early adopters of such innovations. Research by Eric von Hippel suggests lead users adopt an average of seven years before typical users, but the precise lead time will depend on a number of factors, including the technology lifecycle.

Video Clip of Eric von Hippel describing lead user methods and their application in the 3M company is available on the Innovation Portal at **www.innovation-portal.info**

One empirical study identified a number of characteristics of lead users:[11]

- Recognize requirements early – are ahead of the market in identifying and planning for new requirements.
- Expect high level of benefits – owing to their market position and complementary assets.
- Develop their own innovations and applications – have sufficient sophistication to identify and capabilities to contribute to development of the innovation.
- Perceived to be pioneering and innovative – by themselves and their peer group.

This has two important implications. First, those seeking to develop innovative complex products and services should identify potential lead users with such characteristics to contribute to the co-development and early adoption of the innovation. Second, lead users, as early adopters, can provide insights to forecasting the diffusion of innovations. For example, a study of 55 development projects in telecommunications computer infrastructure found that the importance of customer inputs increased with technological newness and, moreover, the relationship shifted from customer surveys and focus groups to co-development because 'conventional marketing techniques proved to be of limited utility, were often ignored, and in hindsight were sometimes strikingly inaccurate'[12]

Video Clip of Catharina van Delden, founder Innosabi, discussing some impressive examples of user innovation is available on the Innovation Portal at www.innovation-portal.info

Extreme Users

We mentioned extreme users as a source of innovation in Chapter 6 and it is clear this can give us valuable clues about what could be mainstream innovations in the future. For example, the whole concept of 'mobile money' is of interest around the world but in the extreme conditions of emerging countries in Africa, Asia and Latin America it is being brought to life because of

Case Study of M-PESA highlighting some of these issues is available on the Innovation Portal at www.innovation-portal.info

the needs of extreme users. M-PESA developed as a system to help provide more security for people not wishing to carry cash in Kenya and has since grown to become a powerful engine for mobile payments across the region and beyond.

In the field of mobile communications this is only one of hundreds of new applications being developed in extreme conditions and by underserved users, and represents a powerful laboratory for new concepts which companies like Nokia and Vodafone are working closely to explore. The potential exists to use this kind of extreme environment as a laboratory to test and develop concepts for wider application, for example Citicorp has been experimenting with a design of ATM based on biometrics for use with the illiterate population in rural India. The pilot involves some 50 000 people but as a spokesman for the company explained, 'We see this as having the potential for global application.'

Extreme users are important but the question again is around how we can engage with them. How can we build effective networks of extreme users? One approach is the setting-up of 'living labs'; places where experimentation and experience sharing can go on in the context of extreme users and from whom valuable insights can be developed.

Case Study of Instituto Nokia de Tecnologia (INdT), Brazil which has helped set up a 'living lab' to identify and meet the needs of rural populations in the Amazonas region is available on the Innovation Portal at www.innovation-portal.info

INNOVATION IN ACTION 10.5

Experience-based Design with Patients

As we saw in Chapter 6, an area where extreme users can play a significant role is in healthcare and patients are increasingly seen as a key part of the innovation system.[13] For example, work

(continued)

at the Luton and Dunstable hospital in the UK involves using design methods to create a user-led solution to the challenge of improving patient care amongst neck and head cancer sufferers. The approach involves patients and carers telling stories about their experience of the service. These stories provide insights which enable the team of co-designers to think about designing experiences rather than designing services. The range of people involved as co-designers made for an unusual mix of expertise in the context of traditional healthcare improvement efforts by taking into consideration the different skills, views and life experiences of the patients, carers and others involved.

In the L&D, such co-design has led to changes, for example patients and carers have changed project documentation so that it better reflects their needs, and clinical staff and patients have worked together to redesign the flow of outpatients in the consulting room. Various methodologies were used to encourage patient involvement in the process, including patient interviews, logbooks and film-making. This enabled patients to show their experience of the service through their own lens, and bring their story to life for others.

 Audio Clip of an interview with Lynne Maher describing this patient-centred approach is available on the Innovation Portal at **www.innovation-portal.info**

The initial co-design group identified 38 different actions to be taken, all based on user experiences.

 Video Clip of introduction to the network Patient Innovation which is trying to draw users more actively into innovation around their care is available on the Innovation Portal at **www.innovation-portal.info**

Another way of building such networks is via online communities, for example a significant innovation community has been pulled together around the experience of living with or caring for those with rare diseases. User experiences of this kind can not only diffuse across the community to everyone's benefit but also surface new directions for innovation.

Co-Development

The potential for users, either as individuals or as groups, to become involved in the design and production of products has clearly been recognized for some time. However, these conceptions of user–supplier innovation all tend to depict a relationship in which suppliers are able, in some way or another, to harness the experience or ideas of users and apply them to their own product development efforts. Many now argue that we are seeing a dramatic shift towards more open, democratized forms of innovation that are driven by networks of individual users, not firms.[14] Users are now visibly active within all stages of the innovation process, from concept generation to development and diffusion. They may now be actively engaged with firms in the co-development of products

 Case Study of Lego demonstrating the building of a community around co-creation is available on the Innovation Portal at **www.innovation-portal.info**

and services and the innovation agenda may no longer be entirely controlled by firms.

Case Study of Local Motors which represents a user community increasingly working with major companies as an innovation partner is available on the Innovation Portal at **www.innovation-portal.info**

Some forms of user activity represent the emergence of a parallel system of innovation that does not share the same goals, drivers and boundaries of mainstream commercial activity. Users are seen as having an active role in seeking to shape or reshape their relationship with innovation, beyond the prescribed application or use, or developing an agenda that may conflict with the producer. In this way the boundary between producers and users becomes less distinct, with some users able to develop and extend technologies or use them in entirely novel and unexpected ways. Innovation can become far more open and democratized. Such lack of compliance by users with producers and promoters of innovations need not be viewed as a deviant activity but can become more central to the processes of innovation and diffusion. This has potentially significant implications for market relationships, business models and intellectual property.

Crowdsourcing

We saw in Chapter 6 the emergence of the crowd as a source of innovation. Crowdsourcing can be implemented in many ways, but it is typically enabled by information and communication technology which can extend the reach without losing some of the richness of user engagement.

One approach is to organize a competition where a problem or challenge is set and potential solutions or ideas are invited. Rewards range from peer or public recognition and community status, but more commonly feature some extrinsic motivation such as free products or cash prizes. For example, Dell's crowdsourcing platform Idea Storm received more than 15 000 ideas, of which over 400 were implemented. Contributions and rewards tend to be more individual and competitive than in peer or user communities.

Another approach is to make extensive use of users as co-developers. For example, Adidas has taken the model and developed its 'mi Adidas' concept where users are encouraged to co-create their own shoes using a combination of website (where designs can be explored and uploaded) and in-store mini-factories (where user-created and customized ideas can then be produced).

Facebook chose to engage its users in helping to translate the site into multiple languages rather than commission an expert translation service. Its motive was to try to compete with Myspace, which in 2007 was the market leader, available in five languages. The Facebook crowdsource project began in December 2007 and invited users to help translate around 30 000 key phrases from the site. Eight thousand volunteer developers registered within two months and within three weeks the site was available in Spanish, with pilot versions in French and German also online. Within one year Facebook was available in over 100 languages and dialects and, like Wikipedia, continues to benefit from continuous updating and correction via its user community.

Audio Clips of a talk by Wikipedia founder Jimmy Wales and of Charles Leadbeater talking about the power of the crowd in innovation are available on the Innovation Portal at **www.innovation-portal.info**

INNOVATION IN ACTION 10.6

Netflix and Open Collective Innovation

Netflix is a major player in the growing film rental business in the USA; the business works by online and mail-order distribution of DVDs and other media. Its business model depends on having a good understanding of what people want and, like Amazon, trying to tailor advertising and offers to their preferences. It was already a successful business but in 2006 decided to try to improve the algorithm it used to develop these recommendations by opening up the challenge to the wider community. It offered a $1m reward – the Netflix Prize – to anyone who could improve the performance of its algorithm by 10% or better.

In running the competition, it had to open up its current customer database of around 100 million people to anyone registering for the competition. The work involved was complex. The data file which contestants had to work with was around 10 gigabytes and the statistical techniques needed to work with it were sophisticated. Within three months over 18 000 contestants from 125 countries had registered, effectively creating a temporary R&D laboratory on a huge and globally distributed scale.

In addition to the $1m prize, Netflix offered 'progress prizes' where it would pay $50 000 for a non-exclusive licence to use any interesting new algorithms. Importantly, it published these so that others in the competition would have access to them and employ them to make their own efforts even better.

After one year it became clear that 'not all the smart guys work for us' – Netflix found over 7000 people had a better algorithm than the one the company had originally been using. Within three years, 51 000 contestants had joined the competition from 186 countries, and they had created 44 000 valid entries. A winner was announced which demonstrated a better than 10% improvement; significantly, the strategy employed was not one of lone expertise but rather continuous co-creation, in which groups of developers learnt from each other and improved on a continuing basis.

In work with colleagues at the University of Erlangen-Nuremburg in Germany and at the Centre for Leading Innovation and Change at Leipzig Business School, Kathrin Moeslein has developed a framework for viewing such developments.[15]

It involves five complementary sets of tools which enable networks to be built and operated drawing on inputs from the crowd:

● *Innovation contests.* Not a new idea (Napoleon's offer of a prize led to the development of margarine as a substitute for butter, while in the UK the development of the maritime chronometer was as a result of an open contest won by Thomas Harrison). The basic principle is to offer a prize and then invite ideas via a Web 2.0 portal on which others can vote, make comments, etc. A 21st-century example is the $20m prize Lunar X competition to develop a robot which can explore the surface of the moon; it must travel at least 500 miles and send pictures back to earth. Many public- and private-sector organizations are using versions of innovation contests to increase the front-end flow of ideas, ranging from jewellery design (Swarovski), car design (Smart) and even public service design (Bavarian state government).

- *Innovation markets.* These essentially work by bringing 'seekers' and 'solvers' together via an eBay-style marketplace enabled by Web 2.0. The pioneer of this approach and still widely used is InnoCentive.com (which brings together 165 000 innovators in 175 countries), but many others now exist. Research suggests that such markets are particularly valuable in dealing with persistent problems which internal innovation teams have been unable to solve.

- *Innovation communities.* Unite interested and often experienced and skilled innovators sharing common interests. User groups and online communities are examples and such groups are often a rich source of cooperative innovation in which ideas from one member are built on by others. Linux is a good example of this process, as is the growing developer community around Apple's iPhone platform.

- *Innovation toolkits.* Enable users to engage with developing their ideas, e.g. through configuration and self-build toolkits. Lego Factory offers a good example of this approach where users are encouraged to create their own designs which software on the Web helps them work with.

- *Innovation technologies.* Offer tools to realize design and production by user creators, e.g. through online computer-aided design and rapid prototyping technologies. Examples include Quirky (www.quirky.com) and Ponoko (www.ponoko.com).

Case Studies of Adidas and Threadless.com which build on models of user configuration and co-creation are available on the Innovation Portal at **www.innovation-portal.info**

Audio Clip with David Overton illustrating how the UK's Ordnance Survey organization uses a similar approach is available on the Innovation Portal at **www.innovation-portal.info**

Case Study of using online crowdsourcing to improve health innovation in dealing with rare diseases is available on the Innovation Portal at **www.innovation-portal.info**

Networks as Purposeful Constructions

If networking is becoming the dominant mode for managing knowledge flows in innovation then it is worth looking at how we can construct them. Putting together networks for a purpose – what Steward and Conway call 'engineered networks' – is not trivial.[16] It requires finding relevant partners, forming a network around them and finally operating that network – and finding, forming and performing is not always easy.

We have enough difficulties trying to manage within the boundaries of a typical business. So, the challenge of innovation networks takes us well beyond this. The challenges include:

- how to manage something we don't own or control
- how to see system-level effects not narrow self-interests

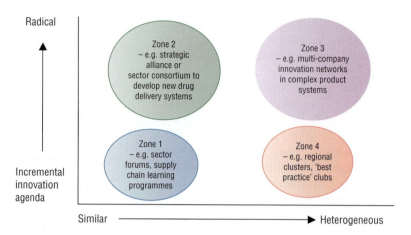

FIGURE 10.3 Types of innovation network

- how to build trust and shared risk taking without tying the process up in contractual red tape
- how to avoid 'free riders' and information 'spillovers'.

It's a new game and one in which a new set of management skills becomes important. For example, there is a big difference between the demands for an innovation network working at the frontier where issues of intellectual property management and risk are critical and one where there is an established innovation agenda. But the challenges are about building trust and sharing key information – as may be the case in using supply chains to enhance product and process innovation. We can map some of these different types of innovation network onto a simple diagram (Figure 10.3) which positions them in terms of:

- how radical the innovation target is with respect to current innovative activity
- the similarity of the participating companies.

By making this distinction, we can see that different types of networks have different issues to resolve. For example, in zone 1 we have individuals and organizations with a broadly similar orientation working on tactical innovation issues. Typically, this could be a cluster or sector forum concerned with adopting and configuring 'good practice' manufacturing or a group of innovation managers in the health sector trying to improve productivity. Issues here would involve enabling them to share experiences, disclose information, develop trust and transparency and build a system-level sense of shared purpose around innovation.

Zone 2 activities could involve players from a sector working to explore and create new product or process concepts, for example the emerging biotechnology/pharmaceutical networking around frontier developments and the need to look for interesting connections and synthesis between these adjacent sectors. Here, the concern is exploratory and challenges existing boundaries but will rely on a degree of information sharing and shared risk taking, often in the form of formal joint ventures and strategic alliances.

In zone 3, the players are highly differentiated and bring different key pieces of knowledge to the party. Their risks in disclosing can be high so ensuring careful intellectual property management and establishing ground rules will be crucial. At the same time, this kind of innovation is likely to involve considerable risk and so putting in place risk- and benefit-sharing arrangements will also be critical.

Zone 4 involves the kind of shared learning across organizations which we saw earlier – essentially building on regional or sectoral links to focus a shared learning effort.

INNOVATION IN ACTION 10.7

High Value Innovation Networks

In a review of such innovation networks in the UK, researchers from the Advanced Institute of Management Research (AIM) found the following characteristics to be important success factors:[17]

- *Highly diverse*. Network partners from a wide range of disciplines and backgrounds who encourage exchanges about ideas across systems.
- *Third-party gatekeepers*. Science partners such as universities but also consultants and trade associations, who provide access to expertise and act as neutral knowledge brokers across the network.
- *Financial leverage*. Access to investors via business angels, venture capitalists and corporate venturing, which spreads the risk of innovation and provides market intelligence.
- *Proactively managed*. Participants regard the network as a valuable asset and actively manage it to reap the innovation benefits.

Building networks involves three steps: finding, forming and performing. The 'finding' stage is essentially about setting up the network. Key issues here are around providing the momentum for bringing the network together and clearly defining its purpose. It may be crisis triggered, for example perception of the urgent need to catch up via adoption of innovation. Equally, it may be driven by a shared perception of opportunity, the potential to enter new markets or exploit new technologies. Key roles here will often be played by third parties, that is network brokers, gatekeepers, policy agents and facilitators.

'Forming' a network involves building a kind of organization with some structure to enable its operation. Key issues here are about trying to establish some core operating processes (about which there is support and agreement) to deal with:

- *Network boundary management*. How the membership of the network is defined and maintained.
- *Decision making*. How (where, when, who) decisions get taken at the network level.

- *Conflict resolution.* How conflicts are resolved effectively.
- *Information processing.* How information flows among members and is managed.
- *Knowledge management.* How knowledge is created, captured, shared and used across the network.
- *Motivation.* How members are motivated to join/remain within the network.
- *Risk/benefit sharing.* How the risks and rewards are allocated across members of the network.
- *Coordination.* How the operations of the network are integrated and coordinated.

Finally, the 'performing' stage is about operating the network and allowing it to evolve. Networks need not last for ever. Sometimes they are set up to achieve a highly specific purpose (e.g. development of a new product concept), and once this has been done the network can be disbanded. In other instances, there is a case for sustaining the networking activities for as long as members see benefits. This may require periodic review and 're-targeting' to keep the motivation high.

For example, CRINE, a successful development programme for the offshore oil and gas industry, was launched in 1992 by key players in the industry, such as BP, Shell and major contractors (and with support from the government), with the target of cost reduction. Using a network model, it delivered extensive innovation in product/services and processes over a ten-year period. Having met its original cost-reduction targets, the programme moved to a second phase with a focus aimed more at capturing a bigger export share of the global industry through innovation.

INNOVATION IN ACTION 10.8

Building Entrepreneurial Networks

A study in 2000 by Iain Edmondson looked at three Cambridge companies and the benefits they gained from networking at three different stages in their development:

- Conceptualization (the ideas)
- Start-up
- Growth.

The benefits fell into two categories:

- *'Harder' benefits.* Lead to customers, investors, partners, suppliers, employees and technical and market knowledge/information.
- *'Softer' benefits.* Credibility/legitimacy, advice and problem solving, confidence and reassurance, motivation/inspiration, relaxation/interest.

At the conceptualization stage, entrepreneurs tended to cast their net widely to try to establish themselves and their ideas in the entrepreneurial community and pave the way for the development of future business relationships. The role of networking groups here is in providing the softer benefits.

At the start-up stage, there is a shift towards using networks to gain more tangible benefits to develop new business relationships. Establishment of trust is crucial at this stage in sharing problems and solutions. The role of networking groups here is to provide both softer and harder benefits.

During the growth stage there is no role for networking groups in providing the softer benefits, the focus for the entrepreneur is on PR, gaining new investors, suppliers, customers and development partners.

Source: Edmondson, I. (2000) *The role of networking groups in the creation of new high technology ventures: The case of the Cambridge high tech cluster*, Cambridge Judge Business School MBA Individual Project.

Chapter Summary

- Innovation is not a solo act but a multiplayer game. Be it the entrepreneur who spots an opportunity or an established organization trying to renew its offerings or sharpen up its processes, making innovation happen depends on working with many different players. This raises questions about relationships *between* organizations, developing and making use of increasingly wide networks.

- The ways knowledge actually flows around an innovation project are complex and interactive, woven together in a kind of social spaghetti where different people talk to each other in different ways, more or less frequently, and about different things. As the innovation becomes more complex so the networks have to involve more and different players, many of whom may lie outside the firm.

- Increasingly, the networks we have to learn to deal with are becoming more virtual, a rich and global set of human resources distributed and connected by the enabling technologies of the Internet, broadband and mobile communications and shared computer networks.

- Innovation networks are more than just ways of assembling and deploying knowledge in a complex world. They can also have what are termed 'emergent properties', that is the potential for the whole to be greater than the sum of its parts. These include getting access to different and complementary knowledge sets, reducing risks by sharing them, accessing new markets and technologies and otherwise pooling complementary skills and assets.

- Open innovation is a very broad and therefore popular concept, but needs to be applied with care as its relevance is sensitive to the context. The appropriate choice of partner and specific mechanisms will depend on the type of innovation project and environmental uncertainty.

- Users can contribute to all phases of the innovation process, acting as sources, designers, developers, testers and even the main beneficiaries of innovation.

- Lead users are by definition atypical, but anticipate the needs of the majority and recognize requirements early, expect high level of benefits and have sufficient sophistication to identify and capabilities to contribute to the development of the innovation.

- Operating within an innovation network is not easy. It needs a new set of management skills and it depends on the starting point. The challenges include:
  ○ how to manage something we don't own or control
  ○ how to see system-level effects not narrow self-interests
  ○ how to build trust and shared risk taking without tying the process up in contractual red tape
  ○ how to avoid 'free riders' and information 'spillovers'.

Key Terms Defined

Clusters   networks which form because of the players being close to each other, for example in the same geographical region. Silicon Valley is a good example of a cluster which thrives on proximity – knowledge flows amongst and across the members of the network but is hugely helped by the geographical closeness and the ability of key players to meet and talk.

Collective efficiency   where a group of (often small) players work together to share resources, risks, etc.

Communities of practice   networks which can involve players inside and across different organizations. What binds them together is a shared concern with a particular aspect or area of knowledge.

Emergent properties   principle in systems that the whole is greater than the sum of the parts.

Learning network   a network formally set up for the primary purpose of increasing knowledge.

Network   a complex, interconnected group or system, and networking involves using that arrangement to accomplish particular tasks.

Open innovation   approach which seeks to mobilize innovation sources inside and outside the enterprise.

Supply chain learning   developing and sharing innovative good practice and possibly shared product development across a value chain.

Discussion Questions

1. Michael Dell didn't invent the computer, but he built one of the most successful businesses selling them. Discuss how he makes use of a networking approach to build and sustain a competitive edge in his business.

2. Why would Joe Bloggs, famous inventor, need help in getting his great idea into widespread use? And how could a networking approach help him?

3. Is innovation a solo act – the product of the lone genius? Show how successful entrepreneurs make use of networks to help take their ideas forward.

4. List three advantages of cooperating across networks in innovation as opposed to a 'go it alone' approach.

5. Jane Wilson has come up with a great new idea for a medical sensor to help in monitoring babies while they sleep. How could she improve her chances of success with her new product idea by using a networking approach to taking it forward?

Further Reading and Resources

Conway and Steward's 'Mapping innovation networks' (1998, *International Journal of Innovation Management*, **2**, 165–96) looks at the concept of innovation networks. This theme is also picked up by Swan, Newell, Scarborough and Hislop's 'Knowledge management and innovation: networks and networking' (1999, *Journal of Knowledge Management*, **3**(4): 262). Learning networks are discussed in John Bessant *et al.*'s 'Constructing learning advantage through networks' (Bessant, Alexander, Rush *et al.*'s 'Constructing learning advantage through networks' (2012, *Journal of Economic Geography*, **12**, 1087–112), and their use in sectors, supply chains and regional clusters in Morris, Bessant *et al.*'s 'Using learning networks to enable industrial development: Case studies from South Africa' (2006, *International Journal of Operations and Production Management*, **26**(5), 557–68). High-value innovation networks are discussed in several reports from AIM – the Advanced Institute for Management Research (www.aimresearch.org).

The open innovation movement includes a lot of relevant work on collaboration and networks, and Henry Chesbrough, Wim Vanhaverbeke and Joel West have edited a good overview of the main research themes in *Open Innovation: Researching a New Paradigm* (Oxford University Press, 2008). See also Anne Huff, Kathrin Möslein and Ralf Reichwald's *Leading Open Innovation* (MIT Press, 2013). There are two useful journal special issues: *R&D Management*, 2010, **40**(3) and *Technovation*, 2011, **31**(1). For more critical accounts of open innovation, see: Paul Trott and Dap Hartmann's 'Why open innovation is old wine in new bottles' (2009, *International Journal of Innovation Management*, **13**(4), 715–36) and David Mowery's 'Plus ca change: Industrial R&D in the third industrial revolution' (2009, *Industrial and Corporate Change*, **18**(1), 1–50) and our own review: Joe Tidd, *Open Innovation Research, Management and Practice* (Imperial College Press, 2014).

For user-innovation, the classic text is Eric von Hippel's *The Sources of Innovation* (Oxford University Press, 1995), and his website (http://web.mit.edu/evhippel/). For more recent and broader reviews see Steve Flowers and Flis Henwood's *Perspectives on User Innovation* (Imperial College Press, 2010) and the Special issue on user innovation in the *International Journal of Innovation Management*, 2008, **12**(3). Frank Piller, Professor at Aachen University in Germany, has a rich website around the theme of mass customization with extensive case examples and other resources (www.mass-customization.de); the original work on the topic is covered in Joseph Pine's *Mass Customisation: The New Frontier in Business Competition* (Harvard University Press, 1993). For crowdsourcing, a good place to begin is the pioneer piece by James Surowiecki, *The Wisdom of Crowds: Why the Many Are Smarter Than the Few* (Abacus, 2005) and for a more recent overview, see *Crowdsourcing*, by Daren Brabham (MIT Press, 2013)

The work of Andrew Hargadon has highlighted the importance of networks and brokers going back to the days of Edison and Ford, *How Breakthroughs Happen* (Harvard Business School Press, 2003). One of the strong examples of this approach today is IDEO, the design consultancy which Kelley and colleagues have described in detail (Kelley, Littman *et al.*, *The Art of Innovation: Lessons in Creativity from IDEO: America's Leading Design Firm*, New York, Currency, 2001).

References

1. Rothwell, R. (1992) Successful industrial innovation: Critical success factors for the 1990s, *R&D Management*, **22**(3): 221–39.

2. Wenger, E. (1999) *Communities of Practice: Learning, Meaning, and Identity*, Cambridge: Cambridge University Press; Brown, J.S. and P. Duguid (2000) Knowledge and organization: A social-practice perspective, *Organization Science*, **12**(2): 198.

3. Bessant, J., A. Alexander, G. Tsekouras and H. Rush (2012) Developing innovation capability through learning networks, *Journal of Economic Geography*, **12**(5): 1087–112; Cooke, P. (2007) *Regional Knowledge Economies: Markets, Clusters and Innovation*, Cheltenham: Edward Elgar.

4. Seely Brown, J. and J. Hagel (2005) Innovation blowback: Disruptive management practices from Asia, *The McKinsey Quarterly*, **February**: 35–45.

5. Best, M. (2001) *The New Competitive Advantage*, Oxford: Oxford University Press.

6. Bessant, J., R. Kaplinsky and R. Lamming (2003) Putting supply chain learning into practice, *International Journal of Operations and Production Management*, **23**(2): 167–84.

7. Dyer, J. and K. Nobeoka (2000) Creating and managing a high-performance knowledge-sharing network: The Toyota case, *Strategic Management Journal*, **21**(3): 345–67.

8. Snow, C., D. Strauss and D. Kulpan (2009) Community of firms: A new collaborative paradigm for open innovation and an analysis of Blade.org, *International Journal of Strategic Business Alliances*, **1**(1): 53.

9. Bessant, J. and G. Tsekouras (2001) Developing learning networks, *A. I. and Society*, **15**(2): 82–98; Marshall, N. and G. Tsekouras (2010) The interplay between formality and informality in managed learning networks, *International Journal of Strategic Business Alliances*, **1**(3): 291–308.

10. Von Hippel, E. (1986) Lead users: A source of novel product concepts, *Management Science*, **32**: 791–805.

11. Morrison, P., J. Roberts and D. Midgley (2004) The nature of lead users and measurement of leading edge status, *Research Policy*, **33**: 351–62.

12. Callahan, J. and E. Lasry (2004) The importance of customer input in the development of new products, *R&D Management*, **34**(2): 107–17.

13. Pickles, J., E. Hide and L. Maher (2008) Experience based design: A practical method of working with patients to redesign services, *Clinical Governance*, **13**(1): 51–8.

14. Flowers, D. and F. Henwood (2010) Perspectives on user innovation, *International Journal of Innovation Management*, **12**(3): 5–10.

15. Bessant, J. and K. Moeslein (2011) *Open Collective Innovation*, London: Advanced Institute of Management Research.

16. Conway, S. and F. Steward (1998) Mapping innovation networks, *International Journal of Innovation Management*, **2**(2): 165–96.

17. AIM (2004) *I-works: How High Value Innovation Networks Can Boost UK Productivity*, London: Advanced Institute of Management Research.

Deeper Dive explanations of innovation concepts and ideas are available on the Innovation Portal at **www.innovation-portal.info**

Quizzes to test yourself further are available online via the Innovation Portal at **www.innovation-portal.info**

Summary of online resources for Chapter 10 –
all material is available via the Innovation Portal at
www.innovation-portal.info

Cases	Media	Tools	Activities	Deeper Dives
• 3M • P&G • NSN • Volvo • Supply chain learning • Alibaba • M-PESA • Instituto Nokia de Tecnologia (INdT) • Lego • Local Motors • Adidas • Threadless.com • Online crowdsourcing	• Victor Cui • Honey Bee • Blackstone Entrepreneur Networks • Chris Anderson • Roy Sandbach • Fabian Schlage • David Simoes-Brown • Eric von Hippel • Catharina van Delden • Lynne Maher • Patient Innovation • Jimmy Wales • Charles Leadbeater • David Overton	—	—	• Collective efficiency • Learning networks

PART IV

DEVELOPING
THE VENTURE

How do we go about taking a concept from a gleam in the eye to a fully fledged process, product, service or business? It's not just a matter of project management – balancing resources against time and budget – but of doing so against a backdrop of uncertainty. We need to understand the factors that influence the success and failure of innovations and new ventures. Even if we can steer a project between the rocks to make it real, there's no guarantee that people will use it or that it will diffuse widely. This often demands alliance to promote acceptance and widespread adoption.

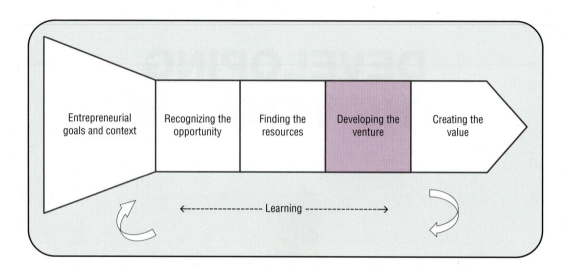

Chapter 11

Developing New Products and Services

LEARNING OBJECTIVES

By the end of this chapter you will develop an understanding of:

- a formal process to support new product development, such as stage-gate and the development funnel
- product and organizational factors which influence success and failure
- choosing and applying relevant tools to support each stage of product development
- the differences between products and services and how these influence development
- applying the lessons of diffusion research to promote the adoption of innovations.

The New Product/Service Development Process

The process of new product or service development – moving from idea through to successful products, services or processes – is a gradual one of reducing uncertainty through a series of problem-solving stages, moving through the phases of scanning and selecting and into implementation – linking market- and technology-related streams along the way.

At the outset anything is possible, but the increasing commitment of resources during the life of the project makes it increasingly difficult to change direction. Managing new product or service development is a fine balancing act between the costs of continuing with projects which may not eventually succeed (and that represent opportunity costs in terms of other possibilities) and the danger of closing down too soon and eliminating potentially fruitful options. With shorter lifecycles and demand for greater product variety, pressure is also placed on the development process to work with a wider portfolio of new product opportunities and to manage the risks associated with progressing these through development to launch.

These decisions can be made on an ad hoc basis, but experience and research suggests some form of structured development system – with clear decision points and agreed rules on which to base go/no-go decisions – is a more effective approach. Attention on internal mechanisms for integrating and optimizing the process is critical, such as concurrent engineering, cross-functional working, advanced tools, early involvement, etc. To deal with this, attention has focused on systematic screening, monitoring and progression frameworks, such as Cooper's stage-gate approach (Figure 11.1).[1]

As Cooper suggests, successful product development needs to operate some form of structured, staging process. As projects move through the development process, there are a number of discrete stages, each with different decision criteria, or 'gates', they must pass. Many variations to this basic idea exist (e.g. 'fuzzy gates'), but the important point is to ensure there is a

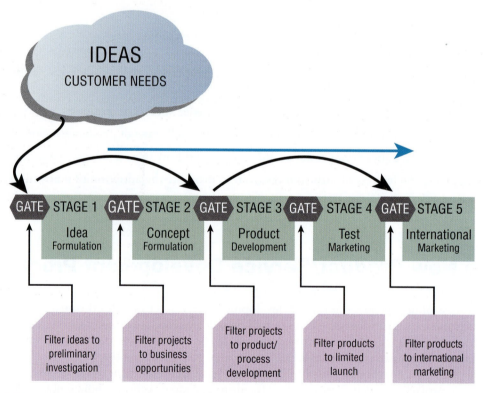

FIGURE 11.1 Stage-gate product development process

Sources: Derived from Cooper, R., *Winning at New Products: Accelerating the Process from Idea to Launch*, 2001, Cambridge, MA: Perseus Books; Doing it right: Winning with new products, 2000, Ivey *Business Journal,* **64**(6), 1–7.

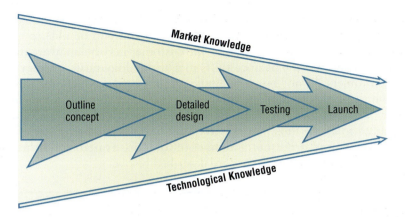

FIGURE 11.2   Product development funnel

Source: Derived from Wheelwright, S.C. and K.B. Clark (1992) *Revolutionizing Product Development*, New York: Free Press.

structure in place which reviews both technical and marketing data at each stage. A common variation is the **development funnel**, which takes into account the reduction in uncertainty as the process progresses, and the influence of real resource constraints (Figure 11.2).[2]

There are numerous other models in the literature, incorporating various stages ranging from three to 13. Such models are essentially linear and unidirectional, beginning with concept development and ending with commercialization. Such models suggest a simple, linear process of development and elimination. However, in practice the development of new products and services is inherently a complex and iterative process, and this makes it difficult to model for practical purposes. For ease of discussion and analysis, we adopt a simplified four-stage model which we believe is sufficient to discriminate between the various factors that must be managed at different stages:[3]

1. *Concept generation.* Identifying the opportunities for new products and services.
2. *Project assessment and selection.* Screening and choosing projects which satisfy certain criteria.
3. *Product development.* Translating the selected concepts into a physical product (we'll discuss services later).
4. *Product commercialization.* Testing, launching and marketing the new product.

Concept Generation

Much of the marketing and product development literature concentrates on monitoring market trends and customer needs to identify new product concepts. However, there is a well-established debate in the literature about the relative merits of 'market-pull' versus 'technology-push' strategies for new product development. A review of the relevant research suggests that the best strategy to adopt is dependent on the relative novelty of the new product. For incremental adaptations or product line extensions, 'market pull' is likely to be the preferred route, as customers are familiar with the product type and will be able to express preferences easily. However, there are many 'needs' the customer may be unaware of, or unable to articulate, and in these cases the balance shifts to a 'technology-push' strategy. Nevertheless, in most cases customers do not buy a technology: they buy products for the benefits they can receive from them; the 'technology push' must provide a solution for their needs. Thus, some customer or market analysis is also important for more novel technology. This stage is sometimes referred to as the 'fuzzy front end' (see Entrepreneurship in Action 8.1) because it often lacks structure and order, but a number of tools are available to help systematically identify new product concepts, and these are described below.

INNOVATION IN ACTION 11.1

Samsung and the Rise of the Smartphone

Smartphones are a good example of continuous product development and innovation, often with lifecycles measured in months rather than years. Apple's entry into the mobile phone market with its various iPhone generations has received most attention, but Samsung is an equally interesting example of a product-development-led success strategy.

There is no accepted definition of a smartphone, or distinction between these and feature-rich phones. However, many accept that Samsung entered the global smartphone market in October 2006 with its BlackJack phone, which at that time was similar in name, appearance and features to the RIM BlackBerry (and indeed resulted in a legal challenge from RIM, similar to the legal disputes between Apple and Samsung in 2012). The BlackJack smartphone was launched first in the USA, via the operator AT&T, and ran Windows Mobile, and in 2007 won the Best Smart Phone award at CTIA in the USA. Just over a year later, the imaginatively named BlackJack II was launched in December 2008, followed by the third-generation Samsung Jack in May 2009, which became the highest-selling Windows Mobile phone series to date.

Another major milestone was in November 2007 when Samsung became a founding member of the Open Handset Alliance (OHA), which was created to develop, promote and license Google's Android system for smartphones and tablets. Another member company, HTC, launched the first Android smartphone in August 2008, but Samsung followed with its own in May 2009, the I7500, which included the full suite of Google services, 3.2" AMOLED display, GPS and a five-megapixel camera. However, Samsung has been promiscuous in its choice of operating systems, and in addition to adopting Windows and Android systems developed and uses its own. In May 2010, Samsung launched the Wave, its first smartphone based on its own Bada platform, designed for touchscreen interfaces and social networking. Six more Wave phones were launched the following year, with sales in excess of ten million units.

The real success story is Samsung's Android-based Galaxy S sub-brand, introduced in March 2010, followed by the Galaxy S II in 2011 and S II in 2012, as a direct competitor to Apple's iPhone. In the first quarter of 2012 Samsung sold more than 42 million smartphones worldwide, which represented 29% of global sales, compared to Apple with 35 million (24% market share).

By 2012, the OHA had 84 member firms, and the Android system accounted for around 60% of global sales, compared to Apple's OS with 26%. However, estimates of market share differ between analysts, depending on whether they measure share of new sales or existing user-base, and market shares also fluctuate significantly with new product launches. For example, in the month of the launch of the new iPhone, Apple's share of new sales in the USA leaped from 26 to 43%, and Android collapsed from 60 to 47%.[4] This clearly demonstrates the impact of a new product launch.

Moreover, this product-led strategy is not easy to sustain. Nokia and BlackBerry were past leaders in their respective markets for many years, but suffered significant declines in sales and profitability. Despite high levels of research and development and strong brands, these two past market-leaders have failed to maintain their lead through new product development. In a single year, 2011–2012, Nokia's market share fell from 24 to just 8%, and RIM, makers of the BlackBerry, from 14 to below 7%. In part, this decline reflects its proprietary operating systems failing to add new features and functions, such as Cloud storage, and providing access to far fewer apps than Apple's iTunes store or Google's Play for Android does.

Project Selection

This stage includes the screening and selection of product concepts prior to subsequent progress through to the development phase. Two costs of failing to select the 'best' project set are: the actual cost of resources spent on poor projects and the opportunity costs of marginal projects which may have succeeded with additional resources.

There are two levels of filtering. The first is the aggregate product plan, in which the new product development portfolio is determined. The aggregate product plan attempts to integrate the various potential projects to ensure the collective set of development projects will meet the goals and objectives of the firm, and help to build the capabilities needed. The first step is to ensure resources are applied to the appropriate types and mix of projects. The second step is to develop a capacity plan to balance resource and demand. The final step is to analyse the effect of the proposed projects on capabilities, to ensure this is built up to meet future demands.

The second lower level filters are concerned with specific product concepts. The two most common processes at this level are the development funnel and the stage-gate system. The development funnel is a means to identify, screen, review and converge development projects as they move from idea to commercialization. It provides a framework in which to review alternatives based on a series of explicit criteria for decision making. Similarly, the stage-gate system provides a formal framework for filtering projects based on explicit criteria. The main difference is that where the development funnel assumes resource constraints the stage-gate system does not.

Product Development

This stage includes all the activities necessary to take the chosen concept and deliver a product for commercialization. It is at the working level, where the product is actually developed and produced, that the individual R&D staff, designers, engineers and marketing staff must

Video Clip of an interview with Armin Rau of SICAP exploring some of these issues is available on the Innovation Portal at www.innovation-portal.info

work together to solve specific issues and to make decisions on the details. Whenever a problem appears, a gap between the current design and the requirement, the development team must take action to close it. The way in which this is achieved determines the speed and effectiveness of the problem-solving process. In many cases this problem-solving routine involves iterative design–test–build cycles, which make use of a number of tools.

Product Commercialization and Review

In many cases the process of new product development blurs into the process of commercialization. For example, customer co-development, test marketing and use of alpha, beta and gamma test sites yield data on customer requirements and any problems encountered in use, but also help to obtain customer buy-in and prime the market. It is not the purpose of this section to examine the relative efficacy of different marketing strategies, but rather to identify those factors which influence directly the process of new product development. We are primarily interested in what criteria firms use to evaluate the success of new products and how these criteria may differ between low- and high-novelty projects. In the former case we would expect more formal and narrow financial or market measures, but in the latter case we find a broader range of criteria are used to reflect the potential for organizational learning and future new product options.

Success Factors

Numerous studies have investigated the factors affecting the success of new products (Figure 11.3). Most have adopted a 'matched-pair methodology', in which similar new products are examined, but one is much less successful than the other. This allows us to discriminate between good and poor practice, and helps to control for other background factors.[5]

These studies have differed in emphasis and sometimes contradicted each other, but despite differences in samples and methodologies it is possible to identify some consensus of what the best criteria for success are:

- *Product advantage.* Product superiority in the eyes of the customer, real differential advantage, high performance-to-cost ratio, delivering unique benefits to users appears to be the primary factor separating winners and losers. Customer perception is the key.
- *Market knowledge.* The homework is vital: better development preparation including initial screening, preliminary market assessment, preliminary technical appraisal, detailed market studies and business/financial analysis. Customer and user-needs assessment and understanding are critical. Competitive analysis is also an important part of the market analysis.
- *Clear product definition.* This includes defining target markets, clear concept definition and benefits to be delivered, clear positioning strategy, a list of product requirements, features and attributes or use of a priority criteria list agreed before development begins.

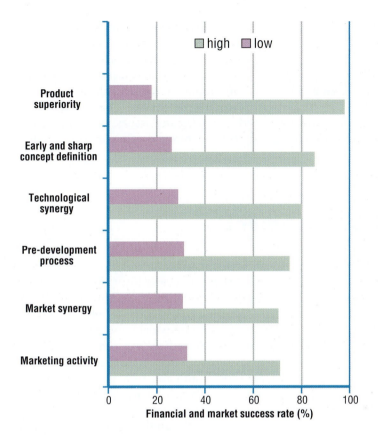

FIGURE 11.3   Factors influencing new product success

- *Risk assessment.* Market-based, technological, manufacturing and design sources of risk to the development project must be assessed, and plans made to address them. Risk assessments must be built into the business and feasibility studies so they are appropriately addressed with respect to the market and the firm's capabilities.
- *Project organization.* The use of cross-functional, multidisciplinary teams carrying responsibility for the project from beginning to end.
- *Project resources.* Sufficient financial and material resources and human skills must be available; the firm must possess the management and technological skills to design and develop the new product.
- *Proficiency of execution.* Quality of technological and production activities, and all pre-commercialization business analyses and test marketing; detailed market studies underpin new product success.
- *Top management support.* From concept through to launch, management must be able to create an atmosphere of trust, coordination and control. Key individuals or champions often play a critical role during the innovation process.

Video Clip of Eric von Hippel describing 3M's processes for seeking out breakthrough products and services is available on the Innovation Portal at **www.innovation-portal.info**

These factors have all been found to contribute to new product success, and should therefore form the basis of any formal process for new product development. Note that successful new product and service development requires the management of a blend of product or service characteristics, such as product focus, superiority and advantage, and organizational issues, such as project resources, execution and leadership. Managing only one of these key contributions is unlikely to result in consistent success.

Service Development

Employment trends in all the so-called advanced countries indicate a move away from manufacturing, construction, mining and agriculture towards a range of services, including retail, finance, transportation, communication, entertainment, and professional and public services. This trend is in part because manufacturing has become so efficient and highly automated, and therefore generates proportionately less employment and because many services are characterized by high levels of customer contact and are reproduced locally, and are therefore often labour-intensive. In the most advanced service economies, such as the USA and the UK, services create up to three-quarters of the wealth and 85% of employment, and yet we know relatively little about managing innovation in this sector. The critical role of services, in the broadest sense, has long been recognized, but service innovation is still not well understood.

Innovation in services in much more than the application of information technology (IT). In fact, the disappointing returns for IT investments in services has resulted in a widespread debate about its causes and potential solutions – the so-called productivity paradox in services. Frequently, service innovations, which make significant differences to the ways customers use and perceive the service delivered, will demand major investments in process innovation and technology by service providers, but also demand investment in skills and methods of working to change the business model, as well as major marketing changes. Estimates vary, but returns on investment on IT alone are around 15%, with a typical lag of two to three years, when productivity often falls, but when combined with changes in organization and management these returns increase to around 25%.[6]

In the service sector the impact of innovation on growth is generally positive and consistent, with the possible exception of financial services. The pattern across retail and wholesale

Case Study of the BBC highlighting some of these issues is available on the Innovation Portal at **www.innovation-portal.info**

distribution, transport and communication services, and the broad range of business services, is particularly strong. Research has identified the 'hidden innovation' in the creative industries and media, for example film and TV programme development, which is not captured by traditional policy or measures such as R&D or patents, as the case of the BBC shows.

Most research and management prescriptions have been based on the experience of manufacturing and high-technology sectors. Most simply assume that such practices are equally applicable to managing innovation in services, but some researchers argue that services are fundamentally different. There is a clear need to distinguish what, if any, of what we know about managing innovation in manufacturing is applicable to services, what must be adapted and what is distinct and different.

We will argue that generic good practices do exist, which apply to the development of both manufactured and service offerings, but that these must be adapted to different contexts, specifically the scale and complexity, degree of customization of the offerings and the uncertainty of the technological and market environments. It is critical to match the configuration of management and organization of development to the specific technology and market environment. For example, service development in retail financial services is very similar to product development for consumer goods.

The service sector includes a very wide range and a great diversity of different activities and businesses, ranging from individual consultants and shopkeepers to huge multinational finance firms and critical non-profit public and third-sector organizations such as government, health and education. Therefore, great care needs to be taken when making any generalization about the service sectors. We will introduce some ways of understanding and analysing the sector later, but it is possible to identify some fundamental differences between manufacturing and service operations:

- *Tangibility.* Goods tend to be tangible, whereas services are mostly intangible, even though you can usually see or feel the results.
- *Perceptions* of performance and quality are more important in services, in particular the difference between expectations and perceived performance. Customers are likely to regard a service as being good if it exceeds their expectations. Perceptions of service quality are affected by:
  - tangible aspects: appearance of facilities, equipment and staff
  - responsiveness: prompt service and willingness to help
  - competence: ability to perform the service dependably
  - assurance: knowledge and courtesy of staff and ability to convey trust and confidence
  - empathy: provision of caring, individual attention.
- *Simultaneity.* The lag between the production and consumption of goods and services is different. Most goods are produced well in advance of consumption, to allow for distribution, storage and sales. In contrast, many services are produced and almost immediately consumed. This creates problems of quality management and capacity planning. It is harder to identify or correct errors in services, and more difficult to match supply and demand.
- *Storage.* Services cannot usually be stored, for example a seat on an airline, although some, such as utilities, have some potential for storage. The inability to hold stocks of services can create problems matching supply and demand – capacity management. These can be dealt with in a number of ways. Pricing can be used to help smooth fluctuations in demand, for example by providing discounts at off-peak times. Where possible, additional capacity can be provided at peak times by employing part-time workers or outsourcing. In the worst cases, customers can simply be forced to wait for the services, by queuing.

- *Customer contact.* Most customers have low or no contact with the operations which produce goods. Many services demand high levels of contact between the operations and ultimate customer, although the level and timing of such contact varies. For example, medical treatment may require constant or frequent contact but financial services only sporadic contact.

- *Location.* Because of the contact with customers and near simultaneous production and consumption of services, the location of service operations is often more important than for operations which produce goods. For example, restaurants, retail operations and entertainment services all favour proximity to customers. Conversely, manufactured goods are often produced and consumed in very different locations. For these reasons the markets for manufactured goods also tend to be more competitive and global, whereas many personal and business services are local and less competitive. For example, only around 10% of services in the advanced economies are traded internationally.

Case Study of Bank of Scotland highlighting some of these issues is available on the Innovation Portal at **www.innovation-portal.info**

These service characteristics should be taken into account when designing and managing the organization and processes for new service development, as some of the findings from research on new product development will have to be adapted or may not apply at all. Also, because of the diversity of service operations, we need to tailor the organization and management to different types of service context (Table 11.1).

In terms of performance, innovation and quality appear to be improved by cross-functional teams and sharing information, raised by involvement with customers and suppliers, and by encouraging collaboration in teams.[7] Service delivery is improved by customer focus and project management, and by knowledge sharing and collaboration in teams. Time to market is reduced by knowledge sharing and collaboration, and customer focus and project organization, but cross-functional teams can prolong the process. Costs are reduced by setting standards for projects and products, and by the involvement of customers and suppliers, but can be increased by using cross-functional teams. Although individual practices can make a significant contribution to performance

Tool for developing new services, the SPOTS tool, is available on the Innovation Portal at **www.innovation-portal.info**

TABLE 11.1 Characteristics of service 'high innovators'

Business descriptor	Low innovators	High innovators
Innovation outcomes		
• % sales from services introduced < 3 years ago	<1%	17%
• % new services versus competitors	>0%	5%

TABLE 11.1 *(Continued)*

Business descriptor	Low innovators	High innovators
Customer base		
• Focus on key customers	Average	High
• Relative customer base	Similar to competitors	More focused than competitors
Value chain		
• Focus on key suppliers	Average	High/strategic
• Value-added/sales %	72%	60%
• Operating cost added/sales	36%	25%
• Vertical integration versus competitors	Same or more	Same or less
Innovation input		
• 'What' R&D	0.1% sales	0.7% sales
• 'How' R&D	0.1% sales	0.5% sales
• Fixed assets/sales	growing at 10% p.a.	growing at >20% p.a.
• Overheads/sales %	8%	11%
Innovation context		
• Recent technology change	20%	40%
• Time to market	>1 year	<1 year
Competition		
• Competitor entry	10%	40%
• Imports/exports versus market	2%	12%
Quality of offer		
• Relative quality versus competitors	Declining	Improving
• Value for money	Just below competitors	Better than competitors
Output		
• Real sales	9%	15%

Source: Clayton (2003) in Tidd, J. and Hull, F.M., eds, *Service Innovation: Organizational Responses to Technological Opportunities and Market Imperatives,* Imperial College Press, London. Copyright Imperial College Press/World Scientific Publishing Co.

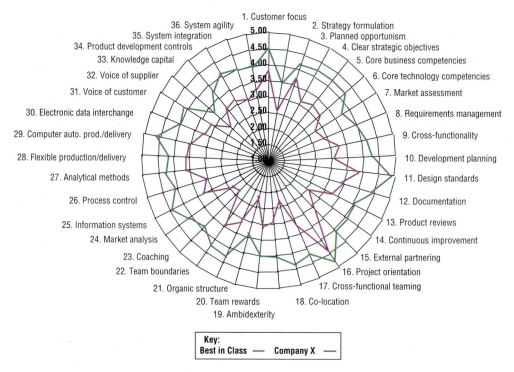

FIGURE 11.4 A framework for assessing new service development

Source: Tidd, J. and F.M. Hull (2006) Managing service innovation: the need for selectivity rather than 'best practice'. *New Technology, Work and Employment* **21**(2): 139–161. Reproduced by permission of John Wiley & Sons, Ltd.

(Figure 11.4), it is clear that the coherent combination of practices and their interaction creates superior performance in specific contexts. These research findings can be used to help assess the effectiveness of existing strategies, processes, organization, technology and systems (SPOTS), and to identify where and how to improve.

Tools to Support New Product Development

There are a very large number of tools to support product development, but these vary in popularity and effectiveness (Table 11.2). Here we identify the key tools by stage of the process.

Concept Generation

Most studies have highlighted the importance of understanding users' needs. Designing a product to satisfy a perceived need has been shown to be an important discriminator of commercial success. Common approaches include:

TABLE 11.2 Use and usefulness of techniques for product and service development

	High Novelty		Low Novelty	
	Usage (%)	Usefulness	Usage (%)	Usefulness
Segmentation*	89	3.42	42	4.50
Market experimentation	63	4.00	53	3.70
Industry experts	63	3.83	37	3.71
Surveys/focus groups*	52	4.50	37	4.00
User-practice observation	47	3.67	42	3.50
Partnering customers*	37	4.43	58	3.67
Lead users*	32	4.33	37	3.57
Probability of technical success	100	4.37	100	4.32
Probability of commercial success	100	4.68	95	4.50
Market share*	100	3.63	84	4.00
Core competencies*	95	3.61	79	3.00
Degree of internal commitment	89	3.82	79	3.67
Market size	89	3.76	84	3.94
Competition	89	3.76	84	3.81
Gap analysis	79	2.73	84	2.81
Strategic clusters*	42	3.63	32	2.67
Prototyping*	79	4.33	63	4.08
Market experimentation	68	4.31	63	4.08
QFD	47	3.33	37	3.43
Cross-functional teams*	63	4.47	37	3.74
Project manager (heavyweight)*	52	3.84	32	3.05

Usefulness Scale: 1–5, 5 = critical, based on manager assessments of 50 development projects in 25 firms. * denotes difference in usefulness rating is statistically significant at 5% level.

Source: Adapted from Tidd, J. and K. Bodley (2002) The effect of project novelty on the new product development process, *R&D Management,* **32**(2), 127–38.

Tools to support product development, including conjoint analysis and the Kano method, are available on the Innovation Portal at **www.innovation-portal.info**

- *Surveys and focus groups:* where a similar product exists surveys of customers' preferences can be a reliable guide to development. Focus groups allow developers to explore the likely response to more novel products where a clear target segment exists.
- *Latent needs analysis:* is designed to uncover the unarticulated requirements of customers by means of their responses to symbols, concepts and forms.
- *Lead users:* are representative of the needs of the market, but some time ahead of the majority, and so represent future needs. Lead users are one of the most important sources of market knowledge for product improvements.
- *Customer developers:* in some cases new products are partly or completely developed by customers. In such cases the issue is how to identify and acquire such products.
- *Competitive analysis:* of competing products, by reverse engineering or benchmarking features of competing products.
- *Industry experts or consultants:* who have a wide range of experience of different users' needs. The danger is they may have become too immersed in the users' world to have the breadth of vision required to assess and evaluate the potential of the innovation. The use of 'proxy experts' to help overcome the problem. They suggest selecting a specific group of respondents who have knowledge of the product category or usage context.
- *Extrapolating trends:* in technology, markets and society to guess the short- to medium-term future needs.
- *Building scenarios:* alternative visions of the future based on varying assumptions to create robust product strategies. Most relevant to long-term projects and product portfolio development.
- *Market experimentation:* testing market response with real products, but able to adapt or withdraw rapidly. Only practical where development costs are low, lead-times short and customers tolerant of product underperformance or failure. Sometimes referred to as 'expeditionary marketing', or more modestly 'test marketing'.

Project Selection

Different combinations of criteria are used to screen and assess projects prior to development. The most common are based on discounted cash flows, such as net present value/internal rate of return, followed by cost–benefit analysis, and simple calculations of the payback period. In addition to these financial criteria, most organizations also use a range of additional measures:

- *Ranking.* A means of ordering a list of candidate projects in relative value or worthiness of support, broken down into several factors, so both objective and judgemental data can be assessed. These techniques are likely to be of most use in the early stages of the process, since they are fairly 'rough cut' methods.
- *Profiles.* Projects are given scores on each of several characteristics, and are rejected if they fail to meet some pre-determined threshold. The projects which dominate on all or most of the factor scores are selected. These methods can be used at all stages of the development process.

- *Simulated outcomes.* Alternative outcomes to which probabilities can be attached, or alternative paths depending on chance outcomes and when the projects have different payoffs for different outcomes. The range of possible outcomes and the likelihood of a specific outcome are found. It is used especially in the analysis of sets of projects which are interdependent (the aggregate project plan).
- *Strategic clusters.* Projects not selected solely for maximization of some financial measure but for the support they give to the strategic position. Groups are clustered according to their support for specific objectives, and then these groups are rated according to strategic importance and funded accordingly (again, this is important at the aggregate project plan level).
- *Interactive.* An iterative process between the R&D director and project managers, where project proposals are improved at each stage to more closely align with the objectives. The aim of this is to develop projects that more nearly fit the strategic and tactical objectives of the firm. These methods are used mainly at the aggregate project plan level, or at the early stages of specific projects.

Product Development

There are a number of tools, or methodologies, which have been developed to help solve the problems, and most require the integration of different functions and disciplines. The most significant tools and methods used are:

- *Design for manufacture (DFM):* the full range of policies, techniques, practices and attitudes that cause a product to be designed for the optimum manufacturing cost, the optimum achievement of manufactured quality, and the optimum achievement of lifecycle support (serviceability, reliability and maintainability). It includes design for assembly (DFA), design for producibility (DFP) and other design rule approaches. Studies from the car industry indicate that up to 80% of the final production costs are determined at the design stage.
- *Rapid prototyping:* is the core element of the design–build–test cycle, and can increase the rate and amount of learning that occurs in each cycle. The first design is unlikely to be complete, and so designers go through several iterations learning more about the problem and alternative solutions each time. The number of iterations will depend on the time and cost constraints of the project. One study found that frequent prototyping proved useful for intra-team communication, obtaining customer feedback and manufacturing process development. Having an actual prototype as a visual model enables a more reliable assessment of preferences and suggestions.
- *Computer-aided techniques:* potential benefits include reduction in development lead times, economies in design, ability to design products too complex to do manually and the combination of computer-aided design (CAD) with production automation computer-aided manufacture (CAM) to achieve the benefits of integration. However, these benefits are not always realized, owing to organizational shortcomings.

- *Quality function deployment (QFD):* is a set of planning and communications routines used to identify critical customer attributes and create a specific link between these and design parameters. It focuses and coordinates the skills within the organization to design, manufacture and then market products that customers. The aim is to answer three primary questions: What are the critical attributes for customers? What design parameters drive these attributes? What should the design parameter targets be for the new design?

INNOVATION IN ACTION 11.2

Tata's Transformation of Jaguar Land Rover

The Indian company Tata is probably best known overseas for its ill-fated Nano micro-car. However, less well documented is its success at the other end of the automotive market. In March 2008, Tata bought Jaguar Land Rover (JLR) from Ford for $2.3 billion, around half of what Ford had paid for the group of companies. Since then, Tata has grown JLR through a sustained investment in new product development. By 2012, JLR's annual sales had risen by 37%, during an economic recession, helped by sales of its new 2011 Range Rover Evoque and increased demand in Russia and China, which accounted for almost a quarter of sales, and contributed to the 57% increase in the profits of JLR. The profit margin of 20% was three times that of parent Tata's domestic business. The two British luxury car brands were valued at over £14 billion in 2012.

Tata acquired JLR cheaply because Ford had failed to develop the company and its products. In 2007, Ford contributed about £400 million into the two brands towards R&D, before they were sold to Tata Motors, and the first of the new product range had been developed and announced under ownership of Ford. The mid-size luxury January XF was revealed in August 2007, with first customer deliveries in March 2008. The more radical, aluminium full-size luxury Jaguar XJ was launched in late 2009, with the first deliveries in April 2010. By 2011, Tata had tripled this annual R&D spend to £1.2 billion, representing about 10% of the two brands' annual revenue (4% is a more typical R&D intensity in the auto industry). The design-led and segment-spanning SUV Range Rover Evoque was launched in 2011, and quickly had a six-month order book, despite the economic recession and premium pricing. All three cars won numerous industry and consumer awards.

In December 2010, 1500 new jobs were created as the Halewood factory ramped up its operations to launch the new Range Rover Evoque, which began production in July 2011. By April 2012, the company needed to recruit more than 1000 additional staff for its advanced manufacturing plant in Solihull, to take the workforce to almost 4500 at the Halewood plant, trebling the number employed there compared to three years before. The company announced an investment of £355 million for new engine plant, which will create 750 new jobs. JLR is now the

UK's largest automotive design, engineering and manufacturing employer, accounting for 20% of the UK's total exports to China.

Tata already builds some Land Rover models in India, and in 2012 selected a joint venture partner in China, Chery Automobile. In 2012, Tata's chief financial officer, C. R. Ramakrishnan, committed to further investments in JLR: 'Over the past five to six years, Jaguar Land Rover has spent around £700 million to £800 million annually on capital expenditure and product development. Going forward, we will double that', and further said that JLR aimed to develop forty new products and variants over the next five years. The new Jaguar F-type sports car was launched in 2013, following a £200 million investment at the Bromwich facility, and another 1000 new staff.

Case Study describing the development of the Lexus brand highlighting some of these issues is available on the Innovation Portal at **www.innovation-portal.info**

Quality function deployment (QFD) is a useful technique for translating customer requirements into development needs, and encourages communication between engineering, production and marketing. Unlike most other tools of quality management, QFD is used to identify opportunities for product improvement or differentiation, rather than to solve problems. Customer-required characteristics are translated or 'deployed' by means of a matrix into language which engineers can understand. The construction of a relationship matrix – also known as 'the house of quality' – requires a significant amount of technical and market research (Figure 11.5). Great emphasis must be placed on gathering market and user data in order to identify potential design trade-offs, and to achieve the most appropriate balance between cost, quality and performance. The construction of a QFD matrix involves the following steps:

1. Identify customer requirements, primary and secondary, and any major dislikes.
2. Rank requirements according to importance.
3. Translate requirements into measurable characteristics.
4. Establish the relationship between customer requirements and technical product characteristics, and estimate the strength of the relationship.
5. Choose appropriate units of measurement and determine target values based on customer requirements and competitor benchmarks.

Symbols are used to show the relationship between customer requirements and technical specifications, and weights attached to illustrate the strength of the relationship. Horizontal rows with no relationship symbol indicate that the existing design is incomplete. Conversely, vertical columns with no relationship symbol indicate that an existing design feature is redundant as it is not valued by the customer. In addition, comparisons with competing products, or benchmarks, can be included. This is important because relative quality is more relevant

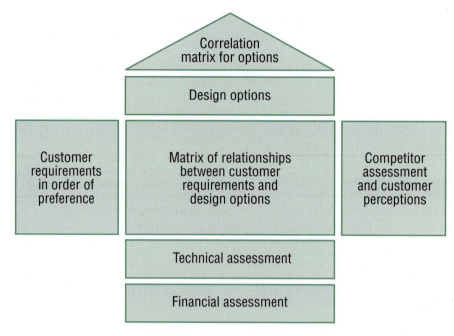

FIGURE 11.5   Quality function deployment (QFD) matrix

than absolute quality: customer expectations are likely to be shaped by what else is available, rather than by some ideal.

QFD was originally developed in Japan, and it is claimed that it has helped Toyota reduce its development time and costs by 40%. More recently, many leading American firms have adopted QFD, including AT&T, Digital and Ford, but results have been mixed: only around a quarter of projects have resulted in any quantifiable benefit. In contrast, there has been relatively little application of QFD by European firms.[8] This is not the result of ignorance but rather a recognition of the practical problems of implementing QFD.

Tool for enabling this approach, quality function deployment, is available on the Innovation Portal at **www.innovation-portal.info**

Activity to help you explore QFD, QFD at Lexus, is available on the Innovation Portal at **www.innovation-portal.info**

Clearly, QFD requires the compilation of much marketing and technical data, and more importantly the close cooperation of the development and marketing functions. Indeed, the process of constructing the relationship matrix provides a structured way of getting people from development and marketing to communicate, and therefore is as valuable as any more quantifiable outputs. It is particularly powerful in identifying and overcoming trade-offs in customer requirements.[9] However, where relations between the technical and marketing groups are a problem, which is too often the case, the use of QFD may be premature.

Diffusion: Promoting the Adoption of Innovations

A better understanding of why and how innovations are adopted (or not) can help us develop and implement more realistic business plans and public policies.

Diffusion is the means by which innovations are translated into social and economic benefits. We know that the impact of the *use* of innovations is around four times that of their generation.[10] And especially the widespread adoption of process innovations has the most significant benefit.[11] Technological innovations are the source of productivity and quality improvements; organizational innovations are the basis of many social, health and educational gains; and commercial innovations create new services and products. However, the benefits of innovations can take 10–15 years to be fully effected,[12] and in practice most innovations fail to be adopted widely, so have limited social or economic impact.[13]

Conventional marketing approaches are adequate for promoting many products and services, but are not sufficient for the majority of innovations. Marketing texts often refer to 'early adopters' and 'majority adopters', and even go so far as to apply numerical estimates of these, but these simple categories are based on the very early studies of the state-sponsored diffusion of hybrid-seed varieties in farming communities, and are far from universally applicable. To better plan for innovations we need a deeper understanding of what factors promote and constrain adoption, and how these influence the rate and level of diffusion within different markets and populations.

Rogers' definition of diffusion is used widely: 'the process by which an innovation is communicated through certain channels over time among members of a social system. It is a special type of communication, in that the messages are concerned with new ideas' (p. 5).[14] The economist's view of the innovation process begins with the assumption that it is simply the cumulative aggregation of individual, rational calculations. These individual decisions are influenced by an assessment of the costs and benefits, under conditions of limited information and environment uncertainty. However, this perspective ignores the effects of social feedback, learning and externalities. The initial benefits of adoption may be small, but with improvement, re-invention and growing externalities the benefits can increase over time and the costs decrease.

In contrast, Rogers conceptualizes diffusion as a social process, in which actors create and share information through communication. Therefore a focus on the relative advantage of an innovation is insufficient, as different social systems will have different values and beliefs, which will influence the costs, benefits and compatibility of an innovation, and different social structures, which will determine the most appropriate channels of communication and the type and influence of opinion leaders and change agents. Rogers distinguishes between three types of decision-making relevant to adoption of an innovation:

- *Individual*, in which the individual is the main decision-maker, independent of peers. Decisions may still be influenced by social norms and interpersonal relationships, but the individual makes the ultimate choice, e.g. the purchase of a consumer durable such as a mobile phone.
- *Collective*, where choices are made jointly with others in the social system, and there is significant peer pressure or formal requirement to conform, e.g. the sorting and recycling of domestic waste.

- *Authoritative*, where decisions to adopt are taken by a few individuals within a social system, owing to their power, status or expertise, e.g. adoption of enterprise resource planning (ERP) systems by businesses or MRI scanning technology by hospitals.

There is much evidence that opinion leaders are critical to diffusion, especially for changes in behaviour or attitudes (see Innovation in Action 11.3). Therefore, they tend to be a central feature of social and health change programmes, such as sex education. However, they are also evident in more routine examples of product diffusion, ranging from sports shoes to hybrid cars. Opinion leaders carry information across boundaries between groups, much like knowledge bridges. They operate at the edge of groups, rather than from the top, not leaders within a group but brokers between groups. In the language of networks, they have many weak ties, rather than a few strong ties. They tend to have extended personal networks, be accessible and have high levels of social participation. They are recognized by peers as being both competent and trustworthy. They have access and exposure to mass media.

The time dimension is important, and many studies are particularly interested to understand and influence the rate of adoption. It can take years for a new drug to be prescribed after licence, a decade for a new crop variety or fifty years for educational or social changes. This leads to a focus on the communication channels and decision-making criteria and process. Generally, mass-marketing media channels are more effective for generating awareness and disseminating information and knowledge, whereas interpersonal channels such as social media are more important in the decision-making and action stages.

INNOVATION IN ACTION 11.3

The Diffusion of Electric and Hybrid Cars

The car industry is an excellent example of a large complex socio-technical system which has evolved over many years, such that the current system of firms, products, consumers and infrastructure interact to restrict the degree and direction of innovation. Since the 1930s, the dominant design has been based around a petrol- or diesel-fuelled reciprocating combustion engine/ Otto cycle, mass produced in a wide variety of relatively minimally differentiated designs. This is no industrial conspiracy, but rather the almost inevitable industrial trajectory, given the historical and economic context. This has resulted in car companies spending more on marketing than on research and development. However, growing social and political concerns over vehicle emissions and their regulation have forced the industry to reconsider this dominant design, and in some cases to develop new capabilities to help develop new products and systems. For example, zero- and low-emissions targets and legislation have encouraged experimentation with alternatives to the combustion engine, while retaining the core concept of personal, rather than collective or mass, travel.

For example, the zero-emission law passed in California in 1990 required manufacturers selling more than 35 000 vehicles a year in the state to have 2% of all vehicle sales zero-emission by 1998, 5% by 2001 and 10% by 2003. This most affected GM, Ford, Chrysler, Toyota, Honda and Nissan, and potentially BMW and VW, if their sales increased sufficiently over that period. However, the US automobile industry subsequently appealed, and had the quota reduced to a maximum of 4%. As fuel cells were still very much a longer-term solution, the main focus was on developing electric vehicles. At first sight this would appear to represent a rather 'autonomous' innovation, that is the simple substitution of one technology (combustion engine) for another (electric). However, the shift has implications for related systems such as power storage, drive-train, controls, weight of materials used and the infrastructure for refuelling/recharging and servicing. Therefore, it is much more of a 'systemic' innovation than it first seems. Moreover, it challenges the core capabilities and technologies of many of the existing car manufacturers. The US manufacturers struggled to adapt, and early vehicles from GM and Ford were not successful. However, the Japanese were rather more successful in developing the new capabilities and technologies, and new products from Toyota and Honda have been particularly successful.

However, zero-emissions legislation was not adopted elsewhere, and more modest emission-reduction targets were set. Since then, hybrid petrol–electric cars have been developed to help to reduce emissions. These are clearly not long-term solutions to the problem but do represent valuable technical and social prototypes for future systems such as fuel cells. In 1993, Eiji Toyoda, Toyota's chairman, and his team embarked on the project codenamed G21. 'G' stands for global and '21' the twenty-first century. The purpose of the project was to develop a small hybrid car that could be sold at a competitive price in order to respond to the growing needs and eco aware-ness of many consumers worldwide. A year later a concept vehicle was developed called the Prius, taken from the Latin for 'before'. The goal was to reduce fuel consumption by 50%, and emissions by more than that. To find the right hybrid system for the G21, Toyota considered 80 alternatives before narrowing the list to four. Development of the Prius required the integration of different technical capabilities, including, for example, a joint venture with Matsushita Battery.

The prototype was revealed at the Tokyo Motor Show in October 1995. It is estimated that the project cost Toyota $1 billion in R&D. The first commercial version was launched in Japan in December 1997, and after further improvements, such as battery performance and power source management, introduced to the US market in August 2000. For urban driving the economy is 60 MPG, and 50 for motorways – the opposite consumption profile of a conventional vehicle, but roughly twice as fuel efficient as an equivalent Corolla. From the materials used in production, through driving, maintenance and finally its disposal, the Prius reduced CO_2 emissions by more than a third, and has a recyclability potential of approximately 90%. The Prius was launched in the USA at a price of $19 995, and sales in 2001 were 15 556 in the USA and 20 119 in 2002. However, industry experts estimate that Toyota was losing some $16 000 for every Prius it sold because it costs between $35 000 and $40 000 to produce. Toyota did make a profit on its second-generation Prius launched in 2003, and other hybrid cars such as the Lexus range in 2005, because of improved technologies and lowered production costs.

Hollywood celebrities soon discovered the Prius: Leonardo DiCaprio bought one of the first in 2001, followed by Cameron Diaz, Harrison Ford and Calista Flockhart. British politicians took rather longer to jump on the hybrid bandwagon, with the then leader of the opposition

(continued)

David Cameron driving a hybrid Lexus in 2006. In 2005, 107 897 cars were sold in the USA, about 60% of global Prius sales, and four times more than the sales in 2000 and twice as many in 2004. By 2013, Toyota had sold over 6 million hybrids globally, representing about two-thirds of all hybrid sales.

In addition to the direct income and indirect prestige the Prius and other hybrid cars have created for Toyota, the company has also licensed some of its 650 patents on hybrid technology to Nissan and Ford. Mercedes-Benz showed a diesel-electric S-class at the Frankfurt auto show in autumn 2005 and Honda has developed its own technology and range of hybrid cars and is also probably the world leader in fuel cell technology for vehicles.

Sources: A. Pilkington and R. Dyerson (2004) Incumbency and the disruptive regulator: The case of the electric vehicles in California, *International Journal of Innovation Management*, 8(4), 339–54; *The Economist* (2004) Why the future is hybrid, 4th December; *Financial Times* (2005) Too soon to write off the dinosaurs, 18th November; *Fortune* (2006) Toyota: The birth of the Prius, 21st February; Toyota (2014), Worldwide Sales of Toyota Hybrids Top 6 Million Units, http://corporatenews.pressroom.toyota.com/releases/worldwide+toyota+hybrid+sales+top+6 +million.htm, accessed 20th December 2014.

Research on diffusion attempts to identify what influences the rate and direction of adoption of an innovation. The diffusion of an innovation is typically described by an S-shaped (logistic) curve (Figure 11.6).

Hundreds of marketing studies have attempted to fit the adoption of specific products to the S-curve, ranging from television sets to new drugs. In most cases mathematical techniques can provide a relatively good fit with historical data, but research has so far failed to identify robust generic models of adoption. In practice the precise pattern of adoption of an innovation will depend on the interaction of demand-side and supply-side factors:

- *Demand-side factors*. Direct contact with or imitation of prior adopters, adopters with different perceptions of benefits and risk.
- *Supply-side factors*. Relative advantage of an innovation, availability of information, barriers to adoption, feedback between developers and users.

The basic epidemic S-curve model is the earliest and still the most commonly used. It assumes a homogeneous population of potential adopters, and that innovations spread by information transmitted by personal contact, observation and the geographical proximity of existing and potential adopters. This model suggests that the emphasis should be on communication, and the provision of clear technical and economic information. However, the epidemic model has been criticized because it assumes that all potential adopters are similar and have the same needs, which is unrealistic.

The most influential marketing model of diffusion was developed by Frank Bass in 1969, and has been applied widely to the adoption of consumer durables.[15] The **Bass model** assumes that potential adopters are influenced by two processes: individual independent adopters,

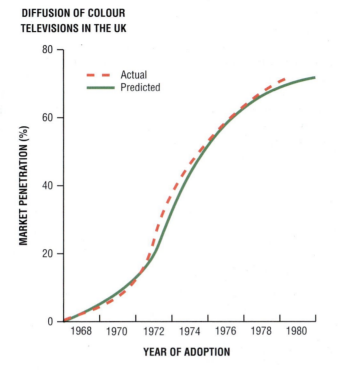

**DIFFUSION OF COLOUR
TELEVISIONS IN THE UK**

FIGURE 11.6   Typical diffusion curve

Source: Mead, N. and T. Islam (2006) Modeling and forecasting the diffusion of innovation: A 25-year review, *International Journal of Forecasting*, **22**(3), 519–532.

influenced mostly by personal, private assessment and trials, and later adopters, more influenced by interpersonal communication, social media and mass-marketing channels. Combining these two types of adopters produces a skewed S-curve because of the early adoption by innovators, and suggests that different marketing processes are needed for the innovators and subsequent imitators. The Bass model is highly influential in economics and marketing research, and the distinction between the two types of potential adopters is critical in understanding the different mechanisms involved in the two user segments.

Tool to help you explore this, accelerating diffusion, is available on the Innovation Portal at **www.innovation-portal.info**

Bandwagons may occur where an innovation is adopted because of pressure caused by the sheer number of those who have already adopted an innovation, rather than by individual assessments of the benefits of an innovation. In bandwagons, beyond a certain threshold of adopters, diffusion continues despite no demonstrated relative advantage of the innovation. This process allows technically inefficient innovations to be widely adopted, or technically efficient innovations to be rejected. Examples include the QWERTY keyboard, originally designed to prevent professional typists from typing too fast and jamming typewriters, and the DOS operating system for personal computers, designed by and for computer enthusiasts.

Bandwagons occur because of a combination of competitive and institutional pressures.[16] Where competitors adopt an innovation, a firm may adopt it also because of the threat of lost competitiveness, rather than as a result of any rational evaluation of benefits. For example, many firms adopted business process re-engineering in the 1980s in response to increased competition, but most failed to achieve significant benefits with it. The main institutional pressure is the threat of lost legitimacy, for example being considered by peers or customers as less progressive or competent.

The critical difference between bandwagons and other types of diffusion is that they require only limited information to flow from early to later adopters. Indeed, the more ambiguous the benefits of an innovation, the more influential the bandwagon effect is on the level of adoption. It is driven more by peer pressure and a need for legitimacy, rather than rational evaluation of any costs and benefits.

Factors Influencing Adoption

Characteristics of an innovation found to influence adoption include relative advantage, compatibility, complexity, observability and trialability. Individual characteristics include age, education, social status and attitude to risk. Environmental and institutional characteristics include economic factors such as the market environment and sociological factors such as communications networks. However, while there is general agreement regarding the relevant variables, there is very little consensus on the relative importance of the different variables of, and in some cases disagreements over, the direction of relationships.

In predicting the rate of adoption of an innovation, five factors explain 49–87% of the variance:

- relative advantage
- compatibility
- complexity
- trialability
- observability.

Activity to explore this theme, accelerating diffusion, is available on the Innovation Portal at **www.innovation-portal.info**

However, the contextual or environmental factors are also important, as demonstrated by the fact that diffusion rates of different innovations are highly variable, and the rates for the same innovation in different contexts also vary significantly.

Relative Advantage

Relative advantage is the degree to which an innovation is perceived as better than the product it supersedes, or competing products. Relative advantage is typically measured in narrow economic terms, for example cost or financial payback, but non-economic factors such as convenience, satisfaction and social prestige may be equally important. In theory, the greater the perceived advantage, the faster the rate of adoption.

It is useful to distinguish between the primary and secondary attributes of an innovation. Primary attributes, such as size and cost, are invariant and inherent to a specific innovation irrespective of the adopter. Secondary attributes, such as relative advantage and compatibility, may vary from adopter to adopter, being contingent upon the perceptions and context of adopters. In many cases, a so-called attribute gap will exist. An attribute gap is the discrepancy between a potential user's perception of an attribute or characteristic of an item of knowledge and how the potential user would prefer to perceive that attribute. The greater the sum of all attribute gaps, the less likely a user is to adopt the knowledge. This suggests that preliminary testing of an innovation is desirable in order to determine whether significant attribute gaps exist. The idea of pre-testing information for the purposes of enhancing its value and acceptance is not widely practised.

> **Case Study** highlighting some of these issues, Gordon Murray Design, is available on the Innovation Portal at **www.innovation-portal.info**

Compatibility

Compatibility is the degree to which an innovation is perceived to be consistent with the existing values, experience and needs of potential adopters. There are two distinct aspects of compatibility: existing skills and practices, and values and norms. The extent to which the innovation fits the existing skills, equipment, procedures and performance criteria of the potential adopter is important, and relatively easy to assess.

However, compatibility with existing practices may be less important than the fit with existing values and norms.[17] Significant misalignments between an innovation and an adopting organization will require changes in the innovation or organization, or both. In the most successful cases of implementation, mutual adaptation of the innovation and organization occurs. However, few studies distinguish between compatibility with value and norms, and compatibility with existing practices. The extent to which the innovation fits the existing skills, equipment, procedures and performance criteria of the potential adopter is critical. Few innovations initially fit the user environment into which they are introduced. Significant misalignments between the innovation and the adopting organization will require changes in the innovation or organization, or, in the most successful cases of implementation, mutual adaptation of both. Initial compatibility with existing practices may be less important, as it may provide limited opportunity for mutual adaptation to occur.

In addition, so-called network externalities can affect the adoption process. For example, the cost of adoption and use, as distinct from the cost of purchase, may be influenced by: the availability of information about the technology from other users, of trained skilled users, technical assistance and maintenance and of complementary innovations, both technical and organizational.

> **Case Study** highlighting some of these issues, gunfire at sea, is available on the Innovation Portal at **www.innovation-portal.info**

Complexity

Complexity is the degree to which an innovation is perceived as being difficult to understand or use. In general, innovations which are simpler for potential users to understand will be adopted more rapidly than those which require the adopter to develop new skills and knowledge.

However, complexity can also influence the direction of diffusion, not only the rate of adoption. Evolutionary models of diffusion focus on the effect of 'network externalities', that is the interaction of consumption, pecuniary and technical factors which shape the diffusion process. For example, for a specific target market segment or user group, the perceived complexity of an innovation may be influenced by: the level of user education, training and experience; availability of technical demonstrations or trials; and reviews and feedback from early adopters, peers or social networks.

Tool to help you explore these ideas, the risk assessment matrix, is available on the Innovation Portal at **www.innovation-portal.info**

Trialability

Trialability is the degree to which an innovation can be experimented with on a limited basis. An innovation that is trialable represents less uncertainty to potential adopters, and allows learning by doing. Innovations which can be trialled will generally be adopted more quickly than those which cannot. The exception is where the undesirable consequences of an innovation appear to outweigh the desirable characteristics. In general, adopters wish to benefit from the functional effects of an innovation, but avoid any dysfunctional effects. However, where it is difficult or impossible to separate the desirable from the undesirable consequences, trialability may reduce the rate of adoption.

Developers of an innovation may have two different motives for involving potential users in the development process. First, to acquire knowledge from the users needed in the development process, to ensure usability and to add value. Second, to attain user 'buy-in', that is user acceptance of the innovation and commitment to its use. The second motive is independent of the first, because increasing user acceptance does not necessarily improve the quality of the innovation. Rather, involvement may increase the user's tolerance of any inadequacies. In the case of point-to-point transfer, typically both motives are present.

Audio Clip of an interview with Richard Reed of Innocent Smoothies exploring some of these issues is available on the Innovation Portal at **www.innovation-portal.info**

However, in the case of diffusion it is not possible to involve all potential users, and therefore the primary motive is to improve usability rather than attain user buy-in. But even the representation of user needs must be indirect, using surrogates such as specially selected user groups. These groups can be problematic for a number of reasons. First, because they may possess atypically high levels of technical knowledge and therefore will not be representative. Second, where the group must represent diverse user needs, such as both experienced and novice users, the group may not work well together. Finally, when user representatives work closely with developers over a long period of time they may cease to represent users and instead absorb the developer's viewpoint. Thus, there is no simple relationship between user involvement and user satisfaction. Typically, very low levels of user involvement are associated with user dissatisfaction, but extensive user involvement does not necessarily result in user satisfaction.

Observability

Observability is the degree to which the results of an innovation are visible to others. The easier it is for others to see the benefits of an innovation, the more likely it will be adopted. The simple epidemic model of diffusion assumes that innovations spread as potential adopters come into contact with existing users of an innovation.

Peers who have already adopted an innovation will have what communication researchers call 'safety credibility', because potential adopters seeking their advice will believe they know what it is really like to implement and utilize the innovation. Therefore, early adopters are well positioned to disseminate 'vicarious learning' to their colleagues. Vicarious learning is simply learning from the experience of others rather than direct personal experimental learning. However, the process of vicarious learning is neither inevitable nor efficient because, by definition, it is a decentralized activity.

Audio Clip of Minimonos founder Melissa Clark-Reynolds discussing some of these issues is available on the Innovation Portal at **www.innovation-portal.info**

Demonstrations of innovations are highly effective in promoting adoption. Experimental, private demonstrations or pilots can be used to assess attributes of an innovation and the relative advantage for different target groups and to test compatibility. Exemplary public demonstrations can improve observability, reduce perceived complexity and promote private trials. However, note the different purpose and nature of experimental and exemplary demonstrations. Resources, urgency and uncertainty should determine the appropriate type of demonstration. Public demonstrations for experimental purposes are ill advised and likely to stall diffusion.

On the demand side, the uncertainty of potential adopters, and communication with and between them, also needs to be managed. While early adopters may emphasize technical performance and novelty above other factors, the mainstream mass market is more likely to be concerned with factors such as price, quality, convenience and support. This transition from the niche market and needs of early adopters, through to the requirements of more mass markets, has been referred to as 'crossing the chasm' by Moore.[18] Moore studied the successes and many more failures of Silicon Valley, and other high-technology products, and argued that the critical success factors for early adopters and mass markets were fundamentally different, and most innovations failed to make this transition. Therefore, the successful launch and diffusion of a systemic or network innovation demands attention to traditional marketing issues such as the timing and positioning of the product or service, but also significant effort to demand-side factors such as communication and interactions between potential adopters.

INNOVATION IN ACTION 11.4

Why Innovations Fail to Be Adopted

This research examined the factors which influence the adoption and diffusion of innovations drawing upon case studies of successful and less successful consumer electronics products, such as the Sony PlayStation and MiniDisc, the Apple iPod and Newton, the TomTom GO, TiVo and RIM's BlackBerry.

The study finds that a critical factor influencing successful diffusion is the careful management of acceptance by the early adopters, which in turn influences the adoption by the main market. Strategic issues such as positioning, timing and management of the adoption network are identified as being important. The adoption network is defined as a configuration of users, peers, competitors and complementary products, services and infrastructure. However, the positioning, timing and adoption networks are different for the early and main market adopters, and failure to recognize these differences is a common cause of the failure of innovations to diffuse widely. Also, innovation contingencies such as the degree of radicalness and discontinuity affect how these factors interact and how these need to be managed to promote acceptance. The relevant assessment of the radicalness and discontinuity of an innovation is not based on the technological aspects but rather the effects on user behaviour and consumption.

To promote use by early adopters, the research recommends that four enabling factors need to be managed: legitimate the innovation through reference customers and visible performance advantage, trigger word of mouth within specialist communities of practice, stimulate imitation to increase the user base and peer pressure and collaborate with opinion leaders. Significantly, the study argues that the subsequent successful diffusion of an innovation into the mainstream market has very little to do with the merits of the product itself and much more to do with the positive acceptance of early adopters and repositioning and targeting for the main market by influencing the relevant adoption network.

Source: Frattini, F. (2010) Achieving adoption network and early adopters acceptance for technological innovations, in J. Tidd (editor) *Gaining Momentum: Managing the Diffusion of Innovations*, London: Imperial College Press.

Chapter Summary

- There is a vast amount of management research on the subject of new product and service development, and we are now pretty certain what works and what does not.

- There are no guarantees that following the suggestions in this chapter will produce a blockbuster product, service or business, but if these elements are not managed well, your chances of success will be much lower. This is not supposed to discourage experimentation and calculated risk taking, but rather to provide a foundation for evidence-based practice.

- Research suggests that a range of factors affect the success of a potential new product or service:
  - Some factors are product-specific, e.g. product advantage, clear target market and attention to pre-development activities.
  - Other factors are more about the organizational context and process, e.g. senior management support, formal process and use of external knowledge.
  - A formal process for new product and service development should consist of distinct stages, such as concept development, business case, product development, pilot and commercialization, separated by distinct decision points, or gates, which have clear criteria such as product fit and product advantages.
  - Different stages of the process demand different criteria and different tools and methods. Useful tools and methods at the concept stage include segmentation, experimentation, focus groups and customer-partnering; at the development stage useful tools include prototyping, design for production and QFD.
  - Services and products are different in a number of ways, especially intangibility and perceived benefits, so will demand the adaptation of the standard models and prescriptions for new product development.
  - The relative advantage, compatibility, complexity, trialability and observability of an innovation all affect the rate of diffusion.

Key Terms Defined

Bandwagons occur during the diffusion of an innovation when an innovation is adopted because of the cumulative volume of previous adoptions, through peer pressure and expectations, rather than by any individual rational assessment of costs and benefits.

Bass model this model of diffusion assumes that potential adopters are influenced by two processes: by individual independent decisions and by interpersonal communications and channels.

Development funnel   an alternative to the stage-gate model, which takes into account the reduction in uncertainty as the process progresses, and the influence of real resource constraints.

Diffusion   is the process by which a focal innovation is adopted by a focal social system or market segment, and includes the rate and direction of change.

Quality function deployment (QFD)   is a set of planning and communications routines which are used to identify critical customer attributes and create a specific link between these and design parameters. It aims to answer three primary questions: What are the critical attributes for customers? What design parameters drive these attributes? What should the design parameter targets be for the new design?

Discussion Questions

1. What are the key differences between managing operations in services and manufacturing? Think of a business, and identify the relative contributions to value-added of the service and physical product components.

2. To what extent do you think manufacturing and services are converging? Try to think of an example of a manufacturing operation that increasingly features a service. Conversely, identify a service operation that is becoming more product-based.

3. In what ways do you think the development of new products differs from the development of new services?

4. Identify the relative importance of product/service attributes and organizational factors in successful development.

5. What effect does the novelty of the new product or service have on the development process?

6. What factors influence the adoption of innovations, and which of these can be managed?

Further Reading and Resources

The classic texts on new product development are those by Robert Cooper, for example, *Winning at New Products: Accelerating the Process from Idea to Launch* (Perseus Books, 2001) and Robert Cooper (2000) 'Doing it right: winning with new products', *Ivey Business Journal*, 64(6), 1–7, or anything by Kim Clark and Steven Wheelwright, such as 'Creating project plans to focus product development' (*Harvard Business Review*, 1997,

September–October) or their book *Revolutionizing Product Development* (Free Press, 1992). Paul Trott provides a good review of research in his text *Innovation Management and New Product Development* (5th edn, FT Prentice Hall, 2012), but for a more concise review of the research see Gerben van der Panne, Cees Beers and Alfred von Kleinknecht (2003) 'Success and failure of innovation: A literature review', *International Journal of Innovation Management*, 7(3), 309–38. A useful and practical handbook is *The PDMA Handbook of New Product Development*, edited by Abbie Griffin (3rd edn, John Wiley & Sons Ltd, 2012), which is particularly strong on process and tools. An excellent guide to applying QFD is *Quality Function Deployment and Six Sigma: A QFD Handbook* by Joseph Ficalora and Louis Cohen (Prentice-Hall, 2012).

The challenges of forecasting the future development, adoption and diffusion of innovations are dealt with by many authors in the innovation field. Everett Roger's classic text the *Diffusion of Innovations*, first published in 1962, remains the best overview of this subject, the most recent and updated edition being published in 2003 (Simon & Schuster). More up-to-date accounts can be found in *Determinants of Innovative Behaviour*, edited by Cees van Beers, Alfred Kleinknecht, Roland Ortt and Robert Verburg (Palgrave, 2008) and our own *Gaining Momentum: Managing the Diffusion of Innovations*, edited by Joe Tidd (Imperial College Press, 2009). The chapter by Paul Stoneman and Giuliana Battisti in the *Handbook of the Economics of Innovation*, volume 2, on the 'Diffusion of New Technology' provides a solid introduction (edited by Bronwyn H. Hall and Nathan Rosenberg, Elsevier, 2010).

References

1. Cooper, R.G. (2000) Doing it right: Winning with new products, *Ivey Business Journal*, **64**(6): 1–7.

2. Wheelwright, S.C. and K.B. Clark (1997) Creating project plans to focus product development, *Harvard Business Review*, **September–October.**

3. Tidd, J. and K. Bodley (2002) The influence of project novelty on the new product development process, *R&D Management*, **32**(2): 127–38.

4. NPD Group, 2012, https://www.npd.com/wps/portal/npd/us/news/press-releases/, accessed 20th December 2014.

5. Panne, van der, G., C. Beers and A. van Kleinknecht (2003) Success and failure of innovation: A literature review, *International Journal of Innovation Management*, 7(3): 309–38.

6. Crespi, G., C. Criscuolo and J. Haskel (2006) Information technology, organisational change and productivity growth: Evidence from UK firms, *The Future of Science, Technology and Innovation Policy: Linking Research and Practice*, SPRU 40th Anniversary Conference, Brighton, UK.

7. Tidd, J. and F.M. Hull (2006) Managing service innovation: The need for selectivity rather than 'best-practice', *New Technology, Work and Employment*, **21**(2): 139–61; (2003) *Service Innovation: Organizational Responses to Technological Opportunities and Market Imperatives*, London: Imperial College Press.

8. Griffin, A. (1992) Evaluating QFD's use in US firms as a process for developing products, *Journal of Product Innovation Management*, **9**: 171–87.

9. Pullman, M.E., W.L. Moore and D.G. Wardell (2002) A comparison of quality function deployment and conjoint analysis in new product design, *Journal of Product Innovation Management*, **19**: 354–64.

10. Geroski, P.A. (2000) Models of technology diffusion, *Research Policy*, **29**: 603–25; Geroski, P. (1991) Innovation and the sectoral sources of UK productivity growth, *Economic Journal*, **101**: 1438–51; Geroski, P. (1994) *Market Structure, Corporate Performance and Innovative Activity*, Oxford: Oxford University Press.

11. Griliches, Z. and A. Pakes (1984) *Patents R&D and Productivity*, Chicago: University of Chicago Press; Stoneman, P. (1983) *The Economic Analysis of Technological Change*, Oxford: Oxford University Press.

12. Jaffe, A.B. (1986) Technological opportunity and spillovers of R&D: Evidence from firms' patents, profits and market values, *American Economic Review*, **76**: 948–99.

13. Ortt, J.R. (2009) Understanding the pre-diffusion phases, in: Tidd, J. (ed.) *Gaining Momentum: Managing the Diffusion of Innovations*, London: Imperial College Press, 47–80.

14. Rogers, E.M. (2003) *Diffusion of Innovations*, New York: Free Press.

15. Bass, F.M. (1980) The relationship between diffusion rates, experience curves, and demand elasticities for consumer durable technological innovations, *Journal of Business*, **53**: 51–67; Bass, F.M. and A.V. Bultez (1982) A note on optimal strategic pricing of technological innovations, *Marketing Science*, **1**: 371–8; Bass, F.M., T. Krishnan and D. Jain (1994) Why the Bass model fits without decision variables, *Marketing Science*, **13**(3): 203–23; Bass, F.M. (1969) A new product growth model for consumer durables, *Management Science*, **15**: 215–27.

16. Abrahamson, E. and L. Plosenkopf (1993) Institutional and competitive bandwagons: Using mathematical modelling as a tool to explore innovation diffusion, *Academy of Management Journal*, **18**(3): 487–517; Lee, Y. and G. C. O'Connor (2003) New product launch strategy for network effects products, *Journal of the Academy of Marketing Science*, **31**(3): 241–55.

17. Chakravorti, B. (2003) *The Slow Pace of Fast Change: Bringing Innovation to Market in a Connected World*, Boston: Harvard Business School Press;

Chakravorti, B. (2004) The new rules for bringing innovations to market, *Harvard Business Review*, **82**(3): 58–67; Leonard-Barton, D. and D.K. Sinha (1993) Developer–user interaction and user satisfaction in internal technology transfer, *Academy of Management Journal*, **36**(5): 1125–39.

18. Moore, G. (1991) *Crossing the Chasm: Marketing and Selling Technology Products to Mainstream Customers*, New York: HarperBusiness; Moore, G. (1998) *Inside the Tornado: Marketing Strategies from Silicon Valley's Cutting Edge*, Chichester: Capstone.

Deeper Dive explanations of innovation concepts and ideas are available on the Innovation Portal at **www.innovation-portal.info**

Quizzes to test yourself further are available online via the Innovation Portal at **www.innovation-portal.info**

Summary of online resources for Chapter 11 –
all material is available via the Innovation Portal at
www.innovation-portal.info

Cases	**Media**	**Tools**	**Activities**	**Deeper Dives**
• BBC • Bank of Scotland • Lexus • Gordon Murray Design • Gunfire at sea	• Armin Rau • Eric von Hippel • Richard Reed • Melissa Clark-Reynolds	• SPOTS • Kano method • Conjoint analysis • Quality function deployment • Accelerating diffusion • Risk assessment matrix	• QFD at Lexus • Accelerating diffusion	• Cross-functional teams

Chapter 12

Creating New Ventures

LEARNING OBJECTIVES

By the end of this chapter you will develop an understanding of:

- the contextual factors which influence the creation of new ventures
- the process of creating an innovative new venture
- distinguishing the challenges of each of the stages of new venture development.

Types of New Venture

In the UK, around 500 000 new businesses are created each year. At the same time, each year around 300 000 firms fail, suggesting a net annual rate of new business creation of some 200 000 firms. However, most of these surviving new businesses are not very creative or innovative, and very few grow. Moreover, entrepreneurship is much more than the creation of a new business.

Contrary to popular belief, the majority of small firms are not particularly innovative. The goal of most entrepreneurs is to achieve independence of employment rather than the creation of innovative businesses. However, here we focus on the creation and development of *innovative* new ventures, those which aim to offer new products or services, or are based on novel processes or ways of creating value. These are not necessarily, or even frequently, based on inventions, new technology or scientific breakthroughs. Instead, the entrepreneur has chosen or been forced to create a new business in order to exploit the innovation.

People create new ventures for many different reasons, and it is critical to understand the different motives and mechanisms of entrepreneurship:

- *Lifestyle entrepreneurs.* Those who seek independence, and wish to earn a living based around their personal circumstances and values, e.g. individual professional consulting practices or home-based craft businesses. Statistically speaking, these are the most common type of new venture, and are an important source of self-employment in almost all economies. Contrary to popular belief, the majority of such small firms are not particularly creative or innovative, and instead are simply exploiting an asset (e.g. a shop) or expertise (e.g. IT consulting).
- *Growth entrepreneurs.* Those who aim to become wealthy and powerful through the creation and aggressive growth of new businesses (plural, as they are often serial entrepreneurs who create a string of new ventures). They are more likely to measure their success in terms of wealth, influence and reputation. Although we tend to think of people like Bill Gates or Steve Jobs, more typical examples are in relatively conservative, capital-intensive and well-understood sectors such as retail, property and commodities. Successful growth entrepreneurs tend to create very large corporations through acquisitions, which may dominate national markets, and the founders may become very wealthy and influential.
- *Innovative entrepreneurs.* Individuals who are driven by the desire to create or change something, whether in the private, public or third sectors. Independence, reputation and wealth are not the primary goals in such cases, although they are often achieved anyway. Rather, the main motivation is to actually change or create something new. Innovative entrepreneurs include technological entrepreneurs and social entrepreneurs, but such ventures are rarely based on inventions, new technology or scientific breakthroughs. Instead, the entrepreneur has chosen or been forced to create a new venture in order to create or change something. These are the focus of this chapter.

ENTREPRENEURSHIP IN ACTION 12.1

Marc Koska and Star Syringe

Marc Koska founded Star Syringe in 1996 to design and develop disposable, single-use 'auto-disable syringes' (ADS) to help prevent the transmission of diseases like HIV/AIDS. For example, over 23 million infections of HIV and hepatitis are given to otherwise healthy patients through syringe reuse every year.

Marc had no formal training in engineering, but had relevant design experience from previous jobs in modelling and plastics design. He designed the ADS according to the following basic principles:

- *Cheap.* Has the same price as a standard disposable plastic syringe.
- *Easy.* Manufactured on existing machinery, to reduce setup costs.

- *Simple*. Used as closely as possible in the same way as a standard disposable plastic syringe.
- *Scalable*. Licensed to local manufacturers, leveraging resources in a sustainable way.

The ADS is not manufactured in-house, but by Star licensees based all over the world. The company now licenses the technology to international aid agencies and is recognized by UNICEF and the World Health Organization. Star alliance is the network which connects the numerous manufacturing licensees to the global marketplace. The alliance includes 19 international manufacturing partners, and serves markets in over 20 countries. The combined capacity of the alliance licensees is close to one billion annual units.

His dedication and persistent drive over the last 20 years have earned him respect from leaders in state health services as well as industry: in February 2005, for example, the Federal Minister for Health in Pakistan presented Marc with an award for Outstanding Contribution to Public Health for his work on safer syringes, and in 2006 the company won the UK Queen's Award for Enterprise and International Trade.

Sources: www.starsyringe.com.

Audio Clip of Carmel McConnell discussing how business skills can be applied to social enterprises is available on the Innovation Portal at **www.innovation-portal.info**

Technology Entrepreneurs

The creation of a technology venture is the interaction of individual skills and disposition and technological and market characteristics. US studies emphasize the role of personal characteristics, such as family background, goal orientation, personality and motivation,[1] whereas European studies stress the role of the environment, including institutional support and resources.[2] The decision to start a technology venture typically begins with a desire to gain independence and to escape the bureaucracy of a large organization, whether it is in the public or private sector. Thus, the background, psychological profile, and work and technical experience of a technical entrepreneur all contribute to the decision to create a new venture.

Education and training are major factors that distinguish the founders of technology ventures from other entrepreneurs. The median level of education of technical entrepreneurs is a master's degree, and with the important exception of biotechnology-based ventures, a doctorate is superfluous. Significantly, the levels of education of technical entrepreneurs do not differentiate them from other scientists and engineers. However, potential technical entrepreneurs tend to have higher levels of productivity than their technical work colleagues, measured in terms of papers published or patents granted. This suggests that potential entrepreneurs may be more driven than their corporate counterparts.

In addition to a master's-level education, on average, a technical entrepreneur will have around 13 years of work experience before establishing a new venture. In the case of Route 128, the entrepreneur's work experience is typically with a single **incubator organization**, whereas technical entrepreneurs in Silicon Valley tend to have gained their experience from a larger number of firms before establishing their own business. This suggests that there is no ideal pattern of previous work experience. However, experience of development work appears to be more important than work in basic research.

As a result of the formal education and experience required, a typical technical entrepreneur will be aged between 30 and 40 years when establishing his or her first technology venture. This is relatively late in life compared to other types of venture, and is due to a combination of ability and opportunity. On the one hand, it typically takes between 10 and 15 years for a potential entrepreneur to attain the necessary technical and business experience. On the other hand, many people begin to have greater financial and family responsibilities at this time. Thus, there appears to be a window of opportunity to start a technology venture, some time in the mid- to late thirties. Although teenage app developers attract most press attention, the median age of technology entrepreneurs in the USA is 39.[3]

Unlike general entrepreneurs, technology entrepreneurs appear to have only moderate n-Ach, but a low need for affiliation (n-Aff). This suggests that the need for independence, rather than success, is the most significant motivator for technical entrepreneurs. Technology entrepreneurs also tend to have an internal locus of control. In other words, they believe they have personal control over outcomes, whereas someone with an external locus of control believes outcomes are the result of chance, powerful institutions or others. More sophisticated psychometric techniques such as the Myers–Briggs type indicators (MBTI) confirm the differences between technology entrepreneurs and other scientists and engineers.

Numerous surveys indicate that most technology entrepreneurs claim to have been frustrated in their previous job. This frustration appears to result from the interaction of the psychological predisposition of the potential entrepreneur and poor selection, training and development by the parent organization. Specific events may also trigger the desire or need to establish a technology venture, such as a major reorganization or downsizing of the parent organization.

ENTREPRENEURSHIP IN ACTION 12.2

Mike Lynch and Autonomy

Mike Lynch founded the software company Autonomy in 1994, a spin-off from his first start-up Neurodynamics. Lynch, a grammar-school graduate, studied information science at Cambridge where he carried out PhD research on probability theory. He rejected a conventional research career as he had found his summer job at GEC Marconi a 'boring, tedious place'. In 1991, aged 25, he approached the banks to raise money for his first venture, Neurodynamics, but 'met a nice chap who laughed a lot and admitted that he was only used to lending money to people to open newsagents'. He subsequently raised the initial £2000 from a friend of a friend. Neurodynamics developed pattern-recognition software which it sold to specialist niche users such as the UK police force for matching fingerprints and identifying disparities in witness statements, and banks to identify signatures on cheques.

Autonomy was spun off in 1994 to exploit applications of the technology in the Internet, intranet and media sectors, and received the financial backing of venture capitalists Apax, Durlacher and ENIC. Autonomy was floated on the EASDAQ in July 1998 and on the NASDAQ in 1999. In February 2000, it was worth $5 billion, making Lynch the first British software billionaire. Autonomy creates software which manages unstructured information, which accounts for 80% of all data. The software applies Bayesian probabilistic techniques to identify patterns of data or text, and compared to crude keyword searches can better take into account context and relationships. The software is patented in the USA, but not in Europe, as patent law does not allow patent protection of software. The business generates revenues through selling software for cataloguing and searching information direct to clients such as the BBC, Barclays, BT, Eli Lilly, General Motors, Merrill Lynch, News Corporation, Nationwide, Procter & Gamble and Reuters. In addition, it has more than 50 licence agreements with leading software companies to use its technology, including Oracle, Sun and Sybase. A typical licence will include a lump sum of $100 000 plus a royalty on sales of 10–30%. By means of such licence deals, Autonomy aims to become an integral part of a range of software and the standard for intelligent recognition and searching. In the financial year ending March 2000, the company reported its first profit of $440 000 on a turnover of $11.7 million. The company employed 120 staff, split between Cambridge in the UK and Silicon Valley, and spent 17% of its revenues on R&D. In 2004, sales reached around $60 million, with an average licence costing $360 000, and high gross margins of 95%. Repeat customers accounted for 30% of sales. In 2011, the company was sold to HP for $10.3 billion, and in May 2012 Mike Lynch left the company he created and grew.

> **Case Studies** of Ihavemoved.com and Threadless.com, two very different examples of Internet start-ups, are available on the Innovation Portal at **www.innovation-portal.info**

Context for Entrepreneurship

Most of what we know about innovative new ventures is based on the experience of start-up firms in the USA, in particular the growth of biotechnology, semiconductor and software firms. Many of these originated from a parent or incubator organization, typically either an academic institution or large, well-established firm. Examples of university incubators include Stanford University, which spawned much of Silicon Valley; Massachusetts Institute of Technology (MIT), which spawned Route 128 in Boston; and Imperial College and Cambridge University in the UK. MIT in particular has become the archetype academic incubator, and in addition to the creation of Route 128 its alumni have established some 200 new ventures in northern California and account for more than a fifth of employment in Silicon Valley. The so-called MIT model has been adopted worldwide, so far with limited success.

ENTREPRENEURSHIP IN ACTION 12.3

Boston's Route 128

The cluster of universities in Boston and Cambridge in the USA, which includes MIT, Harvard, Boston and 70 other colleges and universities, has a long tradition of spawning spin-off firms.

The success of the region can be traced back to the defence-related investments in computing and software which helped to create incubator firms such as Compaq, Digital, Data General, Lucent, Lotus, Raytheon and Wang in the 1970s, and more recently the creation of many life-sciences-based ventures in biotechnology and medical devices.

For several decades now, the venture capital industry has consistently funded the creation or growth of around 200 to 300 new firms each year with annual funding of around $2 billion (this more than quadrupled during the Internet boom/bubble of 1998/2000). By the first decade of the new millennium MIT alone had helped to create 4000 new firms worldwide with total revenues of $232 billion, with more than a thousand of these firms still based in Massachusetts.

Source: Wonglimpiyarat, J. (2006) The Boston Route 128 model of high-tech industry development, *International Journal of Innovation Management*, **10**(1), 47–64.

ENTREPRENEURSHIP IN ACTION 12.4

Spin-off Companies from Xerox's PARC Labs

Xerox established its Palo Alto Research Center (PARC) in California in 1970. PARC was responsible for a large number of technological innovations in the semiconductor lasers, laser printing, Ethernet networking technology and Web indexing and searching technologies, but it is generally acknowledged that many of its most significant innovations were the result of individuals who left the company and firms which spun-off from PARC, rather than those developed via Xerox itself. For example, many of the user-interface developments at Apple originated at Xerox, as did the basis of Microsoft's Word package. By 1998, Xerox PARC had spun out 24 firms, including ten which went public, such as 3Com, Adobe, Documentum and SynOptics. By 2001, the value of the spin-off companies was more than twice that of Xerox itself.

A debate continues as to the reasons for this, most attributing the failure to retain the technologies in-house to corporate ignorance and internal politics. However, most of the technologies did not simply leak out but instead were granted permission by Xerox, which often provided non-exclusive licences and an equity stake in the spin-off firms. This suggests that Xerox's research and business managers saw little potential for exploiting these technologies in its own businesses. One of the reasons for the failure to commercialize these technologies in-house was that Xerox had been highly successful with its integrated product-focused strategy, which made it more difficult to recognize and exploit potential new *businesses.*

Source: Chesbrough, H. (2003) *Open Innovation: The new imperative for creating and profiting from technology*, Boston: Harvard Business School Press.

Innovative SMEs exhibit broadly similar characteristics across sectors. They:

- are more likely to involve product innovation than process innovation
- are focused on products for niche markets, rather than mass markets
- will be more common amongst producers of final products, rather than producers of components
- will frequently involve some form of external linkage
- tend to be associated with growth in output and employment, but not necessarily profit.

Unlike large firms, small firms tend to be specialized rather than diversified in their technological competencies and product range. However, as with large firms, it is impossible to make robust generalizations about their technological trajectories and innovation strategies. Kurt Hoffman and his colleagues have recently pointed out that relatively little research has been undertaken on innovation in small firms; what research has been done tends to concentrate on the small group of spectacular high-tech successes (or failures) rather than the much more numerous run-of-the-mill small firms coping (say) with the introduction of IT into their distribution systems.[4]

Table 12.1 tries to categorize these differences. Until recently, attention has been focused on the left-hand side of the table, the spectacular and visible successes amongst small innovating firms, in particular the superstars that became big and those of the technology-based firms that often want to become big. As we have seen earlier in this chapter, recent, more systematic surveys of innovative activities and of small firms show two other classes of small firm with less-spectacular innovation strategies but of far greater importance to the overall economy: specialized suppliers of production inputs and firms whose sources of innovation are mainly their suppliers.

Superstars are large firms that have emerged from small beginnings, through high rates of growth based on the exploitation of a major invention (e.g. instant photography, reprography), or a rich technological trajectory (e.g. semiconductors, software), enabling small firms to exploit first-mover advantages like patent protection (see Chapter 15). Successful innovators often either accumulated their technological knowledge in large firms before leaving to start their own or offered their invention to large firms but were refused (examples: Polaroid, Xerox). Few superstars have emerged either in the chemical industry over the past 50 years or – contrary to expectations – out of biotechnology firms over the past 15 years, probably because the barriers to entry (in R&D, production or marketing) remain high.

New technology-based firms (NTBFs) are small firms that have emerged recently from large firms and large laboratories in such fields as electronics, software and biotechnology. They are

TABLE 12.1 Types of innovative new ventures

	Superstars: small firms into big since 1950	New technology-based firms (NTBFs)	Specialized	Supplier-dominated
Examples	Polaroid, DEC, Texas Instruments, Xerox, Intel, Microsoft, Compaq, Sony, Casio, Benetton	Start-ups in electronics, biotechnology and software	Producer of goods (machines, components, instruments, software)	Traditional products (e.g. textiles, wood products, food products) and many services
Sources of competitive advantage	Successful exploitation of major invention or technological trajectory	1. Product or process development in fast-moving and specialized area 2. Privatizing academic research	Combining technologies to meet users' needs	Integration and adaptation of innovations by suppliers
Main tasks of innovation strategy	Preparing replacements for the original invention (or inventor)	1. Superstar or specialized supplier? 2. Knowledge or money?	Links to advanced users and pervasive technologies	Exploiting new IT-based opportunities in design, distribution and coordination

usually specialized in the supply of a key component, subsystem, service or technique to larger firms, who may often be their former employers. Contrary to a widespread belief, most of the NTBFs in electronics and software have emerged from corporate or government laboratories involved in development and testing activities. It is only with the advent of biotechnology (and more recently software) that university laboratories have become regular sources of NTBFs, thereby strengthening the strong direct links that have always existed between university-based research and the pharmaceutical industry. However, some observers criticize this trend and fear that the 'privatization' of university research in biotechnology will in the long term reduce the rate of scientific progress and innovation and their contribution to economic and social welfare.

The management of NTBFs faces two sets of strategic challenges:

- The first relates to long-term prospects for growth. Very few technology-based small firms can become superstars, since they provide mainly specialized 'niche' products with no obvious or spectacular synergies with other markets. How far the firm will grow, or how long it will survive, will often depend on its ability to negotiate the transition from the first to the second (improved) generation of products, and to develop the supporting managerial competencies.
- How far the NTBF will grow depends on the second strategic choice: whether the management is aiming to maximize long-term value of the business or merely seeking an increase

in income and independence. Thus, owners of small firms often sell their firms after a few years and live off their investments. And university researchers set up consultancy firms, either to increase their personal income (the BMW effect) or to find supplementary income for their university-based research and teaching activities in times of increasing financial stringency.

Specialized supplier firms design, develop and build specialized inputs into production, in the form of machinery, instruments and (increasingly) software, and interact closely with their (often large) technically progressive customers. They perform relatively little formal R&D but are nonetheless a major source of the active development of significant innovations, with major contributions being made by design and production staff.

Finally, most small firms fall into the 'supplier-dominated' category, which indicates that their main sources of innovation are technological inputs provided by suppliers, such as equipment and components. These firms depend heavily on their suppliers for their innovations, and therefore are often unable to appropriate firm-specific technology as a source of competitive advantage. Technology will become more important in future, with the growing range of potential IT applications offered by suppliers, especially in service activities like distribution and coordination. An increasing range of small firms will therefore need to obtain the technological competencies to be able to specify, purchase, install and maintain software systems that help increase their competitiveness.

Role of University Incubators

The creation and sharing of intellectual property is a core role of a university, but managing it for commercial gain is a different challenge. Most universities with significant commercial research contracts understand how to license, and the roles of all parties – the academics, the university and the commercial organization – are relatively clear. In particular, the academic will normally continue with the research while possibly having a consultancy arrangement with the commercial company.

However, forming an independent company is a different matter. Here both the university and the scientist must agree that **spin-out** is the most viable option for technology commercialization and must negotiate a spin-out deal. This may include questions of, for example, equity split, royalties, academic and university investment in the new venture, academic secondment, identification and transfer of intellectual property and use of university resources in the start-up phase. In short, it is complicated. As Chris Evans, founder of Chiroscience and Merlin Ventures notes: 'Academics and universities … have no management, no muscle, no vision, no business plan and that is 90% of the task of exploiting science and taking it to the marketplace. There is a tendency for universities to think, "We invented the thing so we are already 50% there". The fact is they are 50% to nowhere.'[5] A characteristically provocative statement, but it does highlight the gulf between research and successful commercialization.

Many universities have accepted and followed the fashion for the commercial exploitation of technology, but typically put too much emphasis on the importance of the technology and ownership of the intellectual property, and 'fail to recognize the importance and sophistication of the business knowledge and expertise of management and other parties who contribute to the non-technical aspects of technology shaping and development … the linear model gives no insight into the interplay of technology push and market pull'.[6]

Changes in funding and law in the 1980s clearly encouraged many more universities to establish licensing and technology transfer departments, but the impact of these has been relatively small. For example, there is strong evidence that the scientific and commercial quality of patents has fallen since the mid-1980s as a result of these policy changes, and that the distribution of activity has a very long tail. Measured in terms of the number of patents held or exploited, or by income from patent and software licences, commercialization of technology is highly concentrated in a small number of elite universities which were highly active prior to changes to funding policy and law: the top 20 US universities account for 70% of patent activity. Moreover, at each of these elite universities a very small number of key patents account for most of the licensing income: the five most successful patents typically account for 70–90% of total income.[7] This suggests that a (rare) combination of research excellence and critical mass is required to succeed in the commercialization of technology. Nonetheless, technological opportunity has reduced some of the barriers to commercialization. Specifically, the growing importance of developments in the biosciences and software present new opportunities for universities to benefit from the commercialization of technology.

University spin-outs are an alternative to exploitation of technology through licensing, and involve the creation of an entirely new venture based upon intellectual property developed within the university. Estimates vary, but between 3 and 12% of all technologies commercialized by universities are via new ventures. As with licensing, the propensity for success of these ventures varies significantly. For example, MIT and Stanford University each create around 50 new start-ups each year, whereas Columbia and Duke rarely generate any start-up companies. These significant differences are partly due to location, scale, policy and technical disciplines taught and researched. Note from Table 12.2 that venture capitalists tend to fund larger and later stage ventures, needing capital of $8–$15 million. We discuss the role and limitations of venture capital in Chapter 14.

Studies in the USA suggest that the financial returns to universities are much higher from spin-out companies than from the more common licensing approach. One study estimated that the average income from a university licence was $63 832, whereas the average return from a university spin-out was more than ten times this ($692 121). When the extreme cases were excluded from the sample, the return from spin-outs was still $139 722, more than twice that for a licence.[8] Apart from these financial arguments, there are other reasons why forming a spin-out company may be preferable to licensing technology to an established company:

- No existing company is ready or able to take on the project on a licensing basis.
- The invention consists of a portfolio of products or is an 'enabling technology' capable of application in a number of fields.
- The inventors have a strong preference for forming a company and are prepared to invest their time, effort and money in a start-up.

As such they involve the 'academic entrepreneur' more fully in the detail of creating and managing a market entry strategy than is the case for other forms of commercialization. They also require major career decisions for the participants. Consequently, they highlight most

TABLE 12.2   Examples of venture-capital-funded university spin-offs, 2011–2014

University	Number of VC-funded university entrepreneurs	Number of VC-funded new ventures	Mean VC capital funding per new venture ($m)
Stanford, USA	378	309	11.388
UC Berkeley, USA	336	284	8.493
MIT, USA	300	250	9.666
Indian Institute of Technology	264	205	15.36
Harvard, USA	253	229	14.13
Tel Aviv, Israel	169	141	8.89
Waterloo, Canada	122	96	10.50
Technion, Israel	119	98	8.133
McGill, Canada	74	72	7.458
Toronto, Canada	71	66	14.06
London, UK	71	67	15.94

Source: Derived from Pitchbook (2014) *Venture Capital Monthly August/September 2014 Report*, http://pitchbook.com/.

clearly the dilemmas faced as the scientist tries to manage the interface between academia and industry. The extent to which an individual is motivated to attempt the launch of a venture depends upon three related factors: antecedent influences, individual incubator experiences and environmental factors.

- *Antecedent influences.* Often called the 'characteristics' of the entrepreneur, including genetic factors, family influences, educational choices and previous career experiences, all contribute to the entrepreneur's decision to start a venture.
- *Individual incubator experiences.* Immediately prior to start-up include the nature of the physical location, the type of skills and knowledge acquired, contact with possible fellow founders, the type of new venture or small business experience gained.
- *Environmental factors.* Include economic conditions, availability of venture capital, entrepreneurial role models, availability of support services.

There are relatively few data on the characteristics of the academic entrepreneur, partly owing to the low numbers involved, but also because the traditional context within which they have operated, particularly as they apply to intellectual property rights (IPR) and equity sharing, has meant that many have been unwilling to be researched. It is also probable that this is compounded by inadequate university data capture systems. Nevertheless, it is clear that in the USA scientists and engineers working in universities have long become disposed towards the commercialization of research. Studies in the USA reveal an increasing legitimization of university–industry research interactions. However, academic entrepreneurs are still not the norm, even in the USA. A study of 237 scientists working in three large national laboratories in the USA found clear differences between the levels of education in inventors in national laboratories and those in a study of technical entrepreneurs from MIT. The study found significant differences between entrepreneurs and non-entrepreneurs in terms of situational variables such as the level of involvement in business activities outside the laboratory or the receipt of royalties from past inventions.[9] Studies of academic scientists and engineers in the UK identify similar relationships between attitudes to industry, number of industry links and commercial activity.[10] This raises the question: what is the direction of causation? Do entrepreneurial researchers seek more links outside the organization or do more links encourage entrepreneurial behaviour?

ENTREPRENEURSHIP IN ACTION 12.5

WhatsApp

In February 2014, WhatsApp was sold to Facebook for $19 billion. Since its launch in 2009, WhatsApp has quietly grown to almost half the size of Facebook, with 450 million users.

Founders Jan Koum and Brian Acton are not typical of Silicon Valley technology entrepreneurs. Both were well over 30 years old when they launched their messaging app in 2009. They met while working at Yahoo in 1997.

After almost ten years at Yahoo, in September 2007 Koum and Acton left to take a year out, travelling around South America, funded by Koum's $400 000 savings from Yahoo. In early 2009, Koum realized that the seven-month-old App Store could create a whole new industry of apps. He could develop the backend of applications, but recruited Igor Solomennikov, a iPhone developer from Russia, for the front-end development. WhatsApp Inc. was registered on 24th February 2009, although the app had not yet been developed.

In October 2009, Acton convinced five ex-Yahoo friends to invest $250 000 in seed funding, and as a result was granted co-founder status and a stake. The two founders had a combined stake in excess of 60%, a large proportion for a technology start-up. By 2011, the app was in the Apple top ten, and attracted the attention of many potential investors. Sequoia partner Jim Goetz promised not to push advertising models on them, and they agreed to take $8 million from Sequoia. WhatsApp raised additional funding of $50 million in 2013, from Sequoia Capital, but with little publicity, valuing the company at $1.5 billion.

In 2012, Koum tweeted 'People starting companies for a quick sale are a disgrace to the Valley,' he tweeted. 'Next person to call me an entrepreneur is getting punched in the face by my bodyguard. Seriously.'

Unlike most Internet start-ups, they charged for their service, rather than giving it away for free and relying on advertising. WhatsApp does not collect any of the personal or demographic information that Facebook, Google and their rivals use to target ads. 'No ads! No games! No gimmicks! The simplicity and the utility of our product is really what drives us' – Jan Koum, WhatsApp founder. 'The simplicity and the utility of our product is really what drives us,' Koum said at DLD, joking that WhatsApp was 'clearly not doing that good a job' because it has not yet reached its goal of being on every smartphone in the world.

WhatsApp remains a lean operation, even by Silicon Valley standards. In early 2014, WhatsApp still had only 50-odd employees, 30 of whom were engineers like its founders. Its funding of some $60 million is half as much as the much smaller Snapchat. In 2014, it moved to a new building, and plans to double staff to 100.

Sources: Tim Bradshaw (2014) What's up with the WhatsApp founders? *Financial Times*, 20th February 2014; Olson, P. (2014) The Rags-To-Riches Tale Of How Jan Koum Built WhatsApp Into Facebook's New $19 Billion Baby, *Forbes*, 19th February 2014.

Entrepreneurs, academic or otherwise, require a supportive environment. Surveys indicate that two-thirds of university scientists and engineers now support the need to commercialize their research, and half the need for start-up assistance. There are two levels of analysis of the university environment: the formal institutional rules, policies and structures, and the 'local norms' within the individual department. There are a number of institutional variables which may influence academic entrepreneurship:

- Formal policy and support for entrepreneurial activity from management.
- Perceived seriousness of constraints to entrepreneurship, e.g. IPR issues.
- Incidence of successful commercialization, which demonstrates feasibility and provides role models.

Formal policies to encourage and support entrepreneurship can have both intended and unintended consequences. For example, a university policy of taking an equity stake in new start-ups in return for paying initial patenting and licensing expenses seems to result in a higher number of start-ups, whereas granting generous royalties to academic entrepreneurs appears to encourage licensing activity, but tends to suppress significantly the number of start-up companies.[11] In addition, some very common university policies appear to have little or no positive effect on the number or subsequent success of start-ups, including university incubators and local venture capital funding. Moreover, badly targeted and poorly monitored financial support may encourage 'entrepreneurial academics', rather than academic entrepreneurs – scientists in the public sector who are not really committed to creating start-ups but are seeking alternative support for their own research agendas. This can result in start-ups with little or no growth prospects remaining in incubators for many years. Simply encouraging commercially oriented or industry-funded research also appears to have no effect on the number of start-ups, whereas a university's intellectual eminence has a very strong positive effect.[12] There are two explanations for this effect: more prestigious universities typically attract better researchers and higher funding and other commercial investors use the prestige or reputation of the institution as a signal or indicator of quality.

Formal policies may send a signal to staff, but the effect on individual behaviour depends very much on whether these policies are reinforced by behavioural expectations. Individual characteristics and local norms appear to be equally effective predictors of entrepreneurial activity, but only provide weak predictions of the forms of entrepreneurship. Where successful, this can create a virtuous circle, the demonstration effect of a successful spin-out encouraging others to try. This leads to clusters of spin-outs in space and time, resulting in entrepreneurial departments or universities rather than isolated entrepreneurial academics. Local norms or culture at the departmental level will influence the effectiveness of formal policies by providing a strong mediating effect between the institutional context and individual perceptions. Local norms evolve through self-selection during recruitment, resulting in staff with similar personal values and behaviour, and reinforced by peer pressure or behavioural socialization resulting in a convergence of personal values and behaviour. However, there is a real potential conflict between the pursuit of knowledge and its commercial exploitation, and a real danger of lowering research standards exists. Therefore, it is essential to have guidelines for the conduct of business in a university environment:

- specific guidelines on the use of university facilities, staff and students and IPR
- specific guidelines for, and periodic reviews of, the dual employment of scientist-entrepreneurs, including permanent part-time positions
- mechanisms to resolve issues of financial ownership and the allocation of research contracts between the university and the venture.

ENTREPRENEURSHIP IN ACTION 12.6

License or Spin-out? The Lambert Review of Business: University Collaboration in the UK

In the UK, the Lambert Review of Business: University Collaboration reported in December 2003. It reviewed the commercialization of intellectual property by universities in the UK and made international comparisons of policy and performance. The UK has a similar pattern of concentration of activity to the USA. In 2002, 80% of UK universities made no patent applications, whereas 5% filed 20 or more patents; similarly, 60% of universities issued no new licences, but 5% issued more than 30. However, in the UK there has been a bias towards spin-outs rather than licensing, which the Lambert Review criticizes. It argues that spin-outs are often too complex and unsustainable, and of low quality – a third in the UK are fully funded by the parent university and attract no external private funding. In 2002, universities in the UK created over 150 new spin-out firms, compared to almost 500 by universities in the USA; the respective figures for new licences that year were 648 and 4058. As a proportion of R&D expenditure, this suggests that British universities place greater emphasis on spin-outs than their North American counterparts, and less on licensing. Lambert argues that universities in the UK may place too high a price on their intellectual property and that contracts often lack clarity of ownership. Both of these problems discourage businesses from licensing intellectual property from universities, and may encourage universities to commercialize their technologies through wholly owned spin-outs.

Process and Stages for Creating a New Venture

Typical stages of creating a new venture include:

1. Assessing the opportunity for a new venture – generating, evaluating and refining the business concept.
2. Developing the business plan and deciding the structure of the venture.
3. Acquiring the resources and funding necessary for implementation – including expert support and potential partnerships.
4. Growing and harvesting the venture – how to create and extract value from the business.

A new venture will face different challenges at different stages in order to make a successful transition to the next stage, what the researchers call 'critical junctures':

- *Opportunity recognition.* At the interface of the research and opportunity framing phases. This requires the ability to connect a specific technology or know-how to a commercial application, and is based on a rather rare combination of skill, experience, aptitude, insight and circumstances. A key issue here is the ability to synthesize scientific knowledge and market insights, which increases with the entrepreneur's social capital – linkages, partnerships and other network interactions.
- *Entrepreneurial commitment.* Acts and sustained persistence that bind the venture champion to the emerging business venture. This often demands difficult personal decisions to be made, e.g. whether to remain an academic, as well as evidence of direct financial investments to the venture.
- *Venture credibility.* This is critical for the entrepreneur to gain the resources necessary to acquire the finance and other resources for the business to function. Credibility is a function of the venture team, key customers and other social capital and relationships. This requires close relationships with sponsors, financial and other, to build and maintain awareness and credibility. Lack of business experience and failure to recognize their own limitations are a key problem here. One solution is to hire the services of a 'surrogate entrepreneur'. As one experienced entrepreneur personally communicated to us: 'The not-so-smart or really insecure academics want their hands over everything. These prima donnas make a complete mess of things, get nowhere with their companies and end up disappointed professionally and financially.'

Assessing the Opportunity

One of the failures of many discussions of entrepreneurship is that they assume that the opportunity has already been identified, and all that remains is to develop and resource this. However, in practice a budding entrepreneur may have only a vague idea of the basis of a new venture. Research confirms that the ability to recognize and assess opportunities is a critical determinant of new venture success.[13]

Common sources of ideas for new ventures include:

- Extensions or adaptations of existing products or services.
- Application of existing products or services in different or newly created market segments, or at different price points, e.g. low-cost airlines such as Ryanair and easyJet, or Dyson's household cleaner, which adapted centrifugal technology from industrial applications.
- Adding value to an existing product or service, e.g. Web search engines for specialist fields like travel and insurance, such as TravelJungle.co.uk or Confused.com.
- Developing a completely new product or service.

The more fundamental drivers of opportunities for new ventures are:

- Economic factors, e.g. changes in disposable income.
- Technological developments – which may reduce (or increase) barriers to entry.
- Demographic trends, e.g. the ageing population, more leisure time.
- Regulatory changes, e.g. environmental requirements, health and safety.

All of these potential sources can be more readily identified and assessed by using the systematic approaches to scanning and searching that we advocate in Chapters 6 and 7.

INNOVATION IN ACTION 12.1

Learning from Users at IDEO

IDEO is one of the most successful design consultancies in the world. Based in Palo Alto, California, and London, UK, it helps large consumer and industrial companies worldwide design and develop innovative new products and services. Behind its rather typical Californian wackiness lies a tried-and-tested process for successful design and development:

1. Understand the market, client and technology.
2. Observe users and potential users in real-life situations.
3. Visualize new concepts and the customers who may use them, using prototyping, models and simulations.
4. Evaluate and refine the prototypes in a series of quick interactions.
5. Implement the new concept for commercialization.

The first critical step is achieved through close observation of potential users in context. As Tom Kelly of IDEO argues: 'We're not big fans of focus groups. We don't much care for traditional market research either. We go to the source. Not the "experts" inside a [client] company, but the actual people who use the product or something similar to what we're hoping to create … we believe you have to go beyond putting yourself in your customers' shoes. Indeed we believe it's not even enough to *ask* people what they think about a product or idea … customers may lack the vocabulary or the palate to explain what's wrong, and especially what's *missing*.'

The next step is to develop prototypes to help evaluate and refine the ideas captured from users: 'an iterative approach to problems is one of the foundations of our culture of prototyping … you can prototype just about anything – a new product or service, or a special promotion. What counts is moving the ball forward, achieving some part of your goal.'

Source: Kelly, T. (2002) *The Art of Innovation: Lessons in Creativity from IDEO*, London: HarperCollins Business.

Developing the Business Plan

We discussed this in detail in Chapter 8, so here we only review the main considerations when developing a plan. The primary reason for developing a formal business plan for a new venture is to attract external funding. However, it serves an important secondary function. A business plan can provide a formal agreement between founders regarding the basis and future development of the venture. A business plan can help reduce self-delusion on the part of the founders, and avoid subsequent arguments concerning responsibilities and rewards. It can help to translate abstract or ambiguous goals into more explicit operational needs, and support subsequent decision-making and identify trade-offs. Of the *controllable* factors by entrepreneurs, business planning has the most significant positive effect on new venture performance. However, there are of course many *uncontrollable* factors, such as market opportunity, which have an even more significant influence on performance. Pasteur's advice still applies: 'chance favours only the prepared mind'.

A typical formal business plan will include the following sections:

- details of the product or service
- assessment of the market opportunity
- identification of target customers
- barriers to entry and competitor analysis
- experience, expertise and commitment of the management team
- strategy for pricing, distribution and sales
- identification and planning for key risks
- cash-flow calculation, including break-even points and sensitivity
- financial and other resource requirements of the business.

No standard business plan exists, but in many cases venture capitalists will provide a pro forma for the business plan. Typically, a business plan should be relatively concise, say no more than 10 to 20 pages, begin with an executive summary and include sections on the product, markets, technology, development, production, marketing, human resources, financial estimates with contingency plans and the timetable and funding requirements. Most business plans submitted to venture capitalists are strong on the technical considerations, often placing too much emphasis on the technology relative to other issues. As Ed Roberts notes: 'entrepreneurs propose that they can do *it* better than anyone else, but may forget to demonstrate that anyone wants *it*'.[14] He identifies a number of common problems with business plans submitted to venture capitalists: marketing plan, management team, technology plan and financial plan. The management team will be assessed against their commitment, experience and expertise, normally in that order. Unfortunately, many potential entrepreneurs place too much emphasis on their expertise but have insufficient experience in the team and fail to demonstrate the passion and commitment to the venture.

There are common serious inadequacies in all four of these areas, but the worst are in marketing and finance. Less than half of the plans examined provide a detailed marketing strategy, and just half include any sales plan. Three-quarters of the plans fail to identify or analyse any potential competitors. As a result, most business plans contain only basic financial forecasts, and just 10% conduct any sensitivity analysis on the forecasts. The lack of attention to marketing and competitor analysis is particularly problematic as research indicates that both factors are associated with subsequent success.

Tool to support risk assessment, the risk assessment matrix, is available on the Innovation Portal at **www.innovation-portal.info**

For example, in the early stages many new ventures rely too much on a few major customers for sales and are therefore very vulnerable commercially. As an extreme example, around half of technology ventures rely on a single customer for more than half of their first-year sales. This overdependence on a small number of customers has three major drawbacks:

- vulnerability to changes in the strategy and health of the dominant customer
- a loss of negotiating power, which may reduce profit margins
- little incentive to develop marketing and sales functions, which may limit future growth.

New Venture Structure

One of the early decisions an entrepreneur will have to make is the type of business structure to use. When deciding what type of company to form, you need to ask yourself the following questions:

- How much capital is needed to start the business?
- How much control and ownership do I want?
- How much risk am I willing to take on, in the case of failure?
- How large could the business become, and how fast?
- What are the registration, reporting and tax implications of different structures?
- What are the proposed harvest strategies or exit routes?
- Who could become the beneficiary of the business?

The basic options are:

- *Sole proprietorship.* The advantages are relatively light regulation and reporting, autonomy of decision-making and total control, direct personal incentive to succeed and ease of exit. However, this exposes the owner to unlimited personal liability, provides only limited access to external capital and development and relies on the skills and talent of only one person.
- *Partnership.* The advantages are easy to establish, larger pool of expertise and capital, partners share all profits and having flexibility to extend partnerships as the business develops. However, potential for personality and decision-making conflicts, buying out partners who wish to leave and joint unlimited liability of partners are some of the downsides. In the UK, a hybrid partnership-company structure is popular, the LLP – limited-liability partnership.
- *Company.* Easy and cheap to establish, better access to capital for growth, and exposes owners to only a limited liability. The disadvantages are the reporting requirements, rules of operations, different shareholder interests and restrictions on the sale and transfer of assets.

Acquiring the Resources and Funding

The potential sources of initial funding for creating a new venture include (Figure 12.1):

- self-funding
- family and friends
- business angels
- bank loans
- government schemes
- crowdfunding.

The initial funding to establish a new venture is rarely a major problem. Almost all are funded from personal savings or loans from family or friends. At this stage few professional sources of capital will be interested, with the possible exception of government support schemes. However, a new venture is likely to require financial restructuring every three years, if it is to develop and grow. Studies identify stages of development, each having different financial requirements:

- Initial financing for launch
- Second-round financing for initial development and growth
- Third-round financing for consolidation and growth
- Maturity or exit.

In general, professional financial bodies are not interested in initial funding, because of the high risk and low sums of money involved. It is simply not worth their time and effort to

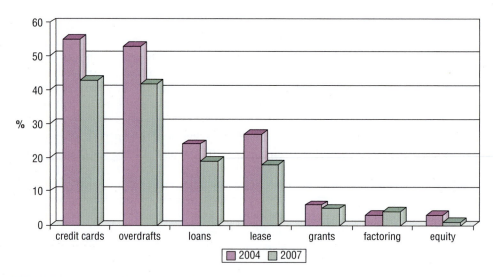

FIGURE 12.1   Source of finance for starting new ventures

Source: Centre for Business Research (2008) *Financing UK Small and Medium-sized Enterprises,* Cambridge: CBR.

evaluate and monitor such ventures. However, as the sums involved are relatively small, typically of the order of tens of thousands of pounds, personal savings, re-mortgages and loans from friends and relatives are often sufficient. In contrast, third-round finance for consolidation is relatively easy to obtain, because by that time the venture has a proven track record on which to base the business plan and the venture capitalist can see an exit route.

ENTREPRENEURSHIP IN ACTION 12.7

UnLtd: The UK Foundation for Social Entrepreneurs

UnLtd aims to support social entrepreneurs by providing funding and support to help these individuals start up and run projects that deliver social benefit.

It was established in 2000 through a partnership between seven leading UK non-profit organizations, including the School for Social Entrepreneurs, Ashoka, Senscot, the Scarman Trust, the Community Action Network, Comic Relief and Changemakers, and funded by an endowment of £100 million from the UK Millennium Commission Award Scheme. The Foundation invests the money awarded to generate an income of £5 million a year to provide grants to individuals with projects to improve their community. These individual grants were launched in 2002, and range from £2500 to £15 000.

In addition to funding, UnLtd provides advice, training and support, using its extensive network of resources and partner organizations throughout the UK. It has formed an Institute for

Social Entrepreneurs to help raise the effectiveness of the sector by building a deeper understanding of what works and what does not, translating that understanding into tools and performance measures, and promoting public and media awareness.

UnLtd plans to establish a Social Venture Fund to link social investors to more mature social entrepreneurs, whose projects have the potential to develop in scope and/or geography with significant financial backing. Current plans range from becoming a broker between different venture philanthropy funds to establishing its own VP fund.

Sources: www.unltd.org.uk, www.aworldconnected.org, www.howtochangetheworld.org, www.socialent.org.

Given their strong desire for independence, most entrepreneurs seek to avoid external funding for their ventures. However, in practice this is not always possible, particularly in the later growth stages. The initial funding required to form a new venture includes the purchase of accommodation, equipment and other start-up costs, plus the day-to-day running costs such as salaries, heating, light and so on – usually referred to as the 'working capital'. For these reasons, many ventures begin life as part-time businesses and are funded by personal savings, loans from friends and relatives and, finally, banks, in that order. Around half also receive some funding from government sources, but in contrast receive next to nothing from venture capitalists. Venture capital is typically only made available at later stages to fund growth on the basis of a proven development and sales record.

Technology ventures are different from other new ventures in that there is often no marketable product available before or shortly after formation. Therefore, initial funding of the venture cannot normally be based on cash flow derived from early sales. The precise cash flow profile will be determined by a number of factors, including development time and cost and the volume and profit margin of sales. Different development and sales strategies exist, but to some extent these factors are determined by the nature of the technology and markets. For example, biotechnology ventures typically require more start-up capital than electronics or software-based ventures, and have longer product development lead times. Therefore, from the perspective of a potential entrepreneur, the ideal strategy would be to conduct as much development work as possible within the incubator organization before starting the new venture. However, there are practical problems with this strategy, in particular ownership of the intellectual property on which the venture is to be based.

The extent of the need for external funding will depend on the nature of the technology and the market strategy of the venture. For example, software-based ventures typically require less start-up capital than either electronics or biotechnology ventures – it is more common for such firms to rely solely on personal funding – but an electronics or software-based venture will also demand high initial funding if a strategy of aggressive growth is to be achieved. Biotechnology firms tend to have the highest R&D costs, and consequently most require some external funding. In contrast, software firms typically require little R&D investment and are less likely to seek external funds. Almost three-quarters of software start-ups were funded by profits after three years, whereas only a third of the biotechnology firms had achieved this.

Venture capitalists are keen to provide funding for a venture with a proven track record and strong business plan, but in return will often require some equity or management involvement. Moreover, most venture capitalists are looking for a means to make capital gains after about five years. However, almost by definition technical entrepreneurs seek independence and control, and there is evidence that some will sacrifice growth to maintain control of their ventures. For the same reason, few entrepreneurs are prepared to go public to fund further growth. Thus, many entrepreneurs will choose to sell the business and found another. In fact, the typical technical entrepreneur establishes an average of three new ventures. Therefore, the biggest funding problem is likely to be for the second-round financing to fund development and growth. This can be a time-consuming and frustrating process to convince venture capitalists to provide finance. The formal proposal is critical at this stage. Professional investors will assess the attractiveness of the venture in terms of the strengths and personalities of the founders, the formal business plan and the commercial and technical merits of the product, probably in that order.

ENTREPRENEURSHIP IN ACTION 12.8

Reuters' Corporate Venture Funds

Reuters established its first fund for external ventures, Greenhouse 1, in 1995. It has since added a further two venture funds, which aim to invest in related businesses such as financial services, media and network infrastructure. By 2001, it had invested $432 million in 83 companies, and these investments contributed almost 10% to its profits. However, financial return was not the primary objective of the funds. For example, it invested $1 million in Yahoo! in 1995, and consequently Yahoo! acquired part of its content from Reuters. This increased the visibility of Reuters in the growing Internet markets, particularly in the USA, where it was not well known, and resulted in other portals following Yahoo!'s lead with content from Reuters. By 2001, Reuters' content was available on 900 Web services, and had an estimated 40 million users per month.

Source: Loudon, A. (2001) *Webs of Innovation: The Networked Economy Demands New Ways to Innovate*, Harlow: Pearson Education.

Venture Capital

An important issue is the influence of venture capitalists on the success of new ventures. They can play two distinct roles. The first is to identify or select those ventures that have the best potential for success, that is 'picking winners' or 'scouting'. The second role is to help develop the chosen ventures, by providing management expertise and access to resources other than financial, that is a 'coaching' role. Distinguishing between the effects of these two roles is critical for both the management of and policy for business. For managers, it will influence the choice of venture capital firm and, for policy, the balance between funding and other forms of support.

Information asymmetry between entrepreneurs and potential professional investors can make external funding difficult – entrepreneurs have information potential investors lack, are reluctant to fully disclose this and may engage in opportunistic behaviour. Analysis of a survey of 136 venture capitalists, each with an average of 17 years' investment experience, identified five factors that influence funding: direct or indirect social ties between entrepreneur and potential investor, the business plan, the technology, size of funding and sector. The average size of the seed-stage funding was just under $1 million (in 1998).[15] This demonstrates the critical importance of social ties, direct and indirect, to promote the flow of 'private' knowledge from entrepreneurs to potential investors; 'while VCs receive many cold deals (without introduction), they rarely invest in them … most funded proposals come by referral'.[16] However, these social ties become less significant when the knowledge becomes more public, for example through the reputation of the entrepreneur or venture.

When selecting start-ups to invest in, the most significant criteria used by venture capitalists are a broad, experienced top management team, a large number of recent patents and downstream industry alliances (but not upstream research alliances, which generally speaking have a negative effect on selection). The strongest effect on the decision to fund was the first criterion, and the human capital in general. However, subsequent analysis of venture performance indicates that this factor has limited effect on performance, and that the few significant effects are split equally between improving and impeding the performance of a venture. The effects of technology and alliances on subsequent performance are much more significant and positive. In short, in the selection stage, venture capitalists place too much emphasis on human capital, specifically the top management team. In the development or coaching stages, venture capitalists do contribute to the success of the chosen ventures, and tend to introduce external professional management much earlier than if the venture is not funded by venture capital. Taken together, this suggests that the coaching role of venture capitalists is probably as important, if not more so, than the funding role, although policy interventions to promote the creation of a venture often focus on the latter.

While there is general agreement about the main components of a good business plan, there are some significant differences in the relative weights attributed to each component. General venture capital firms typically only accept 5% of the ventures they are offered, and the specialist technology venture funds are even more selective, accepting around 3%. The main reasons for rejecting proposals are the lack of intellectual property, the skills of the management team and the size of the potential market. The criteria are similar to those discussed earlier, grouped into five categories:

- the entrepreneur's personality
- the entrepreneur's experience
- characteristics of the product
- characteristics of the market
- financial factors.

Overall, a bundle of personal, market and financial factors are consistently ranked as being most significant: a proven ability to lead others and sustain effort, familiarity with the market and the potential for a high return within ten years. The personality and experience of the entrepreneurs are consistently ranked as being more important than either product or market characteristics, or even financial considerations. However, there were a number of significant differences between the preferences of venture capitalists from different regions. Those from the USA place a greater emphasis on a high financial return and liquidity than their counterparts in Europe or Asia, but less emphasis on the existence of a prototype or proven market acceptance. Perhaps surprisingly, all venture capitalists are averse to techno-logical and market risks. Being described as a 'high-technology' venture was rated very low in importance by the US venture capitalists, and the European and Asian venture capitalists rated this characteristic as having a negative influence on funding. Similarly, having the poten-tial to create an entirely new market was considered a drawback because of the higher risk attached. In short, venture capitalists are not particularly adventurous.

Venture capital in the UK invests relatively little in technology-based ventures. Over the 1990–2005 period, investment in technology-based firms as a percentage of total venture capital remained stable at around 10% of the total by value. In absolute terms this still represents a significant sum, almost £7 billion in 2005, as the UK has a very large venture capital market. Of the total venture capital investment in the UK of £6.8 billion in 2005 (Table 12.3), only 5% was for early stage funding (by value, or 38% by number of firms), 29% for expansion (by value, or 44% by number of firms) and the rest for management buy-outs or buy-ins (MBO/MBI). The average funds for a start-up or early stage venture was £800 000 (in 2005). The USA has the largest venture capital industry with investments of around $33 billion in 2014, compared to $7.4 billion in Europe and $3.5 billion in China (Figure 12.2).

As venture capital firms have gained experience of this type of funding, and the opportu-nities for flotation have increased because of the new secondary financial markets in Europe such as the AIM, TechMARK and Neuer Markt, their returns on investment have increased significantly.

TABLE 12.3   Median venture capital funding per venture by stage ($ million)

	Seed funding	First round	Second round	Late stage
USA	0.5	2.5	5.7	10.0
Europe	0.3	1.3	3.3	6.7
China	0.4	4.0	10.0	20.0
Canada	0.1	1.6	5.3	5.0
Israel	0.7	2.6	9.5	8.1
India	0.2	1.5	6.0	10.0

Source: Data derived from EY (2014) Global venture capital insights and trends 2014, EY.com.

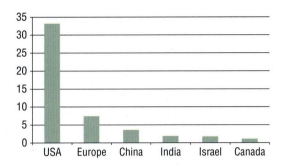

FIGURE 12.2   Venture capital funding by country ($ billion)

Sources: Based on data from OECD (2013), Commercialising Public Research: New Trends and Strategies, OECD Publishing. http://dx.doi.org/10.1787/9789264193321-en

ENTREPRENEURSHIP IN ACTION 12.9

Alternative Investment Market

The **Alternative Investment Market (AIM)** was established in London, UK, in 1995 as an alternative to the London Stock Exchange. It is designed to be more simple and cheaper than the main market, and to have a less restrictive regulatory regime than the main exchange, and therefore is more suited to smaller firms at an earlier stage of development. AIM began with just 10 UK-based companies in 1995, but by 2006 it had 1500 firms listed, including 250 from overseas. The total market capitalization was £72 billion in 2006. About half of all firms on the AIM have a market capitalization of less than £15 million, and a quarter of firms less than £5 million.

Listing on AIM is easier and cheaper than on most other exchanges, and costs around 5% of the funds raised on flotation. Admission to AIM takes around four months and involves a number of prescribed steps:

1. Development of the business plan.
2. Appointment of the advisers – Nomad (nominated adviser, a unique and critical feature of AIM, regulated by the London Stock Exchange), broker, accountant and lawyer.
3. Nomad prepares the timetable for admission.
4. Accountants prepare financial due diligence, including historical trading record.
5. Lawyers conduct the legal due diligence, including a review of all contracts, titles and any litigation.
6. Accountants prepare the 18-month working capital requirements for the admission document.
7. Formal Admission Document is developed.
8. Marketing and completion, including institutional roadshow and public relations.

(continued)

There is no minimum capitalization or trading record requirement, and no minimum proportion of shares which have to be held by the public. Institutional investors have been attracted to invest in AIM companies because of the many tax breaks available to investors, such as Venture Capital Trusts. However, a listing on AIM requires greater transparency than a private company, for example in terms of accounting standards, corporate governance and communication with investors.

In 2005, 29 Chinese or China-focused firms were listed on the London AIM, but regulation, language and distance can make this more difficult and expensive than local firms. The cost of listing is typically between £500 000 and £1 million, around twice that of a UK-based firm. AIM-style markets have been launched in Asia, including the SESDAQ in Singapore, Growth Enterprise Market in Hong Kong, and Mother Market in Japan.

Business Angels

Business angels are successful entrepreneurs who wish to re-invest in others' new ventures, usually in return for some management role. The sums involved are usually relatively small (by venture capital standards), ranging from £100,000 to £250,000, but in addition they can bring experience and expertise to a new venture. They are usually able to introduce a venture to an established network of professional advisers and business contacts. In this way they can provide a critical knowledge bridge between the venture and potential customers and investors.

Government Funding

There are a number of reasons why governments become involved in promoting and providing resources for new ventures:[17]

- There is an 'equity gap' between the costs and risks involved in assessing and funding a new venture, and its potential return. The costs associated with the due diligence of assessing a venture and its subsequent management are relatively high and fixed, therefore professional venture capitalists are unlikely to consider proposals below a certain threshold, typically around £500 000 to £1 million. Similarly, where the risk of a new venture exceeds the expected return, professional venture capital is unlikely to be available. Table 12.4 indicates that this is a common problem, particularly in the UK and the rest of Europe. This suggests that government schemes may provide support and funding for smaller or higher-risk ventures.
- Professional venture capital tends to gravitate to fashionable fields, e.g. IT or biotechnology, and favour established centres of excellence, e.g. Cambridge and Oxford in the UK and Boston in the USA. Table 12.4 indicates that this is a common problem, particularly in the USA and some emerging economies, where venture capital quickly follows technology trends and fads. This suggests there is a role for policy to broaden the availability of funding for ventures in a wider range of fields and regions.[18]

TABLE 12.4 Comparative venture capital structures

Country	% funding for seed/start-up	% funding for technology ventures
Singapore	40	85
USA	31	80
EU	13	26
UK	8	13

• Broader need to promote an entrepreneurial culture within a country or region, to provide management support and to establish equity funding (as opposed to debt) as a legitimate source of venture funding. This includes the non-financial support often provided by venture capitalists, including advice and mentoring.[19]

Crowdfunding

Crowdfunding is a relatively recent potential source of resources. Typically, this is mediated by a Web portal on which projects can be posted to attract investors, often multiple non-professional investors who have some interest in the focus of the project. One of the largest crowdfunding services is kickstarter.com. In the first five years from its launch in 2009, Kickstarter mediated the funding of 64 000 projects with pledges of $1 billion from 6.5 million investors. This suggests a mean investment of around $16 000 per project. The focus is on creative and media, rather than high-technology, projects. Seedups.com is another example, but it has a greater focus on technology start-ups. As a result, the sums raised are larger, in the range of $25 000–$500 000, and investors have six months to review and bid for a stake in projects.

Chapter Summary

- In this chapter we have explored the rationale, characteristics and management of innovative new ventures.

- Typically, an innovative entrepreneur will establish a venture primarily to create something new or to change something, rather than as a means to achieve independence or wealth, although both of these may follow as a consequence.

- A range of factors influences the creation of innovative new ventures, some contextual, such as institutional support and availability of capital and culture, others more personal, such as personality, background and relevant skills and experience.

- Entrepreneurship is not just simply an individual act, driven by psychology, but also a profoundly social process. Therefore innovative entrepreneurs need to be able to identify and exploit a broader range of external resources and sources of knowledge than their more conventional counterparts, including diverse networks of those in the private, public and third sectors.

Key Terms Defined

Alternative Investment Market (AIM)   was established as a simpler and cheaper alternative to the London Stock Exchange.

Business angels   successful entrepreneurs who wish to re-invest in new ventures, usually in return for some management role. They are usually able to introduce a venture to an established network of professional advisers and business contacts.

Incubator organization   a private firm, university or public organization which provides resources and support for the generation of spin-out firms.

New technology-based firms (NTBFs)   small firms that have emerged recently from large firms or public laboratories in such fields as electronics, software and biotechnology. They are usually specialized in the supply of a key component, subsystem, service or technique to larger firms, who may often be their former employers.

Spin-out or **spin-off venture**   originates from a parent organization, usually a private firm or university. However, there is no agreement whether the parent organization has to retain an interest in the spin-out to satisfy this definition. Moreover, there is no agreement on the time lag, so universities routinely include all enterprises created by alumni.

Superstars   large firms that have grown rapidly from small beginnings, through high rates of growth based on the exploitation of a major invention.

Discussion Questions

1. In what ways do social entrepreneurs and technology entrepreneurs differ from other types of entrepreneur?

2. What are the main funding options for a new venture, and what are the advantages and disadvantages of each?

3. What should be included in a business plan, and what do venture capitalists look for?

4. In each of the different stages in the development of a new venture, what are the different management requirements?

5. What factors affect the decision of what type of company to form?

6. What are the relative advantages and drawbacks of different sources of finance?

Further Reading and Resources

There are many books and journal articles on the subject of entrepreneurship, but relatively little has been produced on the more specific subject of innovative new ventures. We believe one of the best general texts on entrepreneurship is Jack Kaplan's *Patterns of Entrepreneurship*, written with A. C. Warren (4th edn, John Wiley & Sons, Inc., 2014), which adopts a very practical approach. Also relevant is the special issue of *Research Policy*, **43**(7), on 'Entrepreneurial innovation: The importance of context', edited by Erkko Autio, Martin Kenney, Philippe Mustar, Don Siegel and Mike Wright (2014).

For a more specialist treatment of technology-based entrepreneurship, Ed Roberts's *Entrepreneurs in High Technology: Lessons from MIT and Beyond* (Oxford University Press, 1991) is an excellent study of the MIT experience, albeit a little dated, but it perhaps places too much emphasis on the characteristics of individual entrepreneurs rather than the unique context. For a more recent analysis of technological entrepreneurs, see *Inventing Entrepreneurs: Technology Innovators and Their Entrepreneurial Journey*, by Gerry George and Adam Bock (Prentice Hall, 2008). Ray Oakey's *High-Technology Entrepreneurship* (Routledge, 2012) is a similar study of NTBFs in the UK, but it places greater emphasis on how different technologies constrain the opportunities for establishing NTBFs, and affect their management and success.

For studies of the influence of venture capital, Simon Barnes, with Rupert Pearce, gives a rare practitioner's account of the workings of venture capital in *Raising Venture Capital* (John Wiley & Sons Ltd, 2006). For a more critical assessment of the role of venture capital and in particular the limitations of venture capitalists, see any of Scott Shane's various accounts, such as *The Illusions of Entrepreneurship* (Yale University Press, 2009).

References

1. Wonglimpiyarat, J. (2006) The Boston Route 128 model of high-tech industry development, *International Journal of Innovation Management*, **10**(1): 47–64; Kenny, M. (2000) *Understanding Silicon Valley: Anatomy of an Entrepreneurial Region*, Palo Alto, CA: Stanford University Press; Roberts, E. (1991) *Entrepreneurs in High Technology: Lessons from MIT and Beyond*, Oxford: Oxford University Press.

2. Oakey, R. (2012) *High-Technology Entrepreneurship*, London: Routledge; Hirsch-Kreinsen, H. and I. Schwinge (2014) *Knowledge-intensive Entrepreneurship in Low-tech Industries*, London: Edward Elgar.

3. Wadhwa, V., R.B. Freeman and B.A. Rissing (2008) Education and technology entrepreneurship, *Social Science Research Network*, working paper 1127248.

4. Hoffman, K., M. Parejo, J. Bessant and L. Perren (1998) Small firms, R&D, technology and innovation in the UK: A literature review, *Technovation*, **18**(1): 39–55.

5. 'Money man makes serial killings', *Times Higher Education*, 30th March 1998.

6. 'Money man makes serial killings', *Times Higher Education*, 30th March 1998.

7. Mowery, D.C., R.R. Nelson, B.N. Sampat and A.A. Ziedonis (2001) The growth of patenting and licensing by U.S. Universities: An assessment of the effects of the Bayh–Dole Act of 1980, *Research Policy*, 30; Henderson, R., A.B. Jaffe and M. Trajtenberg (1998) Universities as a source of commercial technology: A detailed analysis of university patenting 1965–1988, *The Review of Economics and Statistics*, **80**(1): 119–27.

8. Bray, M.J. and J.N. Lee (2000) University revenues from technology transfer: Licensing fees versus equity positions, *Journal of Business Venturing*, **15**: 385–92.

9. Kassicieh, S.K., R. Radosevich and J. Umbarger (1996) A comparative study of entrepreneurship incidence among inventors in national laboratories, *Entrepreneurship Theory and Practice*, Spring: 33–49.

10. Meyer, M. (2004) Academic entrepreneurs or entrepreneurial academics? Research-based ventures and public support mechanisms, *R&D Management*, 33(2): 107–15; Butler, S. and S. Birley (1999) Scientists and their attitudes to industry links, *International Journal of Innovation Management*, **2**(1): 79–106.

11. Lee, Y.S. (1996) Technology transfer and the research university: A search for the boundaries of university–industry collaboration, *Research Policy*, **25**: 843–63.

12. Di Gregorio, D. and S. Shane (2003) Why do some universities generate more start-ups than others? *Research Policy*, **32**: 209–27.

13. Niammuad, D., K. Napompech and S. Suwanmaneepong (2014) The mediating effect of opportunity recognition on incubated entrepreneurial innovation, *International Journal of Innovation Management*, **18**(3): doi: 1440005.

14. Roberts, E. (1991) *Entrepreneurs in High Technology: Lessons from MIT and Beyond*, Oxford: Oxford University Press.

15. Shane, S. and D. Cable (2002) Network ties, reputation and the financing of new ventures, *Management Science*, **48**(3): 364–81.

16. Harding, R. (2000) *Venturing Forward: The Role of Venture Capital in Enabling Entrepreneurship*, London: Institute for Public Policy Research.

17. Lockett, A., G. Murray and M. Wright (2002) Do UK venture capitalists still have a bias against investment in new technology firms? *Research Policy*, **31**: 1009–30.

18. Baum, J.A.C. and B.S. Silverman (2004) Picking winners or building them? Alliance, intellectual and human capital as selection criteria in venture financing and performance of biotechnology startups, *Journal of Business Venturing*, **19**: 411–36.

Deeper Dive explanations of innovation concepts and ideas are available on the Innovation Portal at **www.innovation-portal.info**

Quizzes to test yourself further are available online via the Innovation Portal at **www.innovation-portal.info**

Summary of online resources for Chapter 12 –
all material is available via the Innovation Portal at
www.innovation-portal.info

Cases	**Media**	**Tools**	**Activities**	**Deeper Dives**
• Ihavemoved.com • Threadless.com	• Carmel McConnell	• Risk assessment matrix	• Costs and revenues in business models	• Business model canvas

Chapter 13

Developing Businesses and Talent through Corporate Venturing

LEARNING OBJECTIVES

By the end of this chapter you will develop an understanding of:

- the motives and management of corporate ventures
- the advantages and drawbacks of different structures for corporate ventures
- the likelihood of success of corporate venture outcomes.

Internal Venturing and Entrepreneurship

Samsung began life as a noodle-processing company, Nokia was originally a manufacturer of rubber galoshes and 3M's first business was sandpaper. By a process of strategic diversification, experimentation, innovation and a little luck, each has evolved and continuously created new businesses.

Corporate ventures, broadly defined, are a range of different ways of developing innovations, alternative to conventional internal processes for new product or service development, which often go beyond product development towards the creation of a new business development. We discussed in Chapter 11 the many benefits of using structured approaches to new product and service development, such as stage-gate and development funnel processes, but these approaches also have a major disadvantage, because decisions at the different gates are likely to favour those innovations close to existing strategy, markets and products, and are likely to filter out or reject potential innovations further from the organization's comfort zone. For this reason we need different mechanisms to identify, develop and exploit innovations which do not fit current businesses or markets.

An internal corporate venture attempts to exploit the resources of the large corporation and provide an environment more conducive to radical innovation. The key factors that distinguish a potential new venture from the core business are risk, uncertainty, newness and significance. However, it is not sufficient to promote entrepreneurial behaviour within a large organization. Entrepreneurial behaviour is not an end in itself, but must be directed and translated into desired business outcomes. Entrepreneurial behaviour is not associated with superior organizational performance, unless it is combined with an appropriate strategy in a heterogeneous or uncertain environment.[1] This suggests the need for clear strategic objectives for corporate venturing and appropriate organizational structures and processes to achieve those objectives.

Figure 13.1 suggests a range of venture types that can be used in different contexts. Corporate ventures are likely to be most appropriate where the organization needs to exploit some internal competencies and retain a high degree of control over the business. Joint ventures and alliances, discussed in Chapter 10, involve working with external partners to introduce additional competencies, but will demand some release of control and autonomy. Spin-out or new venture businesses are the extreme case, often necessary where there is little **relatedness** between the core competencies and new venture business. Note that these options are not mutually exclusive, for example a spin-out business can become an alliance partner, or a corporate venture can spin out. Also, all types of venture require a venture champion, a strong business case and sufficient resources to be successful.

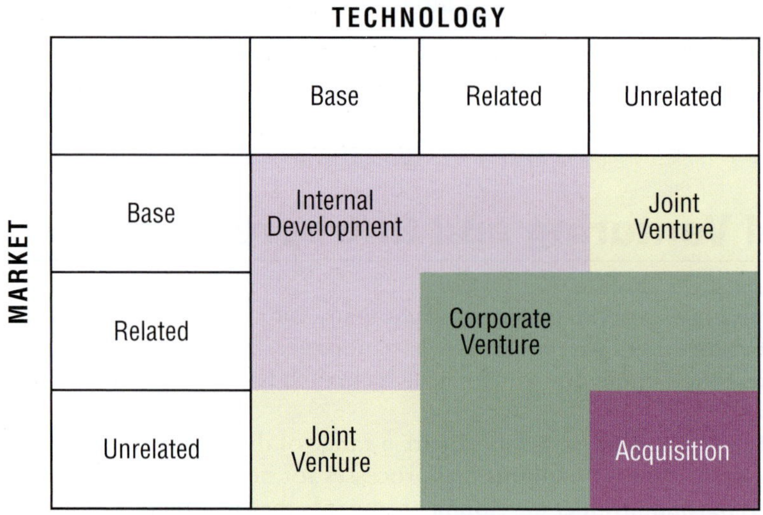

FIGURE 13.1 The role of corporate ventures

Source: Burgelman, R. (1984) Managing the internal corporate venturing process. *Sloan Management Review*, **25**(2): 33–48. © 1984 from MIT Sloan Management Review/Massachusetts Institute of Technology. All rights reserved. Distributed by Tribune Content Agency.

ENTREPRENEURSHIP IN ACTION 13.1

Google[x], Corporate Venture or Skunk Works?

Google[x] was created by Google in 2010 to explore innovations which were outside Google's core business or research labs. There is some disagreement over what the [x] stands for, but a plausible interpretation is it represents innovations which provide 10x (Roman numeral for ten) the potential benefit, or alternatively have a ten-year timeframe.

The very broad brief for Google[x] is to tackle large-scale challenges, relevant to billions of people. It is based on the edge of the Google campus, but in separate buildings to the research labs. It began as a means to develop the concept for the driverless car, but has been central to the development of Google Glass, has experimented with Wi-Fi weather balloons (Project Loon), and in 2014 acquired airborne wind-energy company Makani, and design-house Gecko Design.

By 2014, it had grown to 250 employees, including scientists, engineers, designers and artists. For comparison, Google Research has some 19 000 staff, representing almost 40% of all employees.

The challenge, as with all such ventures, will be to translate such concepts and prototypes into businesses which create real value.

Rather ironically, Google[x] has no website, so don't try to google it!

Why Do It?

There are a wide range of motives for establishing corporate ventures:[2]

- Grow the business
- Exploit underutilized resources
- Introduce pressure on internal suppliers
- Divest non-core activities
- Satisfy managers' ambitions
- Spread the risk and cost of product development
- Combat cyclical demands of mainstream activities
- Learn about the process of venturing
- Diversify the business
- Develop new technological or market competencies.

We discuss each of these motives in turn, and provide examples. The first three are primarily operational; the remainder are more strategic.

ENTREPRENEURSHIP IN ACTION 13.2

Corporate Venturing at Nortel Networks

Nortel Networks is a leader in a high-growth, high-technology sector, and around a quarter of all its staff are in R&D, but it recognizes that it is extremely difficult to initiate new businesses outside the existing divisions. Therefore, in December 1996 it created the Business Ventures Programme (BVP) to help to overcome some of the structural shortcomings of the existing organization, and identify and nurture new business ventures outside the established lines of business: 'The basic deal we're offering employees is an extremely exciting one. What we're saying is "Come up with a good business proposal and we'll fund and support it. If we believe your business proposal is viable, we'll provide you with the wherewithal to realize your dreams."' The BVP provides:

- guidance in developing a business proposal
- assistance in obtaining approval from the board
- an incubation environment for start-ups
- transition support for longer-term development.

The BVP selects the most promising venture proposals, which are then presented jointly by the BVP and employee(s) to the advisory board. The advisory board applies business and financial criteria in its decision whether to accept, reject or seek further development, and if accepted the most appropriate executive sponsor, structure and level of funding. The BVP then helps to incubate the new venture, including staff and resources, objectives and critical milestones. If successful, the BVP then assists the venture to migrate into an existing business division, if appropriate, or creates a new line, business or spin-off company:

> The programme is designed to be flexible. Among the factors determining whether or not to become a separate company are the availability of key resources within Nortel, and the suitability of Nortel's existing distribution channels ... Nortel is not in this programme to retain 100% control of all ventures. The key motivators are to grow equity by maximizing return on investment, to pursue business opportunities that would otherwise be missed, and to increase employee satisfaction.

In 1997, the BVP attracted 112 business proposals, and given the staff and financial resources available aimed to fund up to five new ventures. The main problems experienced were the reaction of managers in established lines of business to proposals outside their own line of:

> At the executive council level, which represents all lines of business, there is a lot of support ... where it breaks down in terms of support is more in the political infrastructure, the middle to low management executive level where they feel threatened by it ... the

first stage of our marketing plan is just titled 'overcoming internal barriers'. That is the single biggest thing we've had to break through.

Initially, there was also a problem capturing the experience of ventures that failed to be commercialized:

Failures were typically swept under the rock, nobody really talked about them ... that is changing now and the focus is on celebrating our failures as well as our successes, knowing that we have learned a lot more from failure than we do from success. Start-up venture experience is in high demand. Generally, it's the projects that fail, not the people.

Source: Quotations taken from transcripts of unpublished interviews conducted by author.

To Grow the Business

The desire to achieve and maintain expected rates of growth is probably the most common reason for corporate venturing, particularly when the core businesses are maturing. Depending upon the timeframe of the analysis, between only 5 and 13% of firms are able to maintain a rate of growth above the rate of growth in gross national product. However, the pressure to achieve this for publically listed firms is significant, as financial markets and investors expect the maintenance or improvement of rates of growth. The need to grow underlies many of the other motives for corporate venturing.

> **Video Clip** highlighting this issue, Tesco Goes West, is available on the Innovation Portal at **www.innovation-portal.info**

To Exploit Underutilized Resources in New Ways

This includes both technological and human resources. Typically, a company has two choices where existing resources are underutilized – either to divest and outsource the process or to generate additional contribution from external clients. However, if the company wants to retain direct and in-house control of the technology or personnel, it can form an internal venture team to offer the service to external clients.

> **Case Study** highlighting this issue, SPIRIT, is available on the Innovation Portal at **www.innovation-portal.info**

To Introduce Pressure on Internal Suppliers

This is a common motive, given the current fashion for outsourcing and market testing internal services. When a business activity is separated to introduce competitive pressure, a choice has to be made: whether the business is to be subjected to the reality of commercial competition or just to learn from it. If the corporate clients are able to go so far as to withdraw a contract, which is not conducive to learning, the business should be sold to allow it to compete for other work.

To Divest Non-core Activities

Much has been written of the benefits of strategic focus, of getting back to basics and of creating the 'lean' organization, all of which prompt the divestment of activities that can be outsourced. However, this process can threaten the skill diversity required for an ever-changing competitive environment. New ventures can provide a mechanism to release peripheral business activities, but to retain some management control and financial interest.

To Satisfy Managers' Ambitions

As a business activity passes through its lifecycle, it will require different management styles to bring out the maximum gain. This may mean that the management team responsible for a business area will need to change, whether between conception to growth, growth to maturity or maturity to decline phases. A paradoxical situation can arise as previously high-growth businesses begin to mature. As a result, ambitious senior managers who seek growth opportunities can become frustrated, or their skills inappropriate. To retain the commitment of such managers the corporation will have to create new opportunities for change or expansion. For example, Intel has long had a venture capital programme that invests in related external new ventures, but in 1998 it established the New Business Initiative to bootstrap new businesses developed by its staff: 'They saw that we were putting a lot of investment into external companies and said that we should be investing in our own ideas...our employees kept telling us they wanted to be more entrepreneurial.'[3] The initiative invests only in ventures unrelated to the core microprocessor business, and in 1999 attracted more than 400 proposals, 24 of which are being funded.

Audio Clip of David Hall discussing the challenges of entrepreneurship is available on the Innovation Portal at **www.innovation-portal.info**

To Spread the Risk and Cost of Product Development

Two situations are possible in this case: (1) where the technology or expertise needs to be developed further before it can be applied to the mainstream business or sold to current external markets or (2) where the volume sales on a product awaiting development must sell to a target greater than the existing customer groups to be financially justified. In both cases, the challenge is to understand how to venture outside current served markets. Too often, when the existing customer base is not ready for a product, the research unit will just continue its development and refinement process. If intermediary markets were exploited these could contribute to the financial costs of development, and to the maturing of the final product.

To Combat Cyclical Demands of Mainstream Activities

In response to the problem of cyclical demand, Boeing set up two groups, Boeing Technology Services (BTS) and Boeing Associated Products (BAP), specifically to keep engineering and laboratory resources more fully employed when its own requirements waned between major development programmes. The remit for BTS was 'to sell off excess engineering laboratory capacity without a detrimental impact on schedules or commitments to major Boeing product-line activities';[4] it has stuck carefully to this charter, and been careful to turn off such activity when the mainstream business requires the expertise. BAP was created to commercially exploit Boeing inventions that are usable beyond their application to products manufactured by Boeing. About 600 invention disclosures are submitted by employees each year, and these are reviewed in terms of their marketability and patentability. Licensing agreements are used to exploit these inventions, and 259 agreements were made as a result of the venture programme. Beyond the financial benefits to the company and to the employees of this programme, it is seen to foster the innovation spirit within the organization.

To Learn about the Process of Venturing

Venturing is a high-risk activity because of the level of uncertainty attached, and we cannot expect to understand the management process as we do for the mainstream business. If a learning exercise is to be undertaken, and a particular activity chosen for this process, it is critical that goals and objectives are set, including a review schedule. This is important not just for the maximum benefit to be extracted but also for the individuals who will pioneer that venture. For example, NEES Energy, a subsidiary of New England Electric Systems Inc., was set up to bring financial benefits, but was also expected to provide a laboratory to help the parent company learn about starting new ventures.

To Diversify the Business

While the discussion so far has implied that business development should be on a relatively small scale, this need not be the case. Corporate ventures are often formed in an effort to create new businesses in a corporate context, and therefore represent an attempt to grow via diversification. Such diversification may be vertical (i.e. downstream or upstream of the current process in order to capture a greater proportion of the value added) or horizontal (i.e. by exploiting existing competencies across additional product markets).

Case Studies of Kodak and Fujifilm highlighting some of these issues are available on the Innovation Portal at **www.innovation-portal.info**

To Develop New Competencies

Growth and diversification are generally based on the exploitation of existing competencies in new products markets, but a corporate venture can also be used as an opportunity for learning new competencies.[5] An organization can acquire knowledge by experimentation, which is a central feature of formal R&D and market research activities. However, different functions and divisions within a firm will develop particular frames of reference and filters based on their experience and responsibilities, and these will affect how they interpret information. Greater organizational learning occurs when more varied interpretations are made, and a corporate venture can better perform this function as it is not confined to the needs of existing technologies or markets.

TABLE 13.1   Objectives of corporate venturing

Objective	Mean rank*
1. Long-term growth	4.58
2. Diversification	3.50
3. Promote entrepreneurial behaviour	2.68
4. Exploit in-house R&D	2.23
5. Short-term financial returns	2.08
6. Reduce/spread cost of R&D	1.81
7. Survival	1.76

(n = 90). * Scale: 1 = minimum, 5 = maximum importance.

Source: Gebbie, D. (1997) *Window on Technology: Corporate Venturing in Practice*, London: Withers Solicitors.

In practice, the primary motives for establishing a corporate venture are strategic: to meet strategic goals and long-term growth in the face of maturity in existing markets (Table 13.1). However, personnel issues are also important. Sectorial and national differences exist. In the USA, new ventures are also used to stimulate and develop entrepreneurial management, and in Japan they help provide employment opportunities for managers and staff relocated from the core businesses (Table 13.2). Nonetheless, the primary objectives are strategic and long term, and therefore warrant significant management effort and investment.

TABLE 13.2   Motives, structure and management of corporate ventures

Primary motive	Preferred structure	Key management task
Satisfy managers' ambitions	Integrated business team	Motivation and reward
Spread cost and risk of development	Integrated business team	Resource allocation
Exploit economies of scope	Micro-venture department	Reintegration of venture
Learn about venturing	New venture division	Develop new skills
Diversify the business	Special business unit	Develop new assets
Divest non-core activities	Independent business unit	Management of intellectual property rights

Source: Adapted from Tidd, J. and S. Taurins (1999) Learn or leverage? Strategic diversification and organisational learning through corporate ventures, *Creativity and Innovation Management*, **8**(2), 122–9.

INNOVATION IN ACTION 13.1

Identifying New Opportunities at QinetiQ

Businesses tend to limit their strategic vision to the conventional boundaries of the existing industry. This they believe is an immutable given. When challenged to think outside of the box or to be more creative in their business models, because they do not explicitly acknowledge the boundaries in which they operate they continue competing in traditional spaces.

Companies that do not permit themselves to be limited by current industry boundaries more often create new profitable spaces. In traditional strategy, pain points would be identified and solutions found. Here we use pain points to find the non-customer.

For each boundary type, we apply the 'Rule of Opposites', which is a set of specific critical questions performed to extract insight into potential new market spaces. Not all boundaries will yield new market opportunities, but may reveal insight which can be exploited across other boundaries.

Critical to identifying new market opportunities will be the ability to visualize and articulate the emergent previously ignored customer, to which a reconstructed value proposition has to be offered.

The process undertaken includes:

1. Articulate the current bounds of the industry the product operates in across the dimensions of industry definition – strategic groups, chain of buyers, proposition, appeal, and time and trends.
2. For each existing customer, map out their buyer experience cycle to identify pain points.
3. Explicitly identify the core customer, then remove this customer from any further consideration.
4. Apply 'Rule of Opposites' to each boundary in turn to unearth whether new customer groups exist beyond the current boundary of the industry.
5. Once a new customer is articulated and brought to life undertake fieldwork to find this person and prove the new opportunity.
6. Hypothesize a set of offerings that would meet this person's needs.
7. From the full range of new opportunities, distil down a set of propositions that minimally meet the needs of the largest catchment of non-customers.

Be aware that this process might initially feel strange, more like opening 'Pandora's box' than a structured analysis. The outcome of the market boundary analysis is a set of non-customer spaces. It is important to acknowledge that not all of the six dimensions of alternative market-places will yield results, typically two to four of the paths will present significant insight.

Source: Carlos de Pommes, Director Innovation and Investment Gatekeeper at QinetiQ, www.qinetiq.com.

Managing Corporate Ventures

There are two critical dimensions to managing ventures: who owns them and who funds them? These two dimensions suggest four different combinations:[6]

- *Opportunistic.* No dedicated ownership or resources for venturing. This approach relies on a supportive organizational climate to encourage proposals which are developed and evaluated locally on a project-by-project basis. For example, Zimmer Medical Devices responded to a new hip replacement proposed by a trauma surgeon by creating the Zimmer Institute to train more than 6000 surgeons in the new minimally invasive procedure.
- *Enabling.* No formal corporate ownership, but the provision of dedicated support, processes and resources. This approach works best where new ventures can be owned by existing divisions in the business. For example, Google provides time, funding and rewards for the development of ideas which extend the core business.
- *Advocacy.* Organizational ownership is clearly assigned, but little or no special funding is provided. This works when there are sufficient resources in the business but insufficient specialist skills or support for venturing. For example, DuPont created the Market Driven Growth initiative which includes four-day business planning training, workshops and agreed access to and mentoring by senior staff.
- *Producer.* Includes both formal ownership and dedicated funding of ventures. This demands significant corporate resources and commitment to venturing, and therefore a critical mass of potential projects to justify this approach. Examples include IBM's Emerging Business Opportunities programme and Cargill's Emerging Business Accelerator initiative. In such cases the goal is to build new businesses, rather than just new products or services.

A corporate venture is rarely the result of a spontaneous act or serendipity. Corporate venturing is a process that has to be managed. The management challenge is to create an environment that encourages and supports entrepreneurship, and to identify and support potential entrepreneurs. In essence, the venturing process is simple, and consists of identifying an opportunity for a new venture, evaluating that opportunity and subsequently providing adequate resources to support the new venture. There are six distinct stages, divided between definition and development.[7]

Definition Stages

1. Establish an environment that encourages the generation of new ideas and the identification of new opportunities, and establish a process for managing entrepreneurial activity.
2. Select and evaluate opportunities for new ventures, and select managers to implement the venturing programme.
3. Develop a business plan for the new venture, decide the best location and organization of the venture and begin operations.

Development Stages

4. Monitor the development of the venture and venturing process.
5. Champion the new venture as it grows and becomes institutionalized within the corporation.
6. Learn from experience in order to improve the overall venturing process.

Creating an environment which is conducive to entrepreneurial activity is the most important, but most difficult, stage. Superficial approaches to creating an entrepreneurial culture can be counterproductive. Instead, venturing should be the responsibility of the entire corporation, and top management should demonstrate long-term commitment to venturing by making available sufficient resources and implementing the appropriate processes.

The conceptualization stage consists of the generation of new ideas and the identification of opportunities that may form the basis of a new business venture. The interface between R&D and marketing is critical during the conceptualization stage, but the scope of new venture conceptualization is much broader than the conventional activities of the R&D or marketing functions, which understandably are constrained by the needs of existing businesses. At this stage three basic options exist:

1. Rely on R&D personnel to identify new business opportunities based on their technological developments, essentially a 'technology-push' approach.
2. Rely on marketing managers to identify opportunities, and direct the R&D staff into the appropriate development work, essentially a 'market-pull' approach.
3. Encourage marketing and R&D personnel to work together to identify opportunities.

Having identified the potential for a new venture, a product champion must convince higher management that the business opportunity is both technically feasible and commercially attractive and therefore justifies development and investment. Potential **corporate entrepreneurs** face significant political barriers:

Audio Clip of an interview with Roy Sandbach of Procter and Gamble highlighting some of these issues is available on the Innovation Portal at **www.innovation-portal.info**

- They must establish their legitimacy within the firm by convincing others of the importance and viability of the venture.
- They are likely to be short of resources but will have to compete internally against established and powerful departments and managers.
- As advocates of change and innovation, they are likely to face at best organizational indifference and at worst hostile attacks.

To overcome these barriers a potential venture manager must have political and social skills, in addition to a viable business plan. In addition, the product champion must be able to work effectively in a non-programmed and unpredictable environment. This contrasts with much of the R&D conducted in the operating divisions which is likely to be much more sequential and systematic. Therefore, a product champion requires dedication, flexibility and luck to manage the transition from product concept to corporate venture, in addition to sound technical and market knowledge. The product champion is likely to require a complementary organizational champion who is able to relate the potential venture to the strategy and structure of the corporation. A number of key roles must be filled when a new venture is established:

- *the technical innovator*, who was responsible for the main technological development
- *the business innovator* or venture manager, who is responsible for the overall progress of the venture
- *the product champion*, who promotes the venture through the early critical stages
- *the executive champion* or organizational champion, who acts as a protector and buffer between the corporation and venture
- *a high-level executive*, who is responsible for evaluating, monitoring and authorizing resources for the venture, but not the operation of specific ventures.

A checklist for assessing the proximity of the venture proposal to existing skills and capabilities would include:

- What are the key capabilities required for the venture?
- Where, how and when is the firm going to acquire the capabilities, and at what cost?

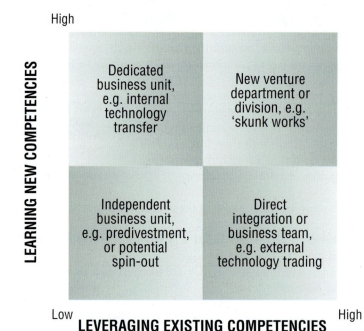

FIGURE 13.2   The most effective structure for a corporate venture depends on the balance between leverage or learning (exploit versus explore)

Source: Tidd, J. and S. Taurins (1999) Learn or leverage? Strategic diversification and organisation learning through corporate ventures, *Creativity and Innovation Management,* **8**(2), 122–9.

- How will these new capabilities affect current capabilities?
- Where else could they be exploited?
- Who else may be able to do this, perhaps better?

In particular, the strategic importance will determine the degree of administrative control required, and the proximity to existing skills and capabilities will determine the degree of operational integration that is desirable. In general, the greater the strategic importance, the stronger the administrative linkages between the corporation and venture (Figure 13.2). Similarly, the closer the skills and capabilities are to the core activities, the greater the degree of operational integration necessary for reasons of efficiency (Table 13.3). Design options for corporate ventures include:

- direct integration with existing business
- integrated business teams
- a dedicated staff function to support efforts company-wide
- a separate corporate venturing unit, department or division
- divestment and spin-off.

Each structure will demand different methods of monitoring and management, that is procedures, reporting mechanisms and accountability. These choices are illustrated by studies of venturing in Europe and the USA.[8]

TABLE 13.3 Type of new venture and links with parent

Venture type	Relatedness of:			Focal activity of venture	Linkages with parent firm
	Product technology	Process technology	Product market		
Product development	Low	Low	High	Development and production	Marketing
Technological innovation	Low	High	High	R&D	Research, marketing and production
Market diversification	High	High	Low	Branding and marketing	Development and production
Technology commercialization	High	Low	Low	Marketing and production	Development
Blue-sky	Low	Low	Low	Development, production and marketing	Finance

Direct Integration

Direct integration as an additional business activity is the preferred choice where radical changes in product or process design are likely to immediately affect mainstream operations and if the people involved in that activity are inextricably involved in day-to-day operations. For example, many engineering-based companies have introduced consultancy to their business portfolio, and in other technical organizations with large laboratory facilities these too have been sold out for analysis of samples, testing of materials, etc. In such cases it is not possible to outsource such activities, because the same personnel and equipment are required for the core business.

Integrated Business Teams

Integrated business teams are most appropriate where the expertise will have been nurtured within the mainstream operations, and may support or require support from those operations for development. Strategically, the product is sufficiently related to the mainstream business's key technologies or expertise that the centre wishes to retain some control over. This control may be either to protect the knowledge that is intrinsic in the activity or to ensure a flow-back of future development knowledge. A business team of secondees is established to coordinate sourcing of both internal and external clients, and is usually treated as a separate accounting entity in order to ease any subsequent transition to a special business unit.

New Ventures Department

A new ventures department is a group separate from normal line management that facilitates external trading. It is most suitable when projects are likely to emerge from the operational business on a fairly frequent basis and when the proposed activities may be beyond current markets or the type of product package sold is different. This is the most natural way for the trading of existing expertise to be developed when it lies fragmented through the organization, and each source is likely to attract a different type of customer. The group has responsibility for marketing, contracting and negotiation, but technical negotiation and supply of services take place at the operational level.

New Ventures Division

A new ventures division provides a safe haven where a number of projects emerge throughout the organization, and it enables separate administrative supervision. Strategically, top management can retain a certain level of control until greater clarity on each venture's strategic importance is understood, but the efficiency of the mainstream business needs to be maintained without distraction, so some autonomy is required. Operational links are loose enough to allow information and know-how to be exchanged with the corporate environment. The origins of such a division vary:

- An effort to bring together existing technologies and expertise throughout the company for adaptation to new or existing markets.
- To combine research from different fields or locations to accelerate the development of new products.
- To purchase or acquire expertise currently outside of the business for application to internal operations or to assist new developments.

- To examine new market areas as potential targets for existing or adapted products within the current portfolio.

Where a critical mass of projects exists, a separate new venture division allows greater focus on the external environment, and the distance from the core corporation enables a global and cross-divisional view to be taken. Unfortunately, the division can often become a kind of dustbin for every new opportunity, and therefore it is critical to define the limits of its operation and its mission, in particular the criteria for termination or continued support of specific projects.

Special Business Units

Special dedicated new business units are wholly owned by the corporation. High strategic relevance requires strong administrative control. Businesses like this tend to come about because the activity is felt to have enough potential to stand alone as a profit centre, and can thus be assessed and operated as a separate business entity. The requirement is that key people can be identified and extracted from their mainstream operational role.

For the business to succeed under the total ownership and control of a large corporate it must be capable of producing significant revenue streams in the medium term. On average, the critical mass appears to be around 12% of total corporate turnover, but in some cases the threshold for a separate unit is much higher. A potential new business must be judged not only on its relative size or profitability but also, and more importantly, on its ability to sustain its own development costs. For example, a profitable subsidiary may never achieve the status of a separate new business if it cannot support its own product development.

However, physically separating a business activity does not ensure autonomy. The greatest impediment to such a unit competing effectively in the market is a cosy corporate mentality. If the managers of a new business are under the impression that the corporate parent will always assist, provide business and second its expertise and services at non-market rates, that business may never be able to survive commercial pressures. Conversely, if the parent plans to retain total ownership, it cannot realistically treat that unit independently.

Independent Business Units

Differing degrees of ownership will determine the administrative control over independent business units, ranging from subsidiary to minority interest. Control would only be exercised through a board presence if that were held. There are two reasons for establishing an independent business as opposed to divisionalizing an activity: to focus on the core business by removing the managerial and technical burden of activities unrelated to the mainstream business or to facilitate learning from external sources in the case of enabling technologies or activities. This structure has benefits for both the parent and the venture:

- Defrayed risk for parent, greater freedom for venture.
- Less supervisory requirement for parent, less interference for venture.
- Reduced management distraction for parent, greater focus for venture.
- Continued share of financial returns for parent, greater commitment from managers of the venture.

• Potential for flow-back or process improvements or product developments for parent and learning for the venture.

The assignment of technical personnel is one of the most difficult problems when establishing an independent business unit. If the individuals necessary to coordinate future product development are unwilling to leave the relative security and comfort of a large corporate facility, which is understandable, the new business may be stopped in its tracks. It is critical to identify the most desirable individuals for such an operation, assessed in terms of their technical ability and personal characteristics. It is also important to assess the effect of these individuals leaving the mainstream development operations, as the capability of the parent's operations could be easily damaged.

Nurtured Divestment

Nurtured divestment is appropriate where an activity is not critical to the mainstream business. The product or service has most likely evolved from the mainstream, and while supporting these operations it is not essential for strategic control. The design option provides a way for the corporate to release responsibility for a particular business area. External markets may be built up prior to separation, giving time to identify which employees should be retained by the corporate and providing a period of acclimatization for the venture. The parent may or may not retain some ownership.

Complete Spin-off

No ownership is retained by the parent corporation in the case of a complete spin-off. This is essentially a divest option, where the corporation wants to pass over total responsibility for activity, commercially and administratively. This may be due to strategic unrelatedness or strategic redundancy, as a consequence of changing corporate strategic focus. A complete spin-off allows the parent to realize the hidden value of the venture, and allows senior management of the parent to focus on their main business.

ENTREPRENEURSHIP IN ACTION 13.3

Lucent's New Venture Group

Lucent Technologies was created in 1996 from the break-up of the famous Bell Labs of AT&T. Lucent established the New Venture Group (NVG) in 1997 to explore how better to exploit its research talent by exploiting technologies which did not fit any of Lucent's current businesses; its mission was to 'leverage Lucent technology to create new ventures that bring innovations to market more quickly … to create a more entrepreneurial environment that nurtures and rewards speed, teamwork, and prudent risk-taking'. At the same time it took measures to protect the mainstream research and innovation processes within Lucent from the potential disruption NVG could cause.

To achieve this balance, at the heart of the process were periodic meetings between NVG managers and Lucent researchers, where ideas were 'nominated' for assessment. These nominated ideas were first presented to the existing business groups within Lucent, and this created pressure on the existing business groups to make decisions on promising technologies, as the vice president of the NVG noted: 'I think the biggest practical benefit of the group was increasing the clockspeed of the system.'

If the nominated idea was not supported or resourced by any of the businesses, the NVG could develop a business plan for the venture. The business plan would include an exit strategy for the venture, ranging from an acquisition by Lucent, external trade sale, IPO (initial public offering) or licence. The initial evaluation stage typically took two to three months and cost $50 000–$100 000. Subsequent stages of internal funding reached $1 million per venture, and in later stages in many cases external venture capital firms were involved to conduct due diligence assessments, contribute funds and management expertise. By 2001, 26 venture companies had been created by the NVG and included 30 external venture capitalists who invested more than $160 million in these ventures. Interestingly, Lucent re-acquired at market prices three of the new ventures NVG had created, all based on technologies that existing Lucent businesses had earlier turned down. This demonstrates one of the benefits of corporate venturing – capturing false negatives – projects which were initially judged too weak to support and were rejected by the conventional development processes. However, following the fall in telecom and other technology equity prices, in 2002 Lucent sold its 80% interest in the remaining ventures to an external investor group for under $100 million.

Source: Chesbrough, H. (2003) *Open Innovation*, Boston: Harvard Business School Press.

Strategic Impact of Ventures

It is very difficult in practice to assess the success of corporate venturing. Simple financial assessments are usually based on some comparison of the investments made by the corporate parent and the subsequent revenue streams or market valuation of the ventures. Both of the latter are highly sensitive to the timing of the assessment. For example, at the height of the Internet bubble, financial market valuations suggested corporate venture returns of 70% or more, whereas a few years later these paper returns no longer existed. A study of 35 spin-offs from Xerox over a period of 22 years reveals that the aggregate market value of these spin-offs exceeded those of the parent by a factor of two by 2001, and by a factor of five at the peak of the previous stock market bubble.[9]

An historical analysis of the development and commercialization of superconductor technologies at General Electric between 1960 and 1990 reveals how the technology began in internal research and development, but reached a point at which there was deemed to be insufficient market potential to justify any further internal investment. Two GE operating businesses were offered the technology, but declined to fund further development. Rather than abandon the technology altogether, in 1971 GE established a 40% owned venture called Intermagnetics General Corporation (IGC) to develop the technology further. GE became a major customer of IGC as demand for the technology grew in its medical systems business owing to the growth of

MRI (magnetic resonance imaging). However, by 1983 the need for the technology has become so central to GE's business that GE had to redevelop its own core competencies in the field.[10]

A longitudinal study of 1527 internal corporate venture projects between 1996 and 2009 suggests that the determinants of survival are highly sensitive to their stage of development.[11] In another study of 48 corporate ventures, the authors conclude that corporate venturing is on the rise, but that success depends on 'well-defined strategic objectives for the corporate venture unit' to 'avoid misplaced expectations and disappointing outcomes'.[12]

INNOVATION IN ACTION 13.2

Bob Noyce, the Pod-father

Robert (Bob) Noyce was one of the pioneers of microelectronics, whose contribution can be traced all the way forward to current entrepreneurs such as Steve Jobs of Apple fame. He has been referred to as both the Thomas Edison and the Henry Ford of Silicon Valley: Edison for his invention and technological innovations, including the co-invention of the integrated circuit; Ford for his process and corporate innovations, including the creation of Fairchild Semiconductor and Intel.

He had a first degree in Physics and Maths, followed by a PhD in Physics from MIT. Upon graduation in 1953, he gained three years' experience as a research engineer, and then at age 29 he joined the then newly established but prestigious Shockley Semiconductor Laboratory in California. William Shockley had won the Nobel Prize for his co-development of the transistor. However, Noyce was very unhappy with the management style at Shockley, and left in 1957 with the so-called Traitorous Eight to form Fairchild Semiconductor, a new division of Fairchild Camera and Instruments.

Sherman Fairchild agreed to fund the Traitorous Eight's new venture on the basis of Noyce's reputation and vision. Noyce convinced Fairchild that the key was the manufacturing process, and that silicon-based components could become low-cost and widely used in a range of electronic devices. At Fairchild, Noyce created a climate in which talent thrived. Everything was much less structured, more relaxed, team based and less hierarchical than at Shockley. Arguably, this was the archetype for the future culture of Silicon Valley.

In 1958, the new venture developed the key planar technology which made higher-performance transistors easier and cheaper to manufacture. In July 1959, he filed for the patent for the integrated circuit, essentially multiple transistors on a single wafer of silicon, which was the next significant technological breakthrough. Between 1954 and 1967, he accumulated sixteen patents. The first sales were to IBM, and sales of Fairchild's semiconductor division doubled each year until the mid-1960s, by which time the company had grown from twelve to twelve thousand employees, and was earning $130 million a year. By 1966, the sales of Fairchild were second to Texas Instruments', followed in third place by Motorola. Noyce was rewarded with the position of corporate vice-president, and was recognized as the de facto head of the semiconductor division.

These devices were analogue, but Fairchild was less successful with its digital devices. Some of its early digital circuits were used in the Apollo Space Guidance computer, but generally these were not suited to other military applications and were not a commercial success. Texas Instruments and a number of new start-up companies offered superior designs, and in 1967 Fairchild suffered its first loss, of $7.6 million. When the CEO resigned, the board did not promote Noyce. As a consequence, in 1968 Noyce left Fairchild to form a new venture with Gordon Moore (also one of the original Traitorous Eight from Shockley, and originator of Moore's Law). Five of the original founders of Fairchild Semiconductor funded the creation of Intel (**Int**egrated **El**ectronics). Intel's third employee was Andy Grove, a chemical engineer credited as its key business and strategic leader.

For the first few years, Intel's business was based on the low-cost manufacture of random access memory (RAM) devices. Noyce oversaw the development of the next major milestone in the industry, the microprocessor, invented by Ted Hoff in 1971. The processor was developed to replace a number of components for an electronic calculator developed for a Japanese client. However, the microprocessor did not become central to Intel's business until much later. Increasing competition from Japan reduced the profitability of memory devices, and Intel changed strategy to pursue the development microprocessor which would be critical to the growth of the nascent PC industry. In July 1979, Intel launched its 8088 processor, a new variant of its 8086, accompanied by a major marketing and sales campaign, Operation Crush, to promote widespread adoption and application. An early win was as a supplier to IBM. In August 1981, IBM launched its PC based upon the Intel processor. In 1982, Intel introduced the 80286 processor, and the 80386 in 1985, first used by Compaq in its PC clones and later by IBM. The 386 was also a milestone as it was the first processor to be single-sourced from Intel. Before this, customers would source critical components from several competing manufacturers to ensure deliveries and reduce risk, but for the 386 Intel refused to license its design and instead manufactured the chips at three separate sites. This strategy established Intel at the heart of the PC industry.

Noyce's charisma and powers of persuasion made him an inspiring leader, but he was a less effective manager. He was criticized by Grove and others for his indecisiveness and dislike of confrontation, a trait that kept him from making difficult decisions and taking tough actions. He resigned as president in 1975, transferring the role to Moore. However, Noyce maintained a mentoring role at Intel and more broadly, and provided advice and seed capital to promising entrepreneurs.

One of these aspiring entrepreneurs was Steve Jobs, who Noyce met during the first year of Apple Computer, in 1977. Jobs deliberately sought out Noyce as a mentor. 'Steve would regularly appear at our house on his motorcycle … he and Bob were disappearing into the basement, talking about projects.' Noyce answered Jobs's phone calls – which invariably began with, 'I've been thinking about what you said' or 'I have an idea' – even when they came at midnight. This relationship continued for over a decade.

Clearly then, Bob Noyce has contributed to almost all aspects of innovation in Silicon Valley – technological, process, product, corporate and cultural. As Noyce advised budding entrepreneurs: 'Optimism is an essential ingredient for innovation … go off and do something wonderful.'

Sources: BBC Productions (2009) *The Podfather;* Berlin, L. (2007) Focus on Robert Noyce, *Core,* Spring/Summer (www.computerhistory.org/core/backissues/pdf/core_2007.pdf); Berlin, L. (2005) *The Man Behind the Microchip: Robert Noyce and the Invention of Silicon Valley.* Oxford: Oxford University Press; Reid, T.R. (2001) *The Chip: How Two Americans Invented the Microchip and Launched a Revolution,* New York: Random House.

Chapter Summary

- There are a wide range of motives for establishing corporate ventures, including to attract, motivate and retain talent, to grow the business, diversify or to develop and exploit new technological or market capabilities.

- The best structure for a corporate venture depends on a number of factors, such as who owns and funds these, and the proximity of the technological or market capabilities to the core businesses.

- The outcomes and success of corporate venturing should be assessed in broad terms, including the long-term survival, growth and evolution of the organization rather than only by narrow financial evaluations of specific projects. It represents a process of corporate experimentation and evolution.

Key Terms Defined

Corporate entrepreneur   is the internal equivalent to an entrepreneur. However, in practice the characteristics of each are quite different, for example the need for autonomy, and degree of social skills and political sensitivity.

Corporate venture   is the equivalent of a new business start-up, but owned by a parent corporation. Strictly speaking, these can be either internal (within the organization) or external ventures, but the terms 'internal venturing' and 'corporate venturing' are often used interchangeably.

Relatedness   refers to how close strategically and operationally the venture is to the core business or technology. This influences the choice of governance and structure for the corporate venture.

Discussion Questions

1. What are the differences between corporate venturing and new product development?

2. In what ways could strategic and operational goals create conflicts?

3. What are the main management challenges in the relationships between the parent organization and its ventures?

4. What are the advantages and disadvantages of the different approaches to resourcing and structuring corporate ventures?

Further Reading and Resources

For an academic review of the field, start with V.K. Narayanan, Yi Yang and Shaker Zahra's 'Corporate venturing and value creation: A review and proposed framework' (2009, *Research Policy*, **38**(1), 58–76). Robert Burgelman and Leonard Sayles's *Inside Corporate Innovation* (Macmillan, 1986) remains the classic combination of theory and case studies, but the more recent book by Zenus Block and Ian MacMillan, *Corporate Venturing: Creating New Businesses within the Firm* (Harvard Business School Press, 1995), provides a better review of research on internal corporate ventures.

Other books which include some interesting examples of venturing in the information and telecommunications sectors are *Webs of Innovation* by Alexander Loudon (FT.com, 2001), which despite its title has several chapters related to venturing, and Henry Chesbrough's *Open Innovation* (Harvard Business School Press, 2003), which includes case studies of the usual suspects such as IBM, Xerox, Intel and Lucent. The book *Inventuring: Why Big Companies Must Think Small* by William Buckland, Andrew Hatche and Julian Birkinshaw (McGraw-Hill, 2003) is also a good review of corporate venture initiatives, including those at GE, Intel and Lucent, which suggest a range of successful venture models and common reasons for failure. The text *Corporate Entrepreneurship* by Paul Burns provides a useful framework and case examples (Palgrave Macmillan, 2008), and for a more practical approach see Robert Hisrich and Claudine Kearney's *Corporate Entrepreneurship* (McGraw-Hill, 2011).

References

1. Dess, G., G. Lumpkin and J. Covin (1997) Entrepreneurial strategy making and firm performance, *Strategic Management Journal*, **18**(9): 677–95.

2. Tidd, J. and S. Taurins (1999) Learn or leverage? Strategic diversification and organisational learning through corporate ventures, *Creativity and Innovation Management*, 8(2): 122–9.

3. Tidd, J. and S. Taurins (1999) Learn or leverage? Strategic diversification and organisational learning through corporate ventures, *Creativity and Innovation Management*, 8(2): 122–9.

4. Tidd, J. and S. Taurins (1999) Learn or leverage? Strategic diversification and organisational learning through corporate ventures, *Creativity and Innovation Management*, 8(2): 122–9.

5. Tidd, J. (2012) *From Knowledge Management to Strategic Competence*, 3rd edn, London: Imperial College Press.

6. Wolcott, R.C. and M.J. Lippitz (2007) The four models of corporate entrepreneurship, *MIT Sloan Management Review*, **Fall**: 74–82.

7. Block, Z. and I. MacMillan (1993) *Corporate Venturing: Creating New Businesses Within the Firm*, Boston: Harvard Business School Press.

8. Wolcott, R.C. and M.J. Lippitz (2007) The four models of corporate entrepreneurship, *MIT Sloan Management Review*, **49**(1): 74–82; Buckland, W., A. Hatche and J. Birkinshaw (2003) *Inventuring*, New York: McGraw-Hill; Campbell, A., J. Birkinshaw, A. Morrison and R.V. Batenburg (2003) The future of corporate venturing, *MIT Sloan Management Review*, **45**(1): 30–37; Dushnitsky, G. (2011) Riding the next wave of corporate venture capital, *Business Strategy Review*, **22**(3): 44–9.

9. Chesbrough, H. (2002) The governance and performance of Xerox's technology spin-off companies, *Research Policy*, **32**: 403–21.

10. Abetti, P. (2002) From science to technology to products and profits: Superconductivity at General Electric and Intermagnetics General (1960–1990), *Journal of Business Venturing*, **17**: 83–98.

11. Masucci, M. (2013) Uncovering the determinants of initiative survival in corporate venture units: A multistage selection perspective, SPRU Seminar, June 2013.

12. Battistini, B., F. Hacklin and P. Baschera (2013) The state of corporate venturing, *Research Technology Management*, **56**(1): 37.

Deeper Dive explanations of innovation concepts and ideas are available on the Innovation Portal at **www.innovation-portal.info**

Quizzes to test yourself further are available online via the Innovation Portal at **www.innovation-portal.info**

Summary of online resources for Chapter 13 –
all material is available via the Innovation Portal at
www.innovation-portal.info

Cases	**Media**	**Tools**	**Activities**	**Deeper Dives**
• SPIRIT • Kodak • Fujifilm	• Tesco Goes West • David Hall • Roy Sandbach	• Selection approaches for radical innovation	• Strategic planning for implementation	• Role of venture capital

Chapter 14

Growing the Enterprise

LEARNING OBJECTIVES

By the end of this chapter you will develop an understanding of:

- identifying the factors which contribute to the success and growth of new ventures
- differentiating the factors which entrepreneurs can influence from those which are more contextual
- implementing proven strategies for new venture success and growth.

Estimates vary, but most studies confirm that around half of start-ups survive no more than four years, and less than 4% of the remaining new ventures grow.[1] In this chapter we identify the factors which contribute to the success and growth of new ventures, and we try to differentiate the factors which entrepreneurs can influence from those which are more contextual.

Factors Influencing Success

A study of 11 259 new technology ventures in the USA over a period of five years found that 36% survived after four years and 22% after five years. To try to explain the success and failure of these ventures, the researchers reviewed 31 other key studies of technology ventures, and found only eight factors that were consistently found to influence success:[2]

- *Value chain management*. Cooperation with suppliers, distribution, agents and customers.
- *Market scope*. Variety of customers and market segments, and geographic reach.

- *Firm age.* Number of years in existence.
- *Size of founding team.* Likely to bring additional and more diverse expertise to the ventures and better decision making.
- *Financial resources.* Venture assets and access to funding.
- *Founders' marketing experience.* But not technical experience, or prior experience of start-ups (see below).
- *Founders' industry experience.* In related markets or sectors.
- *Existence of patent rights.* In product or process technology, but R&D investment was not found to be significant.

The first three factors were by far the most significant predictors of success. However, clearly there is also some interaction between these effects, for example the founders' marketing and industry experience is likely to influence the attention to market scope and the value chain, and patent rights make raising finance easier, and vice versa. In addition, they found that some commonly cited factors had no effect, including founders' experience of R&D or prior start-ups. The importance of other factors depended on the precise context of the venture, for example for independent start-ups R&D alliances and product innovation both had a negative effect on performance, but for ventures of mixed origins R&D alliances and product innovation both had a positive effect on performance.

Despite these relatively high rates of survival, very few firms grow significantly or consistently, the so-called **gazelles**, typically less than 4%.[3] Although these high growth ventures are atypical, they account for a disproportionate proportion of new employment, between 12 and 33% in Europe. The founding conditions appear to have a very significant and persistent effect on the subsequent success and growth of a new venture, but it is difficult to separate the effects of business planning, strategy and context (Table 14.1). Most, but not all, studies suggest that formal business planning contributes to success, as we discussed in Chapter 8.[4]

ENTREPRENEURSHIP IN ACTION 14.1

High-, Low- and No-growth Ventures

Most focus in management and policy for entrepreneurship is on the performance and contribution of the high-growth, so-called gazelle, companies. There is a predilection for animal terms, such as the even rarer billion-dollar **unicorns** (see Enterprise in Action 14.2, below). However, our colleagues Paul Nightingale and Alex Coad argue that we need to have a much finer distinction to disaggregate small firms, in particular the 96% no-growth firms.

They develop the term **muppets** (all rights reserved) to describe the more typical economically 'Marginal, Under-sized, Poor Performance Enterprises'. They argue that the performance and contribution of small firms has been exaggerated significantly, and in fact by most measures such firms are less productive and innovative than larger firms, and contribute less to wealth and employment creation.

Source: Derived from Nightingale, P. and A. Coad (2014) Muppets and gazelles: Political and methodological biases in entrepreneurship research, *Industrial and Corporate Change*, **23**(1), 113–143.

The most significant controllable factors shown in Table 14.1 all help to build credibility for a new venture, what our colleague Sue Birley refers to as the 'credibility carousel': factors which help to recruit and convince other stakeholders of the viability of a venture.[5] This can be a slow, painful process, but an essential one to attract the necessary talent, resources and initial customers.

Studies consistently find that the age, educational level, number of founders and starting capital all have a positive effect on venture success. The effects of age on the success and growth of a new venture are probably the best understood, and shown to be significant in almost every research study. The consensus is that the most common age of successful founders is between 35 and 50 years old, the median age being 39.[6] The explanation for

TABLE 14.1   Initial conditions influencing the success of new ventures

Significance	Condition
Most significant (5% level)	Size of target market
	Industrial experience of founders
	Strength of social networks
	Business management skills
Significant (10% level)	Product attractiveness to target market
	Ownership structure and governance
Not found to be significant	Profit potential
	Entrepreneurial attitude
	Leadership skills
	R&D and production planning
	Market development
	Financial forecast

Source: Adapted from Gao, J., J. Li, Y. Cheng and S. Shi (2010) Impact of initial conditions on new venture success, *International Journal of Innovation Management*, **14**(1), 41–56.

this clustering is that younger founders tend to lack the experience, resources and credibility, whereas older founders may lack the drive and have too much to lose. Of course there are many examples of successful entrepreneurs outside of this age range, but the association between age of founders and success is very significant.

To understand the influence of education, one study tracked 118 070 new start-up firms over ten years and found that human capital at foundation, measured by university degree, had a strong and persistent positive effect on subsequent success. In addition, four structural factors at the time of foundation were predictors of success: firm size at foundation (positive), rate of firm entry into the same sector (negative), concentration of the sector (positive) and GDP growth (positive).[7] Other research examined 622 young or new small firms over five years, and found human and financial capital available at start-up was a strong predictor of survival and growth, specifically the founder's education (degree or above) and access to bank finance.[8] As with age, there are many examples of successful entrepreneurs who chose not to go to college or dropped out early, but the research does consistently demonstrate a strong association between level of education and venture success and growth, especially in more knowledge- or technology-intensive businesses.

Access to sufficient capital is another widely cited founding condition for success and growth. However, the evidence is more mixed than for the effects of age and education. Some studies suggest that access to external capital is associated with higher growth, especially in the case of more high-technology ventures,[9] but others find no such effect or even the exact opposite relationship: that higher growth is associated with maintaining internal funding and ownership.[10] The conflicting evidence and advice may be due to methodological differences, such as definition of high growth, time period studied and so on, but may also reflect the influence of more fundamental moderating factors, for example the type of venture and market or the roles and control needs of founders.

These founder effects are even stronger for **new technology-based firms (NTBFs)**. This is partly because of the human capital necessary, especially the high education of founders:[11]

- 85% have degree, almost half a PhD
- 12 or more years of experience in large private-sector firm
- Founders' ages cluster mid-30s, two-thirds aged 30–50.

However, NTBFs are diverse, and the type of technology will also have an influence of the trajectory of growth (Figure 14.1).

Finally, companies competing on price, rather than by differentiation, are much less likely to survive. Contrary to the popular folklore of the poorly educated, disadvantaged entrepreneur, this study confirms that the more typical profile of a successful new venture is a rare combination of human capital in the form of the university education of founders, availability of sufficient finance and a strategy of growth by product or service differentiation. Similarly, the caricature of the lone, risk-taking entrepreneur is unfounded. The growth of a new venture in terms of sales and employment depends upon planning skills and experience, and profitability flows from developing and exploiting networks.[12]

Innovative firms are more likely to grow, in terms of sales and employment, but are not necessarily more profitable than non-innovators.[13] Funding by venture capital has no effect

(a) Research-based venture e.g. biotechnology

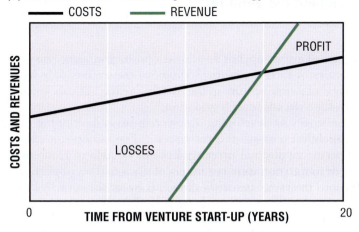

(b) Development-based venture e.g. electronics

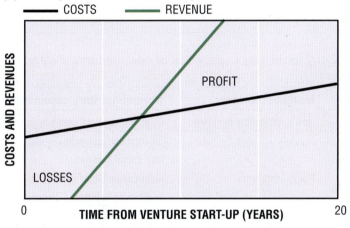

(c) Production-based venture e.g. software

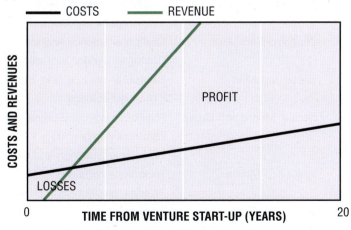

FIGURE 14.1   Influence of technology on the profitability and cash-flow profile of a new venture

on the innovativeness of a start-up, but does have a positive influence on profitability, perhaps reflecting the priorities of such investors.[14] Financial constraints only have an effect on the likelihood of survival of a new venture in the first few years, but continue to constrain profitability and growth for a decade after foundation.[15]

One of the challenges of developing a new venture is developing or gaining access to **complementary capabilities**, assets and resources.[16] For example, a start-up may have the technical know-how or intellectual property but not be able to reach or support potential customers, or conversely an entrepreneur may identify a market opportunity but not be able to provide the product or service to satisfy this. This is one reason why firms created by pairs or small groups of founders are significantly more likely to be successful than those formed by individual entrepreneurs.[17] The contrasting capabilities and perspectives of multiple founders provide a stronger basis to identify, develop and deliver innovative offerings (Table 14.2).

TABLE 14.2   Complementary capabilities of new ventures created by multiple founders

Case company	Multiple founders	Complementary capabilities
Apple	Jobs, Wozniak and Ive	Graphic design and showmanship Computer science Industrial design
Google	Page and Brin	Computer Science (PhD) Mathematics and Computer Science (PhD)
Facebook	Zuckerberg and Saverin	Computer science and psychology Business studies and finance
Netflix	Randolph and Hastings	Engineering and Marketing Mathematics and Computer Science (MSc)
Skype	Zennström and Friis	Computer science and telecommunications Customer service and sales
Microsoft	Gates and Allen	Computer science, and intellectual property Computer science
Intel	Noyce, Moore and Grove	Physics, maths and organisation Electrical engineering Process engineering and strategy
Sony	Ibuka and Morita	Telecommunications R&D Physics, electronics and family business.
Rolls-Royce	Royce and Rolls	Engineering Sales and finance

TABLE 14.2   *(Continued)*

Case company	Multiple founders	Complementary capabilities
Marks & Spencer	Marks and Spencer	Retail sales Finance and supply networks
Formula One	Ecclestone and Mosley	Maths, car sales, motor racing Physics, law and motor racing
Electrification	Tesla and Westinghouse	Science, maths and showmanship Business and finance
Steam power	Watt and Boulton	Engineering Business and manufacturing

Source: Derived from Tidd, J. (2014) Conjoint innovation: Building a bridge between innovation and entrepreneurship, *International Journal of Innovation Management*, **18**(1), 1–20.

ENTREPRENEURSHIP IN ACTION 14.2

European Internet Unicorns

Most of the attention is attracted to the Internet giants which originated in the USA, such as Google and Facebook. However, Europe has created its own Internet superstars. Since 2000, 30 European Internet ventures have grown to be worth more than $1 billion each. This compares favourably with the USA, with 39 $1 billion new ventures over the same period.

These are often referred to as 'unicorns', because they are so rare. The UK leads Europe, with 11, for example property website Zoopla and food delivery site Just Eat. Russia is the next most successful, with five unicorns, third is Sweden with four cases, including Spotify, while France and Finland each have two, but Germany, Spain, Italy, Ireland, Luxembourg and Israel have only one each. The Anglo-Swedish group King, developer of the smartphone game Candy Crush, completes the European unicorns.

As in the USA, most the unicorns were formed by pairs or teams of two to three entrepreneurs, with an average age of 33 at foundation. This is consistent with Table 14.2. Only half of European unicorns have reached a trade sale or an IPO, compared with two-thirds in the USA.

Source: Derived from GP Bullhound (2014) *Can Europe Create Billion Dollar Tech Companies?* http://www.gpbullhound.com/en/research/, accessed 20th December 2014.

Funding

The initial funding to establish a new venture is rarely a major problem, as most are self-funded. However, Peter Drucker suggests a new venture requires financial restructuring every three years.[18] Different stages of development each have different financial requirements:

- Initial financing for launch.
- Second-round financing for initial development and growth.
- Third-round financing for consolidation and growth.
- Maturity or exit.

ENTREPRENEURSHIP IN ACTION 14.3

Seedcamp

Seedcamp was established in 2007 by Index Ventures partners Saul Klein and Reshma Sohoni. It provides early-stage mentoring and micro-seed investment, and networking and advice through monthly Seedcamp days and an annual Seedcamp week. Each year around 2000 entrepreneurs and businesses compete for seed funding of up to €50 000, but only 20 or so are successful. Seedcamp offers a standard investment of €50 000 in return for a 8–10% stake in the business, but one of the main benefits is the access to an extensive network of mentors, including entrepreneurs, business angels and professional services. The main business areas supported are in relatively low-capital technology ventures in Internet, mobile, gaming, software and media.

Source: www.seedcamp.com.

In general, professional financial bodies are not interested in initial funding, because of the high risk and low sums of money involved. It is simply not worth their time and effort to evaluate and monitor such ventures. However, as the sums involved are relatively small – typically of the order of tens of thousands of pounds – personal savings, re-mortgages and loans from friends and relatives are often sufficient. The initial funding required to form a new venture may include the purchase of accommodation, equipment and other start-up costs, plus the day-to-day running costs such as salaries, utilities and so on. Research in the USA and the UK suggests that most begin life as part-time ventures and are funded by personal savings, loans from friends and relatives and then bank loans, in that order. Around half also receive some funding from government sources, but in contrast receive next to nothing from venture capitalists.[19]

Venture capital is typically only made available at later stages to fund growth on the basis of a proven development and sales record. Given their strong desire for independence, most entrepreneurs seek to avoid external funding for their ventures. However, in practice this is not always possible, particularly in the later growth stages.

Venture capitalists are keen to provide funding for a venture with a proven track record and strong business plan, but in return will often require some equity or management involvement. Moreover, most venture capitalists are looking for a means to make capital gains after about five years. However, almost by definition entrepreneurs seek independence and control, and there is evidence that some will sacrifice growth to maintain control of their ventures. For the same reason, few entrepreneurs are prepared to go public to fund further growth. Thus, many entrepreneurs will choose to sell the business and found another. For example, the typical technology entrepreneur establishes an average of three ventures in their lifetime. Therefore, the biggest funding challenge is likely to be for the second-round financing to fund development and growth. This can be a time-consuming and frustrating process to convince venture capitalists to provide finance. The formal proposal is critical at this stage. Professional investors will assess the attractiveness of the venture in terms of the strengths and personalities of the founders, the formal business plan and the commercial and technical merits of the product, typically in that order. As we discussed in the previous chapter, general venture capital firms typically only accept 5% of the technology ventures they are offered, and the specialist technology venture funds are even more selective, accepting around 3%. The main reasons for rejecting technology proposals compared to more general funding proposals are the lack of intellectual property, the skills of the management team and the size of the potential market.

ENTREPRENEURSHIP IN ACTION 14.4

The Role of Venture Capital in Innovation

I was recently asked by a friend who works in the R&D group at a large corporation to summarize the role of venture capital in innovation. Trying to make it relevant to his own experience, I explained that we simply provide the R&D budget for companies that would not ordinarily have one! I explained further that the companies we back are, on the whole, small self-contained R&D organizations generating intellectual property and ultimately new products that threaten the incumbents in any particular industry. Venture capitalists believe that to create value a small firm should follow a strategy that means it will be needed by or become a threat to global corporations. That way, such corporations may be forced to bid against each other to acquire the small firm and obtain the new innovations (or remove the threat) thus providing the venture capitalist with a high-value exit from its investment.

This goes to the very heart of the venture capital business model. Venture capitalists are professional fund managers who invest cash in early-stage high-risk ventures in return for shares, with the aim of selling those shares at a later date through some form of exit event. The golden rule of investment – 'buy low, sell high' – is modified in the realm of venture capital to 'buy very low sell very high' to account for the extreme risk profile of the early-stage ventures they back.

(continued)

The follow-up question to what venture capitalists do is usually about whether they provide value to early-stage ventures beyond pure financial investment. The question usually provokes a debate, sometimes heated, about the pros and cons of having venture capitalists involved in running a business. In my view the answer is simple – and is based around a philosophy within the venture capital industry to kill failure early. By allocating their capital only to companies that continue to demonstrate success, venture capitalists deprive underperforming ventures of cash and usually bring about their rapid demise. This is often not the case within the R&D groups of large corporations where underperforming or low-potential projects can struggle on for years protected by managerial indecision and political sensitivity. Thus, venture capitalists provide a rigorous and ongoing selection process for the innovation process holding the companies they back to strict targets and tight deadlines… there is no hiding place.

In short, venture capital investment provides the cash to drive innovation forward within small companies at a faster rate than would ordinarily be possible and provides a rigorous and ongoing monitoring process that responds by killing failure early. Ultimately, this is underpinned by the very simplest of selection criterion: will this investment make a significant financial return within 3–5 years' time? Answering that question clarifies even the most difficult of investment decisions.

Source: Simon Barnes is managing partner of Tate & Lyle Ventures LP, an independent venture capital fund backed by Tate & Lyle, a global food ingredients manufacturer.

ENTREPRENEURSHIP IN ACTION 14.5

Andrew Rickman and Bookham Technology

Andrew Rickman founded Bookham Technology in 1988, aged 28. Rickman has a degree in mechanical engineering from Imperial College London, a PhD in integrated optics from Surrey University, an MBA and has worked as a venture capitalist. Unlike many technology entrepreneurs, he did not begin with the development of a novel technology and then seek a means to exploit it. Instead, he first identified a potential market need for optical switching technology for the then fledgling optical fibre networks and then developed an appropriate technological solution. The market for optical components is growing fast as the use of Internet and other data-intensive traffic grows. Rickman aimed to develop an integrated optical circuit on a single chip to replace a number of discrete components such as lasers, lenses and mirrors. He chose to use silicon rather than more exotic materials to reduce development costs and exploit traditional chip production techniques. The main technological developments were made at Surrey University and the Rutherford Appleton Laboratory, where he had worked, and 27 patents were granted and a further 140 applied for. Once the technology had been proven, the company raised $110 million over several rounds of funding from venture capitalist 3i, and leading electronics firms Intel and Cisco. The most difficult task was scale-up and production: 'Taking the technology out of the lab and into production is unbelievably tough in this area. It is infinitely more difficult than dreaming up the technology.' Bookham Technology floated in London and on the NASDAQ in New York in April 2000 with a market capitalization of more than £5 billion, making Andrew Rickman, with 25% of the equity, a paper billionaire. Bookham is based in Oxford, and employs 400 staff. The company acquired the optical component businesses of Nortel and Marconi in 2002, and in 2003 the US optical companies Ignis Optics and New Focus, and the latter included chip production facilities in China. In 2009, Bookham merged with the Californian company Avanex, to create a new company called Oclaro, a combination of the words Optica and Clarity, which achieved revenues of more than $0.5 billion in 2013.

Venture capitalists can play two distinct roles. The first is to identify or select those NTBFs that have the best potential for success, that is 'picking winners' or 'scouting'. The second role is to help develop the chosen ventures, by providing management expertise and access to resources other than financial, that is a 'coaching' role. Distinguishing between the effects of these two roles is critical for both the management of and policy for NTBFs. For managers, it will influence the choice of venture capital firm, and, for policy, it will influence the balance between funding and other forms of support. A study of almost 700 biotechnology firms over ten years provides some insights into these different roles.[20] It found that when selecting start-ups to invest in the most significant criteria used by venture capitalists were a broad, experienced top management team, a large number of recent patents and downstream industry alliances (but not upstream research alliances, which had a negative effect on selection). The strongest effect on the decision to fund was the first criterion, and the human capital in general. However, subsequent analysis of venture performance indicates that this factor has limited effect on performance, and that the few significant effects are split equally between improving and impeding the performance of a venture. The effects of technology and alliances on subsequent performance are much more significant and positive.

In short, in the selection stage, venture capitalists place too much emphasis on human capital, specifically the top management team. In the development or coaching stages, venture capitalists do contribute to the success of the chosen ventures, and tend to introduce external professional management much earlier than in NTBFs not funded by venture capital. Taken together, this suggests that the coaching role of venture capitalists is probably as important, if not more so, than the funding role, although policy interventions to promote NTBFs often focus on the latter.

Case Study of Internet start-up Ihavemoved.com, which raised its initial venture capital and then faced the challenge of growing the new business, is available on the Innovation Portal at **www.innovation-portal.info**

Video Clip of an interview with Melissa Clark-Reynolds, founder of Minimonos, giving insights into the entrepreneurial process and the challenges of growing an idea into a successful business is available on the Innovation Portal at **www.innovation-portal.info**

Growth and Performance of New Ventures

There has been a great deal of economic and management research on small firms, but much of this has been concerned with the contribution all types of small firms make to economic, employment or regional development. Relatively little is known about innovative new ventures.

In most developed economies, around 10% of the economically active population engage in new venture creation each year, a slightly higher proportion (15% or so) in the USA and Asia and a little lower in Europe (excluding the UK) – 6%. However, the rate of churn (i.e. new ventures closed less those created) is high. Closure does not necessarily indicate failure, as a founder may choose to change business or seek alternative employment. Survival rates are quite high, in the UK after two years 80% survive, and 54% after four years (Barclays Capital, 2008).[21] In the USA there are more short-term failures, probably owing to the ease of establishing a business there, but similar rates of longer-term survival: 66% survive two years, 50% four years and 40% more than six years.[22]

A study of 409 SMEs examined the differences between the highest-growing, the gazelles, and the lowest-growing companies over a four-year period, to identify how innovation contributed to the growth. It found that, in addition to high growth, the highest-growing companies also showed higher profitability, increased number of employees and significantly higher market shares locally, nationally and internationally than the lowest-growing companies. Several traits were found to contribute to this:[23]

- The high growers had significantly ($p < 0.001$) younger CEOs than the low growers, but the average of 47 years for the high growers clearly indicates that several of their CEOs were over 50 years of age.
- The high growers had a significantly higher portion of new products as part of the turnover.
- The high growers perceived themselves as better than their competitors at understanding customer needs, offering better products, being agile but also at keeping costs low.
- The high growers prioritized growth rather than profitability ($p < 0.001$), market share rather than profitability ($p < 0.001$) and reinvesting rather than showing profit ($p < 0.001$).

Much of the research on innovative small firms has been confined to a small number of high-technology sectors, principally microelectronics and biotechnology. A notable exception is the survey of 2000 SMEs conducted by the Small Business Research Centre in the UK. The survey found that 60% of the sample claimed to have introduced a major new product or service innovation in the previous five years.[24] While this finding demonstrates that the management of innovation is relevant to the majority of small firms, it does not tell us much about the significance of such innovations, in terms of research and investment, or subsequent market or financial performance.

Audio Clip of Simon Murdoch describing the development, growth and sale of his business BookPages is available on the Innovation Portal at **www.innovation-portal.info**

Research over the past decade or so suggests that the innovative activities of SMEs exhibit broadly similar characteristics across sectors.[25] They:

- are more likely to involve product innovation than process innovation
- are focused on products for niche markets, rather than mass markets
- will be more common amongst producers of final products, rather than producers of components
- will frequently involve some form of external linkage
- tend to be associated with growth in output and employment, but not necessarily profit.

The limitations of a focus on product innovation for niche or intermediate markets were discussed earlier, in particular problems associated with product planning and marketing, and relationships with lead customers and linkages with external sources of innovation. Where an SME has a close relationship with a small number of customers, it may have little incentive or scope for further innovation, and therefore will pay relatively little attention to formal product development or marketing. Therefore, SMEs in such dependent relationships are likely to have limited potential for future growth and may remain permanent infants or subsequently be acquired by competitors or customers.[26] Moreover, an analysis of the growth in the number of NTBFs suggests that the trend has as much to do with negative factors, such as the downsizing of larger firms, as it does with more positive factors, such as start-ups.[27]

Innovative SMEs are likely to have diverse and extensive linkages with a variety of external sources of innovation, and in general there is a positive association between the level of external scientific, technical and professional inputs and the performance of an SME.[28] The sources of innovation and precise types of relationship vary by sector, but links with contract research organizations, suppliers, customers and universities are consistently rated as being highly significant, and constitute the 'social capital' of the firm. However, such relationships are not without cost, and the management and exploitation of these linkages can be difficult for SMEs and overwhelm their limited technical and managerial resources.[29] As a result, in some cases the cost of collaboration may outweigh the benefits,[30] and in the specific case of collaboration between SMEs and universities there is an inherent mismatch between the short-term, near-market focus of most SMEs and the long-term, basic research interests of universities.[31]

Activity to help you explore the need for external expertise and partners, Partner Search, is available on the Innovation Portal at **www.innovation-portal.info**

In terms of innovation, the performance of SMEs is easily exaggerated. Early studies based on innovation counts consistently indicated that when adjusted for size smaller firms created more new products than their larger counterparts did. However, methodological shortcomings appear to undermine this clear message. When the divisions and subsidiaries of larger organizations are removed from such samples,[32] and the innovations weighted according to their technological merit and commercial value, the relationship between firm size and innovation is reversed: larger firms create proportionally more significant innovations than SMEs do.[33] The amount of expenditure by SMEs on design and engineering has a positive effect on the share of exports in sales,[34] but formal R&D by SMEs appears to be only weakly associated with profitability,[35] and is not correlated with growth.[36] Similarly, the high growth rates associated with NTBFs are not explained by R&D effort,[37] and investment in technology does not appear to discriminate between the success and failure of NTBFs. Instead, other factors have been found to have a more significant effect on profitability and growth, in particular the contributions of technically qualified owner managers and their scientific and engineering staff, and attention to product planning and marketing.[38]

A large study of start-ups in Germany found that the founder's level of management experience was a significant predictor of the growth of a venture. However, innovation, broadly defined, was found to be statistically three times more important to growth than founder attributes or any other of the factors measured.[39] Another study, of Korean technology start-ups, also found that innovativeness, defined as a propensity to engage in new idea generation, experimentation and R&D, was associated with performance. So was proactiveness, defined as the firm's approach to market opportunities through active market research and the introduction of new products and services.[40] The same study also found that what it referred to as 'sponsorship-based linkages' had a positive effect on performance. This included links with venture capital firms, which reinforces the developmental role these can play, as discussed earlier.

The size and location of a venture also has an effect on performance. Geographic closeness increases the likelihood of informal linkages and encourages the mobility of skilled labour across firms. However, the probability of a start-up benefiting from such local knowledge exchanges appears to decrease as the venture grows.[41] This growing inability to exploit informal linkages is a function of organizational size, not the age of the venture, and suggests that as ventures grow and become more complex they begin to suffer from many of the barriers to innovation, and therefore the explicit processes and tools to help overcome these become more relevant. Larger SMEs are associated with a greater spatial reach of innovation-related linkages and with the introduction of more novel product or process innovations for international markets. In contrast, smaller SMEs are more embedded in local networks, and are more likely to be engaged in incremental innovations for the domestic market.[42] It is always difficult to untangle cause and effect relationships from such associations, but it is plausible that as the more innovative start-ups begin to outgrow the resources of their local networks they actively replace and extend their networks, which creates both the opportunity and demand for higher levels of innovation. Conversely, the less-innovative start-ups fail to move beyond their local networks, and therefore are less likely to have either the opportunity or the need for more radical innovation.

However, different contingencies will demand different innovation strategies. For example, a study of 116 software start-ups identified five factors that affected success: level of R&D expenditure, how radical new products were, the intensity of product upgrades, use of external technology and management of intellectual property.[43] In contrast, a study of 94 biotechnology start-ups found that three factors were associated with success: location within a significant concentration of similar firms, quality of scientific staff (measured by citations) and the commercial experience of the founder.[44] The number of alliances had no significant effect on success, and the number of scientific staff in the top management team had a negative association, suggesting that scientists are best kept in the laboratory. Other studies of biotechnology start-ups confirm this pattern, and suggest that maintaining close links with universities reduces the level of R&D expenditure needed, increases the number of patents produced and moderately increases the number of new products under development. However, as with more general alliances, the *number* of university links has no effect on the success or performance of biotechnology start-ups, but the *quality* of such relationships does.[45]

ENTREPRENEURSHIP IN ACTION 14.6

Intelligent Energy

The company was founded by a group of academics at Loughborough University in 2001, but can be traced back to Advanced Power Sources Ltd, formed in 1995 by Paul Adcock, Phillip Mitchell, Jon Moore and Anthony Newbold. The company was based on research since 1988 in the departments of chemistry, aeronautical and automotive engineering. Intelligent Energy Ltd acquired APS Ltd in 2001, and a private fund-raising also allowed the new company to acquire an irrevocable, worldwide licence to exploit all fuel cell know-how which had been developed at Loughborough University.

The company develops compact, air-cooled fuel cells. It uses a technology licensing model, similar to ARM, and licenses its 500+ patent portfolio to a number of automotive firms, including Nissan, Toyota, Suzuki, Vauxhall, Daimler, Ricardo, Hyundai and Tata (Jaguar Land Rover), consumer electronics companies and distributed power projects. The company employs 350 people and has offices in Japan, India and the US.

The company has been highly effective in promoting itself through high-profile projects and partnerships: the World's First Fuel Cell Motorbike in 2005; first manned fuel cell power flight, in an EU venture with Boeing in 2008; and in collaboration with Manganese Bronze to develop and operate a fleet of 15 zero-emission black cabs for the 2012 London Olympic Games. Intelligent Energy was awarded the 2013 Barclays Social Innovation Award by *The Sunday Times* Hiscox Tech Track 100.

Through a second fundraising in 2003, the company expanded through the acquisition of Element One Enterprises, based in California. The company raised further funding of £22 million in 2012 and £32.5 million in 2013. It was floated in London in July 2014, raising a further £40 million, and valuing the company at more than £600 million. Singaporean sovereign wealth fund GIC owns about 10% of the company and Philip Mitchell, one of the founders, now owns less than 1% having divested shares at the 2014 issue of new shares.

Such sector-specific studies confirm that the environment in which small firms operate significantly influences both the opportunity for innovation, in a technological and market sense, and the most appropriate strategy and processes for innovation. For example, a venture may have a choice of whether to use its intellectual assets by translating its technology into product and services for the market or alternatively it may exploit these assets through a larger, more established firm, through licensing, sale of IPR or by collaboration. More specifically, the venture needs to consider two environmental factors:[46]

- *Excludability.* To what extent can the venture prevent or limit competition from incumbents who develop similar technology?
- *Complementary assets.* To what extent do the complementary assets – production, distribution, reputation, support, etc. – contribute to the value proposition of the technology?

Combining these two dimensions creates four strategy options:

- *Attacker's advantage.* Where the incumbent's complementary assets contribute little or no value, and the start-up cannot preclude development by the incumbent (e.g. where formal intellectual property is irrelevant or enforcement poor), the venture will have an opportunity to disrupt established positions, but technology leadership is likely to be temporary as other new ventures and incumbents respond, resulting in fragmented niche markets in the longer term. This pattern is common in computer components businesses.
- *Ideas factory.* In contrast, where incumbents control the necessary complementary assets, but the venture can preclude effective development of the technology by incumbents, cooperation is essential. The new venture is likely to focus on technological leadership and research, with strong partnerships downstream for commercialization. This pattern tends to reinforce the dominance of incumbents, with the ventures failing to develop or control the necessary complementary assets. This pattern is common in biotechnology.
- *Reputation-based.* Where incumbents control the complementary assets, but the venture cannot prevent competing technology development by the incumbents, ventures face a serious problem of disclosure and other contracting hazards from incumbents. In such cases, a venture will need to seek established partners with caution, and attempt to identify partners with a reputation for fairness in such transactions. Cisco and Intel have both developed such a reputation, and are frequently approached by ventures seeking to exploit their technology. This pattern is common in capital-intensive sectors such as aerospace and automobiles. However, these sectors have a lower 'equilibrium', as established firms have a reputation for expropriation, therefore discouraging start-ups.
- *Greenfield.* Where incumbents' assets are unimportant, and the venture can preclude effective imitation, there is the potential for the venture to dominate an emerging business. Competition and cooperation with incumbents are both viable strategies, depending upon how controllable the technology is, e.g. through establishing standards or platforms, and where value is created in the value chain.

A high proportion of new ventures fail to grow and prosper. Estimates vary by type of business and national context, but typically 40% of new businesses fail in their first year and 60% within the first two. In other words, around 40% survive the first two years. Common reasons for failure include:

- poor financial control
- lack of managerial ability or experience
- no strategy for transition, growth or exit.

TABLE 14.3 Some of the fastest-growing private firms in the UK

Company	Annual growth, % (3-year mean)	Sales 2013/14 (£ million)	Business
Anesco	374.94	106.7	Energy efficiency consultancy
Missguided	191.17	51.0	Online fashion retailer
G2 Energy	178.61	12.8	Electrical and civil engineer
Ovo Energy	140.14	171.7	Energy supplier
AlphaSights	139.73	18.8	Business information provider
LSE Retail	120.17	6.8	Online lighting retailer
Concrete Canvas	118.33	5.1	Concrete impregnated fabrics manufacturer
Earthmill	112.58	13.4	Wind turbine installer

Source: Sunday Times Virgin Fast Track League Table 2014.

There are many ways a new venture can grow and create additional value:

- organic growth through additional sales and diversification
- acquisition of or merger with another company
- sale of the business to another company, or private equity firm
- an initial public offering (IPO) on a stock market.

For example, UK *Sunday Times* Profit Track estimates that of the 500 fastest-growing private firms in the UK, over five years around 100 have merged with or been acquired by other companies or private equity firms, but only ten or so have been floated (Table 14.3). Some of the best-performing ones have been in ICT; others, in service innovation. A separate survey of technology-based start-ups reveals a dominance of Web-based businesses, which demonstrates how much has changed since the Internet bubble burst.

ENTREPRENEURSHIP IN ACTION 14.7

Technology-based High-growth Ventures

Since 2001, the Oxford-based research company Fast Track has compiled a report for the *Sunday Times* newspaper on the top 100 technology-based new ventures in the UK, sponsored by consultants PricewaterhouseCoopers and Microsoft.

(continued)

Following the collapse of the dotcom bubble, the annual survey has provided an excellent barometer of the more robust and consistent technology-based new ventures, which, without reaching the headlines, continue to be created, grow and prosper.

Of the 100 firms studied between 2001 and 2006, 48 had been funded by venture capital or private equity funds. As may be expected, many of the most successful new ventures were based on software or telecommunications technologies, so-called information communication telecommunications (ICT) technologies, but the commercial applications were increasingly dynamic and diverse, including gaming, gambling, music, film, fashion and education. Although most of these firms were only five or six years old, annual sales averaged £5 million, with annual growth of 60%. Examples include:

- Gamesys, a gaming website operator created in 2001, with 50 staff and sales of £9.4 million by 2006
- The Search Works, an advertising consultant for search engines, founded in 1999, eventually employing more than 50 staff, with sales of $18.6 million
- REDTRAY, an e-learning software developer, formed in 2002, reaching 30 staff and sales of £4.5 million
- Ocado, the delivery business for online orders to supermarket Waitrose, created in 2000, and within six years employing almost 1000 staff, with three million deliveries each week and a turnover of $143 million
- Wiggle, an online retailer of sports goods, founded in 1998, and by 2006 with 50 staff and sales of £9.2 million
- Betfair, an online bookmaker and betting website, established in 1999, that seven years later had a turnover of £107 million and employed more than 400 staff.

Source: Sunday Times Tech Track 100, 24th September 2006, www.fasttrack.co.uk, www.pwc.com.

A lack of managerial experience and credibility in their founders can also be a major barrier to funding and growing new ventures. In the early stage, developing relationships with potential customers and suppliers is the most critical, but as the venture grows the relationship and role of partners in the network of a new venture will change. Later, external sources of funding need to be cultivated, which can result in changes of ownership and the dissolution of some of the initial relationships, and substitution for more mature partners in more stable networks. Over time, the roles of different actors in the venture network become more specialized and professional.[47] Individual skills are essential in building and developing such relationships and networks. These skills include:[48]

- *social and interpersonal communication.* To build credibility and promote knowledge sharing

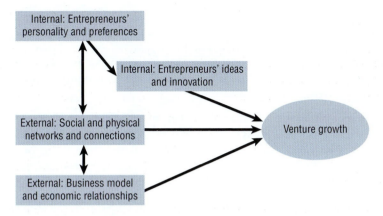

FIGURE 14.2   Internal and external factors influencing new venture growth

Source: Derived from Tove Brink (2014) The impact on growth of outside-in and inside-out innovation, *International Journal of Innovation Management*, **18**(4), doi 1450023.

- *negotiating and balancing skills.* To balance cooperation and competition, and to develop awareness, trust and commitment
- *influencing and visioning skills.* To establish roles, and shares of responsibilities and rewards.

Therefore, the challenge is not only to simultaneously manage the more mature firm and its relations but also to maintain the early focus on innovation. To conclude, new venture growth is a consequence of the interaction of internal factors, such as the entrepreneurs' personalities and capabilities, and external factors such as social and physical network connections. However, as Figure 14.2 indicates, an entrepreneurial disposition is necessary but is not by any means a sufficient condition for innovation or success.

Chapter Summary

- A new venture represents an opportunity to develop and deliver new technology, products or services. However, the majority of new ventures fail after a few years, and very few continue to grow.

- The mythology of the lone risk-taking entrepreneur is unfounded. Internal and external factors contribute to the success and growth of a new venture. Internal factors include the education, experience and capabilities of founders, and a focus on innovation and planning. External factors include access to complementary resources, social and business networks, and the regional and national context.

- The availability of financial resources is a significant constraint, not so much at the initial stages but for subsequent development and growth. However, innovation promotes the development and growth of a new venture, and this demands access to complementary resources and capabilities within the new venture and throughout its external networks.

Key Terms Defined

Complementary capabilities the mixture of diverse experience, expertise and resources that ventures need to grow, partly achieved through multiple founders and partly through external networks.

Gazelles are extremely fast-growing firms, typically double-digit, in terms of sales and employment over a prolonged period. Rare, most estimate less than 5% of all firms.

Muppets (marginal, under-sized, poor performance enterprises) which are more typical, and by most measures such firms are less productive and innovative than larger firms, and contribute less to wealth and employment creation.

NTBFs (new technology-based firms) which are formed around a focal technology, but not necessarily novel, radical or science-based, e.g. any Internet business would qualify. These are different from the majority of new ventures in terms of the founder characteristics and resources required.
Plus, a menagerie:

Unicorns are ventures that have grown to be worth more than $1 billion, even rarer than gazelles!

Discussion Questions

1. What individual founder characteristics influence the success of a new venture?

2. How does innovation affect the growth and profitability of a new venture?

3. Why are complementary resources critical to the development and growth of a new venture?

4. What contribution do the external context and networks make to success?

Further Reading and Resources

There are thousands of books and journal articles on the more general subject of entrepreneurship, but relatively little has been produced on the more specific subject of innovative or technology entrepreneurship. Ed Roberts's *Entrepreneurs in High Technology: Lessons from MIT and Beyond* (Oxford University Press, 1991) is an excellent study of the MIT experience, although perhaps places too much emphasis on the characteristics of individual entrepreneurs. For a broader analysis of technology ventures in the USA, see Martin Kenny's (ed.) *Understanding Silicon Valley: Anatomy of an Entrepreneurial Region* (Stanford University Press, 2000). For a more recent analysis of technological entrepreneurs, see *Inventing Entrepreneurs: Technology Innovators and their Entrepreneurial Journey* by Gerry George and Adam Bock (Prentice Hall, 2008). Ray Oakey's *High-Technology Entrepreneurship* (Routledge, 2012) is a similar study of technology ventures in the UK, but places greater emphasis on how different technologies constrain the opportunities for establishing new ventures, and affect their management and success. For more accessible how-to books, try Ben Horowitz's *The Hard Thing about Hard Things: Building a Business When There Are No Easy Answers* (HarperBusiness, 2014) or *The Lean Startup: How Constant Innovation Creates Radically Successful Businesses*, by Eric Ries (Portfolio Penguin, 2011).

For more academic approaches, a special issue of the *Strategic Management Journal* (volume 22, July 2001) examines entrepreneurial strategies, and includes a number of papers on technology-based firms, and a special issue of the journal *Research Policy* (volume 32, 2003) features papers on technology spin-offs and start-ups. A special issue of the *Journal of Product Innovation Management* examines technology commercialization and entrepreneurship (volume 25, 2008), and a special issue of *Industrial and Corporate Change* focuses on university spin-outs (**16**(4), 2007). Most texts on entrepreneurship and new business fail to cover the factors which influence the success and growth of new ventures, in particular the role of innovation, but the worthy exception is the work by our colleagues David Storey and Francis Green entitled *Small Business and Entrepreneurship* (Financial Times/Prentice Hall, 2010), which provides a thorough review of the research on venture growth. For more succinct but excellent reviews of the research on the initial conditions which influence subsequent success and growth, see Gao, Li, Cheng and Shi's (2010) 'Impact of initial conditions on new venture Success' (*International Journal of Innovation Management*, **14**(1), 41–56) and Geroski, Mata and Portugal's (2010) 'Founding conditions and the survival of new firms' (*Strategic Management Journal*, **31**, 510–29). For a comprehensive empirical overview, see Alex Coad's *The Growth of Firms: A Survey of Theories and Empirical Evidence* (Edward Elgar, 2009). A recent special issue on high-growth firms was published in the journal *Industrial and Corporate Change* (**23**(1), 2014).

References

1. Storey, D. and F. Greene (2010) *Small Business & Entrepreneurship*, Upper Saddle River, NJ: Prentice Hall; Coad, A. (2009) *The Growth of Firms: A Survey of Theories and Empirical Evidence*, Cheltenham: Edward Elgar.

2. Song, M., K. Podoynitsyna, H. van der Bij and J.I.M. Halman (2008) Success factors in new ventures: A meta-analysis, *Journal of Product Innovation Management*, **25**: 7–27.

3. Storey, D. and F. Green (2010) *Small Business and Entrepreneurship*, Upper Saddle River, NJ: Prentice Hall; Storey, D. (1994) *Understanding the Small Business Sector*, Boston: Thomson Learning; Mason, G., K. Bishop and C. Robinson (2009) *Business Growth and Innovation*, London: NESTA.

4. Barr, S.H., T. Baker, S.K. Markham and A.I. Kingon (2009) Bridging the Valley of Death: Lessons learned from 14 years of commercialization of technology education, *Academy of Management Learning and Education*, **8**(3): 370–88; Beaver, G. (2007) The strategy payoff for smaller enterprises, *Journal of Business Strategy*, **28**(1): 9–23; Lyles, M.A., I.S. Baird, B. Orris, B. and K. Kuratko (1993) Formalised planning in business: Increasing strategic choice, *Journal of Small Business Management*, **31**(2): 38–51.

5. Birley, S. (2002) Universities, academics and spin-out companies: Lessons from Imperial, *International Journal of Entrepreneurship Education*, **1**(1): 133–54.

6. Coad, A. (2009) *The Growth of Firms: A Survey of Theories and Empirical Evidence*, Cheltenham: Edward Elgar; Capelleras, J.L. and F.J. Greene (2008) The determinants and growth implications of venture creation speed, *Entrepreneurship and Regional Development*, **20**(4): 317–43; Koeller, C.T. and T.G. Lechler (2006) Employment growth in high-tech new ventures, *Journal of Labor Research*, **27**(2): 135–47; Persson, H. (2004) The survival and growth of new establishments in Sweden, *Small Business Economics*, **23**(5): 423–40.

7. Geroski, P.A., J. Mata and P. Portugal (2010) Founding conditions and the survival of new firms, *Strategic Management Journal*, **31**: 510–29; Gao, J., J. Li, Y. Cheng and S. Shi, S. (2010) Impact of initial conditions on new venture success, *International Journal of Innovation Management*, **14**(1): 41–56; Wadhwa, V., R.B. Freeman and B.A. Rissing (2008) Education and technology entrepreneurship, *Social Science Research Network*, working paper 1127248.

8. Saridakis, G., K. Mole and D.J. Storey (2008) New small firm survival in England, *Empirica*, **35**: 25–39.

9. Birley, S. and P. Westhead (1994) A taxonomy of business start-up reasons and their impact on firm growth and size, *Journal of Business Venturing*, **9**(1): 7–31;

Davila, A., G. Foster and M. Gupta (2003) Venture capital financing and the growth of start-up firms, *Journal of Business Venturing*, **18**(6): 689–708.

10. Cosh, A., A. Hughes, A. Bullock and I. Milner (2009) *SME Finance and Innovation in the Current Economic Crisis*, Cambridge: Centre for Business Research, University of Cambridge.

11. Storey, D. and B. Tether (1998) New technology-based firms in the European Union, *Research Policy*, **26**: 933–46; Tether, B. and D. Storey (1998) Smaller firms and Europe's high technology sectors: A framework for analysis and some statistical evidence, *Research Policy*, **26**(9): 947–71.

12. Koellinger, P. (2008) The relationship between technology, innovation, and firm performance: Empirical evidence from e-business in Europe, *Research Policy*, **37** (8): 1317–28.

13. Mayer-Hauga, K., S. Read, J. Brinckmann *et al.* (2013) Entrepreneurial talent and venture performance: A meta-analytic investigation of SMEs, *Research Policy*, **42**(6): 1251–73; Delmar, F. and S. Shane (2003) Does business planning facilitate the development of new ventures? *Strategic Management Journal*, **24**: 1165–85.

14. Arvanitis, S. and T. Stucki (2014) The impact of venture capital on the persistence of innovation activities of start-ups, *Small Business Economics*, **42**(5): 849–70.

15. Stucki, T. (2013) Success of start-up firms: The role of financial constraints, *Industrial and Corporate Change*, **23**(1): 25–64.

16. Agarwal, R. and S.K. Shah (2014) Knowledge sources of entrepreneurship: Firm formation by academic, user and employee innovators, *Research Policy*, **43**(7): 1109–33.

17. Tidd, J. (2014) Conjoint innovation: Building a bridge between innovation and entrepreneurship, *International Journal of Innovation Management*, **18**(1): 1–20; Tidd, J. (2012) It takes two to tango: How multiple entrepreneurs interact to innovate, *European Business Review*, **24**(4): 58–61.

18. Drucker, P. (1985) *Innovation and Entrepreneurship*, New York: Harper & Row.

19. Oakey, R. (2012) *High-Technology Entrepreneurship*, Oxford: Routledge; Lockett, A., G. Murray and M. Wright (2002) Do UK venture capitalists still have a bias against investment in new technology firms? *Research Policy*, **31**(6): 1009–30.

20. Baum, J. and B. Silverman (2004) Picking winners or building them? Alliance, intellectual and human capital as selection criteria in venture financing and performance of biotechnology start-ups, *Journal of Business Venturing*, **19**(5): 411–36.

21. Frankish, J., R. Roberts and D. Storey (2008) *Measuring Business Activity in the UK*, Poole: Barclays Bank.

22. Head, B. (2003) Redefining business success: Distinguishing between closure and failure, *Small Business Economics*, **21**(1): 51–9.

23. Grundstrom, C., R. Sjöström, A. Uddenberg and A. Öhrwall Rönnbäck (2012) Fast-growing SMEs and the role of innovation, *International Journal of Innovation Management*, **16**(3): 1–19.

24. Small Business Research Centre (1992) *The State of British Enterprise: Growth, Innovation and Competitiveness in Small and Medium Sized Firms*, Cambridge: SBRC.

25. Hoffman, K., M. Parejo, J. Bessant and L. Perren (1998) Small firms, R&D, technology and innovation in the UK: A literature review, *Technovation*, **18**(1): 39–55.

26. Calori, R. (1990) Effective strategies in emerging industries, in: R. Loveridge and M. Pitt (eds) *The Strategic Management of Technological Innovation*, Chichester: John Wiley & Sons Ltd, 21–38; Walsh, V., J. Niosi and P. Mustar (1995) Small firms formation in biotechnology: A comparison of France, Britain and Canada, *Technovation*, **15**(5): 303–28; Westhead, P., D. Storey and M. Cowling (1995) An exploratory analysis of the factors associated with survival of independent high technology firms in Great Britain, in: F. Chittenden, M. Robertson and I. Marshall (eds) *Small Firms: Partnership for Growth in Small Firms*, London: Paul Chapman, 63–99.

27. Tether, B. and D. Storey (1998) Smaller firms and Europe's high technology sectors: A framework for analysis and some statistical evidence, *Research Policy*, **26**: 947–71.

28. MacPherson, A. (1997) The contribution of external service inputs to the product development efforts of small manufacturing firms, *R&D Management*, **27**(2): 127–43.

29. Rothwell, R. and M. Dodgson (1993) SMEs: Their role in industrial and economic change, *International Journal of Technology Management*, **Special Issue**: 8–22.

30. Moote, B. (1993) *Financial Constraints to the Growth and Development of Small High Technology Firms*, Cambridge: Small Business Research Centre, University of Cambridge; Oakey, R. (1993) Predatory networking: The role of small firms in the development of the British biotechnology industry, *International Small Business Journal*, **11**(3): 3–22.

31. Storey, D. (1992) United Kingdom: Case study, in: *Small and Medium Sized Enterprises, Technology and Competitiveness*, Paris: OECD; Tang, N. *et al.* (1995) Technological alliances between HEIs and SMEs: Examining the current evidence, in: D. Bennett and F. Steward (eds), *Proceedings of the European Conference on the Management of Technology: Technological Innovation and Global Challenges*, Birmingham: Aston University.

32. Tether, B. (1998) Small and large firms: Sources of unequal innovations? *Research Policy*, **27**: 725–45.

33. Tether, B., J. Smith and A. Thwaites (1997) Smaller enterprises and innovations in the UK: The SPRU Innovations Database revisited, *Research Policy*, **26**: 19–32.

34. Strerlacchini, A. (1999) Do innovative activities matter to small firms in non-R&D-intensive industries? *Research Policy*, **28**: 819–32.

35. Hall, G. (1991) *Factors associated with relative performance amongst small firms in the British instrumentation sector*, Working Paper No. 213, Manchester: Manchester Business School.

36. Oakey, R., R. Rothwell and S. Cooper (1988) *The Management of Innovation in High Technology Small Firms*, London: Pinter.

37. Keeble, D. (1993) *Regional Influences and Policy in New Technology-based Firms: Creation and Growth*, Cambridge: Small Business Research Centre, University of Cambridge.

38. Dickson, K., A. Coles and H. Smith (1995) Scientific curiosity as business: An analysis of the scientific entrepreneur, paper presented at the 18th National Small Firms Policy and Research Conference, Manchester; Lee, J. (1993) Small firms' innovation in two technological settings, *Research Policy*, **24**: 391–401.

39. Bruderl, J. and P. Preisendorfer (2000) Fast-growing businesses, *International Journal of Sociology*, **30**: 45–70.

40. Lee, C., K. Lee and J. Pennings (2001) Internal capabilities, external networks, and performance: A study of technology-based ventures, *Strategic Management Journal*, **22**: 615–40.

41. Almeida, P., G. Dokko and L. Rosenkopf (2003) Startup size and the mechanisms of external learning: Increasing opportunity and decreasing ability? *Research Policy*, **32**: 301–15.

42. Freel, M. (2003) Sectoral patterns of small firm innovation, networking and proximity, *Research Policy*, **32**: 751–70.

43. Zahra, S. and W. Bogner (2000) Technology strategy and software new ventures performance, *Journal of Business Venturing*, **15**(2): 135–73.

44. Deeds, D., D. DeCarolis and J. Coombs (2000) Dynamic capabilities and new product development in high technology ventures: An empirical analysis of new biotechnology firms, *Journal of Business Venturing*, **15**(3): 211–29.

45. George, G., S. Zahra and D. Robley Wood (2002) The effects of business–university alliances on innovative output and financial performance: A study of publicly traded biotechnology companies, *Journal of Business Venturing*, **17**: 577–609.

46. Gans, J. and S. Stern (2003) The product and the market for 'ideas': Commercialization strategies for technology entrepreneurs, *Research Policy*, **32**: 333–50.

47. Oberg, C. and C. Grundstrom (2009) Challenges and opportunities in innovative firms' network development, *International Journal of Innovation Management*, **13**(4): 593–614.

48. Ritala, P., L. Armila and K. Blomqvist (2009) Innovation orchestration capability, *International Journal of Innovation Management*, **13**(4): 569–91.

Deeper Dive explanations of innovation concepts and ideas are available on the Innovation Portal at **www.innovation-portal.info**

Quizzes to test yourself further are available online via the Innovation Portal at **www.innovation-portal.info**

Summary of online resources for Chapter 14 –
all material is available via the Innovation Portal at
www.innovation-portal.info

Cases	Media	Tools	Activities	Deeper Dives
• Ihavemoved. com	• Melissa Clark-Reynolds • Simon Murdoch	—	• Partner Search • Business model innovation	• Guide to building learning networks

PART V

CREATING VALUE

There is a significant difference between generating an innovation or new venture and creating and capturing the value from it. How do we ensure the social gains are there if we are trying to change the world? How do we make sure there is a stream of income from its widespread use? How do we recover our – and other people's – investment of time, energy and money? How do we protect ourselves from people copying our idea and capitalizing on all our pioneering? And even if we fail, how do we capture the learning about how the innovation process works so that next time we try something we can increase our chances of success?

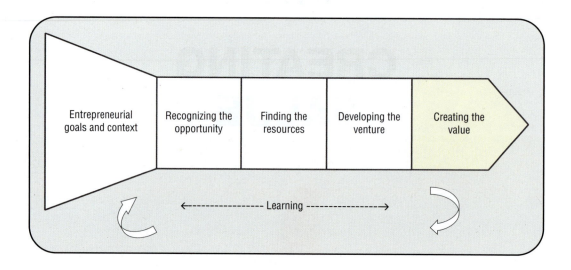

Chapter 15

Exploiting Knowledge and Intellectual Property

LEARNING OBJECTIVES

By the end of this chapter you will develop an understanding of:

- identifying different types of knowledge and intellectual property
- choosing and applying appropriate methods of knowledge management
- developing a strategy for licensing intellectual property.

Innovation and Knowledge

In this chapter we discuss how individuals and organizations identify 'what they know' and how best to exploit this. We examine the related fields of knowledge management, organizational learning and intellectual property. Key issues include the nature of knowledge, for example explicit versus tacit knowledge; the locus of knowledge, such as individual versus organizational; and the distribution of knowledge across an organization. More narrowly, knowledge management is concerned with identifying, translating, sharing and exploiting the knowledge within an organization. One of the key issues is the relationship between individual and organizational learning, and how the former is translated into the latter, and ultimately into new processes, products and businesses. Finally, we review different types of formal intellectual property, and how these can be used in the development and commercialization of innovations.

In essence, managing knowledge involves five critical tasks:

- generating and acquiring new knowledge
- identifying and codifying existing knowledge
- storing and retrieving knowledge
- sharing and distributing knowledge across the organization
- exploiting and embedding knowledge in processes, products and services.

Generating and Acquiring Knowledge

Organizations can acquire knowledge by experience, experimentation or acquisition. Of these, learning from experience appears to be the least effective. In practice, organizations do not easily translate experience into knowledge. Moreover, learning may be unintentional or it may not result in improved effectiveness. Organizations can learn incorrectly, and they can learn that which is incorrect or harmful, such as learning faulty or irrelevant skills or self-destructive habits. This can lead an organization to accumulate experience of an inferior technique, and may prevent it from gaining sufficient experience of a superior procedure to make it rewarding to use, sometimes called the 'competency trap'.

Experimentation is a more systematic approach to learning. It is a central feature of formal R&D activities, market research and some organizational alliances and networks. When undertaken with intent, a strategy of learning through incremental trial and error acknowledges the complexities of existing technologies and markets, as well as the uncertainties associated with technology and market change and with forecasting the future. The use of alliances for learning is less common and requires the intent to use them as an opportunity for learning, a receptivity to external know-how and partners of sufficient transparency. Whether the acquisition of know-how results in organizational learning depends on the rationale for the acquisition and the process of acquisition and transfer. For example, the cumulative effect of outsourcing various technologies on the basis of comparative transaction costs may limit future technological options and reduce competitiveness in the long term.

A more active approach to the acquisition of knowledge involves scanning the internal and external environments. As we discussed in Chapter 7, searching consists of looking for, filtering and evaluating potential opportunities from outside the organization, including related and emerging technologies, new markets and services, which can be exploited by applying or combining with existing competencies. Opportunity recognition, which is a precursor to entrepreneurial behaviour, is often associated with a flash of genius, but in reality is probably more often the result of a laborious process of environmental scanning. External scanning can be conducted at various levels. It can be an operational initiative, with market- or technology-focused managers becoming more conscious of new developments within their own environments, or a top-driven initiative, where venture managers or professional capital firms are used to monitor and invest in potential opportunities.

Identifying and Codifying Knowledge

It is useful to begin with a clearer idea of what we mean by 'knowledge'. It has become all things to all people, ranging from corporate IT systems to the skills and experience of individuals. There is no universally accepted definition, but the following hierarchy is helpful:

- *Data* are a set of discrete raw observations, numbers, words, records and so on. Typically easy to structure, record, store and manipulate electronically.
- *Information* is data that have been organized, grouped or categorized into some pattern. The organization may consist of categorization, calculation or synthesis. This organization of data endows information with relevance and purpose, and in most cases adds value to data.
- *Knowledge* is information that has been contextualized, given meaning and therefore made relevant and easier to operationalize. The transformation of information into knowledge involves making comparisons and contrasts, identifying relationships and inferring consequences. Therefore, knowledge is deeper and richer than information, and includes framed expertise, experience, values and insights.

The concept of disembodied knowledge can become a very abstract idea, but it can be assessed in practice. Here are some types of knowledge identified in a study of the biotechnology and telecommunications industries:[1]

- variety of knowledge
- depth of knowledge
- source of knowledge, internal and external
- evaluation of knowledge and awareness of competencies
- knowledge management practices, the capability to identify, share and acquire knowledge
- use of IT systems to store, share and reuse knowledge
- identification and assimilation of external knowledge
- commercial knowledge of markets and customers
- competitor knowledge, current and potential
- knowledge of supplier networks and value chain
- regulatory knowledge
- financial and funding stakeholder knowledge
- knowledge of intellectual property (IPR), own and others'
- knowledge practices, including documentation, intranets, work organization and multidisciplinary teams and projects.

There are essentially two different types of knowledge, each with different characteristics:

- **Explicit knowledge,** which can be codified, that is expressed in numerical, textual or graphical terms, and therefore is more easily communicated, e.g. the design of a product.

- **Tacit or implicit knowledge**, which is personal, experiential, context-specific and hard to formalize and communicate, e.g. how to ride a bicycle.

Note that the distinction between explicit and tacit is not necessarily the result of the difficulty or complexity of the knowledge but rather how easy it is to express that knowledge. Each of these contribute to the intellectual assets and innovative performance of companies, but in different ways. For example, the tacit knowledge of individuals and groups may be necessary to exploit the more explicit types of knowledge, such as R&D and IPR. In this way the interaction and combination of explicit and tacit knowledge can strengthen the position and reputation of an organization.

 Video Clip exploring Xerox and its range of knowledge management programmes is available on the Innovation Portal at **www.innovation-portal.info**

It is also useful to distinguish between learning *how* and learning *why*. Learning how involves improving or transferring existing skills, whereas learning why aims to understand the underlying logic or causal factors with a view to applying the knowledge in new contexts.

As we have seen, knowledge can be embodied in people, organizational culture, routines and tools, technologies, processes and systems. Organizations consist of a variety of individuals, groups and functions with different cultures, goals and frames of reference. Knowledge management consists of identifying and sharing knowledge across these disparate entities. There is a range of integrating mechanisms which can help to do this. Nonaka and Takeuchi argue that the conversion of tacit to explicit knowledge is a critical mechanism underlying the link between individual and organizational knowledge. They argue that all new knowledge originates with an individual, but that through a process of dialogue, discussion, experience sharing and observation such knowledge is amplified at the group and organizational levels. This creates an expanding community of interaction, or 'knowledge network', which crosses intra- and inter-organizational levels and boundaries. Such knowledge networks are a means to accumulate knowledge from outside the organization, share it widely within the organization and store it for future use. This transformation of individual knowledge into organizational knowledge involves four cycles:[2]

- *Socialization.* Tacit to tacit knowledge, in which the knowledge of an individual or group is shared with others. Culture, socialization and communities of practice are critical for this.
- *Externalization.* Tacit to explicit knowledge, through which the knowledge is made explicit and codified in some persistent form. This is the most novel aspect of Nonaka's model. He argues that tacit knowledge can be transformed into explicit knowledge through a process of conceptualization and crystallization. Boundary objects are critical here.
- *Combination.* Explicit to explicit knowledge, where different sources of explicit knowledge are pooled and exchanged. The role of organizational processes and technological systems are central to this.
- *Internalization.* Explicit to tacit knowledge, whereby other individuals or groups learn through practice. This is the traditional domain of organizational learning.

Storing and Retrieving Knowledge

Storing knowledge is not a trivial problem, even now that the electronic storage and distribution of data is so cheap and easy. The biggest hurdle is the codification of tacit knowledge. The other common problem is to provide incentives to contribute, retrieve and reuse relevant knowledge. Many organizations have developed excellent knowledge intranet systems, but these are often underutilized in practice.

INNOVATION IN ACTION 15.1

Knowledge Management at Arup

Arup is an international engineering consultancy firm which provides planning, designing, engineering and project management services. The business demands the simultaneous achievement of innovative solutions and significant time compression imposed by client and regulatory requirements.

Since 1999, the organization has established a wide range of knowledge management initiatives to encourage sharing know-how and experience across projects. These initiatives range from organizational processes and mechanisms, such as cross-functional communications meetings and skills networks, to technology-based approaches, such as the Ovebase database and intranet.

To date, the organizational processes have been more successful than the technology-based approaches. For example, a survey of engineers in the firm indicated that in design and problem solving discussions with colleagues were rated as being twice as valuable as knowledge databases, and consequently engineers were four times as likely to rely on colleagues. Two primary reasons were cited for this. First, the difficulty of codifying tacit knowledge. Engineering consultancy involves a great deal of tacit knowledge and project experience which is difficult to store and retrieve electronically. Second, the complex engineering and unique environmental context of each project limits the reusing of standardized knowledge and experience.

In practice, there are two common but distinct approaches to knowledge management. The first is based on investments in IT, usually based on groupware and intranet technologies. These are the favoured approach of many management consultants. But introducing knowledge management into an organization consists of much more than technology and training. It can require fundamental changes to organizational structure, processes and culture. The second approach is more people- and process-based, and attempts to encourage staff to identify, store, share and use information throughout the organization. However, the storage, retrieval and reuse of knowledge demands much more than good IT systems. It also requires incentives to contribute to and use knowledge from such systems, whereas many organizations instead encourage and promote the generation and use of new knowledge.

Richard Hall goes some way towards identifying the components of organizational memory. His main purpose is to articulate intangible resources and he distinguishes between intangible assets and intangible competencies. Assets include **intellectual property rights** and reputation. Competencies include the skills and know-how of employees, suppliers and distributors, as well as the collective attributes which constitute organizational culture. His empirical work, based on a survey and case studies, indicates that managers believe that the most significant of these intangible resources are the company's reputation and employees' know-how, both of which may be a function of organizational culture. These include:[3]

- *Intangible*, off balance sheet assets, such as patents, licences, trademarks, contracts and protectable data.
- *Positional*, which are the result of previous endeavour, i.e. with a high path dependency, such as processes and operating systems, and individual and corporate reputation and networks.
- *Functional*, which are either individual skills and know-how or team skills and know-how, within the company, at the suppliers or distributors.
- *Cultural*, including traditions of quality, customer service, human resources or innovation.

The key questions in each case are:

Activity to help you explore this theme, identifying innovation capabilities, is available on the Innovation Portal at **www.innovation-portal.info**

1. Are we making the best use of this resource?
2. How else could it be used?
3. Is the scope for synergy identified and exploited?
4. Are we aware of the key linkages which exist between the resources?

Sharing and Distributing Knowledge

In practice, large organizations often do not know what they know. Many organizations now have databases and groupware to help store, retrieve and share data and information, but such systems are often confined to 'hard' data and information, rather than more tacit knowledge. As a result, functional groups or business units with potentially synergistic information may not be aware of where such information could be applied.

Knowledge sharing and distribution is the process by which information from different sources is shared and, therefore, leads to new knowledge or understanding. Greater organizational learning occurs when more of an organization's components obtain new knowledge and recognize it as being of potential use. Tacit knowledge is not easily imitated by competitors, because it is not fully encoded, but for the same reasons it may not be fully visible to all members of an organization. As a result, organizational units with potentially synergistic information may not be aware of where such information could be applied. The speed and extent to which knowledge is shared between members of an organization is likely to be a function of how codified the knowledge is.

This process of connecting different knowledge and people is underpinned by communities of practice. A **community of practice** is a group of people related by a shared task or process or by the need to solve a problem, rather than by formal structural or functional relationships.[4] Through practice, a group within which knowledge is shared becomes a community of practice through a common understanding of what it does, of how to do it and how it relates to other communities of practice.

Within communities of practice, people share tacit knowledge and learn through experimentation. Therefore, the formation and maintenance of such communities represents an important link between individual and organizational learning. These communities naturally emerge around local work practice and so tend to reinforce functional or professional silos, but also can extend to wider, dispersed networks of similar practitioners.

The existence of communities of practice facilitates the sharing of knowledge within a community, owing to both the sense of collective identity and the existence of a significant common knowledge base. However, the sharing of knowledge between communities is much more problematic, owing to the lack of both these elements. Thus, the dynamics of knowledge sharing within and between communities of practice are likely to be very different, with the sharing of knowledge between communities typically being much more complex, difficult and problematic.

Many factors can prevent the sharing of knowledge between communities of practice, such as the distinctiveness of different knowledge bases and the lack of common knowledge, goals, assumptions and interpretative frameworks. These differences significantly increase the difficulty not just of sharing knowledge between communities but also of appreciating the knowledge of another community.

However, there are some proven mechanisms to help knowledge transfer between different communities of practice:[5]

- An organizational **knowledge translator** is an individual who is able to express the interests of one community in terms of another community's perspective. Therefore, the translator must be sufficiently conversant with both knowledge domains and trusted by both communities. An example of a translator would be a 'heavyweight product manager' in new product development who bridges different technical groups, or bridges the technical and marketing groups.
- A **knowledge broker** differs from a translator in that they participate in different communities rather than simply mediate between them. They represent overlaps between communities, and are typically people loosely linked to several communities through weak ties who are able to facilitate knowledge flows between them. An example could be a quality manager responsible for the quality of a process that crosses several different functional groups.
- A **boundary object or practice** is something of interest to two or more communities of practice. Different communities of practice will have a stake in it, but from different perspectives. A boundary object could be a shared document, e.g. a quality manual; an artefact, e.g. a prototype; a technology, e.g. a database; or a practice, e.g. a product design. A boundary object provides an opportunity for

Video Clip of an interview with Francisco Pinheiro of Atos highlighting some of these themes is available on the Innovation Portal at **www.innovation-portal.info**

discussion and debate (and conflict) and therefore can encourage communication between different communities of practice.

For example, formally appointed knowledge brokers can be used to systematically scavenge the organization for old or unused ideas, to pass these around the organization and imagine their application in different contexts. Hewlett-Packard, for instance, created a SpaM group to help identify and share good practice among its 150 business divisions. Before the new group was formed, divisions were unlikely to share information, because they often competed for resources and were measured against each other. Similarly, Skandia, a Swedish insurance company active in overseas markets, attempted to identify, encourage and measure its intellectual capital, and appointed a 'knowledge manager' who was responsible for this. The company developed a set of indicators that it used both to manage knowledge internally and for external financial reporting.

 Case Study of Joint Solutions Ltd, an intermediary between medical professionals and companies that make medical devices, is available on the Innovation Portal at **www.innovation-portal.info**

More generally, cross-functional team working can help to promote this intercommunal exchange. Functional diversity tends to extend the range of knowledge available and increase the number of options considered, but it can also have a negative effect on group cohesiveness. The cost of projects and efficiency of decision making. However, a major benefit of cross-functional team working is the access it provides to the bodies of knowledge that are external to the team. In general, a high frequency of knowledge sharing outside of a group is associated with improved technical and project performance, as gatekeeper individuals pick up and import vital signals and knowledge. In particular, cross-functional composition in teams, it could be argued, permits access to disciplinary knowledge outside. Therefore, cross-functional team working is a critical way of promoting the exchange of knowledge and practice across disciplines and communities.

INNOVATION IN ACTION 15.2

Profiting from Digital Media

The business model for capturing the value from video was simple but conservative: own and enforce the copyright, global cinema release, followed by DVD rental and sale and, lastly, TV and other broadcast. The DVD stage was critical, as it generated income of $23.4 billion in the USA in 2007, compared to $9.6 billion from cinema release. Note that when DVD was introduced in 1997, three of the major studios initially refused to publish on it, as they feared losing revenue from the existing proven VHS tape format.

In 2013, the value of digital movie purchases grew to more than $1 billion, video streaming to more than $3 billion, but despite a decline of 10%, physical DVD and Blu-ray sales and rentals still accounted for almost $10 billion, demonstrating the slow pace of substitution.[6] Therefore, the industry has begun to promote the successor to DVD, the high-definition DVD. After a stupid format war, Blu-ray became the new standard for high-definition disks early in 2008. Initial sales of the new format have been slow, not helped by uncertainty of the format war, with nine million

Blu-ray disks shipped in 2007, compared to nine billion conventional DVDs – just 0.1% of the market (in addition some 40 million Blu-ray PS3 games were sold – since its launch in 2006 the Sony PlayStation 3 has sold some 11 million games consoles which also play Blu-ray disks). Surveys in the USA and Europe suggest that 80% of consumers are happy with the picture and sound quality of DVD and standard definition broadcast. Therefore, formats such as Blu-ray and high-definition satellite and cable broadcasts are aimed at the 20% 'early adopters' who value (i.e. are prepared to pay a premium for) higher-definition pictures and sound, primarily for films and sports coverage.

However, for the majority who favour cost and convenience over quality, the Internet is the current preferred medium, legal or otherwise. Illegal sites lead the way, such as ZML which offers 1700 movies for (illegal) download, whereas to date the legal services like MovieFlix and FilmOn tend to be restricted to independent or amateur content. Hollywood has been slow to adapt its business model, and still relies on cinema releases, followed by DVD rental and sales, and finally broadcast. Legal download and streaming offer the potential for lower cost (and prices), as this removes much of the cost of creating, distributing and selling physical media, as well as greater convenience for consumers in terms of choice and flexibility. However, DVD sales depend on the major chain stores for distribution, for example in the USA Wal-Mart accounts for around 40% of sales, and this represents a powerful resistance to change. As a result, in 2008 legal online film distribution was only around $58 million in the USA, less than 5% of total film sales. Television broadcasters have been faster to adopt such services, such as the BBC iPlayer in the UK, mainly because their current business model is based on subscription or advertising, without the film studios' legacy of reliance on physical media and retail distributors. In the USA, Apple iTunes and TV and the Microsoft Xbox have begun to dominate the emerging market for download video rental, but copyright issues have restricted the legal sale of video by download.

As a result of the growing importance of Internet sales of video material, in 2007 the Writers' Guild of America went on strike for better payment terms for electronic distribution and sales. The Hollywood studios' offer was for the payments for Internet sales to be based on the precedent set by DVD – 1.2% of gross receipts – whereas the writers wanted something closer to book or film publishing – 2.5% of gross. The final settlement, reached in February 2008, was a compromise, with a royalty on download rentals of 1.2% of gross, and 0.36–0.70% of gross on download sales, and up to 2% where video streaming is part-funded by advertising. A partial victory for the authors, but this compares with 20% of gross receipts claimed by some leading actors of blockbusters. Clearly, there is work to be done on the final business model for the creation, sale and distribution of digital video. Greater clarity of the regime for managing intellectual property is a start, and faster broadband will soon make higher-quality download practical for the mass markets, so all that remains is a little innovation in the business model.

Tool to help you explore knowledge management, absorptive capacity audit, is available on the Innovation Portal at **www.innovation-portal.info**

Sources: *The Economist*, 23rd February 2008, **386**(8568); *ALCS News*, Spring 2008.

Exploiting Intellectual Property

In some cases, knowledge, and in particular its more explicit or codified forms, can be commercialized by licensing or selling the intellectual property rights (IPR), rather than the more difficult and uncertain route of developing new processes, products or businesses.

For example, in one year IBM reported licence income of $1 billion, and in the USA the total royalty income of industry from licensing is around $100 billion. Much of this is from payments for licences to use software, music or films. For example, in 2005 the global sales of legal music downloads exceeded $1 billion (although illegal downloads are estimated to be worth three to four times this figure), still only around 5% of all music company revenue, with music downloaded to mobile phones accounting for almost a quarter of this. Patterns of use vary by country. For example, in Japan 99.8% of all music downloads are to mobile phones rather than to dedicated MP3 players. However, despite the growth of legal sites for downloading music and an aggressive programme of pursuing users of illegal file-sharing sites, the level of illegal downloads has not declined.

This clearly demonstrates two of the many problems associated with intellectual property: these may provide some legal rights, but such rights are useless unless they can be effectively enforced; and once in the public domain, imitation or illegal use is very likely. For these reasons, secrecy is often a more effective alternative to seeking IPR. However, IPR can be highly effective in some circumstances and, as we argue later, can be used in less obvious ways to help to identify innovations and assess competitors. A range of IPR exists, but those most applicable to technology and innovation are patents, copyright and design rights and registration.

Patents

All developed countries have some form of patent legislation, the aim of which is to encourage innovation by allowing a limited monopoly, usually for 20 years, and more recently many developing and emerging economies have been encouraged to sign up to the TRIPS (Trade Related Intellectual Property System). Legal regimes differ in the detail, but in most countries the issue of a **patent** requires certain legal tests to be satisfied:

- *Novelty*. No part of 'prior art', including publications, written, oral or anticipation. In most countries the first to file the patent is granted the rights, rather the first to invent.
- *Inventive step*. 'Not obvious to a person skilled in the art.' This is a relative test, as the assumed level of skill is higher in some fields than others. For example, Genentech was granted a patent for the plasminogen activator t-PA, which helps to reduce blood clots, but despite its novelty, a Court of Appeal revoked the patent on the grounds that it did not represent an inventive step because its development was deemed to be obvious to researchers in the field.
- *Industrial application*. Utility test requires the invention to be capable of being applied to a machine, product or process. In practice a patent must specify an application for the technology, and additional patents be sought for any additional application. For example, Unilever developed Ceramides and patented their use in a wide range of applications.

However, it did not apply for a patent for application of the technology to shampoos, which was subsequently granted to a competitor.

- *Patentable subject.* e.g. discoveries and formula cannot be patented, and in Europe neither can software (the subject of copyright) or new organisms, although both these are patentable in the USA. For example, contrast the mapping of the human genome in the USA and Europe: in the USA the research is being conducted by a commercial laboratory which is patenting the outcomes, and in Europe by a group of public laboratories which is publishing the outcomes on the Internet.
- *Clear and complete disclosure.* Note that a patent provides only certain legal property rights, and in the case of infringement the patent holder needs to take the appropriate legal action. In some cases secrecy may be a preferable strategy. Conversely, national patent databases represent a large and detailed reservoir of technological innovations which can be interrogated for ideas.

Patents can also be used to identify and assess innovation, at the firm, sector or national level. However, great care needs to be taken when making such assessments, because patents are only a partial indicator of innovation.

The main advantages of patent data are that they reflect the corporate capacity to generate innovation, are available at a detailed level of technology over long periods of time, are comprehensive in the sense that they cover small as well as large firms and are used by practitioners themselves. However, patenting tends to occur early in the development process, and therefore can be a poor measure of the output of development activities, telling us nothing about the economic or commercial potential of the innovation. (See Figure 15.1 and Figure 15.2.)

Crude counts of the number of patents filed by a firm, sector or country reveal little, but the quality of patents can be assessed by a count of how often a given patent is cited in later patents. This provides a good indicator of its technical quality, albeit after the event, although not necessarily commercial potential. Highly cited patents are generally of much greater importance than patents which are never cited, or cited only a few times. The reason for this is that a patent which contains an important new invention – or major advance – can set off a stream of follow-on inventions, all of which may cite the original, important invention upon which they are building.

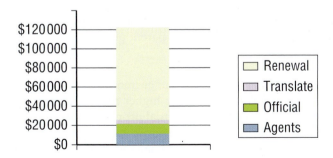

FIGURE 15.1 Typical lifetime cost of a single patent from the European Patent Office

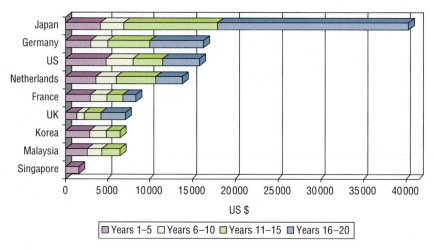

FIGURE 15.2   Lifetime patent costs in different national markets

The most useful indicators of innovation based on patents are (Table 15.1):

- *Number of patents*. Indicates the level of technology activity, but crude patent counts reflect little more than the propensity to patent of a firm, sector or country.
- *Cites per patent*. Indicates the impact of a company's patents.
- *Current impact index (CII)*. This is a fundamental indicator of patent portfolio quality. It is the number of times the company's previous five years of patents, in a technology area, were cited from the current year, divided by the average citations received.
- *Technology strength (TS)*. Indicates the strength of the patent portfolio, and is the number of patents multiplied by the current impact index, i.e. patent portfolio size inflated or deflated by patent quality.
- *Technology cycle time (TCT)*. Indicates the speed of invention, and is the median age, in years, of the patent references cited on the front page of the patent.
- *Science linkage (SL)*. Indicates how leading edge the technology is, and is the average number of science papers referenced on the front page of the patent.
- *Science strength (SS)*. Indicates how much the patent applies basic science, and is the number of patents multiplied by science linkage, i.e. patent portfolio size inflated or deflated by the extent of science linkage.

Companies whose patents have above-average current impact indices (CII) and science linkage (SL) indicators tend to have significantly higher market-to-book ratios and stock-market returns. However, having a strong intellectual property portfolio does not, of course, guarantee a company's success. Many additional factors influence the ability of a company to move from quality patents to innovation and financial and market performance. The decade of troubles at IBM, for example, is certainly illustrative of this, since IBM has always had very high quality and highly cited research in its laboratories.

TABLE 15.1 Patent indicators for different sectors

	Current impact index (expected value 1.0)	Technology life cycle (years)	Science linkage (science references/patents)
Oil and gas	0.84	11.9	0.8
Chemicals	0.79	9.0	2.7
Pharmaceuticals	0.79	8.1	7.3
Biotechnology	0.68	7.7	14.4
Medical equipment	2.38	8.3	1.1
Computers	1.88	5.8	1.0
Telecommunications	1.65	5.7	0.8
Semiconductors	1.35	6.0	1.3
Aerospace	0.68	13.2	0.3

Source: Narin, F. (2012) Assessing technological competencies, in: J. Tidd (ed.) *From Knowledge Management to Strategic Competence*, 3rd edn, London: Imperial College Press, pp. 179–219.

There are major inter-sectoral differences in the relative importance of patenting in achieving its prime objective, namely to act as a barrier to imitation. For example, patenting is relatively unimportant in automobiles, but critical in pharmaceuticals. Moreover, patents do not yet fully capture technological activities in software since copyright laws are often used as the main means of protection against imitation, outside the USA.

Examples of the strategic value of patents include recent acquisitions of complete patent portfolios, and legal battles for alleged infringements of intellectual property rights:

- Apple aggressively defends its patents against alleged infringements, including HTC and Samsung in 2011, seeking to ban sales of competing mobile devices.
- Nokia won a patent dispute regarding touch-screen technology with Apple in 2011, and now receives 2% of iPhone revenues, in excess of $30 billion annually.
- Oracle launched a case against Google, alleging Android infringes Java patents, claiming $6.1 billion in damages.
- Nortel sold its entire patent portfolio in 2011 for $4.5 billion to a consortium of firms: Apple, Microsoft, Sony, Ericsson and RIM (BlackBerry).
- In response, Google acquired Motorola's mobile telephony patents in 2011 for $12.5 billion, because of the vulnerability of its Android platform.

Using 'international patents', where a single patent filing can include up to 144 countries, in 2009 the USA filed 487 000 patents, Euro 6 group 387 000

Case Study illustrating the tension created by using intellectual property to protect innovation rather than preventing broader competition and innovation, Apple versus Android, is available on the Innovation Portal at **www.innovation-portal.info**

and Japan 218 000. Compare this to emerging economies such as China (48 000) and India (32 000) and this suggests at current relative growth rates China will catch up in 20–30 years.[7]

INNOVATION IN ACTION 15.3

The Goldilocks Patent Strategy: Exploiting (Nearly) New Technologies

A study of the relationships between the age of patents and financial performance appears to provide some additional support for a 'fast-follower' strategy, rather than a 'first-mover' approach. It found that the median age of the patents of a firm is correlated with its stock-market value, but not in a linear way. For firms utilizing very recent patents or older patents, the relationship is negative, resulting in below-average performance over time, whereas firms using patents close to the median age outperform the average over time.

The study examined 288 firms over 20 years, and 204 000 patents. When patents are filed, they must list the other patents which they cite, by patent number and year of filing. These data allow the median age of the patent to be calculated – the median difference between the patent application date and the dates of the prior patents cited. This provides an indication of the age of the technological inputs used, but needs to be compared to the average within different technology patents classes, as the technology lifecycle varies significantly between the 400 patent classes, from months to decades. This comparison reveals a variation in the median ages of technologies used by different firms operating in the same technical fields, indicating different technology strategies. Finally, these data are compared with the financial performance, in this case share performance, of the firms over time. The results show that firms at the technological frontier, defined as one or more standard deviations ahead of their industry, or for those using mature technologies, that is 1.3 or more standard deviations behind the industry average, the stock returns underperform. However, the stock-market returns outperform for firms exploiting median-age technologies.

One interpretation of this observed relationship is that the firms with the very new patents face the very high costs and uncertainty associated with emerging technology, including development and commercialization. Conversely, the firms using mature patent portfolios face more limited opportunity to exploit these commercially. However, the firms with patents closer to the median age (in the relevant patent classes) have reduced much of the very high cost and uncertainty associated with the newer patents, but retain significant scope for further development and commercialization. Therefore, one lesson may be for firms to more carefully manage the age profile of their patents, and to focus exploitation on a specific time window. This is not simply about being a fast follower, which implies some degree of imitation, but another argument for closer integration between technological and market strategies.

Source: Heeley, M. B. and R. Jacobson (2008) The recency of technological inputs and financial performance, *Strategic Management Journal*, **29**, 723–44.

Copyright

Copyright is concerned with the expression of ideas, and not the ideas themselves. Therefore, the copyright exists only if the idea is made concrete, for example in a book or recording. There is no requirement for registration, and the test of originality is low compared to patent law, requiring only that 'the author of the work must have used his own skill and effort to create the work'. Like patents, copyright provides limited legal rights for certain types of material for a specific term. For literary, dramatic, musical and artistic works copyright is normally for 70 years after the death of the author, 50 in the USA, and for recordings, film, broadcast and cable programmes 50 years from their creation. Typographical works have 25 years of copyright. The type of materials covered by copyright include:

• 'original' literary, dramatic, musical and artistic works, including software and in some cases databases
• recordings, films, broadcasts and cable programmes
• typographical arrangement or layout of a published edition.

Design Rights

Design rights are similar to copyright protection, but mainly apply to three-dimensional articles, covering any aspect of the 'shape' or 'configuration', internal or external, whole or part, but specifically excluding integral and functional features, such as spare parts. Design rights exist for 15 years and 10 years if commercially exploited. Design registration is a cross between patent and copyright protection; it cheaper and easier than patent protection but more limited in scope. It provides protection for up to 25 years, but covers only visual appearance – shape, configuration, pattern and ornament. It is used for designs that have aesthetic appeal, for example consumer electronics and toys (the knobs on top of Lego bricks are functional, and would therefore not qualify for design registration but were also considered to have 'eye appeal' and were therefore granted design rights).

INNOVATION IN ACTION 15.4

Using Patents Strategically

Each year, some 400 000 patents are filed around the world. However, only a small proportion of these are ever exploited by the owners, and many are not renewed. Based on a review of the research and case studies of 14 firms from different sectors, the study identified a range of different patent strategies:

• *Offensive*. Multiple patents in related fields to limit or prevent competition.
• *Defensive*. Specific patents for key technologies which are intended to be developed and commercialized, to minimize imitation.

(*continued*)

- *Financial.* Primary role of patents are to optimize income through sale or licence.
- *Bargaining.* Patents designed to promote strategic alliances, adoption of standards or cross-licensing.
- *Reputation.* To improve the image or position of a company, e.g. to attract partners, talent or funding, or to build brands or enhance market position.

In practice, firms may combine different strategies, or more likely have no explicit strategy for patenting (which is our experience outside the pharmaceutical and biotechnology sectors). The European Patent Office (EPO) suggest only two alternatives: patenting as a cost centre, i.e. to provide the necessary legal support, or as a profit centre, to generate income. However, this ignores the more strategic positioning possibilities patents can provide if they are viewed as more than just a legal or income issue.

Source: Gilardoni, E. (2007) Basic approaches to patent strategy, *International Journal of Innovation Management,* **11**(3), 417–440.

Licensing IPR

Once you have acquired some form of formal legal IPR, you can allow others to use it in some way in return for some payment (a licence) or you can sell the IPR outright (or assign it). Licensing IPR can have a number of benefits:

- reduce or eliminate production and distribution costs and risks
- reach a larger market
- exploit in other applications
- establish standards
- gain access to complementary technology
- block competing developments
- convert competitor into defender.

Considerations when drafting a licensing agreement include degree of exclusivity, territory and type of end use, period of licence and type and level of payments – royalty, lump sum or cross-licence. Pricing a licence is as much an art as a science, and depends on a number of factors such as the balance of power and negotiating skills. Common methods of pricing licences are:

- *Going market rate.* Based on industry norms, e.g. 6% of sales in electronics and mechanical engineering.
- *25% rule.* Based on licensee's gross profit earned through use of the technology.
- *Return on investment.* Based on licensor's costs.
- *Profit sharing.* Based on relative investment and risk.

First, estimate total lifecycle profit. Next, calculate relative investment and weight according to share of risk. Finally, compare results to alternatives, for example return to licensee, imitation or litigation.

There is no 'best' licensing strategy, as it depends on the strategy of the organization and the nature of the technology and markets. For example, Celltech licensed its asthma treatment to Merck for a single payment of $50 million, based on sales projections. This isolated Celltech from the risk of clinical trials and commercialization, and provided a much-needed cash injection. Toshiba, Sony and Matsushita license DVD technology for royalties of only 1.5% to encourage its adoption as the industry standard. Until the recent legal proceedings, Microsoft applied a 'per processor' royalty to its OEM (original equipment manufacturer) customers for Windows to discourage them from using competing operating systems.

INNOVATION IN ACTION 15.5

ARM Holdings

ARM Holdings designs and licenses high-performance, low-energy-consumption 16- and 32-bit RISC (reduced instruction set computing) chips, which are used extensively in mobile devices such as mobile phones, cameras, electronic organizers and smart cards. ARM was established in 1990 as a joint venture between Acorn Computers in the UK and Apple Computer. Acorn did not pioneer the RISC architecture, but it was the first to market a commercial RISC processor in the mid-1980s. Perhaps ironically, the first application of ARM technology was in the relatively unsuccessful Apple Newton PDA (personal digital assistant). One of the most successful applications was in the Apple iPod. ARM designs but does not manufacture chips, and receives royalties of between 5 cents and $2.50 for every chip produced under licence. Licensees include Apple, Ericsson, Fujitsu, Hewlett-Packard, NEC, Nintendo, Sega, Sharp, Sony, Toshiba and 3Com. In 1999, it announced joint ventures with leading chip manufacturers such as Intel and Texas Instruments to design and build chips for the next generation of hand-held devices. It is estimated that ARM-designed processors were used in ten million devices in 1996, 50 million in 1998, 120 million devices sold in 1999 and a billion sold in 2004, and more than two billion in 2006, and 20 billion by 2012, representing around 80% of all mobile devices. The company now employs around 2000 people, headquartered in Cambridge, UK, with design centres in Taiwan, India and the USA. It has sold 800 processor licences to more than 250 companies, and has created 30 millionaires amongst its staff. In 2014, ARM achieved sales of more than £700 million, reflecting the growing demand for mobile devices.

The main strategic motives for licensing are:[8]

- strategic freedom to operate
- access to knowledge
- entry to new markets

- establishing technological leadership
- enhancing reputation.

The benefits of licensing depend very much on the absorptive capacity of an organization and its complementary assets.[9] Absorptive capacity such as internal R&D and know-how allow an organization to more easily identify, evaluate and adapt external knowledge, whereas complementary assets allow an organization to create additional value by combining internal and external knowledge, for example applying technology to a new market segment.[10]

However, the successful exploitation of IPR also incurs costs and risks, such as the:

- cost of search, registration and renewal
- need to register in various national markets
- full and public disclosure of your idea
- need to be able to enforce.

In most countries the basic registration fee for a patent is relatively modest, but in addition applying for a patent includes the cost of professional agents, such as patent agents, translation for foreign patents, official registration fees in all relevant countries and renewal fees. Pharmaceutical patents are much more expensive, up to five times more, owing to the complexity and length of the documentation. In addition to these costs, firms must consider the competitive risk of public disclosure and the potential cost of legal action should the patent be infringed. Costs vary by country, because of the size and attractiveness of different national markets, and because of differences in government policy. For example, in many Asian countries the policy is to encourage patenting by domestic firms, so the process is cheaper. There are still significant regional differences in the rates of patenting (Figure 15.3). Patents are only a partial indicator of innovation, and tend to lag R&D, but at this rate of growth, China will catch up with the USA and Europe in 20–30 years.

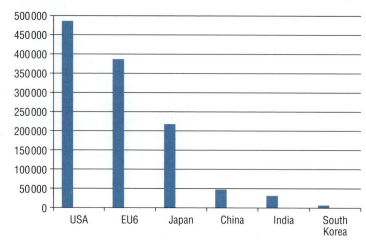

FIGURE 15.3   International patents by region

EU6 = Germany, France, the UK, the Netherlands, Sweden and Italy.
Source: Derived from Godinho, M. M. and V. Ferreira, V. (2012) Analyzing the evidence of an IPR take-off in China and India, *Research Policy*, **41**, 499–511.

Chapter Summary

- The generation, acquisition, sharing and exploitation of knowledge are central to successful innovation, but there is a wide range of different types of knowledge, and each plays a different role.

- One of the key challenges is to identify and exchange knowledge across different groups and organizations, and a number of mechanisms can help, mostly social in nature, but supported by technology.

- Tacit knowledge is critical but is difficult to capture, and draws upon individual expertise and experience. Therefore, where possible, tacit knowledge needs to be made more explicit and codified to allow it to be more readily shared and applied to different contexts.

- Codified knowledge can form the basis of legal IPR, and these can form a basis for the commercialization of knowledge. However, care needs to be taken when using IPR, as these can divert scarce management and financial resources and expose organizations to imitation and illegal use of IPR.

Key Terms Defined

Boundary object or practice   something of interest to two or more communities of practice. Different communities of practice will have a stake in it, but from different perspectives. A boundary object may be a shared document, for example a quality manual; an artefact, for example a prototype; a technology, for example a database; or a practice, for example a product design.

Community of practice   a group of people related by a shared task, process or the need to solve a problem, rather than by formal structural or functional relationships.

Copyright   legal rights associated with the *expression* of ideas, and not the ideas themselves, only available if the idea is made explicit or codified, for example in a book or recording, and can demonstrate some effort or skill used. There is no requirement for registration, and the test of originality is low compared to patent law.

Design rights   only apply to the shape and configuration of objects. They do not require registration and automatically protect a qualifying design for ten years after the design was first sold or 15 years after it was created, whichever is earlier.

Explicit knowledge   can be codified, that is expressed in numerical, textual or graphical terms, and therefore is more easily communicated, for example the design of a product.

Intellectual property rights (IPR)   include all formal legal means of identifying or registering rights, including patents, copyright, design rights and trademarks.

Knowledge broker   differs from a translator in that they participate in different communities rather than simply mediate between them. They represent overlaps between communities, and are typically people who are loosely linked to several communities and are able to facilitate knowledge flows between them. An example could be a quality manager responsible for the quality of a process that crosses several different functional groups.

Knowledge translator   an individual able to express the interests of one community in terms of another community's perspective. Therefore, the translator must be sufficiently conversant with both knowledge domains and trusted by both communities.

Patent   a limited legal monopoly, usually for 20 years, provided an invention satisfies certain requirements, including novelty, inventive step and application.

Tacit or implicit knowledge   personal, experiential, context-specific and hard to articulate, formalize and communicate.

Discussion Questions

1. Consider a smartphone. What types of intellectual property are necessary to create value?

2. In what ways can tacit knowledge be made explicit and codified?

3. What mechanisms exist to help the sharing and transfer of knowledge within an organization?

4. What are the advantages and disadvantages of using formal IPR to commercialize an innovation?

Further Reading and Resources

Knowledge management and intellectual property are both very large and complex subjects. For knowledge management, we would recommend the book *Working Knowledge: How Organizations Manage What They Know*, by Thomas H. Davenport and Laurence Prusak (2nd edn, Harvard Business School Press, 2000), which draws upon 30 case studies, and for a more academic approach *Knowledge at Work: Creative Collaboration in the Global Economy* by Robert Defillippi, Michael Arthur and Valerie Lindsay (John Wiley & Sons Ltd, 2006). We provide a good combination of theory, research and practice of knowledge management in *From Knowledge Management to Strategic Competence*, edited by Joe Tidd (3rd edn, Imperial College Press, 2012), which examines the links between knowledge, innovation and performance. Harry Scarbrough edits *The Evolution of Business Knowledge* (Oxford

University Press, 2008), which reports the findings of the UK national research programme on the relationships between business and knowledge (including one of our research projects).

For a comprehensive technical legal overview of intellectual property, see David Bainbridge's *Intellectual Property* (9th edn, Pearson, 2012), or for a much more concise summary try John Palfrey's *Intellectual Property Strategy* (MIT Press, 2011). For understanding the strategic role and limitations of intellectual property, we like the theoretical approach adopted by David Teece, for example in his book *The Transfer and Licensing of Know-how and Intellectual Property* (World Scientific, 2006), or for a more applied treatment of the topic see *Licensing Best Practices: Strategic, Territorial and Technology Issues*, edited by Robert Goldscheider and Alan Gordon (John Wiley & Sons Ltd, 2006), which includes practical case studies of licensing from many different countries and sectors.

References

1. Marques, D.P., F.J.G. Simon and C.D. Caranana (2006) The effect of innovation on intellectual capital: An empirical evaluation in the biotechnology and telecommunications industries, *International Journal of Innovation Management*, **10**(1): 89–112.

2. Nonaka, I. and H. Takeuchi (1995) *The Knowledge Creating Company*, Oxford: Oxford University Press.

3. Hall, R. (2012) What are strategic competencies?, in: J. Tidd (ed.), *From Knowledge Management to Strategic Competence*, 3rd edn, London: Imperial College Press.

4. Brown, J.S. and P. Duguid (2001) Knowledge and organization: A social practice perspective, *Organization Science*, **12**(2): 198–213; Brown, J.S. and P. Duguid (1991) Organizational learning and communities of practice: Towards a unified view of working, learning and organization, *Organizational Science*, **2**(1): 40–57; Hildreth, P., C. Kimble and P. Wright (2000) Communities of practice in the distributed international environment, *Journal of Knowledge Management*, **4**(1): 27–38.

5. Star, S.L. and J.R. Griesemer (1989) Institutional ecology, translations and boundary objects, *Social Studies of Science*, **19**: 387–420; Carlile, P.R. (2002) A pragmatic view of knowledge and boundaries: Boundary objects in new product development, *Organization Science*, **13**(4): 442–55.

6. 'Sales of Digital Movies Surge', *Wall Street Journal*, 7th January 2014.

7. Godinho, M.M. and V. Ferreira (2012) Analyzing the evidence of an IPR take-off in China and India, *Research Policy*, **41**: 499–511.

8. Lichtenthaler, U. (2007) The drivers of technology licensing: An industry comparison, *California Management Review*, **49**(4): 67–89.

9. Mazzola, E., M. Bruccoler and G. Perrone (2012) The effect on inbound, outbound and coupled innovation on performance, *International Journal of Innovation Management*, **16**(6): doi 1240008; Walter, J. (2012) The influence of firm and industry characteristics on returns from technology licensing deals: Evidence from the US computer and pharmaceutical sectors, *R&D Management*, **42**(5): 435–54.

10. Denicolai, S., M. Ramirez and J. Tidd (2014) Creating and capturing value from external knowledge: The moderating role of knowledge-intensity, *R&D Management*, **44**(3): 248–64.

Deeper Dive explanations of innovation concepts and ideas are available on the Innovation Portal at **www.innovation-portal.info**

Quizzes to test yourself further are available online via the Innovation Portal at **www.innovation-portal.info**

Summary of online resources for Chapter 15 –
all material is available via the Innovation Portal at
www.innovation-portal.info

Cases	**Media**	**Tools**	**Activities**	**Deeper Dives**
• Joint Solutions • Apple versus Android	• Xerox • Francisco Pinheiro	• Absorptive capacity audit	• Identifying Innovation Capabilities	• Linking knowledge and innovation management

Chapter 16

Business Models and Capturing Value

LEARNING OBJECTIVES

By the end of this chapter you will develop an understanding of:

- the concept of business models
- their role as a framework for describing how value is created and captured
- the skills to map and build business models and to use these to explore value capture.

What's a Business Model?

What makes a good idea special? What's the secret of translating an insight, a flash of inspiration, into something which changes the lives of millions of people? How does a tiny seed become a strong and flourishing tree, bearing fruit for generations? We've tried in this book to answer some of these questions – by showing that innovation is a process, not simply a new idea, and that shaping and configuring it is something which effective entrepreneurs do. Whatever the context in which they work the same message is clear: making innovations which create value is a craft. It's a set of skills which can be learnt and practised, whether in a small start-up or as part of the way a giant corporation renews itself and what it offers the world.

Throughout the book, we've been concerned not just with ideas but also with how they create value – and how entrepreneurs can capture that value. One helpful approach to the question is the concept of business models, and we explore this here. Put simply, a **business model** is an explanation of how value is created for customers, and making it explicit can help us focus on how we can capture this in innovation. For example:

- A theatre uses scripts, actors, scenery, lighting and music to create a theatrical experience which the audience values.
- A car company mobilizes an extensive supply network to bring together components and services and assemble them into a car which the customer values.
- A supermarket procures various food and non-food products and makes them available on its shelves to customers, who can collect them conveniently. They value this and are prepared to pay more than the supermarket paid for the items because they value the service this collection, storage and display offers them.
- An insurance company provides a guarantee of payment to offset the cost of losses owing to accidental damage, theft or other incident, and customers value the peace of mind which this brings and are prepared to pay for it.
- A smartphone retailer provides a platform across which communications, entertainment and personalized applications traffic can flow and customers are prepared to pay to own or rent the device for the functions it offers them.

Every organization, public or private sector, offers some kind of **value proposition** – a product or service or some combination which end users value. In commercial markets this is something they are prepared to pay for, but in other contexts, such as the public sector, services like education, welfare and healthcare are similarly 'valued' by those who consume them.

Innovation, as we have seen, is all about creating new or better ways of delivering such value and so if we are concerned to capture value it makes sense to begin by making explicit the model we are using to create it and to check whether it does the job well. And importantly, whether it is sustainable in the long term or whether it is vulnerable to replacement or challenge by someone else – the idea of **business model innovation**.

Why Use Business Models?

The purpose of a business model is to provide a clear representation of where and how value is created and can be captured. That's useful for a number of reasons:

- It provides a roadmap for how an innovation can create value. It won't just happen; it needs a framework.
- It provides a way of sharing the idea with others, making the business vision explicit. That can be useful for entrepreneurs trying to pitch their ideas to venture capitalists or to innovation teams trying to win resources and support for an internal innovation project.

- It offers a helpful checklist of areas to consider in making sure the idea and the route to creating value with it is well thought out.

A close relation of the business model is the **business case**, which we have already seen in Chapter 8. The idea of a business case is essentially constructing a story with enough detail about what we are trying to achieve, how we will do it, for whom, when, what the costs and rewards will be, etc. In other words, it

Activity to explore constructing a case, business case development, is available on the Innovation Portal at **www.innovation-portal.info**

is the story about the underlying innovative idea and how we are going to implement it. A business case without a clear and robust underlying business model is likely to be limited in its impact.

Think of any innovation and you can see it as a story which has meaning for people. Henry Ford's was all about 'a car for Everyman at a price everyone could afford'. George Eastman's was about putting photography in the hands of ordinary families: 'You point and shoot and we'll do the rest!' Edwin Land's daughter gave him the idea for his story when he tried to answer her photography question: 'Daddy, why can't I see the picture you just took?' He couldn't answer so he worked on the concept which became instant photography based on the Polaroid process. Muhammad Yunus told a rags-to-riches story about 'ordinary' people having the discipline and courage to create their own businesses if only they were given a financial chance to get started. His Grameen Bank has grown to become one of the world's most important on the back of this business model.

These examples have one thing in common. Their innovations weren't a single idea but a detailed and well-constructed story which gave the idea meaning and direction and helped communicate it to others. Creating value – social or commercial – depends upon getting a good story and telling it in a compelling fashion.

Importantly it is not just a matter of telling the story to potential customers. A key part of any entrepreneur's task is sharing his or her vision with others, to get their support, energy and commitment to the idea. Later the process involves pitching for resources and again this requires compelling storytelling. And each time the story is told it is refined and improved, embellished with new ideas and shaped by feedback and questions from the audience.

A robust business model, like a good story, doesn't just happen; it is shaped and developed in the process of telling and retelling. The plot emerges, the characters take shape, the scenery moves – and each time we tell it the story is refined and changed. Explaining it to others gives us new insights about what to add or take away. People ask questions or make suggestions

Activity to explore this, business model stories, is available on the Innovation Portal at **www.innovation-portal.info**

which change the way the story unfolds the next time we tell it. They pick up the threads and spread the story, telling it to others so that the idea gradually takes on a life of its own and starts to make sense in other people's lives. And as it does so it becomes stronger and clearer.

What's in a Business Model?

Value creation doesn't just happen. It is the result of a structured process which involves:

- A value proposition – what is valued?
- A target market – by whom?
- A supplier – who?
- A set of activities – how?
- A representation of the value – how much?

Figure 16.1 illustrates this simple model and Table 16.1 gives some examples.

This may sound simplistic but understanding how business models create value is a core part of our innovation discussion. If we can't make explicit how value is created and how we will capture it then the best idea in the world may not have an impact. Equally, if we understand how this process works we can improve it – streamline it and reduce the waste and friction in it. We can extend its application to new markets and adapt and shape the innovation for them. If we go back to our idea of innovation strategy then these three concepts – changing what we offer, how we create and deliver that and to whom – are three of the core dimensions on the '4Ps' model which we saw in Chapter 1 (Figure 16.2).

 Activity to explore this, creating value through innovation, is available on the Innovation Portal at **www.innovation-portal.info**

 Video Clip of Finnegan's Fish Bar showing how the idea can be applied to a simple catering business is available on the Innovation Portal at **www.innovation-portal.info**

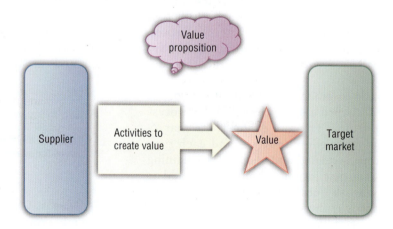

FIGURE 16.1   Outline framework for a business model

TABLE 16.1   Examples of business models

Example	Value proposition?	For whom?	By whom (key players on supply side)?	Core activities to deliver that value
Razor blades	Shaving with a fresh sharp blade every time instead of having to sharpen a razor	Men (and later women)	Manufacturers like Gillette	Design and development Manufacture and distribution of blades, advertising and marketing, etc.
National Health Service (UK)	Healthcare for all free at the point of delivery	All population (as opposed to healthcare for those who could afford it)	Mobilizes entire medical system of primary and secondary care	Healthcare services
Online banking	24/7 bank opening and ability to operate independent of physical banking offices	Customers unable or unwilling to use 'normal' banking hours but who appreciate the convenience Eventually all customers – becomes the dominant model	IT platforms, call centre staff other customer interfaces Back-office systems and providers	Customer service and relationship management
Streaming music services (e.g. Spotify)	Rent a huge collection of music and have it available on many mobile devices	Customers keen to access large volume and variety of music and have it available whenever they want it	IT platforms, IP relationship with music providers	Access control IT distribution and streaming Rights management Rental processing

Activity to explore this, identifying business models, is available on the Innovation Portal at **www.innovation-portal.info**

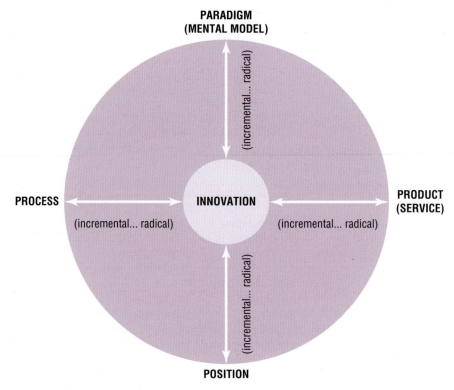

FIGURE 16.2 Exploring innovation space

Business Model Innovation

Crucially, we can also change the business model itself – replacing, for example, a simple grocer's shop with a supermarket or replacing that with an online service. Or shifting between making and selling a product and renting out the functions which it performs – Rolls-Royce no longer sells jet engines but charges customers for the number of useful hours of power which they provide over a thirty-year life is a good example of this. This kind of innovation is our fourth part of the '4Ps' innovation space: 'paradigm innovation'.

ENTREPRENEURSHIP IN ACTION 16.1

The Disruptive Business Model of Skype

Skype successfully combined two emerging technologies to create a new service and business model for telecommunications. The two technologies were voice over Internet protocol (VoIP) and peer-to-peer (P2P) file sharing. The first allowed the transfer of voice over the Internet, rather than conventional telecommunications networks, and the other exploited the distributed computing power of users' computers to avoid the need for a dedicated centralized server or infrastructure.

Skype was created in 2003 by the Swedish serial entrepreneur Niklas Zennström. Zennström was previously (in)famous for his pioneering Web company Kazaa, which provided a P2P service, mainly used for the (illegal) exchange of MP3 music files. He sold Kazaa to the USA company Sharman Networks to concentrate on the development of Skype. He teamed up with the Dane Janus Friis and together they built Skype. Unlike other VoIP firms like Vonage, which charges a subscription for use and is based on proprietary hardware, Skype was available for free download and use for free voice communication between computers. Additional premium pay services were subsequently added, such as Skype-Out to connect to conventional telephones, and Skype-In, to receive conventional calls. The service was made available in 15 different languages which covered 165 countries, and partnerships were made with Plantronics to provide headsets, and Siemens and Motorola for handsets. Happy users quickly recruited family and friends to the service, which grew rapidly.

Given the provision of free software and free calls between computers, the business model had to be innovative. There were several ways in which revenues were generated. The premium services like Skype-In and Skype-Out proved to be very popular with small- and medium-sized firms for business and conference calls, and the licensing of the software to specialist providers and the hardware partnership deals were also lucrative. Later, the large user base also attracted Web advertising.

By 2005, there were 70 million users registered, but despite this rapid growth the core model of providing a free service meant that revenues were a rather more modest $7 million, equivalent to only 10 cents per user. In 2008, Skype had around 310 million registered users, 12 million of whom were online at any one time. Its revenues were estimated to be $126 million, equivalent to 40 cents per user. This does represent an improvement in financial performance, especially as costs remain low, but the business model remains unproven, except for the founders of Skype. They sold the company to eBay Inc. in October 2005 for $2.6 billion, with further performance-based bonuses of $1.5 billion by 2009.

Source: Based on Rao, B., B. Angelov and O. Nov (2006) Fusion of disruptive technologies: Lessons from the Skype case, *European Management Journal*, **24**(2/3), 174–88.

Business model innovation is about creating new models or changing existing ones to maximize the value created and return it to the organization which created it – capturing value. So, for example, a pharmaceutical company spends around 20% of its sales on R&D, funding extensive laboratories and facilities to create new drugs. It pays for testing and approvals, for manufacture and packaging and for marketing across a global network. People value the health benefits which a drug gives them – and they or the agencies (insurance companies, governments, etc. which represent them) pay for this. The flow of revenue funds the direct costs and generates a surplus which can be reinvested.

They can invest in refining the business model, adding improvements to make it work better. But they can also change the fundamental approach – as is now beginning to happen

TABLE 16.2   Examples of the Internet as a route to business model innovation

Old model	Internet-enabled alternative
Airline and travel booking	Disintermediation – DIY or else via online aggregators
Encyclopaedia – expert driven	Wikipedia and open-source options
Printing and publishing – physical networks and specialist	Online coordination, self-publishing, long tail, print on demand
Retailing – physical presence via shops, distribution centres, etc.	Amazon and online, long tail effect, data-base mining, etc.

Activity to explore this, business model canvas, is available on the Innovation Portal at **www.innovation-portal.info**

Audio Clip of a talk by Christian Rangen outlining approaches to BMI is available on the Innovation Portal at **www.innovation-portal.info**

in that industry. A combination of rising costs and problems with tight regulatory frameworks have slowed down innovation and reduced the chances of finding blockbuster drugs successfully to market; instead, the model is shifting to one where research is increasingly being carried out by small entrepreneurial labs working in rapidly changing technological fields like genetics and biotechnology.[1]

Similarly, Procter and Gamble changed its business model for R&D back in 1999, shifting away from the 'closed' innovation model which it had pioneered and used for over a hundred years and opening up new options with its 'connect and develop' approach.[2] Caterpillar, like Rolls-Royce, has moved its model from selling capital equipment to novel ways of offering the functions as part of a service package, which many of its clients prefer to rent from the company.

Table 16.2 gives some examples of business model innovation enabled by entrepreneurs working with the tools of the Internet.

Of course, like all innovation the established players do not have the monopoly on good ideas. The particular problem of 'paradigm' – business model – innovation is that it represents the story an organization tells, not least to itself. So to change that model is very difficult for them because it involves letting go of so much of the past. For entrepreneurs the advantage of coming with a clean sheet and building a new model from scratch is powerful, as Jeff Bezos has found with his approach to reinventing retailing via the Amazon approach.

INNOVATION IN ACTION 16.1

Problems at Polaroid

Polaroid was a pioneer in the development of instant photography. It developed the first instant camera in 1948, the first instant colour camera in 1963 and introduced sonar automatic focusing in 1978. In addition to its competencies in silver halide chemistry, it had technological competencies in optics and electronics, and mass manufacturing, marketing and distribution expertise. The company was technology-driven from its foundation in 1937, and the founder Edwin Land had 500 personal patents.

When Kodak entered the instant photography market in 1976, Polaroid sued the company for patent infringement and was awarded $924.5 million in damages. Polaroid consistently and successfully pursued a strategy of introducing new cameras, but made almost all its profits from the sale of the film (the so-called razor-blade marketing strategy also used by Gillette), and between 1948 and 1978 the average annual sales growth was 23%, and profit growth 17% per year.

Polaroid established an electronic imaging group as early as 1981, as it recognized the potential of the technology. However, digital technology was perceived as a potential technological shift rather than as a market or business disruption. By 1986, the group had an annual research budget of $10 million, and by 1989 42% of the R&D budget was devoted to digital imaging technologies. By 1990, 28% of the firm's patents related to digital technologies. Polaroid was therefore well positioned at that time to develop a digital camera business.

However, it failed to translate prototypes into a commercial digital camera until 1996, by which time there were 40 other companies in the market, including many strong Japanese camera and electronics firms. Part of the problem was adapting the product development and marketing channels to the new product needs. However, other more fundamental problems related to long-held cognitions: a continued commitment to the razor-blade business model, and pursuit of image quality. Profits from the new market for digital cameras were derived from the cameras rather than the consumables (film). Ironically, Polaroid had rejected the development of ink-jet printers, which rely on consumables for profits, because of the relatively low quality of its (early) outputs. Polaroid had a long tradition of improving its print quality to compete with conventional 35mm film.

Source: Tripsas, M. and G. Gavetti (2000) Capabilities, cognition, and inertia: Evidence from digital imaging, *Strategic Management Journal*, **21**, 1147–61.

Case Study highlighting disruption and problems with business model innovation, Polaroid, is available on the Innovation Portal at **www.innovation-portal.info**

Case Study highlighting the difficulties for established players in letting go of their old models, gunfire at sea, is available on the Innovation Portal at **www.innovation-portal.info**

Generic and Specific Business Models

In reality, there are some generic business models; Table 16.3 gives some examples.

Once established, there is competition about finding new and modified ways of deploying these – playing with the '4Ps' in terms of streamlining or changing processes, modifying the product/service offering or changing the positioning in new markets or in the story we tell about our offer.

For example, the basic airline business model is that people pay for the service of transportation. Over the years we have seen competition amongst airlines based on incremental innovations in the service offered – different destinations, different catering, different aircraft, different seating and sleeping options, provisions of lounge accommodation, transportation to/from the terminal, etc. Process innovations have reduced the costs and improved the flow in areas like check-in, reservations, fuel efficiency, terminal turnaround times, etc. Position innovation has segmented the market, first into different classes and experiences and, in recent times, radically opening up the market through low-cost short-haul flying. And this has led to a paradigm innovation: from being seen as a luxury service for the few flying has now become

TABLE 16.3   Some examples of generic business models

Model	Value proposition
Product or service provider	Offers an end-product or service
Ownership of key assets and renting them out	Rental for temporary period of something valuable like space, e.g. car parks, luggage and goods storage businesses
Finance provider	Offers access to money and services around that
Systems integrator	Pulls together components on behalf of an end customer, e.g. building contractors, software service providers, computer builders like Dell
Platform provider	Offers a platform across which others can add value, e.g. smartphones and the various apps which run across them, and Intel whose chipsets enable others to offer computing functions
Network provider	Offers access to various kinds of network service, e.g. mobile phone or broadband company
Skills provider	Sells or rents access to human resources and knowledge, e.g. recruitment agencies, professional consultancies and contract services
Outsourcer	Offers to take over responsibility for management and delivery of key activities, e.g. payroll management, IT services or financial transaction processing

the possible mode of travel for the many, rather as Henry Ford changed the earlier transport paradigm with his Model T.

The generic pattern of innovation is played out by many different players each of whom is trying to compete by modifying some aspect of the business model through innovation. So transatlantic carriers offer flat beds or different customer lounges. Low-cost carriers compete on price, translating their savings through process innovations into lower ticket prices. Niche airlines offer services to remote locations or serving specialist segments, for example helicopters serving oil platforms.

INNOVATION IN ACTION 16.2

Business Model Innovation in the Music Industry

Over time we can see a pattern of occasional breakthroughs in the underlying business model followed by long periods of elaboration – do better innovation – around that. For example, the music industry emerged during the early 20th century when the radio and gramophone made it possible to listen to and own recordings. This dominant model lasted until the late part of the century, where growth in consumer electronics led to the Walkman and other forms of personal music ownership and portability, on a platform of different storage media: cassettes, CDs, etc. The digital revolution, and particularly the invention of compression technology around the mp3, led to the move into virtual space – and the business model challenge became one of delivering value while staying within the bounds of IPR law! After a period in which various illegal but widely used models proliferated – Napster and beyond – the dominant model became iTunes, which orchestrated a very different value network. But that too is being challenged by an alternative business model associated with renting rather than owning music – via online streaming and on device storage.

Case Studies of the changing music industry and the lighting (dimming of the light bulb) and imaging industries are available on the Innovation Portal at **www.innovation-portal.info**

We can see a similar pattern of 'generic' business model innovation strategies – routes along which there may be rich opportunities for entrepreneurs to rewrite the rules of the game. For example:

- *User-driven instead of supplier-led*, in which the role of active and informed users is reshaping the trajectory of innovation.
- **Servitization,** in which manufacturing operations are increasingly being reframed as service offerings. As we've seen, the aircraft engine maker Rolls-Royce redefined its business model as 'power by the hour', recognizing that what its customers actually valued was the provision of power, not the engines themselves. It now charges users for usable hours of power.

Chemical companies are increasingly looking to provide rental models in which they offer services to support the effective use of their products rather than simply delivering bulk chemicals.

- *Rent not own*, in which the value proposition moves to making available the functionality rather than the asset. For example, people are beginning to move to renting music via streaming services like Spotify rather than needing to buy record collections, while in city centres the idea of bicycle and even car rental is displacing the need for ownership.

INNOVATION IN ACTION 16.3

Business Model Innovation

For many years, Costas Markides at London Business School has been researching the links between strategy, innovation and firm performance. He argues for the need to make a clearer distinction between the technological and market aspects of disruptive innovations, and to pay greater attention to business model innovation.

By definition, business model innovation enlarges the existing value of a market, either by attracting new customers or by encouraging existing customers to consume more. Business model innovation does not require the discovery of new products or services, or new technology, but rather the redefinition of existing products and services and how these are used to create value.

For example, Amazon did not invent book selling, and low-cost airlines such as Southwest and easyJet are not pioneers of air travel. Such innovators tend to offer different product or service attributes to existing firms, which emphasize different value propositions. As a result, business model innovation typically requires different and often conflicting systems, structures, processes and value chains to existing offerings.

However, unlike the claims made for disruptive innovations, new business models can co-exist with more mainstream approaches. For example, Internet banking and low-cost airlines have not displaced the more mainstream approaches but they have captured around 20% of the total demand for these services. Also, while many business model innovations are introduced by new entrants, which have none of the legacy systems and products of incumbent firms, the more mainstream firms may simply choose not to adopt the new business models as they make little sense for them. Alternatively, they may make other innovations to create or recapture customers.

Sources: Markides C. (2006) disruptive innovation: In need of a better theory, *Journal of Product Innovation Management*, **23**, 19–25; (2004) *Fast Second: How Smart Companies Bypass Radical Innovation to Enter and Dominate New Markets*, San Francisco: Jossey-Bass.

Building a Business Model

Let's look in more detail at how we could construct a business model as a representation of how value is created and how we could best capture it. There are plenty of models for how to do this, but they have the same underlying architecture, which can be expressed in a small number of key questions:

- What? The value proposition.
- By whom? The supply side.
- For whom? The demand side.
- How? The key activities by the supply side to create value for the demand side.

If it is going to be robust then the 'revenue' from the demand side needs to be greater than the costs on the supply side of doing it.

Beyond that there are important questions about timing (can we ensure the flow of resources out is supported by the flow of revenue in?) and long-term sustainability. How can we protect our model so that others can't instantly copy it, and how can we develop our idea in the long term to counter other competitors coming in to try?

We can build the model in simple fashion; first, what is the core value proposition?

Value Proposition

Here we need to think about the features of the innovation and how it represents something new which people will value over what they currently have. What differentiates it – what is our unique selling proposition (USP)? 'Why hasn't someone already done this?' is often a useful question to ask at this stage. We may be reinventing the wheel or we may be trying to do something which others have found to their cost is

impossible! But we may also find that things have changed and we are now able to do something which was previously impossible, for example the opportunities offered by having GPS positioning in smartphones opens up a whole set of possibilities for location-based services which couldn't have been offered ten years earlier.

Target Market

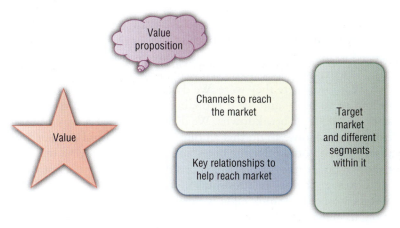

Next, we need to think about the demand side. Who is going to value this? It's important here to think about targeting as precisely as we can, for example not just saying we will offer a bicycle for rent in a big city but specifying for whom (tourists who want to explore, business people who want to avoid congestion of public transport or taxis, etc.). And we need to think about how we would reach those people – which channels would we use to find them and make our offer clear to them? Online advertising? Point of sale – little advertising stations where the bikes can be found? Newspaper or TV advertising? Then we need to think about how we will interact with them: do we have someone in a stall renting the bikes out personally like a shop or do we go for an online booking and self-service unlocking model?

In other words, we need to think hard about the specifics of the demand side and how best to make sure the value we are offering in our proposition reaches and is appreciated by the target market.

Creating and Delivering

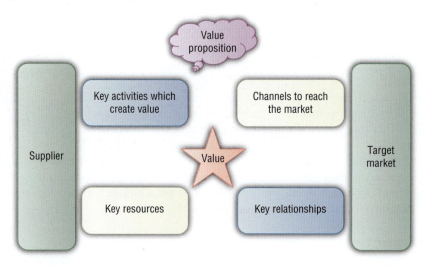

But the offering which we hope they value isn't going to magically appear. We need to create and deliver it. So we also need to think hard about the supply side. What are the key activities we'd need to do to be able to offer our value proposition? For example, we'd need to purchase or build a fleet of bikes, we'd need to distribute them around cities and we'd need to track them so we know where they were. We'd need to maintain them and make sure they were available and fit to use – and we'd probably need some kind of emergency response service in case of accidents or breakdowns. We'd certainly need a way of taking money for the bikes! We might not choose to do this all ourselves – we could partner with others – for example local shops who could offer the bikes and take the money on our behalf, or a local bicycle repair shop to undertake the maintenance side of things for us. But we'd need to build this network and manage the key relationships in it.

In other words, we need to think equally hard about the specifics of the supply side and how we are going to deliver the best version of our value proposition.

Value Capture

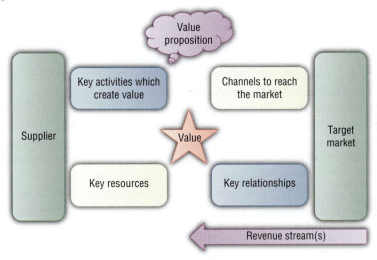

Next, we need to think about how we will capture the value from this. What are the different sources of 'revenue' or reward which flow to us from people in our target segment who value what we offer them? This is certainly the money they are prepared to pay but it may also be information – useful feedback about how to improve our offering. We can also build up information about the kind of people who are using our offering and use that to help design other products and services for them. (For example, Amazon and Google not only provide a service but also gain huge understanding of the people consuming it which can be recycled into a variety of other innovations.)

Cost Structure

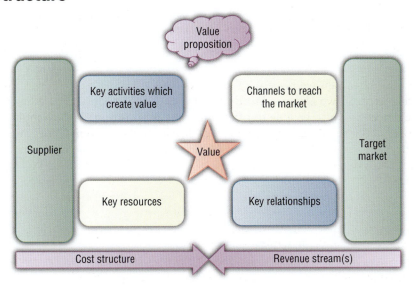

The other side of this equation is, of course, the resources we need to spend – time, energy, money – in creating and delivering our offering: the **cost structure**. What are these and how do they break down? How much of it is fixed and how much varies with the volume of demand? When do these costs kick in – at the start-up stage or through the operation of our model? We also have to think about the timing of these flows and make sure the balance between what we spend and what we get back is positive and we don't spend all our resources before we get something back to help refill the tanks!

Sustainability

Activity to give you the chance to explore this approach to building business models. There is a description of the business model canvas tool and an activity to give you a chance to try using it on the Innovation Portal at **www.innovation-portal.info**

Finally, we need to think about the model in the long term. How easy is it for someone to copy right now – and where are the places where we can protect and defend ourselves from competition? And looking ahead, how could we develop the idea further to add new kinds of value, or do it for more people on the demand side, or with different players on the supply side? In other words, how would we go about business model innovation?

Audio Clip of a talk by Alexander Osterwalder, one of the founders of the BMC approach, is available on the Innovation Portal at **www.innovation-portal.info**

Tool to help with this kind of search strategy for peripheral vision is available on the Innovation Portal at **www.innovation-portal.info**

Chapter Summary

- Innovation is about using change to create value. Business models provide a way of articulating and mapping the ways in which this process happens.

- A robust business model should set out the value proposition, the target market, the supply side and the cost and revenue aspects. Building the model will be the focus of much discussion, but this helps ensure that innovation proposals are robust and well thought through.

- Business cases represent the stories which can be told based on a clear business model about the need for and likely benefits of innovation.

- We can map the benefits from changes in products/service offerings, process changes or position innovations on a business model framework. But changing the business model itself is also a powerful source of innovation, especially since it often involves changing the underlying system/architecture rather than just the components.

Key Terms Defined

Business case   a framework for summarizing the core innovation idea and how it will be developed.

Business model   an explanation of how value is created for customers.

Business model innovation   creating new models or changing existing ones.

Cost structure   a list of the various elements of costs which will be incurred in delivering the value proposition.

Servitization   example of business model innovation in which manufacturing organizations increasingly shift their approach to providing services wrapped around their core product offering.

Value proposition   a statement of what the end user/customer will value and which differentiates your offer from others.

Discussion Questions

1. You have a scientist friend at the university who has been working on a new technology for blood sugar measurement. She's asked you to help develop this into a business idea

for a portable monitor for diabetics. Using the business model framework, develop a coherent story for how this business could develop.

2. Use the business model canvas approach to 'reverse engineer' a successful innovation which you have recently bought. What was the value proposition, how did it identify and develop key activities, key markets, etc.?

3. Spotify is a successful streaming music service which has challenged existing business models in the industry. Using the ideas in this chapter, try to map the business model canvas the original entrepreneurs may have had when they were thinking about starting the business.

4. You are a social entrepreneur with an idea for providing simple low-cost shelters for housing refugees in crisis areas. How could you use the business model approach to develop your story to pitch it successfully to potential supporters?

Further Reading and Resources

Business models are increasingly being discussed in the innovation literature, for example Henry Chesbrough's *Open Services Innovation* (Jossey-Bass, 2011), Costas Markides's *Fast Second: How Smart Companies Bypass Radical Innovation to Enter and Dominate New Markets* (Jossey-Bass, 2004), Robert Galavan's *Strategy, Innovation and Change* (Oxford University Press, 2008) and Julian Birkinshaw's *Reinventing Management* (John Wiley & Sons Ltd, 2012). Alan Afuah's *Business Model Innovation: Concepts, Analysis, and Cases* (Routledge, 2014) offers both methods and case examples of business model innovation and a good review of the field is given by Sabine Schneider and Patrick Spieth's 'Business model innovation: Towards an integrated future research agenda' (*International Journal of Innovation Management*, 2013, **17**(1)).

Kaplan's *The Business Model Innovation Factory: How to Stay Relevant When the World is Changing* (John Wiley & Sons Ltd, 2012) offers a series of examples of business model change as a source of strategic advantage. Other case examples include Procter and Gamble (Lafley, A. and R. Charan, *The Game Changer*, New York: Profile, 2008) and Google (Iyer, B. and R. Davenport, 'Reverse engineering Google's innovation machine', *Harvard Business Review*, 2008, 83(3): 102–11). Tools for developing and working with business models include the business model canvas (Osterwalder, A. and Y. Pigneur, *Business Model Generation: A Handbook for Visionaries, Game Changers, and Challengers*, New York: John Wiley & Sons Ltd, 2010) and blue ocean strategy (Kim, W. and R. Mauborgne, *Blue Ocean Strategy: How to Create Uncontested Market Space and Make the Competition Irrelevant*, Boston: Harvard Business School Press, 2005).

References

1. Bohlin, N., J. Brennan, T. Kaltenbach and F. Thomas (2014) *Innovation in the Healthcare Space*, Frankfurt: Arthur D. Little Consultants, http://www.adlittle.com/prism-articles.html?&no_cache=1&view=414, accessed 20th December 2014.

2. Lafley, A. and R. Charan (2008) *The Game Changer*, New York: Profile.

Deeper Dive explanations of innovation concepts and ideas are available on the Innovation Portal at **www.innovation-portal.info**

Quizzes to test yourself further are available online via the Innovation Portal at **www.innovation-portal.info**

Summary of online resources for Chapter 16 –
all material is available via the Innovation Portal at
www.innovation-portal.info

Cases	**Media**	**Tools**	**Activities**	**Deeper Dives**
• Polaroid • Gunfire at sea • Dimming of the lightbulb	• Finnegan's Fish Bar • Christian Rangen • Alexander Osterwalder	• Business model canvas • Search strategy for peripheral vision	• Business case development • Business model stories • Identifying business models • Creating value through innovation • Business model canvas	• Servitization

Chapter 17

Learning to Manage Innovation and Entrepreneurship

LEARNING OBJECTIVES

By the end of this chapter you will develop an understanding of:

- reviewing and consolidating the key themes in the book
- exploring key influences on how to manage the innovation process effectively
- identifying key skills at individual, team and organizational level associated with effective innovation
- developing the ability to review how well individuals and organizations manage the process
- practising taking an audit approach to improving innovation and entrepreneurship.

Introduction

Let's try to summarize the key themes in the book. In Part I we introduced the idea of innovation not as some luxury to be thought about occasionally but as a business and social imperative. Unless established organizations change what they offer the world and the ways they create and deliver that offering, they are likely to fall behind their competitors and even disappear. On a more positive side, creating new business through coming up with and deploying ideas is well established as a powerful source of economic growth – not to mention a great way to make the successful entrepreneurs behind those ideas very wealthy!

The energy and passion which drives through the process is entrepreneurship: the seeing and making real of opportunities. It is clearly involved in a start-up where a new business requires an individual/small group to channel their creative energy and drive to make something new. But it's also needed in an established company where renewal comes through stimulating and enabling the same drive and creativity to deliver both a stream of improvement innovations and also the occasional inspired leap which helps reinvent the business. And increasingly such drive, energy and enthusiasm is being harnessed to more than economic growth – in start-ups and established organizations where the challenges of sustainability are being picked up. Social entrepreneurship is literally about changing the world, but it uses the same basic engine.

This process works right across the economy, whether we are talking about cars, clothes or silicon chips. It isn't confined to manufacturing; it works just as powerfully for the services which make up the majority of most economies – banks, insurance companies, shops and airlines all have to look hard and often at the innovation challenge if they are to stay ahead.

For public services and in social enterprises the same is true, but here we begin to see that it isn't always money which turns the entrepreneurial wheels. Innovation here is targeted at improving education, saving lives, making people more secure and addressing other basic needs. And while some innovation is about taking costs and waste out of established service delivery processes, much is about coming up with new and better ways of improving the quality of human life. Whether in a start-up or across a large public sector department, there is a strong thread of social entrepreneurship running through driven less by a desire for profits than literally wanting to change the world.

But whatever drives innovation and wherever it happens – big firm, small firm, start-up business, public-sector department – one thing is clear: successful innovation won't happen simply by wishing for it. This complex and risky process of transforming ideas into something which makes a mark needs organizing and managing in a strategic fashion. Passion and energy aren't enough. If we are to do more than just gamble enthusiastically then we need to organize and focus the process. And we need to be able to repeat the trick (anyone can get lucky once but being able to deliver a steady stream of innovations requires something a bit more structured and robust).

This chapter looks at the key lessons learnt about organizing and managing the process of innovation and entrepreneurship – and how we can use these lessons to review and strengthen our capability.

Making Innovation Happen

Innovation is a generic process, running from ideas through to their implementation. Despite the many different ways in which we see it playing out in manufacturing or services, at heart the process is about weaving knowledge and resources together. And it's this creative tapestry that we have to organize and manage as we move through finding opportunities, mobilizing resources, developing the venture and capturing the value.

We know that this process is influenced along the way by several things which can help or hinder it, for example having a clear sense of direction (an **innovation strategy**) or working within a creative network of players. We looked particularly at some of the levers we could use as architects and managers of the process. For example, how can an entrepreneur channel his or her energy, passion and idea in such a way that it motivates others and gets them to buy into the vision? How can we construct innovative organizations which allow creative ideas to come through, let people build on and share knowledge and feel motivated and rewarded for doing so? How can we harness the power of networks, making rich and extensive connections to deliver a stream of innovations?

Learning and Building Capability

No organization or individual starts with a fully developed version of Figure 17.1. We learn and adapt our approach, building capability through a process of trial and error, gradually improving our skills as we find what works for us. These 'behavioural routines' become embedded in 'the way we do things around here'; they reflect our approach to managing innovation.

We need to recognize the importance of failure in this. Innovation is all about trying new things out – and they may not always work. Experimentation and testing, prototyping and pivoting are all part and parcel of the innovation story, and it is through this process that we gradually build capability.

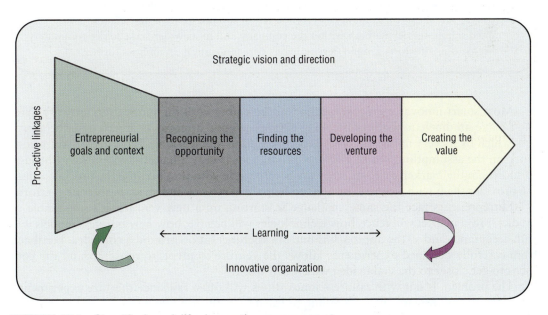

FIGURE 17.1 Simplified model for innovation management

INNOVATION IN ACTION 17.1

Failure at 3M

Next time you scrawl a message on a Post-it note you should pause for a moment to reflect on the value of failure in innovation. Because Post-its – like many of the breakthrough innovations produced in over a century by the 3M company – actually evolved from a failed innovation. Spencer Silver, a polymer chemist, was working on adhesives when he came up with glue which was not particularly sticky. Viewed through the single lens of developing glue, this represented bad news – but change the lens, reframe the problem and the question becomes: 'What other uses might there be for non-sticky glue?' And the answer they came up with led to a thriving new business.

3M is a company which has learnt from its very beginnings that innovation is all about taking risks and learning from failure. Its origins as the Minnesota Mining and Manufacturing Company (hence 3M) were less than glorious since the mine it bought for the purpose of extracting carborundum abrasives turned out to contain the wrong kind of rock! It took some rapid reframing to recover, but it did and has grown consistently on the back of a relentless commitment to innovation.

Its history is based on recognizing that mistakes happen and failures occur but that these are opportunities for finding out what works and what doesn't. They fuel a culture of experimentation and learning which still operates today. For example, the company was for many years in the top three of *Business Week*'s list of innovative companies. But following a change in CEO and a shift in emphasis away from breakthrough innovation and towards incremental improvement linked to a 'Six Sigma' programme, its position fell to seventh in 2006 and 22nd in 2007. This prompted significant debate both within the company and in its wider stakeholder community and a refocusing of efforts around developing its core innovation capabilities further.

Most smart innovators recognize that failure comes with the innovation territory. 'You can't make an omelette without breaking eggs' is as good a motto as any to describe a process which by its very nature involves experimentation and learning. Typically, organizations work on the assumption that of 100 new product ideas only a handful will make it through to success in the marketplace, and they are comfortable with that because the process of failing provides them with rich new insights to help them refocus and sharpen their next efforts.

Entrepreneurs face the same challenge in starting up a new venture. It's impossible to predict how a market will react, how technologies will behave, how new business models will gain acceptance and so the approach is one of experimentation around a core idea. Feedback from carefully designed experiments allows the venture to pivot, to move around the core focus to get closer to the viable idea which will work.

The problem is not with failure – innovations will often fail since they are experiments, steps into the unknown – it's with failing to *learn* from those experiences.

Failure is important in at least three ways in innovation:

- *It provides insights about what not to do.* In a world where you are trying to pioneer something new there are no clear paths and instead you have to cut and hack your own way through the jungle of uncertainty. Inevitably, there is a risk that the direction you chose was wrong, but that kind of 'failure' helps identify where not to work, and this focusing process is an important feature in innovation.
- *Failure helps build capability.* Learning how to manage innovation effectively comes from a process of trial and error. Only through this kind of reflection and revision can we develop the capability to manage the process better next time. Anyone can get lucky once but successful innovation is all about building a resilient capability to repeat the trick. Taking time out to review projects is a key factor in this. If we are honest, we learn a lot more from failure than from success. Well-managed post-project reviews where the aim is to learn and capture lessons for the future rather than apportion blame are among the most important tools for improving innovation management.
- *Failure helps others learn and build capability.* Sharing failure stories – a kind of 'vicarious learning' – provides a roadmap for others, and in the field of capability building that's important. Not for nothing do most business schools teach using the case method; stories of this kind carry valuable information which can be applied elsewhere.

Experienced innovators know this and use failure as a rich source of learning. Most of what we've learnt from innovation research has come from studying and analysing what went wrong and how we can do it better next time – Robert Cooper's work on stage gates, NASA's development of project management tools, Toyota's understanding of the minute trial and error learning loops which its kaizen system depends upon and which have made it the world's most productive car-maker.[1] Google's philosophy is all about 'perpetual beta' – not aiming for perfection but allowing for learning from its innovation. And IDEO, the successful design consultancy, has a slogan which underlines the key role learning through prototyping plays in its projects: 'Fail often, to succeed sooner!'

So rather than seeing failure in innovation as a problem we should see it as an important resource – as long as we learn from it. That focuses us on the question of how organizations and individuals learn.

How Learning Happens

The psychologist David Kolb developed a simple model of learning which is worth bringing in here. He used it to talk about how adults learn, but we can adapt it to think of entrepreneurs and organizations.[2] Figure 17.2 gives a simple illustration.

The model suggests that learning is not simply about acquiring new knowledge: it is a cycle with a number of stages. It doesn't matter where we enter but only when the whole cycle

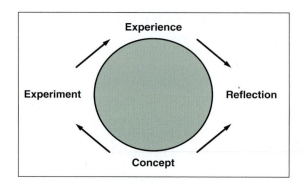

FIGURE 17.2   Simple model of the learning cycle

is complete does learning take place. So to enable effective learning about how to manage innovation better we need to:

- Capture and reflect on our experiences, trying to distil patterns from them about what works and doesn't work.
- Create models of how the world works – concepts – and link these to those we already have.
- Using our revised models engage again in innovation – trying new things out.

There are many ways we can help this process, for example:

- Rather than simply stepping back for a reflective pause we could employ some structured question frameworks. And we could ask others to help us in the process, acting as critical and challenging partners to help us learn.
- We can develop our own concepts, but we can also use, adapt and try out new ideas developed elsewhere. The 'theory' of innovation and entrepreneurship has emerged from many experiences codified into a rich body of knowledge and this is available to draw upon. We don't have to reinvent the wheel.
- Similarly, we don't have to make all the mistakes ourselves. We can learn from others' experiences.

There is growing interest in planned experimentation and learning as a key framework for developing entrepreneurial ventures. Concepts like 'agile software development' and 'lean start-up' essentially build on the idea of setting up high-frequency versions of the above learning cycle so that organizations can quickly learn and adapt their ideas and enhance the chances of succeeding in innovation. Rather than a master plan, they seek to develop the capability for fast learning.[3] To enable such learning we need to pause and reflect and so we'll now briefly revisit the key themes from the book by looking at the core process model and by framing some useful reflective questions for individual and organizational entrepreneurs.

Recognizing the Opportunity

Ideas, as we've seen, can come from anywhere. Some boffin in a lab may have a 'Eureka!' moment. Or someone talking with a customer may see a need which hasn't been met. A competitor may start offering a service we haven't got in our repertoire. A civil servant may change the rules of the particular game our business is playing and force us to rethink what we do. Or a newcomer from a different industry may spot a way to reframe the game and bring in a completely new way of looking at it – as we see every day on the Internet. And social entrepreneurship often arises from individuals looking at the world and seeing ways in which public services could be delivered better, or disadvantaged groups could be enabled or resources more equitably distributed.

Wherever the ideas come from, the challenge for us is to make sure we pick them up and harness them to provide the fuel of the innovation process. Entrepreneurship may give us the drive, but without ideas the engine will be running on empty. So how could we organize and manage this search process? Needless to say there isn't a standard recipe but – as we saw in Chapter 7 – we need to spread the net widely and make sure we cover the spectrum from 'exploit – do what we do better' through to 'explore – do something different'.

It's also not a passive process; successful entrepreneurs don't just bump into opportunities. The evidence is that they actively create them, by looking around but also by reframing, trying new angles and experimenting with new approaches.

So when thinking about this opportunity finding stage, here are some questions…

ASK YOURSELF – REFLECTION QUESTIONS…

…for start-up entrepreneurs

When looking for triggers for innovation, smart players try to cover as many bases as possible. So in reviewing your approach, how far do you:

- Explore the technology space – find opportunities but also check who else is doing it?
- Explore market space – find out if there is a market and how big, how fast it's growing, etc.? And how do you find out about competitors real and potential and about barriers to entry, etc.?
- Explore what others are doing. Who else is or could be playing – and could we learn from them?
- Explore future space – do you look ahead at how threats and opportunities could develop and affect both technical and market space?
- Exploring with others – do you bring different stakeholders into the process, using their perspectives and ideas to enrich the variety and generate new directions?

(continued)

…and for established organizations – how well do we do it?

There are many approaches which an organization could take to managing the challenge of finding opportunities to trigger the innovation process. How well it does it is another matter – but one way we could tell would be to listen to the things people said in describing 'the way we do things around here', in other words the pattern of behaviour and beliefs which creates the climate for innovation. And if we walked around the organization, we'd expect to hear people talking about the methods they actually used. We should hear things like:

Around here:

- We have good win–win relationships with our suppliers and we pick up a steady stream of ideas from them.
- We are good at understanding the needs of our customers/end-users.
- We work well with universities and other research centres to help us develop our knowledge.
- Our people are involved in suggesting ideas for improvements to products or processes.
- We look ahead in a structured way (using forecasting tools and techniques) to try to imagine future threats and opportunities.
- We systematically compare our products and processes with other firms.
- We collaborate with other firms to develop new products or processes.
- We try to develop external networks of people who can help us, for example with specialist knowledge.
- We work closely with 'lead users' to develop innovative new products and services.

Dealing with the unexpected

Of course, part of the search question is about picking up rather weak signals about emerging, and sometimes radically different, triggers for innovation. So people in smart firms may also say things like:

Around here:

- We deploy 'probe and learn' approaches to explore new directions in technologies and markets.
- We make connections across industry to provide us with different perspectives.
- We have mechanisms to bring in fresh perspectives, for example recruiting from outside the industry.
- We use formal tools and techniques to help us think outside of the box.
- We focus on 'next practices' as well as 'best practices'.
- We use some form of technology scanning/intelligence gathering – we have well-developed technology antennae.
- We work with 'fringe users' and very early adopters to develop our new products and services.
- We use technologies like the Web to help us become more agile and quick to pick up on and respond to emerging threats and opportunities on the periphery.

- We deploy 'targeted hunting' around our periphery to open up new strategic opportunities.
- We are organized to deal with 'off-purpose' signals (not directly relevant to our current business) and don't simply ignore them.
- We have active links into the long-term research and technology community – we can list a wide range of contacts.
- We recognize users as a source of new ideas and try to 'co-evolve' new products and services with them.

Finding the Resources

The trouble with ideas is that you can have too much of a good thing. A well-developed search process will throw up all sorts of possible opportunities – interesting ideas which are all waiting to take flight if only they had the resources to help them get off the ground. But no organization, and certainly no individual entrepreneur, has infinite resources, so the next stage in the process involves making some tough decisions about which ideas to back – and why. Inevitably, this is a risky process: we have to take decisions about ideas which are in their earliest stages and could become the best thing since sliced bread, but which could equally crash into oblivion and take us down with them!

For the entrepreneur the challenge is daunting – like taking part in a high-stakes competition. The test is one of working out how to put across your wonderful idea to a panel of judges who seem determined to find fault with everything. Passion and energy are all very well but they are looking for the impossible: guarantees that the idea will work, that people will want to buy and use it when it is developed and, most important, that they will get a return on their investment in you and your idea. Whether you are trying to convince a venture capitalist, a group of business angels or some close friends who may be interested in backing you, the same problem will emerge: can you marshal enough to convince them that they are taking a well-calculated risk rather than a wild gamble? Putting the business plan together is critical – and it doesn't hurt to have a sense of the kind of questions they could be thinking of asking you.

Which brings us to the other side of the fence. How do those responsible for judging ideas and selecting the best for further investment actually think? What are their concerns and how do they go about building an effective and balanced portfolio of ideas? The judges may be venture capitalists specializing in examining and taking risks with innovative ideas. But they could also be the management board reviewing the company's portfolio of new products or services, a department manager considering a new process to implement across their group or a hospital administrator looking for new ways to reduce costs or increase the quality of service delivery.

As with the previous stage we have learnt quite a bit about the ways in which this task of selection can be organized and managed – a 'good practice' model which we can learn from and adapt. Smart organizations don't simply gamble. They make choices on the basis of some clear ground rules:

- Does the idea have promise?
- Is it a good fit with where we are trying to go in our wider business strategy?
- Does it build on things that we know and can take advantage of – or if not, can we get hold of this knowledge to make it work?

They make use of techniques and structures to help them in the selection process, and make sure these are flexible enough to help monitor and adapt projects over time as ideas move towards more concrete innovations. And if they aren't going as well as expected, because of unexpected developments on the technological or market front, they have mechanisms in place to stop the process and either go back to the drawing board or kill it altogether. (Chapter 8 described many of these approaches in more detail.)

Video Clips of live pitches, Dragons' Den, are available on the Innovation Portal at **www.innovation-portal.info**

Activity exploring the challenge of pitching ideas, Dragons' Den, is available on the Innovation Portal at **www.innovation-portal.info**

One interesting development has been the shift to crowdsourcing judgements about innovation. A number of funding websites, like Kickstarter, rely on the 'wisdom of crowds' to attract funding for ideas which enough people are convinced by. While this is increasingly common in start-up ventures, there are examples of using such 'idea markets' within existing organizations, like Intel.

ASK YOURSELF – REFLECTION QUESTIONS...

...for start-up entrepreneurs

How far do you:

- Know what resources you will need to take your opportunity forward?
- Plan ahead to identify the resources which you will need – and work out where and how you will get those you don't have?
- Build rich networks to enable you to access wider resources?
- Build contingency plans (What if I can't get access to these key resources? What other routes can I take to exploit this opportunity?)
- Learn from how others have obtained resources?

...and for established organizations – how well do we do it?

If we visited a smart organization, we'd expect to find evidence that these ways of helping the selection and resource-finding process were widely used. People we approached would tell us things like:

> Around here:
>
> - We have a clear system for choosing innovation projects and everyone understands the rules of the game in making proposals.
> - When someone has a good idea, they know how to take it forward.
> - We have a selection system which tries to build a balanced portfolio of low- and high-risk projects.
> - We focus on a mixture of product, process, market and business model innovation.
> - We balance projects for 'do better' innovation with some efforts on the radical 'do different' side.
> - We recognize the need to work outside of the box and there are mechanisms for handling off-message but interesting ideas.
> - We have structures for corporate venturing.

Developing the Venture

Having decided on which ideas to back, the organization has one small problem left: how to actually make them happen. Moving from a gleam in some entrepreneur's eye to a product or service people use and value, or a business process which employees buy into and work with, can be a somewhat difficult journey! It isn't usually a simple matter of project management, balancing resources against a budget of time and money. The big difference with innovation is that we don't know whether things will work until we start doing them. So it's a case of developing something against a background of uncertainty. The only way we reduce the uncertainty is by trying things out and learning, even if what we learn is that it isn't going to work after all!

We're also weaving together different strands of knowledge about the innovation: the 'technological' (Will it work as an idea?) and the 'market' (Is there a need for this idea and do we understand and meet that need?). So a key aspect of implementation is making sure the threads come together and intertwine successfully, which in practice means making sure the right people get to talk with each other at the right time and for long enough to make something happen.

Innovation is often described in terms of the metaphor of a journey – and this helps us particularly think about the implementation phase. What stages does our idea need to go through before it becomes a successful innovation as a product/service in the marketplace or a process in everyday use within the business? And what structures and techniques do smart entrepreneurs and firms use to help their innovation along this journey – and to check its progress? Chapter 8 explored this theme in detail and highlights the kind of learning which experienced entrepreneurs and organizations bring into play when dealing with this challenge.

In the case of start-ups, the risk of burning through initial cash focuses the mind very quickly. Developing the venture cannot simply be a matter of writing a plan and then implementing it; instead, as we've seen, there is a need for fast learning. Early experiments may identify problems in technology or market and we can use these to adapt – to 'pivot' – around the core idea and come up with a better version to test out next. In this way we go through a series of fast learning loops and at the same time manage the risk in a controlled way.

It's the same in established organizations, and most make use of some kind of risk management as they implement innovation projects. By installing a series of 'gates' as the project moves from a gleam in the eye to an expensive commitment of time and money, it becomes possible to review – and if necessary redirect or even stop something if it is going off the rails. And they employ a variety of project management structures to help balance flexibility, spread of different knowledge inputs and engagement of key stakeholders with the demands of time and budget.

INNOVATION IN ACTION 17.2

What Makes for Success in Product/Service Innovation?

The table contains some examples of the mechanisms, tools and structures which smart firms and entrepreneurs use.

Key needs/issues on the journey	Key mechanisms
Systematic process for progressing new products/services	Stage-gate model Close monitoring and evaluation at each stage
Early involvement of all relevant functions	Bringing key perspectives into the process early enough to influence design and prepare for downstream problems Early detection of problems leads to less rework
Overlapping/parallel working	Concurrent or simultaneous engineering to aid faster development while retaining cross-functional involvement
Appropriate project management structures	Choice of structure (e.g. matrix/line/project/ heavyweight project management) to suit conditions and task
Cross-functional team working	Involvement of different perspectives, use of team-building approaches to ensure effective team working and develop capabilities in flexible problem solving
Advanced support tools	Use of tools – such as CAD, rapid prototyping, computer-supported cooperative work aids – to assist with quality and speed of development
Learning and continuous improvement	Carrying forward lessons learnt – via post-project audits, etc. Development of continuous improvement culture

Source: Belliveau, P., A. Griffin and S. Somermeyer (2002) *The PDMA ToolBook for New Product Development: Expert Techniques and Effective Practices in Product Development*, New York: John Wiley & Sons, Inc.

Managing innovation projects is more than simply scheduling resources against time and budget. Dealing with unexpected and unpredictable events and gradually bringing projects into being requires high levels of flexibility and creativity – and in particular it involves integrating knowledge sets from across organization, functional and disciplinary boundaries. And we've learnt a lot about how to do this, for example through using cross-boundary teams, through various forms of parallel or concurrent working and through the use of simulation and other exploration technologies to anticipate downstream problems and reduce time and resource costs while enhancing innovation quality.

ASK YOURSELF – REFLECTION QUESTIONS...

...for start-up entrepreneurs

How well have you thought through:

- How you will manage the project from your idea to full-scale launch?
- Who will you need to involve – and how will their involvement be timed?
- Is there a clear project plan with a timeline and plans for resources, especially cash flow, throughout the life of the project?
- Do you have criteria for stopping the project if it is going seriously off-track?
- How will you know how well you are doing in terms of project progress? When and how will you review?
- Do you have contingency plans? What if something goes unexpectedly wrong or falls behind schedule?

...and for established organizations – how well do we do it?

We can use the kind of 'good practice' model in Table 17.2 to compare against – and identify where and how we could improve the ways we manage the implementation of innovation. If we visited a smart organization we'd find many of these structures and techniques in use to help make the process happen well – and if we asked people we'd find evidence that they were using them. We'd hear things like:

Around here:

- We have clear and well-understood formal processes in place to help us manage new product development effectively from idea to launch.
- Our innovation projects are usually completed on time and within budget.
- We have effective mechanisms for managing process change from idea through to successful implementation.

(continued)

- We have mechanisms in place to ensure early involvement of all departments in developing new products/processes.
- There is sufficient flexibility in our system for product development to allow small fast-track projects to happen.
- To take innovation forward, our project teams involve people from all the relevant parts of the organization.
- We involve everyone with relevant knowledge from the beginning of the process.
- We'd also expect them to have some provision for the wilder and more radical kind of project which may need to go on a rather different route in making its journey. People could say about that things like:

  Around here:

- We have alternative and parallel mechanisms for implementing and developing radical innovation projects which sit outside the 'normal' rules and procedures.
- We have mechanisms for managing ideas that don't fit our current business, for example we license them out or spin them off.
- We make use of simulation, rapid prototyping tools, etc. to explore different options and delay commitment to one particular course.
- We have strategic decision-making and project-selection mechanisms which can deal with more radical proposals outside of the mainstream.
- There is sufficient flexibility in our system for product development to allow small fast-track projects to happen.

Innovation Strategy: Having a Clear Sense of Direction

Innovation depends on vision. Unless our entrepreneur has a sense of compelling vision, and the ability to communicate this passion to others, then getting the early-stage support for their idea is unlikely to happen. Equally, it is precisely because of their willingness to push the frontiers that major and exciting changes get to happen. George Bernard Shaw, the famous playwright, got pretty close to it when he observed in his *Maxims for Revolutionists* (*Man and Superman*, Penguin Classics, 2000):

> The reasonable man adapts himself to the conditions that surround him... The unreasonable man adapts surrounding conditions to himself... Therefore, all progress depends on the unreasonable man.

It's the same in established organizations: the need here is to balance the day-to-day improvement with a clear sense of what's coming next. And this may need some stretching leadership. As we've seen, challenging the way the organization sees things (the corporate mindset) can sometimes be accomplished by bringing in external perspectives. IBM's recovery was due in no small measure to the role played by Lou Gerstner, who succeeded at least in part *because* he was a newcomer to the computer industry, and was able to ask the awkward questions that insiders were oblivious to. And when Intel was facing strong competition from Far Eastern producers, senior managers like Andy Grove and Bill Noyce reported on the need to 'think the unthinkable', that is to get out of memory production (the business on which Intel had grown up) and to contemplate moving into other product niches. They trace their subsequent success to the point where they found themselves 'entering the void' and creating a new vision for the business.[4]

Doing this may need mechanisms for legitimating challenge to the dominant vision. Often this needs to come from the top – such as Jack Welch's challenge to 'destroy your business' memo within General Electric.[5] Perhaps building on their earlier experiences Intel now has a process called 'constructive confrontation', which essentially encourages a degree of dissent. The company has learnt to value the critical insights which come from those closest to the action rather than assume senior managers have the right answers every time.

Innovation needs clear strategic leadership and direction, plus the commitment of resources to make this happen. Innovation is about taking risks, about going into new and sometimes completely unexplored spaces. We don't want to gamble – simply changing things for their own sake or because the fancy takes us. And passion, drive and energy are critical entrepreneurial characteristics but they carry the risk that we could point them in the wrong direction. No organization has resources to waste in that scattergun fashion. Innovation needs a strategy. But equally we need to have a degree of courage and leadership, steering the organization away from what everyone else is doing or what we've always done and into new spaces.

Again, we've learnt that successful entrepreneurs and innovating organizations use a range of structures, tools and techniques to help them create, articulate, communicate and deploy a clear strategy. For example, many organizations take time – often off-site and away from the day-to-day pressures of their 'normal' operations – to reflect and develop a shared strategic framework for innovation. Start-up entrepreneurs may not have this luxury, but they certainly need to 'look before they leap' and be sure that they have a coherent and clear strategic plan for their venture. Two key questions underpin this:

- Does the innovation we are considering help us reach the strategic goals (for growth, market share, profit margin – or changing the world in some way through creating social value, etc.) which we have set ourselves?
- Do we know enough about this to pull it off (or if not do we have a clear idea of how we would get hold of and integrate such knowledge)?

Much can be gained through taking a systematic approach to answering these questions – a typical approach would be to carry out some form of competitive analysis which looked at the positioning of the organization in terms of its environment and the key forces acting upon competition. Within this picture, questions could then be asked about how a proposed innovation might help shift the competitive positioning favourably – by lowering or raising entry barriers, by introducing substitutes to rewrite the rules of the game, etc.

In carrying out such a systematic analysis, it is important to build on multiple perspectives. This can be done in a variety of ways, for example using tools for competitor and market analysis or looking for ways of deploying competencies – things the individual or organization knows about and is good at. It can build on explorations of the future or use techniques like 'technology road mapping' to help identify courses of action. It's important in all of this to remember that strategy is not an exact science. It's the process of building a shared framework which matters.

For the start-up entrepreneur, the challenge will be to share his/her vision with others and get them excited and engaged with it. And unless people within an established organization understand and commit to the strategy it has developed it will be hard for them to use it to frame their actions. The issue of **innovation strategy deployment** – communicating and enabling people to use the framework – is essential if the organization is to avoid the risk of having know-how but not know-why in its innovation process.

In Chapter 16, we explored the idea of using a business model as a device around which to build the story of an innovation. This gives a framework around which people can contribute, elaborating and challenging the underlying story both to make it stronger and to spread it to a wider population.

ASK YOURSELF – REFLECTION QUESTIONS...

...for start-up entrepreneurs

- Do you have a clear and concise 'story' which you can share with others about your idea?
- Where will you be in a year's time – and how will you know whether or not you have succeeded?
- What comes next if things go well – what will you do to grow or develop the venture further?
- Can you 'paint a picture' – can you make your idea come alive for others to see and share what excites you about what you are trying to do?
- Is there a clear roadmap for how you will get from your idea and exciting vision today to making that dream a reality next year?

...and for established organizations – how well do we do it?

Statements we'd expect to hear around such a strategically focused and led organization would include:

Around here:

- People in this organization have a clear idea of how innovation can help us compete.
- There is a clear link between the innovation projects we carry out and the overall strategy of the business.

- We have processes in place to review new technological or market developments and what they mean for our firm's strategy.
- There is top-management commitment and support for innovation.
- Our top team have a shared vision of how the company will develop through innovation.
- We look ahead in a structured way (using forecasting tools and techniques) to try to imagine future threats and opportunities.
- People in the organization know what our distinctive competence is – what gives us a competitive edge.
- Our innovation strategy is clearly communicated so everyone knows the targets for improvement.

And we'd also expect some stretching strategic leadership, getting the organization to think well outside of its box and anticipate very different challenges for the future – expressed in statements like:

Around here:

- Management create 'stretch goals' that provide the direction but not the route for innovation.
- We actively explore the future, making use of tools and techniques, like scenarios and foresight.
- We have capacity in our strategic thinking process to challenge our current position – we think about 'how to destroy the business'!
- We have strategic decision-making and project-selection mechanisms which can deal with more radical proposals outside of the mainstream.
- We are not afraid to 'cannibalize' things we already do to make space for new options.

Building an Innovative Organization

The key to innovation and entrepreneurship is, of course, people. And the simple challenge is how to enable them to deploy their creativity and share their knowledge to bring about change. For small start-ups the structures may be very loose and informal, and the sense of trust and cooperation high. But, as we saw earlier, being small has limits in terms of resources and so entrepreneurs here need to work hard at building and maintaining rich creative networks.

It's easy to find prescriptions for innovative organizations which highlight the need to eliminate stifling bureaucracy, unhelpful structures, brick walls blocking communication and other factors stopping good ideas getting through. But we must be careful not to fall into the chaos trap. Not all innovation works in organic, loose, informal environments or 'skunk works'. Indeed, these types of organization can sometimes act against the interests of successful innovation. We need to determine *appropriate* organization, that is the most suitable organization given the operating contingencies. Too little order and structure may be as bad as too much.

Successful entrepreneurs and innovative organizations recognize this, and make use of a range of structures, tools and techniques to help them achieve this balance. As we saw in Chapter 9 these include:

- shared vision, leadership and the will to innovate
- appropriate structure
- identifying and supporting key individuals
- effective team working
- high involvement innovation
- creative climate
- external focus.

We can use these as building blocks around which to construct a reflection framework.

ASK YOURSELF – REFLECTION QUESTIONS...

...for start-up entrepreneurs

- Have you the key skills and resources which you need to make the venture succeed?
- Have you identified the key people who will help you achieve your vision?
- How will you motivate them – how will you get them to buy in to what you are trying to do?
- How will you handle conflicts and disagreements?
- How will you take decisions – and make sure everyone sticks to what is decided even if they don't agree?
- How will you communicate – keep everyone in the loop?
- How will you make sure teams perform as greater than the sum of the individual parts, rather than less?

...and for established organizations – how well do we do it?

If we visited such an organization we'd find evidence of these approaches being used widely, and people would say things like:

Around here:

- Our organization structure does not stifle innovation but helps it happen.
- People work well together across departmental boundaries.
- There is a strong commitment to training and development of people.
- People are involved in suggesting ideas for improvements to products or processes.
- Our structure helps us take decisions rapidly.
- Communication is effective and works top down, bottom up and across the organization.

- Our reward and recognition system supports innovation.
- We have a supportive climate for new ideas – people don't have to leave the organization to make them happen.
- We work well in teams.

We'd also find recognition that one size does not fit all and that innovative organizations need the capacity, and the supporting structures and mechanisms, to think and do very different things from time to time. So we'd also expect to find people saying things like:

Around here:

- Our organization allows some space and time for people to explore 'wild' ideas.
- We have mechanisms to identify and encourage 'intrapreneurship' – if people have a good idea they don't have to leave the company to make it happen.
- We allocate a specific resource for exploring options at the edge of what we currently do – we don't load everyone up 100%.
- We value people who are prepared to break the rules.
- We have high involvement from everyone in the innovation process.
- Peer pressure creates a positive tension and creates an atmosphere to be creative.
- Experimentation is encouraged.

Networking for Innovation

We've always known that innovation is not a solo act: successful players work hard to build links across boundaries inside the organization and to the many external agencies that can play a part in the innovation process. These include suppliers, customers, sources of finance, skilled resources and of knowledge, etc. And as we saw in Chapter 10, 21st-century innovation is increasingly about 'open innovation', a multiplayer game where connections and the ability to find, form and deploy creative relationships is of the essence.

On the plus side the explosion in both technological possibility enabled by information and communications tools and the shift towards social networking as a major cultural movement means that there are now powerful tools to help us build networks. One key feature from systems theory is that networks have what are called 'emergent properties', that is the whole can be greater than the sum of the parts.

Table 17.1 summarizes the opportunity landscape opened up by the emergent properties around OCI.

But realizing these emergent properties and capitalizing on the significant opportunities in 'fifth generation innovation' is going to require learning new skills. As

Case Study exploring this, open collective innovation, is available on the Innovation Portal at **www.innovation-portal.info**

TABLE 17.1   Emergent properties around 'open collective innovation'[6]

Emergent property	Comments
Lowering of entry barriers	Widespread cheap communications allows 'democratization' of innovation, bringing many more players into the innovation game fast and easily
Increasing reach	OCI 'enfranchises' many more people, giving them access to the process of innovation and the tools to enable it
Increasing range	OCI spreads the net more widely, and the resulting 'flexibility' offers more different starting points for development of ideas and new insights and inspiration across different worlds – 'recombinant innovation'
Sustainability: innovation communities become thriving ecosystems with long-term identity	Critical mass, emergence of governance rules and structures, development of a culture around a critical mass of players
Mass creation: takes mass customization a stage further because users are directly enabled to design and produce	Extent of user-involvement is deepened – moving from 'cosmetic' customization to deep design involvement
Acceleration of diffusion	Innovation markets, communities and other groupings are simple to establish and quickly reach a scale of connectivity with significant effects in terms of idea generation, idea development and rapid 'viral' spread across communities
Networking the networks	As small local level communities of innovation evolve, it becomes possible to link them, or to mobilize their creation and coordination
	Scale effects and emergent properties across such 'meta-networks'

we saw in Chapter 10, making this happen requires skills in finding network partners, building relationships with them and finally linking their contributions with others so that the whole becomes greater than the sum of the parts.

The challenges include:

- how to manage something we don't own or control
- how to see system-level effects not narrow self-interests
- how to build trust and shared risk taking without tying the process up in contractual red tape
- how to avoid 'free riders' and information 'spillovers'.

ASK YOURSELF – REFLECTION QUESTIONS...

...for start-up entrepreneurs

- Have you identified who you will need to help you in taking your venture forward?
- How will you engage and motivate them to 'buy in' to the project?
- How will you manage conflicts and tensions within the network?
- How will you share information and communicate?
- How will you take decisions – and see that people stick to them?
- How will you find partners for your network and with these people build a sense of shared identity and commitment?

...and for established organizations – how well do we do it?

If we were to visit a successful innovative player, we'd get a sense of how far they had developed these capabilities for networking by asking around. People would typically say things like:

Around here:

- We have good win–win relationships with our suppliers.
- We are good at understanding the needs of our customers/end-users.
- We work well with universities and other research centres to help us develop our knowledge.
- We work closely with our customers in exploring and developing new concepts.
- We collaborate with other firms to develop new products or processes.
- We try to develop external networks of people who can help us, for example with specialist knowledge.
- We work closely with the local and national education system to communicate our needs for skills.
- We work closely with 'lead users' to develop innovative new products and services.

And there would be some evidence of their increasing efforts to create wide-ranging 'open innovation' type links, with statements like:

Around here:

- We make connections across industry to provide us with different perspectives.
- We have mechanisms to bring in fresh perspectives, for example recruiting from outside the industry.
- We have extensive links with a wide range of outside sources of knowledge: universities, research centres, specialized agencies and we actually set them up even if not for specific projects.

(continued)

- We use technology to help us become more agile and quick to pick up on and respond to emerging threats and opportunities on the periphery.
- We have 'alert' systems to feed early warnings about new trends into the strategic decision-making process.
- We practise 'open innovation' – rich and widespread networks of contacts from which we get a constant flow of challenging ideas.
- We have an approach to supplier management which is open to strategic 'dalliances'.
- We have active links into long-term research and technology community – we can list a wide range of contacts.
- We recognize users as a source of new ideas and try to 'co-evolve' new products and services with them.

Learning to Manage Innovation

As we said earlier, no individual or organization is born with the perfect set of capabilities to make innovation happen. Instead, they learn and develop these over time and through trial and error. In this chapter we've looked at a range of 'good practices' which are commonly found across very different entrepreneurial organizations – and some reflection questions to help us think about how well we are doing. But one last set of questions we should ask refers to whether we are good at learning itself – whether we take the time out, use challenging reflection, bring in new concepts and develop our own models for how we will manage innovation in the future. So we should finish with some reflection questions around this theme, and remember that a common characteristic shared by successful serial entrepreneurs and long-running businesses is that they do have an awareness of what it is they do and how they can use their insight to continue to succeed.

ASK YOURSELF – REFLECTION QUESTIONS...

...for start-up entrepreneurs

Looking back on the project (whether it succeeded or failed):

- What could I do more of (because it helped)?
- What could I do less of or even stop doing (because it didn't work or slowed things down or in some other way blocked the project)?
- What new/different things might I try?

- What advice would I give to someone else about to start a new venture, based on what I have learnt?
- What three key dos and three key don'ts would I take away from this venture and apply to my next one?
- What have I learnt?

...and for established organizations – how well do we do it?

Smart firms actively manage their learning – and the kinds of thing people might say in such organizations would be:

Around here:

- We take time to review our projects to improve our performance next time.
- We learn from our mistakes.
- We systematically compare our products and processes with other firms.
- We meet and share experiences with other firms to help us learn.
- We are good at capturing what we have learnt so that others in the organization can make use of it.
- We use measurement to help identify where and when we can improve our innovation management.
- We learn from our periphery – we look beyond our organizational and geographical boundaries.
- Experimentation is encouraged.

Getting Fit for Innovation

Learning isn't easy. Individuals and organizations are usually too busy getting on with building and running their ventures to find time to stop and think about how they could do things better. But assuming they did manage to get offline and reflect on how they might improve their innovation management they would probably find some structured framework for thinking about the process helpful. We can use the idea of comparing against what we've learnt about good practice to develop simple audit frameworks which could be used for diagnosis. How well do we do things compared to what the 'good practice' is? How far would we agree with the kinds of statements we've listed in the chapter associated with good innovators? Where are our strengths? And where would we want to focus our efforts to improve the organization? This kind of audit and review process doesn't carry any prizes but it can help with making the organization more effective in the ways it deals with the innovation challenge. And that may lead to some pretty important outcomes – like survival or growth!

INNOVATION IN ACTION 17.3

Measuring Innovation Performance

In reviewing innovative performance we can look at a number of possible measures and indicators:

- measures of specific outputs of various kinds, for example patents and scientific papers as indicators of knowledge produced or number of new products introduced (and percentage of sales and/or profits derived from them) as indicators of product innovation success
- output measures of operational or process elements, such as customer satisfaction surveys to measure and track improvements in quality or flexibility
- output measures which can be compared across sectors or enterprises, for example cost of product, market share, quality performance
- output measures of strategic success, where the overall business performance is improved in some way and where at least some of the benefit can be attributed directly or indirectly to innovation, for example growth in revenue or market share, improved profitability, higher value added.

We could also consider a number of more specific measures of the internal workings of the innovation process or particular elements within it. For example:

- number of new ideas (product/ service/ process) generated at start of innovation system
- failure rates: in the development process, in the marketplace
- number or percentage of overruns on development time and cost budgets
- customer satisfaction measures: was it what the customer wanted?
- time to market (average, compared with industry norms)
- development man-hours per completed innovation
- process innovation average lead time for introduction
- measures of continuous improvement: suggestions/employee, number of problem-solving teams, savings accruing per worker, cumulative savings.

There is also scope for measuring some of the influential conditions supporting or inhibiting the process, for example the 'creative climate' of the organization or the extent to which strategy is clearly deployed and communicated. And there is value in considering inputs to the process, for example percentage of sales committed to R&D, investments in training and recruitment of skilled staff, etc.

TABLE 17.2   Examples of innovation audit frameworks

Key questions and issues in managing innovation	Reflection and development aids available on Innovation Portal
How well do we manage innovation?	Innovation fitness test
How well do we manage service innovation?	SPOTS framework
Start-up phase for new ventures	Entrepreneur's checklist
Do we engage our employees fully in innovation?	High involvement innovation audit tool
How well do we manage discontinuous innovation?	Discontinuous innovation audit
How widely do we search in an open innovation world?	Search strategies for peripheral vision
Do we have a creative climate for innovation?	Creative climate review
Can we make the most of external knowledge for innovation?	Absorptive capacity audit

Activities based on innovation auditing, including the Innovation management project, are available on the Innovation Portal at **www.innovation-portal.info**

There is no single framework for doing an **innovation audit** – and no 'right' answer at the end of the process. But using such frameworks can be helpful. Table 17.2 gives some examples and you can find full details on the Innovation Portal.

There are audits which look in general terms, those which focus on capabilities to manage the more radical end of innovation, those which deal with sector differences like how to manage innovation in services and there are those which focus on aspects of the organization – like how well it is able to engage its whole workforce in the innovation process. Audits can be targeted at the individual, for example on the Innovation Portal there is a framework for reflecting on 'How creative are you?'

There are also an increasing number of online audit resources available, and a growing consultancy industry built around providing this kind of mirror on how well an organization is doing at innovation together with some advice on how it may do it better. But it's not the audits so much as using them in the *process* of questioning and developing innovation capability which matters. As the quality guru, W. Edwards Deming, pointed out, 'If you don't measure it you can't improve it!'

Managing Innovation and Entrepreneurship

We began the book by talking about innovation as a survival imperative. Quite simply, if organizations don't change what they offer the world, and the ways they create and deliver those offerings, then they may not be around in the long term. But simply saying, 'We believe in innovation' isn't likely to get us very far – it's going to need a considerable amount of action to make it happen. Getting a good idea into widespread and successful use is hard enough, but growing and sustaining a business requires the ability to repeat the trick. Even serial entrepreneurs, whose philosophy is to make this happen and then make their (hopefully wealthy) exit, only do so in order to repeat the process with another good idea.

Success isn't about luck; indeed, often what seems like luck is actually the result of hard work, as the (possibly apocryphal story) of the golfer demonstrates. He had scored a hole in one. When a spectator shouted that it had been a very lucky shot, he muttered to his caddy, 'Yes, and the more I practise, the luckier I get!' Innovation is about managing a structured and focused process, engaging and deploying creativity throughout but also balancing this with an appropriate degree of control. No organization or individual starts out with this. It's essentially something they learn and develop over time. This learning can come through trial and error, but it can also come through learning from others and building on their hard-won experience. And it can come through using tools and models to help understand and engage with managing innovation more effectively. We hope that the lessons we've tried to capture in the book provide some helpful input to this process.

Chapter Summary

- Wherever innovation happens – big firm, small firm, start-up business, social enterprise – one thing is clear: successful innovation won't happen simply by wishing for it. This complex and risky process of transforming an idea into something which makes a mark needs organizing and managing in strategic fashion.

- Entrepreneurship provides the drive, the motive power behind innovation. But force alone won't make effective change – and many entrepreneurs fail. Those who succeed – and especially those who do so repeatedly – understand that innovation is a process to be understood and managed.

- It's a generic process, running through four core stages – recognizing opportunities, finding resources, developing the venture and capturing the value.

- We know that this process is influenced along the way by several things which can help or hinder it. Is there clear strategic leadership and direction? How can we construct innovative organizations which allow creative ideas to come through, let people build on and share knowledge and feel motivated and rewarded for doing so? How can we harness the power of networks, making rich and extensive connections to deliver a stream of innovations?

- A wide range of structures, tools and techniques exist for helping think about and manage these elements of the innovation process. The challenge is to adapt and use them in a particular context, essentially a learning process.

- Developing innovative capability needs to begin with an audit of where we are now – and there are many ways of asking and exploring the core questions:
  - Do we have a clear process for making innovation happen and effective enabling mechanisms to support it?
  - Do we have a clear sense of shared strategic purpose and do we use this to guide our innovative activities?
  - Do we have a supportive organization whose structures and systems enable people to be creative and share and build on each other's creative ideas?
  - Do we build and extend our networks for innovation into a rich open innovation system?

Key Terms Defined

Innovation audit   structured review of innovation capability across an organization.

Innovation strategy   statement of how innovation is going to take the business forward – and why.

Innovation strategy deployment   communicating and enabling people to use the framework.

Discussion Questions

1. Use the reflection questions in this chapter (and additional ones from the online audit frameworks) to carry out a review of innovation management capability in an organization you are familiar with.

2. 'If we don't learn from history, we are condemned to repeat it.' This famous quotation underlines the challenge of learning. What stops organizations learning from their past efforts at innovation – and what can they do to improve their learning capability in the future?

Further Reading and Resources

The idea of organizational learning has been widely explored and there are a number of useful resources, including Chris Argyris's *On Organizational Learning* (Wiley-Blackwell, 1999), David Garvin's 'Building a learning organisation' (*Harvard Business Review*, 1993. **July/ August**: 78–91) and Peter Senge's *The Dance of Change: Mastering the Twelve Challenges to Change in a Learning Organisation* (Doubleday, 1999). Approaches like agile development and 'lean start-up' emphasize the idea of fast cycles of learning as a way of driving innovation. See Ries' *The Lean Startup* (Crown, 2011) and Blank's 'Why the lean start-up changes everything' (*Harvard Business Review*, 2013, **91**(5), 63–72). Measuring innovation is covered in reports in NESTA's *The Innovation Index* (NESTA, 2009) and in articles by Adams (for example Adams, R., R. Phelps, and J. Bessant, Innovation management measurement: A review, *International Journal of Management Reviews*, 2006, 8(1), 21–47) and Kolk, Kyte, van Oene and Jacobs' *Innovation: Measuring It to Manage It* (Arthur D. Little, 2012, http://www. adlittle.com/downloads/tx_adlprism/Prism_01-12_Innovation.pdf).

A wide range of books and online reviews of innovation now offer some form of audit framework, including the Pentathlon model from Cranfield University discussed in Goffin and Mitchell's *Innovation Management* (2nd edn, Pearson, 2010) and von Stamm's 'Innovation wave' model discussed in her *The Innovation Wave* (John Wiley & Sons Ltd, 2003). And also see von Stamm's *Managing Innovation, Design and Creativity* (2nd edn, John Wiley & Sons Ltd, 2008). For other examples, see Dodgson, Salter and Gann's *The Management of Technological Innovation* (2nd edn, Oxford University Press, 2008) or Trott's *Innovation Management and New Product Development* (5th edn, Prentice Hall, 2011).

Websites include www.innovationforgrowth.co.uk, www.innovationexcellence.com and www.cambridgeaudits.com. AIM Practice (www.aimpractice.com) also has a variety of audit tools around innovation and NESTA (www.nesta.org) has a number of reports linked to its major Innovation Index project.

References

1. Cooper, R. (2001) *Winning at New Products*, 3rd edn, London: Kogan Page; Monden, Y. (1983) *The Toyota Production System*, Cambridge, MA: Productivity Press.

2. Kolb, D. and R. Fry (1975) Towards a theory of applied experiential learning, in: Cooper, C. (ed.), *Theories of Group Processes*, Chichester: John Wiley & Sons Ltd.

3. Morris, L., M. Ma and P. Wu (2014) *Agile Innovation: The Revolutionary Approach to Accelerate Success*, New York: John Wiley & Sons, Inc.

4. Groves, A. (1999) *Only the Paranoid Survive*, New York: Bantam Books.

5. Welch, J. (2001) *Jack! What I've Learned from Leading a Great Company and Great People*, New York: Headline.

6. Bessant, J. and K. Moeslein (2011) *Open Collective Innovation*, London: Advanced Institute of Management Research.

Deeper Dive explanations of innovation concepts and ideas are available on the Innovation Portal at **www.innovation-portal.info**

Quizzes to test yourself further are available online via the Innovation Portal at **www.innovation-portal.info**

Summary of online resources for Chapter 17 –
all material is available via the Innovation Portal at
www.innovation-portal.info

Cases	**Media**	**Tools**	**Activities**	**Deeper Dives**
• Open Collective Innovation	• Dragons' Den	—	• Dragons' Den • Innovation management project	• Lean start-up • Agile innovation • Measuring innovation

Index

Note: *Italic* page numbers refer to illustrations.